Contents

KU-120-838

About the Guide

This is the first edition of the *Time Out San Francisco Guide*, one of an expanding series of city guides that includes London, Paris, New York, Berlin, Rome, Madrid, Prague, Budapest and Amsterdam. Our hard-working team of resident writers has striven to provide you with all the information you'll need to take on one of the world's most laid-back yet culturally diverse cities. We offer advice on which sights to see (and which to avoid), where to eat, drink, shop, stay and play in San Francisco and the Bay Area.

PRACTICAL GUIDE

Above all, we've tried to make this book as useful as possible. Addresses, telephone numbers, transport details, opening times, admission times and credit card details are all included in our listings. And, as far as possible, we've given details of facilities, services and events.

ADDRESSES

Apart from the area around Twin Peaks and the outer neighbourhoods, most of San Francisco is laid out on a grid plan, with Market Street bisecting it into north and south segments from the Embarcadero to the Castro. Each block increases its numbering by 100, but we have included cross streets in all our addresses, so you can find your way about more easily. We've also included a fully-indexed street map, as well as a map of the Bay Area and the city's transport network at the back of this guide.

Streets have both names and numbers; it's important not to confuse the numerical avenues (to the west) with the streets (which start at the Embarcadero, in the east). It is also worth noting that in the US, what is called the ground floor of a building in the UK, is the first floor, which makes the first floor the second, and so on.

PRICES

The prices we've supplied should be treated as guidelines, not gospel. Fluctuating exchange rates and inflation can cause prices, in shops and restaurants particularly, to change rapidly. If prices vary wildly from those we've quoted, ask whether there's a good reason. If not, go elsewhere. Then please write and let us know. We aim to give the best and most up-to-date advice, so we always want to know if you've been badly treated or over-charged.

CREDIT CARDS

The following abbreviations have been used for credit cards: **AmEx**: American Express; **DC**: Diners' Club; **JCB**: Japanese credit cards; **MC**: Mastercard (Access); **V**: Visa (Barclaycard). Virtually all shops, restaurants and attractions will accept dollar travellers' cheques issued by a major financial institution (such as American Express).

TELEPHONE NUMBERS

There are two area codes that serve the Bay Area: 415 for San Francisco and the northern peninsular, and 510 for Berkeley, Oakland and the East Bay. All telephone numbers printed in this guide take the 415 code, unless otherwise stated. Numbers preceded by 1-800 can be called free of charge from within the US.

RIGHT TO REPLY

It should be stressed that the information we give is impartial. No organisation has been included in this guide because its owner or manager has advertised in our publications. We hope you enjoy the *Time Out San Francisco Guide*, but we'd also like to know if you don't. We welcome tips for places that you think we should include in future editions and take notice of your criticism of our choices. There's a reader's reply card at the back of this book.

An on-line version of this guide, as well as weekly events listings for San Francisco and other international cities, can be found at http//:www.timeout.co.uk. For a list of on-line sites relating to San Francisco, *see page 9.*

Time Out
San Francisco Guide

Penguin Books

PENGUIN BOOKS

Published by the Penguin Group
Penguin Books Ltd, 27 Wrights Lane, London W8 5TZ, England
Penguin Books USA Inc., 375 Hudson Street, New York, New York 10014, USA
Penguin Books Australia Ltd, Ringwood, Victoria, Australia
Penguin Books Canada Ltd, 10 Alcorn Avenue, Toronto, Ontario, Canada M4V 3B2
Penguin Books (NZ) Ltd, 182–190 Wairau Road, Auckland 10, New Zealand

Penguin Books Ltd, Registered Offices: Harmondsworth, Middlesex, England

First published 1996
10 9 8 7 6 5 4 3 2 1

Copyright © Time Out Group Ltd, 1996
All rights reserved

Colour reprographics by Precise Litho, 34–35 Great Sutton Street, London EC1
Mono reprographics, printed and bound by William Clowes Ltd, Beccles, Suffolk NR34 9QE

Introduction

San Francisco is a city defined by its geography. Its hilly, bayside setting is spectacular, its architecture – much of it carefully restored pastel-painted Victorian houses – charming. A port, surrounded on three sides by water, it sits in close proximity to the ocean, but also the Sierra Nevada mountains, the desert, and the agricultural valleys that make up Northern California.

The city is also divided by geography – the centres of culture and activity separated into distinct neighbourhoods by the hills and valleys. Though it is surprisingly small, it can take some time for the uninitiated to work out when to be where, since many of the neighbourhoods have schizophrenic characteristics. The downtown financial district bustles with business people during the day, for example, but at night is nearly abandoned. South of Market, centre of the city's booming computer technology industry and filled with multimedia types working furiously to stake out the cyber-frontier, shifts to nightclub territory after dark. In Union Square, the city's downtown shopping centre, you can hear the cash register's constant daytime ring, but at night, well-heeled theatre-goers heading for the adjacent theatre district, jostle with the homeless and down and out.

Of course, San Francisco is also defined by its inhabitants. Since the days of the Gold Rush, the golden gateway has beckoned people from all over the world, a diverse collection of individuals who come to map their own lives with others who are doing the same, giving the city both its multicultural and hedonistic reputation. Chinatown is home to both Asian immigrants and Asian Americans, as is the Richmond district, which has more recently embraced a wave of Russian immigrants who have begun to set up shops and businesses in the area. The Castro – world renowned among gay men and lesbians as a mecca for queer culture – used to be home to the city's Irish population, as was the nearby Mission district which today houses most of the city's Latino population. On the east side of the city, by the bay, the Bayview district is where many African Americans live, having gradually migrated from the Fillmore district, which in turn is filling up with young professionals.

Cultural life in San Francisco combines this ethnic diversity with the penchant for experimentation that has always been a part of life here. Don't be surprised if you sit down for a quiet drink at a bar, and are rudely interrupted by arrival of the 'cultural activist' group Those Darn Accordions! who rush in to perform a few tunes and raise awareness of the art of accordion playing. You're as likely to see gay subject matter at the Asian American Theater as in the Castro; or a solo performance on the African American experience in a performance space in the Mission.

San Franciscans pride themselves on being laid-back. You can't spend any time here without hearing some resident utter the phrase, 'only in San Francisco', and with some pride. And if the people don't surprise you, the weather probably will. The climate is famously unpredictable: one day it may be foggy and cold, the next balmy and clear. Only in San Francisco can you walk down the street behind one person wearing a winter coat, while their companion is dressed in shorts and a T-shirt.

Despite all the city's dedicated diversity, there are, of course, some constants – the things that bind the collection of individuals who live here together. You can always count on being chilly on a cable car ride, and on the fact that the clang of its bell, and the view from its seats will conjure up romance and nostalgia. The sea lions will always bark at Pier 39, and just a few docks away, the smell of fresh sourdough will always waft through the air, amidst the clatter of the seafood vendors offering up fresh crab and chowder. And through the bold orange arches of the Golden Gate Bridge, the city on a hill will always beckon, across the sparkling bay, to both the traveller and the settler.
Robin Stevens

Hungry?.....

Tired?........

Sick?........

Homesick?...

Lost?........

Broke?.. **WESTERN UNION MONEY TRANSFER**

Edited and designed by
Time Out Magazine Limited
Universal House
251 Tottenham Court Road
London W1P 0AB
Tel: 0171 813 3000
Fax: 0171 813 6001

Editorial
Managing Editor Peter Fiennes
Editor Caroline Taverne
Consultant Editors Judith Coburn, Robin Stevens
Copy Editor Cath Phillips
Researcher Kath Stanton
Indexer Jacqueline Brind

Design
Art Director Warren Beeby
Art Editor John Oakey
Designers Paul Tansley, James Pretty
Picture Editor Catherine Hardcastle
Ad Make up Carrie Lambe

Advertising
Group Advertisement Director Lesley Gill
Sales Director Mark Phillips
Advertisement Sales (San Francisco) Media Corps

Administration
Publisher Tony Elliott
Managing Director Mike Hardwick
Financial Director Kevin Ellis
Marketing Director Gillian Auld
Production Manager Mark Lamond

Features in this guide were written and researched by:
Introduction Robin Stevens. **Essential Information, Getting Around, Accommodation** Erika Lenkert, Matthew Poole. **San Francisco by Season** Brad Wieners. **Sightseeing, Architecture** Elgy Gillespie. **History** Chris Bohn, Elgy Gillespie. **San Francisco Today** Harriet Swift. **San Francisco by Neighbourhood** Tessa Souter, Shirley Fong-Torres (Chinatown), Ricardo Sandoval (the Mission), Brad Wieners (SoMa). **Bars & Cafés** Brad Wieners. **Restaurants** Howard Karel, Ellen Towell. **Shopping & Services** Susan Lydon (Shopping), Erika Lenkert, Matthew Poole (Services). **Museums & Galleries** Marty Olmstead. **Literary San Francisco** Andrew Moss. **Media, Clubs** Brad Wieners. **Film** Robin Stevens. **Music: Classical & Opera** Elgy Gillespie. **Music: Rock, Roots & Jazz, Sport** Brad Wieners. **Theatre & Dance** Judith Coburn, Robin Stevens. **Business** Ricardo Sandoval. **Children** Elgy Gillespie. **Gay & Lesbian San Francisco** Steven Sassaman, Robin Stevens (Lesbian San Francisco). **Students, Women's San Francisco** Gabriella West. **Trips Out of Town** Marty Olmstead. **Survival** Erika Lenkert, Matthew Poole.

The editors would like to thank the following for their help and information:
Chris Bohn, Debra Chasnoff, Danny Chau Photolabs (for black and white printing), Deveny Dawson, Frank Heaney, Mimi McGurl, Sam Michel, Ravi Mirchandani, Derk Richardson, Claudia Sandoval, Dawn Stranne and the San Francisco Convention & Visitors Bureau, Ben Tollett, Patricia Unterman.

Photographs: page iii **Coit Tower**; page 157 **The Circle Gallery**.
Erratum: the photo on page 35 is the Bay Bridge, not the Golden Gate Bridge, as captioned.

Photography by **Barry J. Holmes** except: pages 32, 74, 201, 213, 236 **San Francisco Convention & Visitors Bureau**; pages 57, 255 **Museum of the City of San Francisco**; pages 59, 61 **Mary Evans Picture Library**; pages 62, 63, 70, 75 **Hulton Deutsch**; pages 64, 65, 68, 71, 73 **Range/ Bettmann/ UPI**; page 214 **Daniel Nicoletta**; pages 239, 242, 244 **Californian Office of Tourism**; pictures on pages 109, 110 were supplied by the featured establishments.

Essential Information

All you need to know about telephones and tipping, currency and the climate in Fog City.

*Feeling lost? You can always ask a policeman, but you're better off at the **Visitor's Center**.*

For more information on surviving the urban jungle, *see chapter* **Survival**. For information on abbreviations used in this guide, *see page vi* **About the Guide**.

If you're phoning from outside San Francisco, dial the area code 415 before the numbers listed in this guide, unless otherwise stated. All 1-800 numbers can be called free of charge, although many hotels add a surcharge for use of their phones, whatever number you call.

Emergency

In case of emergency, for fire brigade, police or ambulance, **dial 911**.

Banks, Bureaux de Change & ATMs

Most banks are open from 9am to 6pm Monday to Friday and a few are open on Saturday until 2pm. You need identification, such as a driver's licence or a passport, to change travellers' cheques. Many banks do not exchange foreign currency, so it's a good idea to arrive with some US dollars. If you're scheduled to arrive in San Francisco after about 6pm, change money at the airport or, if you have US dollars travellers' checks, buy something in order to get some change. If you want to cash travellers' cheques at a shop, ask first – some require a minimum purchase. You can also obtain cash on a credit card account from certain banks; check with your credit card company before you leave, and be prepared to pay daily interest rates. Most banks and shops accept travellers' cheques in US dollars.

San Francisco is brimming with Automated Teller Machines (ATMs). Most accept Visa, Mastercard and American Express, among others. There is a usage fee, of course, although the convenience of cash-on-demand often makes it worth the price. *See chapter* **Survival** for more information on emergency cash.

Exchange Offices

American Express Travel Services

237 Post Street, between Stockton Street and Grant Avenue (981 5533). Muni Metro J, K, L, M, N/2, 3, 4, 30, 45, 76 bus. **Open** 9am-5pm Mon-Fri; 9am-2pm Sat.
AmEx will change money and travellers' cheques and they offer other services such as poste restante and worldwide money transfers. Call for details of other branches within San Francisco. For lost or stolen travellers' cheques, phone 1-800 525 2155.

Thomas Cook

75 Geary Street, between Grant Avenue and Kearny Street (1-800 287 7362). Muni Metro J, K, L, M, N/2, 3, 4, 30, 45, 76 bus. **Open** 9am-5pm Mon-Fri; 9am-5pm Sat.
A complete foreign exchange service is offered here, including money transfer by wire.
Branch: Pier 39, Building M, Level 2, Unit M-10 (1-800 287 7362).

Western Union

Phone 1-800 325 6000 for a recording of your closest branch.
The old standby for bailing cash-challenged travellers out of trouble. Expect to pay a whopping 10% commission, possibly more.

Climate

For daily weather information, phone 936 1212. For more information on seasonal variations in temperature, *see chapter* **San Francisco by Season**.

Clothing

Nothing you pack will be more important than a comfortable pair of walking shoes; San Francisco's infamous hills will wear a wimpy pair of footwear out in minutes. Also

Tipping

You'll find some of the finest and friendliest service in the world in San Francisco, but it comes at a price. The following are basic tipping guidelines (if service is bad, which is rare, don't tip):

Coat check: 50¢-$1 per item.
Concierge: from $5.
Doorman: $1 (for hailing a cab).
Food delivery: $2.
Manicure or pedicure: 10%-20%.
Porters: $2-$5 for unloading; $1 per bag.
Barbers, hairdressers, waiters, bartenders: 15% of bill not including sales tax for adequate service; 20% for excellent service.
Restaurants: 15% of total bill in cheaper restaurants; 20% in fancy ones.
Room maid: 50¢ per night; $1 if double room.
Room service: 20% of bill (minimum $2).
Shoeshine: 25¢.
Taxi: 15% (more for a short trip).
Valet: $1-$2.

Don't tip: gas station attendants, movie ticket takers, ushers and bus/BART/cable car drivers.

strongly recommended is a light jacket, a coat and tie should you wish to dine at a fancy restaurant and a bathing suit (for massaging your wimpy feet in the hotel's jacuzzi). Forget everything you hear about sunny, warm California – San Francisco has its own climate, and will punish any visitor who thinks shorts and a t-shirt will suffice. Bring a warm sweater even if you're arriving in mid-summer.

Credit Cards

You are strongly advised to bring at least one major credit card or you will find yourself strangely handicapped in San Francisco. Credit cards are accepted (and often required) at nearly all hotels, car rental agencies and airlines, as well as most restaurants, shops and petrol stations. The five major credit cards accepted in the US are Visa, Mastercard (Access), Discover, Diners Club, and American Express.

Currency

The US dollar ($) equals 100 cents (¢). Coins range from copper pennies (1¢) to silver nickels (5¢), dimes (10¢), quarters (25¢) and half dollars (50¢). Paper money (or bills) comes in denominations of $1, $5, $10, $20, $50 and $100, which are, confusingly, all the same size and colour. A few $2 bills and $1 coins are in circulation, but are rare. Few small shops or stores will break a $50 or $100 bill.

Disabled Access

Disabled travellers will find San Francisco one of the most accommodating cities in the world. In fact, California is the national leader in providing the disabled with access to facilities and attractions. Privileges include unlimited free parking in designated (blue) parking stalls and free parking at most metered spaces (a visible blue and white disabled 'parking placard' is required), and special prices and arrangements for train, bus, air and sightseeing travel. In addition, all public buildings within the city are accessible to wheelchairs and have wheelchair-accessible toilets; most city buses can 'kneel' to make access easier and have handgrips and spaces designed for wheelchair users; most city street corners have ramped kerbs, and most restaurants and hotels are either designed (or have been redesigned) to accommodate wheelchairs.
Of course, what a building is supposed to have and what it really has can be two different things, so the wheelchair-bound traveller's best bet is to contact the **Independent Living Resource Center** on 863 0581.

Electricity

Throughout the US, electricity voltage is 110-120V 60-cycle AC. If you have electrical appliances – hair dryers, razors, irons – that are not dual voltage with a two-prong tip, you must use a transformer or travel plug, available at department stores, hardware stores and certain airport boutiques.

Immigration & Customs

Standard immigration regulations apply to all visitors, which means you may have to wait (over an hour) when you arrive at Immigration. On the flight over, you will be handed an immigration form, which must be presented to the immigration official when you land. You will be expected to explain the nature of your visit. Expect close questioning if you are planning a long visit, don't have a return ticket, or much money with you. You will usually be granted an entry permit to cover the length of your stay. Work permits are hard to get, and you are not permitted to work without one.

Telephone hotlines

Who to phone when you're bored or desperate.

American Express Travel Agency
(981 5533/1-800 528 4800).
Full financial services including personal cheque cashing, AmEx travellers' cheques and foreign currency exchange. Card member services range from emergency fund transfers to card replacement.

B-AT Line
(626 4087).
The locals' choice for the inside scoop on underground clubs, live performances and hip hop happenings.

eTours
(1-510 284 3183).
On-line services offering a photographic database with information on hotels, shopping, sightseeing and attractions.

Dial-a-Story
(626 6516).
Too tired to read a bedtime story after trudging up all those hills? This free service from the public library offers soothing stories for children of all ages.

Hearing Society Dial-a-Test
(834 1620).
Hearing not what it used to be? Have your eardrums checked out by the experts.

Grateful Dead Hotline
(457 6388).
The great Garcia may be gone, but as far as we know the Dead play on. Phone for tour information and a mail order hotline.

Morrison Planetarium Information Line
(750 7141).
Need to know the date of the next full moon? Call here for details of sunrise, sunset and the phases of the moon.

SF Convention & Visitors Bureau
(391 2001).
Round-the-clock information on the city's events: seasonal and sporting occasions, theatre, music, dance and exhibition details.

Speaking Clock
(767 8900). **Open** 24-hours daily.
Even in San Francisco, this may be useful.

UC Berkeley Seismographic Station
(1-510 642 2160).
The latest information on recent earthquakes.

Weather Forecast
(936 1212).
The National Weather Service updates the forecast daily for San Francisco and the Bay Area.

US Customs allow foreigners to bring in $100 worth of gifts ($400 for returning Americans). One carton of 200 cigarettes (or 100 cigars) and 33.8fl oz (one litre) of spirits is allowed. No plants, fruit, meat or fresh produce can be taken through Customs. A Customs official will mark your declaration card before you leave the baggage claim area.

If you have bought a one-way ticket, phone the Immigrant Assistance Line (554 2444), which provides information on legalisation and referrals to support services. *See chapter* **Survival** for information on work permits.

Any possible questions you could have about United States immigration policies or laws can be answered by calling the INS Ask Immigration System in San Francisco (705 4411).

Insurance

It's best to take out medical and baggage insurance before you leave because it is almost impossible to arrange once you're in the US. It can be very difficult to get treatment at hospitals and emergency rooms without insurance. Make sure that you have adequate medical coverage – medical expenses in the US can be outrageous. *See chapter* **Survival** for a list of San Francisco hospitals and emergency rooms.

Liquor Laws

California has strict drinking laws forbidding any bar, restaurant, nightclub or store from selling alcohol to minors (under-21s). Even if you look 30, bring ID (preferably a driver's licence or passport) with you if you plan to drink – many nightclubs check ID as house policy. Minors are allowed in some clubs that serve alcohol, but it's a good idea to phone first to check.

A major *faux pas* is any 'open container' in your car or any public area that isn't zoned for alcohol consumption. Cops will give you a ticket on the spot for walking down the street with a beer in your hand, or even having an old empty beer can in the back seat of your car. You don't want to know what happens if you're busted driving drunk, so don't do it.

Opening Times

Standard American business hours are 9am to 5pm during the week, and – if the business is open at the weekends – generally from 10am to 6pm on Saturdays and 11am to 4pm on Sundays. Naturally, every business has its own schedule, so always phone to check.

Pacific Standard Time

San Francisco is on Pacific Standard Time, which is three hours behind Eastern Standard Time (New York) and eight hours behind Greenwich Mean Time (Britain). Daylight Savings Time (which runs almost concurrent with British Summer Time) runs from the first Sunday in April to the last Sunday in October when the clocks are rolled ahead one hour.

Going from the west to east coast, Pacific Time is one hour behind Mountain Time (Arizona to Alberta), two hours behind Central Time (Texas to Manitoba) and three hours behind Eastern Time.

Post Office

Post offices are open from 8am to 6pm, Monday to Saturday. Phone 284 0755 for information on your nearest branch and mailing facilities. Stamps can be purchased at any post office and also at some hotel reception desks and vending machines. For information on poste restante and telegrams, *see chapter* **Survival**.

You'll be lucky to get aboard at the Powell-Hyde cable car turnaround.

Safety

Part of the Bay Area's charm lies in the fact that socially, culturally and economically diverse people closely share the tiny peninsula they call home. In some areas of the city you can walk down a street lined with ornate Victorians, turn the corner, and suddenly find yourself at a low-income housing project. Of course, some areas are safer than others and crime is a reality in all big cities, but San Franciscans feel secure in their town and follow one basic rule of thumb – use common sense. If an area doesn't feel safe to you, it probably isn't. If confronted with a shaky situation, either turn around or pass through it and look as if you know where you're going. Don't flaunt purses, shopping bags or cameras, avoid walking through dark streets and alleys and try not to look too much like a gullible tourist.

Areas where you should be particularly alert include the Tenderloin (near the downtown theatres), SoMa (especially around Sixth Street), Golden Gate Park at night and out by Candlestick Park (Hunter's Point). Many tourist areas are sprinkled with the city's homeless (the Union Square shopping area, for example), who beg for change but for the most part are harmless.

If you are unlucky enough to be mugged, your best bet is to give your attacker whatever he wants (which is why you're carrying travellers' cheques and small amounts of cash, right?), then call the police from the nearest payphone by dialling 911. Don't forget to get the reference number on the claim report for insurance purposes and travellers' cheques refunds.

Smoking

Smokers are not particularly welcome in San Francisco, which has some of the stiffest anti-smoking laws in the nation (and probably the world). There is no smoking in lobbies, banks, public buildings, sports arenas, elevators, theatres, restaurants that don't have bars, offices, stores and any form of public transport. Many small hotels and bed-and-breakfast inns don't allow you to light up either (and, boy, do they get cross if you do).

Telephones

The phone system in San Francisco – and the entire US – is very reliable and, and least for local calls, cheap. Americans love their phones and, thanks to the boom in cellular communication, are rarely seen without one stuck to their dashboard or stuffed into their pockets. Tourists, however, will have to rely mostly on public payphones, which are scattered throughout the city, usually within a block of wherever you happen to be. Payphones only accept nickels, dimes and quarters, but check to see if you get a dialling tone before you start feeding them your change. Local calls cost 20¢, and the price rises as the distance between callers increases (an operator or recorded message will tell you how much to add). Long-distance, particularly overseas calls, are best paid for with a phone card or by visiting the calling centre listed below.

Operator assistance dial 0.
Emergency (police, ambulance, fire) dial 911.
Directory enquiries (local) dial 411.
Long-distance directory enquiries dial 1 + area code + 555 1212 (calls are free from payphones).
Toll-free numbers generally start with a 1-800, while pricey **pay-per-call** lines (usually phone-sex numbers) start with 1-900, so don't mix the two up.

Area Codes

San Francisco, Marin and the peninsula cities: 415.
East Bay (including Oakland and Berkeley): 510.
San Jose: 408.
Wine Country: 707.

Direct Dial Calls

Outside your area code, dial 1 + area code + phone number and an operator or recording will tell you how much money to add.

Collect Calls

For collect calls or when using a phone card, dial 0 + area code + phone number and listen for the operator or recorded instructions. If you are completely befuddled, just dial 0 and plead your case with the operator. For assistance with

San Francisco runs on Pacific Standard Time.

international calls, dial 1-800 874 4000 (touch tone phone) or 1-800 225 5288 or 102 880 (rotary phone).

AT&T Global Communication Center

170 Columbus Avenue at Pacific Avenue (693 9520). Bus 12, 15, 41, 83. **Open** 9am-6pm daily. **No credit cards**.

Tourist Information

San Francisco

Visitor's Information Center

Lower level of Hallidie Plaza, corner of Market and Powell Streets (391 2000). BART Powell Street/Muni Metro J, K, L, M/6, 7, 8, 9, 21, 26, 27, 31, 66, 71 bus. **Open** 9am-5.30pm Mon-Fri; 9am-3pm Sat; 10am-2pm Sun.
You won't find any parking here, but you will find tons of free maps, brochures, coupons and advice. For a 24-hour recorded message listing daily events and activities, call 391 2001. Save yourself the trip and write to them in advance for free information about hotels, restaurants and shopping; send a postcard with your address to PO Box 429097, San Francisco, CA 94102, USA.

San Francisco Convention and Visitors Bureau

Suite 900, 201 Third Street, at Howard Street (974 6900). BART Montgomery/Muni Metro J, K, L, M, N/ 12, 30, 45, 76 bus. **Open** 8.30am-5pm Mon-Fri.
Free information on life's essentials: hotels, restaurants and shopping.

Street smart

Not unlike New York, San Francisco has its own pet names for its districts that are bound to confuse newcomers. For example, SoMa means the district South of Market Street. If someone says they live in the Avenues, they're talking about the 48 numerically-ordered streets (for example, 32nd Avenue, 33rd Avenue) that run north-south through the Sunset and Richmond districts on the west side of the city. The Streets, however, are on the opposite side of the city, starting with First Street at SoMa and fanning out through the Mission and Protrero districts. The moral here is 'Don't get the Streets mixed up with the Avenues', or you'll have wasted an hour travelling in exactly the wrong direction.

East Bay

Oakland Convention and Visitors Bureau

Suite 3214, 550 Tenth Street, at Broadway, Oakland (1-510 839 9000). **Open** 8.30am-5pm Mon-Fri.
The centre is aimed at convention-goers but also at tourists. Museums, historical attractions and local events are listed in a free guide.

East Bay Regional Parks District

2950 Peralta Oaks Court, at 106th Street, Oakland (1-510 562 2267). **Open** 8.30am-5pm Mon-Fri.
Maps and information on the 46 parks and 13 trails in the Oakland hills.

Marin County

Marin County Convention and Visitors Bureau

Avenue of the Flags, at Civic Centre Drive, San Rafael (472 7470). **Open** 9am-5pm Mon-Fri.
Covering Muir Woods and Mount Tamalpais State Park, Sausalito, Tiburon and Angel Island.

South Bay

Convention and Visitors Bureau of Santa Clara

1850 Warburton Avenue, at Scott Street, Santa Clara (1-408 296 7111). **Open** 8am-5pm Mon-Fri.

San Jose Convention and Visitors Bureau

150 West San Carlos Street, between Almaden Avenue and Market Street, San Jose (1-408 283 8833). **Open** 8am-5.30pm Mon-Fri; 11am-5pm Sat, Sun.

San Mateo County Convention and Visitors Bureau

Suite 410, 111 Anza Boulevard, Burlingame (348 7600). **Open** 8.30am-5pm Mon-Fri.

Visas

Under the Visa Waiver Scheme, citizens of Japan, the UK and all West European countries (except Ireland, Portugal, Greece and the Vatican City) do not need a visa for stays of less than 90 days for business or pleasure, as long as they have a passport that is valid for the full 90-day period, a visa waiver form (provided by your travel agency, during check-in, or while on the flight), and a return or onward journey ticket (an open standby ticket is acceptable).

Some restrictions, such as for those who have previously been turned down for a visa or have infectious diseases, may apply. For British citizens, the US Embassy in London provides a reasonably comprehensive recorded message for all general visa enquiries (0898 200290).

Canadians and Mexicans do not need visas, but they may be asked for proof of their Canadian or Mexican citizenship. Travellers from American Samoa, Guam, Puerto Rico and the US Virgin Islands are US citizens and do not require visas.

All other travellers, including those from Australia and New Zealand, must have visas. Full information and visa application forms can be obtained from your nearest US embassy or consulate. In general, apply at least three of four weeks before you plan to travel. Visas required urgently should be applied for via the travel agent booking your ticket.

If you're visiting on business or pleasure no inoculations are necessary.

San Francisco on-line

A selection of world wide web sites that relate to San Francisco and the Bay Area. For more on multimedia, *see chapter* **Media**.

Bay Area Backcountry
http://www.sj-coop.net/~mlh/bab.html
Places to hike and camp in the San Francisco Bay Area.

Bay Area Transit Information
http://server.berkeley.edu/Transit/index.html
Instant on-line access to transit information.

Buzznet
http://www.hooked.net/buzznet/index.html
Counterblasts from the SF counter-culture.

C-net
http://www.cnet.com
Indispensable multimedia source.

Cinema Guide
http://www.movietimes.com
Bay Area movie times, with film clips, previews, photos.

City Culture
http://www.cityculture.com
City arts magazine.

Claremont Hotel
http://www.claremnt.com/
Hotel and spa, 20 minutes by car from San Francisco.

Clarion Hotel
http://www.goldpage.com/travel/californ/clarion
At San Francisco Airport.

Classified Flea Market
http://www.cfm.com/cfm/
Published on Wednesdays, covering the Bay Area.

Concerts in the San Francisco Bay Area
http://www.usfca.edu/usf/neufeld/concerts.html
What's on at which Bay Area venue.

de Young Museum
http://www.island.com/famsf/famsf_deyoung.html
The Fine Arts Museums in Golden Gate Park.

Digital Lantern on San Francisco
http://www.sf.net/lantern/
Locate and review every San Francisco restaurant.

Escape Artist Tours Inc
http://www.best.com/~travel/sf-escapes/
Tours of the city, Napa Valley, Lake Tahoe and surrounding Bay Area.

Hostels in America
http://www.ushostel.com/hostels/hostels.htm InterClub
Hostels in San Francisco, Los Angeles and elsewhere.

Hotel Bedford
http://www.cdiguide.com/cdi/415/hotels/bedford.html
Hotel near Union Square.

Hotwired
http://www.hotwired.com/
The essential multimedia source.

Mexican Museum
http://www.folkart.com/~latitude/museums/m_mexsf.html
Art and cultural institution in the Fort Mason Center.

Museum of the City of San Francisco
http://www.slip.net/~dfowler/1906/museum.html
A scrapbook of San Francisco's past.

Pacific Bay Inn
http://www.ernestallen.com/tr/ca/PacificBayInn/
A weekly-rate hotel in downtown San Francisco.

Q San Francisco
http://www.qsanfrancisco.com/
Gay and lesbian magazine.

The Randall Museum
http://www.wco.com/~dale/randall.html
A must for kids.

Rock & Roll Digital Gallery
http://www.hooked.net/julianne/index.html
San Francisco rock concert posters from the 1960s.

San Francisco Ballet
http://www-leland.stanford.edu/~rbeal/sfb.html
Forthcoming productions and ticket information.

San Francisco Bay Area Ski Connection
http://www.jaws.com/baski/home.html
On-line guide to skiing in Northern California.

San Francisco Bicycle Coalition
http://reality.sgi.com/employees/jonim_csd/SFBC.home/sfbc.home.html
Bicycling in SF, discussions and membership details.

SF Gate
http://www.sfgate.com
The combined San Francisco Chronicle and Examiner, including Herb Caen's essential daily column.

San Francisco Exploratorium
http://www.exploratorium.edu/
An unmissable site from the hands-on science museum.

San Francisco 49ers
http://www.yahoo.com/Recreation/Sports/Football__American_/NFL/Teams/San_Francisco_49ers/
Strictly for fans.

San Francisco 49ers Tickets and Packages
http://www.best.com/~travel/sf-49ers/
Packages or game tickets for home games.

San Francisco Giants
http://www.yahoo.com/Recreation/Sports/Baseball/Major_League_Baseball/Teams/San_Francisco_Giants/
The virtual dugout.

San Francisco Hotel Reservations
http://www.hotelres.com
Make your hotel reservations on-line.

San Francisco Symphony
http://www.hooked.net/sfsymphony/sfshome.html
Forthcoming performances.

South San Francisco
http://tcomeng.com/cities/ssf/index.html
City of South San Francisco Police Department site.

Stacey's Professional Bookstores
http://www.staceys.com
The area's largest technical and professional book source.

Theater Bay Area
http://artdirect.com/tba
Play listings, news about half-price tickets, and excerpts from Callboard, the SF theatre magazine.

Thierry's Travelogue
http://www.belgasoft.com/travel.html
Travel information; links to airline and railway sites .

Time Out
http://www.timeout.co.uk
What's on in San Francisco and other world cities.

The Well
http://www.well.com
Short for Whole Earth 'Lectronic Link; long on resources. Considered the birthplace of the virtual community.

Whaler's Inn
http://www.ernestallen.com/tr/ca/whaler'sinn/
A quiet seaside resort between LA and San Francisco.

Wilderness Wanderings
http://www.coastside.net/WhistlerE/wildwan.html
Northern Sierra and Bay Area backpacking trips.

Getting Around

With its grid streetplan, efficient public transport network – and this guide – you'll have no problem exploring the streets of San Francisco.

*Easy riders can get on the road at the **American Scooter and Cycle** shop. See page 15.*

In a nation where the car is king and trains are those things you wait for at railroad crossings, San Francisco is something of an anomaly: it is one of the few cities in the United States where having a car isn't a necessity. In fact, it's more of a hindrance, which is why most locals leave their cars parked for weeks at a time and commute on foot, by taxi or via the city's much maligned yet indisputably reliable public transport system – the San Francisco Municipal Railway, or MUNI.

The best plan for finding your way around the city's transport network is to purchase a MUNI map (available at most bookshops and drugstores, or free from the Visitor's Information Center at Powell and Market Streets). Next to hoofing it, buses are the cheapest and easiest way to get around. The famous cable cars, which ramble along at about a mile every 10 minutes, are mostly for entertainment, and taxis never seem to be around when you need one. Cycling around San Francisco is an option but, be warned, you need superhuman legs to cope with all the steep hills.

To & From the Airports

San Francisco International Airport

For more information about how to get to and from San Francisco Airport, phone 1-800 736 2008.

By Bus

There are three main options for getting to and from the airport. The cheapest method (and least convenient) is by SamTrans **7F** and **7B** buses, which run every 30 minutes between 5.45am and 1.15am from the airport's upper level to the Transbay Terminal at First and Mission Streets. Bus 7B costs $1, takes 35 minutes and has no luggage restrictions. Bus 7F costs $2 and takes 30 minutes, but you're restricted to only one small carry-on bag. Phone 1-800 660 4287 for more information.

There are also two slightly more complicated but cheap routes. From outside the North and South terminals catch a **3X** or **3B** bus to Daly City Station (85¢-$1) and then take a BART train to downtown San Francisco. Or take the free **CalTrain** shuttle from the North and South terminals to Millbrae Station and then a 24-minute train ride ($1.75) to the CalTrain Depot on Fourth and Townsend Streets in the Mission district (not recommended alone at night).

By Shuttle

A definite step up from bussing it is travelling by shuttle. Rates range from $10 to $15 per person and many offer door-to-door service, such as **Lorrie's Airport Service** (334 9000), **SuperShuttle** (558 8500), **Bay Shuttle** (564 3400), **American Airporter Shuttle** (546 6689), **Quake City Airport Shuttle** (255 4899) and **SFO Airporter** (major hotel service only; 495 8404). Most shuttles depart every five to ten minutes from the upper level of the airport terminal at specially marked kerbs – simply walk to the upper level and wait. For the return journey to the airport, book the shuttle at least 24 hours in advance. The shuttles don't run throughout the night so if your plane arrives in the small hours, you might be faced with an expensive taxi ride.

By Taxi or Limousine

The most expensive – but most convenient – option for getting into town may be your only recourse if your plane lands in the wee small hours of the night. Expect to pay about $30-$35 plus tip for the 14-mile trip to the city, and be sure to haggle for a flat rate. Taxis are found at the lower level of the terminal in an area marked with yellow columns. For limousine service, use the toll-free white courtesy phones in the terminal or phone **Limousine 2000** on 877 0333.

Oakland International Airport

Getting to San Francisco from Oakland International is simple. Take the Air-BART shuttle ($2) from the airport terminal (they run every 10 minutes from the central island outside terminals 1 and 2) to the Coliseum/ Oakland BART station, and then catch the next BART train to San Francisco; for schedule information phone 992 2278. Other options include a shared-ride shuttle service via Bayporter Express (phone 467 1800 for a reservation) or a very expensive taxi or limo ride.

Major International Airlines

For more airlines, consult the Yellow Pages.

American Airlines *(1-800 433 7300).*
British Airways *(1-800 247 9297).*
Continental Airlines *(397 8818).*
Delta Air Lines *(1-800 221 1212).*
Northwest Airlines *(domestic 1-800 225 2525; international 1-800 447 4747).*
Trans World Airlines (TWA) *(domestic 864 5731; international 441 1805).*
USAir *(1-800 428 4322).*
United Airlines *(1-800 241 6522).*
Virgin Atlantic *(1-800 862 8621).*

Public Transport

Information

For information on MUNI's schedules, passes, and fares, phone **673 6864** (and expect to be put on hold), or seek out one of the numerous glass-enclosed bus shelters throughout the city, which will have everything you could ever want to know about the MUNI system posted up inside. Much handier is having your own MUNI map. More esoteric transportation questions can be answered at the Visitor's Information Center (*see chapter* **Essential Information**).

Buses

San Francisco's number one mode of public transport is MUNI's homely fleet of orange and white buses. Spewing smog or sparks as they make their perpetually off-schedule rounds, at least they are relatively cheap and can get you within a block of just about anywhere you might want to go.

Fares

Fares are $1 for adults (18-65yrs), 35¢ for kids, and travel is free for children under five. Exact change is required, and paper money is accepted. Place your change or bills in the automatic toll-taker, and ask the driver for a free transfer, which is valid for two changes of vehicle in any direction within two hours.

Bus Stops

These are marked by one or more of the following: a large white rectangle painted on the street with a red kerb; a yellow marking on a telephone or light pole; a glass-walled bus shelter; a brown and orange sign listing the bus or buses that serve that route. Route numbers are posted on the front and rear of the bus (so you know which one you've just missed). On busy lines buses run every 5-10 mins during peak hours. Between 1am and 5pm a skeleton crew called the Owl Service offers just nine lines that run every 30 minutes.

Travel Passes

If you plan to use MUNI often, buy a one-day ($6), three-day ($10), or seven-day ($15) 'passport', which is valid on all MUNI vehicles, including the pricey cable cars. One-day passports can be purchased from cable car conductors; and three- or seven-day passports are available at the Visitor's Information Center, Maritime Market (3098 Polk Street, at Bay Street); MUNI headquarters (949 Presidio Avenue, at Geary Boulevard); the MUNI ticket booth/police kiosk at Powell and Market Streets; the MUNI ticket booth at Hyde and Beach Streets, and the Bay Area TIX booth at Union Square. A MUNI passport also entitles you to discounts at 26 of the city's major attractions. For more information or locations of passport vendors, phone 673 6864.

Outside San Francisco

Bus services operating outside the city include:
AC Transit (1-800 559 4636). Alameda and Contra Costa counties and transbay service between those counties and San Francisco.
Golden Gate Transit (332 6600). Marin and Sonoma counties from Sausalito to Santa Rosa.
Greyhound Bus Line (1-800 231 2222). Long-distance bus routes throughout the US.
SamTrans (1-800 660 4287). San Mateo county with a service to downtown San Francisco and the Hayward BART station.

MUNI Metro Streetcar

A cross between an electric bus and a cable car is the MUNI Metro streetcar (tram). Surprisingly rarely used by tourists, the five lines (J, K, L, M, N and the new 'historic streetcar' line F) run underneath the downtown area and above ground in the outer neighbourhoods. They make the same stops as BART (*see p13*) along Market Street, but past the Civic Center the routes branch off in different directions toward outlying districts such as the Mission, Castro and Sunset. Fares are the same as on the buses, and the same passports apply. For

schedule information phone 673 6864. Lines run between roughly 6am and midnight.

Cable Cars

Brought back to life in 1984 at a cost of more than $60 million, San Francisco's beloved cable cars are without question the most enjoyable ride in town, as the lengthy queues at the cable car turnarounds will attest. There are 44 cable cars in all, with 27 used at peak times, travelling a steady 9.5mph on three lines: California, Powell-Mason and Powell-Hyde. (The Powell-Hyde line has the most thrills, the best scenery and, consequently, the most tourists). All lines run from 6.30am to 12.30am. If you don't have a MUNI pass, buy a $2 non-transferable one-way ticket from the conductor as you board the car (children under five go free). Cable car stops are marked by pole-mounted signs displaying the cable car symbol; their routes are marked on all MUNI bus maps. Hold on tightly, or you're more than likely to get thrown about as the car lurches around a corner and down a precipitous hill.

Bay Area Rapid Transit (BART)

Looking more like a ride at Disneyland than a form of public transport, BART is a $5-billion network of four interconnected high-speed rail lines that serve San Francisco, Daly City and East Bay counties. It's one of the most modern, automated and efficient public transport systems in the world, run by computers at the Lake Merritt BART station in Oakland. Almost everything – trains, ticket dispensers, entry and exit gates, announcements – is automated. Passengers feed money into a vending machine, which dispenses a re-usable ticket encoded with the dollar amount entered. When you reach your destination, the cost of the ride (measured by the distance travelled) is automatically deducted from the ticket as you pass through the exit gate, so don't forget to **save your ticket**! Any remaining value on the ticket can be used toward the next trip.

Though BART is of little use for getting around the city – it only stops at five locations within San Francisco – it's a great way for tourists to get an inexpensive tour of the Bay Area, as much of the rail is elevated above the streets. Special excursion-ride tickets allow passengers to ride all the lines for up to three hours, but they must enter and exit from the same station, and travelling during peak hours (7am-9am and 4pm-6pm weekdays) isn't recommended. BART stations close at around midnight and open at 4am on weekdays, 6am on Saturday and 8am on Sunday. Fares range from 90¢ to $3.45. In downtown San Francisco, four boarding stations are located along Market Street; look out for the blue and white 'ba' signs and the escalators leading down into the station. You can take bicycles on BART, though not during the rush hour and you need a pass to take them on board ($3). For more information, phone 992 2278 (1-510 839 2220 for the hearing-impaired).

Ferries

The completion of the Golden Gate Bridge in 1937 marked the end of the ferry route between San Francisco and Marin – until 1970, when the ferry service resumed to take a load off commuter traffic. Used mainly by 'suits' during the peak commuting hours, the ferries double as wonderful and inexpensive excursions across the Bay and into Sausalito – the ferry docks just steps away from the town's shopping district – or Larkspur, where a footbridge leads you to a popular shopping mall and brewpub.

Ferries run daily from around 7am to 8pm, departing from the south side of the San Francisco Ferry Building at the foot of Market Street on the Embarcadero. One-way fares range from $2.50 to $4.25, depending on your destination (a real bargain compared to the packaged Bay sightseeing trips). For more information, phone the **Golden Gate Transit Ferry Service** (332 6600). The **Red & White Fleet** (705 5444) serves Alcatraz, Angel Island, Alameda, Oakland, Sausalito, Tiburon, and Vallejo; at the time of writing the company had just changed hands, and so may change its name.

Taxis & Limousines

San Francisco is so compact that taxi drivers rarely see their meters hit the $10 mark. Average fares are in the $5-$7 range, with a base fee of $1.70 and $1.50 for each additional mile thereafter. Taxis can be hailed from the street in the downtown area, and most drivers don't seem bothered by a short hop (in fact, the majority of drivers are an altogether more friendly, helpful and articulate bunch than their New York counterparts). On weekend nights it's almost mandatory to call for a cab in

Alternative Transport

So, you've got a handful of dusty dollars, a sackful of Grateful Dead tapes and you're ready for the open road: now's the time to ride the legendary Green Tortoise. Sing, sleep and meditate on an old green bus as it takes you from San Francisco to Los Angeles, New York or even Guatemala. Fares are dirt cheap, but you really have to be a people person to enjoy yourself. Unbelievably, no smoking (of anything) or alcohol is allowed on the bus. Call 1-800 867 8647 or 956 7500 for additional routes and information.

advance. Companies include: **Luxor Cab** (282 4141); **Veteran's Cab** (552 1300); **Yellow Cab** (626 2345); **National Cab** (648 4444); **De Soto Cab** (673 1414), and **City Cab** (468 7200).

Limousine services include **Robertson's** (775 6024); **Pure Luxury** (485 1764), and **Silver Cloud** (1-800 640 3851), which offers an eight-hour Wine Country special for up to six people for $375.

Driving

Renting a car to explore San Francisco is crazy. There's no place to park (and parking garages charge up to $12 per hour), locals honk and curse at you for slowing them down, the steep hills fry your nerves, and you're more than likely to get a parking ticket, the city's favourite source of revenue. The only reason for renting a car is to explore the Bay Area and beyond; otherwise, forget it.

If you must drive in the city, there are a few things you should know. Unless otherwise posted, the speed limit within the city is 25mph (which every local ignores) and Californian law requires that all occupants wear their seatbelts. Cable cars always have the right of way, and should be given a wide berth. When parking in residential neighbourhoods, do not block driveways even slightly, or you'll get fined and towed away. When parking on hills, you must set the hand brake and 'kerb' your front wheels (towards the kerb when facing downhill, away from the kerb when facing uphill) – or you'll get another hefty ticket. Parking meters accept quarters only, so make sure you have plenty in your pocket.

The general rule with parking spaces in San Francisco is that if they look too good to be true, they probably are. Immediately after parking, read the sign on the meter, then read all the signs on your side of the block. One missed sign could lead to a towed car, in which case you'll have to take a taxi to the nearest police station to pay the fine ($100 plus the parking ticket), then take another taxi to the tow garage and pay more money for storage fees. Welcome to San Francisco for drivers.

A white kerb indicates a drop-off zone for passengers with a five-minute maximum, but is usually only in effect when the business it fronts is in operation. A green kerb signifies parking for 10 minutes only, yellow kerbs are for loading and unloading commercial vehicles and blue kerbs are reserved for drivers or passengers with disabilities. (It's usually legal to park in yellow zones after 6pm and on weekends.) Parking – or even waiting – in red zones, particularly bus zones and in front of fire hydrants, is an absolute no-no, and makes metermaids salivate with the thought of writing a $250 ticket. For long-term parking, car parks are usually your only recourse in the downtown area, particularly if you're going to be away from your

Hop on the **SuperShuttle** *for a hassle-free trip into town. See page 11.*

car for more than an hour. For a list of city car parks, *see chapter* **Survival**.

Should you venture outside San Francisco across the Golden Gate or Bay Bridges, make sure you have cash for the toll fee on the return trip ($3 Golden Gate, $1 Bay), and take a map.

Car Rental

When renting a car, you will need a credit card and a driver's licence. There are dozens of car rental companies within the city and at San Francisco International Airport, and it definitely pays to shop around. Before you rent, find out if your own auto insurance or credit card company covers you; otherwise, you might have to pay an additional surcharge. Most car rental companies have minimum and maximum age requirements.

Rental Companies
National companies usually offer the best deals and service. These include **Alamo** (1-800 327 9633); **Hertz** (1-800 654 3131); **Dollar** (1-800 800 4000); **Budget** (1-800 527 0700); **Thrifty** (1-800 367 2277); **Avis** (1-800 831 2847); **Enterprise** (1-800 325 8007); and **Rent-A-Wreck** (851 2627). Local car rental companies include **Ace** (771 7711); **Bay Area Rental** (621 8989); and **A-One** (771 3977).

By Bicycle

There are bike lanes in certain parts of the city and the Bay Area and two marked scenic cycle routes; one from Golden Gate Park south to Lake Merced, the other from the southern end of Golden Gate Bridge north to Marin County. Bicycles can be

hired for around $25 per day or $125 per week. Rental companies include **Park Cyclery** (221 3777) and **Waller's Sports** (752 8383) on the edge of Golden Gate Park; **Karim's Cyclery** in Berkeley (1-510 841 2181); and **Wheel Escapes** in Sausalito (332 0218). *See also chapter* **Sport & Fitness**.

By Motorcycle

What better way to see San Francisco than on a big fat hog? **Dubbelju Motorcycle Rentals** can set you up with a Harley or BMW of your choice, as long as you have a valid driver's licence, cash or credit card deposit and $90 burning a hole in your pocket. The company is open 9am to 1pm, Monday to Saturday (495 2774). **American Scooter and Cycle** (931 0234) is a bit more expensive but also rents out scooters from $45 per day; it's open 9am to 10pm daily.

On Foot

Walking the streets of San Francisco is one of the most enjoyable and entertaining things do to in the world. However, there are some inherent risks involved. For example, San Francisco drivers tend to separate pedestrians between the quick and the dead. And watch out for the electric-powered buses – you can't hear them coming. Also, when walking though the Financial District, look for the pedestrian signal to cross the street, not a green stop light; the two are timed differently.

Accommodation

Whether you're hip or drab, poor or stinking rich, you'll find a hotel that caters for your needs here.

As one of the most popular tourist destinations in the world, San Francisco bends over backwards to make sure it has a room for visitors of every ilk and tax bracket: at the last count there were some 50,000 rooms in 176 different hotels. Competition between hotels is, as you would imagine, fierce, which helps bring down the price and bring up the quality and choice. In fact, many hoteliers have shunned the general market in search of a more specific clientele, such as gay and lesbian, alternative lifestylers, travellers with pets and even teddy bear *aficionados*.

For basic accommodation – double bed, private bathroom, phone and TV – within the city, expect to pay from $70 to $100 a night during the peak season (May to October). This doesn't include a 12 per cent room tax, telephone surcharges and nightly parking fees of around $15. Of course, you can always find a bed for as little as $14 and as

much as $1,400, but for the average visitor the bulk of their budget will be handed over the front desk. Haggling for a better price isn't unheard of, but don't expect much success – if it's a cheap holiday you want, go to Las Vegas.

If you would rather hand over the lodging decision to a reservation service, there are a number of reputable companies that will do the work for you, the best being **San Francisco Reservations** (1-800 667 1550). At no cost to you, they'll find a hotel, motel or bed and breakfast in your price range, and even negotiate for a discounted rate.

When making a hotel reservation, have your credit card handy, and, although this isn't the norm, be prepared to pay for at least one night in advance. Reservations are held until about 6pm, unless you've told the hotel you'll be arriving late; otherwise, you may lose your room. Cash, credit cards and travellers cheques are the preferred methods of payment, but most hotels will ask for an imprint of your credit card upon arrival for 'incidental expenses' and to prevent walk-outs. Service from the staff at most moderate to expensive hotels in San Francisco is usually superb, but don't think for a minute that they're doing it purely out of the kindness of their hearts, so tip accordingly.

All 1-800 numbers can be called free of charge from within the US. However some hotels add a

*The terminally hip **Hotel Triton**. See page 24.*

Pick of the Best

Architecture **Sheraton Palace**
Art Deco digs **Commodore International**
Bed & Breakfast **The Bed & Breakfast Inn**
Big bucks **Sherman House**
Budget **The San Remo**
Budget family **Holiday Lodge**
Business best **Nob Hill Lambourne**
Haight experience **The Red Victorian**
Location **Hotel Bohème**
Party spot **The Phoenix**
Romantic opulence **The Archbishop's Mansion**
Luxurious lobby **Ritz-Carlton**
Star gazing **Hotel Monaco**
View **The Mardarin Oriental**

*Beaux Arts luxury at the newly revamped **Ritz-Carlton**. See page 20.*

surcharge for use of their phones, whatever number you phone.

For a list of gay and lesbian hotels in the city, *see chapter* **Gay & Lesbian San Francisco**.

Top Dollar

Campton Place Hotel

340 Stockton Street, CA 94108, at Post Street (781 5555/1-800 235 4300/fax 955 5536). Bus 2, 3, 4/Powell-Hyde, Powell-Mason cable car. **Rates** *single* from $160; *double* from $220; *one- and two-bedroom suites* $395-$570; *one- and two-bedroom penthouse suites* $680-$850. **Credit** AmEx, DC, MC, V.

After a hefty $18 million retro-fit in 1981, the former Drake-Wiltshire Hotel re-opened as the Campton Place and has attracted a very discreet (and wealthy) following ever since. A nifty use of mirrors in the lobby and the 117 rooms helps to disguise the hotel's surprisingly small size, although some guests may still wonder what their money is paying for. The services, however, are exceptional, and include valet-assisted packing and unpacking, French laundry service, immediate and overnight shoeshine and 24-hour room, concierge, maid and valet service. Two additional enticements are its central location (on the corner of Union Square) and its highly-rated restaurant.

Hotel services *Air-conditioning. Babysitting. Bar. Car park. Conference facilities. Currency exchange. Disabled: access; rooms for disabled. Fax. Laundry. Lifts. Multilingual staff. No-smoking rooms. Restaurant.*
Room services *Hair dryer. Mini-bar. Radio. Refrigerator. Room service. Safe. Telephone. TV. VCR.*

The Mandarin Oriental

222 Sansome Street, CA 94104, between Pine and California Streets (885 0999/1-800 622 0404/fax 986 5667). Muni Metro J, K, L, M, N/30X, 42 bus. **Rates** *rooms* from $275-$395; *suites* from $595-$1,295. **Credit** AmEx, DC, JCB, MC, V.

Few hotels in the world can boast such an extraordinary view as the Mandarin Oriental. Its lobby is on the ground floor of the 48-storey First Interstate Building and all its 158 rooms and suites are on the top 11 floors. The view is phenomenal, particularly when the fog settles below you – it's like being in heaven. In keeping with the Asian-style décor, the rooms contain a sparse selection of blond-wood furnishings and Asian artwork, and rumour has it that the staff-to-guest ratio is 1:1. Adjoining the lobby is the hotel's renowned restaurant, Silks, considered one of the best in the country.

Hotel services *Air-conditioning. Babysitting. Bar. Car park. Conference facilities. Currency exchange. Disabled: access; rooms for disabled. Fax. Laundry. Lifts. Multilingual staff. No-smoking rooms. Restaurant. Safe.*
Room services *Hair dryer. Mini-bar. Radio. Refrigerator. Room service. Telephone. TV. VCR in suites. Video library.*

The Pan Pacific

500 Post Street, CA 94102, at Mason Street (771 8600/1-800 327 8585/fax 398 0267). Bus, 2, 3, 4/Powell-Hyde, Powell-Mason cable car. **Rates** *single* $205-$305; *double* $225-$325; *suites* $350-$1,700. **Credit** AmEx, DC, JCB, MC, V.

Rarely does a hotel get everything right. The Pan Pacific, however, hits the bull's-eye. Rooms? Immaculate. Service? Outstanding. Cuisine? Superb. Architecture? Breathtaking. Guests are supplied with lavish marble bathrooms, personal valet service and a complimentary chauffeur service. Even if you're not staying here, the 330-room hotel is worth visiting just to ride in one of the glimmering glass elevators inside the 17-storey, atrium lobby. Located one block from Union Square, the Pan Pacific is certainly among the finest hotels in San Francisco.

Hotel services *Air-conditioning. Babysitting. Bar. Conference facilities. Currency exchange. Disabled: access; rooms for disabled. Fax. Gym. Laundry. Lifts. Multi-*

lingual staff. No-smoking rooms. Personal valet service. Restaurant.
Room services *Hair dryer. Mini-bar. Radio. Refrigerator. Room service. Safe. Telephone. TV. VCR.*

The Ritz-Carlton

600 Stockton Street, CA 94108, at California Street (296 7465/1-800 241 3333/fax 986 1268). Powell-Hyde, Powell-Mason cable car. **Rates** *rooms from $240-$650; suites from $3,000.* **Credit** AmEx, DC, JCB, MC, V.

There are several fine hotels at the top of Nob Hill – such as the Huntington, the Fairmont and the Mark Hopkins – but it's this newcomer that's getting all the attention, and deservedly so. After a four-year, multi-million dollar renovation, the 336 room Ritz-Carlton opened its doors in 1991 and has continued to wow its guests ever since. Amenities include an indoor spa with swimming pool and sauna; a fully-equipped training room; the excellent Dining Room restaurant; daily piano performances in the Lobby Lounge, and an armada of valets and ushers to assist your every need. The rooms are a bit of a let-down after the fancy façade and lobby, but are quite comfortable and come with all the luxury items you would expect from the Ritz.

Hotel services *Air-conditioning. Babysitting. Bar. Car park. Conference facilities. Disabled: access; rooms for disabled. Fax. Indoor swimming pool and fitness facilities. Laundry. Lifts. Multi-lingual staff. No-smoking rooms. Restaurant.*
Room services *Hair dryer. Mini-bar. Radio. Refrigerator. Room service. Safe. Telephone. TV. VCR in suites.*

Sherman House

2160 Green Street, CA 94123, between Webster & Fillmore Streets (563 3600/1-800 424 5777/fax 563 1882). Bus 12, 22, 24. **Rates** *rooms from $190-$375; suites $575-$825.* **Credit** AmEx, DC, MC, V.

This stately, four-storey, Victorian mansion had its ups and downs over the years until the present owners dumped a small fortune into a four-year restoration project. Now its 14 rooms – each furnished in Jacobean, German Biedermeier or French Second Empire style with fireplaces, tapestries and brocaded bed hangings – are good enough for the likes of Shirley MacLaine, Ted Kennedy and Bill Cosby, which means if you have an equally fat bank account you too can afford to stay here.

Hotel services *Babysitting. Car park. Disabled: access; rooms for disabled. Fax. Laundry. Multi-lingual staff. No-smoking rooms. Restaurant. Safe.*
Room services *Hair dryer. Radio. Refrigerator in suites. Room service. Telephone. TV. VCR on request.*

Still Sumptuous

Hotel Milano

55 Fifth Street, CA 94103, at Mission Street (543 8555/1-800 398 7555/fax 543 5843). BART Powell Street/Muni Metro J, K, L, M, N. **Rates** *queen bed $120; king bed or two queen beds $140; deluxe king bed with queen sofa bed and jet tub $160.* **Credit** AmEx, DC, JCB, MC, V.

Since it opened in 1994, the Milano has been applauded for its contemporary design and simple-yet-tasteful rooms. Strategically located near the ever-bustling San Francisco Shopping Centre, the new Museum of Modern Art and Yerba Buena Gardens, the Milano initially targeted the film and TV industry, enticing guests from Hollywood with its specialised production facilities and private screening room. But its 108 rooms also feature everything a business executive could want – even a Nintendo game system.

Hotel services *Air-conditioning. Babysitting on request. Bar. Car park. Conference facilities. Disabled: access;*

Shirley MacLaine's favourite: **Sherman House.**

rooms for disabled. Fax. Laundry. Lifts. Multi-lingual staff. No-smoking rooms. Sports/fitness facilities. Restaurant.
Room services *Fax/modem hook ups. Hair dryer on request. Mini-bar. Radio. Refrigerator. Room service. Safe. Telephone. TV and in-house movies. VCR on request.*

The Prescott

545 Post Street, CA 94102, at Taylor Street (563 0303/1-800 283 7322/fax 563 6831). Bus 2, 3, 4/Powell-Hyde, Powell-Mason cable car. **Rates** *rooms from $165-$195; suites from $215-$245.* **Credit** AmEx, DC, JCB, MC, V.
There was a time when guests would check into the Prescott solely to get preferential seating at the adjoining Postrio Restaurant (*see chapter* **Restaurants**). While the Postrio has lost some of its divine status (although it's still pretty popular), the Prescott remains one of San Francisco's finer small hotels. The 154 rooms, 11 suites and the penthouse – a lavish affair complete with roof-top jacuzzi, grand piano and twin fireplaces – are decorated with custom-made cherry-wood furnishings, silk wallpaper and wonderfully cushy beds. Highly recommended is the Club Level, a private floor where the deal includes free drinks, hors-d'oeuvres, continental breakfast and a host of other amenities. The Prescott is well located, too, with Union Square a short walk away.
Hotel services *Air-conditioning. Babysitting on request. Bar. Car park. Conference facilities. Disabled: access; rooms for disabled. Fax. Laundry. Lifts. Multi-lingual staff. No-smoking rooms. Restaurant. Safe.*
Room services *Hair dryer. Mini-bar. Radio. Refrigerator. Room service. Telephone. TV. VCR in suites.*

Savoy Hotel

580 Geary Street, CA 94102, between Jones and Post Streets (441 2700/1-800 227 4223/fax 441 2700). Bus 38/Powell-Hyde, Powell-Mason cable car. **Rates** *rooms from $105-$200.* **Credit** AmEx, DC, JCB, MC, V.
Imported French furnishings, billowy feather beds and continental breakfast served in the brasserie add to the European sophistication of this hotel. The 83-room Savoy, built in 1913 for the Panama-Pacific Exposition and resurrected in a profusion of black marble and mahogany, is centrally located in the centre of the Theater District, a few blocks from Union Square, but near enough to the sleazy Tenderloin to keep its prices low. Well worth considering if you're looking for a moderately-priced hotel.
Hotel services *Babysitting on request. Bar. Conference facilities. Disabled: access; rooms for disabled. Fax. Laundry. Lifts. No-smoking rooms. Restaurant. Safe. Valet car park.*
Room services *Hair dryer. Limited room service. Mini-bar. Telephone. TV.*

Tuscan Inn

425 Northpoint Street, CA 94133, at Mason Street (561 1100/1-800 648 4626/fax 561 1199). Bus 32, 39/Powell-Mason cable car. **Rates** *rooms from $138-$178; suites from $198-$218.* **Credit** AmEx, DC, JCB, MC, V.
This may be part of the Best Western motel chain but it's still a classy hotel. It's hard to find fault with the 220-room Tuscan Inn, located in the bowels of Fisherman's Wharf: the rooms are handsome, spacious and comfortable; the staff are exceedingly helpful and the adjoining Café Pescatore – a gleaming Italian trattoria – is as good as it looks for breakfast, lunch or dinner. If you tire of the touristy Wharf, escape is on hand: the Inn is a block away from the cable car turnaround.
Hotel services *Air-conditioning. Babysitting. Bar. Car park. Conference facilities. Disabled: access; rooms for disabled. Fax. Laundry. Lifts. Multi-lingual staff. No-smoking rooms. Restaurant. Safe.*
Room services *Hair dryer. Mini-bar. Radio. Refrigerator. Room service. Telephone. TV. VCR.*

The Chain Gang

Grand Hyatt

345 Stockton Street, CA 94108, between Bush and Sutter Streets (398 1234/1-800 233 1234/fax 392 2536). Bus 45/Powell-Hyde, Powell-Mason cable car. **Rates** *single from $215-$250; double from $240-$275; suites from $350-$850.* **Credit** AmEx, DC, JCB, MC, V.
The 693-room Grand Hyatt offers just about everything the business or pleasure traveller would expect from a four-star hotel – and then some. Its location – at the north-east corner of Union Square – couldn't be better, and the view from most of the 36 floors is spectacular (especially from the roof-top jazz club). Additional perks include use of the spacious health club, a car service to the Financial district, a fully-equipped business centre and surprisingly good (and reasonably-priced) food at the handsome Plaza Restaurant.
Hotel services *Air-conditioning. Babysitting. Bar. Conference facilities. Currency exchange. Disabled: access; rooms for disabled. Fax. Laundry. Lifts. Multi-lingual staff. No-smoking rooms. Fitness centre. Restaurant. Safe. Valet car park.*
Room services *Hair dryer. Mini-bar. Radio. Refrigerator. Room service. Telephone. TV. VCR.*

Marriott Hotel

55 Fourth Street, CA 94103, between Market and Mission Streets (896 1600/fax 777 2799). BART Powell Street/Muni Metro J, K, L, M, N. **Rates** *single from $169-$185; double from $189-$205.* **Credit** AmEx, DC, JCB, MC, V.
Completed in 1989, when it created a storm of controversy over its design (critics likened it to a giant jukebox or parking meter), the 39-storey Marriott is, for better or worse, undoubtedly striking, with its numerous arches of tinted glass and steel (one almost expects to see Batman astride the roof). The 1,500 rooms, however, are more down to earth, with huge beds, large bathrooms and wonderful views of the city and Bay (ask for a room overlooking the Yerba Beuna Gardens). Free unlimited use of the on-site health club, indoor pool and jacuzzi make the Marriott worth considering.
Hotel services *Air-conditioning. Babysitting. Bars. Conference facilities. Currency exchange. Disabled: access; rooms for disabled. Fax. Laundry. Lifts. Multi-lingual staff. No-smoking rooms. Safe. Sports/fitness facilities. Restaurant. Valet car park.*
Room services *Hair dryer on request. Kitchenette. Mini-bar. Radio. Refrigerator. Room service. Telephone. TV. VCR. Video library.*

Sheraton Palace Hotel

2 New Montgomery Street, CA 94105, at corner of Market Street (392 8600/1-800 325 3535/fax 543 0671). BART Montgomery/Muni Metro J, K, L, M, N. **Rates** *single from $255-$315; double from $275-$335; suites from $550-$2,600.* **Credit** AmEx, DC, JCB, MC, V.
It took 27 months and a cool $170 million to restore the Palace Hotel to its original grandeur, but in return the Sheraton can boast one of the most breathtaking dining rooms in the world. The spectacular Garden Court has 80,000 panes of stained glass, and the hotel's glass-domed swimming pool is by far the finest in the city. The 552 rooms, in comparison, are rather modest, but spacious enough, with rich wooden furniture and marble-clad bathrooms.
Hotel services *Air-conditioning. Babysitting. Bar. Car park. Conference facilities. Currency exchange. Disabled: access; rooms for disabled. Fax. Fitness centre. Laundry. Lifts. Multi-lingual staff. No-smoking rooms. Pool. Restaurant.*
Room services *Hair dryer. Mini-bar. Radio. Refrigerator. Room service. Safe. Telephone. TV. VCR on request.*

Romantic

Archbishop's Mansion

1000 Fulton Street, CA 94117, at Steiner Street (563 7872/1-800 543 5820). Bus 5, 22. **Rates** *single* from $115; *suites* from $385. **Credit** AmEx, MC, V.

The Archbishop's Mansion is one of the most opulent small hotels in San Francisco. What's more, despite the ostentation – elaborate chandeliers, gorgeous antiques, canopied beds – the staff are genuinely friendly. Indulge in splendour in the Mansion's 15 wildly elegant rooms, such as the Don Giovanni suite with its hand-carved four-poster bed, two fireplaces and seven-head shower. Built in 1904 for the Archbishop of San Francisco, the Mansion combines romance, history and luxury into a surprisingly affordable package.

Hotel services *Afternoon wine/hors-d'oeuvres. Babysitting. Car park. Concierge. Conference facilities. Continental breakfast. Fax. Laundry. Lifts. No-smoking rooms. Spa.*
Room services *Hair dryer. Radio. Safe. Telephone. TV and VCR.*

Hotel Bohème

444 Columbus Avenue, CA 94133, between Vallejo and Green Streets (433 9111/fax 362 6292). Bus 13, 15, 41, 45/Powell-Mason cable car. **Rates** *single/double* from $95-$115; *up to four guests* $130. **Credit** AmEx, DC, JCB, MC, V.

Small, suave and artistic. If you hate corporate incubators such as the Hyatt and Marriott, you'll love the Bohème, where art, poetry and hospitality collide in a particularly engaging combination. Conveniently located on Columbus Avenue, the aorta of North Beach, the 15-room hotel is surrounded by dozens of small cafés and boutiques and within walking distance of Chinatown and Fisherman's Wharf. Light sleepers should request a room that doesn't face Columbus Avenue.

Hotel services *Fax. Laundry. Multi-lingual staff. No smoking. Safe.*
Room services *Hair dryer. Radio. Telephone and modem hook ups. TV.*

Hotel Majestic

1500 Sutter Street, CA 94019, at Gough Street (441 1100/1-800 869 8966/fax 673 7331). Bus 2, 3, 4. **Rates** *single/double* from $125-$160; *suites* from $250. **Credit** AmEx, DC, MC, V.

The Majestic has long been regarded as one of San Francisco's most romantic hotels. Built in 1902, it was one of the city's first grand hotels, and the owners have obviously spent a fortune keeping it that way. Each of the 51 rooms and nine suites has a canopied four-poster bed with feather quilts, a host of English and French Empire antiques and matching furniture. Many rooms also have fireplaces. The adjoining Café Majestic is also known for its pleasingly romantic setting and good seasonal dishes. After dinner, adjourn to the mahogany bar for a cognac.

Hotel services *Babysitting. Bar. Car park. Conference facilities. Disabled: access; rooms for disabled. Fax. Laundry. Lifts. No-smoking rooms. Restaurant. Safe.*
Room services *Hair dryer. Radio. Refrigerator in suites. Room service. Telephone. TV.*

Union Street Inn

2229 Union Street, CA 94123, between Fillmore and Steiner Streets (346 0424). Bus 22, 41, 45. **Rates** *standard room* from $125-$155; *rooms with double spa tubs and view* from $175-$225. **Credit** AmEx, MC, V.

There are some people – and some places – that it's impossible not to like. Union Street Inn is one of those places, and owner Helen Stewart is one of those people. After an initial greeting by Charlie, the resident golden retriever, Helen and her staff provide a brief tour of their two-storey Edwardian hotel with its five large and luxurious rooms. You can have breakfast or afternoon tea in the splendid garden, then stroll along Union Street, browsing among the trendy shops and cafés. For the ultimate romantic holiday, book the private Carriage House – complete with jacuzzi – hidden in the garden.

Hotel services *Babysitting on request. Car park. Fax. Laundry. Multi-lingual staff. No-smoking.*
Room services *Hair dryer. Radio. Telephone. TV.*

Only in California

Nob Hill Lamborne

725 Pine Street, CA 94108, between Powell and Stockton Streets (433 2287/1-800–274 8466/fax 433 0975). Bus 38/Powell-Hyde, Powell-Mason cable car. **Rates** *rooms* from $145-$225. **Credit** AmEx, DC, JCB, MC, V.

Billed as an 'urban spa' catering to the executive traveller, the 20-room Lamborne has found its niche as a health haven for well-paid business executives. Mints on the pillow? The extras here include beta-carotene tablets, aromatherapy gels and sea salts, as well as your own personal computer, fax machine and voice mail. The $1,200, hand-sewn bedcovers and $300 pillows reek of indulgence, as does the 15-minute free neck-and-shoulder massage during hors-d'oeuvres hour. Even the Ritz-Carlton, located around the corner, sends its guests here when it's overbooked. *See also chapter* **Business**.

Hotel services *Babysitting. Business facilities. Conference facilities. Laundry. Lifts. Massage and facial. No smoking. Safe.*
Room services *Hair dryer. Kitchenette. Mini-bar. Radio. Room service. Telephone. TV. VCR. Voice mail.*

The Archbishop's Mansion.

The best B & B in town: the **Bed and Breakfast Inn**. *See page 29.*

White Swan Inn

845 Bush Street, CA 94108, between Taylor and Mason Streets (775 1755/fax 775 5717). Bus 2, 3, 4. **Rates** *rooms* from $145-$195; *suites* from $250. **Credit** AmEx, MC, V.

If you like the sort of boutique hotel that is decorated with teddy bears and serves platters of fresh-baked cookies, read on. The 26-room White Swan Inn likes to think of itself as a cosy English inn, right down to the 'English' wallpaper and prints, working fireplaces and fresh flower arrangements in each room. Afternoon is, of course, tea time, served in a large parlour decorated with old teapots and yet more teddy bears. The entire hotel is as twee as can be and not to everyone's taste, but its location near Union Square is hard to beat.

Hotel services *Babysitting. Car park. Conference facilities. Fax. Laundry. Lifts. No smoking. Safe.* **Room services** *Hair dryer. Mini-bar. Radio. Refrigerator. Telephone. TV.*

Hip Hotels

Commodore International Hotel

825 Sutter Street, CA 94019, at Jones Street (923 6800/1-800 338 6848/fax 923 6804). Bus 27. **Rates** *single/double* from $69-$109. **Credit** AmEx, DC, MC, V.

Are you cool? Are you contemporary? Are you wearing black? If the answer is yes, then you're Commodore material. From the company that raised the legendary Phoenix Hotel from its ashes comes the most far out, curvaceous and unquestionably cool hotel to hit the San Francisco scene since the Triton. Billed as an 'urban adventure' hotel, the Commodore's young and chic staff has all the tips for touring the far side of San Francisco, and will even take you there by van or on foot. Of the 113 spacious rooms – all with large walk-in closets and bathtubs – request one of the 'post-modern deco' rooms with custom furnishings fashioned by local artists.

Hotel services *Bar. Car park. Coffee shop. Conference facilities. Disabled: access; rooms for disabled. Fax.*

Laundry. Lifts. Multi-lingual staff. No-smoking rooms. Safe.
Room services *Telephone. TV. VCR.*

Hotel Monaco

501 Geary Street, CA 94102, at Taylor Street (292 0100/1-800 214 4220/fax 292 0111). Bus 38. **Rates** *rooms* from $125-$195; *suites* from $295. **Credit** AmEx, DC, JCB, MC, V.

Few hotels offer the romantic and larger-than-life ambience of the spanking-new Monaco. The remodelled Beaux Arts building, built in 1910 and previously known as the Hotel Bellevue, opened in June 1995 after a $24-million dollar facelift, and is the latest addition to the collection of Union Square luxury hotels. Everything about the Monaco is big: from the hand-painted ceiling domes and grandiose common areas juxtaposing antique nicknacks with local contemporary art, to the 201 rooms with canopy-draped beds surrounded by a jumble of vibrant patterns. If you tire of gawping at the details, wander next door to the Grand Café and get a load of the fantastic 1920s and 1930s' décor accented by more local art – including a three storey-high bunny sculpture.

Hotel services *Air-conditioning. Bar. Car park. Conference facilities. Currency exchange. Disabled: access; rooms for disabled. Fax. Laundry. Lifts. Multi-lingual staff. No-smoking rooms. Fitness club. Restaurant. Shoeshine. Safe.*
Room services *Hair dryer. Kitchenette. Mini-bar. Radio. Refrigerator. Room service. Telephone. TV. VCR. Voice mail.*

Hotel Triton

342 Grant Avenue, CA 94108, at Bush Street (394 0500/1-800 433 6611). Bus 9X, 45/Powell-Hyde, Powell-Mason cable car. **Rates** *single* from $110; *double* from $125. **Credit** AmEx, DC, MC, V.

Hotel Bohème – *in the heart of North Beach. See page 23.*

Everything about the Hotel Triton screams hip, from the glimmering dervish chairs in the lobby to the bellmen's Chairman Mao uniforms. Designed by a team of Bay Area artisans, the 140-room hotel is a visual smorgasbord of stylish eccentricities including mythological 3-D murals, inverted-pyramid podiums and gilded floor-to-ceiling pillars. Add a prime location (steps away from the entrance to Chinatown) and the adjoining Café de la Presse, a small 'European' coffee house, and you have San Francisco's version of Alice in Wonderland's hotel.
Hotel services *Concierge. Business and limousine service. Fitness centre. Free wine and coffee. Valet car parking.*
Room services *24-hour room service. TV. Telephone.*

The Phoenix
601 Eddy Street, CA 94109, at Larkin Street (776 1380/1-800 248 9466/fax 885 3109). Bus 19. **Rates** *single from $69; double from $99.* **Credit** AmEx, DC, JCB, V.
What do Ziggy Marley, Johnny Depp, John F Kennedy Jr, and Pearl Jam have in common? They've all stayed at the funky Phoenix, one of San Francisco's hippest hostelries, located, oddly enough, in one of the city's worst neighbourhoods. Forty-four bungalow-style rooms equipped with bamboo furniture and tropical plants help to create that oasis atmosphere, particularly when guests bask by the pool on a sunny day. The adjoining Miss Pearl's Jam House (*see chapter* **Bars & Cafés**) provides great Jamaican food and live music to help everyone get together and feel alright.
Hotel services *Bar. Car park. Conference facilities. Disabled: access. Fax. Laundry. Multi-lingual staff. Pool. Restaurant. Safe.*
Room services *Hair dryer. Kitchenette in suites. Radio. Refrigerator optional. Telephone. TV. VCR.*

The Red Victorian
1665 Haight Street, CA 94117, at Cole Street (864 1978/fax 863 3293). Muni Metro N/33, 37 bus. **Rates** *single from $59-$134; double from $76-$200.* **Credit** AmEx, MC, V.
Nothing comes as close to offering the quintessential Haight-Ashbury experience as a night at the Red Vic. Haight Street's only hotel offers 18 wildly decorated rooms, each with its own thematic twist, such as the rainbow-coloured Flower Child room or the tie-dyed Summer of Love double. A continental

breakfast is included in the room price, as is free use of the meditation room. Highly recommended for hippy-loving souls.
Hotel services *Multi-lingual staff. No-smoking. Continental breakfast.*
Room services *Telephone.*

Home From Home

Edward II Inn & Pub
3155 Scott Street, SF, CA 94123, at Lombard Street (922 3000/toll-free 1-800 473 4666). Bus 28, 43, 76. **Rates** *single or double with shared bath from $69; single or double with private bath from $89; suites from $160-$225.* **Credit** AmEx, DC, JCB, MC, V.
A self-styled 'English Country' inn. Its Lombard Street location is a little over congested with traffic, but nearby Chestnut and Union Streets offer some of the best shopping and dining in the city. You can choose from fancy suites with whirlpool baths (from $160) or the more basic pension rooms with shared baths (from $69).
Hotel services *Bar. Fax. Limited car park. No smoking.*
Room services *Hair dryer on request. Radio. Refrigerator in suites. Telephone. TV.*

Washington Square Inn
1660 Stockton Street, CA 94133, at Filbert Street (981 4220/1-800 388 0220/fax 397 7242). Bus 39, 41, 45/Powell-Mason cable car. **Rates** *room with shared bath from $85-$95; room with private baths from $95-$180.* **Credit** AmEx, DC, JCB, MC, V.
You can't ask for a better hotel location in San Francisco – across from Washington Square in the heart of North Beach and within walking distance of Chinatown. The smoke-free, 16-room hotel has a European flavour, and each room is decorated with French and English antiques. The overall feeling is of casual, quiet elegance. A continental breakfast and afternoon tea complete with finger sandwiches are included in the room price.
Hotel services *Babysitting. Car park. Fax. Continental breakfast. Laundry. No smoking. Safe.*
Room services *Hair dryer. Radio. Telephone. TV on request.*

Take a dip at the funky **Phoenix***.*

Bed & Breakfast

Bed and Breakfast Inn
4 Charlton Court, CA 94123, at Union Street (921 9784). Bus 41, 45. **Rates** *room with shared bath* from $70-$90; *room with private bath, telephone & TV* from $115-$140; *penthouse flat* from $190-$275. **Credit** TC.
The Bed and Breakfast Inn is a real charmer. A forerunner of the B&B craze, this small 11-room inn is awash with fresh flowers, antiques and the sort of personal touches that create the American version of an old English hostelry. Tucked into a tiny cul-de-sac off Union Street, the inn consists of three immaculate Victorian houses and one exquisite garden – a good place to enjoy breakfast on sunny mornings. It's in a great location, too, with some of the city's best shopping and dining steps away.
Hotel services *Car park. Disabled: access; rooms for disabled. Multi-lingual staff. No smoking. Safe.*
Room services *Hair dryer. Telephone & TV in rooms with private bath.*

Jackson Court
2198 Jackson Street, CA 94115 at Buchanan Street (929 7670/fax 929 1405). Bus 12, 24. **Rates** *rooms* from $113-$165. **Credit** AmEx, MC, V.
Not many people know about Jackson Court, a nineteenth-century brownstone mansion that has been converted into a superb ten-room bed-and-breakfast inn. Located on a quiet residential stretch of Pacific Heights – one of San Francisco's more prestigious neighbourhoods – the inn is as quiet as a church and as elegant as, well, a mansion. All rooms have private baths, antiques and contemporary furnishings – and surprisingly reasonable rates. If you don't mind walking five or six blocks (or getting a cab), there are some wonderful shops and restaurants on Union Street.
Hotel services *Fax. No smoking.*
Room services *Hair dryer on request. Kitchen access. Radio. Telephone. TV.*

Practical

The Andrews
624 Post Street, CA 94109, between Jones and Taylor Streets (563 6877/1-800 263 7397/fax 928 6919). Bus 2, 3, 4. **Rates** *single* from $82; *double* from $92; *suites* from $119. **Credit** AmEx, DC, JCB, MC, V.
Finding a decent hotel room within two blocks of Union Square for under $100 is as hard as finding a taxi when you need one. The seven-storey Andrews Hotel offers 48 small-but-comfortable rooms, each decorated in a pleasant pastel and floral theme with the usual TV, radio and telephone amenities. A bonus is the free continental breakfast served in the hallway with additional trays if you want breakfast in bed. The adjoining Fino restaurant is highly recommended for its moderately priced Italian dishes.
Hotel services *Air-conditioning. Babysitting. Bar. Car park. Conference facilities. Currency exchange. Disabled: access; rooms for disabled. Fax. Laundry. Lifts. Multi-lingual staff. No-smoking rooms. Sports/fitness facilities. Restaurant.*
Room services *Hair dryer. Kitchenette. Mini-bar. Radio. Refrigerator. Room service. Safe. Telephone. TV. VCR.*

Holiday Lodge
1901 Van Ness Avenue, CA 94109, between Jackson and Washington Streets (776 4469/1-800 367 8504/fax 474 7046). Bus 12. **Rates** *rooms* from $99-$109; *suites* from $145-$165. **Credit** AmEx, DC, JCB, V.
This weathered motor lodge looks out of place among San Francisco's boutique and high-rise hotels, but it serves a purpose: to house families and visitors who otherwise couldn't afford to stay in the city. The large garden courtyard and

heated swimming pool are perfect for children (all that's missing is the pink flamingo), while the room rates will please most parents. Despite the funky façade, the 77 rooms are clean and modern. Free parking and a great location are further bonuses.
Hotel services *Car park. Fax. Laundry. Lifts. No-smoking rooms. Pool. Safe.*
Room services *Hair dryer. Radio. Telephone. TV.*

The New Abigail
246 McAllister Street, CA 94102, between Hyde & Larkin Streets (861 9728/toll-free 1 800–243 6510/fax 861 5848). BART Civic Center/Muni Metro J, K, L, M, N/5 bus. **Rates** *single* from $59; *double* from $79. **Credit** AmEx, DC, JCB, MC, V.
Another so-called 'European' hotel, due in part to the European antiques, down quilts and turn-of-the-century English lithographs and paintings adorning each room. Located in Civic Center, within walking distance of the Opera House and Symphony Hall but in an otherwise not very prepossessing area, the 60-room Abigail is a safe bet for visitors looking for a clean, comfortable room at a reasonable price. The weekly and monthly rates are a bargain.
Hotel services *Bar. Car park. Disabled: access. Fax. Lifts. Multi-lingual staff. No-smoking rooms. Restaurant. Safe.*
Room services *Radio. Room service (by outside company). Telephone. TV.*

Budget

Grant Plaza Hotel
465 Grant Avenue, CA 94108, at Pine Street (434 3883/1-800 472 6899/fax 434 3886). Bus 9X/Powell-Hyde, Powell-Mason cable car. **Rates** *single* from $42; *double* from $55-$73. **Credit** AmEx, MC, V.
As long as you don't have a car – the Grant Plaza is located smack-bang in Chinatown – you'd be hard pressed to find a better deal anywhere in the city. As little as $42 buys you a night in an immaculately clean (albeit small) room complete with contemporary furnishings, private bath, colour TV and even a phone. If you split one of the larger rooms four ways then you'll pay less than hostel rates – definitely a bargain.
Hotel services *Car park. Disabled: access. Fax. Lifts. Multi-lingual staff. Safe.*
Room services *Hair dryer. Telephone. TV.*

Hyde Plaza
835 Hyde Street, CA 94109, between Bush and Sutter Streets (885 2987/fax 921 1648). Bus 27. **Rates** *room with shared bath* $29.95; *room with private bath* $34.95. **Credit** AmEx, MC, V.
In the running with Grant Plaza Hotel as one of the best budget hotels in the city, the newly-renovated Hyde Plaza is a European-style hotel with 50 small, plain but comfortable rooms, most of which share a bath (an extra $6 buys a private bath). The hotel is in a good spot, within walking distance of Union Square and two blocks from the California Street cable car line.
Hotel services *Fax. Laundry. Lifts. Restaurant/espresso bar. Safe.*
Room services *Radio. Telephone. TV. Voice mail.*

San Remo
2337 Mason Street, CA 94133, at Chestnut Street (776 8688/1-800 352 7366/fax 776 2811). Powell-Mason cable car. **Rates** *single* from $35-$65; *double* from $45-$65; *triple* from $75; *penthouse* from $85. **Credit** AmEx, DC, JCB, MC, V.
Originally a boarding house for dock workers displaced in the Great Fire of 1906, this meticulously restored three-storey Italianate Victorian is one of San Francisco's best bargains. Though the rooms are small and the baths (showers, actually) shared, you will not find finer accommodation at this price anywhere in the city. The spotless bathrooms are

practically a work of art, and all the 62 rooms have brass or cast-iron beds, wicker furniture and antique armoires. Ask for a room on the upper floor facing Mason Street if you can, or if the penthouse is free, book it – you'll never want to leave.
Hotel services *Car park. Conference facilities. Fax. Laundry. Multi-lingual staff. Restaurant (breakfast only). Safe.*
Room services *Hair dryer.*

Youth Hostels

Globe Hostel/Inter-Club

10 Hallam Place, CA 94103, off Folsom Street between Seventh and Eighth Streets, (431 0540/fax 431 3286). BART Civic Center/Muni Metro J, K, L, M, N/12 bus. **Rates** *single* from $10-$15; *double* from $35 (available off-season only). **Credit** TC.
Although the SoMa (South of Market) district can be shady at times, there's no closer location to the area's many hopping bars and clubs. Open around the clock, the hostel's 33 rooms offer 140 beds (five beds per room) and – hallelujah! – each room has a private bath. No reservations are taken during peak season, but there are no curfews or chores either. Breakfast and dinner are available on the premises.
Hotel services *Café. Cigarette and sweet vending machines. Community lounge. E-mail. Fax. Free coffee. Free safe deposit boxes. Laundry. Multi-lingual staff. No-smoking rooms. Pay phones (hallway 626 0385, stairway 626 0396). Pool table. Sports/fitness facilities. Sun deck. TV.*

Globetrotter's Downtown Hostel

225 Ellis Street, CA 94102, at Mason Street (346 5786/fax 346 5786). BART Powell Street/Muni Metro J, K, L, M, N/27 bus. **Rates** *bed* $12; *private room* $24. **Credit** TC.
Located in Union Square next to all the big hotels (as well as near the seedy Tenderloin district), the two-storey Globetrotter has 30 beds, shared baths, a laundry room and a common kitchen and room with TV/VCR. It is open 24 hours a day – with no curfew or lockout – and amenities include free linen, tea and coffee. It shouldn't be your first choice, but you can't beat the location or the price.
Hotel services *Fax. Kitchen. Laundry. Multi-lingual staff. No-smoking areas. Pay phone. TV. VCR.*

Green Tortoise Guesthouse

494 Broadway, CA 94102, at Kearny Street (834 1000/1-800 867 8647/fax 956 4900). Bus 12, 15, 83. **Rates** *dorm* from $10-$15; *single* from $19-$20; *double* from $29-$35. **Credit** TC.
Known throughout San Francisco and beyond as a funky bus tour company for earthy psychedelic types (*see chapter Getting Around*), Green Tortoise extends its services to the mellow traveller in search of friendly accommodation. Perched on prime North Beach real estate, the guesthouse is in the middle of Broadway's burlesque action and a short walk from the centre of North Beach and Chinatown. Dorm rooms equipped with twin beds, linen and a desk accommodate two to six people. There's no curfew here so you'll have ample time to explore the area's wild and infamous night life.
Hotel services *Free breakfast and coffee. Kitchen. Laundry. Lounge with TV and weekly movies. Multi-lingual staff. No-smoking except in TV lounge. Pay phones. Safe deposit boxes. Sauna. TV. VCR.*

Hostel at Union Square (AYH)

312 Mason, CA 94102, between Geary and O'Farrell Streets (788 5604/fax 788 3023). BART Powell Street/Muni Metro J, K, L, M, N/27, 38 bus. **Rates** *members* from $14-$15; *non-members* from $17-$18; under-18s with parent half-price. **Credit** MC, V.
Make your reservation at least five weeks in advance during the high season (between June and September) to stay at this downtown 230-bed hostel. The four year-old hostel prides itself on privacy and security (apparently more than

192,000 guests have stayed here but only 27 claimed that something went missing). Guests are accommodated in small two-, three-, four- or five-person rooms, with their own lock and key (the four- and five-person rooms also have their own bathroom). AYH membership is required, but don't worry – you can buy it on the spot. There are always beds for walk-ins on a first-come-first-served basis, but remember to bring ID or you'll be turned away at the door.
Hotel services *Dining room. Disabled: access; rooms for disabled. Free linen. Free nightly movies. Library. Lifts. Multi-lingual staff. No-smoking rooms. Pay phones. Safe. Self-serve kitchen. TV. VCR.*

San Francisco International Hostel (AYH)

Fort Mason Building, 240 Fort Mason, CA 94123 (771 7277/fax 771 1468). Bus 28, 47, 49. **Rates** $14. **Credit** MC, V.
Many San Franciscans would kill for the bay view from this affordable vacation spot. One of the most desirable locations in the city is available for under $15 per night – and you don't even have to be an AYH member (though you do have to book at least 24-hours in advance). Located on National Park property, the hostel's dorm-style accommodation sleeps 155 souls in rooms fitting three to four people. Guests have easy access to the Marina's shops, restaurants, and sweeping vistas. Unlike some hostels where, if you're not asleep, you'd rather be elsewhere, here you'll might actually want to stick around to enjoy the fireplace, pool table, dining room, coffee bar, complimentary movies and the rarest of San Francisco amenities – free parking. There's no curfew either.
Hotel services *Car park. Disabled: access; rooms for disabled. Information desk. Kitchen. Laundry. Lifts. Multi-lingual staff. No-smoking rooms.*
Room services *Hair dryer. Kitchenette. Mini-bar. Radio. Refrigerator. Room service. Safe. Telephone. TV. VCR.*

Accommodation Agencies

American Property Exchange

(863 8484/1-800 747 7784). **Open** 9am-5pm Mon-Fri.
Provides luxury accommodation in apartments and condos (studios start at $1,500 a month). The exchange also offers long-term furnished accommodation (studios start at $1,000 a month).

Bed & Breakfast Reservations

(696 1690/fax 696 1699). **Open** 9am-4pm Mon-Fri; 9am-noon Sat.
An organisation which claims it has something for everyone, whether they want to spend $65 or $125 a night. Apartments are also available.

California Reservations/ Discount Hotel Rates

(252 1107/1-800 576 0003). **Open** 8am-7pm Mon-Fri; 9am-5pm Sat; 9am-8pm Sun.
A California hotel broker which provides great deals on over 1,000 hotels in the state (with up to 50% off the hotels' usual price).

Central Reservation Services (CRS)

(1-407 339 4116/1-800 548 3311). **Open** 24-hours daily.
Budget-minded travellers should contact this service offering accommodation for under $100 a night, with prices up to 70% off hotels' published rates.

Trinity Properties

(433 3333). **Open** 9am-5pm Mon-Fri.
Specialises in furnished and unfurnished apartments (for three months rental, or longer) ranging from $500-$5,000 per month. Trinity runs the rental gamut, from luxury apartments in Pacific Heights to less pricey, unfurnished apartments starting at $500 a month.

San Francisco by Season

Whether it's Hallowe'en in drag, fireworks at Chinese New Year, or jazz in the park, there's always an excuse for a party in San Francisco.

Seasons in San Francisco, at least in terms of climate, can seem to come and go in the space of a week, or even within the week. During the summer, for example, two or three hot days will be punished by a chilling fog. In mid-January, when everyone's spirits are low from constant rain, a week of brilliant sunshine will suddenly pack the beaches. Then, the sun will just as abruptly disappear and the grey will seem infinite. Tourists shivering in sweatshirts and jackets obviously purchased while visiting the Bay Area are a never-ending source of amusement for locals.

Rain or shine, San Francisco remains a city that knows how to throw a civic party and, along with the national holidays, there's almost always some kind of celebration hitting the streets. For the most up-to-date information on events, consult the **San Francisco Visitor Information Center** (391 2000) or call the 24-hour tourist information line devoted to festivals and fairs (837 6191).

The seasons

Bob Hope called San Francisco the 'city of four seasons – every day'. Because of its coastal location, the city has a temperate marine climate all year round, usually hovering somewhere between 40ºF and 70ºF (4ºC-21ºC), but the temperature can change dramatically during the day, as chilly afternoon offshore winds whip up. **Winter** months tend to be wet and cold, although hardly ever downright freezing. **Spring** offers more direct sunlight (and brilliant floral displays in Golden Gate Park) but not enough to shed your sweater. While the rest of California suffers through typically sweltering **summers**, San Francisco normally remains a balmy 70ºF-75ºF (21ºC-24ºC) during the day, although Mark Twain's famous remark about the coldest winter being a summer spent in San Francisco rings just as true, despite global warming. This is the season for the city's famous blankets of fog, which usually burn off in the course of the day, but can sometimes remain for weeks. **Autumn** is everyone's favourite season, when temperatures sometimes reach the eighties and the fog is much more forgiving. If you came to California to work on your tan but the fog won't let up, your best bet is to head 30 miles in any direction – to Marin, Napa, San Jose, Berkeley – away from the city and out of the fog.

National Holidays

New Year's Day (1 Jan); Martin Luther King Jr Day (3rd Mon, Jan); President's Day (3rd Mon, Feb); Memorial Day (last Mon, May); Independence Day (4 July); Labor Day (1st Mon, Sept); Columbus Day (2nd Mon, Oct); Election Day (1st Tue, Nov); Veteran's Day (11 Nov); Thanksgiving Day (4th Thur, Nov); Christmas Day (25 Dec).

Spring

St Patrick's Day
Information (661 2700). Parade goes from Fifth and Market Streets to the Embarcadero Center. BART Powell Street/Muni Metro F, J, K, L, M, N/5, 9, 14, 26, 27, 31 bus. **Date** Sunday before 17 March.
Like everywhere in the world where St Patrick's Day is celebrated, this is a long day of shamrocks, parades and booze. Most Irish pubs celebrate long into the night.

Tulip Mania
Information (981 7437). Pier 39, Embarcadero. Bus 32. **Date** March.
To get the feeling that spring has really arrived, go to Pier 39 and gaze at the 35,000 tulips planted for this annual flower festival.

St Stupid's Day Parade
From Transamerica Pyramid building, on Washington and Montgomery Streets. Bus 1, 15, 41. **Date** 1 April.
On April Fools' Day for the past 17 years, Bishop Joey of the First Church of the Last Laugh has led the St Stupid's Day Parade, a zany, parodic assembly that snakes through San Francisco's Financial District. The parade concludes on the steps of the Pacific Stock Exchange, where sermons are

*Carmen Miranda wannabes should save their posh frocks for **Carnival**.*

given and everyone removes a sock for the 'Pacific Sock Exchange'. It should come as no surprise to learn that many go home sockless, as the exchange degenerates into a sock fight. The starting point may not be the same each year; details are usually passed by word of mouth nearer the time.

Cherry Blossom Festival

Information (563 2313). Japan Center, Geary Boulevard, between Fillmore and Laguna Streets. Bus 2, 3, 4, 22, 38L. **Date** 13/14 and 20/21 April 1996; usually mid/late April.
Held over two weekends in April, this is a celebration of traditional Japanese arts and crafts, including a parade, dance and drumming performances.

San Francisco International Film Festival

Information (931 3456/929 5000). Kabuki 8 Cinema at Post and Fillmore Streets, and other cinemas around town. Bus (to Kabuki) 4, 22, 38. **Date** Mid April-early May.
Featuring two weeks of events, the San Francisco Film Festival may not be the largest, but it definitely screens enough films to make a run at being the world's most eclectic cinematic experience. It is particularly strong on independent documentaries and Third World films rarely shown at other American festivals. Booking in advance is advised.

Cinco de Mayo

Information (826 1401). Civic Center Plaza. BART Civic Center/Muni Metro F, J, K, L, M, N/5, 19, 26, 42, 47 bus. **Date** around 5 May.
A weekend of parades, fireworks and music celebrates the day that marks Mexican general Ignazio Zaragoza's famous victory over the French army at Puebla in 1862.

Bay to Breakers

Information (777 7770/808 5000 ext 2222). Starts at corner of Howard and Spear Streets. BART Embarcadero/1, 30X, 41 bus. **Date** third Sunday in May.
The *San Francisco Examiner* and a host of other sponsors encourage 100,000 or more athletes, weekend warriors, jog-walkers, joggers-for-a-day and just plain freaks to run to

Ocean Beach. The course is about 12km/7.6 miles, a perfect length since most can make it without much training. Famous for its costumes, nudity (there's always a few running free and bouncy), and the occasional beer jock, who runs alongside his keg in a shopping cart.

Carnaval

Information (826 1401). Mission District. BART 16th/24th Streets/9, 12, 14, 22, 49, 53 bus. **Date** Memorial Day weekend.
Part of what makes Carnaval so special is its location in the heart of the lively Mission district. The Mission sees more than its share of strife but Carnaval transforms it into a centre of mirth and whimsy. Unmissable.

Festival at the Lake

Information (510 464 1061). Lake Merritt, Oakland. BART Lake Merritt. **Date** early June.
Held over a long weekend, Oakland's Festival at the Lake is the city's largest annual shindig, with food stalls, arts and crafts, water sports and several stages with bands.

Lesbian and Gay Freedom Day Parade and Celebration

Information (864 3733). Phone for venues and information. **Date** 30 June 1996; usually fourth Sunday in June.
One of the most famous and popular of San Francisco's celebrations. This being San Francisco, you don't need to be proud-to-be-gay to attend. In 1995, Newt Gingrich's half-sister made quite a splash, taking a turn as Grand Marshall of the parade, but the event, for all its entertainment value, is also about countless numbers of private lives going public with their desire.

Summer

Fourth of July

Information (550 0560). Crissy Field. Golden Gate Transit 10, 50/28, 29 bus.
On Independence Day, even San Francisco admits that it is part of the US, with firework displays shortly after dark all around the Bay and especially at Crissy Field, in the Presidio.

Mime Troupe in the Park

Information (285 1717). Dolores Park, at 18th and Dolores Streets. Muni Metro J/33 bus. **Date** *around 4 July.*
For more than 30 years, the San Francisco Mime Troupe has developed and performed shows in the parks of San Francisco – free of charge. Between the wit of the Mime Troupe, the sun, the grass, the dogs and the views of the city, the festival goes a long way toward restoring one's sanity.

San Francisco Shakespeare Festival

Information (666 2221). Golden Gate Park. Bus 5, 6, 21, 33, 66, 71. **Date** *September.*
The Bard knows no chronological or geographical limits, especially in northern California. No less than five theatre companies produce Shakespeare plays during the summer, but the one closest to home – and free – is the San Francisco Shakespeare Festival, performed on outdoor stages in Golden Gate Park at weekends throughout September. Alternatively, the **California Shakespeare Festival**, held at the Bruns Amphitheater, Orinda, in the East Bay (1-510 548 9666), is a better funded, 23 year-old event, which is also better received by the critics.

Autumn

A la Carte, A la Park

Information (383 9378). JFK and Kezar Drives, Golden Gate Park. Bus 7, 21, 33, 66. **Date** *Labor Day weekend; 11am-6pm.* **Tickets** *$8.*
At this huge outdoor food fair, you can sample an impressive array of cuisine from over 40 restaurants in the San Francisco and Bay Area in just three days. And with all the Californian wine that pours, plan to take a bus or cab home.

Burning Man

Burning Man, PO Box 420572, San Francisco, CA 94142-0572 (985 7471). Black Rock Desert, Nevada. **Date** *first weekend in September.* **Tickets** *$35 from clothes shops Held Over (864 0818) and Clothes Contact (621 3212).*
Hundreds of San Franciscans ride in convoy out to the Black Rock Desert – the largest continuous flat space in the US – for a weekend of bizarre fun. For three days, a camp forms for parties, fashion shows, neo-pagan rituals, live music, pirate radio stations, drive-by shooting ranges and just about any game you'd care to invent. The climax is the immolation of a 12m/40ft wooden figure, laced with neon and packed with explosives. After it collapses in flames, circle dances begin. For some, the Burning Man has replaced Christmas as the main ritual of the year.

Festival de las Americas

Information (821 1401). 24th and Mission Streets. BART 24th Street/14, 48, 49, 67 bus. **Date** *around 15 September.*
The Mission district can't go more than a few weeks without some kind of fiesta and at the Festival de las Americas (formerly the Mexican Day of Independence) many of the newest *Norte Americanas* celebrate the nation of their birth. There's music and parades, dancing and food.

San Francisco Blues Festival

Information (826 6837). Great Meadow, Fort Mason Center, at Marina Boulevard and Laguna Street. Bus 28. **Date** *third or fourth weekend in September.* **Tickets** *Advance $17 per day; $30 two days; on the door $20 per day; free under-6s.*
Traditionally kicking off at noon on a Friday, this weekend-long festival blurs into one eternal afternoon, exposing blues fans to the elements and set after set of broken-hearted chords. Wear your shades and bring a blanket and a cooler full of refreshments. Tickets are available in advance from BASS Tickets (1-510 762 2277).

Solo Mio Festival

Information (626 9196). Climate Theater, 252 Ninth Street, between Folsom and Howard Streets. Bus 12, 19. Also Fort Mason Center, Buchanan Street and Marina Boulevard. Bus 22, 28. **Date** *mid-September to mid-October.* **Tickets** *$14-$22 from City Tickets (392 4400) or BASS Tickets (1-510 762 2277).*
Although a form that can attract egocentric hacks, performance art lives up to its name at the annual Solo Mio Festival, devoted to one-person shows. Started in 1989, the festival already has a rich history including infamous shows from Karen Finley, Spalding Gray and John Waters.

Artists' Open Studios

Information (861 9838). Phone for venues. **Date** *October.*
Local artists invite the public to visit their studios, on every weekend during October. A map ($1) and directory of studios ($10) are available from bookshops; a map is also published in the *Sunday Examiner & Chronicle* on the last Sunday in September.

Día de los Muertos

Information (826 8009). Evening procession starts from Mission Cultural Center, 2868 Mission Street, between 24th and 25th Streets. BART 24th Street/14, 48, 49, 67 bus. **Date** *2 November.*
A celebration of Mexican Hallowe'en – the Day of the Dead – a traditional holiday for welcoming the spirits of the dead with a feast and a night-time procession.

Fleet Week

Information (395 3928). Pier 39, Embarcadero. Bus 32. **Date** *Columbus Day weekend.*
The US Navy's Blue Angels tear up the heavens in a *Top Gun*-like display of speed, daring and tax payer abuse. Plus free tours of various American and foreign ships.

San Francisco Jazz Festival

Information (788 7353/outside California 1-800 627 5277). Phone for venues. **Date** *11-27 October 1996; usually second and third weeks in October.* **Tickets** *$3-$50 from City Box Office (392 4400) or BASS Tickets (1-510 762 2277).*
Growing every year, the San Francisco Jazz Festival attracts some of the biggest names in jazz and usually concludes with a performance or two at Grace Cathedral on Nob Hill.

Outdoor music

San Francisco has no shortage of music for those who like to take their tunes alfresco. The **San Francisco Blues Festival** takes place on two outdoor stages near the Fort Mason Center on what is known as the Great Meadow (*see above*). At Golden Gate Park, look for banners announcing **Opera in the Park** (861 4008) in early September and **Reggae in the Park** (381 2425) in October. Stern Grove, an amphitheatre sequestered among eucalyptus trees, plays host to a number of free shows including the **Stern Grove Midsummer Music Festival** (252 6252), from June to August (*see chapter* **Music: Classical & Opera**).

Hallowe'en in the Castro

Venue to be confirmed; check the gay press nearer the time. **Date** 31 October.

Hallowe'en in the Castro is for anyone who considers spooky, scary and/or sexy trick-or-treating a serious, adult activity. Previously convened in the blocks where Market, 17th, 18th and Castro Streets intersect, the event has become so huge that there are plans, as yet unconfirmed, to move it to the Embarcadero or the Civic Center. *See also chapter* **Gay & Lesbian San Francisco**.

Winter

Christmas Tree Lighting Ceremonies

Ghirardelli Square (775 5500). Bus 19. **Date** day after Thanksgiving, around 7.30pm.
Pier 39 (981 8030). Bus 42. **Date** day before Thanksgiving, 6pm.
Fell and Stanyan Streets (666 7107). Bus 6, 7, 33, 66, 71. **Date** second week of December (phone for exact date), around 5.30pm.

Run to the Far Side

Information (864 2243). Golden Gate Park. Bus 5, 7, 21, 33, 66, 71. **Date** weekend after Thanksgiving.
A 5km/3 mile walk and 10km/6 mile run through Golden Gate Park, where participants dress as their favourite characters from Gary Larson's cartoons.

Martin Luther King Jr Birthday Celebration

Information (771 6300). Start of parade varies; ends with rally at Yerba Buena Gardens, Fourth and Mission Streets. BART Powell Street/Muni Metro F, J, K, L, M, N/14, 26 30, 45 bus. **Date** Monday after 15 January (King's birthday).
In honour of the great civil rights leader, the US takes a day off and holds birthday parades. Phone for more information.

Tet Festival

Information (885 2743). Larkin Street, between Eddy and O'Farrell Streets. Bus 19, 31, 38. **Date** January-February (phone for exact date).
San Francisco has a sizeable population of Vietnamese-Americans and at Vietnamese New Year they transform the Civic Center and Tenderloin areas with a multi-cultural festival, joined by many Cambodian, Latino and African-American San Franciscans.

Chinese New Year

Information (982 3000). Parade starts from Market and Second Streets, and goes through Chinatown. BART Montgomery Street/Muni Metro F, J, K, L,M, N/2, 3, 4, 9, 30, 45, 71, 76 bus. **Date** January, February or March (phone for exact date).
With a huge parade through Chinatown and plenty of fireworks, Chinese New Year turns San Francisco jubilant and upside-down. If you're in town, don't miss it.

Street fairs

The street fair season runs from late May until early October. Each fair has its own official theme and a few, such as the Haight Street and Folsom Street events, have unofficial themes as well (acid punch and leather fetishes, respectively). All provide plenty of ways to spend money on arts and crafts and food, much of it from stalls on the street. Bands are hired and play on stages throughout the day, usually for free.

Union Street Spring Festival and Arts and Crafts Fair

Information (346 4446). Union Street, between Gough and Steiner Streets. Bus 12, 22, 24. **Date** first weekend in June.
One of the city's more frou-frou streets gathers some of its most accomplished artisans together for this event. Includes an arts and crafts fair, a waiters' race and a tea dance.

Haight Street Fair

Information (661 8025). Haight Street, between Masonic and Stanyan Streets. Bus 6, 7, 43, 66, 71. **Date** second Sunday in June.
A themepark version of the Summer of Love, set to a contemporary vibe, with 230 stalls offering food from around the world.

North Beach Fair

Information (403 0666). Grant Avenue and Green Street, around Columbus Avenue, and Washington Square Park. Bus 14, 30, 45, 51. **Date** second weekend in June.
There's no shortage of music and Italian food, plus street painting in the Italian tradition.

Jazz and All that Art on Fillmore

Information (346 4446). Fillmore Street, between Post and Jackson Streets. Bus 2, 3, 4, 22, 24, 38. **Date** weekend before 4 July.
Long the bandstand for Frisco jazz, Fillmore Street sponsors what may be the most vibrant of the city's street fairs.

Blues and Art on Polk

Information (346 4446). Polk Street, between Bush and Jackson Streets. Bus 1, 19, 27, 42, 47, 49. **Date** second weekend in July.
The blues is an apt choice for Polk Street which runs the gamut of socio-economic lifestyles. On this day, everyone – rich and poor, john and hustler – boogies on down.

Folsom Street Fair

Information (861 3247). Folsom Street between Seventh and 11th Streets. Bus 9, 12, 19, 27, 42. **Date** September.
Leather and mace and everything nice. The Folsom Street Fair has a naughty edge to it – but that's part of its charm.

Castro Street Fair

Information (467 3354). Castro and Market Streets. Muni Metro F, K, L, M/8, 24, 33, 35, 37 bus. **Date** first Sunday in October.
In the gay capital of the world, the Castro Street party can't help but also be a gay and lesbian fiesta.

Potrero Hill Festival

Information (826 8080). In and around Daniel Webster Elementary School, 465 Missouri Street, between 19th and 20th Streets. Bus 22, 48, 53. **Date** mid-October.
Still mainly a neighbourhood thing, the Potrero Hill festival does boast views that the other street fairs don't have.

Sightseeing

Gravity-defying bridges, windswept beaches, civic monuments and those hills: 'when you get tired of walking around San Francisco, you can always lean against it'.

San Francisco's geographic restrictions – namely, the Pacific Ocean and the Bay – mean that most of the city is squeezed into a relatively small area, a blessing for the visitor keen to explore its sights. Tramping the streets is probably the best way to experience it, but if the shockingly steep hills become too much, you can always turn to the efficient public transport system and hop on a bus or cable car. Listed below are some major attractions, ranging from buildings and beaches to parks and plazas; for more information on where to explore off the beaten track, *see chapter* **San Francisco by Neighbourhood**.

Islands & Bridges

Alcatraz

San Francisco Bay. Ferry from Pier 41, Fisherman's Wharf (546 2700/1-800 229 2784). **Admission** $9 adults; $4.50 children; $8 senior citizens.

Alcatraz means 'pelican' in Spanish, after the birds whose nesting ground the island originally was, but to Al Capone,

Machine Gun Kelly and Robert 'the Birdman' Stroud, it was 'the Rock'. The first lighthouse on the West Coast was built here in 1854, but Alcatraz became a prison island when crude stockades were built to house convicted criminals in the 1870s, then quarantined soldiers after the Spanish-American Civil War and finally prisoners from city jails that crumbled in the 1906 earthquake. Now the craggy outcrop lures 4,000 willing tourists a day – well over a million each year – and is San Francisco's single biggest draw. Park rangers escort visitors around the semi-derelict concrete cell blocks where the incorrigible maximum security lifers were sent between 1934 and 1963, when the cost of supporting an island jail without its own water supply forced its closure. The jokey tour guides describe Capone's fondness for the banjo ('he did hard time, got beaten up by young punks, had syphilitic dementia'), and the Birdman's similarity to Hannibal Lecter – creating a distinctly surreal atmosphere. The views of the city from the island are also unreal, so tantalisingly near that 'you can smell the spicy shrimp in Chinatown', as Ranger John says, yet a bone-freezing swim away. No wonder 36 prisoners tried it, among the last Frank Morris and the Anglin brothers, who escaped without trace in 1962, fuelling speculation that their attempt was successful. (*Escape From Alcatraz* is the Clint Eastwood version of events; the official version is that they drowned.) Every Thanksgiving, boats of Native Americans land on the island to commemorate

*The **Golden Gate Bridge**, the city's luminous symbol. See page 37.*

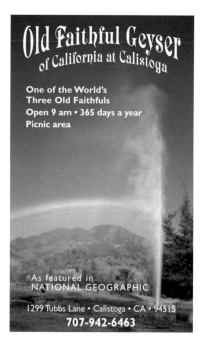

Mission Dolores, *the city's sole survivor of 200 years of 'quakes and fires. See page 41.*

their 1969 Alcatraz occupation with an Unthanksgiving ceremony. The island also boasts one of the only foghorns left in the Bay Area that *doesn't* emit a high-pitched, satellite- and radar-friendly 'beep', restored by the Coast Guard in 1992 after local outrage at the replacement of the traditional deep-pitched ones. *See also chapter* **History**.

Angel Island

San Francisco Bay, off Tiburon. Ferry from Pier 43½, Fisherman's Wharf (546 2628). **Tickets** *$9 adults; $8 12-18s; $4.50 5-11s.*

Blinding hangover? A ramble and a bicycle ride around this rocky island – the largest in the Bay – is a 20-minute ferry ride away, and the ozone breezes have a way of clearing your head. The boats arrive at Ayala Cove, where you can rent bikes. The top of Mount Livermore (238m/781ft) has a great view; and the five-mile Perimeter Trail brings you to the deserted Camp Reynolds, with its picturesque Civil War barracks – the only remaining garrison of its type. Now part of the Golden Gate Park Recreation Area, Angel Island has been both internment camp (the West Coast's answer to Ellis Island between 1910 and 1940), quarantine area for immigrants and American soldiers with tropical diseases, and prisoner of war camp for Italians and Germans in World War II. Today, ghostly quarantine barracks are scattered on the island among the volleyball courts. A visitors' centre at Ayala Cove offers 20-minute video tours, and a bus goes to Quarry Beach on the other side – a sheltered, sandy, sunbathing strip, popular with kayakers. The island offers nine 'environmental' campsites (running water, pit toilets and barbecues, but no showers) with stunning views of the Bay and city skyline; telephone 1-800 444 7275 for reservations.

Bay Bridge

Linking the East Bay and Oakland with downtown, near Rincon Annex. Bus 5, 6, 32, 38 to the bridge/AC Transit F, O, N across the bridge.

For a brief moment in October 1989, the Bay Bridge became more famous than the Golden Gate, its rival and the older structure by a year. Part of the upper storey collapsed during the Loma Prieta earthquake and the world forever associates the bridge that joins the city to the East Bay with that disaster. Before it, the Bay Bridge was distinguished as the longest high-level steel bridge in the world (13.52km/8.4 miles). Designed by Charles H Purcell, its piers are bigger than the highest pyramid and more concrete was poured to

build them than for New York's Empire State Building. It has two levels and five lanes of traffic which tunnel through **Yerba Buena Island**, where tourists stop off for the spectacular views of the West Bay section. Road exits here lead to **Treasure Island**, the point where the two halves of the bridge meet, and site of the 1939 World Fair held to celebrate its completion, and later a naval base. A small museum here covers the World Fair as well as the history of the island's military heyday.

Golden Gate Bridge

Linking the Toll Plaza near the Presidio with Marin County. Bus 28, 29, 76 to the bridge/Golden Gate Transit 10, 20, 30, 50, 60, 70, 80, 90 across the bridge.

Luminous symbol of the city and star of countless films, the bridge took 13 years to plan, five to build, and 11 lives by the time the controversial design, overseen by chief engineer Joseph Strauss, neared completion in 1937. It takes its name from the mile-wide span of bay first christened by US army captain John Frémont in the 1840s, and is continuously repainted with red rust-proof paint (5,000 gallons of 'International Orange' per year), rendering it fiery at sunset and apparently surreally suspended when foggy. Walk across it for the best views of how the unique metal gussets allow flexibility in high winds. When the city threw a party in 1987 to celebrate the bridge's 50th anniversary, a third of the city came, and the construction swayed visibly. Over 1,000 suicides have jumped from it, all facing a city of dashed dreams – but it's a statistic the police try not to publicise, naturally enough. A film on its construction can be seen at Fort Point on the south side (556 1693; 3.30pm, Wed-Sun).

Hills, Streets & Squares

Alamo Square

On Steiner Street, between Hayes and Fulton Streets. Bus 5, 21, 24.

As well as being 'postcard row', thanks to the six picture-perfect restored Queen Anne houses ranged along the eastern side (the famous **Painted Ladies**), the square is one of several in the city that afford grand views, as well as a tennis court, picnic area and children's playground. Similar attractions can be found at **Alta Plaza Park** in Pacific Heights (also on Steiner Street, between Jackson and Clay

Streets), and at **Lafayette Park** just to the east (on Gough Street, at Sacramento Street). All three leafy havens are patronised by dog owners, children, pensioners sunning themselves and joggers.

Jackson Square

Bounded by Jackson, Montgomery, Gold and Sansome Streets. Bus 30X, 42, 83.

All that remains of the once-notorious Barbary Coast, where the Sydney Ducks and Hounds sallied forth from their saloons on raiding parties up Telegraph Hill to the area known as 'Little Chile', is the renovated block bounded by Jackson, Montgomery, Gold and Sansome Streets. In its heyday back in the 1860s, Pacific Avenue (known as 'terrific') harboured many a brothel and bar where young girls were reputedly spirited into white slavery and boys force-fed drink until they passed out – only to wake up on board ship, as reluctant sailors. Much of the area perished in the 1906 Great Fire; what remains are small-scale, elegant and rather chic buildings. Oscar Wilde once visited the infamous criminal attorney Melvin Belli in his ornately furnished offices at 722 Montgomery Street. Today the square is the symbol of the city's elegant northern Californian mode, with turn-of-the-century red brick offices lovingly restored and antique, furniture and book shops lining the alleys and side streets.

Lombard Street

Between Hyde and Leavenworth Streets. Cable car Powell-Hyde.

San Francisco's so-called 'crookedest street', designed in 1920, snakes steeply down the edge of Russian Hill from Hyde Street, packing in nine hairpin bends in the space of one brick-paved and landscaped block. In the summer tourists queue up for the thrill of driving down its hazardous 27 per cent gradient at 5mph – you'll have to arrive early or late to avoid them and their cameras. For more on the surrounding streets of Russian Hill, and Telegraph Hill at the far end of Lombard Street, *see chapter* **San Francisco by Neighbourhood**. For further thrills, try negotiating the steepest street in the city: Filbert Street descends at a whopping 31.5 per cent gradient between Hyde and Leavenworth.

Nob Hill

Bounded by Bush, Larkin, Pacific and Stockton Streets. Bus 1, 27, 30, 45, 83/Powell-Hyde cable car.

A short but fantastically steep walk or cable car ride up from Union Square, this is where the 'Big Four' Boom Era spenders – robber barons Charles Crocker, Leland Stanford, Mark Hopkins and Collis P Huntington – built their palaces. The mansions all perished in the fire that razed the city after the 1906 earthquake. The hill stands at 103m/338ft above the Bay, and it wasn't until after the opening of the cable car line in the 1870s that its steep slopes began to attract wealthy residents. Sole survivor after the earthquake was the mansion built for James C Flood in 1886, which was remodelled, and is now the exclusive Pacific-Union 'gentlemens'' club. The grand residences were replaced after the earthquake with what are now the city's most élite hotels, many of which have enticing bars. They include the **Fairmont**, with its plush marble lobby and infamous ersatz islander Tongo Room, complete with simulated tropical rainstorm; the **Huntington Hotel** (it has a Big Four bar), and the **Mark Hopkins Inter-Continental**, where the Top of the Mark bar has fabulous views over the city (*see chapter* **Bars & Cafés**). Local lore has it that Nob Hill is the safest place to stand in an earthquake.

Union Square

Geary Street, between Powell and Stockton Streets. Bus 2, 3, 4, 38/Powell-Hyde, Powell-Mason cable car.

The leafy Filbert Steps, beneath the Coit Tower.

The small square, surrounded by lush shops and grand hotels, takes its name from the pro-Union rallies held here on the eve of the Civil War of 1861-65. It's the heart of the downtown district's hotels and upmarket shopping – from Tiffany and Hermès to Cartier – and so usually packed with tourists. Palm trees shelter the buskers, mime artists and street musicians – such as the World Saxophone Quartet, who perform in white tie to lunching secretaries and clerks and a determined army of panhandlers who congregate here. Kerbside flower stalls add a Parisian touch. On the Stockton Street side, TIX (433 7827) has its half-price theatre tickets stall. At the centre stands the **Dewey Monument**, a 30m/97ft-high Corinthian column that commemorates the 1898 US naval victory at Manila during the Spanish-American war. It was dedicated by Theodore Roosevelt in 1904 and not touched by the Great Quake two years later, when the square became a tent refuge for the VIPs who had been staying in the nearby hotels.

Washington Square

On Columbus Avenue at Union Street. Bus 15, 30, 39, 41.

This grassy park, anchored by the Romanesque church of **Sts Peter and Paul**, is the heart of North Beach, San Francisco's oldest Italian community, where the Beats' raucous poets, jazz musicians and free sexers put down roots in the 1950s. With Chinatown only a block away, tai chi practitioners and Chinese grandmas mix in the park with young mothers and kids, elderly gents chatting in Italian, poets hurrying from one *caffè latte* to another and the lawyers and accountants who've moved into the increasingly gentrified neighbourhood. The statue in the centre is of Benjamin Franklin (1879). It was donated by a prohibitionist who wanted to offer water to the thirsty citizens to keep their minds off booze, although now it is the taps which are dry rather than the people.

Civic Symbols

Balmy Alley

Off 24th Street, between Treat and Harrison Streets. BART 24th Street.

The Mission district is famed for its exuberant, brilliantly-coloured murals. There are hundreds of them, decorating everything from restaurants, banks and buildings, to garage doors. Subjects range from Carnaval to the building of the BART system, covering the political and social preoccupations of the neighbourhood which was once populated by working-class Italian, German and Irish residents, and is now

Drop in for a cuppa at the **Japanese Tea Garden** *in Golden Gate Park. See page 48.*

Sts Peter and Paul. *See page 39.*

home to the thousands of Hispanic families who began emigrating from central America in the 1960s. The small cut-through that is Balmy Alley contains some of the best murals. *See also chapter* **San Francisco by Neighbourhood**; and for details of tours of the Mission Murals, *see p51* **Tours**.

Cable Cars

Lines: California; Powell-Hyde; Powell-Mason (route information 673 6864).

If the cable cars are a legendary part of the city, so is the hassle of getting a ticket to board one at the downtown Powell Street terminus during working hours. Scotsman Andrew Hallidie's quaint invention was originally intended to take passengers to the top of Nob Hill, but the story about how he got the idea – after watching a hapless horse-drawn vehicle being dragged backwards down the steep hill – is probably apocryphal. As it happened, he owned the patent on a wire cable grip developed by his father and wanted a market for his cables. His invention was first tested along five steep blocks of Clay Street in 1873. An amusing photograph of this maiden voyage can be seen at the **Cable Car Barn Museum** (*see chapter* **Museums & Galleries**), where you can also see the engines and wheels that operate the cables in operation. Only three cable car lines survive out of the original 30: the Powell-Mason, Powell-Hyde and California lines. The California-Van Ness line is rarely crowded, although the tourist-jammed Powell-Hyde line to Fisherman's Wharf affords the best views. *See also chapter* **Getting Around**.

Chinatown Gateway

Grant Avenue at Bush Street. Bus 2, 3, 4, 15, 30, 45.

This ornate, three-arched gateway marks the southern entrance to Chinatown, and was a gift from Taiwan in 1970. The design of the Dragons' Gate, as it's known, is based on the ceremonial entrances traditional in Chinese villages, and its three green-tiled roofs are topped by various good-luck symbols, including two dragons and two large carp. The gateway leads onto Grant Avenue, Chinatown's main, and usually most tourist-thronged, thoroughfare. For more information on what to see in Chinatown, *see chapter* **San Francisco by Neighbourhood**.

City Hall

200 Polk Street, at Van Ness Avenue (554 4000). Bus 5, 42, 47, 49. **Closed to visitors until 1997.**

Currently being repaired in the wake of the 1989 earthquake, the 1915 City Hall was originally built under the auspices of Mayor 'Sunny Jim' Rolph, to replace the one that collapsed during the 1906 'quake. Designed by architect Arthur Brown in the Beaux Arts style, at a cost of $3.5 million, it boasts a huge dome modelled on St Peter's in Rome and higher than the Capitol's in Washington DC by just over 4.9m/16ft. The centrepiece of the Civic Center complex, there are regular wedding processions up the magnificent central sweeping stairs. It was here that Dan White assassinated Mayor George Moscone and gay Supervisor Harvey Milk in 1978, and was

later the scene of the violent 'White Night Riot' after White was found guilty of manslaughter, not murder (*see chapter* **History**). In recent years, the plaza around City Hall has been the subject of a battle between the Mayor and the homeless who have set up encampments only to be roused by police.

Coit Tower

Telegraph Hill (362 0808). Bus 39. **Open** 10am-6.30pm daily. **Admission** (elevator) $3 adults; $1 children; $2 senior citizens.

Shaped like a firehose's nozzle, this 64m/210ft-high concrete tower, built by City Hall architect Arthur Brown in 1933, was a gift from Lillie Hitchcock Coit to the city. Lillie, a fun-loving crossdresser, was snatched as a child from a blaze by a fireman, became a lifelong fan of fire fighters and when she died in 1929 left San Francisco $118,000 to build a monument to them. Telegraph Hill, where Coit Tower stands, is so named because it was the site of the first telegraph on the West Coast, which tapped out bulletins of ships arriving from across the Pacific. Before taking the lift to the top, inspect the terrific murals at the bottom, which were supervised by Diego Rivera for the WPA (Works Project Administration), the agency set up by Roosevelt to create employment during the Depression. The Socialist Realist images of muscle-bound Californian workers were deemed subversive at the time of their completion in 1934; a hammer and sickle was erased from one, and the nervous authorities delayed the opening of the tower.

Palace of Fine Arts

3601 Lyon Street, between Jefferson and Bay Streets (Exploratorium 561 0360). Bus 22, 28, 30, 43.

The only surviving piece of finery left from the 1915 Panama-Pacific Exposition, the Palace was the centrepiece of a mile-long swathe of temporary buildings that stretched as far as Fort Mason, and included an astonishing, multi-coloured, 132m/432ft-high Tower of Jewels. Bernard Maybeck's *pièce de résistance* – his ode to the 'mortality of grandeur' – is a Neo-Classical domed rotunda supported by a curved colonnade topped with friezes and statues of weeping women, and is one of the most romantic spots in the city. Its lifespan was intended to be short, and the original plaster structure was mortal indeed. It was expensively replaced by a more permanent concrete version in the 1960s, finished in time for the 1969 opening of the famous **Exploratorium** hands-on science museum, which lies behind the Palace (*see chapter* **Museums & Galleries**). The Palace is flanked by a lagoon full of lily pads, ducks and swans, set in a small park at the foot of the pastel-painted Marina district, an area still recovering from damage inflicted by the 1989 earthquake.

San Francisco Main Library

Larkin Street, at McAllister Street (557 4400). Bus 5, 19. **Open** 10am-6pm Mon; 9am-8pm Tue-Thur; 11am-5pm Fri; 9am-5pm Sat; noon-5pm Sun.

The enormous grey Beaux Arts building that houses the city's main public library was criticised for its prodigal waste

Turn and turn again. The famous cable cars.

of space when it opened in 1917. Designed by George Kelham, its monumental interior includes a grand staircase, checkout desks designed in the shape of classical temples, and some didactic murals of life in pioneering times by Frank DuMond. The **San Francisco History Room** on the third floor exhibits objects and documents from the city's past. The library took some hard knocks during the 1989 earthquake and is currently undergoing much-needed renovation. The nearby **New Main Library** (on Larkin Street, at Fulton) is due to open in spring 1996 and has much more in the way of space and facilities; the old building will eventually become the Asian Art Museum, relieving the pressure on the overcrowded collection in Golden Gate Park.

Transamerica Pyramid

600 Montgomery Street, between Clay and Washington Streets. Bus 1, 15, 42. **Open** 8.30am-4.30pm Mon-Fri.
William Pereira's 260m/853ft-high building provoked public outrage when it opened in 1972, but has since become an accepted if not loved element of the city skyline, and probably San Franciso's most recognisable building. Built to be earthquake-proof, the exterior is covered with panels which are designed to move laterally; something must work because the building was undamaged by the 1989 Loma Prieta quake. The public observation area on the 27th floor, about halfway up, gives spectacular views of the Golden Gate Bridge and Alcatraz.

Churches & Cathedrals

Glide Memorial United Methodist Church

330 Ellis Street, at Taylor Street (771 6300). Muni Metro F, J, K, L, M, N/27 bus.
Glide's Sunday morning services at 9am and 11am are a San Francisco institution: multi-cultural and liberationist, packed with worshippers of every age and race (although increasingly white and middle-class), drawn by the exuberance of the gospel choir and the exhortations to do good by the minister Cecil Williams. Williams, whose roots go back to the early days of the civil rights movement, is a major player in left-of-centre politics and anti-poverty efforts in the city. Glide runs major drug treatment initiatives, a soup kitchen for the homeless and self-help programmes for people who are HIV-positive.

Grace Cathedral

1051 Taylor Street, at California Street (776 6611). Bus 1/California cable car. **Open** 7am-6pm daily.
With a façade modelled on Notre Dame in Paris, gilded bronze doors made from casts of the Doors of Paradise in Florence's Baptistry, a gorgeous rose window and a magnificent organ, the city's Episcopalian cathedral is a mock-Gothic extravaganza. Midnight mass here, sung by the celebrated boys' choir, is a Christmas ritual, but sung eucharist is heavily attended too, and there's always plenty of action in between, from concerts by Jan Garbarek to appeals by Archbishop Desmond Tutu, as well as the biggest weddings and funerals in town. The cathedral stands on what was once the site of Charles Crocker's family mansion on Nob Hill: he donated the land for the cathedral after his house burned to the ground in the 1906 fire. It took 54 years to build and work is still going on in a $13.3 million refit.

Mission Dolores

Dolores Street, at 16th Street (621 8203). Muni Metro J/BART 16th Street/22 bus. **Open** *summer* 9am-4.30pm daily; *winter* 9am-4pm daily. **Admission** $2 adults; $1 5-12s.
Small wonder that the cool, dim interior of the Mission San Francisco de Assisi looks authentically Spanish Colonial. In a city of *faux* Colonial, this is the lone example of the real thing, as well as the oldest standing structure in the city, its four foot-thick adobe walls having withstood the test of time

You can't escape the **Transamerica Pyramid***.*

(and earthquakes) relatively undamaged. Dedicated on 2 August 1791, it was the sixth of 21 Franciscan missions built by Spanish settlers, and was known as Dolores after the nearby Laguna de los Dolores (Lake of Our Lady of Sorrows). Now it's attached to a basilica (rebuilt in 1918) where most of the religious services take place, including the traditional midnight mass at Christmas, complete with choir and trumpets. There's a tiny museum and a flower-filled cemetery containing the remains of the city's first mayor as well as Spanish settlers, and the mass grave of thousands of the unfortunate Indians who died in their service.

Old St Mary's Cathedral

660 California Street, at Grant Street (288 3800). Bus 1, 15, 30/California cable car. **Open** 7am-3.30pm Mon-Fri, Sun; 11am-6pm Sat.
When the city's first-ever Catholic cathedral was built in 1854, it represented the most solid structure yet built on the West Coast, and, miraculously, its brick survived the 1906 earthquake and fire, although its bell and altars melted. Constructed of granite imported across the Pacific from China, the rest of the materials made the longer journey by ship round the Horn from Europe. When it was built, all this brick, metalwork and stone stood in a particularly seedy neighbourhood, filled with Chinese and European brothels and opium parlours – which explains the message on the clock tower, which reads 'Son, observe the time and fly from evil'. The church offered the city's first English language school for the Chinese community, although now many worshippers have deserted it for mass in Chinese.

St Mary's Cathedral

1111 Gough Street, at Geary Boulevard (567 2020). Bus 2, 3, 4, 38. **Open** 6.30am-5.30pm daily.
The city's new Catholic cathedral (designed by Pietro Belluschi and finished in 1971) is a huge white concrete structure that resembles a washing machine (some say a food mixer) and dominates the skyline for miles around. Even its soaring, 61m/200ft-high, stained glass windows look dated, although the interior is light, plain and simple. These days, the church, which seats 2,500, is popular for large funerals.

Views & vistas

There's an embarrassment of views in this city, with its plummeting hills and Bay vistas. One of the most clichéd viewpoints is on Nob Hill, where the **Top of the Mark** 'skyroom' bar on the 19th floor of the Mark Hopkins Inter-Continental Hotel offers panoramic views of the night sky (*see chapter* **Bars & Cafés**). One of the best cheap thrills to be had in the downtown area is a ride in one of the great glass elevators of the **Westin St Francis Hotel** (335 Powell Street, at Union Square). Framed like a vanity mirror with light bulbs, the lifts shoot up the outside of the hotel tower, providing stunning views and a roller-coaster adrenaline rush.

Another popular night view is from the slopes of **Twin Peaks** (bus 37 takes you to the top) that overlook the Castro and Cole Valley at the start of the often fog-bound Sunset district in the west. The Costanoan Indians thought that this was where a quarrelling couple were separated by a clap of thunder from the Great Spirit; the Spanish later dubbed the hills 'Los Pechos de la Chola' (The Breasts of the Indian Girl).

Further north and to the west of the Castro, is a much better scramble onto a rocky outcrop called **Tank Hill** (bus 33, 37). Here, you'll find an old water tank and an exhilarating vista that puts you in mind of Batman's view of Gotham City (and indeed, it's not a good idea to go at night).

Take the lift to the top of the **Coit Tower**, on top of Telegraph Hill (bus 39), for Robert Louis Stevenson's favourite view, from where you can see all the little piers and jetties poking out into the Bay. Descend by the secluded trail at the back, down the Filbert Steps (*see page 39*), with its flower bedecked paths and earth-quake cottages, and past the eccentric Julius Castle Italian restaurant perched at the top of Montgomery Street, overlooking the Bay, and from which there are more splendid views (*see chapter* **Restaurants**).

*Most people make the trek up to **Twin Peaks** for a stunning sweep of the city...*

Buena Vista Park (bus 6, 7, 66, 71) is the Haight's own park, with plentiful forestation – eucalyptus, pine and cypress – supplied by the Golden Gate Park's gardener John McLaren in the 1890s. It offers fabulous views and especially good hiking, with courts, a playground and a good panorama from Buena Vista Avenue.

Stoll along the **Golden Gate Promenade** (bus 19, 22, 28, 30), past Marina Green and Crissy Field from Aquatic Park for more Bay- and bridge-scapes and continue round the famous coastal path in the **Presidio** for more of the same. **Fort Point** (bus 28, 29) also provides a top-storey view of the Golden Gate Bridge. Further to the west, the **Cliff House** (bus 18, 31, 38) in Sutro Heights Park is another tourist-packed spot but nonetheless a good one for gazing out over the Seal Rocks at sunset.

South of this along the coast past the San Francisco Zoo, is **Fort Funston** (bus 18), a promontory which makes a handy jumping-off point for hang-gliders, surfers and other fool-hardy types. You can gaze out to sea with them, or lie on the sand underneath staring up at them.

The **Marin Headlands**, just north of the Golden Gate Bridge off Highway 101 (bus 28, 76 and all Golden Gate Transit buses), provides another much-loved viewpoint. There's almost nothing you can do to spoil an outing here, other than drive off the cliff. The usual stop-off point for tourists is Vista Point, just across the bridge; a much better option is to cross under the highway to the Marin Headlands, and then take the short, winding and windswept cliff-top path north-east past defunct gun emplacements and hidden coves. On foggy days – it's more than likely to roll in on summer mornings and evenings – head across the Golden Gate Bridge to **Mount Tamalpais** (bus Golden Gate Transit 20 to Marin City, then 63), whose half-mile-high summit gives a 360-degree view of the fog-bound Bay below.

*… but Robert Louis Stevenson reckoned **Coit Tower** gave the city's best views.*

Waterfront & Wharf

Aquatic Park

Between Hyde Street and Van Ness Avenue. Bus 19, 30, 32, 42/Powell-Hyde cable car.

Only hardy regulars from the nearby Dolphin Club, wearing matching Speedo swimming costumes, plunge into the sea here on a daily basis. The water is choppy and swimming to (or from) Alcatraz is dangerous – fortunately, only professionals with back-up boats attempt the Bay crossing these days. This is one of the best strolls in the city, offering a panorama of the Golden Gate Bridge, Alcatraz, windsurfers, sailing boats, wildly-coloured kites and dogs catching fris-bees. Along the Municipal Pier, fishermen, many of them Vietnamese, try their luck. There are historic ships moored at Hyde Pier, to the east, including the *Eureka*, an 1890 steam-powered ferry. This is where the 2.17km/3¼-mile Golden Gate Promenade begins, continuing along the bay past the defunct gun emplacements of **Fort Mason** (*see below*) to Crissy Field (where Fourth of July fireworks and open-air concerts are held) and the **Golden Gate Bridge**. The entire waterfront as far west as Ocean Beach was incorporated into the Golden Gate National Recreation Area in 1972, and the authorities have studiously barred the tourist kitsch that ruins Fisherman's Wharf from what is the world's largest urban park.

The Embarcadero

Between Pier 41 and China Basin. BART Embarcadero/32 bus.

Once obscured by a hideous freeway overpass which cracked in the 1989 earthquake and was cleared away, San Francisco's most gorgeous promenade and its anchor, the **Ferry Building**, has been opened up and framed with stately palm trees. The clock on the Ferry Building's tower – an 1894 replica of Seville cathedral's campanile – stopped at the minute the earthquakes of 1906 and 1989 struck, but although the spire leaned, on neither occasion did it fall. Before the bridges were built in the 1930s, the building on the Embarcadero was the world's busiest terminus, handling 50 million people annually. Ferries made a genteel comeback recently, particularly after the 1989 quake when the Bay Bridge was closed for a month, but they now carry less than 2 million people annually, to the Marin suburbs of Sausalito, Tiburon and Larkspur, or sunny East Bay communities like Alameda and Vallejo. Justin Herman Plaza, outside the Ferry Building, with a walk-through water sculpture by French-Canadian sculptor Armand Vaillancourt, is the rallying point of most big demon-strations from anti-war to pro-choice, and the centre of an ebullient farmers' market every Saturday morning.

Fisherman's Wharf

Jefferson and Beach Streets, between Kearny and Hyde Streets. Bus 15, 30, 32, 39, 42/Powell-Hyde cable car.

San Francisco's port was once the soul of the city, but as the shipping and fishing business moved on, the Wharf was con-verted into a garish and tacky tourist trap amusing only to those with a taste for kitsch or the macabre. The magic of its history survives only at 5am when the few fishermen still working unload their catch and fish buyers for the city's gourmet restaurants and markets swarm. The **Maritime Museum** on Beach Street, at the foot of Polk Street (929 0202) remembers that past. Among the 'amusements' on offer are **Ripley's Believe It Or Not! Museum** (175 Jefferson Street; 771 6188), with its two-headed calf, croco-dile totem and nasty photos of people doing nasty things. The **Wax Museum** (145 Jefferson Street; 1-800 439 4305) displays more than 300 life-size wax figures, including var-ious US presidents, members of the Royal Family, Elvis Presley and William Shakespeare. The World War II *Pampanito* submarine is docked at Pier 45, and there are countless restaurants, cafés and souvenir shops. Further to the west (at 2801 Leavenworth Street) is **The Cannery** –

once a Del Monte canning factory and now a renovated shop-ping centre – and **Ghirardelli Square** (900 North Point Street, between Polk and Larkin Streets), a collection of care-fully restored red-brick buildings that once belonged to the celebrated chocolate-makers and are now occupied by a series of chi-chi shops and restaurants.

Fort Point

Marine Drive (556 1693). Bus 28, 29. **Open** 10am-5pm Wed-Sun. **Admission** free.

A spectacular brick fortress with a melodramatic setting beneath the southern edge of the Golden Gate Bridge, that resembles a vast outdoor stage crying out for some good open-air theatre. Interestingly, the performances here are historic re-enactments of the Civil War, by and for children. The fort was built between 1853 and 1861 to protect the city from a sea attack which never came, and its 126 cannons remained idle until the fort was closed in 1900. The four-storey vaulted building houses a giant 10-inch Rodman gun and various military exhibitions, and the pier is famous as the location where Kim Novak attempts suicide in Hitchcock's *Vertigo*.

The Arts

For details of the Asian Art Museum, another city landmark, *see chapter* **Museums & Galleries**.

California Palace of the Legion of Honor

Lincoln Park, at Legion of Honor Drive (750 3600). Bus 18, 38. **Open** 10am-5pm Wed-Sun. **Admission** $5 adults; $3 children. **Credit** MC, V.

Spectacularly placed on a promontory overlooking the Golden Gate Bridge, just north of Land's End, the Palace is architect George Applegarth's homage to the Palais de la Legion d'Honneur in Paris. Built in the 1920s, it was donated to the city as a memorial to California's World War I dead. The museum originally only displayed French works of art, but today lesser paintings by Fra Angelico, Titian, El Greco, Rubens, Rembrandt, Renoir, Degas, Monet and Cézanne are all on view. The Palace has recently re-opened following three years of renovation and seismic upgrading after the Loma Prieta quake wreaked its worst. The **Rodin Collection** contains the finest collection outside the Musée Rodin in Paris, including a cast of 'Le Penseur', and some fine works by Camille Claudel, and the vast **Achenbach Foundation** is devoted to works of graphic art. Scrambling north of the car park, you can make your way down a rocky path to a tiny, secluded beach, although swimming is for-bidden. *See also chapter* **Museums & Galleries**.

Fort Mason Center

Marina Boulevard (entrance at Buchanan Street) (441 5706). Bus 28.

Home to cultural organisations such as the Magic Theater (which has premiered several plays of Sam Shepard), the Cowell and Hearst Theaters, various restaurants, shops, gal-leries and several small museums, Fort Mason is a water-front complex of reconditioned military buildings that served as a command post for the US Army in the 1850s. It was converted to peaceful use in 1972, and now forms part of the Golden Gate National Recreation Area – a windswept site with magnificent views towards the Golden Gate Bridge and Alcatraz. Among the museums on site is the delightful **Mexican Museum**, which exhibits Mexican art and sells handcrafted jewellery and embroidery; the **San Francisco African-American Historical and Cultural Society**; the **Museo Italo-Americano**, which displays works by Italian artists and craftsmen (Italian-made motorbikes were a hit here); and the **San Francisco Craft and Folk Art Museum**, which has exhibitions covering anything from book binding to furniture. The Book Bay Bookstore run by Friends of the San Francisco Public Library sells second-hand

Life's a beach

Because of cold currents and rare Great White sightings, only wetsuited surfer nuts enjoy Beach Culture in the southern Californian sense here. Yet to the south and north of the city, along Highway 1, runs a glorious string of beaches, each a protected pearl guarded by conservationists, and sinfully under-utilised. To the north are several with nudist corners, including Kirby Cove, Black Sand, Red Rock, Bonita, Bolinas, Rodeo and Muir beaches. To the south unfold endless miles of ravishing sands, including Devil's Slide (recently re-opened after storm damage), Gray Whale Cove, and continuing past San Gregorio and Pomponio to Bonny Doon and Monterey.

In the city there are three great beaches accessible by public transport:

Baker Beach

To the south-west of the Golden Gate Bridge. Bus 1, 29.
Part of the fun of Baker Beach is getting there; if you're driving, take Lincoln Boulevard through the Presidio to Bowley Street, or cycle or walk the Coastal Trail from Golden Gate Bridge, flanked by the Presidio and overlooking some breathtaking views of the coastline. Running for almost a mile along the craggy shoreline, the beach is the former hiding place of a huge cannon, hidden here by the army in 1905 to protect the bay, although it never saw active service. A replica of the original 95,000-pounder has been installed for the curious, although picnic tables, sunbathing and fishing are the real lure now (as with Ocean Beach, Baker isn't recommended for

swimmers). There's a northern nudist section of the beach towards the Golden Gate Bridge, which is predominantly gay, and recommended only for those really keen to connect with nature.

China Beach

Seacliff Avenue. Bus 29.
Slotted between Baker Beach and Lincoln Park, in the salubrious Sea Cliff part of town, is the beautifully sheltered and windproof China Beach, which took its name from the settlement of Chinese fisherman who camped here in the last century. It's the nicest of all the beaches, and indeed, local residents wanted to keep it for themselves, but public demand prevails, and it's still open to all. Despite the free sundeck, showers and changing rooms, the beach remains uncrowded, although no running around in the altogether is allowed, as it's a bookable spot for barbecues and weddings.

Ocean Beach

Great Highway. Muni Metro N/18, 31, 38 bus.
The city's biggest beach is a three mile-long sandy strip along the Pacific coast at the end of the fog-bound Sunset district, where people stroll, walk dogs, paddle and have illicit midnight revels. If nature had its way, the Sunset would revert to sand up as far as Twin Peaks, but is prevented by a large wall along the Great Highway, added in the 1920s. A cycle path runs along it as far as Sloat Avenue and the zoo, from where you can stroll to Fort Funston ('Fort Fun') and to Mussel Rocks, headquarters of hang-gliders and windsurfers. However, the currents are strong, especially at Point Lobos, where a number of experienced surfers drown every year, and swimming is not advised.

Baker Beach, *for anglers, sunbathers, armaments fetishists, naturalists and naturists.*

Golden Gate Park's **Conservatory of Flowers.**

books for a mere quarter. Fort Mason also houses one of the city's favourite restaurants, Green's, which serves gourmet vegetarian meals in a spectacular dining room overlooking the Marina and the Golden Gate Bridge. *See also chapter* **Museums & Galleries**.

San Francisco Museum of Modern Art

151 Third Street, between Mission and Howard Streets (357 4000). BART Montgomery/Muni Metro F, J, K, L, M, N/12, 30, 45, 76 bus. **Open** 11am-6pm Tue, Wed, Fri-Sun; 11am-9pm Thur. **Admission** $7 adults; $3.50 13-18s, students, senior citizens; free under-13s. **Credit** (café and bookstore only) AmEx, MC, V.

A symbol of the city's would-be status as a leading centre for modern culture, the Museum of Modern Art's new $62-million home opened with a fanfare in 1995. Red brick dominated by a huge cylindrical skylight trimmed with a stunning play of black and white striped stone, the museum

is America's first design by Swiss architect Mario Botta. It is the centrepiece of the Yerba Buena Gardens complex, which also contains a theatre, a convention centre and other exhibition halls and galleries. So far, the SFMOMA has attracted huge crowds, lured by the building itself as much as its collection of abstract, expressionist and post-modern artists (from Wassily Kandisky to Sigmar Polke). Especially strong is the photography collection and the Cultural Center's programme of live, contemporary music. *See also chapter* **Museums & Galleries**.

War Memorial Opera House

301 Van Ness Avenue, at Grove Street (621 6600/box office 864 3330). Muni Metro F, J, K, L, M, N/21, 26, 47, 49 bus.

San Francisco has been an opera buff's paradise since the 1850s, and has never had any trouble in attracting world-class performers. Enrico Caruso gave a triumphant performance here the night before the 1906 earthquake and then fled the next day. In 1923 Gaetono Merola founded the San Francisco Opera and in 1932 the company moved into its permanent home, another Beaux Arts gem designed by Arthur Brown, and dedicated to solders who fought in World War I. It was here in June 1945 that 51 nations signed the United Nations Charter and gave birth to the UN. Next door is the **Veteran's Building**, constructed at the same time, which used to house the Museum of Modern Art. *See also chapter* **Music: Classical & Opera**.

Gardens & Parks

See also **Hills, Streets & Squares** *above.*

Golden Gate Park

Between Fulton and Stanyan Streets, Lincoln Way and the Great Highway. Bus 5, 7, 21, 33, 66, 71. **Open** sunrise to sunset.

One of the world's largest parks – its 1,017 acres range from the Haight to the Pacific – is an oasis of lakes, landscaped vistas, flower beds, meadows, trails and forest, much of it seemingly completely removed from the city. In 1871, landscape architect William Hammond Hall took up the challenge of turning a barren stretch of sand dunes into a park respecting the land's natural contours. A million trees were planted over the years under the tutelage of wizard gardener John McLaren and, as the park's fame spread, horticulturalists from all over the world sent him seeds and cuttings. A Japanese tea garden, a Chinese pavilion, an arboretum, a

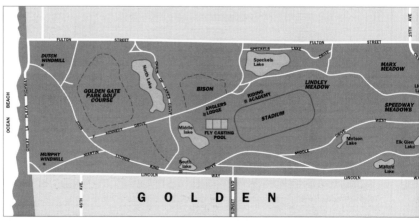

Waiting patiently for lunch at the **Golden Gater Park**.

Victorian conservatory modelled on London's Palm House in Kew Gardens, an antique carousel, a Dutch windmill and fountains grace the park. There are also two museums, an academy of sciences, an aquarium, a planetarium, a laserium, stables and trails for horses and a pasture for a herd of buffalo, lakes for boating, miles of bike trails and swooping concrete paths for roller-bladers. Over the years the park has hosted everything from encampments for earthquake victims and the homeless, free rock concerts in the 1960s, free Shakespeare and opera performances, the annual Bay to Breakers running race and, most recently, a funeral for Grateful Dead icon Jerry Garcia, attended by 10,000 heartbroken fans. *See also chapters* **History**, **Children** *and* **Museums & Galleries**.

The Presidio

Main entrances at Lombard Street (at Lyon Street); Presidio Boulevard (at Broadway), Arguello Boulevard (at Jackson Street), Lincoln Boulevard (at 25th Avenue) and Golden Gate Bridge Toll Plaza (556 1874). Bus 3, 29, 43.

Covering 1,480 acres of fabulous bayside views and rolling green hills by the Golden Gate Bridge, the Presidio was a military outpost from 1776 when Captain de Anza planted the Spanish flag here, making it Spain's northernmost outpost on the West Coast. Later it became a US army outpost which it remained until 1993, when the 11 miles of hiking trails, 14 miles of bike routes and three miles of beaches became part of the Golden Gate National Recreation Area. Its future use is still in question, although current opinion is favouring prestigious social and cultural bodies (Mikhail Gorbachev has already rented the Coast Guard Lifesaving Station just along the Bay for his Peace Foundation), and commercial developers clamour for the $2 billion-plus real estate in vain.

Among the 500-odd buildings, from Civil War mansions to simple barracks dating from the 1890s, is the old-fashioned **Presidio Museum**, Lincoln Boulevard at Funston Avenue; 556 0856. It is based in the old station hospital (built in 1864), and is now a repository of documents and artefacts from the city's military and political past.

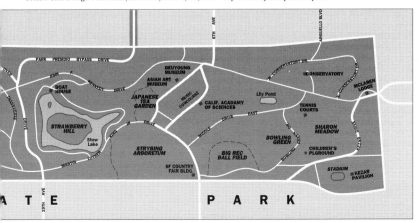

Game on in **Chinatown**.

Tours

The city offers visitors an astonishing variety of customised tours – from boat or bus trips to tours on foot with a literary, artistic or culinary bent. There are tours that cover specific areas, such as Chinatown, the Mission, the Castro or North Beach; and those that focus on architecture, film locations, views or crime scenes, whether real (the Patty Hearst bank robbery) or fictitious (the murder of Miles Archer, Sam Spade's partner in *The Maltese Falcon*).

We've listed a rough selection of what's on offer below; for more suggestions, visit the San Francisco Visitor Information Center, at the corner of Market and Powell Streets under Hallidie Plaza (*see chapter* **Essential Information**), or consult the pink Datebook section of the Sunday *San Francisco Chronicle/Examiner*.

Walking Tours

Architectural Tours
Heritage Tours, Foundation for San Francisco's Architectural Heritage (441 3004). **Tickets** $5 adults; $3 under-12s.
Among the neighbourhoods covered in depth are Chinatown, the Presidio and Pacific Heights, long the preserve of the city's wealthiest residents.

The Castro
Cruisin' the Castro from an Historical Perspective (550 8110). **Tickets** $30.
Trevor Hailey leads walking tours around the Castro, emphasising the history and development of the gay movement as well as points of architectural interest. A special visit is made to The NAMES Project on Market Street, where part of the AIDS Memorial Quilt is on display (the rest is stored on Townsend Street, where they are fast running out of storage space). The tour takes 3-4 hours and includes a stopover at the Castro Cinema and Harvey Milk's Camera Store, as well as a longer one for brunch.

Chinatown
Chinatown Discovery Tours (982 8839). **Tickets** $25 adults; $10 under-17s; *Wok Wiz Chinatown Tours & Cooking Co (355 9657).* **Tickets** $25 walk only; $35 with lunch; *Glorious Food Culinary Tours (441 5637).* **Tickets** $35 with lunch.
Among the many tours of the 24-block enclave is one lead by television chef and writer Shirley Fong-Torres, who runs Wok Wiz, which covers historical alleyways, Chinese herbalists and groceries, dim sum restaurants and fortune cookie factories. Another possibility worth investigating is Ruby Tom's Chinatown Culinary Walk.

Dashiell Hammett Walking Tour
Tour details (1-707 939 1214). Starts from San Francisco Main Library, Larkin Street, at McAllister Street. Muni Metro F, J, K, L, M, N/5, 8 19, 21, 26, 47, 49 bus. **Time** noon Sat. **Tickets** $10.
If Dashiell Hammett were alive today, he'd be just over 100, which is a good enough excuse to follow writer-guide Don

Herron around the Tenderloin in his hero's footsteps, and eat Hammett's meal at his regular restaurant, John's Grill at 63 Ellis Street. As Herron's tour proves, it's hard not to trip over Hammett's ghost; but even if you don't fancy Wild Turkey, pork chops or the Reading Room at the Main Library, go and see the placard near the Stockton Tunnel which reads 'On approximately this spot, Miles Archer, partner of Sam Spade, was done in by Brigid Shaughnessy'. Or visit Spade's apartment at 811 Post Street, where Sam clamped his teeth together and said to Brigid, 'I won't play the sap for you'. *See also chapter* **Literary San Francisco**.

Golden Gate Park

Friends of Recreation and Parks (information 221 1311). Free walking tours of the 1,017-acre green giant, led by the Friends of Recreation and Parks, take in all the major points such as the Strybing Arboretum and Botanical Gardens, the museums and the Conservatory of Flowers, as well as more flora and fauna and history besides.

Neighbourhood Walks

The City Guides, Friends of the San Francisco Public Library (information 557 4266). Voluntary guides steer visitors around town between May and October, shedding light on some unusual corners of the city. Most popular are their tours of North Beach, Victorian San Francisco, Pacific Heights and Japantown. Other tours cover the Beaux Arts Buildings and City Hall, Chinatown, Cityscapes and Roof Gardens. The Mission and its Murals takes in the entire area around 24th Street, where city artists following in the footsteps of Diego Rivera have produced an unparalleled number of building-sized murals (*see also chapter* **San Francisco by Neighbourhood**).

Other Tours

49-Mile Scenic Drive

This is a driving tour signposted throughout the city by blue-and-white seagull markers, designed to take tourists through the most scenic or historic parts of the city in less than a day (the San Francisco Visitor Information Center provides a map of the tour).

Bus Tours

Gray Line (558 7300); Golden City Tours (692 3044); Golden Gate Tours (788 5775); Super Sightseeing Tours (362 7808). Gray Line offers six bus tours daily that pick up passengers at central hotels; its Cable Car Tours send motorised cable cars from Union Square to Fisherman's Wharf, or to the Golden Gate Bridge, the Presidio and Japantown. Among the many other tour companies is Golden City Tours, which runs an enjoyable series of five-hour city tours, half-day trips out of town or Bay cruises, picking up tourists from their hotels. City tours cost around $25 for adults and are usually half-price for children.

Further Afield

For a tour of the beauty spots outside the city, try the **Great Pacific Tour**, which offers trips in the Bay Area and Wine Country (phone 626 4499 for more details). For more information on exploring beyond the bounds of the city, *see chapter* **Trips Out of Town**.

The peace pagoda in **Japantown**.

Trails of the City

If you're a fan of Armistead Maupin's 'Tales of the City' series, it's possible to discover all of the places he lovingly describes. Check out the **Buena Vista** bar where Mary Ann Singleton phoned her mother in Cleveland to tell her she was never coming back (2765 Hyde Street, near Fisherman's Wharf). Drop into **Perry's** in Pacific Heights (1944 Union Street, between Laguna and Buchanan Streets) to eye up the talent, just as Brian Hawkins did when he was a waiter there. Go cruising in **Marina Safeway**, where people still pick each other up as Mary Ann tried to when she first arrived in the city (15 Marina Boulevard). Go clubbing down **The End-Up** (995 Harrison Street) where Michael Tulliver won the jockey shorts contest, much to the shame of on-off lover Jon Fielding who happened to be in the audience. This is the place where all-night clubbers hang out on Sunday mornings. Go upmarket and wander into ritzy clothes shop **Wilkes Bashford** (375 Sutter Street) where Beauchamp bought all his suits. And finally, find **Macondry Lane** on Russian Hill, the street that inspired Barbary Lane and the house presided over by Mrs Madrigal.

Architecture

Exploring the city's skyline, from pastel-painted 'Victorians' to Post-Modern pyramids.

One of the city's many 'painted ladies'.

When architects talk of San Francisco's powerful sense of place, they invariably mention its 'dominant physiography' – in other words, hills steep enough to lean against, which create a unique stacking effect and, combined with the surrounding waterscape of the Bay, give San Francisco its spectacular appearance. The city's topography is the challenge that draws architects to it, inspired by the opportunity to perform at peak.

Since the first buildings were put up, San Francisco's citizens have fought to save the city from sand dunes, fires, earthquakes and the visually banal – and they struggle on with mixed results. Twenty years ago, they voted $25 million to beautify Market Street, which now boasts palm trees and restored Muni trolley tracks, although there is still some way to go. But by and large San Francisco has avoided 'Manhattanisation', resisting any move to build concrete boxes a mile high,

helped by the threat of earthquakes and the success of the conservation lobbies.

EARLY ARCHITECTURE

The Ohlone Indians, the first inhabitants of the Bay Area, left no permanent structures, so the settlement of Yerba Buena is represented by the simplicity of the thick adobe walls and painted hammer beams of the chapel of **Mission Dolores** (Dolores Street, at 16th Street) founded in 1776, and containing a poignant cemetery of Indian and outlaw graves mingled with those of the city's first Irish and Hispanic mayors. It is the oldest building in San Francisco and was one of 21 missions built in California by the Spanish. Only two others, at Carmel and Monterey, rival it for authentic atmosphere. Together with a portion of the original walls of the **Officers' Club** in the Presidio, the Mission is the only remaining piece of colonial architecture to have outlived the city's steep progress from hamlet to metropolis.

The 'Forty-Niners' or 'Argonauts', as the Gold Rush immigrants were called, suffered the city's scourge of fire after fire. Tiny **Portsmouth Square** (in present-day Chinatown) was the heart of the early outpost but it was razed by successive fires, and the surrounding streets all perished in the fire which followed the 1906 earthquake. The best examples of buildings surviving from the Gold Rush era are preserved in the nearby **Jackson Square Historical District** and are now used as design showrooms, law offices and antique shops.

THE PAINTED LADIES

It was the sudden burst of nineteenth-century prosperity and the *arriviste* urge to spend, spend, spend, that quickly filled San Francisco's once-empty slopes with its characteristic Victorian terraced houses. Built by middle-class tradesmen in the Mission and Lower Haight districts and by rich merchants in Presidio Heights and around Alamo Square, these 'Painted Ladies' provide the most distinctive architectural face of San Francisco. One of the city's most familiar views is of the row of five painted 'Victorians' along **Steiner Street** on the east side of Alamo Square in the Lower Haight; although these are sparkling examples, over 14,000 equally pleasing versions of the city's architectural vernacular rival them in ornamentation.

There are four distinct styles of Victorian, although all share similarities in having wooden frames decorated with mass-produced ornament. The earliest Gothic Revival houses have pointed arches over their windows and are often painted white, rather than the bright colours of the later styles. The Lower Haight area, notably Grove Street around Webster Street, contains versions of the later Italianate style, with its tall cornices, Neo-Classical elements and add-on porches. Perfect examples can be found at **1900 Sacramento Street** (near Lafayette Park) and at the 1876 **Lilienthal-Pratt House**, at 1818 California Street.

The Italianate style was succeeded by the Stick-Eastlake style, with square bay windows framed by angular, carved, redwood ornamentation, perhaps the most common among Victorian houses left in the city, and named after London furniture designer Charles Eastlake. A shining 'Stick' glory is the over-the-top extravaganza at **1057 Steiner Street**, at the corner of Golden Gate Avenue.

The so-called Queen Anne style, the last and most ornate of the form, with its turrets, towers and curvaceous, corner bay windows, is amply demonstrated by the **Wormser-Coleman** house in Pacific Heights (1834 California Street, at Franklin Street). Fans of this style will find no more extravagant example than the **Haas-Lilienthal House** (2007 Franklin Street, near Washington Street), built in 1886 by Bavarian grocer William Haas. He treated himself to 28 rooms and 6½ bathrooms with bay windows, as well as an upstairs bathroom with bidet, gas jet for curling tongs and Victorian Gothic shower head. The house has been turned into a museum and is one of the few Victorians open to the public (noon-4pm Wed, 11am-5pm Sun).

You can also visit the **Octagon House** at 2645 Gough Street, near Union Street (open noon-3pm on second Sun and second and fourth Thur of each month except Jan). Built in 1861, when the latest craze dictated that an eight-sided building was better for one's health, it's one of just two octagon-shaped buildings left in the city. Furnished in Early Colonial style, with Chippendale and Hepplewhite furniture, the upper floors have been restored to their original state with a central staircase leading to a domed skylight.

HOTELS & MANSIONS

Another example of the ostentation that was part and parcel of San Francisco's booming late nineteenth-century lifestyle, can be seen at the **Sheraton Palace Hotel** (at Market and New Montgomery Streets), where everyone from Rudyard Kipling to royalty stayed. Opened in 1875, it epitomised local entrepreneur Billy Ralston's dreams – and his inability to resist Italian marble and solid gold dinner services (still on display in the lobby). The original building was

greatly mourned after it burnt down in the Great Fire of 1906 and the city rebuilt it, glassing in the atrium for elegant dining and adding fashionable Art Deco murals in the bar, now painstakingly and splendidly restored. It's still a wonderful time-tunnel to the past, dropping you down somewhere between Old Vienna and the Prohibition Era (*see chapters* **Accommodation** *and* **Bars & Cafés**).

Ralston's friend, engineer Adolph Sutro, was his equal in ambition in buying a sandy wasteland at the very western edge of San Francisco in 1881 for his elaborate **Sutro Baths** (now in ruins) and the elegant **Cliff House**. Freshly annexed and civilised by the new Golden Gate Park, Sutro's property provided the city with the most elaborate baths in the western world. Much in need of repair by the 1960s and badly burnt in a fire, the baths were sold to developers for high-rise apartments that were never built. The adjoining Cliff House was twice burnt to the ground. The eight-storey 'castle' that was destroyed in 1907 was rebuilt in an unremarkable style, and is now open to the public (10am-5pm daily). It offers spectacular views of the Seal Rocks and the ocean, and also houses a Camera Obscura and Musée Méchanique, containing a collection of vintage mechanical games.

The 'Big Four' names in San Francisco business – Mark Hopkins, Leland Stanford, Collis P Huntington and Charles Crocker – also added their mark to the burgeoning city. Their mining investments funded railroads and public transport, banks and businesses, and their baronial mansions on Nob Hill, victims of the 1906 fire, have since been restored as the city's finest luxury hotels, among them the **Mark Hopkins Inter-Continental Hotel** (1 Nob Hill, at California and Mason Streets) and the **Stouffer Stanford Court Hotel** (905 California Street). One house that has not been turned into a hotel is the **Spreckels Mansion** (2080 Washington Street), an impressive Beaux Arts building occupying an entire block, built in 1912 for sugar baron Adolph Spreckel and now owned by best-selling novelist Danielle Steele.

PUBLIC BUILDINGS

The city has more than its share of oddities, among them the **Columbarium** (1 Loraine Court, off Anza Street, open 10am-1pm daily). Built in 1898, this tubby Neo-Classical temple houses the ashes of thousands of San Franciscans and has Portuguese mosaic tiling and elaborate urns in imaginatively decorated niches – a china football and photo of Candlestick Stadium in one, doll's furniture in another.

Another eccentricity is the **Vedanta Temple** (2963 Webster Street), where Oriental promise meets Occidental vulgarity. Built in 1905 for the Vedanta Society, its bizarre mix of architectural styles includes a Russian Orthodox onion-shaped

*East collides with West at the eccentic **Vedanta Temple**.*

dome, a Hindu cupola, castle-like crenellations and Moorish arches. It is open to the public for Friday night services only.

When the growing city began to burst at the peninsular seams, a ferry network evolved to carry passengers to and from the Bay Area cities. In 1896 the Embarcadero **Ferry Building** was built, inspired by Saville Cathedral's Moorish campanile, and it became the heart of the city's commuter network.

AFTER THE 1906 EARTHQUAKE

After the earthquake, a passion for engineering spurred an interest in Chicago architect Daniel Burnham's City Beautiful project; this proposed a heroic new Civic Center planted below a terraced Telegraph Hill, enlaced with tree-lined boulevards that traced the city's contours, rather than riding roughshod up and down the hills. The plan was the result of Burnham's two-year consultations with leading city architects Bernard Maybeck and Willis Polk – but it never came to fruition.

In the event, the city was hastily rebuilt on a grid plan. Under Mayor 'Sunny Jim' Rolph, the main thrust of the 1915 $8.5 million **Civic Center** complex came from public contests, many won by Arthur Brown, architect of the mighty-domed **City Hall** (200 Polk Street, at Van Ness Avenue). Other Civic Center buildings built at this time include the **Main Library** (Larkin Street at McAllister), the **War Memorial Opera House** (301 Van Ness Avenue) and the **Bill Graham Civic Auditorium** (99 Grove Street). All were built in the imperial style named after the Ecole des Beaux Arts in Paris and sometimes described as French Renaissance or Classical Baroque, distinguished by their grandiose proportions and ornamentation, theatrical halls and stairways.

It was largely Sunny Jim's idea to host the huge Panama-Pacific Exposition in 1915, for which he commissioned Bernard Maybeck to build the romantic Tower of Jewels, **Palace of Fine Arts** and myriad pavilions. Originally made of wood and plaster, the Palace (3601 Lyon Street, on the eastern edge of the Presidio) is the only building to survive, having been rebuilt in reinforced concrete in the 1960s.

Around the same time, Arts and Crafts architect Julia Morgan was at work on much of the East Bay, and on the extravagant Hearst Castle, home of San Francisco newspaper magnate William Randolph Hearst, located roughly 322 kilometres/200 miles down the coast at San Simeon.

Passionate rebuilding continued during the Depression, resulting in the **Bay Bridge** (1936) and the **Golden Gate Bridge** (1937) and a slew of WPA projects such as the **Coit Tower** on Telegraph Hill and **Alcatraz prison**. The Works Project Administration – introduced as part of President Roosevelt's New Deal job-creation scheme – had a hand in everything from murals

The unmistakable – and earthquake-proof – **Transamerica Pyramid.**

by Mexican artist Diego Rivera, to the organisation of community archives. The best examples of projects from this period include the 1932 **Herbst Theater** with its 1915 murals by Frank Brangwyn (inside the Veteran's Building at 401 Van Ness Avenue), the 1930 **Pacific Coast Stock Exchange** with its Rivera mural (301 Pine Street) and the old **Rincon Annex Post Office Building** (now part of the Rincon Center, on Spear Street). The last is a wonderful example of steel-trimmed marble, built in 1940; the entire building, including Anton Refregier's murals of Californian history, was a WPA project.

The only Frank Lloyd Wright building in the city is the red brick, oval-entranced **Circle Gallery**, at 140 Maiden Lane off Union Square. Designed in 1948 – a prototype of the Guggenheim in New York – it is now a private gallery.

RECENT ARCHITECTURE
St Mary's Cathedral (1111 Gough Street), designed by Pietro Belluschi, is, with its 61 metre/200 foot-high concrete structure supporting a cross-shaped, stained-glass ceiling, a 1970s' symbol of anti-quake defiance. So is the 260 metre/853 foot-high **Transamerica Pyramid** (600 Montgomery Street), built in 1972 and one of the most well-known buildings in San Francisco. Its $34-million seismic-proofed structure boasts internal suspension to protect it against tremors. Successfully, it would seem: the 48 stories and 65

metre/212 foot spire did not suffer in the 1989 quake. Originally unpopular, the tower now has few enemies and is regularly lampooned in the *Beach Blanket Babylon* revue and at Hallowe'en in the Castro: a sure sign of affection.

Along with John Portman's spectacularly glassy **Hyatt Regency Hotel** in the Embarcadero Center and the Post-Modern 'Juke-box' **Marriott Hotel** (55 Fourth Street), which opened on the day the 1989 earthquake struck, a preponderance of suspended glass panels has dominated the buildings of the last decade. Exceptions are the largely underground **Moscone Convention Center** and the nearby brick-trimmed **San Francisco Museum of Modern Art** (both part of the $87 million Yerba Buena arts complex), the latter by Swiss architect Mario Botta, which opened to great acclaim in 1995 (*see chapters* **Sightseeing** *and* **Museums & Galleries**).

The new **New Main Library** (on Larkin and Fulton Streets), designed by Cathy Simon of architects Pei Cobb Freed and due to open in the spring of 1996, is a discreet marriage of Beaux Arts and new design. One side links the building to the more contemporary Marshall Plaza while the other, with grandiose, grey-corniced, Neo-Classical columns, echoes the old Main Library, next door. The interior is just as theatrical, centred around a five-storey atrium beneath a 15 metre/50 foot domed skylight designed to let natural light filter throughout the building.

History

Key Events

The Ohlone Age

10,000 BC The Ohlone and Miwok – or 'Costanoan' – Indians begin to settle the Bay Area.

In Search of Eldorado

1542 Juan Cabrillo sails up the California coastline.
1579 Sir Francis Drake lands just north of San Francisco Bay, claiming the land he finds for Queen Elizabeth I as New Albion.
1769 Gaspar de Portola and Father Junípero Serra lead an expedition overland of 300 men to establish a mission at San Diego. An advance party under José Francisco Ortega is sent to scout out the coast. He becomes the first white man to see San Francisco Bay.
1775 The *San Carlos* is the first foreign ship to sail into the Bay.
1776 On 4 July 13 American colonies declare their independence from Great Britain.
In the autumn, a Spanish Presidio is founded near Fort Point and Father Junípero establishes the religious Mission Dolores to convert the Ohlone to Christianity.

Frontiersmen & Trappers

1821 Mexico declares its independence from Spain and annexes California.
1828 Fur trapper Jedediah Smith becomes the first white man to reach California across the Sierra Nevada.
1835 William Richardson founds the Yerba Buena settlement, later renamed San Francisco.
1846 The 'Bear Flag Revolt' against Mexican dominion.
1847 Yerba Buena is renamed San Francisco. It has 800 inhabitants.
1848 US-Mexican treaty confirms American dominion over California.

Gold!

1848 Gold discovered in the low Sierras just above Sacramento.
1849 The Gold Rush swells the city's population from 800 to 25,000 in less than a year. On Christmas Eve a huge fire levels the tent city.
1850 California becomes the 31st State of the Union. But lawlessness still rules in San Francisco.
1851 Vigilantes hang four men in Portsmouth Square.

1859 The Comstock Lode is discovered in western Nevada, triggering the Silver Rush.
1861 Civil War breaks out between the Union and the Confederacy in the US. Being so far west, California remains largely untouched by hostilities.
1868 The University of California is established at Berkeley.
1869 The Central Pacific Railroad reaches San Francisco.
1873 Andrew Hallidie builds the first cable cars.

The Great Quake Strikes

1906 The Great Earthquake strikes and the fire that follows razes the city.

Building Bridges

1913 The Los Angeles aqueduct opens.
1915 San Francisco celebrates the opening of the Panama Canal with the Panama-Pacific Exhibition.
1932 San Francisco Opera House opens.
1934 On 'Bloody Thursday', police open fire on striking longshoremen, leaving two dead, and prompting a three-day general strike that brings the Bay Area to a standstill.
1936 The Bay Bridge (*pictured*) is completed, joining San Francisco and Oakland.
1937 The city's most prominent landmark, the Golden Gate Bridge, is completed.
1941 The Japanese attack Pearl Harbour, bringing America into World War II.
1945 Fifty nations meet at San Francisco Opera House to sign the United Nations Charter.

From the Beats to the Present Day

1955 Allen Ginsberg reads *Howl* at the Six Gallery, with other members of the Beat Generation cheering him on. The first Disneyland opens in California.
1961 UC Berkeley students stage a sit-in protest against a HUAC meeting at City Hall.
1964 Student sit-ins and mass arrests grow as the Civil Rights, Free Speech and anti-Vietnam War movements gain momentum. John Steinbeck receives the Nobel Prize for literature.
1967 The Human Be-in, organised by Ginsberg, starts San Francisco's long Summer of Love. The San Francisco sound is defined by groups like Jefferson Airplane and the Grateful Dead. *Rolling Stone* magazine is founded by Jann Wenner.
1968 Seventeen year-old Bobby Hutton is killed in a Black Panther shoot-out with Oakland police.
1972 The Bay Area Rapid Transit (BART) system opens.
1978 Gay supervisor Harvey Milk and Mayor George Moscone are killed by former supervisor Dan White. Dianne Feinstein becomes Mayor.
1981 First cases of AIDS are recorded.
1989 An earthquake measuring 7.1 on the Richter Scale strikes San Francisco.
1992 Fire sweeps through the Oakland hills killing dozens and destroying 3,000 homes.
1995 Jerry Garcia, icon of the Grateful Dead, dies and his funeral is attended by 10,000 heart-broken fans.

The Ohlone Age

The hunter-gatherer existence of the early inhabitants of California is brought to an end with the arrival of European explorers.

San Francisco Bay began to take shape through the melting of the last glacial ice sheet a couple of millennia ago. The swelling waters of the Sacramento River and successive earthquakes created what we now call northern California, giving it roughly the outline it has today. Forty-three prominent hills jostle around two sandy peninsulas that almost meet at either end of the Golden Gate, like a forefinger and thumb crooked around towards each other, and this natural bay protects three islands – Alcatraz, Angel and Yerba Buena.

DANCING ON THE BRINK OF THE WORLD

Until the eighteenth century, the sand-swept, fault-striped peninsulas and surrounding area had scarcely changed in thousands of years. After the Ice Age had scooped out the deep gouge of the Bay and dappled the marshes with reeds and the hilly banks with meadows, the area came to sustain more than 10,000 north Californian Indians of different tribes, collectively known as the Costanoans – or 'coast-dwellers' as they were later dubbed by the Spanish.

The people who inhabited the site of the future San Francisco were the Ohlone. They seemed to live in harmony both with their Miwok neighbours and the land, which provided them with such rich pickings of game, fish, shellfish, fruit and nuts that they were scarcely forced to develop an agriculture. On the contrary, they were able to survive with little effort in a land of 'inexpressible fertility' in the words of a later French explorer.

Protected by the Bay's seeming inaccessibility, the Ohlone and their neighbours lived a successful hunter-gatherer existence – so an Ohlone song went – 'dancing on the brink of the world' – until their disastrous introduction to 'civilisation' at the hands of over-zealous Spanish missionaries. Up to this moment, their rare contacts with Europeans had been friendly.

In fact, the visiting Europeans had also been rather impressed by the welcome the Costanoans afforded them. But the Spanish returned their hospitality with the dubious gifts of God, 'civilising' hard labour in the fields, and diseases like smallpox, which would all but annihilate their number in a matter of 200 years.

Spanish Jesuits busy destroying a culture.

THE LONG GOODBYE

The tragic destruction of their culture has been largely ignored because the Ohlone and other tribes had no tradition of recording their history, orally or otherwise. Indeed, in Ohlone culture it was impolite to mention the past, the dead or your ancestors. The efforts of historian Malcolm Margolin (author of *The Ohlone Way*), and film-maker Pam Roberts, who restored ancient film footage and recordings for a documentary about the last Yahi Indian to speak his own language, *Ishi, the Last Yahi*, were an attempt to prevent much of northern Californian Indian culture disappearing without trace. Their work aside, the only surviving traces of the north Californian Indians feature in the records of their colonisers and destroyers.

In Search of El Dorado

The Spanish claim California as another colony, and set about 'civilising' it.

*The **Mission Dolores**, set up to consolidate Spanish control over northern California.*

Looking at the Golden Gate Bridge today, it's hard to imagine how anyone could miss the mile-wide opening into a bay that was twice as large back then as it is now. The Bay and its Indians were hidden from view by 'stynkinge fogges' (as Drake later complained) and a lush green island.

THE COLONISATION OF CALIFORNIA

The series of Spanish missions sent up the coast by Hernando Cortés, notorious conqueror of Mexico and the Aztecs, never got as far as Upper California. But in 1542, under the flag of Cortés' successor Antonio de Mendoza, the Portuguese Juan Cabrillo became the first European to visit the area. The Spanish named their new-found land El Dorado, after a mythical island in an ancient book, and hoped they would find gold there as they

had done further south. Yet, though he passed it both on his way north and back again, Cabrillo failed to discover the Bay's large natural harbour.

An Englishman got even closer, yet still managed to miss it. In 1579, during a foraging and spoiling mission in the name of the Virgin Queen Elizabeth, the then-unknighted Francis Drake landed in Miwok Indian territory just north of the Bay. His state-sanctioned pirate party was down to one ship, the *Golden Hind*, and his crew was in dire need of rest and recreation, when he put in for a six-week berth somewhere along the Marin coastline, probably near Point Reyes. Long before the Pilgrims landed at Plymouth Rock or the English settled Cupid's Cove at Newfoundland in 1609, Drake dropped anchor and claimed California for Queen Elizabeth I, naming it Nova Albion or New Britain.

But Drake's land-grab didn't stick, and details of his landing are vague and disputed. Drake's Bay on Point Reyes peninsula is the usual claim; but a counter-claim is made for San Quentin, near the present-day prison, thanks to the mention of a 'plate of brasse' made by Drake's logkeeper-chaplain, Francis Fletcher, which was unearthed there in 1936. Though it's very probably a fake, you can inspect it yourself in Berkeley's Bancroft Library.

It would take another 190 years for a white man to set eyes on the Bay. Under increasing pressure from the British colonial ambitions in America, the Spanish sent northbound missions to stake out their own territories, with a view to converting the 'bestias' (Spanish for 'savages') and claiming land for the Spanish crown. In 1769, the so-called Sacred Expedition of Gaspar de Portola, a Spanish aristocrat who would become the first governor of California, and the Franciscan priest Father Junipéro Serra, set off with 300 men on a gruelling march across the Mexican desert to establish a mission at San Diego. The expedition then worked its way north to Monterey, the area lavishly praised by the seventeenth-century explorer Vizcaíno, to claim it for Spain, building missions and baptising the Indians as they went. In November, a small advance party under José Francisco Ortega discovered the unexpectedly

Sir Francis Drake, with ruff.

wide bay 100 miles further up the coast. But since the expedition's brief was only to claim Monterey, Ortega's party returned to San Diego.

It was not until August 1775 that the first European ship, the Spanish supply vessel *San Carlos* under the command of Juan Manuel de Ayala, actually docked inside the Bay. Meanwhile, a mission under Juan Bautista de Anza and Father Pedro Font set off to establish a safer land route to what would eventually become San Francisco.

MISSION ACCOMPLISHED

Roughly concurrent with the American declaration of independence on 4 July 1776, which plunged American colonials into a revolutionary war against Britain, a Spanish military Presidio, or garrison, was begun near Fort Point to strengthen Spain's western claims. It was completed on 17 September 1776. The Mission San Francisco de Asis, named after the holy order operating in Upper California, but popularly known as Mission Dolores, was established by Father Junipéro Serra on 9 October 1776.

Father Serra's Mission was catastrophic for the Ohlone and their fellow tribes. Their friendliness was their downfall. Intrigued by the curious ways of the strangers, the 'bestias' were easily led into harsh servitude at the Mission, where their numbers were savagely reduced by illness and hard labour in the fields.

Drake's ship, the Golden Hind.

Frontiersmen & Trappers

The tiny hamlet of Yerba Buena is founded and finally, after the Spanish colonies crumble, becomes US territory.

Mexicans and Americans settle an argument.

Just as elsewhere in Latin America, the combination of Spanish favouritism, authoritarianism and religious fervour helped sow seeds of resentment and resistance in all the territories they colonised. Their hold on their American empires first began to crumble in Mexico, which declared itself a republic in 1821. The Mexican annexation of California in the same year meant that it became more open to foreign settlers, among them American pioneers like fur trapper Jedediah Smith, who in 1828 became the first white American to reach California over the Sierra Nevada. His feat might have been the more impressive, but the sedate arrival, by whaler ship, of an Englishman had a more lasting impact. He was Captain William Richardson, who pioneered the settlement of Yerba Buena Cove when, in 1835, he built the first dwelling on the site of the future San Francisco. He is credited with its first name: Yerba Buena, named after the sweet mint the Spanish used to make tea.

That same year the United States bid unsuccessfully to buy the whole Bay Area from the Mexicans. But in the long run they got California for free. The Texan declaration of independence, and its consequent annexation by the United States, triggered the Mexican-American war in June 1846. The resulting Guadaloupe-Hidalgo treaty of 1848 officially granted the Union all the land from Texas to California, and the Rio Grande to Oregon. But before the treaty could be nailed down, a few American hotheads decided to 'liberate' the territory from Mexico.

THE BEAR FLAG REVOLT

The short-lived Mexican rule of California was also the era of idealistic frontiersmen like the 'Bear Flaggers' John Frémont and Kit Carson. By the time of their arrival, the Presidio (fort) had fallen into such an obvious state of disrepair that Frémont, an American army captain, believed he could seize it with half a dozen volunteers. In June 1846, Frémont convinced his motley crew to take over the abandoned Presidio in Sonoma, in the valley to the north of the Yerba Buena, and with it the Spanish General Vallejo's ranch, where the victors drank wine with the defeated, yet polite general. Captain Frémont proclaimed his new state The Bear Flag Republic after the ragged bear flag he raised over Sonoma's adobe square (the design was eventually adopted as California's state flag). Frémont also christened the mouth of San Francisco Bay the 'Golden Gate', after Istanbul's Golden Horn, insisting it would some day become glorious. A few weeks after the Bear Flaggers annexed Sonoma, Yerba Buena's Presidio was captured without a struggle by the US Navy, and the whole of California became US territory.

At this point, the infant Yerba Buena was just a sleepy trading post of 800 people. On 30 January 1847, the newly appointed Mayor, Lieutenant Washington A Bartlett, officially renamed it San Francisco. But the tiny settlement was about to change beyond all recognition. Days before the 1848 treaty ending the Mexican War was signed, a man named James Marshall found something glittering at the bottom of the stream in John Sutter's sawmill, up in the foothills of the Sierras. It was gold....

Out for a day's hunting in about 1850.

Gold!

The nascent city is flooded with prospectors, and fortunes are won and lost in the era of lawlessness and expansion that follows.

In the early 1840s former Swiss citizen Johann – or John – Sutter was running New Helvetia, a large ranch, as if it were his own dukedom. With the consent of the Mexican Governor of California, he encouraged American citizens to settle the land. One such was James Marshall, who built a sawmill for his landlord at Coloma, near Sacramento. Returning from the Bear Flag adventure, Marshall discovered gold in the water at the sawmill. Naturally enough, the pair attempted to keep their discovery secret, but word got out, and once the news hit town, 'boosters' – the San Francisco equivalent of town criers – and newspapermen quickly spread the word around the world, prompting the 1849 Gold Rush.

CALIFORNIA OR BUST

Every kind of drifter and fortune seeker made their way around Cape Horn to California – in windjammers, whalers, sloops and steamships. The Bay was white with sail. Soon, hundreds of ships lay abandoned in Yerba Buena Cove, deserted by crews gone to pan for gold in the hills. Others arrived after a treacherous trek across malarial Panama, and yet more headed west by land, crossing prairies in covered wagons – Prairie Schooners

– with 'California or Bust!' emblazoned on their sides. The journey meant months of exposure to blizzards, mountains, deserts and hostile Indians. Their raging fever had been fanned by people like local shopkeeper Sam Brannan of Portsmouth Square, whose *California Star* newspaper told of men extracting fortunes within an hour up at the diggings, and who marched down Market Street with a jar of gold dust, shouting: 'Gold! Gold!' But in reality, the accessible riverbed gold quickly dried up and the seams that were left were too difficult for solitary prospectors to exploit.

The prospectors' port of arrival was a city of confusion with no clear name – Yerba Buena or San Francisco – no identity and no planned structure. Thousands of young men (who became known as the Forty-Niners), milled about its non-existent streets looking for release from the miseries and hardships they found instead of gold. On their way through San Francisco to the mines they were fleeced by predatory merchants who charged a glass of gold dust per shot of whisky, and they found the basics hadn't got any cheaper by the time they got back, broke. So they were left to grub mean existences from the mud that passed for the city's undoubtedly mean streets, seeking refuge in brothels, gambling dens and bars.

Within a year of the Sutter discovery, 100,000 men passed through the city, swelling the tiny settlement into a giant muddy campsite. The population leapt from 800 to 25,000, with a transient population four times as large. It was not a place for the faint-hearted. Lawlessness and arson ruled. A huge fire levelled the settlement on Christmas Eve in 1849, but just as quickly a new camp rose up to take its place.

DUCKS, HOUNDS AND HOODLUMS

Eyewitness accounts of San Francisco abound at the time of the Gold Rush – and the Silver Rush of the 1860s. Mark Twain and Bret Harte, and, later, visitors Robert Louis Stevenson, Oscar Wilde and Anthony Trollope, all reported on its exciting, if lurid reputation. They described an anarchic boomtown where guns, violence, gambling and prostitution were commonplace. Unburied corpses littered the streets, while the living sheltered in tents or shacks on roads which were little more than muddy canals. Even so, Twain was taken with the place, calling the nascent city 'the liveliest, heartiest community in the continent'. Elsewhere he observed: 'A wild, free, disorderly, grotesque society! Men – only swarming hosts of stalwart men – nothing juvenile, nothing feminine visible anywhere'.

The men charged with administrating the city viewed its anarchy with horror. In August 1849, the future Mayor John White Geary wrote: 'At this time we are without a dollar in the public treasure and it is to be feared the city is greatly in debt'. Geary had been appointed First Postmaster by President James Knox Polk as a reward for fighting Mexicans at the Battle of Vera Cruz. Upon arrival, his first act was to find a room for the city's post office. Eventually he rented one at the corner of Montgomery and Washington, where he marked out squares for the alphabet and began filing letters for the newcomers under each. This crude set-up was the first postal system for San Francisco's 10,000 souls. The opening of the post office was the city's first optimistic stab at improving communications with the rest of the continent and the world.

His first task successfully discharged, Geary established a council to furnish the city with proper streets. The council bought the brig *Euphemia* and turned it into San Francisco's first jail. It was a sound investment.

In April 1850 – the year California became the 31st State of the Union – San Francisco's city charter was approved. Elections for mayor were called, which Geary won. The council's first concern was to impose law and order on San Francisco's massive squatter town. Vicious hoodlums controlled certain districts between them. One gang, called the Ducks, was led by tough Australian convicts, who lived at a spot known as Sydney Town. Together with a bunch of New York toughs called the Hounds, they roamed Telegraph Hill to rape and pillage among the more orderly community of Chilean merchants who occupied 'Little Chile'. Eventually, their outrages incurred the wrath of right-minded citizens, who decided to take the law into their own hands.

FRONTIER JUSTICE

Whipped into a fury by the rabble-rousing newspaperman Sam Brannan, the vigilantes established a Committee of Vigilance headquarters and lynched their first victim, John Jenkins, at a Portsmouth Square 'necktie party' in June 1851. Three more thieves were lynched during the following weeks by way of warning to the other Ducks and Hounds, who immediately cut out for the Sierras. If the vigilantes' frontier justice temporarily curbed the lawless excesses of the area, they were still as much part of the problem as the solution to Mayor Geary.

Their crusade against lawlessness was hardly helped when the riverbed gold started running dry. By 1853 boom had turned to bust. The resulting depression set the cyclical boom and bust pattern which would be repeated through the city's history. By the mid-1860s, the city was $2 million in debt and was forced to declare itself bankrupt.

The first cable car, Clay Street at Kearny.

NOBS, SNOBS AND SLOBS

But then came the Silver Rush. The discovery in 1859 by prospector Henry Comstock of a rich blue vein of ore (the 'Comstock Lode') in western Nevada triggered another invasion by the world's fortune seekers. This time, though, the nature of the ore demanded more elaborate methods of extraction. Businessmen set up companies to raise the capital necessary to get at the metal. Individual prospectors scarcely got a look in and the initially high yields went instead to a relatively small number of companies and tycoons. Before the seams ran dry, they'd made enough money to transform the face of San Francisco. By 1870, it was no longer just a town of seething brothels. Its *nouveaux riches* had established a millionaire quarter of mansions on Nob Hill.

If the nobs atop the hill took the moral and geographical high ground, the city's easy money went on sluicing the vice dens dotting the city's waterfront at the bottom of Telegraph Hill, earning it the nickname Barbary Coast. Naïve newcomers and drunken sailors alike were viewed as fair game by the gamblers and hoods waiting to 'shanghai' them (like 'hoodlum', 'shanghai' is a San Francisco expression). As were the immigrant girls who'd find themselves waking up to a life of prostitution or slavery having been given spiked drinks.

Family life was as rare as women with unblemished reputations. At one low point, the female population numbered just 22, and none of them respectable, according to a French visitor who lavished $300 on a whore. No wonder the mere sight of a woman could reduce the city's roughnecks to a state of silent awe. Many a brothel madam made enough of a fortune to buy her way onto Nob Hill.

WIND FROM THE EAST

The roots of San Francisco's present-day multiculturalism reside in this period, when a deluge of immigrants poured in from all over the world for its gold and silver rushes. The rapidly growing Chinatown was later expanded with the coming of the transcontinental railroad, which brought in thousands of Chinese labourers at criminally low pay rates.

Naturally enough, in common with the city's other ethnic districts, not all of Chinatown's 4,000 inhabitants were gainfully employed: the Tongs (or affiliations) controlled the opium dens and other rackets.

Their obviously different culture and appearance made the Chinese easy targets for the first wave of racist anti-immigrant activity perpetrated by so-called Nativists, who used the existence of the opium dens as the excuse for their attacks. But San Francisco would have been a far dirtier place without the Chinese. A Chinaman, Wah Lee, opened the city's first proper laundry in Chinatown. The success of Chinese laundry and restaurant businesses did little to improve the Chinese standing in the community, however. Proscriptive anti-Chinese legislation, which restricted the numbers of immigrants and all but prohibited their families from accompanying them, would persist right through until 1938. The unfairness of their treatment was finally officially acknowledged in a speech by President Kennedy to Congress in 1962.

The Chinese weren't the only nationality adding to the city's growing culinary reputation. Miners washed up in San Francisco Bay from all over the world yearning for home-cooking provided a ready market for the enterprising cooks and waiters who came to feed them. Sourdough bread was invented by French immigrants vying with the Italians for the Best Bread vote in North Beach. Necessity bred invention in other fields, too. Young immigrant Levi Strauss used rivets to strengthen the jeans he made for miners to stop them from tearing so easily when they stuffed their pockets with gold.

Entertainment was always high on the agenda for San Franciscans, be they writers like Mark Twain holed up at Lick's Hotel, gold miners, silver barons, prostitutes, poets, bankers, traders, hoodlums or city officials. In 1853, the city boasted five theatres, 27 consulates, 250 streets, 38 water cisterns for fire hoses and two squares. It was divided into eight public wards and split into ghettos of Germans, Mexicans, Chileans, Chinese and a growing black population. Some 600 saloons and taverns served 42,000 customers, and citizens downed seven bottles of champagne for every bottle swallowed in Boston. When Lola Montez, entertainer to European monarchs and thieves, arrived on a paddle-steamer from Panama in 1853, her 'Spider Dance' became an instant hit at the American Theater.

COME WEST, YOUNG MAN

The Ohlone Indians sang of 'dancing on the brink of the world' and indeed, San Francisco's relative isolation from the rest of the continent had its advantages. The city was hardly affected by the Civil War that devastated the South in the first part of the 1860s. But as the masses who raced across country and round Cape Horn to participate in the Gold Rush ruefully learnt, getting to San Francisco was at the very least very uncomfortable, and more

often than not hazardous in the extreme. And once they got there, the six-month wait for letters consolidated their sense of isolation.

Communications were slowly improving, however. Telegraph wires were gradually progressing across the continent, and where the telegraph poles ran out at St Joseph, the Pony Express would pick up the message, providing a relay of up to 75 despatch riders across the West to get the mail to the Pacific Coast. By the mid-1860s, however, the telegraph had all but rendered the Pony Express obsolete. Its *coup de grâce* was provided by the coming of the transcontinental railroads built to transport cattle and human cargo. An important turning point in San Francisco's history came with the arrival of the Central Pacific Railroad in 1869.

The completion of the railroad was the signal for runaway consumption in the city, and the biggest spenders were the 'Big Four', the mighty millionaires who were the powerful and influential principal investors behind the Central Pacific Railroad – Charles Crocker, Collis P Huntington, Mark Hopkins and Leland Stanford. Their eagerness to impress the West with their flamboyantly successful business practices manifested itself in the mansions they built on Nob Hill.

The Big Four were highly adept at making money for themselves and their favoured partners, and cutting out the competition. By 1871, 121 businessmen controlled $146 million, according to one newspaper. But others did get in on their act. Four legendary Irishmen who'd chipped their fortunes from the silver Comstock Lode, came to be known as the Bonanza Kings. James Flood, William O'Brien, James Fair and John W Mackay were rough-hewn miners and barmen, yet their money was good enough to buy their way onto Nob Hill.

Of course, there were also casualties, like the Scottish-Irish banker and industrialist Billy Ralston, who opened the Bank of California on Sansome Street in 1864. Partnered by a Prussian engineer called Adolph Sutro (later famous for the first Cliff House and the Sutro Baths), Ralston was hellbent on the idea of tunnelling into Sun Mountain to extract every last ounce of silver. Unfortunately, he was left high and dry when the precious ore ran out before he and Sutro had recouped their investment, leading to the collapse of Ralston's bank. Smiling to the last in an effort to calm his investors, Ralston was later found drowned after he went bathing off the jetty – and his wife collected on his insurance.

Apart from his wife, Ralston left behind the luxurious 7,000-room Palace Hotel; but he also had a hand in the development of the Golden Gate Park, which became the symbol of San Francisco's new civic pride. Ralston's company provided the water for designer William Hammon Hall's audacious project, which ultimately turned the sand dunes of the 'Outside Lands' into 1,017 magnificent acres of trees, plants, flowers and lakes.

The Great Quake Strikes

The city is ripped apart and then burnt to the ground by the Great Earthquake and Fire of 1906.

Keeping up appearances in the face of disaster.

The city continued to grow, and by 1900 its population had reached more than a third of a million, making it the ninth largest city in the Union. But on 18 April 1906, shortly after 5am, dogs began howling and horses whinnying and prancing – noises, along with glasses tinkling and windows rattling, that marked the few tense and unnerving seconds before an earthquake. The sun was rising, when out at sea a schooner approaching the city suddenly leapt two feet in the air. A rip in the tectonic plates 25 miles beneath the ocean bed had triggered the shifting of billions of tons of rock, generating more energy than all the explosives used in World War II.

The rip snaked inland, tearing a gash down the coastline that is now known as the San Andreas Fault. Cliffs appeared from nowhere, cracks yawned, ancient redwoods were toppled and the fine dome of the 29 year-old City Hall collapsed like a soufflé. The streets began to undulate and church bells pealed crazily. A second tremor struck, ripping the walls out of buildings. A ghastly pause

followed, then half-naked people ran into the street, some in nightgowns or pyjamas, or less.

Tragically, one of the earthquake's many victims was a man the city direly needed just then: the popular Fire Chief Dennis Sullivan. He was not long back from fighting a cannery fire when the earthquake struck. He was found in the rubble of the firehouse and died some days later. The fire brigade seemed lost without him. The second tremor had destroyed the city alarms and disrupted the water pipes feeding the fire hydrants, leaving the famous fire-fighters of the West absolutely helpless.

The Great Fire of 1906, which compounded the disaster of the earthquake, was started when a Hayes Valley woman defied an order not to cook. The breakfast she was preparing for her family proved costly to the city when the cracked stove set her roof alight. The fire spread, until Mayor Eugene Schmitz and General Frederick Funston were forced to carry out a desperate plan to blow up the houses along Van Ness Avenue to make a fire-break. The mansions belonged to the very rich folk that any politician would be loathe to alienate, but in this instance necessity spoke louder than money.

RISING FROM THE ASHES

On the third day the wind changed direction, bringing rain. By 21 April 1906, the fire was out. The earthquake and 74-hour inferno was initially thought to have accounted for some 700 dead, though military records now reveal that the figure probably ran into several thousand. At least 500 people suspected of looting were shot dead in the chaos that followed the quake and fire. Three-quarters of a million people were left homeless, and 3,000 acres of buildings were destroyed. Yet even before the ashes had time to cool, the citizens set about rebuilding their city. Within 10 years the San Francisco phoenix had risen from the ashes. Some claimed that in the rush to rebuild, city planners passed up the chance to replace its street grid system with a more sensible one that followed the natural contours of the area. But there's no doubt that San Francisco was reborn as a cleaner, more attractive city and, furthermore, one that, within three years of the fire, could boast that it contained half the United States' concrete and steel buildings. Such

A grandstand view of the Great Fire.

statistical boastfulness was not out of keeping with the 'boosterism' that accelerated its post-gold rush growth from tiny settlement to the large, rumbustious, anarchic and exciting city of opportunity now ready to meet the twentieth century full on.

The quake at first hand

Edna Laurel Calhan, an 18 year-old who lived with her mother and grandmother on Fillmore Street, had been to a church revival meeting the night before; and thought it was the end of the world when she woke to see the folding doors slamming and the glass in the window actually bend. One of many San Franciscans who wound up in a tent in Golden Gate Park, in later life Edna ran for office as San Francisco's first woman Supervisor.

We had rented a room upstairs to a young man and he came down pulling on his pants. I said, 'If you could see how you look you'd go back and put some more clothes on'. He said, 'If you could see how you looked you'd do the same!' I had all these pigtails, I had picked up my long black opera cloak and put it on over my nightgown and I was barefooted... We went to the front door and the electric wires were broken in the street, and the water main had broken and the water was shooting in a geyser up in the air... We decided we had to get out.

I went down to the corner of McAllister and Fillmore. There was a grocery store; the grocer had a lot of buggies, because it was a large store. I went down to ask him if I could borrow one of his buggies to get Mother and Grandma out. He was wringing his hands and said he didn't know one end of a horse from the other. I said: 'Well, I do'. He gave me the keys. I went out on Baker Street near Presidio Avenue. There was a large

wooden barn with horses. I picked out a buggy and hitched it up and went over to get my mother and my grandmother. I filled a jug with some water from the broken main and I took the perishable things. Then I drove them out to Ninth and Fulton where my brother lived.

Before I had left the house, when I was deciding what to do, I was watching people go by. A woman came by in a beautiful evening gown with her Japanese houseboy. She didn't have a thing and he didn't have a thing either. They just walked by. A young man came by with a wheelbarrow and on it was a large looking glass. Tied with a string to his leg he had a rooster. The rooster was on top of the barrow fighting the rooster in the glass. Another man went by carrying a bird cage with a cat in it. I said, 'What have you got a cat in the cage for?'. He said, 'The cat ate the canary so I thought I'd keep the cat'.

When I was walking in the Panhandle I met a young couple. They had a very young baby and they were just frantic. The wife was crying. The man had gotten a baby bottle. He had milk in it and was trying to heat it... People were so helpless: they just didn't know what to do...

Taken from 1906 Remembered: Eye Witness Accounts of the Great Quake, *and reproduced by kind permission of the Friends of the San Francisco Public Library.*

Building Bridges

The city is hard-hit by the Depression, but still manages to build two revolutionary bridges and celebrate their opening with a World Fair, as war breaks out in Europe.

The San Franciscans set about rebuilding their city with a vengeance. The most potent symbol of their restored civic pride was the new City Hall, for the construction of which they secured an $8 million city bond. It wasn't good enough simply to take their architectural cue from the Capitol building in Washington DC – by the time it was completed in 1915, City Hall rose some 16 feet higher than the building it was modelled on.

Between 1913 and 1915 two new waterways important to the economic vitality of California were opened. In 1913 the Los Angeles aqueduct was completed, thereby beginning the transformation of that once sleepy cowtown into the urban sprawl of modern LA. And in 1915, the opening of the Panama Canal considerably shortened the shipping times connecting the Atlantic and Pacific coasts. San Francisco celebrated the achievement by hosting the hugely successful Panama-Pacific Exposition. Not even the outbreak of World War I in Europe dampened the city's party spirits. On the contrary, the war provided a boost to California's mining and manufacturing industries. But the good times were quickly swallowed up in the world depression signalled by the Wall Street Crash of 1929.

BLOODY THURSDAY

As elsewhere in America, the Depression brought to an end the economic well-being of the 1920s. It hit San Francisco port especially badly and three-quarters of the workforce was laid off. As a result, on 9 May 1934, under the leadership of its charismatic Australian-born organiser Harry Bridges, the International Longshoremen's Association declared a coast-wide strike. Other unions came out in sympathy, including the powerful Teamsters. They succeeded in shutting down work in the Bay for three months. A crew of black-leg workers did manage to break the picket on 5 July – Bloody Thursday – but with disastrous results. As the violence escalated, the police opened fire, killing two strikers and wounding 30. A general strike was called for 14 July, when 150,000 people stopped work and brought San Francisco to a standstill for three days. The strike ground to a halt when its leaders couldn't agree on how to end the stalemate, but the action wasn't completely futile: the longshoremen won a wage

increase and a degree of control in the hiring halls, though Harry Bridges later fell foul of Senator McCarthy's anti-Communist witchhunts.

BRIDGING THE BAY

Despite this black chapter in the city's labour relations, San Francisco still managed an extraordinary amount of construction. In 1932 the San Francisco Opera House was completed. In 1933 the notorious prison island of Alcatraz was transferred from the army to the Federal Bureau of Prisons, which set about building high security accommodation for 370 'incorrigible' convicts.

The decade's two other landmark constructions were the San Francisco-Oakland Bay and Golden Gate bridges. The former, completed in 1936, consists of two back-to-back suspension bridges connected by a tunnel though Yerba Buena Island. Six months after the Bay Bridge was finished, the russet-orange, pure suspension Golden Gate Bridge began to rise from the Bay with its revolutionary gusset-ribbed design. Its opening meant that people could drive the full eight and a quarter miles across the Bay. The bridges had their downside, however. Their impact on the ferry traffic that had served the city and its suburbs so well was devastating. Commuter trains also suffered – at least until the completion of the Bay Area Rapid Transit (BART) subway system in 1972 encouraged some drivers to leave their cars at home.

To celebrate the new era ushered in by the opening of the bridges, the city hosted another fair in 1939, on new landfill off Yerba Buena Island: the Treasure Island Golden Gate International Exposition. It was described as a 'Pageant of the Pacific' and those who went were dubbed the Thirty-Niners by local wits. It was to be San Francisco's last big celebration for a while; in 1941 the Japanese attacked Pearl Harbour, bringing America into World War II.

THE FORTUNES OF WAR

World War II changed the city almost as much as the Gold Rush or the Great Quake. More than one and a half million men and thousands of tons of material were shipped out from the Presidio, Travis Air Force Base or Treasure Island, to the Pacific. Between 1941 and 1945, the entire Pacific war effort passed under the Golden Gate. Oakland's shipyard

workers worked overtime to keep the war effort going, and the massed ranks of troops and some half a million wartime civilian workers flooding San Francisco turned the city into a milling party town hellbent on giving its boys a last good time before they departed for battle.

Towards the end of the war in Europe, in April 1945, representatives of 50 nations met at San Francisco Opera House to draft the United Nations Charter, which was eventually signed on 26 June 1945 and formally ratified in October at the General Organisation of the United Nations in London. Many people felt – and still do – that San Francisco was the ideal location for the UN headquarters, strategically and racially. But the British and French thought it was too far to travel, and the headquarters moved to New York, much to the city's disappointment.

From the Beats to the Present Day

The post-war generation dances to a new Beat and then discovers radical politics, while the city establishes itself as the centre of the counter-culture.

Just as San Francisco during the war was characterised by mass troop mobilisation, the immediate post-war period was coloured by the return of the demobilised GIs. One such GI was poet Lawrence Ferlinghetti. While studying at the Sorbonne on his GI scholarship in the early 1950s, Ferlinghetti discovered Penguin paperbacks and was inspired to open his tiny wedge-shaped bookshop at 261 Columbus Avenue. Called City Lights, it became the natural mecca for the bohemians later known as the Beat Generation, many of whose works he published in his City Lights Pocket Poets series.

BEAT BUT NOT BEATEN

The Beat Generation, so named by novelist Jack Kerouac, reflected the angst and ambition of a post-war generation attempting to escape both the shadow of the Bomb and the rampant consumerism of ultra-conformist 1950s America. In Kerouac's definition, Beat could stand for beatific or being beat – as in exhausted. The condition is most enthusiastically explained in his most famous novel *On the Road*, which charted the restless coast-to-coast odysseys of San Francisco-based Beat saint Neal Cassady (thinly disguised as Dean Moriarty), poet Allen Ginsberg and Kerouac himself (named Sal Paradise). Another novel, *The Dharma Bums*, chronicles the impact of the Beat movement on the West Coast. It also vividly reports the poetry reading of 13 October 1955 at the Six Gallery on Fillmore Street, when Allen Ginsberg read his famous poem *Howl*, with Jack Kerouac and the 150-strong crowd shouting 'Go! Go! Go!'.

Other notable poets Philip Whalen, surrealist Philip Lamantia, Michael McClure and Gary Snyder were also introduced to the wildly enthusiastic audience by the bow-tied senior poet and literary guru Kenneth Rexroth, but of all the poems read that night, it was Ginsberg's *Howl* which

Peter Orlovsky and Allen Ginsberg (right).

made the deepest impression. When City Lights printed it in England, it was seized by the US Customs, who prosecuted publisher Ferlinghetti for obscenity. The lengthy trial focused the eyes of the world on San Francisco's poetry renaissance.

'The emergence of the Beat Generation made North Beach the literary centre of San Francisco – and it nurtured a new vision that would spread far beyond its bounds,' reflected Ferlinghetti, 40 years on. 'The Beats prefigured the New Left evolution and the impulse for change that swept eastward from San Francisco.'

The attention of the world might have been on the beret-clad artists and poets populating North Beach cafés, but the opening of Disney's first theme park, Disneyland, at Anaheim in 1955 was perhaps more truly reflective of mainstream America.

SUMMER OF LOVE AND HAIGHT

Kerouac, Ginsberg and mass media exposure had established the Bay Area as a mecca for the burgeoning counter-culture. If the Beats renewed American suspicions that San Francisco was the muesli capital of the US, where the landmass ran out for drifters and all the continent's fruits and nuts fetched up, then their fears were about to be confirmed by the hippie explosion of the 1960s.

The Beats and the hippies might have shared a love of marijuana and a common distaste for 'the system', but a generation gap formed even here in the counter-culture. The Beats sometimes mocked their juniors as part-time bohemians, and Kerouac – by the 1960s an embittered alcoholic – abhorred what he perceived as the hippies' anti-Americanism. His distaste for the new bohemians pouring into California was shared by John Steinbeck, winner of the Nobel Prize for Literature in 1964, who shied away from the recognition he was now receiving in the streets.

Where the Beats were never interested in converting their dissatisfaction with the system into political action, the newer generation were prepared to tackle it full on. A sit-in protest against a closed session of the House of Representatives Un-American Activities Committee at the City Hall in 1961 drew ranks of protesters from San Francisco State University and Berkeley's University of California. It quickly degenerated into a riot, establishing the pattern of counter-cultural protest and police response to come. In the following years, the civil rights movement and America's involvement in the Vietnam war added urgency to the voices of dissent; Berkeley students were at the forefront of protests on campuses around the country. By the mid-1960s, the counter-culture was split between the politically conscious students behind the Free Speech movement and the hippies who'd chosen to opt out of the system altogether.

The spreading popularity of LSD, boosted in San Francisco by such events as the Human Be-in organised by Allen Ginsberg in 1967, and the Acid Tests overseen by Owsley Stanley and the Grateful Dead, drew an estimated 8,000 hippies from across America. Some 5,000 of them stayed, occupying the cheap old Victorian houses round the Haight-Ashbury district (later dubbed 'the Hashbury') not far from Golden Gate Park – the scene of the Be-in. The combination of San Francisco's laissez faire attitude, sun, drugs and the acid-induced psychedelic music explosion produced one golden Summer of Love that year. By 1968, the spread of hard drugs, notably heroin, had taken the shine off the hippie movement. Shuffling around the Haight-Ashbury district strung out on hard drugs or burnt out altogether, the flower children were no longer the beautiful people of their self-projection.

THE BLACK PANTHERS

The politics were getting harder too. Members of the Black Panther movement, the radical black organisation founded in the predominantly Afro-American suburb of Oakland by Huey Newton and

Bobby Seale, asked themselves why they should ship out to Vietnam and shoot South-east Asians they'd never met when the real enemy was at home. Around Oakland, the Panthers took to exercising the purportedly basic American right to bear arms. Gunfights inevitably followed. In April 1968, Panther leader Eldridge Cleaver was wounded in the leg and 17 year-old Bobby Hutton was killed in a shoot-out with Oakland police. By the early 1970s, the Black Panther movement had petered out, its leaders either dead, imprisoned or, like Cleaver, on the run. The kidnapping of the Hearst newspaper empire's heir Patty by the tiny radical outfit the Symbionese Liberation Army in 1974 was perhaps the point where the 1960s revolution turned to deadly farce. Hearst was eventually captured, along with the SLA, after being brainwashed or converted into joining their cause.

THE LSD LEGACY

Despite the violence that characterised the student and anti-war protests, black radicalism and failed revolutions, the enduring memory of 1960s' San Francisco is as the host city to the Summer of Love. The psychedelic blasts of the Grateful Dead, Big Brother and the Holding Company with and without Texan *émigrée* Janis Joplin, Country Joe and the Fish, Jefferson Airplane and Quicksilver Messenger Service defined both the San Francisco sound and counter-cultural attitude. Jann Wenner founded *Rolling Stone* magazine in 1967 to explain and advance the counter-cultural cause, and later document its growth into a multi-million dollar mass entertainment industry, helping to invent New Journalism in the process. The extent of its impact can be partly measured by the seriousness with which it was taken: *Rolling Stone*'s most demented writer, Hunter S Thompson, was an accredited journalist on the 1972 campaign trail that returned Richard Nixon to the White House.

THE KILLING OF HARVEY MILK

San Francisco's radical baton was taken up in the 1970s by the Gay Liberation Movement. Local gays insisted that strong gay traditions had always existed in San Francisco, first of all among the Ohlone Indians, and later out of necessity, during the 1849 Gold Rush, when women in the West were scarcer than gold. Early homophile groups like the Daughters of Bilitis, the Mattachine Society and the Society for Individual Rights (SIR) had paved the way for more radical political movements of the 1970s.

In 1977, gay activists made successful forays into mainstream politics. Jim Foster of SIR became the first openly gay delegate at a Democratic Convention. For the ninth year running, the Gay Pride Parade drew participants from all over the world. And Harvey Milk was elected onto the city's

Tuning in and dropping out.

Board of Supervisors. Then, on 28 November 1978, Dan White, a former supervisor, climbed into City Hall via a basement window to escape the metal detector, and shot and killed Milk and Mayor George Moscone. The killings stunned San Francisco.

White was a former policeman from an Irish Catholic working-class background, who had run for supervisor as an angry young blue-collar populist and won. But he suffered poor mental health and had to resign under the strain of office. He quickly changed his mind and asked Mayor Moscone to reinstate him. But Milk, who held the deciding vote, persuaded the Mayor not to let the unstable White back in – with catastrophic consequences. White turned himself in after the killings. In the subsequent poorly prosecuted court case, the jury returned two verdicts of voluntary manslaughter instead of first-degree murder counts. White was sentenced to seven years.

The sentence prompted a journalist to wonder jokingly why the jury had not posthumously convicted the slain Milk of 'unlawful interference with a bullet fired from the gun of a former police officer'. The outraged gay community responded to the verdict by storming City Hall and hurling rocks through its windows. The disturbance escalated into a full-blown battle, known as the White Night Riot.

For his part, White committed suicide not long after his release from prison.

THE AIDS CURSE

Gay life and politics changed radically and irrevocably when the first cases of AIDS were diagnosed in 1981.

The onset of the HIV virus tore the gay community apart and initially caused controversy when the bath houses – symbol of gay liberation and promiscuity – were closed in panic over the disease's spread. Gay activist Randy Shilts was branded a 'fascist Nazi, traitor and homophobe' by gay radicals when he ran a story in the *San Francisco Chronicle* criticising bath house owners

who refused to post safe sex warnings.

To date, there have been some 15,000 AIDS-related deaths in San Francisco. The city is home to the most efficient volunteer activists in the country, who've taken charge of housing, food and legal problems for many thousands of people diagnosed as HIV positive, and San Francisco General Hospital is still the country's number one AIDS care centre.

STRIKE TWO

Because of its location on the San Andreas Fault, San Francisco has always lived in expectation of a major earthquake to match the 1906 disaster. One came in October 1989, while Oakland was playing the San Francisco Giants during the World Baseball Series. The Loma Prieta earthquake (named after the ridge of mountains at its epicentre) hit 7.1 on the Richter Scale in the middle of the play-offs. A section of the West Oakland Freeway collapsed, crushing many drivers beneath the concrete and arousing fears that hundreds more had been killed. The Marina district and Bay Bridge were hit hard, but in the final count, damage was relatively slight and the number of casualties was less than 70. Far worse than the damage itself, from the survivors' point of view, was the incompetence of the city's rebuilding programme, which compared unfavourably with the clean-up following the LA earthquake of 1987.

INTO THE 1990S

As it approaches the end of the millennium, San Francisco suffers the same social problems that blight many major American cities in the wake of the economic and welfare cutbacks exercised by President Reagan's administration in the 1980s. Homelessness is particularly severe in the city. More than 12,000 destitute men and women overwhelm the 44 under-funded downtown agencies set up to help them.

Roughly a fifth of these are former asylum inmates, homeless since Ronald Reagan – when Governor of California – emptied the mental hospitals. Others have drink problems or are drug users, but some are simply those who fell behind with the rent.

On a more positive note, the city is still a magnet for the world's economic migrants dreaming of a better life. With an Asian community that makes up one fifth of its population, San Francisco is set to remain America's most Asian city at the turn of the century, and the Hispanic community is almost as large. Immigrants from Russia and Eastern Europe pour in at the rate of 1,000 or more each month, and Americans, too, continue to flock to the US city where it's still possible to reinvent yourself. Multicultural San Francisco continues to function as a crucible for new trends and influences as it looks forward to a new century of 'dancing on the brink of the world'.

San Francisco Today

'If you're alive, you can't be bored in San Francisco. If you're not alive, San Francisco will bring you to life.' (William Saroyan).

In some ways the Gold Rush never ended for San Francisco, despite earthquake, fire, depression and the advent of Los Angeles as the capital of the Pacific Rim. Magical life-changes, and the discovery and reworking of the past, continue to be the frame of reference for the city.

This is at once San Francisco's greatest asset and its greatest problem. Like Peter Pan, San Francisco retains its magic because it won't grow up, leave Neverland and admit that life cannot be endlessly re-invented. As one would expect, this makes the city alternately winning and maddening, as it continues down its idiosyncratic path, usually oblivious to the rest of the world. Certainly in 1996 the city is marching to its own drummer, whose beat reverberates to themes such as multiculturalism, feminism, gay rights, pluralism in the arts and an addiction to being amused. This is in

stark contrast to most of the United States, which continues to turn grimly to the right. San Francisco remains politically left-of-centre, fighting rearguard actions on every issue to maintain the city's quality of life and *sui generis* personality.

Despite its free-spirited ways, San Francisco hasn't been able to escape the disheartening problems of late twentieth century urbania: crime, homelessness, AIDS, declining literacy and erosion of the infrastructure. And it hasn't been able to solve them, either. Like other US cities, San Francisco has had budget cuts curtailing some city services and diminishing others. San Franciscans, generally a hip, consumer-oriented population, carefully track the political movements (political 'alerts' run in one weekly paper like entertainment listings and are just as avidly read). Citizens complain loudly and bitterly over everything from AIDS funding to treatment of the homeless to reduction of funding for the arts. Indeed, visitors often look askance at the level of vitriol splashed around during elections and in complaints by the citizenry.

The physical beauty of San Francisco remains undimmed, however, while the variety and scale of amusements are among the nation's best. This is all the more surprising when one considers that San Francisco is far away from the days when it reigned as the unquestioned capital of the American West. Today, San Francisco isn't even the largest city in the Bay Area. That crown goes to San Jose, bustling with Silicon Valley energy.

RADICAL POLITICS

Yet 'The City', as its populace and newspapers insist on calling it (capital T, capital C), has a far more powerful impact than mere numbers would suggest. San Francisco consistently produces political leaders who move into statewide and national leadership. San Jose and the Los Angeles suburbs, the genuine population hot-spots, seem to put forward only bland candidates who fail to capture the imagination of the voters. In 1992 Californian – and American – political traditions were turned upside down when two Bay Area women became California's US senators. Dianne Feinstein, who had been the city's first woman mayor, was elected to one seat, while Barbara Boxer, a congresswoman from Marin, won the other. It's hard to overstate how inconceivable this election was until it happened. Women have only made the barest inroads into the US Senate, often called the most powerful men's club on earth. In California, it was unheard of for both senators to come from the same part of the state, let alone the same party. Southern California-Northern California rivalry is intense and unforgiving. For two women, both Democrats, both from the San Francisco Bay Area, to capture two of the biggest prizes in US politics, says a great deal about the level of politics and sense of entitlement practised in San Francisco.

CITY OF DREAMS

San Francisco's energy and excitement about itself is constantly renewed by an endless stream of new residents. The city is a magnet to the young and adventurous. Gays of all ages look on San Francisco as a kind of Mecca, but the allure goes beyond sexual preference. Like the Forty-Niners who came to make their fortunes, the regular waves of newcomers are seeking a new kind of life. The wildly ambitious go to New York, the fameseekers go to Los Angeles, the cautiously ambitious go to Chicago, but the dreamers, hopers and visionaries come to San Francisco. This uncategorisable yearning for otherness has yielded the Beats, Allen Ginsberg, Jack Kerouac and company; the American Zen Buddhist movement; 1960s acid rock; hippies; the Summer of Love; the modern

Fans mourn the passing of Jerry Garcia.

dance of Isadora Duncan; Levi's; the United Nations; the gay liberation movement; California cuisine, and Danielle Steel's romance novels.

San Francisco has a significantly higher proportion of never married people under the age of 35 in its population than most major cities. It's a place where people go to begin their lives and follow their dreams. When their lives are well underway and their dreams have been achieved or substantially altered, they will often move on. The cost of living in the city is among the highest in the US. When these bright, busy young people marry (or if gay, declare themselves domestic partners at City Hall), they often find it impossible to afford to buy a home and raise a family in San Francisco. There's a steady movement outward to the suburbs, even among gay couples.

HOMELESSNESS

Because San Francisco is a city of renters, many of whom deeply resent their status, the homeless issue takes on a particular edge here. Some are fond of saying that everyone is only a couple of paychecks away from being homeless. San Franciscans often make what would be considered princely salaries in other cities, yet live like undergraduates in the city they love. Rent control and affordable housing are volatile issues that stir up tremendous political debate, but no clear mandate

San Francisco by numbers

723,959 official city population (1990 US census: 338,917 white; 207,457 Asian or Pacific Islander; 96,640 Latino; 76,944 African American; 4,001 other).

6,023,577 population of the nine Bay Area counties (ibid.).

207,469 estimated gay and lesbian population (1994, Horizons Foundation).

11,000-16,000 estimated homeless population (1994, City of San Francisco, Comprehensive Housing Affordability Strategy, Final Report).

46.38 square miles area of San Francisco (SF Convention & Visitors Bureau).

15,609.2 number of San Franciscans per square mile (extrapolated).

8.4 miles of shoreline (SF Convention & Visitors Bureau).

3,038,000 annual visitors (1993, ibid.).

9,555,142 annual flights in and out of San Francisco International Airport (1994, ibid.).

30,575 number of hotel rooms (ibid.).

$150 million annual economic impact of the arts and cultural activity in San Francisco (San Francisco Hotel Tax Fund).

9 per cent workforce in arts-related jobs (San Francisco Art Commission).

3,372 number of eating establishments (California Restaurant Association).

11 miles of cable car track (SF Convention & Visitors Bureau).

2,252 total AIDS cases in San Francisco in 1994 (San Francisco Department of Public Health AIDS Office).

1,142 in 1995 (as of August, ibid.).

726 new AIDS cases in 1995 (as of August, ibid.).

1,829 in 1994 (ibid.).

115,982 reported crime in 1994 (San Francisco Police Department).

124,033 in 1993 (ibid.).

53 murders and non negligent manslaughters in 1994 (ibid.).

93 in 1993 (ibid.).

1,114,754 total annual visitors to Alcatraz (1994, SF Convention & Visitors Bureau).

42 average age of a San Francisco tourist (ibid.).

14,000 number of Victorian houses (ibid.).

45 number of professional mystery writers living in SF (Mystery Readers International).

125 number of outdoor monuments, sculptures, and statues (San Francisco Art Commission).

5,000 gallons of paint used annually to paint the Golden Gate Bridge (the official colour is International Orange, SF Convention & Visitors Bureau).

7,601 marriage licences issued in 1994 (San Francisco Recorder's Office).

2,928 same sex couples registering as domestic partners in 1994 (ibid.).

21 earthquakes of magnitude 2.0 or more in San Francisco (1994, United States Geological Survey, National Earthquake Information Centre, Denver, Colorado; 2.0 is usually the minimum for a quake to be felt).

13 in 1995 (up to October, ibid.).

67 per cent possibility of San Francisco experiencing an earthquake of 7.0 or more before the year 2020 (USGS, Information Centre, Menlo Park, California).

emerges. Renters are a powerful voting block, but they are counterbalanced by the deep pockets of real estate interests. The situation lurches toward one plan and then another.

All the while the homeless, believed to number anywhere from 11,000 to 16,000, haunt the streets and parks. City programmes have been some help in providing health care and temporary shelters for the homeless, but dealing with the root problems has proved elusive. The city is understandably nervous about the impact the homeless have on visitors, as tourism is now San Francisco's number one industry. But the city's deeply held ideas about

The San Francisco Museum of Modern Art: symbol of a new cultural era?

tolerance and democracy clash with programmes that aim to sweep the homeless off the streets.

Not as visible to the visitor, but even more troubling is the AIDS crisis. As a centre of gay life, San Francisco has inevitably been at the centre of dealing with AIDS. San Francisco's AIDS death total was approaching an estimated 15,000 at the end of 1995. The loss and destruction is really too enormous to comprehend, but it is in this holocaust that the gay community has shown its steel. From the early days of rag-tag fundraisers in Castro Street bars organised by healthy friends to help sick friends, gay men and lesbians have forged an AIDS support infrastructure that has served as a model for the rest of the US. San Francisco hospitals provide the world's most comprehensive and sensitive care for people with AIDS, bracketed by a sophisticated political lobby and a deep-seated concern for the quality of life of people with AIDS. In this San Francisco interpretation of tragedy, it's not just the body that must be ministered to but the spirit as well. Consequently, there is a volunteer group that delivers beautifully prepared healthy meals to AIDS households (free), while another organisation helps sick people with their pets. There is also a proliferation of support groups, alternative medicine healers and economic counsellors. In spite of the crisis, gay men and lesbians have emerged as an ever more powerful voting and cultural block in the city.

A FEAST OF FOOLS

Underlying San Francisco's political obsessions, AIDS tragedies and urban angst, is an irrepressible *joie de vivre*, unmatched in other US cities. Crusty old William Saroyan got it exactly right when he said 'San Francisco is the genius of American cities'. The genius is most clearly seen in the city's ability to transform everything from a foot race to city government to public transport into pageantry and drama. The annual Bay to Breakers Run, for instance, isn't so much an athletic event as a slow-moving Feast of Fools that features runners in costumes so bizarre that Rio's Carnival pales in comparison. A gay stand-up comic is one of the 11 members of the Board of Supervisors, but is widely considered to be one of the more constrained members. And then there are the cable cars, those antiques that trundle up and down the city's steep inclines, still attended by a grip (driver) and a conductor. Against all odds the cable cars have survived and even flourished, as other US municipalities routinely gutted their public transport systems after World War II.

There's a populist attitude about the arts in San Francisco, which makes little distinction between pop culture and traditional culture. The opening night of the opera in September, for example, is celebrated on the same scale as the first day of the baseball season. When the San Francisco Ballet decided to ditch popular artistic director Michael Smuin a few years ago, the move was as hotly debated as when the 49ers traded football hero Joe Montana a few years later.

With dire cutbacks in arts funding on the horizon, San Francisco has continued to marshal energy and money for major projects. The new San Francisco Museum of Modern Art is one of the world's most important new art buildings. It is hoped that the striking Mario Botta postmodern pile will signal a new era in the Northern California art scene. Certainly, its opening has created a new arts district almost overnight, around Yerba Buena Gardens in the hitherto drab South of Market area. At the same time, a splendid new public library has been built at the Civic Centre and the earthquake-damaged Geary Theater is being brought back to life despite a huge pricetag.

James Joyce presides over Vesuvio's Café.

San Francisco supports an internationally-renowned opera, symphony and ballet, yet has a population of under a million. Although the population of the Bay Area numbers something over six million, the city's commitment to the arts is still remarkable. One of the mainstays of the arts is the Hotel Tax Fund, an agency that allocates money from tourist dollars to arts groups. Though it has been galling for San Franciscans to see the city become dependent on tourism, the tourist has protected many of the city's treasures. Armed with facts and figures showing that a hefty dose of the tourist horde is made up of the much-loved 'cultural tourist' (well-educated, well-heeled, prone to stay longer and spend more), arts administrators are able to make powerful arguments for the city continuing to support its institutions in a big way.

One of the most vibrant cultural innovations in the 1990s has been the mushrooming of 'spoken word' events. Almost imperceptibly, arid poetry readings by the unpublished evolved into spirited performances, often with music. This crystallised into the poetry slam – an Olympic-esque event with judges, scorecards and Muhammad Ali-style posturing by the participants. The phenomenon has slowly percolated above street-level, mostly taking place in cafés and bars in the Haight, the Mission and SoMa. When the mainstream press began to tune in, a reporter ventured to interview one of the organisers. When the subject of Beat poets and their jazz readings was broached, the spoken word spokesman was offended. 'That's like expecting Bing Crosby to be at Woodstock', he said.

It was the perfect comment. In the great San Francisco tradition of hubris, the young poet was convinced that his generation had invented its own wheel, one unrelated to the primordial efforts of earlier wheelwrights. It is also the perfect illustration of what's good and enduring about San Francisco. Few of the inhabitants actually believe that there's nothing new under the sun. Even fewer believe that the sun doesn't orbit around San Francisco. It's this half-mad attitude that keeps the energy churning and the wild ideas flowing. San Francisco wills itself to be larger than the sum of its parts – and it is.

SF by Neighbourhood

Downtown

Explore the chic shops of Union Square, the gleaming towers of the Financial district and an abundance of cafés and bars in which to adopt the recovery position.

San Francisco, unlike most major cities in the world, doesn't have a true centre, but is composed of various neighbourhoods, each with its own distinct character and style. It's not so much a melting pot, as a presentation of individual dishes. For example, downtown is the place for mainstream shopping, South of Market is for music, eating and clubbing. The Marina has been colonised by the mostly single yuppie set, while the Castro is almost entirely gay, and the Haight is a mix of grunge and gentrification. Pacific Heights' inhabitants are nearly all Getty-style rich. The Western Addition is predominantly black, North Beach is Italian, the Mission is Mexican. Such diversity would be exhausting if it were not for the fact that San Francisco is relatively small, enabling you to explore the neighbourhoods on foot, by car or using public transport, with relative ease.

For more information on many of the places and sights mentioned in the following chapters, *see chapters* **Sightseeing**, **Museums & Galleries**, **Bars & Cafés** *and* **Restaurants**.

Around Union Square

As with so many American cities, the downtown area of San Francisco, centred along Market Street from about Second to Fifth Streets, and north as far as Pine, is rarely crowded. Aside from a few overenthusiastic sales assistants, who invariably pounce on you before you've even crossed the threshold, and some similarly zealous panhandlers, exploring is therefore relatively stress-free. Within a short walk of Union Square (where much of Francis Ford Coppola's movie *The Conversation* was shot), are the **San Francisco Shopping Center**, a nine-storey shopping mall of department stores, boutiques and shoe shops; the **Crocker Galleria** shopping complex; department stores **Macy's** and **I Magnin**; toy shop **FAO Schwartz**; and enough clothing stores, from Banana Republic and The Gap to Tiffany and Chanel, to keep most shopaholics busy for weeks.

If you get tired of shopping, **Union Square** itself, named after the Union rallies that were held there during the American Civil War, is a nice enough place from which to watch passers-by. There are also several interesting art galleries in the area, including the **Erika Meyerovich**

Gallery (on Grant Avenue), with its permanent collection of pieces by Picasso, Chagall, Warhol and Matisse, and the **Joseph Dee Camera Museum** (above Brooks Camera shop on Kearny Street). Not far away, between Stockton Street and Grant Avenue, lies **Maiden Lane**, once one of San Francisco's most dangerous and seedy alleyways (famous for having the cheapest prostitutes). It has been transformed into an exclusive shopping street, the centrepiece of which is the exquisite **Circle Gallery** at 140 Maiden Lane, designed by Frank Lloyd Wright in 1949.

There is a huge choice of coffee shops and restaurants in the area but most are either prohibitively expensive or uninspired tourist-trap fast food joints. There are some exceptions, however. **Café de la Presse** (next door to the Hotel Triton on Grant Avenue) sells a broad selection of international magazines and newspapers to browse through, and is a good place to sit outside on a sunny morning and watch the people wandering in and out of the nearby gateway to Chinatown. Tucked away in an alley (Claude Lane, near Union Square), bustling **Café Claude** feels like a Parisian sidewalk café, with chairs and tables outside and live jazz on most evenings.

It would be hard to miss the **Powell Street cable car turnaround**, where there is always a long line of tourists waiting to get on board. If you want to take a cable car ride, do what the locals do, and get on a block or two further up the hill. At the end of the day pay a visit to **Club 36** inside the Grand Hyatt Hotel on Union Square. This jazz venue on the 36th floor has fabulous views of the city and has been called one of 'the best places to kiss in California'.

Local buildings of particular interest include the **Humboldt Savings Bank Building** (783 Market Street, at Fourth Street). Under construction when the 1906 earthquake hit, work on it had to be started all over again; now newly restored, it is a beautiful example of one of San Francisco's earliest skyscrapers. It would be hard to miss the **Phelan Building**. Built in 1908 by Mayor James Phelan (the 'honest politician') as part of his famous reconstruction programme, it is San Francisco's largest flatiron building (so-called because of its triangular shape) and takes up most of the block on Market Street between Third and Fourth Streets.

City Hall, *the centrepiece of Civic Center. See page 82.*

The Financial District

The Financial District, which roughly covers the area along Market Street from Second Street to the Embarcadero, and north to Jackson Street, has been the commercial centre of San Fmrancisco for over a century, since the establishment of the first bank there in the 1850s. Nowadays it is ruled by the **Transamerica Pyramid** on Montgomery Street, which looms 260 metres/853 feet above the area's earliest buildings. Sadly, one of its best, the original building of the Bank of California (400 Market Street), which was inspired by St Mark's Library in Venice, was demolished in 1906 to make way for expansion; the present Classical structure was built in 1908. One of the most interesting buildings is the **Merchant's Exchange** (465

California Street), rebuilt in 1906 after the Great Fire and which houses an impressive collection of William Coulter seascapes.

Wannabe financial wizards can practise their skills at the **Federal Reserve Bank Building** (101 Market Street) on computer games that simulate the stock market. To catch the flavour of the Gold Rush days, visit the **Wells Fargo History Museum** (420 Montgomery Street). Mementoes of the Wild West include paintings, photographs, gold nuggets and a real stage coach.

However, this being famously liberal San Francisco, the Financial District also has some incongruously non-financial landmarks, including the **Transamerica Redwood Park**, next to the Transamerica Pyramid and notable for its free jazz and blues concerts, and the **American Indian**

Contemporary Arts Gallery, upstairs at 685 Market Street, which also has a gift shop.

There are many excellent restaurants in the area but particularly noteworthy are the **Rubicon** (558 Sacramento Street) – which is part owned by Robert de Niro, Robin Williams and Francis Ford Coppola – and the magnificent **Tommy Toy's Cuisine Chinoise**, opposite the Transamerica Pyramid. Consistently voted the best Chinese restaurant in the city, it is as famous for its excellent service (a convoy of elegantly dressed waiters delivers every course) as for its signature menu, which is so popular that it that hasn't changed in ten years.

Geographically within the bounds of the Financial District is the area known as **Jackson Square Historical District**, a brick-built oasis of low-rise buildings dating from the 1850s, which used to be one of the city's most notorious red-light districts in the late nineteenth century. In the 1930s it became popular among artists and writers, including John Steinbeck and William Saroyan, who used to drink at the now non-existent Black Cat Café, and socialist artist Diego Rivera who had a studio on Gold Street. Nowadays, the area retains a slightly artsy feel, partly because so many creative advertising agencies are based there.

Two interesting restaurant-bars popular with after-work drinkers are **Bix** (56 Gold Street) – which has live jazz most evenings and a reputation for brilliant martinis – and just around the corner at 500 Jackson Street, the **Cypress Club**, where the bizarre, 1940s-inspired interior might make you wonder if your Martini has been spiked with acid.

Civic Center

The once-grand Civic Center is a popular homeless hang-out overlooked by the splendour of **City Hall**, designed by Arthur Brown, also the architect of Coit Tower. The magnificent **War Memorial Opera House** and **Louise M Davies Symphony Hall** are reminders of the Civic Center's former opulence but the area is now mostly deserted, except on Wednesdays and Sundays when it comes to life for a superb **Farmers' Market**.

Just up Van Ness Avenue, at Opera Plaza, **A Clean Well-Lighted Place For Books** is regarded as one of the city's best bookstores; pick up a programme to find out which famous authors will be giving readings while you're in town. Next door, at **Max's Opera Cafe** you can request operatic turns from your waiter or waitress. The appropriately named **Stars** restaurant (150 Redwood Street) is the place for celebrity spotting. If that's too pricey for you, check out the **California Culinary Academy**, on Polk and Turk Streets, for bargain meals made by tomorrow's famous chefs.

The **History Room at the San Francisco Public Library** (on the corner of Larkin and McAllister Streets) contains a mine of information. There is a browsing section, changing exhibits, an archive of a quarter of a million photographs of San Francisco history and the staff are knowledgeable and helpful. For even more history, don't miss the **Society of California Pioneers** at 456 McAllister Street, whose members are the descendants of the first settlers – but you'll have to make an appointment first (861 5278).

The Tenderloin

The Tenderloin, the downtown area roughly bordered by Larkin, Mason, O'Farrell and Market Streets, is San Francisco's red-light district and much is made of its potential for danger. One of the most politically organised – and active – neighbourhoods in the city, it has been settled by poor immigrants, especially from Indochina, and most recently by artists. During the daytime, Cambodian grandmothers in sarongs policing their grandchildren blend in amongst the homeless and crack dealers. At night it is sensible to know where you're going, and take a cab if necessary, for there are plenty of good reasons to explore the Tenderloin.

The jazz and blues venue, the **Blue Lamp** (561 Geary Street) is one reason, as is **The Edinburgh Castle** pub down the road which serves fish and chips wrapped in newspaper. Also look up **Miss Pearl's Jam House** (601 Eddy Street), where you can eat brunch on a Sunday and shake it off to the tune of a live steel band; **Biscuits and Blues** on Mason Street (for live blues), and the **Mason Street Wine Bar** (for live jazz) are also worth checking out. Hearing someone sing *Love for Sale* is given a new poignancy by the fact that you can see prostitutes doing business outside on the street.

If you're up late, **The Grub Stake** on Pine and Polk Streets is open until 4am every morning, serving delicious greasy spoon fare to a variety of customers. Exotic dancers from the local nude revues, transvestite singers and transsexual prostitutes with their 'dates' mingle with tourists and hungry clubbers. Don't miss the **Glide Memorial United Methodist Church** (330 Ellis Street), which serves food to around 3,000 homeless a day, and sponsors several drug rehabilitation programmes, and where the Reverend Cecil Williams conducts uplifting sermons on Sundays.

The Tenderloin is also home to San Francisco's theatre district. Within a few blocks of each other are the **Theater on the Square** (on Post Street), the **Improvisation Theater** (on Mason), the famous **American Conservatory Theater** (on Geary), and the **Golden Gate Theater** (on Taylor). Check local papers for what's playing while you're in town. *See also chapter* **Theatre & Dance**.

Chinatown & North Beach

Sample the chow mein in Chinatown, follow the Beats in North Beach or track down the mythical 'Barbary Lane' on Russian Hill.

*Former site of Chinatown's telephone exchange, now the **Bank of Canton**. See page 84.*

Hemmed in by the gleaming towers of the Financial district to the east and the affluent hotels of Nob Hill to the west, **Chinatown** is one of the oldest ethnic neighbourhoods in America. Before the discovery of gold in the Sierra foothills, there were only a few hundred people living here. Today, it's home to over 8,500 residents and forms part of the largest Asian community outside Asia. **North Beach**, San Francisco's predominantly Italian neighbourhood, is most famous for being home to the Beat poets in the 1950s and 1960s. Bordered by Bay, Washington, Montgomery and Leavenworth Streets, nowadays the area is an odd mixture of Italian, Bohemian, touristy and sleazy, with strip joints and clubs doing business alongside some of the city's best restaurants and coffee shops. Surrounding these enclaves are three of the city's most famous hills, Russian Hill, Telegraph Hill and Nob Hill.

Chinatown

The influx of the Cantonese began in the late 1840s, fuelled by the dream of striking it rich and the need to escape the Opium Wars and famine at home, and later by the prospect of work on America's transcontinental railway. The area the Chinese had settled was completely destroyed by the 1906 earthquake and fire, but despite attempts by city politicians to confiscate what had become premium land, the community managed to rebuild on the same area before anything could be done. The new Chinatown was as cramped as the old – and today the crowded streets are thronged with tourists and shoppers, lured by the scent of herbal shops, Chinese food markets and hundreds of restaurants offering regional Chinese cuisine.

A few blocks from Union Square, the dragon-topped **Chinatown Gateway** – a gift, in 1970, from Taiwan – opens (at Bush Street) onto **Grant Avenue**. Once called Dupont Street and a notorious thoroughfare of gambling and opium dens, it was patrolled by *tongs*, the secret groups formed in the late 1870s and 1880s to combat racial attacks, but which quickly developed into mafia-style gangs fighting to control the gambling and prostitution rackets. Today it's the official main drag of Chinatown, clogged with souvenir shops peddling tacky T-shirts, sweatshirts, cameras, Chinese art, china, ceramics and toys.

Several blocks north of Grant Avenue (and one block east) is **Portsmouth Square**, the historical centre and pulse of Chinatown. Bounded by Washington Street to the north and Clay to the south, the square has been unprepossessingly rebuilt over an underground car park. This is where the small village of Yerba Buena was first claimed for the United States (from Mexico) in 1846, and where Sam Brannan, owner of the city's first newspaper, the *California Star*, announced the discovery of gold two years later. The surrounding streets were the first to be settled by the Chinese in the 1840s and 1850s. From around 7am each morning locals gather in the square to practice *tai chi* and, later, Chinese men congregate on the east side to play hotly-contested games of Russian poker or Chinese chess. **Robert Louis Stevenson** spent some time in San Francisco in 1879, and a monument on the north-west side of the square – the galleon *Hispaniola* – stands in his honour.

Across the square, on the third floor of the Holiday Inn at 750 Kearny Street, is the **Chinese Culture Center**, linked to Portsmouth Square by a concrete footbridge. The Center puts on art exhibitions throughout the year, sponsors cultural events and stocks a useful collection of books in its gift shop. Two blocks south, at 650 Commercial Street, the **Chinese Historical Society Museum** traces the history of the Chinese people in America in pictures and documents, and also houses the original – handwritten – Chinatown telephone book.

It's worth exploring the surrounding network of side streets and alleyways. In the days when Chinatown was confined to a five-block area, you didn't need a map to get around – a good nose was enough. The street now called **Wentworth Alley**, off Washington Street, was known as 'Salted Fish Alley', and was the place to buy fresh and preserved fish. Refrigerators were a rarity in the cramped conditions where several families had to share one tiny kitchen, and fish was salted and 'sun-dried' on the rooftops. Eggs were preserved in large jars of salted water for 40 days or more.

Walk back along Washington Street, and follow the scent of the **Golden Gate Fortune Cookie Factory**, at 56 Ross Alley (between Grant Avenue and Stockton Street) to watch the cookies being made by hand. On the south side of Washington Street is 'Fifteen Cent Street', named after the price

of a haircut in the 1930s, and officially called **Waverly Place**. It's a wide, picturesque street that stretches between Washington and Sacramento Streets, parallel to Grant and Stockton. On the fourth floor of one of its brightly-painted buildings, at number 125, is the **Tien Hau Temple**, dedicated to the Queen of Heavens and Goddess of the Seven Seas. Opening times vary, but if you're lucky you'll be able to peep into the incense-filled sanctuary.

The **Bank of Canton**, at 743 Washington Street, almost directly across the street from Waverly Place, is probably one of the most photographed buildings in the area. The *California Star*'s offices originally occupied the site, but the present pagoda-like creation was built for the Chinatown Telephone Exchange.

The small alley to the west of Ross Alley, off Washington Street, is called **Old Chinatown Lane** (and used to be known as the 'Street of Gamblers'). It was once home to **Donaldina Cameron**, the determined New Zealander who devoted her life to saving young Chinese girls from slavery and prostitution. **Cameron House** at 920 Sacramento Street – a youth centre that also offers social services to immigrants in Chinatown – is her legacy to the neighbourhood.

The **Chinese herbalists** are one of the pleasures of Chinatown. There's a string of them on Jackson and Clay Streets, their entire walls filled with hundreds of drawers containing various herbs, purchased not just to cure ill-health but also to maintain good health. Look in at the famous **Li Po** bar (916 Grant Avenue), decorated with Asian kitsch and one of San Francisco's more outlandish spots. At 949 Grant Avenue is the **Ten Ren Tea Shop**, the largest in San Francisco, where you can choose from 40 different types of Chinese tea.

To the west of Grant Avenue, running the length of Chinatown, is **Stockton Street**, where the locals shop daily. The street is lined with Chinese fish markets, supermarkets, grocery stores, windows displaying roast duck, soy sauce chicken and roast pig with crackling skin, and dim sum restaurants. If you are in a hurry, duck into one of the many takeaway restaurants to pick up an order of chow mein or a cha sil bow (steamed barbecued pork bun).

North Beach

Despite being a popular tourist attraction as much for its Beat heritage as for its thriving Italian bars, cafés and restaurants, North Beach retains a sense of authenticity – no doubt because 'real' people still live and work here as well as because of all the genuine reminders of its past.

The bars on the back windows of the Italian pottery store **Biordi** on Columbus Avenue, for example, are a reminder of the days when it was a

Eating in Chinatown

Chinatown is a paradise for food lovers. The following is a list of restaurants worth investigating in the area. For more places to eat in Chinatown, and in the Chinese enclave in the Richmond district, *see chapter* **Restaurants**.

Bow Hon
850 Grant Avenue (362 0601).
A funky, small café which specialises in noodles and claypot dishes.

Chef Jia
925 Kearny Street (398 1626).
This tiny – and popular – Szechuan restaurant serves hot and spicy food.

Kowloon Vegetarian
909 Grant Avenue (362 9888).
Tasty vegetarian dim sum in a brightly-lit, narrow, two-level restaurant.

Lucky Creation
854 Washington Street (989 0818).
Small, inexpensive Chinese vegetarian hot spot. Generous use of fresh vegetables, beans and whole-grain products.

Royal Jade
675 Jackson Street (392 2929).
Three-level Chinese restaurant – like a typical teahouse – which offers dim sum by day, dinner and banquets in the evening.

Sun Hung Heung
744 Washington Street (982 2319).
One of the oldest, but just-renovated, Cantonese restaurants. Excellent won ton and noodle dishes, and fresh seafood; famous for its Salt 'n' Pepper prawns or crab.

Dim sum menu

Many of San Francisco's Chinese restaurants specialise in dim sum, a Cantonese cuisine of bite-sized, steamed dumplings, pastries and other snacks. Usually served at lunchtime, in many restaurants the food is wheeled from table to table on a trolley and diners choose whatever takes their fancy. The bill is calculated by counting the number of plates and steamer baskets on each table.

Cha sil bow: steamed barbecued pork bun.
Cha sil or **ha cheung fun**: rice noodles with roast pork or shrimp steamed in a roll. Served cold or fried.
Chern goon: spring or egg rolls.
Don todd: custard egg tart.
Faw op: roast duck.
Fun gor: pork, mushrooms and bamboo shoots in a wheat starch wrapper.
Gee bow gai: paper- or foil-wrapped chicken.
Ghow nom: beef tripe.
Gai bow: steamed chicken bun.
Gai guerk: braised chicken feet.
Ghow yuk sil mi: steamed beef and Chinese parsley dumpling.

Har gow: steamed shrimp and bamboo shoots in a wheat starch wrapper.
Ho yow gai lon: Chinese broccoli with oyster sauce.
Jin dooey: sesame seed ball filled with lotus paste.
Leen yoong bow: sweet lotus bean steamed bun.
Lo bok go: turnip cake.
Lot jui ha: pan-fried shrimp stuffed in pepper quarters.
No mi gai: lotus leaf stuffed with sticky rice, chicken, pork and shrimp.
Op guerk: braised duck feet.
See jup pai gwut: steamed spare ribs.
See jup pi gwut: steamed black bean and garlic spare ribs.
Sil mi: steamed pork dumplings, often with shrimp meat as well.
Woo tow go: deep-fried, mashed taro root rice cakes with meat stuffing.

drugstore and people were constantly breaking in to steal their next fix. The **City Lights** bookstore (261 Columbus Avenue) is still owned by Beat poet Lawrence Ferlinghetti and is open until midnight every day. **Vesuvio's** next door (once frequented by literary drunks Jack Kerouac and Dylan Thomas) still has a booth upstairs set aside for lady psychiatrists.

Most of the people on the streets and in the cafés and bars live and work in the area, including Francis Ford Coppola, who has an office in Columbus Tower – the green building on the corner of Columbus Avenue and Kearny Street. Across the street, **Tosca's** café has opera on the juke box, and the nearby **Tattoo Art Museum** (841 Columbus Avenue) is also worth investigating.

The array of excellent coffee shops is truly dazzling. It would be hard to find bad coffee anywhere in North Beach but particular landmarks include **Caffè Trieste** at Vallejo Street and Grant Avenue – the oldest coffee shop in San Francisco, where Francis Ford Coppola is supposed to have discussed the script of *The Godfather* with Mario Puzo (a claim made by most of the area's cafés), and where there are mini concerts on Saturday afternoons. Also try **Caffè Roma**, (414 Columbus Avenue) where the coffee is roasted on the premises and John Lee Hooker is an occasional customer, and **Mario's Bohemian Cigar Store** (566 Columbus Avenue, at Union Street), which sells delicious foccacia sandwiches but not cigars.

You can't go wrong in this neighbourhood, and simply wandering the streets at random is always rewarding. Pretty **Washington Square** is a lovely place to sit and watch people walk their dogs, play frisbee or practise juggling, overlooked by the **Church of Sts Peter and Paul**, where Marilyn Monroe and Joe DiMaggio had their wedding photos taken (since both were divorcees, they got married at City Hall). Nearby Grant Avenue, the oldest street in the city, is packed with interesting and idosyncratic shops, including **Figoni Hardware**, owned and run by Mel Figoni since 1 March 1924. It is the only place in San Francisco to sell *bocce* balls, for the Italian version of lawn bowls which is still played at North Beach Playground, two blocks north-east of Washington Square.

Continuing along Grant Avenue, **Prudente**, on the corner of Union Street, is the oldest butcher in the city and a good place to get exotic picnic ingredients such as own-cured cheeses and home-made sausages. There are also several good music bars on the street, including **Grant and Green Blues Club** (at Green Street) and **The Gathering Cafe**, (between Green and Vallejo Streets), the street's newest free venue for live jazz. Don't miss the rustic Spanish restaurant **La Bodega** at 1337 Grant Avenue; the food is average but the flamenco dancing is great.

There are so many Italian restaurants in the area, it almost seems unfair to highlight any in particular. However, **Enrico's Sidewalk Café** on Broadway has good quality live jazz and a heated outdoor section set back from the street, perfect for people-watching, and if you want to pretend you're really in Italy you can eat at the **Bocce Cafe** at 478 Green Street. The food is plain Italian but it's cheap, and on sunny days or one of San Francisco's rare warm evenings, the garden at the back is a Tuscan-like haven dripping with bougainvillaea, asparagus ferns and fig trees.

Two hotels sum up the different sides of North Beach. The aptly-named **Hotel Bohème** (444 Columbus Avenue) celebrates its Beat heritage with framed photographs of bohemian North Beach scenes from the 1950s and 1960s. On the other hand, the *pension*-like **San Remo Hotel**, a pretty Italianate Victorian (2237 Mason Street) is more suitable if you want to soak up the area's Italian ambiance.

Russian Hill

Russian Hill, the quiet, residential neighbourhood roughly bordered by Van Ness Avenue, Broadway, Powell and Chestnut Streets, is most famous for having the crookedest (and surely most photographed) street in the world, **Lombard Street**. Named after a group of Russian sailors thought to be buried here, the area is also home to the **San Francisco Art Institute** (800 Chestnut Street, at Jones Street), which houses the Diego Rivera Gallery.

Take a stroll up Vallejo Street to **Ina Coolbrith Park** at Taylor Street and have a secluded picnic; arrive early if you want to see Chinese elders practising *tai chi*. Walk back down the **Vallejo Street Stairway**, designed by San Francisco architect Willis Polk and surrounded on each side by pretty gardens. Landmark addresses include **29 Russell Street**, where Jack Kerouac lived with Neal and Carolyn Cassady in the 1950s, and the octagon-shaped house at **1067 Green Street**, one of the oldest houses in the city.

One of the best views of the city can be seen from the **Vallejo Crest** at Vallejo and Jones Streets. If you turn right here and continue across Green Street, you'll get to **Macondray Lane** – immortalised as Barbary Lane in Armistead Maupin's 'Tales of the City' series. And at 1088 Green Street is a two-storey **Fire Station** built in 1907, which has a fire museum on the ground floor.

Polk Street, from Sacramento to Greenwich Streets, is a busy little area with a number of bars, shops and restaurants worth checking out. **The Real Food Deli** (2164 Polk Street) has a phenomenal selection of salads – perfect for a picnic in Ina Coolbrith Park. **Shanghai Kelly's** (2064 Polk Street) is a popular bar with locals who just want a quiet beer. The biggest straight pick-up joint in San Francisco has to be **Johnny Love's** at 1500 Broadway where the 'bridge and tunnel' (out-of-town) crowd is raucous, rowdy and randy. This is also where Virgin's Richard Branson likes to hang out when he's in town, so don't be surprised to find him behind the bar pulling pints.

The so-called **Polk Gulch** area (Gulch describes Polk Street from Sacramento to around Chestnut Streets) used to be quite downmarket. The Tenderloin (east) side of Polk is still patrolled by transvestite prostitutes but the Gulch is far from dangerous and there are some wonderful shops, gay bars, restaurants and bookstores to investigate. In early July the **Blues and Art on Polk** street fair brings the gay leather crowd out in droves; be prepared to see more than you thought it was legal to show.

Telegraph Hill

Telegraph Hill covers the area bordered by Grant Avenue, Green, Bay and Sansome Streets. Its main claim to fame is that it is home to **Coit Tower** (at the top of Filbert Street), which contains some magnificent murals by protégés of Diego Rivera and has spectacular vistas of the city and Bay. Just down from Coit Tower, the **Julius' Castle** restaurant is small and intimate but with views rivalling those of any tower block. From here you can take the steep wooden **Filbert Steps**, which run down from Montgomery to Sansome Streets; walk them at night, when the blooms from the surrounding gardens smell especially gorgeous. At the bottom head for **Levi's Plaza**, where you can walk across specially-constructed steps and platforms which follow a path through a fountain designed by Lawrence Halprin. In the modern Levi offices, you can see some of the first jeans ever bolted and stitched by Levi Strauss for the Forty-Niners back in the gold rush days (the Levi Strauss factory, which you can tour (565 9153), is in what is now an unsalubrious block at 250 Valencia near 13th Street).

Nob Hill

Nob Hill, named after the wealthy 'nabobs' who built their mansions in the area, was once described by Robert Louis Stevenson as 'the hill of palaces'. Bordered by Bush, Larkin, Pacific and Stockton Streets, it is still one of San Francisco's smartest (and highest) neighbourhoods with beautiful views over the city and many of its grandest hotels.

If you're suffering from hill overkill, take the California cable car which runs up from the bottom of Market Street. In the midst of the area's crusty refinement are two kitsch gems – both in the basement of the otherwise smart **Fairmont Hotel**, on California and Mason Streets. In the **Tonga Room** cocktail bar, indoor tropical

rainstorms occur every few minutes and old biddies fight it out on the dance floor to the tune of a live band, which plays on a raft in the middle of a huge pool. Have dinner first at the **Bella Voce** restaurant where the waiters and waitresses are dressed like extras from a Gilbert and Sullivan opera and take regular breaks to sing; whatever you think of the music, the food is excellent. Just across the street, the **Mark Hopkins Inter-Continental Hotel** houses the great **Top of the Mark** bar, with its fabulous views of the city.

Grace Cathedral (1051 Taylor Street), a beautiful mock-Gothic concrete structure modelled on Notre Dame in Paris, is well worth visiting for its concert performances, from choral to jazz; a specially commissioned piece by Duke Ellington was performed here in 1965. It also houses the **Labyrinth Walk** – a meditative walk on a carpet copied from the one laid in the floor of Chartres Cathedral in France. There is a free guided tour at 1pm daily or you can take the tour on your own at any time from 7am-6pm.

SoMa & the Mission

Two of the city's liveliest neighbourhoods are the non-stop Latin-American Mission, and the multi-media and clubbing mecca, South of Market.

The area south of Market Street is known as SoMa, and like New York's SoHo it was for many years a neglected area, occupied by warehouses and sweatshops; the current moniker was first adopted to help overcome the sketchy reputation of the district. It is now an emerging centre for multi-media businesses, the visual arts and all-night parties. To the south and west of it is the buzzing **Mission** district. Entering San Francisco's oldest neighbourhood is like jumping into South America without a passport.

SoMa

Today, much of SoMa (formerly known as South-of-the-Slot) has been transformed into a trendy and artistic area. It has huge arts centres; a newish convention centre; reconditioned towers with loft spaces that double as residences and offices, and a new waterfront plaza, made possible by the removal of the overhead freeway damaged in the 1989 earthquake.

SoMa changes rapidly from block to block and provides scores of interesting nooks worth exploring for anyone wanting to investigate emergent San Francisco. There are at least three distinct areas worth exploring: Mario Botta's recently-completed $60-million modernist **San Francisco Museum of Modern Art** (SFMOMA, *see chapter* **Museums & Galleries**), a hidden square that features a lawn, playground and all the favourite lunch spots for the movers and shakers of multi-media; and the intersection of **11th and Folsom Streets**, the epicentre of the city's music clubs.

Across the street from SFMOMA at Third and Howards Streets, the **Yerba Buena Center for the Arts** set in the new $87-million Yerba Buena Gardens arts complex, has several permanent exhibitions as well as touring shows. Its first major show, The Art of Star Wars, and the space devoted to mixed and multimedia presentations have signalled the YBC's commitment to new media. At 250 Fourth Street, facing the YBC and SFMOMA

from the west, is the unmissable **Ansel Adams Center for Photography**.

But there's more to this area than large-scale, civic museums. Nearby, at 816 Folsom, is **Lulu**, one of the city's best restaurants, while the Basque-owned **Fringale** restaurant also bears investigation (570 Fourth Street, between Bryant and Brannan Streets). And if you prefer to seek out the raw, experimental and up-and-coming players in the arts, several small studios and independent galleries, some no bigger than a one-person flat, have sprung up like mushrooms in the alleys and above the retail spaces near the more established venues. A handy guide to the smaller galleries, some of which last no longer than a new dance craze, can be found in the free *City Culture* magazine, available at SFMOMA, the **Moscone Convention Center** (747 Howard Street) and at a number of local cafés. Three galleries worth investigating are the **Blasthaus** (217 Second Street, near Howard Street), which is run by the publishers of *City Culture*; the **Capp Street Project** (525 Second Street, near Bryant Street), and the **Gallery on the Rim** (333 Third Street near Folsom).

South Park

A pioneer residential development designed by a Brit during the Gold Rush, this area is now a sylvan haven from the three-lane boulevards just outside its oval enclave. For many years after World War II, South Park was home to African-Americans and, as in too many American cities, this fact was coincidental with a drop-off in city services. If the city authorities overlooked its value, however, its potential was not lost on the private sector, which began renovating garages, workshops and houses in the area in the early 1980s; the developers have been rewarded handsomely for their efforts in the 1990s.

Perhaps more significantly, a few investors saw South Park as a perfect spot for urbane dining. First to open was the **South Park Café** (108

Serving caffeine to the multimedia élite: **Caffè Centro**.

South Park Avenue). Encouraged by its success, its owners opened **Ristorante Ecco** (101 South Park Avenue), specialising in northern Italian fare. Other lively venues are **Caffè Centro** (102 South Park) and **Pepito's Parrilla** (24 South Park), serving burritos and grilled food.

The more recent and headline-grabbing element of the South Park story is the multimedia explosion, since the area is the centre of the so-called 'Multimedia Gulch' (*see chapter* **Media**). Though there isn't much of a gulch, actually, the name has stuck and come to represent the area and the multimedia industry as a whole, just as Madison Avenue stands for the advertising world or Hollywood for the movies. Many of the customers jamming South Park's cafés and picnic tables are employed by telecommunications firms, multimedia developers or other media, such as the magazines *Wired* and *PCWorld*. Go there to see the starry-eyed youth behind America's latest cultural fantasy/profit motive.

If this all proves too much, just around the corner from South Park are several unpretentious saloons serving tasty, straightforward fare, like the fish sandwiches at **Butterfield's** (202 Townsend Street). Shoppers can browse in the several discount outlets on Third Street (*see also chapter* **Shopping & Services**). The **660 Center** has an impressive array of them and the **Isda & Co Outlet** (29 South Park Avenue) specialises in women's clothing from name designers, discounted by up to 70 per cent.

11th & Folsom Streets

SoMa after dark is definitely no place to go walking with an expensive camera or wristwatch on show. There's not much need to brave Sixth Street between Market and Folsom Streets after sunset anyway, and although SoMa has its edge, don't be daunted, for it offers several nightlife attractions.

The conjunction of 11th and Folsom Streets is the area for the hottest clubs, and is packed with restaurants. Start at the corner with the **Paradise Lounge** (1501 Folsom Street). Or try **20 Tank Brewery** (316 11th Street); **Slim's** (333 11th Street); the **DNA Lounge** (375 11th Street), and **Eleven** (374 11th Street), which are all on the same block. Just around the corner, there's the **Ace Café** (1539 Folsom Street), **Holy Cow** (1531 Folsom Street) and **Hamburger Mary's** (1582 Folsom Street). The **Acorn Tea & Griddle** (1256 Folsom Street) specialises in organic ingredients, artistically arranged.

From here, a number of off-beat attractions not found on many picture postcards are within five minutes' walk. Check out the stretch of sidewalk on Seventh Street just north of Harrison Street – you could call it a poor man's Hollywood Stars. In front of the **San Francisco Studios** (375 Seventh Street) several large- and small-screen celebrities – among them comedians Whoopi Goldberg and Bobcat Goldthwait, and James Doohan (Scotty) and George Takei (Sulu) of the original *Star Trek* team – made impressions of their hands and signed their names in the concrete before it dried.

Finally, at the **Old Mint Museum** (88 Fifth Street) you can see where American bank notes were first printed in San Francisco.

If you feel in need of a cake or a bottle of wine, SoMa has two excellent resources: the **Wine Club** (953 Harrison Street) and the notorious **Cake Gallery** (290 Ninth Stree) whose speciality is genitalia gateaux. For a laundry stop and a cappuccino drop into **Brainwash** (1122 Folsom Street), a full-service bar, café and laundromat. Just around the corner is **Pink Tarantula** (71 Langton Street, off Seventh Street), a hair salon that can make your hair *look* like a pink tarantula (if that's what you want), although less outlandish styles, extensions and colourings are also available. A couple of doors down from Brainwash is **Neurotic**, which has a hip magazine rack, vintage clothing and music, much of it still on vinyl.

An additional area of activity within SoMa lies along the front of the Bay, an area that real estate brokers call **South Beach** (although the handle hasn't really caught on yet). Among the waterfront attractions are **Gordon Biersch** (2 Harrison Street), an upscale brewpub with a swish restaurant upstairs; **One Market** (1 Market Street) and **Boulevard** (1 Mission Street), both five-star dining rooms; and the **Rincon Annex** (at the corner of Mission and Spear Streets), a huge residential tower and shopping mall. Inside, you will find one of San Francisco's coolest fountains, a 26 metre/85 foot-high atrium with a cascade of water.

The Mission

The atmosphere is different in San Francisco's historic Mission district – the city's oldest neighbourhood. The weather is drier and warmer than elsewhere in the city and the smells are different, too: a mix of chilli peppers, garlic and onion, tomatoes, coriander and seared beef. Food is king here, and the flashy yet cheap burrito and taco restaurants started a trend that has taken San Francisco by storm in recent years.

This *barrio* – as it's known to its dominant Mexican and Latin American population – invites exploration beyond the charming Mission Dolores, the only stop on the tourist bus routes. Its history is one of tolerance; it has always been the first port of call for a steady influx of newcomers waiting to enter the American mainstream. It is also home to a dazzling array of political and spiritual art: there are more than 200 murals in the Mission, painted on the walls of banks, schools and restaurants, many celebrating the struggles and achievements of its Latino residents.

You can also find pretty much anything – legal or illegal – here. Want your very own palm tree? A corner nursery sells them at the intersection of Cesar Chavez and Valencia Streets. At night, the district offers diverse entertainments, from

traditional *mariachi* at **La Rondalla** and salsa dancing at **Cesar's Latin Palace** to the grunge rock mosh pits of the **Kolidescope** nightclub.

But the Mission is also afflicted with the ills of modern urban life. It has more than its share of prostitutes, drug addicts and gangs, so take the precautions you would in any big city, while remembering that for decades the newspaper and television headlines have overstated the neighbourhood's rough edges – and ignored its hidden treasures.

There's a lot to see in the Mission, so consider taking a couple of day-long walking tours to explore the wordless storytelling of its murals, rambling Victorian buildings and unadvertised second-hand shops and antique stores. From the BART station at the corner of 16th and Mission Streets, you can embark on a four-mile jaunt through the heart of the neighbourhood.

16th Street to Dolores Street

On **16th Street**, face west, toward the imposing radio towers above nearby Twin Peaks. The western stretch between Mission and Dolores Streets is a short three blocks, but packed with goodies. You'll pass crowded restaurants dispensing anything from French crêpes and crudités (**Ti Couz**), to Spanish *tapas* and *sangria* (**El Picaro**). At Rondel Alley is one of the district's most visited *taqueria*, the **Pancho Villa**, where the machine-gun rat-tat-tat of cleavers bouncing on butcher blocks is matched with the smell of searing tomatoes, onions and cilantro (coriander). The **Casa Lucas La Hacienda** produce store at Valencia Street, with its fresh Latin groceries, is alone worth half an hour's exploration. Across the street is the **Roxie Theater**, with an eclectic playbill of offbeat American and foreign films.

At Dolores Street turn left to see San Francisco's oldest building, the 225-year-old **Mission Dolores**, founded when a zealous *conquistador* planted a simple white cross on the edge of what was once a lake. The lake is now filled with asphalt and concrete, but the church, its peaceful flower garden and ornate cemetery remain, and offer a quiet insight into the region's history. Look at the names on the tombstones, then compare them with the names of many San Francisco streets.

Continue south for two blocks until you reach **18th Street**. On the right is **Dolores Park**, worth a few minutes' stroll, if only for the view of San Francisco and the Bay from the park's apex at 20th and Church Streets, and of the mélange of people and dogs who frequent the park. At the same intersection, there is a small, **bronze-painted fire plug**, which in 1906 provided the only working water source for beleaguered firefighters battling the fire that gutted most of the city after the infamous earthquake. The little hydrant did its

On this stretch, funky boutiques and coffee houses – except for the old favourite **Café Nidal** and the new **Java City** franchise – are scarce, but Mission Street offers some of the best people-watching in the city. Look out for local notables such as the Red Man and the White Lady, neighbourhood residents who for years have strolled the district's streets, their skin painted a flaming red and pallid white, respectively.

Since San Francisco's founding, immigrants have been drawn to it in search of an economic toehold in the country. Mission Street is fascinating in its role as a mixing tank for the latest waves of economic and political refugees from around the world, many of whom settle here first. Each wave has left its mark. **La Traviata** near 25th Street, an upmarket Italian restaurant – once the favoured dining house for visiting opera singers – has endured fires and a gradual deterioration of its surrounding neighbourhood, yet still offers a cosy, quiet retreat from the crowds outside.

Despite Mission Street's overt commercialism, there are some unusual sights. You can explore **Ritmo Latina**, with its huge selection of Latin music, or the **Cigarettes Cheaper** and **Mission Smoke Shop** outlets that cater to a stubborn population of tobacco *aficionados* resisting the Californian disapproval of smoking. Inside the **Bank of America** (at 23rd Street), a powerful mural depicts the area's history. Near 24th Street, the **King Bakery** offers a living example of how different cultures have met and melded in this neighbourhood: the Korean owner sells Mexican pastries to a stream of Anglo, Asian and Central American customers, in three languages.

job, keeping the flames away from homes in the Noe Valley district.

Walk downhill back to 18th and Dolores Streets and head east on **18th**. A block and a half down, you'll see a curious juxtaposition: the grimy **Dovre Bar** – a hangover from the days when Irish, German and Italian working men dominated the neighbourhood – tucked into the corner of the **Women's Building**, which houses a refuge, recreation centre and theatre workshop. You can't miss the building: local women artists have adorned it with the newest and grandest of the Mission's murals, a larger-than-life retelling of woman's history in the New World, topped off with a portrait of Guatemalan Nobel Laureate Rigoberta Menchu.

Walk another block east (to reach Mission Street) and explore the expansive **18th and Mission Produce and Meat Market**, which, like Casa Lucas, sells mainly Latino goods.

Mission Street

The Mission Street corridor is the economic lifeline of the neighbourhood. It is a river of commercialism, catering primarily to the neighbourhood's middle-to-low-income residents with its cheque-cashing operations, banks and shops crammed with cheap clothes, kitchen appliances, second-hand goods and groceries.

24th Street

At **24th Street**, head east; this is the Mission District at its diverse, traditional best. Like the neighbourhood's other main streets, 24th is lined with murals. One of the biggest is near **South Van Ness Avenue**: an illustration of Mexican-American rockstar Carlos Santana surrounded by plumed participants in the Mission's annual carnival. The street's most famous murals, however, are found at **Balmy Alley**, which, with adjacent **Lucky Alley**, looks back to the turn of the century when racehorse tracks and an amusement park dominated the area (both alleys bear the names of famous racehorses from that era). Before the 1906 earthquake, the Mission was the Bay Area's primary recreation destination. Today's Balmy Alley murals were the district's first public art effort, put up two decades ago as an artistic counterpoint to rampant youth-gang graffiti.

Further down 24th Street, on the north wall of **St Peter's Catholic Church**, another imposing mural describes the catastrophic meeting of the Old and New Worlds, from the perspective of

Mayan scholars. At the intersection with Bryant Street, you'll find **Galeria de la Raza**, the wellspring of the district's fantastic art where ever-changing exhibitions by local artists draw visitors from around the country. The adjoining **Studio 24** supports the gallery by selling contemporary and traditional Latin American crafts; its brightly painted grocery store calendars are very popular.

If you're still hungry, 24th Street has more produce stands, offering a variety of tastes from different Latin American countries. Unfortunately, many restaurants seem tired after decades of serving the same Latino-flavoured fare. However, there are still some outstanding ones: the Caribbean-spiced **Frutilandia** (near Florida Street); **El Farolito** (at Alabama Street), which serves simple but good Mexican food, spiced up with free tubs of hot salsa and a wonderful avocado-tomatillo sauce; **Casa Sanchez** (near Hampshire Street), which specialises in traditional Mexican dishes; **La Palma** (at Bryant Street), which sells the only authentic, hand-made Mexican corn tortillas in the district, and **Pollo Supremo** (at Harrison Street), a fast-food outlet whose fruit-juice-and-garlic-marinated chicken is sold by the bucket-load to Financial district business types and local families alike.

A local favourite is the **St Francis Ice Cream and Candy Shop** at York Street. Founded in 1917 by Greek immigrants, the store is flamingo-pink and chrome on the inside, and has achieved unofficial landmark status as San Francisco's oldest soda fountain, and as the birthplace of the city's beloved 'Niners football team.

At the Mission's eastern boundary is the old **York Theater** and the adjacent **Café Fanari**, at the forefront of the street's artistic renaissance. By mid-1996, the York's conversion from an abandoned movie house into an expansive live theatre and film centre should be complete. At Café Fanari Argentine immigrant Oscar Rocha serves up espresso, pastries and a selection of Italian dishes to young and hip Latinos and Anglos discussing politics and art.

Valencia Street

On Valencia Street, the curious will find off-beat bookshops like **La Casa de Libros/Books on Wings** (near 20th Street), hip novelty shops such as the **Yahoo Herban Ecology** store (near 19th Street) and the long-standing women's sex shop **Good Vibrations** (at 23rd Street). There's even the **Botanica Yoruba** (at 21st Street), selling traditional Caribbean religious items, and, near 24th Street, the **Chinese and Alternative Medicines** shop does brisk business.

On Valencia, you can measure your walk by checking out the two **Muddy Waters** cafés, set nearly a mile apart on 24th and 17th streets. The atmosphere is busy, with people standing in early morning queues trying to decide between lattes and café mochas, while beleaguered cashiers race to steam milk and keep pace.

Over the past two decades, the bohemian feel of 16th Street has spread to Valencia Street. Near 19th Street is the colourful **Dal Jeets** clothing and accessories store. A block away, a video store goes by the outlandish name of **Leather Tongue Videos** and a greasy spoon called the **Burger Joint** is disguised as a 1950s' hangout with brightly coloured leather booths and stools. Across the street, the **Marsh**, a popular, well-off-Broadway theatre, poses as a drab, olive-coloured building.

This mix of shops is perhaps an economic response to the nightly arrival of insatiable San Franciscans in search of good restaurants. Just try to get a table at **Esperpento's** Spanish hideaway, or the eclectic **Rooster** next door. **Val 21**, an upmarket experiment in fine food science, is always packed, as is the expensive **Flying Saucer**, a block west on Guerrero Street, at 22nd Street. Even the bars serve good food: **La Rondalla** (901 Valencia Street) is a favourite for its margaritas and *mariachi* performances, while **Timo's** near 18th Street offers Spanish tapas and seafood plates.

Off Valencia, you can also take a detour up **Liberty Street** to ogle the row of old Victorian houses, including some pre-1906 earthquake survivors, and check out the former Jewish synagogue, on 19th and Lapidge Streets, next to a recreation centre splashed with a surrealist mural.

Potrero Hill

Potrero Hill, like the nearby Mission district, is nearly always sunny, even when the rest of the city is shrouded in fog. Bordered by Potrero Avenue, Army Street, 17th Street and the docks, it is a predominantly residential area, but there are still things for the traveller to do and see.

Have an alfresco lunch at **Sally's** on De Haro and 16th Streets or next door at **Rustico** – mini-oases in the virtual wasteland of their surroundings. The **Anchor Brewing Company** (1705 Mariposa Street) gives free group tasting tours by appointment only; book at least two weeks in advance to sample some of California's best brews.

Farleys café on 18th and Texas Streets is a favourite hang-out. Just a few blocks away is the **Esprit** outlet store (499 Illinois Street, at 16th Street) for marked-down Esprit designs. The old Caffe Esprit is now called **42 Degrees** and is an excellent spot for lunch or a reviving cup of coffee after a hard morning's shopping. Its owners also run the famously excellent **Slow Club** bar and restaurant on Mariposa where you can hear live music twice a week; Tuesday night is tapas night. The **Bottom of the Hill** club (1233 17th Street) has good local live bands and an outdoor patio where barbecues are sometimes held.

The Haight
& the Castro

Cruise the cafés of the Castro, or hang out in the 'Hashbury', once the capital of the hippies, and now torn between grunge and gentrification.

The Haight-Ashbury

The Haight's fame as 1967 Summer of Love hang-out of the Beautiful People has obscured its original incarnation as late-nineteenth century weekend resort. Only the fabulous Victorian and Edwardian architecture remains as evidence of the days when people came to play in the park or take the steam train three miles down to Ocean Beach, and the wealthy had weekend homes or stayed at the Stanyan Park Hotel.

Nowadays the young panhandlers on the street who jokingly ask for 'spare change for drugs and alcohol' are following the ethos of the 1960s when many of the shops gave away clothes and food and several of the restaurants went bust because they let so many people eat without paying. To 1960s-pop star *aficionados* the historical value of this neighbourhood is vast. The **Grateful Dead** lived at 710 Ashbury Street; **Janis Joplin** at 122 Lyon Street, and **Jefferson Airplane** at 2400 Fulton Street. The address of the Red House referred to in the Jimi Hendrix song was 1524 Haight Street, now the **Ashbury Tobacco Center**. Less appealing landmarks include 636 Cole Street, **Charlie Manson's** house in the mid-1960s.

To stay in the thick of things you can't do better than **The Red Victorian** hotel (1665 Haight Street, between Cole and Belvedere Streets). The rooms are decorated in hippy style and everyone has breakfast together in the morning. Just wander the length of Haight Street from Stanyan Street (where the entrance to Golden Gate Park is a homeless hangout) to around Central Avenue to soak up the atmosphere. Get a huge breakfast at **The Pork Store Cafe** (1451 Haight Street), then work it off rollerblading in the park. You can rent blades from **Skates on Haight** (at number 1818) and bicycles from **Park Cyclery** (at number 1865).

The **Rock 'n' Bowl** (1855 Haight Street) is a fabulous evening out – if you like bowling and loud rock music. The more sedate might prefer an evening watching independent movies at the **Red Vic** cinema (at number 1727) which has church

pew seating (with cushions) and serves home-made snacks and popcorn in big wooden bowls. Next door, the **Cafe Paradiso** has an excellent vegetarian menu and a good bar. However, **Cha Cha Cha** (1801 Haight Street) is the place to go for atmosphere; it's cheap, always packed and the sangria is excellent. Guaranteed to break the ice on the chilliest first date. **The Booksmith** (at number 1644) is an excellent bookstore which also sells international newspapers and magazines. It's worth checking out the listings to see which authors will be giving readings there.

The Haight is a rare neighbourhood mix of black and white, rich and poor, young and old. In line with its gentrification, there are even celebrities. Danny Glover moved into the other

Spreckels Mansion, on Beuna Vista Avenue West, next door to Bobby McFerrin's house. (There are two Spreckels Mansions in San Francisco; Danielle Steele lives in the grander one in Pacific Heights.) If you don't want to miss a thing take local girl Rachel Heller's Haight-Ashbury Flower Power Walking Tour (221 8442).

Lower Haight

The Lower Haight is the name given to the area at the seedier, eastern end of Haight Street. Here the body-pierced, skateboarding crowd mixes uneasily with crack-sellers and street vendors selling junk from rugs on the pavement. It's a young and hip area, and there are gems to be found there, including some great bars and cafés.

On Haight Street itself, don't miss the British-owned **Mad Dog in the Fog** pub (at number 530), where you can buy British as well as American beer, eat bangers-and-mash and shepherd's pie and play darts with the locals. At number 557 is the self-consciously hip bar **Noc Noc**, and just a few doors away is **Spaghetti Western**, which some say does the best breakfasts in San Francisco. Definitely one of the best dancing venues in town is **Nickie's Barbecue** (460 Haight). Small and intimate, it used to be a black club but is getting more mixed, and the music is always fabulous.

It's best to avoid the housing projects on the eastern end of Haight past Fillmore Street, especially at night. Instead, turn right down Fillmore. **Body Manipulations** (254 Fillmore Street) is a famous tattoo parlour where you can also be scarred, branded and, the latest fashion, have small parts of your fingers amputated.

At the bottom of Fillmore turn left and then right for Church Street; the **Safeway** there is known as the gay pick-up equivalent of the Marina Boulevard Safeway. Just across the street, **Art's Café** is the place to go for delicious soul food and jolly service. Then turn left onto Market Street to get to the **Mint Karaoke Bar** where some of the best amateurs in town (as well as some of the worst) do their thing nightly.

Cole Valley

Cole Valley used to be called Upper Haight. Roughly covering the small area bordered by Cole Street, Parnassus Street, Hill Point Avenue and Waller Street, it's very easy to walk to from the Haight. On the way up Cole Street keep an eye out for the local character who sits on the steps outside his house wearing a viking helmet or a huge golden crown, chatting with passers-by.

This area is mainly known for its cafés and bars. Pick up a magazine or newspaper at the drugstore **Val-Grin** and pop next door to **Spinelli's** (919 Cole Street) to read it over a cup of coffee. There

are so many coffee shops in San Francisco that it's a wonder they all stay in business, but they're all packed. Admittedly, the coffee's not great at the **Tassajara Bakery** (on the corner of Cole and Parnassus Streets) but the bread and pastries are out of this world.

Zazie Cafe (941 Cole Street) is small and stylish and open for breakfast, lunch and dinner. There are two crêpe cafés – **Crêpes on Cole** and **The Crêpery** – almost opposite each other on the corner of Carl and Cole Streets, both of which are always busy. At the same junction, **The Kezar** is a friendly local bar that also does food; if you're feeling more raucous, **Finnegan's Wake** (937 Cole Street) has a pool table and is loud and noisy.

If you want some peace and quiet, walk south up Stanyan Street and turn left on Belgrave Avenue to reach **Tank Hill**. This secluded area of grass and rocks is nearly always empty and has a very romantic view of San Francisco at night; on the way up keep your eyes open for raccoons exploring the rubbish bins. **UCSF Hospital** on Parnassus Avenue holds free lunch-time lectures on subjects as diverse as 'How and why we age' and 'Being your own psychic'; phone 330 5353 for more information.

The Castro

The Castro, bordered by 20th, Market, Diamond and Church Streets, was once the city's capital of Catholicism. Originally a Mexican ranch, the land was broken into lots and sold off in the 1880s to mainly working-class Irish families. Rumour has it that the opening of **Twin Peaks** (at Castro and Market Streets), the first gay bar in the area, caused a mass exodus of Catholics; subsequently, the cheap but beautiful housing was bought and fixed up by gays who gradually re-established the area as the capital of gay San Francisco – if not the whole of the US. See also chapter **Gay & Lesbian San Francisco**.

Its geographical focus is the huge neon sign of the beautiful **Castro Theater** (at Castro and Market Streets), where all the movies are preceded by entertaining renditions on a Wurlitzer organ which eventually disappears slowly underground to the whoops and cheers of the audience. The main thoroughfare is Castro Street, between Market and 20th Streets, probably one of San Francisco's busiest neighbourhoods. The people are friendly, open and relaxed and you are almost guaranteed to start a conversation in any one of the coffee shops in the area. **The Cafe** (2367 Market Street) is one of the few lesbian pick-up bars; the rest of the bars are predominantly male-oriented.

There are plenty of interesting little shops on Castro. Look out for **Cliff's Variety** which sells fabrics, gifts and general hardware; it gets absolutely packed around Hallowe'en when everyone flocks to

Twin Peaks

The Twin Peaks are the two hills (275 metres/903 feet and 278 metres/913 feet, respectively) that overlook the Castro and Cole Valley. The slightly taller hill is always swarming with tourists by day but it's still a nice place to sit on a windy day or evening. The other peak, only a short walk away, is always deserted (perhaps because it has no parking) and the view from the top is just as beautiful.

Further south, *Dirty Harry* fans will recognise **Mount Davidson**. At 286 metres/938 feet, it is the highest spot in San Francisco; originally named Blue Mountain in 1852 by city surveyor George Davidson, it was subsequently renamed after him. It is topped by a distinctive 31m/103ft-high white concrete cross, under which Easter sunrise services are held every year.

See chapter **Sightseeing** for where to go to find more good views of the city and the Bay.

buy accessories for their costumes. Just a few doors away, **A Different Light Bookstore** sells books and magazines by, for and about gays. Take a walk up 18th Street to see even more shops. One of the most unusual is **Southwest Tradewinds** on 18th and Sanchez Streets which sells jewellery, pottery, Native American artefacts, Himalayan antiques, rugs, clothing and unusual cacti.

On Market Street itself, heading towards downtown, stop by **The NAMES Project** at number 2362, which serves as a memorial museum to all those who have died of AIDS. Central to the exhibits is the AIDS quilt, each square of which was created in memory of a dead friend or family member. At number 2335, **Crystal Way** sells New Age books, crystals and incense and offers tarot and psychic readings.

Take advantage of the many outdoor cafés and restaurants along Market Street. **La Mediterranée** (on the corner of Market and Noe Streets) serves delicious Middle Eastern food and is always busy – especially in the evenings when you'll probably have to leave your name on a list and wait for up to an hour for a table. Just across the street, the pretty garden of **Café Flore** is a good people-watching spot and the food is cheap but good.

Carry on down Market Street towards downtown to find one of the very best used clothes stores in town. At **Crossroads Trading Co** (2231 Market) you can pick up second-hand Levi's for $12 or a suede jacket for only $22. Just before Church Street, **Café Du Nord** is popular with twenty- and thirtysomething heterosexuals. Go

there for salsa dancing lessons and to hear bands play several nights a week. Almost next door, **Centrium**, which sells furniture, lighting and decorative arts from the 1930s to the 1970s, is a museum of modern classics.

The two social high spots of gay San Francisco based in the Castro are **Gay Pride Week** and the **Freedom Day Parade**, which attract up to 500,000 visitors every June, and **Hallowe'en in the Castro**, an extravagant and outrageous display of wildly imaginative costumes (*see chapter* **San Francisco by Season** for more information).

Noe Valley

Noe Valley, the area roughly bordered by 20th, Dolores, 30th and Douglass Streets, was, like nearby Castro, once populated by Irish families. Still a predominantly residential area, nowadays it is peopled by young families and yuppies who flock to the area because the architecture is splendid and it's so quiet and sunny.

Activity in Noe Valley is centred around 24th Street, which has an excellent selection of clothes shops, book and magazine stores and cafés. Starting at the top of the hill, at Douglass Street, the **Firefly** restaurant serves enormous portions in intimate, romantic surroundings. On the way east towards Guerrero Street is **Déjà Vu** (4156 24th Street) which sells second-hand wedding dresses, vintage clothing, American pottery and dinnerware, as well as small pieces of furniture. **The San Francisco Mystery Bookstore** on the corner of Diamond and 24th Streets is a tiny gem selling new and second-hand mystery books and magazines; sections of the shop are devoted to staff members' favourite books. **Star Magic** (4026 24th Street) is a must for 'space age' gifts; it sells everything from telescopes to globe-shaped pencil sharpeners.

Continuing along 24 Street, **Just For Fun** at number 3982 sells stick-on tattoos, jewellery, toys and other gifts. Stop off at **Spinelli's** at number 3966, or **Starbucks** (number 3995) for a cup of coffee and a seat outside if it's not too windy. Across the street from Spinelli's, **Chocolate Covered Sweets and Gifts** sells just that – chocolate guitars, animals and telephones and chocolate-coated organic strawberries. The sushi at **Hamano**, at 24th and Castro Streets, is excellent. Nearby, **Peek-a-boutique** (1306 Castro Street) sells second-hand children's clothes, including Osh Kosh at less than half the price they'd be in the UK.

The latest gem to appear in the area is **Lovejoy's Antiques and Tea Room** (1195 Church Street) where you can have a traditional English high tea and then buy the cup and saucer you drank it from, the chair you sat in, the paintings on the wall – in fact, anything you see. **La Sirena Botanica** (1478 Church Street) sells magical herbs, incense and spiritual supplies for fledgling witches.

The Waterfront

We cover the waterfront, from the tacky excesses of Fisherman's Wharf, to the yuppie singles spots of the Marina and the promenades of the Embarcadero.

For more on San Francisco's nearest beaches, *see* chapter **Sightseeing**. *See also chapter* **Sport & Fitness**, for where to go whale watching, hire a windsurfer or surfboard, or go sailing.

The Presidio

The Presidio is a huge, 1,400-acre green area which is currently in the process of turning from an army base into a national park. It stretches from the western tip of the Marina around the Bay to the Golden Gate Bridge, and has forests, hiking trails, a stream and some excellent views of Golden Gate Bridge and the ocean. The entrance in Pacific Heights on Presidio Boulevard and Jackson Streets leads you through fairytale woods to another entrance at Lombard and Lyon Streets in the Marina district. Sights include the **Presidio Army Museum** on Funston Avenue; the **Pet Cemetery** on McDowell Avenue; and the **California Palace of the Legion of Honor** in Lincoln Park, to the west of the Presidio, which is most famous for its Rodin collection. **Baker Beach** on the west side of the Presidio is the city's nearest nude beach, but swimming is discouraged because of the currents. At **China Beach**, at the end of Seacliff Avenue, you can swim – if you don't mind the cold. Or better still, watch the surfers under the Golden Gate Bridge at **Fort Point**.

To find out more about tours and the latest events in the Presidio phone the **Visitor's Information Center** (556 0865); *see also chapter* **Sightseeing**.

The Marina

The Marina district, between Fort Mason and the Presidio, is known to San Franciscans as the neighbourhood of yuppie singles. Unashamedly heterosexual, the local bars are full of young and trendy, bare-midriffed, twentysomethings and even the local **Safeway** at 15 Marina Boulevard is a famous pick-up joint. Built on the rubble of the 1906 earthquake, the Marina was probably the worst hit of San Francisco's neighbourhoods in the 1989 Loma Prieta earthquake. However, little evidence of the disaster remains and there are some interesting bars, restaurants and shops, particularly along the main drag, Chestnut Street.

Don't miss **Pasta Pomodoro** (2027 Chestnut Street) for Italian fast food. Lombard Street, between the Fillmore and Pierce Streets, has little to recommend it except for the bar **Blues**, which showcases the best local bands. Make a detour to **Some Like It Hot!** (3208 Scott Street), a shop which sells 350 varieties of spicy salsa.

Marina Green has grand views of the Golden Gate Bridge and San Francisco Bay, and at the end of the harbour jetty, the amazing **Wave Organ**, a bizarre structure of underwater pipes that produce 'music' with the changing currents. Behind the **Palace of Fine Arts** (at the end of Lyon Street) is the marvellous **Exploratorium** science museum; don't leave without looking at the gift shop with its fabulous array of educational toys. The Palace itself is a Neo-Classical temple constructed for the 1915 Panama-Pacific Exposition and is now an attractive picnic area where locals take their children to feed the ducks in the pond.

From the Palace it's a few blocks south to **Cow Hollow**, a one-time dairy pasture turned popular yuppie shopping area. The crowd here are slightly older and more established than in the rest of the Marina, which is reflected in the relative chicness of the bars, shops and restaurants along **Union Street**, between Broderick and Fillmore Streets, which are mostly housed in tastefully renovated Victorians.

Fort Mason & the Northern Waterfront

The Northern Waterfront unofficially describes the area which runs west of Fisherman's Wharf towards the Marina. Aside from pretty **Marina Green Park**, where the locals go to fly kites, jog or picnic, it also encompasses the **Fort Mason Center** arts complex. Here you can eat at **Greens**, the best vegetarian restaurant in the city; listen to folk music at the **San Francisco Music Center**, which attracts musicians from all over the country; or take in a play at the **Magic Theater**, which showcased the early works of Sam Shepard and continues to produce innovative theatre.

The centre also houses a number of museums and art societies, including the San Francisco Craft

The Presidio Army Museum. *See page 96.*

and Folk Art Museum; the Mexican Museum; the Museo Italo-American; the African-American Historical and Cultural Society and the National Poetry Association. Don't leave the area without making a small detour to 600 Embarcadero to sample the delights of the **Delancey Street Restaurant** – part of the huge Delancey Street rehabilitation organisation which is staffed and run by reformed ex-cons.

Fisherman's Wharf

Fisherman's Wharf is the departure point for day trips to **Alcatraz Island**. Otherwise it doesn't have a great deal to recommend it, unless you actually like tacky, over-priced, souvenir shops and streets chock-a-block with tourists. If tat is your thing, however, you won't want to miss the Wax Museum, Ripley's Believe It Or Not! Museum (both on Jefferson Street) and Pier 39, a 45-acre amusement arcade/shopping complex where you can get anything from fast food and souvenir T-shirts to giant chocolate teddy bears (at Chocolate Heaven they sell 1,200 different chocolate items). Otherwise, do yourself a favour and restrict your Wharf experience to watching the barking seals in the harbour (fun and free).

Other free activities include a trip to the **National Maritime Museum** in Aquatic Park, the interior of which has been done up to resemble an Art Deco ocean liner. If your cash is burning a hole in your pocket, check out **Cost Plus** on Taylor and Northpoint Streets – a huge warehouse selling everything from exotic food and drink to plant pot holders – or **Ghirardelli Square**, once home to the San Francisco chocolate factory and now (yet another) complex of shops and restaurants. Sort through your swag in the central plaza accompanied by the soothing trickle of the lovely Mermaid Fountain designed by local artist Ruth Asawa.

Another reminder of the area's former life is **The Cannery** (2801 Leavenworth Street, at Jefferson Street). Built in 1909 as a fruit-canning factory, it is now a twee shopping mall in the style of London's Covent Garden, complete with street performers. The Cannery also houses **Cobb's Comedy Club**, which showcases some of the top comedians in the country; on Open Mike night, you might even witness the career-baby steps of the next Robin Williams. Another local hangout is **Alioto's** restaurant at the end of Taylor Street near Jefferson Street; one of the best seafood restaurants in town, it has been there since 1938 and is well worth a visit. A bonus is the spectacular view of the Golden Gate Bridge from it.

Avoid the area immediately surrounding the housing projects on Bay and Taylor Streets at night, when you stand a reasonably high chance of being mugged.

The Embarcadero

Before the Bay and Golden Gate Bridges were built in the 1930s, the Embarcadero, which stretches north along the waterfront from Market Street, used to be the landing point for upwards of 50,000 daily commuters from Marin and the East Bay. Subsequently completely overshadowed by an ugly freeway, the area went from being one of San Francisco's busiest places to one of its emptiest. Considerably improved after the 1989 earthquake put paid to the freeway, the vicinity is now light and airy. However, it remains somewhat deserted except for the area immediately surrounding the looming presence of the **Embarcadero Center** – a huge complex of hotels, offices, restaurants and stores, which spans eight city blocks.

Another notable Embarcadero landmark is the 1896 **Ferry Building**, the design of which was inspired by the bell tower of Seville Cathedral, and where the ferry commuters from Marin still disembark. It is also the venue for the popular **Ferry Plaza Farmers' Market**, held every Saturday morning. Take a picnic and, if it's not too windy, join the local office workers on the waterfront promenade and watch the ships coming in.

Pacific Heights & the Central Neighbourhoods

The central swathe of the city contains some of its most up-and-coming neighbourhoods, as well as Pacific Heights – the Beverley Hills of San Francisco.

Pacific Heights

Pacific Heights, north of California Street and west of the Presidio, is the high society neighbourhood of San Francisco, as is evident from the wide, mansion-lined streets. The Mayor has a house here as do the Gettys, rockstar Linda Rondstadt, and best-selling romantic novelist Danielle Steele, who lives in the **Spreckels Mansion**, which spans an entire block between Jackson, Gough, Washington and Octavia Streets.

It's possible to spend hours just wandering the streets marvelling at the opulence. Look out for the **Octagon House** (2645 Gough Street), built for a health fad and now restored to its 1861 splendour, and the 28-room 1886 **Haas-Lilienthal House** (2007 Franklin Street); both are open to the public (*see chapter* **Architecture**). The antiques and clothes shops on Sacramento Street, between Presidio Avenue and Spruce Street are, consequently, pretty expensive but there are some bargains to be had at **Good Buys** (3464 Sacramento Street), a fabulous second-hand clothes store where you might find a Chanel bag or suit for less than half the original price.

Considering the area it serves, the **Vogue Cinema** (at Presido Street) is a surprising flea-pit, but often shows good double bills. If you want to stay in the area, the Victorian **Mansion Hotel** (2220 Sacramento Street) is genuinely eccentric, with life-sized dummies of people lounging in the hallway chairs, a Pianola that plays by itself in one of the many deserted, antique-filled sitting rooms, magic shows every night, live parrots and a good restaurant. There's even a pool table. If you want to eat out, **Pane e Vino**, just down the road at Steiner and Union Streets, is one of the best Italian restaurants in San Francisco (*see chapter* **Restaurants**).

Upper Fillmore

Just east from Pacific Heights, Upper Fillmore Street between Jackson and California Streets, is very smart, with lots of excellent shops and restaurants. **Vivande Porta Via** (2125 Fillmore Street) used to be cookery queen Elizabeth David's favourite restaurant for lunch in San Francisco – quite a recommendation when you consider that there are over 4,500 others to choose from. Or head further south to **Oritalia** (1915 Fillmore Street), which specialises in a magical mixture of Asian and Italian cuisine. For designer furniture, decorating accessories and gifts, check out **Fillamento** (at number 2185). But compare the prices before you buy; the Alessi kettles here cost twice what they do in the UK.

Japantown

Tiny Japantown used to be a much larger area covering about 40 blocks, but the Japanese immigrants who had settled here were forced to move after the bombing of Pearl Harbour; many were interned and treated abominably. In 1968, in a vague spirit of reparation, San Francisco's urban planners created the **Japan Center**, a huge shopping, dining and entertainment complex, which takes up three blocks between Post Street and Geary Boulevard and one block of Buchanan Street.

On Post Street, the eight-screen **Kabuki** cinema complex is the venue for most of the events and films shown during the annual San Francisco International Film Festival in April and May, and for the latest films during the rest of the year. Like many of San Francisco's cinemas, it has cheaper tickets at certain times of day; phone 931 9800 for more information.

To immerse yourself (literally) in the Japanese experience, have a relaxing massage at **Kabuki**

Zuni Café *on Market Street – an essential pitstop. See page 100.*

Hot Spring (1750 Geary Boulevard), a traditional Japanese bathhouse with communal pools, saunas and steam rooms. Spend a restful half an hour or so in the **Buddhist Church of San Francisco** on Pine Street, or just sit in the Peace Plaza garden, overlooked by the five-tiered concrete **Peace Pagoda**, which was given to the community by Japan. You could also attend a Japanese tea ceremony, held monthly at the **Nichi Bei Kai** cultural centre on Sutter Street, and in April the **Cherry Blossom Festival** is a month-long celebration of Japanese culture, with flower-arranging demonstrations, martial arts displays, traditional dance performances and a parade on the last day. Any one of the area's restaurants are excellent for Japanese noodles and sushi but for a sublime culinary experience, purse willing, go to the Japanese-influenced **Yoyo Tsumami Bistro** on Post Street, a very upmarket Japanese tapas restaurant.

The Western Addition

The Western Addition (referred to by some as 'Midtown') is the area roughly bordered by California, Fell, Divisadero and Buchanan Streets. It is a predominantly African-American neighbourhood, once home to the city's jazz clubs but now pretty rundown and certainly not 'hep' anymore. However, it does have some interesting sights. **Alamo Square** is very pretty (although not very safe at night) and has the most photographed row of Victorians in the city on Steiner Street. At 1057 Steiner Street, the **Chateau Tivoli** B&B has been restored to its former Victorian splendour and is filled with enough four poster beds and *objets d'art* to keep Christies in business for 50 years.

At the lower end of Fillmore Street by Geary Boulevard, check out **Jack's Bar**, where Van Morrison and John Lee Hooker have been known to turn up for impromptu gigs; it's also a venue for open mike comedy and lesser-known bands. The nearby **Fillmore Auditorium**, which booked the likes of Jimi Hendrix and The Doors in the 1960s has recently re-opened and books their 1990s equivalents, while **Marcus Books** (1712 Fillmore Street) is a specialist African and African-American bookshop. There are several excellent second-hand clothing stores; just keep on walking and you can't miss them. For a magical Sunday experience go to the **First Union Baptist Church** on Webster Street and Golden Gate Avenue for real gospel singing and a Screamin' Jay Hawkins-style sermon you'll never forget.

Hayes Valley

North of Market Street and west of the Civic Center, San Francisco's most exciting, fastest developing and uncharacteristically flat neighbourhood, Hayes Valley, used to be one of its least salubrious – in spite of its close proximity to the Davies Symphony Hall and War Memorial Opera House (also home to the San Francisco Ballet). Few people came here except to visit the prostitutes and drug dealers who did business under cover of an ugly raised freeway that divided the area in half.

It still isn't wise to wander up Hayes Street much further than Laguna Street after dark. But when the 1989 earthquake brought down the freeway, the area started to improve.

Today, older establishments such as the 20 year-old **Sharp Brothers** (525 Hayes Street), an unruly mound of junk where you can still unearth under-priced treasures, and **Powell's Place** (at number 511), which has been serving delicious fried chicken since 1972, do business alongside the stores owned and run by the talented young fashion and furniture designers who have taken over the area in recent years. Block parties are held four times a year when shops serve wine and hold fashion shows, bands play in the shops, fire-eaters perform and the streets are packed with revellers.

Hayes Valley is best approached from the Van Ness section of Market Street where there are several little streets to check out on the way. At 66 Page Street, between Franklin and Gough, is the oldest Harley Davidson dealership in town, **Dudley Perkins Co**, which has been going since 1914. **Bell'occhio** (8 Brady Street) is worth the minor detour for European toiletries, antique ribbons and jewellery, as is the clothes shop next door, **Salon de Thé**. There are also several large, hard-to-miss, antique shops on this section of Market Street before you head off towards Hayes Valley proper. On your way make time to stop for breakfast or lunch at **Zuni Café** at 1658 Market Street.

Just across the street, check out **New Deal** for one of a kind, new and used furniture and *objets d'art*, before cutting through tiny Rose Street to Gough Street and then turning right for more treasures. This really is San Francisco's nearest equivalent to New York's SoHo, chock-a-block with wonderful shops and restaurants. On Hayes and Laguna Streets don't miss the extremely stylish **Suppencuche** restaurant, which is run along the lines of a German *wirtshaus* (a kind of living room for the community) and is deservedly popular among the locals.

If you like tarot with your tea, get down to **Mad Magda's Russian Tea Room** (579 Hayes Street). The intimate **Momi Toby's Cafe**, just up from Suppencuche on Laguna Street, is the perfect place to relax and read the newspaper over a latte or a light meal and has excellent live music in the evenings. Down the road, **Marlena's** bar is at its best on a Friday night when the pool table is turned into a stage on which sexy transvestites dance and mime to their favourite songs.

Shops worth a special mention are **Zeitgeist** (437B Hayes Street) for vintage watches; **Bella Donna** (539 Hayes) sells wonderful clothes and unusual fabrics; **Vintage Boutique** just across the street is part vintage clothes store, part toy museum; **Goldstein Collection** sells African art, as does **The African Outlet** just around the corner on Octavia Street, where you can also get your body

Mad Magda's Russian Tea Room.

decorated with henna; **Hila Lampshades** (501 Hayes) sells one-off lamps; **Richard Hildert** (330 Hayes) sells new books on every subject but is probably the best source in the US for valuable, second-hand and out-of-print books on interior design.

Just across from Hildert's, the **San Francisco Women Artists Gallery** grew out of the all-women Sketch Club of the 1880s and continues to showcase the work of women artists in the Bay Area. **Star Classics** record store (425 Hayes) stocks a huge selection of classical music and has twice-weekly daytime performances of chamber music and jazz. **Place Pigalle** (at number 520) has live jazz bands seven days a week. The famous jazz venue, **Kimball's West** (on the corner of Grove and Franklin Streets) showcases jazz greats from all over the world.

Nearby, the **San Francisco Performing Arts Library and Museum** (399 Grove Street) has a huge collection of performing arts memorabilia. You can even print from your floppy disk, send international faxes and access your e-mail account at **All Systems Go** (332 Gough Street), a few doors from the popular **Caffe Delle Stelle** Italian restaurant. All this within a four- or five-block radius. Phew.

Golden Gate Park & the West

Go barefoot in the Park, watch the sun set in Sunset and discover the alternative Chinatown in Richmond.

Golden Gate Park

Golden Gate Park, which stretches between Fulton Street and Lincoln Way from Stanyan Street to the Pacific, is extraordinarily diverse. Its 1,000-plus acres include manicured gardens, wild areas, fairy-tale woodlands, illegal homeless encampments, rollerblading paths, bike trails, lakes, rose gardens, a playground, a riding school and several museums. Knowing that its construction didn't begin until the late 1870s makes it almost impossible to walk through the park without marvelling at the imaginations of its creators – civil engineer William Hammond Hall and the long-serving Park Supervisor John McLaren, who worked here from 1887 until 1943.

It is quite a walk from sight to sight. You might want to rent a bicycle (from **Park Cyclery** at 1865 Haight Street) or rollerblades (from **Magic Skates** at 3038 Fulton at Sixth Avenue) to speed things up a bit. Free rock concerts are often held at the Stanyan Street end of the park and **Opera in the Park** is a summer treat when local music lovers get a picnic together and settle down to an afternoon of performances by the stars from the San Francisco Opera. Bored children can be appeased with the promise of a ride on the beautifully restored **carousel**, not far away by the playground just off Kezar Drive.

Don't miss the **de Young Memorial Museum** which has a surprisingly good art collection, including works by Georgia O'Keeffe and Mary Cassatt. Admission to the de Young also gets you into the **Asian Art Museum**, which has the largest collection of Asian art outside Asia. All the park museums are free on the first Wednesday of the month (*see chapter* **Museums & Galleries** for more details). The **California Academy of Sciences** houses a number of scientific exhibitions, including the **Natural History Museum**, the **Morrison Planetarium** and the **Steinhart Aquarium**. The latter includes a beautiful living coral reef, and the popular Fish Roundabout – much loved by children – where a huge and populous fish tank encircles the room.

The **Japanese Tea Garden**, which is also free on the first Wednesday of the month, is an oasis of peace with a little bridge, flowering trees, a huge bronze Buddha and an outdoor tearoom where waitresses in kimonos serve tea. Gardening enthusiasts will love the **Strybing Arboretum**, a huge garden planted with 6,000 species of plants, trees and shrubs from different countries; the ornate **Conservatory of Flowers**, the design of which was inspired by the Palm House glass palace at London's Kew gardens, and the **Queen Wilhelmina Tulip Garden**, which surrounds the windmill by 48th Avenue. Literary gardeners will also love the **Shakespeare Garden**, which is stocked with plants mentioned in William Shakespeare's plays or poetry.

At **Stow Lake,** the largest lake in the park, you can rent a paddle or rowing boat. Or you can have riding lessons at the **Golden Gate Park Riding Academy** at 36th Avenue and Kennedy Drive. If just looking at four-legged beasts is more your kind of thing, **Buffalo Park** always has a small herd of buffalo conveniently clustered around the fence for easy viewing. For a map of the park, *see chapter* **Sightseeing**.

Richmond

The Richmond district borders the northern edge of Golden Gate Park, from Arguello Boulevard to the ocean and from Fulton Street to the Presidio. Once a sandy wasteland, visited at weekends by upper-class San Franciscans when they came to enjoy the once-smart Cliff House restaurant, the 1906 construction of the Geary Boulevard tramway made it a viable residential area. Settled by Russian and Eastern European Jews after World War I, it is now a decidedly mixed neighbourhood, dominated by Russian, Irish and, increasingly, Chinese immigrants.

Clement Street, from Fourth to 20th Avenues, is seen by many as the 'real' Chinatown. Huge shops sell cheap Chinese kitchenware and decorated enamel crockery; acupuncture clinics and small Chinese medicine shops can be found on every block, and there are hundreds of excellent Asian restaurants. Notable ones include **The Fountain Court** (at Fifth Avenue and Clement Street); **Minh's Garden** (208 Clement Street), where you can get a Vietnamese meal for under $5; the more upscale Vietnamese, **Le Soleil**, on the next block; and the vegetarian **Red Crane** (115 Clement Street, at 12th Avenue).

Non-Asian delights on Clement Street include the **Blue Danube** 1960s-style coffee house; **Haig's Delicacies**, which sells British food, Middle Eastern goods and a fabulous selection of Indian spices; and the new and second-hand bookstore **Green Apple Books**. Further down Clement Street towards the beach, look out for **Ernesto's Pizza Restaurant** (at 25th Avenue); **Gordo Taqueria** (at number 2252) for Mexican food, and **Bill's Place** (at 24th Avenue). This local diner has a pretty garden at the back and serves hamburgers named after local celebrities, such as the Carol Doda Burger, in honour of the woman who introduced topless dancing to the city (two hamburger patties each topped with an olive, served side by side).

Across the street, the **Family Sauna Shop** has been providing saunas, massage, facials and beauty treatments since 1975. Almost next door, the **Buddhist Temple** is a relaxing haven from the street. Another gem is the **Four Star Cinema** (2200 Clement Street); it may be a bit of a flea-pit and the films sometimes start later than advertised, but it has character, and often puts on cheap double bills in the afternoon.

At the Ocean Beach end of Richmond, **Sutro Heights Park** is a tiny idyll, virtually empty except for a few Russians playing chess on the benches. By the park entrance at 46th Avenue a statue of the goddess Diana is often decorated with flowers by local believers. At the nearby walled garden you can have a secluded picnic in oddly Mediterranean surroundings and enjoy a spectacular panoramic view of the ocean – fog permitting. Walk down to the beach and stop off for a huge milkshake at **Louis'**, which offers truckstop-style food and a view just as good as the one from the nearby, touristy **Cliff House**. Tobacco magnate Adolph Sutro built the first Cliff House in the 1860s and after a fire in 1894, replaced it with a Victorian turreted palace. When this too burned down, it was replaced by the present architectural muddle.

At the bottom of the Cliff House, check out the antique penny arcade machines at the **Musée Mécanique**, view the Seal Rocks from the nineteenth-century **Camera Obscura** (on a clear day, you can see the Farallon Islands, 30 miles out to sea) and then walk down to the ruins of the **Sutro Baths** in Sutro Heights Park. Built by Sutro in 1896, these were once the world's biggest swimming baths with seven different heated pools under a magnificent glass roof, all sadly destroyed by fire in 1966.

To the right of the old baths is a long cave. A spooky walk through this opens onto the side of the cliffs where the sea crashes against the rocks; don't attempt it at high tide, however, when the cave fills up and you could get trapped. Instead, walk the three-mile wind-swept **Coastal Trail** from the Cliff House to the Golden Gate Bridge.

Don't leave Richmond without visiting the **Columbarium** (1 Loraine Court, off Anza Street), which is open to the public from 10am-1pm daily. This beautiful Victorian building and miniature 'museum' of funeral architecture set in two acres of gardens, is the only cemetery for cremated remains in San Francisco. Come here to admire the lovely stained glass windows and magnificent tiled floor.

Sunset

The Sunset area of San Francisco is a large and mainly residential neighbourhood stretching along the southen length of Golden Gate Park as far as the ocean and south to Rivera Street. Like the Richmond district, it can be extremely foggy in the summer months between June and September; however, on clear days the area enjoys some spectacular sunsets over the ocean.

Start your tour of Sunset on **Irving Street**; the shopping area from Fifth to Tenth Avenues is well worth exploring. **Noah's Bagels** by Ninth Avenue has the best bagels in the city; at weekend lunchtimes it is packed with people heading for picnics in the park. There are several excellent restaurants in the area, including seafood specialist **PJ's Oysterbed** (737 Irving Street) and **Ebisu** (1283 Ninth Avenue), which locals claim serves the best sushi in San Francisco. Coffee shops in the area include **The Beanery** on the corner of Irving and Seventh Streets; the **Java Place** on Ninth and Judah Streets; and **The Owl and Monkey**, which has a garden and live music several times a week. For a greasy spoon breakfast, you can't do much better than **Art's Cafe** on Irving and Eighth Streets.

Ninth Avenue Books (at number 1348) sells new and second-hand books. **Le Video** (1239 Ninth Avenue) is probably the best video store in San Francisco with the broadest selection of films, from mainstream to the downright obscure, and is well worth schlepping across town to visit. Anyone with photo ID, a credit card and a San Francisco address is welcome.

At the northern end of Sunset, **Ocean Beach**, the city's biggest beach, is good for a blustery walk and for watching the surfers. You can then take a coffee break at the **Java Beach** café (at Judah and 47th Streets), where the coffee is famously good. The best restaurant in the immediate vicinity is probably the Vietnamese **Thanh Long** (4101 Judah Street); anything on the menu is good but it's famous for garlic crab. After dinner it's a short

*Check out the windsurfers from **Ocean Beach**, the city's largest.*

walk to back to Ocean Beach to look at the sunset; when the weather allows, the views from here (and Richmond) are the best in the city.

To the south-west of Sunset at the end of the Muni Metro L line, and five blocks beyond Rivera is **San Francisco Zoo**, which is small but exotic, and has a special children's section where kids can feed domestic farm animals. Further east **Stern Grove** (at 19th Avenue and Sloat Boulevard) is a 63-acre oasis of eucalyptus, redwood and fir trees; it's very popular in the summer when San Franciscans brave the fog to attend the free Sunday afternoon jazz and classical concerts. **Stonestown Galleria** shopping mall, a few blocks south on 19th Avenue at Winston Drive, should satisfy most shopaholics in the area.

Eating & Drinking

Eating & Drinking by Area

Downtown

Restaurants: Anjou p115; Café Claude p115; China Moon Cafe p114; Emporio Armani Express p118; Kyo-Ya Restaurant p119; MacArthur Park p113; Masa's p117; Mo's p122; Postrio p112; Rubicon p113; Sears Fine Foods p122; Tadich Grill p119; Yank Sing p115.
Bars: Blue Lamp p123; Garden Court p125; Miss Pearl's Jam House p126; Redwood Room p127.
Cafés: Café Capriccio p130; Café Bastille p130.
Wine Bars: London Wine Bar p125.

Civic Center
Restaurants: Maharani p117; Stars p111; Vicolo Pizzeria p121; Zuni Café p113.
Cafés: Zuni Café p133.

Chinatown & North Beach

Chinatown
Restaurants: House of Nanking p114; Lichee Garden p114; R & G Lounge p114.
Brewpubs: San Francisco Brewing Company p127.

North Beach
Restaurants: Buca Giovanni p117; Cafe Jacqueline p117; Caffè Freddy's Eatery p122; Caffè Macaroni p117; Helmand p122; Il Pollaio p122; Little Joe's p122; Lo Coco's p118; L'Osteria del Forno p118; Moose's p112; Tommaso's p117; Zax p113.
Bars: Green's Sports Bar p126; Mick's Lounge p126; Tosca Cafe p129; Vesuvio's Café p129; Spec's p129.
Cafés: Art Institute Cafe p130; Caffe Greco p132; Caffè Trieste p132; Enrico's p132; Le Petit Cafe p133; Mario's Bohemian Cigar Store p133; Savoy Tivoli p133; Steps of Rome p133.

Nob Hill, Russian Hill & Telegraph Hill
Restaurants: Alfred's p119; Harris' p119; Golden Turtle p121; Julius' Castle p118; La Folie p117; Ristorante Milano p118; Ritz-Carlton Dining Room p113; Swan Oyster Depot p119; Zarzuela p119.
Bars: Tonga Room p129; Top of the Mark p132.

SoMa & the Mission

SoMa
Restaurants: Appam p117; Bizou p112; Fringale p115; Hawthorne Lane p111; Lulu p111; Manora's Thai Cuisine p120; South Park Cafe p117; Woodward's Garden p113; Wu Kong p115.
Bars: Cafe Mars p124; Caribbean Zone p124; Hotel Utah p125; View Lounge p132.
Brewpubs: Gordon Biersch p127; Twenty Tank Brewery p127.
Cafés: Ace Cafe p130; Caffè Centro p132; Josie's Juice Bar and Cabaret p133. **Wine Bars**: Cava 555 p125.

The Mission
Restaurants: Betelnut p114; Esperento's p119; Fina Estampa p121; Flying Saucer p112; La Taqueria p120; Le Trou p117; Pancho Villa Taqueria p120; Ti Couz Crêperie p122; Timo's in the Zanzibar p119; Universal Café p113.
Bars: Albion p123; Cafe Babar p123; Chameleon p124; Dalva p124; Elbo Room p125; The 500 Club p125; Latin American Club p126; Lone Palm p126; The Rite Spot p129.

Brewpubs: Anchor Steam Brewing Company p127.
Cafés: Café la Boheme p132; Slow Club p133.

The Haight & the Castro

The Haight-Ashbury
Restaurants: Cha Cha Cha p113; Hama-Ko p118; Thep Phanom p120.
Bars: Club Deluxe p124; Mad Dog in the Fog p126; Noc Noc p126.
Cafés: Horseshoe Coffee House p132.

The Castro & Noe Valley
Restaurants: Firefly p112.
Bars: The Café p123; Cafe Du Nord p123; Rat & Raven p126; Zeitgeist p129.
Cafés: Cafe Flore p130.

The Waterfront

Restaurants: Aqua p119; Boulevard p109; Fog City Diner p113; Gaylord of India p117; Greens p120; Harbor Village p113; Il Fornaio p117; One Market Reataurant p113; Square One p111.
Bars: Union Ale House p129.

The Marina & Union Street
Restaurants: Cafe Marimba p120; Izzy's Steaks & Chips p120; North India p117; World Wraps p122.

The Central Neighbourhoods

Pacific Heights
Restaurants: The Heights p112; Jackson Fillmore p118; Pane e Vino p117; Vivande Porta Via p118.
Bars: Harry's on Fillmore p125.

Japantown & the Western Addition
Restaurants: Café Kati p117; Isobune Sushi p118; Mifune p119; Sanppo p119.

Hayes Valley
Restaurants: Hayes Street Grill p109.
Wine Bars: Hayes and Vine p125.

Golden Gate Park & the West

Pacific Heights
Hana p118.

Richmond
Restaurants: Alain Rondelli p115; Chiang Mai p120; Hong Kong Flower Lounge p113; Kabuto p118; Laghi p118; Mayflower p114; Socca p113; Ton Kiang p114.
Cafés: The Plough & Stars p126.

Further Afield

Restaurants: Angkor Borei p120; Bay Wolf Cafe p111. Cafe at Chez Panisse p112; Chez Panisse p110; Citron p112; French Laundry p110; Lark Creek Inn p110; Mustards Grill p121; Oliveto p112; Piatti p121; Terra p121; Tra Vigne p121.
Bars: E-Line Ale House p124. **Brewpubs**: Jupiter p127; Marin Brewing Company p127.

Restaurants

Wake up and smell the coffee – the garlic, the freshly baked sourdough and all the other scents that confirm San Francisco as a gourmet paradise.

San Francisco has always been a great place to eat well, inexpensively or at least moderately. Over the past ten or 15 years, with the development of California Cuisine by local chefs and the arrival of several famous chefs, San Francisco has become a gourmet destination on a par with Paris, London, and New York.

A number of factors contribute to making San Francisco one of the world's best restaurant cities. This eater's mecca is an isthmus of different cultures and therefore produces a remarkable diversity of cuisines. It's at the centre of a rich agricultural base, making good quality, fresh produce available to restaurateurs all year round. Its proximity to the wine regions of Napa, Sonoma, Calistoga, Santa Cruz, and Mendocino – which are producing cabernets, merlots, and chardonnays comparable to those produced in Europe – means interesting wine lists at the better restaurants. And since it is a coastal city, fresh seafood is available from the Pacific Ocean. Finally, though a less tangible contribution, there is the aesthetics of the city

itself: people here are accustomed to natural beauty and creative design, and they expect no less when they are dining out.

You only have to spend a short time in San Francisco, to witness the importance of food to its citizens. Wander through the neighbourhoods and smell the garlic in North Beach, the fish in Chinatown and the famous freshly-baked sourdough bread throughout, mixed with the inescapable scent of strong coffee.

Statistics indicate that there are more restaurants per capita in San Francisco than in any other American city. Some of its chefs are renowned celebrities. The open kitchens found in so many restaurants testify to the entertainment value that good cooking has become here. Even the local growers get billing on many menus – as proof that ingredients are fresh and organically grown. Although food is sometimes treated as theatre, you rarely have to dress up for it, except in the grandest of restaurants. It's also worth bearing in mind that locals tend to eat early: 7pm is the usual supper time, and many restaurants stop serving food at 9.30pm or 10pm.

Pick of the best

Cafe Marimba
Boisterous Mexican café in the Marina district.
Chez Panisse
The birthplace of California Cuisine.
Fringale
SoMa bistro serving the best steak frites in town.
Greens
For the complete Californian veggie experience.
Hayes Street Grill
Seafood to die for.
Helmand
Classy but cheap Afghani.
Kyo-Ya
For the best sushi in San Francisco.
Lulu
Outrageously – deservedly – popular Cal-Ital eatery.
Pane e Vino
Tuscan food in a rustic setting.
Stars
Great food, high prices, and guaranteed glitterati.
Ton Kiang
Unmissable dim sum in the Richmond district.
Zuni Café
The archetypal San Fran eating experience.

Brunch

Brunching is a popular weekend activity in San Francisco. Not many people stir in the city at the weekends until after 11am, after which you're likely to bump into many of them in their favourite brunch spots. Some of the snazziest options include **Stars** (*see page 111*), **Campton Place** (in the hotel of that name at 340 Stockton Street; 955 5555), the **Lark Creek Inn**, just across the Golden Gate Bridge in Larkspur (*page 110*), **One Market Restaurant** (*page 113*), **Postrio** (*page 112*), and **Rubicon** (*page 113*). More moderately priced choices include the vegetarian restaurant **Greens** in the Fort Mason Center (*page 121*), **Il Fornaio** (*page118*), **Lulu Café** (*page 111;* in the restaurant of the same name), the ultra hip **Zuni Café** (*page 113*), or, the dim sum favourite, **Yank Sing** (page 115). Choices on the budget side include **Ti Couz Crêperie**, **Sears Fine Foods**, **Caffè Freddy's** (*all listed on page 112*), **Universal Cafe** (*page113*), and dim sum at **Ton Kiang** (*page 114*).

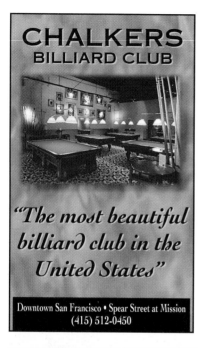

*Where the glitterati go: chef Jeremiah Tower presides over the popular **Stars**. See page 111.*

Celebrity Chefs

Boulevard

1 Mission Street, at First Street (543 6084). BART Embarcadero/Muni Metro F, J, K, L, M, N/15, 24, 41 bus. **Lunch served** 11.30am-2pm, **bistro service** 2.30-5.15pm, Mon-Fri. **Dinner served** 5.30-10.30pm daily. **Average** from $25. **Credit** AmEx, MC, V.

Chef Nancy Oakes teamed up with restaurant designer Pat Kuleto to create this upmarket restaurant in the turn-of-the-century Audifred building, near the Embarcadero. Oakes provides huge, colourful portions that are quite elaborate. This is a good choice for a special occasion when you want to dress up and don't mind your credit card suffering. *Disabled: access; toilet.*

Chez Panisse

1517 Shattuck Avenue, at Cedar Street, Berkeley (1-510 548 5525). BART Berkeley. **Dinner served** (two sittings) 6-6.30pm, 8.30-9.15pm, Mon-Sat. **Set dinners** $35 Mon, $55 Tue-Thur, $65 Fri, Sat, three courses. **Credit** AmEx, DC, MC.

Foodies say that Alice Waters, owner of Chez Panisse, created 'California Cuisine'. This famous prix fixe restaurant, located in Berkeley, remains the Bay Area mecca for food lovers. Chefs Catherine Brandel and Jean-Pierre Moullé offer simply stunning meals in the ground floor restaurant, prepared from ultra-fresh ingredients, down to the last detail. The staff are infectiously knowledgeable and enthusiastic about the food and lengthy wine list. For less expensive fare, try the **Cafe at Chez Panisse**, located upstairs (*see p112* **California Cuisine**).

Hayes Street Grill

320 Hayes Street, between Franklin and Gough Streets (863 5545). BART Van Ness/Muni Metro F, J, K, L, M, N/21, 42, 49 bus. **Lunch served** 11.30-2pm Mon-Fri. **Dinner served** 5-9pm Mon-Thur; 5-10.30pm Fri; 5.30-10.30pm Sat; 5-8.30pm Sun. **Average** $45. **Credit** AmEx, DC, MC, V.

Owner, chef and restaurant critic Patricia Unterman offers some of the best seafood in San Francisco in her simply decorated restaurant. Flawlessly fresh fish comes with a choice of sauces or salsas and the Grill's trademark pomme frites. All the dishes are prepared using local organic produce. The restaurant was opened because there wasn't a good place to eat near the Civic Centre before going to the opera, ballet, or symphony concerts; 16 years later it remains the best place to eat before a performance. *Disabled: access; toilet.*

Lark Creek Inn

234 Magnolia Street, Larkspur (924 7766). Golden Gate Transit ferry to Larkspur. **Lunch served** 11.30am-2.30pm daily. **Dinner served** 5.30-10pm Mon-Thur; 5-10.30pm Fri-Sun. **Average** $40. **Credit** AmEx, MC, V.

Brad Ogden's rustic Marin inn specialises in New American cuisine – robust dishes such as hearty Yankee pot roast to be followed by comfort food like apple pie with ice-cream. Sunday brunch is a popular event here (*see p107* for other popular options). The inn is housed in a converted Victorian mansion set among towering redwood trees, just across the Golden Gate Bridge, and so easily accessible by car or by ferry. *Disabled: access; toilet.*

For some of the freshest seafood in town, head for the **Hayes Street Grill.**

Eat Cal-Ital food in laid-back surroundings at **Lulu**.

Lulu

816 Folsom Street, at Fourth and Fifth Streets (495 5775). Bus 12, 27, 45, 76. **Lunch served** 11.30am-2.30pm Tue-Sun. **Dinner served** 5.30-11pm Mon-Thur, Sun; 5.30pm-midnight Fri, Sat. **Average** $30. **Credit** AmEx, DC, JCB, MC, V.

A huge wood-burning rôtisserie and oven distinguish Reed Hearon's extremely popular restaurant, where excellent Cal-Ital food is served in a jubilant atmosphere. The large room can be quite noisy and the giant plates don't always fit comfortably onto some of the smaller tables. On either side of Lulu are little Lulus – Lulu Bis, tucked away behind the bar, puts out fixed-price wholesome food at long communal refectory tables in a candle-lit room; Lulu Café, opposite, serves coffee, morning pastries, and sandwiches. *Disabled: access; toilet.*

Square One

190 Pacific Avenue, at Front Street (788 1110). BART Embarcadero/Muni Metro F, J, K, L, M, N/12, 83 bus. **Lunch served** 11.30am-2pm Mon-Fri. **Dinner served** 5.30-10pm Mon-Thur, Sun; 5.30-10.30pm Fri, Sat; 5-9pm Sun. **Average** $40. **Credit** AmEx, DC, MC, V.

Globe-trotting cooking with ample vegetarian dishes and low-sodium and low-fat, heart-healthy dishes is what Joyce Goldstein serves up. You'll find dishes from the Middle East, North Africa, Italy and Brazil, among the cuisines represented. A very impressive, well-priced wine list accompanies this international, ethnically inspired menu.

Stars

555 Golden Gate Avenue, at Van Ness Avenue and Polk Street (861 7827). Bus 19, 42, 47, 49. **Lunch served** 11.30am- 2pm Mon-Fri. **Dinner served** 5.30-10pm daily. **Late supper served** 11pm Mon-Thur, Sun; 11.30pm Fri, Sat. **Average** $50. **Credit** AmEx, DC, MC, V.

Jeremiah Tower presides over this favourite of local glitterati. It's the number one eating and drinking spot in the city and therefore very difficult to get into (book well in advance), but it's definitely worth the bother. Expect consistently great food and big-time prices. There's also a great late-night, after-theatre party crowd. The less expensive café nearby serves less interesting food.

Branch: **Stars Café** 500 Van Ness Avenue (861 4344).

California Cuisine

Making its first appearance in the 1970s – many say thanks to Alice Waters of **Chez Panisse** – California Cuisine caught on in the 1980s and continues to evolve in the 1990s. But what is it? Those who produce it emphasise fresh, often locally produced, organic and seasonal ingredients, and cross-cultural influences infused into traditional dishes. Those who eat it, notice a lot of grilling or light sautéing, plenty of salads, and generally healthful dishes artfully presented. Those who criticise it, find tiny portions of simple food, fussily arranged on a plate, and charged at exorbitant prices. (In fact, the small portions were more a criticism of the past, since the cuisine has now evolved into something heartier, served in more generous quantities.)

All agree that California Cuisine is creative and sometimes daring in its novel combinations of flavours and textures. Borrowing from many cuisines, chefs often prefer the term eclectic, especially since early on California Cuisine was labelled 'simple'. In fact, the blending of cuisines has become quite sophisticated. The latest trend within this cuisine is Mediterranean cooking, which melds the flavours of France, Greece, Italy, Spain, Egypt, and Morocco.

Key ingredients include shiitake mushrooms, arugula (rocket), raddicchio, and salsas made of oranges, chillies, mint, lime or ginger; techniques included brief cooking that releases flavours but retains textures and nutrients, and a French or Japanese sensibility when it comes to presentation.

This distinctively American method of cooking began regionally but its spiritedness and casual elegance has spread nationally.

Bay Wolf Cafe

3853 Piedmont Avenue, Oakland (1-510 655 6004).
BART Rockridge. **Lunch served** 11.30am-2pm Mon-
Fri. **Dinner served** 6-9pm Mon-Thur; 6-9.30pm Fri;
5.30-9.30pm Sat; 5.30-9pm Sun. **Average** $30.
Credit MC, V.
After 19 years, this East Bay institution still puts out
inspired, always fresh, French-influenced California
Cuisine. The menu changes frequently, taking advantage
of seasonal ingredients. It's open for lunch or dinner and
has patio seating outside. There's also a strong, well-
conceived wine list.

Bizou

598 Fourth Street, at Brannon Street (543 2222).
Bus 15, 30, 45. **Lunch served** 11.30am-2.30pm Mon-
Fri. **Dinner served** 5.30-10pm Mon-Thur; 5-10.30pm Fri,
Sat. **Average** $30. **Credit** AmEx, MC, V.
A recent addition to the hip SoMa restaurant scene, this is a
cozy spot for a romantic dinner. Beautifully prepared local
catch, like sand dabs and petrale, or delicious pastas and
pizzas are recommended. Moderate prices make it a real find.
Disabled: access; toilet.

Café Kati

1963 Sutter Street, at Fillmore and Webster Street (775
7313). Bus 2, 3, 4, 22. **Dinner served** 5.30-10pm Tue-
Sun. **Average** $25. **Credit** MC, V.
Café Kati serves up delicious food in unassuming surroundings. The 'East meets West' menu is executed in the arty, sculp-
tural style of some California Cuisine; so that spun sugar
towers eight inches over a crème brûlée. But the presentations
are fun and the flavours are delicious. The restaurant is small
and there are enough devoted locals to make booking necessary; try and get a seat in the front room, which is more attractive than the back one.
Disabled: access.

Cafe at Chez Panisse

1517 Shattuck Avenue, at Cedar Street, Berkeley (1-510
548 5049). BART Berkeley. **Lunch served** 11.30am-
3pm Mon-Thur; 11.30am-4pm Fri, Sat. **Dinner served**
5-10.30pm Mon-Thur; 5-11.30pm Fri, Sat. **Average** $30.
Credit AmEx, DC, MC, V.
This is a moderately priced and more casual version of its
downstairs parent (*see p110* **Chez Panisse**). But it's still
the real thing – a dining experience to be savoured, and well
worth the drive from San Francisco.
Disabled: access; toilet.

Citron

5484 College Avenue, at Taft Street, Berkeley (1-510 653
5484). BART Rockridge. **Dinner served** 5.30-10pm
daily. **Average** $30. **Credit** MC, V.
The generous portions of simply prepared classic dishes are
well-executed at this charming neighbourhood bistro in the
tony Rockridge area between Berkeley and Oakland.
Reservations are a must, since it's highly popular. Delicious
desserts and a good-quality wine list are further highlights.
Disabled: access; toilet.

Firefly

4288 24th Street, at Douglass Street (821 7652). Bus 35,
48. **Dinner served** 5.30-10pm daily. **Average** $25.
Credit AmEx, MC, V.
An affordable neighbourhood restaurant that blends a multitude of ethnic cuisines quite well. Share appetisers like Thai
salmon cakes or the popular Caesar salad; the fruit shortcake
is recommended for pudding.

Flying Saucer

1000 Guerrero, at 22nd Street (641 9955). BART 24th
Street/26, 48 bus. **Dinner served** 5.30-9.30pm Tue-Sat;
6-9pm Sun. **Average** $40. **Credit** MC, V.

This popular Mission district restaurant has the reputation
of being on the far side of whimsy in its culinary content.
Eccentric, sophisticated, flamboyant dishes are works of art.
The place has expanded to include the shop next door, but
late diners may still have to wait for a table.
Disabled: access; toilet.

Hawthorne Lane

22 Hawthorne, at Second and Third Streets (777 9779).
Bus 12, 15, 30,45, 76. **Lunch served** 11.30am-2pm
Mon-Fri. **Dinner served** 5.30-10.30pm daily.
Average $15-$25. **Credit** DC, MC, V.
Located near the new Museum of Modern Art, this new
Yerba Buena restaurant was all the rage at the time of
writing. The chefs, who previously worked at Postrio (*see*
below) concoct Asian- and European-influenced dishes. Try
the tempura lobster.
Disabled: access; toilet.

The Heights

3235 Sacramento Street, at Presidio Avenue (474 8890).
Bus 1, 3, 4, 43. **Dinner served** 5.30-9.30pm Tue-Sat.
Average $50. **Credit** AmEx, DC, MC, V.
A well-heeled neighbourhood clientele frequents this charming French-influenced Californian bistro, located in highly
des res Pacific Heights. Expect a refined atmosphere and service. Specialties include roasted glazed duck and squab
served with polenta.
Disabled: access.

Moose's

1652 Stockton Street, at Union and Filbert Streets (989
7800). Bus 15, 30, 39, 41, 45/Powell-Mason cable car.
Meals served 11.30am-11pm Mon-Thur; 11.30am-
midnight Fri, Sat; 10am 10pm Sun. **Average** $30.
Credit AmEx, DC, MC, V.
Ed Moose presides over this bustling, 'in' North Beach
restaurant near Washington Square. The place gets incredibly crowded and noisy but no one seems to care – that's half
the fun. The food can also be inconsistent, so stick to the
basic bistro fare.
Disabled: access; toilet.

Oliveto

5655 College Avenue, at Shafter Avenue, Berkeley (1-510
547 5356). BART Rockridge. **Lunch served** 11.30am-
2pm Mon-Fri. **Dinner served** 5.30-9.30pm Mon-Thur,
Sun; 5.30-10pm Fri, Sat. **Average** $35. **Credit** AmEx,
DC, MC, V.
Tuscan-style food prepared by a former chef from Chez
Panisse (*see p110*) keeps this stylish restaurant busy
upstairs. A less expensive café downstairs always hums. In
the summer you could choose home-made noodles with
chanterelles, fresh peas and a little cream. Skinned chicken
cooked in a brick with garlic mashed potatoes, or squash
gratin and grilled tomatoes are other, suitably satisfying,
options.
Disabled: access; toilet.

Postrio

545 Post Street, at Taylor and Mason Streets (776
7825). BART Powell/Muni Metro all lines/2, 3, 4,76
bus/Powell-Mason cable car. **Breakfast served** 7am-
10am, **lunch served** 11.30am-2pm, **dinner served**
5.30-10.30pm, Mon-Sat. **Brunch served** 9am-2pm Sat,
Sun. **Average** $50. **Credit** AmEx, DC, MC, V.
Los Angeles celebrity chef Wolfgang Puck's entry into the
Northern Californian restaurant wars has been a raging suc-
cess ever since it opened its doors. A truly inspired
Californian/Mediterranean menu and a helpful and knowl-
edgeable staff make this a must on anyone's list. It's close to
Union Square and convenient for a pre-theatre dinner.
Booking is definitely advised.
Disabled: access; toilet.

Ritz-Carlton Dining Room

Ritz-Carlton, 600 Stockton Street, at California Street (296 7465). Powell-Hyde/Powell-Mason cable car. **Dinner served** 6-9.30pm Mon-Sat. **Set dinner** $43 three courses. **Credit** AmEx, DC, MC. V.

The best hotel dining room in the city is in the spectacularly renovated Ritz-Carlton on top of Nob Hill. An impressive menu changes seasonally, but if you see the quail salad with foie gras croûtons and apricot-ginger chutney, try it. The surroundings are ultra-grand and the service impeccable, and the menu has more flair than most traditional luxury hotels. The superb selection of cheeses is an added bonus. *See also chapter* **Accommodation**.
Disabled: access; toilet.

Rubicon

558 Sacramento Street, at Sansome and Montgomery Streets (434 4100). BART Montgomery Street/Muni Metro F, J, K, L, M, N/1, 41, 42 bus. **Lunch served** 11.30am-2.30pm Mon-Fri. **Dinner served** 5.30-10.30pm Mon-Thur; 5.30-11pm Fri, Sat. **Average** from $35. **Credit** AmEx, DC, MC. V.

Backed by Francis Ford Coppola, Robert de Niro, Robin Williams and their friends, this newly opened downtown restaurant serves up lamb, fish, and the best of locally grown vegetables. It's pricey but has a wine list to please the most discriminating of wine enthusiasts.
Disabled: access; toilet.

Socca

5800 Geary Avenue, at 22nd Street (379 6270). Bus 29, 38, 38L. **Dinner served** 5.30-10pm Tue-Sun. **Average** $25. **Credit** AmEx, DC, MC. V.

It's surprising to find this culinary gem nestled among scores of Asian restaurants in San Francisco's working-class Richmond district. This is a good choice if you're museum hopping between the de Young and the newly re-opened Palace of the Legion of Honor. Socca has excellent California Cuisine at moderate prices.
Disabled: access; toilet.

Universal Cafe

2814 19th Street, between Bryant and Florida Streets (821 4608). Bus 27, 33. **Lunch served** 11.30am-2.30pm, **dinner served** 6-10pm, Tue-Sun. **Average** $18. **Credit** AmEx, MC, V.

Designer pizza, focaccia sandwiches and salads are the fare at this hip café run by a semi-industrial block of the Mission district. Italian and Californian wines by the glass are charged at affordable prices and the coffee roasted on the premises is very good.
Disabled: access; toilet.

Woodward's Garden

1700 Mission Street, at Duboce Street (621 7122). Bus 14, 26, 49. **Dinner served** (two sittings) 6-6.30pm, 8-8.30pm, Wed-Sun. **Average** $20. **No credit cards.**

Two women chefs from Postrio (*p112*) and the vegetarian restaurant Greens (*p121*) run this tiny nine-table establishment. The small kitchen dictates a simple menu, but everything that comes out of it is first rate. The only negative aspect is the locale – it's under a noisy freeway. Booking is advisable.

Zax

2330 Taylor Street, at Columbus Street (563 6266). Bus 15, 30, 45/Powell-Mason cable car. **Dinner served** 5.30-10pm Tue-Sat. **Average** $25. **Credit** MC, V.

This Californian/Mediterranean spot is hidden away in a North Beach side street. The fresh tuna and salmon main courses with grilled seasonal vegetables are recommended. It offers a well-chosen but limited wine list.
Disabled: access with assistance; toilet.

Zuni Café

1658 Market Street, between Franklin and Gough Streets (552 2522). Muni Metro F, J, K, L, M, N/6, 22, 47, 49, 66, 71 bus. **Breakfast served** 7.30-11am, **lunch served** 11.30am-5.45pm, Tue-Sun. **Dinner served** 6pm-midnight Tue-Sat; 6-11pm Sun. **Average** from $25. **Credit** AmEx, MC, V.

Ranking among the top San Francisco restaurants is this local treasure, which satisfies on every level and is wildly popular as a result. Roast chicken to die for, a selection of every available West Coast oyster, and home-made ice-creams are a few of the specialties. An archetypal San Francisco experience. *See also chapter* **Bars & Cafés**.
Disabled: access; toilet.

Afghani

Helmand

430 Broadway, at Kearny and Montgomery Streets (326 0641). Bus 12, 15, 30, 41, 42, 83. **Lunch served** 11.30am-2.30pm Mon-Thur. **Dinner served** 6-10pm Mon-Thur; 6-11pm Fri, Sat. **Average** $15. **Credit** AmEx, MC, V.

This favourite North Beach restaurant is an excellent meal for the price. In a classy atmosphere decorated with Afghani artifacts, settle in and try the aushak (leek-filled ravioli topped with a meat sauce, and served with yoghurt and mint), lamb dishes, or soups. Don't skip dessert. The set price dinners are an incredible bargain.
Disabled: access; toilet.

American

Fog City Diner

1300 Battery Street, between Greenwich and Lombard Streets (982 2000). Bus 42, 82X. **Meals served** 11.30am-11pm Mon-Thur; 11.30am-midnight Fri, Sat. **Average** $30. **Credit** DC, MC, V.

The atmosphere buzzes at this upmarket diner opposite Levi Plaza. Ask to sit in one of the luxurious wooden booths, where you can eat burgers and onion rings or several small plates of lighter dishes. Though the sleek green railway carriage-like restaurant is mostly filled with tourists at night, locals know it as a good lunch spot.

MacArthur Park

607 Front Street, at Jackson Street (398 5700). BART Embarcadero/Muni Metro F, J, K, L, M, N/12, 42 bus. **Lunch served** 11.30am-3.30pm Mon-Fri. **Dinner served** 5-10pm Mon-Thur; 5-11pm Fri, Sat; 4.30-10pm Sun. **Average** $30. **Credit** AmEx, DC, MC, V.

Half a slab of baby back ribs is the ticket here. Cobb salad, barbecue chicken, and an expansive list of Californian wines by the glass or bottle can also be had at this noisy but fun after-work hangout.
Disabled: access; toilet.

One Market Restaurant

1 Market Street, at Embarcadero Centre (777 5577). BART Embarcadero/Muni Metro F, J, K, L, M, N/1, 8, 9, 41 bus. **Lunch served** 11.30am-2pm Mon-Fri. **Brunch served** 10am-2pm Sun. **Dinner served** 5.30-9.15pm Mon-Thur; 5.30-9.45pm Fri, Sat; 5-8.45pm Sun. **Average** $35. **Credit** AmEx, DC, MC, V.

Celebrity chef Brad Ogden's New American, Financial District food emporium boasts a big room, hefty prices, and good food and service, though most agree that it's not as stellar as his Lark Creek Inn (*see p110*). This is a favourite of downtown corporate types who aren't price-conscious and like the more formal surroundings.
Disabled: access; toilet.

Caribbean

Cha Cha Cha

1801 Haight Street, at Shrader Street (386 5758). Bus 6, 7, 33, 43, 66, 71. **Lunch served** 11.30am-3pm Mon-Fri; 1-4pm Sat, Sun. **Dinner served** 5-11pm Mon-Thur, Sun; 5-11.30 Fri, Sat. **Average** $20. **No credit cards.**

A spicy Caribbean tapas hot spot in the Haight has people coming in for the huge plates of fried calamares, deep-fried new potatoes, fried plantains, black beans, yellow rice, Cajun-style pan-fried fish, and refreshing sangria. It's festive and reasonably priced but it's also notorious for the long wait before you get your food.

Disabled: access; toilet.

Chinese

Many restaurants in Chinatown offer incredibly cheap deals at lunchtime. For a tour of Chinatown and a dim sum menu, *see chapter* **Chinatown & North Beach.**

Betelnut

2030 Union Street, at Webster and Buchanan Streets (929 8855). Bus 22, 41, 45. **Meals served** 11.30am-11pm Mon-Thur, Sun; 11am-midnight Fri, Sat. **Average** $14. **Credit** DC, MC, V.

One of the newest restaurants to open at the time of writing, Betelnut's creative pan-Asian menu has proved a hit. You might try the dragon balls (light pork and shrimp wun tuns) or an Indonesian influenced curry with rice noodles. The atmosphere is welcoming. A bar area serves food and opens out onto Union Street, a middle section offers a great view of the open kitchen and includes stools around the kitchen's perimeter, and the nicely-lit back dining area has tables for larger parties.

Disabled: access; toilet.

China Moon Cafe

639 Post Street, at Jones and Taylor Streets (775 4789). Bus 2, 3, 4, 38, 76. **Dinner served** 5.30-10pm daily. **Average** from $25. **Credit** AmEx, DC, MC, V.

This downtown Asian diner uniquely blends Northern Chinese and Californian cooking. Egg rolls filled with crab, scallops, clams in a black bean sauce with noodles, and home-made ginger ice-cream with hot fudge are typically cross-cultural dishes. Its detractors complain of uncomfortable bench-type seating and hefty prices.

Disabled: access.

Yank Sing – *for dim sum. See page 115.*

Harbor Village

4 Embarcadero Centre (398 8883). BART Embarcadero/Muni Metro F, J, K, L, M, N. **Lunch served** 11am-2.30pm Mon-Fri; 10.30am-2.30pm Sat; 10am-2.30pm Sun. **Dinner served** 5.30-9.30pm daily. **Average** $25. **Credit** AmEx, DC, MC, V.

A Californian branch of a respected Hong Kong restaurant with polished service and prices, Harbor Village caters particularly to a lunchtime business crowd. The huge array of delicious dim sum or fresh fish from the tank are good bets.

Disabled: access; toilet.

Hong Kong Flower Lounge

5322 Geary Boulevard, between 17th and 18th Avenues (668 8998). Bus 29, 38, 38L. **Lunch served** 11am-2.30pm Mon-Fri; 10.30am-2.30pm Sat, Sun. **Dinner served** 5-9.30pm daily. **Average** $20. **Credit** AmEx, DC, JCB, MC, V.

Bustling and overcrowded, this Cantonese restaurant consistently serves exquisitely prepared seafood, fresh seasonal vegetables, and delectable dim sum. It satisfies hundreds of diners daily.

Disabled: access; toilet.

House of Nanking

919 Kearny Street, at Columbus Avenue (421 1429). Bus 12, 18, 53. **Meals served** 11am-10pm Mon-Fri; noon-10pm Sat; 4-10pm Sun. **Average** $20. **No credit cards.**

Barely larger than a closet, this grungey Chinese restaurant has nevertheless become a San Francisco landmark, straddling North Beach and Chinatown. Although the place looks like a health risk, the food served here is inexpensive and some of the best to be found in town, so there's usually a queue.

Lichee Garden

1416 Powell Street, at Broadway (397 2290). Bus 30, 83, 12, 45/Powell-Hyde, Powell-Mason cable car. **Meals served** 7am-9.30pm daily. **Average** $15. **Credit** MC.

A soulful Hong Kong style Chinese dinner house serves quality ingredients in comfortable surroundings. It's very popular among the local Chinese. The dim sum is unbelievably good and cheap as well.

Mayflower

6255 Geary Boulevard, at 27th Avenue (387 8338). Bus 29, 38, 38L. **Lunch served** 11am-2.30pm Mon-Fri; 10am-2.30pm Sat, Sun. **Dinner served** 5-9.30pm daily. **Average** $12. **Credit** MC, V.

This family-run Cantonese restaurant specialises in earthy clay pot and simply prepared Chinese seafood. Steamed rock cod is as good as anywhere in the city. Like many of the better Chinese places, the crowds of diners eating or waiting for a table can be a problem.

R & G Lounge

631 Kearny Street, between Clay and Sacramento Streets (982 7877). Bus 1, 15, 41. **Meals served** 11am-9.30pm daily. **Average** $12. **Credit** AmEx, DC, MC, V.

For fine seafood in the restaurant-packed Chinatown, head to this affordable restaurant where you can choose your live lobster, shrimp, and fish and have them pulled from tanks. Salt-and-pepper fried shrimp or steamed flounder are good choices. Vegetables are fresh.

Disabled: access; toilet.

Ton Kiang

5827 Geary Boulevard, between 22nd and 23rd Avenues (387 8273). Bus 29, 38, 38L. **Meals served** 10.30am-10pm Mon-Fri; 10am-10.30pm Sat, Sun. **Average** $20. **Credit** AmEx, MC, V.

Quality, fresh food and low prices have made this restaurant one of the best in the new Chinatown of the Richmond

Join the movers and shakers of multimedia gulch at the **South Park Café**. *See page 117.*

district. Prawns with lobster sauce, and crab in a black bean sauce are delicious, as is the steamed fish with ginger and the ever popular dim sum. For vegetables, ask what's in season. This branch has more amenities than the one on Spruce Street.
Disabled: access; toilet.
Branch: 3148 Geary Boulevard, at Spruce Street (752 4440).

Wu Kong

101 Spear Street, between Mission and Howard Streets (957 9300). BART Embarcadero/Muni Metro F, J, K, L, M, N/1, 2, 7, 8, 41 bus. **Lunch served** 11am-2.30pm Mon-Fri; 10.30am-2.30pm Sat, Sun. **Dinner served** 5.30-10pm daily. **Average** $20. **Credit** AmEx, DC, MC, V.
This is the number one Shanghai-style restaurant in San Francisco. The vast menu can be a challenge for the uninitiated or for ditherers. Try the delicious, exotic sounding dishes such as jellyfish salad, fried bean curd wrapped around a mushroom stuffing, or the yellow fish fritters with seafood.
Disabled: access; toilet.

Yank Sing

427 Battery Street, between Clay and Washington Streets (781 1111). BART Embarcadero/Muni Metro F, J, K, L, M, N/1, 12, 41, 42 bus. **Lunch served** 11am-3pm Mon-Fri; 10am-4pm Sat, Sun. **Average** $20. **Credit** AmEx, DC, MC, V.
The variety of mouth-watering little plates carted around the large dining areas on trolleys during brunch, make this one of the best places for dim sum in the city. In fact, dim sum is the only meal served here. The dumplings – filled with shrimp, pork, pea shoots or black mushrooms among other fillings – are particularly worth trying. The bill is calculated by the total number of plates on your table at the end of the meal.
Disabled: access; toilet.
Branch: 49 Stevenson Street, between First and Second Streets (495 4510).

French

Alain Rondelli

126 Clement Street, between Second and Third Avenues (387 0408). Bus 33, 38. **Dinner served** 5.30-10pm Tue-Thur, Sun; 5.30-10.30pm Fri, Sat. **Average** $40. **Credit** MC, V.
The talented, Provençe-trained Alain Rondelli presides over this shopfront Richmond district restaurant, which serves inventive contemporary French food. The single page menu always includes an entrée to be shared and a special vegetarian dish. All of the specially selected French and Californian wines are available by the glass or by the bottle.
Disabled: access; toilet.

Anjou

44 Campton Place, between Sutter and Post, Stockton and Grant Streets (392 5373). BART Montgomery Street/Muni Metro F, J, K, L, M, N/2, 3, 4, 30, 45 bus. **Lunch served** 11.30am-2.30pm, **dinner served** 5.30-10pm, Tue-Sat. **Average** $25. **Credit** AmEx, DC, JCB, MC, V.
For an echo of Paris, visit this reasonably priced downtown bistro. A bit cramped (all the more authentic), Anjou offers classic bistro fare. Favourites include home-made seafood sausage, duck-leg confit with endive and watercress, calf's liver with bacon and onions, and creamy chicken liver sauté.

Café Claude

7 Claude Lane, at Bush Street, between Grant and Kearny Streets (392 3505). BART Montgomery Street/Muni Metro F, J, K, L, M, N/2, 3, 4, 15, 30, 45 bus. **Meals served** 8am-10pm Mon-Fri; 10am-11pm Sat. **Average** $15. **Credit** AmEx, DC, JCB, MC, V.
For lunch or, later, for dinner and live jazz, Café Claude is a good scene. All the furnishings, the fresh baguettes, and the 'attitude' are authentically Gallic. Wonderful sandwiches and a very good salade niçoise can be complemented by glasses of inexpensive Rhône, Beaujolais, and Mâcon Blanc.
Disabled: access; toilet.

Cafe Jacqueline

*1454 Grant Avenue, between Green and Union Streets
(981 5565). Bus 41, 45, 83.* **Dinner served** 5.30-11pm
Wed-Sun. **Average** $20. **Credit** AmEx, DC, JCB, MC, V.
Savour creamy, mouthwatering soufflés at this cosy North
Beach French bistro. Wooden floors, high ceilings, white
linen clothed tables each with a rose, create the right ambience at this romantic little hideaway. The chocolate soufflé
is a wonderful way to complete dinner.

Fringale

*570 Fourth Street, between Bryant and Brannon Streets
(543 0573). Bus 15, 30, 42, 45, 76.* **Lunch served**
11.30am-3pm Mon-Fri. **Dinner served** 5.30-10.30pm
Mon-Sat. **Average** $25. **Credit** AmEx, MC, V.
A sophisticated crowd usually frequents this top-rated SoMa
bistro. Fish is a good choice here, but then, so is the steak
frites or roast rack of lamb. The chef started out as a pastry
chef, so save room for dessert.
Disabled: access; toilet.

La Folie

*2316 Polk Street, at Union and Green Streets (776
5577). Bus 19, 41, 45, 47, 49, 76.* **Dinner served** 5.30-
10pm Mon-Sat. **Average** $25. **Credit** AmEx, DC, JCB,
MC, V.
Chef Roland Passot presides over this delightful Californian
French eatery on Russian Hill. The Provençal-inspired décor
and attentive staff add to its charm. The prices are surprisingly under control. Especially noteworthy is the bargain
prix fixe dinner.

Le Trou

*1007 Guerrero Street, at 22nd Street (550 8167). BART
24th Street/14, 26, 48, 49 bus.* **Dinner served** 5.30-9pm
Tue-Thur; 5.30-10pm Fri, Sat. **Set dinner** $22.50 three
courses. **Credit** AmEx, MC, V.
This quaint Mission district café dishes out inspired French
country cooking. The menu consists of approximately five
main courses and changes daily. It has a small but well
chosen wine list.
Disabled: access; toilet.

Left Bank

*507 Magnolia Street, at Ward Street, Larkspur (927
3331). Golden Gate Transit ferry to Larkspur.* **Meals
served** 11.30am-11pm Mon-Thur; 11.30am-midnight Fri,
Sat; 10am-10pm Sun. **Average** $25. **Credit** DC, MC, V.
Drive across the Golden Gate Bridge and sit outside under
the covered verandah of this historic building in tiny downtown Larkspur and enjoy a hearty Parisian meal. The interior is nice, too. Portions of coq au vin, steak frites, lovely
vegetable salads, and everything else here are enormous.
Disabled: access; toilet.

Masa's

*648 Bush Street, between Powell and Stockton Streets
(989 7154). Bus 2, 3, 4, 45, 76/Powell-Mason cable car.*
Dinner served (two sittings) 6-6.30, 9.30pm, Tue-Sat.
Set dinners $68, $75. **Credit** AmEx, DC, MC, V.
Long rated the top French restaurant in the city, Masa's
offers the ultimate dining experience to those with the highest standards, at the highest prices. An excellent choice for
purists with a thick wallet. Oddly, reservations are for sittings at either 6-6.30 pm (early) or after 9pm (late).
Disabled: access; toilet.

South Park Cafe

*108 South Park Avenue, between Second, Third, Bryant
and Brannon Streets (495 7275). Bus 15, 30, 76.*
Meals served 7.30am-10pm Mon-Fri; 6am-10pm Sat.
Average $25. **Credit** AmEx, MC, V.
This lively, moderately-priced, narrow bistro is popular with
those who have found it, especially designers, architects, and

those from nearby 'multimedia gulch'. The menu is limited,
but strong, featuring, for example, tempting roast pork loin
and excellent roast chicken. A good wine list is augmented
by a blackboard listing inexpensive wines by the glass.
Disabled: access; toilet.

Indian

Appam

*1261 Folsom Street, between Eighth and Ninth Streets
(626 2798). Bus 12, 19, 42.* **Dinner served** 5.30-10pm
daily. **Average** $18. **Credit** AmEx, MC, V.
Located in the heart of hip SoMa, Appam serves Indian cuisine
with a Californian accent. The savoury tandoori, along with
other more unique and creative dishes, is always a good bet.

Gaylord of India

*900 North Point, at Ghiradelli Square (771 8822). Bus
19, 30, 42, 47, 49, 76/Powell-Hyde cable car.* **Lunch
served** 11.45am-1.45pm Mon-Sat; noon-2.45pm Sun.
Dinner served 5-10.45pm daily. **Average** $25. **Credit**
A, AmEx, DC, JCB, V.
This is probably your best choice in the city for Indian food,
although it's pricey. This Ghiradelli Square branch has an elegant dining room overlooking the Bay (it's one of the few places
in town where you can have both a great view and an excellent
meal). Ordering à la carte will run your bill up amazingly fast.
Branch: 1 Embarcadero Centre (397 7775).

Maharani

*1122 Post Street, between Polk Street and Van Ness
Avenue (775 1988). Bus 2, 3, 4, 19, 42, 47, 49, 76.*
Lunch served 11.30am-2.30pm daily. **Dinner served**
5-10pm Mon-Fri. **Average** $20. **Credit** A, AmEx, DC,
JCB, V.
This North Indian restaurant emphasises healthy cuisine
with reduced amounts of oil and salt in many of the dishes.
House specialties include fabulous breads and vegetarian
main courses.
Disabled: access; toilet.

North India

*313 Webster Street, at Lombard Street (931 1556). Bus
22, 28, 30, 43, 76.* **Lunch served** 11.30am-2.30pm Mon-
Fri. **Dinner served** 5-10.30pm daily. **Average** $25.
Credit MC, V.
Try the tandooris or any of the lamb dishes at this friendly,
family-run establishment. It caters to an upmarket
Marina/Pacific Heights clientele. Prices are on the high side.
Disabled: access; toilet.

Italian

Buca Giovanni

*800 Greenwich Street, at Columbus Avenue (776 7766).
Bus 30, 41, 45/Powell-Mason cable car.* **Dinner served**
5.30-10.30pm Tue-Sat. **Average** $25. **Credit** AmEx, DC,
JCB, MC, V.
The cave-like downstairs dining room adds to the ambience
of this North Beach trattoria. Hearty northern Italian pastas
and game duck are the specialties. Italian wines are mostly
from Piedmont.

Caffè Macaroni

*59 Columbus Street, at Jackson Street (956 9737). Bus
12, 15, 41, 83.* **Lunch served** 11.30am-2.30pm Mon-Fri.
Dinner served 5.30-10pm Mon-Sat. **Average** $25.
No credit cards.
You can feel claustrophobic inside this small, friendly trat-
toria-like North Beach restaurant, especially upstairs where
the ceilings are low. But the southern Italian cooking is good,
the antipasti and gnocchi in particular.

Emporio Armani Express Restaurant

*1 Grant Avenue, between O'Farrell and Market Streets
(677 9010). BART Montgomery Street/Muni Metro F, J,
K, L, M, N/8, 30, 38 bus.* **Meals served** 11am-7pm
Mon-Fri; 10am-6pm Sat; noon-6pm Sun. **Average** $15.
Credit AmEx, DC, MC, V.

Would you like a tie with that sandwich? In the centre of
designer Giorgio Armani's retail emporium is a café and bar,
serving tasty pizzas, salads and foccacia sandwiches. The
atmosphere is a bit strange, but it is a useful pitstop if you
need sustenance while you're shopping around Union Square.
Disabled: access; toilet.

Il Fornaio

*1265 Battery Street, between Union and Greenwich
Streets (986 0100). Bus 12, 32, 42.* **Meals served** 7am-
11pm Mon-Thur; 7am-midnight Fri, Sat; 9am-11pm Sun.
Average $15-$25 (dinner). **Credit** AmEx, DC, MC, V.

Reliable contemporary Italian food is served in tasteful surroundings in this Embarcadero branch of the Fornaio chain.
In addition to the extensive varieties of pasta dishes, good
choices are the pizzas, roast chicken from the wood-burning
oven, fresh bread, and cookies.
Disabled: access; toilet.

Jackson Fillmore

*2506 Fillmore Street, at Jackson Street (346 5288).
Bus 1, 3, 22, 24.* **Dinner served** 5.30-10pm Mon; 5.30-
10.30pm Tue-Thur; 5.30-11pm Fri, Sat; 5-10pm Sun.
Average $25-$30. **Credit** AmEx, MC, V.

A trendy, yuppie crowd hangs out at this busy Southern
Italian spot. Large portions of pasta and fresh fish dishes are
served in an austere, cramped dining room. Counter seating
is usually a good option, as reservations can be difficult to
obtain. Be warned that parking here is nearly impossible.
Disabled: access.

Julius' Castle

*1541 Montgomery Street, at Union Street (362 3042).
Bus 12, 39, 42, 83.* **Dinner served** 5-10.30pm daily.
Average $25-$35. **Credit** AmEx, DC, JCB, MC, V.

The pink castle you're likely to spot on top of Telegraph Hill
is this landmark restaurant. The awesome view of the Bay
– not necessarily the food – draws in the punters. It's a
supremely romantic spot nonetheless.

Laghi

*1801 Clement Street, at 19th Avenue (386 6266).
Bus 1, 2, 38, 38L.* **Dinner served** 5-10pm Tue-Sun.
Average $20. **Credit** MC, V.

This quaint husband-and-wife-owned restaurant in the
Richmond district specialises in authentic Northern Italian
cooking. It offers wonderful pastas and risottos. The entrées
are on the robust side – there are plenty of lamb and other
meat dishes. Desserts are splendid and the service is friendly.
Disabled: access; toilet.

Lo Coco's

*510 Union Street, between Grant and Kearny Streets
(296 9151). Bus 30, 39, 41, 45.* **Dinner served** 5-10pm
Tue-Thur; 5-11pm Fri, Sat; 4-10pm Sun. **Average** $20.
Credit MC, V.

The pappardelle with porcini mushrooms, pungent pasta con
sarde, and great pizzas with flaky crusts are all recommended at this comfortable and moderately priced Sicilian-
style restaurant in the heart of North Beach. There's a choice
of good Sicilian wines.
Disabled: access; toilet.

L'Osteria del Forno

*519 Columbus Street, at Green and Union Streets (982
1124). Bus 12, 15, 30, 41, 45, 83/Powell-Mason cable
car.* **Meals served** 11.30am-10pm Wed-Sat; 1-10pm Sun.
Average $15. **No credit cards.**

It's easy to overlook this pocket-size shopfront in North Beach,
but don't if you want an unpretentious, delicious, and inexpensive Italian lunch or dinner. Thin-crust pizzas, sumptuous pastas of the day, excellent espresso, and friendly service are among
the magic that two Italian women owner-chefs work here.
Disabled: access.

Pane e Vino

*3011 Steiner Street, at Union Street (346 2111). Bus 22,
41, 45.* **Lunch served** 11.30am-2.30pm Mon-Sat.
Dinner served 5-10pm Mon-Thur, Sun; 5-10.30pm Fri,
Sat. **Average** $25-$30. **Credit** MC, V.

A delightful place to dine, this Union Street restaurant is usually overcrowded without a comfortable place to wait, which
you often have to do even if you have booked a table. Terra-
cotta floors and wood-beam ceilings lend a rustic feel to this
intimate dining spot and well-chosen regional Italian and
Californian wines complement the Tuscan menu.
Disabled: access; toilet.

Ristorante Milano

*1448 Pacific Avenue, between Hyde and Larkin Streets
(673 2961). Bus 12, 83/Powell-Hyde cable car.* **Dinner
served** 5.30-10.30pm Tue-Sat; 5-10pm Sun. **Average**
$25. **Credit** AmEx, MC, V.

There's a no-booking policy at this locally popular Northern
Italian restaurant, which usually means a 30-45 minute wait
for a table. Most agree it's worth it, though, for the outstanding gnocchis and raviolis or perfectly prepared veal
dishes. Arrive early.

Vivande Porta Via

*2125 Fillmore Street, between Sacramento and California
Streets (346 4430). Bus 1, 3, 22, 24.* **Meals served**
10am-10pm daily. **Average** from $30. **Credit** AmEx,
DC, MC, V.

The place to have lunch in the busy, boutique-filled Upper
Fillmore district. This trattoria/delicatessen serves quintessential Southern Italian fare. It's also known for its salads
and desserts.
Disabled: access; toilet.

Japanese

Hama-Ko

*108 Carl Street, at Cole Street (753 6808). Muni Metro N/
6, 43 bus.* **Dinner served** 6-10pm Tue-Sun. **Average** $25.
Credit MC, V.

Impeccably fresh raw fish is served at this tiny, somewhat
secret restaurant. It's essential to phone ahead to secure one
of the few tables or a spot at the small sushi bar. Expect gra-
cious Japanese service.
Disabled: access.

Hana

*408 Irving Street, between Fifth and Sixth Avenues (665
3952). Muni Metro N/6, 43, 66 bus.* **Lunch served**
11.30am-2pm Mon-Fri. **Dinner served** 5-9.30pm Mon-
Sat. **Average** $15. **Credit** MC, V.

Inexpensive, hearty Japanese cooking draws students from
the nearby University of California Medical School.
Yosemabe, a seafood stew with vegetables, or gyoza, those
Japanese ribstickers, are recommended.

Isobune Sushi

*Restaurant Mall, Kintetsu Building, 1737 Post Street, at
Webster Street (563 1030). Bus 2, 3, 4, 28, 32 bus.*
Meals served 11.30am-10pm daily. **Average** $15-$25.
Credit MC, JCB, V.

One of the most popular restaurants in the city, regardless of
cuisine, this is the perfect place for a quick fix sushi lunch or
dinner. Assorted raw fish float by on little wooden boats for
the plucking.

Kabuto
5116 Geary Boulevard, between 15th and 16th Avenues (752 5652). Bus 28, 38, 38L. **Dinner served** 5.30-11pm Tue-Sat. **Average** from $25. **Credit** MC, V.
You won't be disappointed by the exquisite sushi at this Richmond district restaurant. Securing a chair at the sushi bar can be difficult because the chefs always put on quite a show and they are only too glad to create special sushi for their customers. Unlike most Japanese places, this one is open late – past midnight, though you have to arrive by 11pm.

Kyo-Ya Restaurant
Sheraton Palace Hotel, 2 New Montgomery Street, at Jesse Street (392 8600). BART Montgomery Street/ Muni Metro F, J, K, L, M, N/5, 8, 9, 14, 30 bus. **Lunch served** 11.30am-2pm Mon-Fri. **Dinner served** 6-10pm Mon-Sat. **Average** from $30. **Credit** AmEx, DC, MC, V.
A favourite haunt of visiting Japanese businessmen, this is by far the best sushi house in San Francisco, with prices to match. Meticulous service and opulent surroundings help to create the total dining 'experience'.
Disabled: access; toilet.

Mifune
1737 Post Street, at Buchanan Street (922 0337). Bus 2, 3, 4, 22. **Meals served** 11am-9.30pm Mon-Thur, Sun; 11am-10pm Fri, Sat. **Average** $15. **Credit** MC, V.
Slurp splendid udon or soba noodles at this popular Japantown spot. Although the menu presents more, most people come here for a quick bowl of noodles before or after a movie at the Kabuki cinema next door. There's often a queue to get in, but it moves fairly quickly.
Disabled: access.

Sanppo
1702 Post Street, at Buchanan Street (346 3486). Bus 2, 3, 4, 22. **Meals served** 11.30am-9.50pm Tue-Sun. **Average** $15. **Credit** MC, V.
Situated in the heart of Japantown, Sanppo serves up lightly battered tempura and always fresh seafood dishes. Communal seating and the open kitchen help create a relaxed atmosphere, and the sushi and sashimi are also worth trying here.

Seafood

Aqua
252 California Street, between Front and Battery Streets (956 9662). BART Embarcadero/Muni Metro F, J, K, L, M, N/12, 42, 76 bus. **Lunch served** 11.30am-2.15pm Mon-Fri. **Dinner served** 5.30-11pm Sat. **Average** $45. **Credit** AmEx, DC, MC, V.
For a full-scale meal of fresh seafood, try this luxurious restaurant, the grand setting accented by huge floral arrangements. It's one of the most popular top-ranking restaurants in town. Beautiful ingredients are artfully presented. Prices are high.
Disabled: access; toilet.

Swan Oyster Depot
1517 Polk Street, at California and Sacramento Streets (673 1101). Bus 1, 19, 42, 49, 76/California cable car. **Meals served** 8am-5.30pm Mon-Sat. **Average** $15-$25. **Credit** MC, V.
Half fish market and half counter-service hole-in-the-wall, Swan's has been serving some of the best seafood in San Francisco since 1912. The best time of year to visit is between May and November, when the local Dungeness crab is in season. Classic clam chowder, the smoked salmon plate or a tray of blue point oysters are specialties of the house.
Disabled: access; toilet.

Tadich Grill
240 California Street, at Battery Street (391 1849). BART Embarcadero/Muni Metro F, J, K, L, M, N/12, 30, 41, 42 bus. **Meals served** 11am-9pm Mon-Sat. **Average** $30. **Credit** MC, V.
Tourists and locals have been flocking to this landmark restaurant for over a century, seemingly waited upon by the same grandfatherly staff. Grilled or pan-fried sand dabs or Rex sole with French fries are two of the better entrées from an extended menu that changes daily. Eating in one of Tadich's private wood-panelled dining compartments is like stepping back in time.
Disabled: access; toilet.

Spanish

Esperpento
3295 22nd Street, at Valencia Street (282 8867). **Lunch served** 11am-3pm, **dinner served** 5-10.30pm, daily. **Average** $15. **No credit cards**.
Tapas and paellas are the main attractions at this funky, bohemian café in the Mission district. Service is somewhat erratic, but the laid-back clientele couldn't care less.
Disabled: access.

Timo's in the Zanzibar
842 Valencia Street, between 19th and 20th Streets (647 0558). Bus 14, 26, 33, 49. **Dinner served** 5-10.30pm Mon-Thur, Sun; 5-11.30pm Fri, Sat. **Average** $10. **Credit** AmEx, MC, V.
Unexpectedly good tapas show up at what appears to be a dive bar in the Mission. In addition to the bar in front, there is a dance floor at the back and the whole interior is painted purple and green. If you don't mind the faint odour of stale beer, there are some inventive tapas to be had. Recommended is the salt cod and potato cake.
Disabled: access.

Zarzuela
2000 Hyde Street, at Union Street (346 0800). Bus 41, 45/Powell-Hyde cable car. **Meals served** noon-10.30pm Mon-Thur, Sun; noon-11pm Fri, Sat. **Average** $14. **Credit** MC, V.
Delicious hot and cold tapas and fantastic paella can be enjoyed in the front room, which has a view of the Russian Hill cable car line, or in the Mediterranean, cave-like, and more private, back room. Inexpensive Spanish wines complement the terrific fare.

Steak Houses

Alfred's
886 Broadway, at Powell and Mason Streets (781 7058). Powell-Hyde, Powell-Mason cable car. **Lunch served** 11.30am-2.30pm Thur. **Dinner served** 5.30-9.30pm Mon-Thur, Sun; 5.30-10pm Fri, Sat. **Average** $40. **Credit** AmEx, MC, V.
Not too much has changed over the past 60 years at this San Francisco institution. Stay away from the Italian dishes and stick with the steaks. Tender, dry-aged T-bone, Porterhouse, and New York steaks are expertly grilled over mesquite coals. A meat-eater's paradise.
Disabled: access; toilet.

Harris'
2100 Van Ness Avenue, at Pacific Avenue (673 1888). Bus 42, 47, 49. **Dinner served** 6-10pm Mon-Fri; 5-10pm Sat, Sun. **Average** $40. **Credit** AmEx, DC, MC, V.
This excellent steakhouse harks back to an earlier era with its Martinis, club-like wood panelling, and silver-haired clientele. The large booths are a comfortable place to enjoy the

Manora's Thai Cuisine: for Thai food that won't strain your wallet.

juicy steaks from the famous Harris Ranch. The rest of the menu is pretty simple – potatoes, creamed spinach and a couple of seafood or poultry dishes.
Disabled: access; toilet.

Izzy's Steaks & Chops

3345 Steiner Street, between Lombard and Chestnut Streets (563 0487). Bus 22, 28, 30, 43, 76. **Dinner served** 5-10.30pm Mon-Sat; 5-10pm Sun. **Average** $20. **Credit** AmEx, DC, MC, JCB, V.

An excellent steak, priced fairly, and a friendly and attentive staff make this the best steak option in town. Thirtysomethings congregate at the bar of this hot spot every evening, entertained by a gregarious, storytelling bartender.

Thai/Cambodian

Angkor Borei

3471 Mission Street, between Cortland and 30th Street (550 8417). Bus 14, 24, 26, 49, 67. **Lunch served** 11am-3pm, **dinner served** 5-10.30pm, Mon-Sat. **Average** $15. **Credit** AmEx, MC, V.

Even newcomers to Cambodian cuisine will appreciate these fine dishes. Try the Cambodian spring rolls, omelette-like crêpes, or the authentic curry dishes. Although the food is inexpensive and tasty, it's a bit of a trek to the outer Mission.

Chiang Mai

5020 Geary Boulevard, at 14th Avenue (387 1299). Bus 28, 38, 38L. Lunch served 11.30am-3pm Mon-Fri. **Dinner served** 5-10pm Mon-Thur, Sun; 5-10.30pm Fri, Sat. **Average** $10. **Credit** AmEx, MC, V.

Pleasant waitresses in sarongs welcome diners to this small, inexpensive but well-appointed Thai restaurant in the Richmond district. There are no surprises on this menu, but everything is fresh and well-executed.
Disabled: access; toilet.

Manora's Thai Cuisine

1600 Folsom Street, at 12th Street (861 6224). Bus 9, 12. **Dinner served** 5.30-10.30pm Mon-Sat; 5-10pm Sun. **Average** from $25. **Credit** MC, V.

Curries and dishes with nicely blended spices pack in the customers at this attractive and popular Thai restaurant. It's the sort of place where you can feel you've been out on the town and had a good meal, without having to splurge.
Branch: 3226 Mission Street, at Valencia Street (550 0856).

Thep Phanom

400 Waller Street, at Fillmore Street (431 2526). Bus 6, 7, 22, 66, 71. **Dinner served** 5.30-10.30pm daily. **Average** $20. **Credit** AmEx, MC, V.

Venture over to the Lower Haight for some excellent Thai food at reasonable prices, if you don't mind waiting in line for a table. The neighbourhood can be dicey late at night, but once inside the cosy restaurant decked out with Thai artifacts, you'll be transported to Bangkok. Try the angel wings – fried chicken wings stuffed with glass noodles – which are particularly good.

Mexican

Cafe Marimba

2317 Chestnut Street, between Divisadero and Scott Streets (776 1506). Bus 28, 30, 43, 76. **Meals served** 11.30am-11pm Tue-Thur, Sun; 11.30pm-midnight Fri, Sat. **Average** $25. **Credit** AmEx, MC, V.

You can dine on authentic Oaxacan and Yucatan specialties, amid colourful and festive decorations at the Cafe Marimba. The mole sauces here aren't the usual chocolate versions, but a marvellous blend of exotic spices. Excellent fresh fruit juices complement some of the spicy offerings. Reed Hearon (from Lulu, *see p111*) is behind this successful café which is often boisterous at the weekends, and attracts a young Marina clientele.

La Taqueria

2889 Mission Street, at 25th Street (285 7117). BART 16th Street/14, 48, 49 bus. **Meals served** 11am-9pm Mon-Sat; 11am-8pm Sun. **Average** $7. **No credit cards.**
Hundreds of large burritos and soft tacos are served daily at this clean and efficient taqueria, which many consider the best in San Francisco. The carnitas is especially good here.

Pancho Villa Taqueria

3071 16th Street, between Mission and Valencia Streets (864 8840). BART 16th Street/14, 22, 26, 33, 49 bus. **Meals served** 10am-midnight daily. **Average** $4-$8. **No credit cards.**
If it's not La Taqueria that San Franciscans believe make the best burrito, then it's Pancho Villa. The queue moves quickly here. Wash down one of these filling meat or bean and cheese rolls with one of the refreshing aguas frescas (fruit drinks).
Disabled: access, toilet.

Peruvian

Fina Estampa

2734 Mission Street, between 19th and 20th Streets (824 4437). BART 24th Street/14, 33, 49 bus. **Lunch served** 11.30am-3.30pm, **dinner served** 5-9pm, Tue-Sun. **Average** $18. **Credit** MC, V.
A husband and wife run this modest Mission Street café. Locally available fish are perfectly presented in traditional Peruvian-style paellas and soups. Grilled steaks on toast with onions and tomatoes, and the deep-fried chicken with salsa are also worth investigating.
Disabled: access; toilet.

Pizza

Tommaso's

1042 Kearny Street, at Broadway (398 9696). Bus 12, 15, 30, 41, 45, 83. **Dinner served** 5-11pm Tue-Sat; 4-10pm Sun. **Average** $25. **Credit** AmEx, MC, V.
There is always a queue of people stretching out of the door here, waiting for perhaps an hour to bite into the delicious pizzas and calzones cooked in the woodfired, brick oven. The super deluxe pizza with mushrooms, peppers, ham, and Italian sausage is enough to feed a family. The cave-like dining room creates a cosy atmosphere at this North Beach trattoria.

Vicolo Pizzeria

201 Ivy Street, at Franklin Street (863 2382). BART Van Ness/Muni Metro F, J, K, L, M, N/21, 42, 47, 49 bus. **Meals served** 11.30am-11pm Mon-Thur; 11.30am-11.30pm Fri, Sat; noon-10pm Sun. **Average** $15. **Credit** MC, V.
The cornmeal crust and inventive toppings make these pizzas addictive. Located down an alley just by Civic Centre, Vicolo can be hard to find, but once you've tracked it down, you'll be glad you did. It's an inexpensive alternative when searching for a place to eat before a performance. Alternatively, consider it for lunch if you're exploring the shops in Hayes Valley (*see chapter* **San Francisco by Neighbourhood**). The creative salads are a perfect complement to a Vicolo pizza.
Disabled: access; toilet.

Vegetarian

As you might expect from health-conscious Californians, it is rare to find a restaurant menu in San Francisco that doesn't contain one, if not several, meat-free options. But for the complete veggie experience, try Greens.

Greens

Building A, Fort Mason Centre, Marina Boulevard at Buchanan Street (771 6222). Bus 28. **Brunch served** 10am-2pm Sun. **Lunch served** 11.30am-2pm Tue-Fri; 11.30am-2.30pm Sat. **Dinner served** 5.30-9pm Tue-Fri; 6-9.30pm Sat. **Average** $25. **Credit** DC, MC, V.
Many consider this Zen Centre-run operation to be the quintessential veggie restaurant in the United States and it's certainly a wonderful place to have brunch at the weekends. Greens offers a magnificent view of the Bay and Golden Gate Bridge, and satisfying meals which even meat-eaters will appreciate. The fresh ingredients in the lively dishes are all locally grown, and if you like the cooking, you can buy a copy of one of their best-selling cookbooks. A counter in the front of the restaurant sells fresh bread, pastries, sandwiches, and soups.
Disabled: access; toilet.

Vietnamese

Golden Turtle

2211 Van Ness Avenue, between Broadway and Vallejo Street (441 4419). Bus 12, 42, 47, 49, 76, 83. **Lunch served** 11.30am-3pm, **dinner served** 5-10pm, Tue-Sun. **Average** $20. **Credit** AmEx, MC, V.
The bargain prices and gourmet food make this place among the best value in San Francisco dining. Try the five spice roast chicken, one of many fine dishes. The staff are happy to explain the menu to the uninitiated and the good selection of French wines is a further plus.
Branch: 308 Fifth Avenue, between Geary Boulevard and Clement Street (221 5285).

Wine Country Restaurants

For more on the wine country, and details of how to get there by car or by other means, *see chapter* **Trips Out of Town**.

French Laundry

6640 Washington Street, Yountville, Napa (1-707 944 2380). **Lunch served** noon-1.30pm Wed-Sat. **Dinner served** 5.30-10.30pm Tue-Sun. **Set Menu** $57 five courses. **Credit** MC, V.
The idyllic setting – a wood and stone French country house surrounded by lush gardens – is as much a part of the experience as the celebrated food at this Napa Valley restaurant. The five-course fixed price menu can take four hours from start to finish, but few diners have any regrets.
Disabled: access; toilet.

Mustards Grill

7399 St Helena Highway, Yountville, Napa (1-707 944 2424). **Meals served** 11.30am-10pm daily. **Average** $35. **Credit** DC, MC, V.
This popular roadside café is constantly busy with both tourists and locals. Baby back ribs, Chinese chicken salad, world class onion rings, and grilled rabbit are just a few of the highlights on the eclectic Californian menu.
Disabled: access; toilet.

Piatti

6480 Washington Street, Yountville, Napa (1-707 944 2070). **Meals served** 11.30am-10pm Mon-Thur, Sun; 11.30am-11pm Fri, Sat. **Average** $40. **Credit** AmEx, MC, V.
The Italian chain began here. Pizzas, pastas, and chicken or rabbit cooked on the rôtisserie are its specialties. The food isn't always consistent, however, so it's best to find out what the daily specials are.
Disabled: access; toilet.
Branch: 405 First Street West, Sonoma (996 2351).

Terra

1345 Railroad Avenue, St Helena, Napa (1-707 963 8931). **Dinner served** 6pm-9.30pm Mon-Thur; 6pm-10pm Fri, Sat. **Average** $45. **Credit** DC, MC, V.

From traditional Japanese dishes to Tuscan-inspired fare, this Californian eclectic restaurant is considered one of the top dinner spots in the valley. The chef, Hiro Sone, from Los Angeles' Spago, daringly combines multiple exotic ingredients on a single dish and brings it off. Desserts such as tiramisu, shortcakes with crème fraîche, and fresh fruit sorbets are by Lissa Doumani, also from the famous Spago.

Disabled: access; toilet.

Tra Vigne

1050 Charter Oak Avenue, St Helena, Napa (1-707 963 4444). **Meals served** 11.30am-10pm daily. **Average** $45. **Credit** DC, MC, V.

This is a great place to eat on a sunny day in Napa Valley. You can dine on fried calamare appetisers, delicious pasta dishes, and top it all off with fresh figs and prosciutto. The large, outside terrace dining area will transport you to the Italian countryside. As you might expect from a wine country eatery, an excellent selection of local wines is available by the glass or bottle.

Disabled: access; toilet.

Cheap eats

Unlike the rest of the country, fast food chains are not that popular in San Francisco. Those eating on a budget usually frequent ethnic restaurants, typically inexpensive taquerias – there are lots in the Mission district – where a full stomach can be had at little expense, or the many economical Chinese restaurants that pack Chinatown. Café fare – mostly consisting of sandwiches and snazzy pizza slices – are also popular options and can be found throughout the city. A budget meal can be had a most of the places listed below for under $15.

Caffè Freddy's Eatery

901 Columbus Avenue, at Lombard Street (922 0151). Bus 30/Powell-Mason cable car. **Open** 11am-10.30pm Mon-Thur; 10am-10.30pm Sat; 10am-10pm Sun. **Credit** AmEx, MC, V.

Halfway between Fisherman's Wharf and North Beach proper on the cable car line, this pleasant café frequented by students from the nearby Art Institute. In two cheerful rooms – one with diner-style booths, the other with small tables – you can be served pizzas with toppings such as pancetta, new potatoes, mozzarella and spinach, as well as salads, open sandwiches, and bowls of chilli. The lattes and cappuccinos are good, too.

Il Pollaio

555 Columbus Avenue, between Union and Green Streets (362 7727). Bus 15, 30, 39, 41, 45/Powell-Mason cable car. **Open** 11.30am-9pm Mon-Sat. **Credit** AmEx, MC, V.

Succulent grilled chicken is what Il Pollaio does and does well. In fact, it's the best – and most popular – of the local chicken rôtisseries. You can sit in the small unadorned dining room and watch the comings and goings along Columbus Avenue in North Beach. Takeaways are also available.

Disabled: access; toilet.

Little Joe's

523 Broadway, at Columbus Avenue (433 4343). Bus 15, 30, 41, 45, 83/Powell-Mason cable car. **Open** noon-10pm daily. **Credit** AmEx, DC, JCB, MC, V.

Giant-size portions of basic Italian food can be had at very cheap prices at this family dining hall and San Francisco institution. Expect a lot of garlic, tomatoes, fresh bread, and cheap house red wine served in carafes – and not a lot of service.

Disabled: access; toilet.

Mo's

1322 Grant Avenue, at Vallejo Street (788 3779). Bus 12, 15, 30, 41, 45, 83. **Open** 11.30am-10.30pm Mon-Thur; 11.30am-11.30pm Fri; 9am-11.30pm Sat; 9am-2pm Sun. **Credit** MC, V.

Big Macs are scorned in gastronomic San Francisco, so if you need a burger fix in the city which boasts more than 2,000 different ethnic restaurants, this little joint is an excellent choice. The scrumptious, juicy slabs of ground beef are grilled to perfection and served with french fries and a thick old-fashioned milkshakes. The perfect comfort food.

Disabled: access; toilet.

Sears Fine Foods

439 Powell Street, between Sutter and Post Streets (986 1160). Bus 2, 3, 4, 30, 45, 76/Powell-Mason cable car. **Open** 6.30am-3.30pm Wed-Sun. **No credit cards.**

A trip to San Francisco is not complete without breakfast at Sears. Pancakes or waffles stacked high with strawberries accompanied by either Canadian bacon or specially made breakfast sausages will satisfy the most demanding eater. And it's handy if you're staying in one of the many downtown hotels. Service can be rushed during peak hours.

Disabled: access.

Ti Couz Crêperie

3108 16th Street, between Guerrero and Valencia Streets (252 7373). BART 16th Street/14, 22, 26, 33, 49 bus. **Open** 11am-11pm Mon-Fri; 10am-11pm Sat; 10am-10pm Sun. **Credit** MC, V.

The thin buckwheat pancakes here – authentic and delicious – come stuffed with a variety of different ingredients, so they can be eaten for lunch, dinner and dessert. Cheese, ratatouille, almond butter, chocolate and ice-cream are a few of the many options to chose from. The popularity of Ti Couz means that there can be a queue in the evenings.

World Wrapps

2257 Chestnut Street, between Scott and Pierce Streets (563 9727). Bus 22, 28, 30, 43, 76. **Open** 8am-11pm daily. **No credit cards.**

The concept of the burrito is extended to cuisines of the world at this small shopfront eatery. Most of the business is 'to-go' (takeaway), because there are few seats, but since its recent opening, people have lined up for the huge tortilla-wrapped meals. The Thai chicken wrap is particularly recommended.

Disabled: access; toilet.

Bars & Cafés

Our pick of the best watering-holes in town: from those with views to those with the best brews.

Bars

San Francisco, they say, has the best bars in the world – or at least plenty that would make any cosmopolitan barfly's top 100. As you might expect, several are part of restaurants and for these you should refer to the **Restaurants** chapter. Most restaurants with bars will serve drinks and snacks to those who aren't staying for a meal (although it can't hurt to confirm this over the phone before setting out).

Like the city itself, San Francisco bars are a diverse and often peculiar lot – one that defies the sort of generalisations helpful to travellers. But at least this variety means that there is something for everyone: there are 'rooms' (frou-frou bars too posh to be called mere bars); pubs (including brewpubs, establishments that brew their own beer, of which San Francisco has three and the Bay Area upwards of a dozen); sports bars (dominated by TVs, pennants on the wall, rowdy fans); wine bars (refined

Booze and the law

All bars are subject to California's alcohol laws: you have to be over 21 to buy and consume the stuff (take ID even if you look a bit older), and it can be sold between the hours of 6am and 2am. Last orders vary between 1.15am and 1.30am, and technically staff are obliged to confiscate unconsumed alcoholic drinks after 2am.

Smokers searching for a place to light up with their coffee will be hard pressed in San Francisco. In fact, if you're determined to smoke while you sip your morning joe, the best advice is to go to a café with a patio or sidewalk seating, as local ordinances have forbidden smokers from indulging indoors at cafés and restaurants. Bars, however, remain exempt from the health conscious legislation of the city's Board of Supervisors – a final reprieve where one can guiltily enjoy both liquor and tobacco.

settings for serving the official soft drink of the Bible); upscale dives (joints with pathos and the scent of hard luck, but spruced up with white tablecloths, candles and the occasional piano); and saloons (too Western to be called pubs, they come complete with all the alcoholic bells and whistles: juke-boxes, pinball games and dartboards).

For bars serving a specifically gay or lesbian clientele, *see chapter* **Gay & Lesbian San Francisco**.

Albion
3139 16th Street, at Albion Street, between Valencia and Guerrero Streets (552 8558). Bus 22. **Open** 2pm-2am daily. **No credit cards.**
Almost too much of a dive to recommend to non-residents, the Albion's disposition is summarised well by the sign above the bar, which says in large, pink neon, capital letters: 'Service for the sick'. With a loud juke-box, pool table and sketchy characters loitering outside, the Albion is just the place for drinkers who like an edge to their surroundings.

Blue Lamp
561 Geary Street, between Taylor and Jones Streets (885 1464). Bus 38. **Open** 11am-2am daily. **No credit cards.**
Over-dressing for the Blue Lamp is as easy as putting on a dress or tie. It serves as an antidote to nearby Union Square, with its quilted wall panels, stale fireplace, ear-ringing blues and cheap drinks. The clientele, as you might surmise from the offerings, tends to be drunks, fans of the blues or post-collegiates who hate their jobs.

The Café
2367 Market Street, at Castro Street (861 3846). Bus 35, 37. **Open** 12.30pm-2am daily. **Credit** MC, V.
The Café – officially, or at least formerly, called the Café San Marcos – is an infamous singles scene in the Castro, a must for gays and lesbians in the mood for a bit of cruising without wheels. Cruise un-control can and does happen while unwinding on the dance floor, playing billiards or people-watching on the patio overlooking bustling Market Street. (*See also chapter* **Gay & Lesbian San Francisco**.)

Cafe Babar
994 Guerrero Street, at 22nd Street (282 6789). Bus 26. **Open** 5pm-2am daily. **No credit cards.**
Recently renovated, the Cafe Babar has a unique floor plan, made up of narrow passages, steps and four distinct rooms, each a bit more sequestered. With a pool table, Internet access, aperitifs, a juke-box and Guinness on tap, Babar attracts a youngish crowd of artists, artisans and office workers in equal number – and is distinctly not a pick-up joint.

Cafe Du Nord
2170 Market Street, between Church and Sanchez Streets (861 5016). Muni Metro F, K, L, M/8, 22, 37 bus. **Open** 3.30pm-2am daily. **Credit** AmEx, MC, V.
A subterranean speakeasy, Du Nord has two elegant bars in two large rooms, ruby carpets, plenty of solid, mahogany tables and chairs, and a reputation for attracting folks who

look as if they've just come off the set of the latest period picture. This den of vamps and post-mods also stages one of the city's only cabarets and one of its more consistent jazz bills. (*See also chapter* **Music: Rock, Roots & Jazz**.)

Cafe Mars

798 Brannan Street, at Seventh Street (621 6277). Bus 19, 27, 41. **Open** *4pm-2am Mon-Fri; 5pm-2am Sat.* **Credit** AmEx, MC, V.

Drawing a true SoMa crowd – graphic artists, Contract Designer Center indies, the fashionably pierced – the Mars has a vogue chartreuse-and-red colour-scheme and vibe (as befits the planet). For the munchies, it offers personal pizzas and other hot and cold dishes. An excellent pitstop, rather than a destination.

Caribbean Zone

55 Natoma Street, between First and Second Streets (541 9465). Bus 12, 15, 76. **Lunch served** *11.30am-2.30pm Mon-Fri.* **Dinner served** *5-10pm Mon-Sat.* **Credit** AmEx, DC, MC, V.

What makes the Caribbean Zone attractive isn't hard to suss: it feels like a theme party inside, mainly due to the centrepiece – the cabin of a 'crash-landed' passenger aeroplane, that serves as a cocktail lounge. The drinks – tropical, blended and mostly frozen – are pricey, but come with keep-sake swivel sticks. A little hard to find (the entrance is off an alley under a freeway), it's probably a good idea to take a cab to and from the CZ, which, according to the proprietors is 'safer than heaven'.

Chameleon

853 Valencia Street, between 19th and 20th Streets (821 1891). Bus 26. **Open** *10am-2am daily.* **No credit cards.**

It doesn't get any grungier than this. Offering a free cig with your coffee and pints for $2.25 from 4pm-7.30pm, the Chameleon fronts local and touring punk bands and (on Monday evenings) a spoken word event that can only be described as hit or miss. The perfect place for those who

don't tuck in their shirts, wash their hair or think twice about sleeping in their car.

Dalva

3121 16th Street, between Valencia and Guerrero Streets (252 7740). Bus 22, 26. **Open** *5pm-2am Mon-Thur, Sat; 2pm-2am Fri.* **No credit cards.**

Named after the female lead in a Jim Harrison novel, Dalva has grown from a locals-only watering hole to a hideout for refugees from the raucous *Animal House* scenes on the north side of town. With its high ceilings and cement floors, however, this is one hideout where you'll have to speak up to be heard. It's near the Kilowatt, Jack's Elixir (which serves 65 beers) and Albion bars, which are all within one block on 16th Street.

Club Deluxe

1511 Haight Street, at Ashbury Street (552 6949). Bus 7, 33, 43, 66, 71. **Open** *4pm-2am Mon-Fri; 3pm-2am Sat; 2pm-2am Sun.* **No credit cards.**

Spend much time here and you may leave town with the impression that San Franciscans all yearn to be back in the swing era. A swing pianist and medium-sized swing bands often sit in and employees and patrons alike show up in vintage threads. Fittingly, the Deluxe does martinis and gimlets especially well. Sundays find the place serving raw oysters and arguably the city's best Bloody Mary.

E-Line Ale House

5612 College Avenue, Oakland (1-510 547 8786). BART Rockridge. **Open** *11.30am-12.30am Mon-Thur; 11.30am-1.30am Fri, Sat; 10am-12.30am Sun.* **Credit** AmEx, MC, V.

High ceilings, a vintage handle-shaped bar and a few posters – and that's about it at this Oakland bar. So what's the draw? An excellent location, some of the friendliest bar service in the state and a mature taste in draught beers. The E-Line is a microbrew draught bar, which means it doesn't brew its own but taps the product of lots of small brewers whose beers are distinctive and rich in flavour, and have 'cute'

Don't be alarmed, but Tuesday night is salsa night at **Café Du Nord**. *See page 123.*

Wine Bars

San Francisco boasts any number of hospitable locations to taste and buy wine. The **Wine Impression** (3641 California Street, 221 9463), **SRO** (4 Embarcadero Center, 986 5020) and the **Wine Club** (953 Harrison Street, 512 9086) are all retail outlets with wine bars attached, so you can taste before you buy. As places to relax and meet friends, however, they can't compete with the wine bars listed below.

Cava 555

555 Second Street, between Bryant and Brannan Streets (543 2282). Bus 76. **Open** 5pm-midnight Mon-Fri; 5pm-2am Sat, Sun. **Credit** AmEx, MC, V.
Specialising in sparkling wines and champagnes from Spain, Cava 555 was one of the first on the block to play jazz over dinner. Cool, dark and modern inside, it feels better if you're wearing nice threads and is best enjoyed with a small party who can command a booth. Book ahead or arrive early and watch the crowd ease in.

Hayes and Vine

377 Hayes Street, at Gough Street (626 5301). Bus 16, 21, 42, 47. **Open** 4pm-midnight Mon-Fri; 4pm-1am Sat, Sun. **Credit** MC, V.
Truly global, Hayes and Vine has an active list of more than 350 wines from around the world and an exceptionally well-informed staff who have tried almost everything they serve. Situated just behind the major performing arts venues in Hayes Valley, the interior design is refined with-

Hayes and Vine.

out being pretentious. If you take a 'flight', you can try several different wines for a fixed price.

London Wine Bar

415 Sansome Street, between Sacramento and Clay Streets (788 4811). Bus 1, 41, 42. **Open** 11.30am-9pm Mon-Fri. **Credit** AmEx, MC, V.
A few doors down from the Pacific Stock Exchange, the London Wine Bar draws a lively lunch and after-work crowd, who can make it seem less of a place to learn about wines than to just drink them down. Still, the bar serves two- to three-dozen different wines at any given time, mainly from California.

names to match such as Twist of Fate bitter, Death and Taxes Black (a black lager) and Downtown Brown.

Elbo Room

647 Valencia Street, between 17th and 18th Streets (552 7788). Bus 22, 26. **Open** 5pm-2am daily. **No credit cards.**
The Elbo Room is always a good call for youthful night owls. Upstairs it has a well-attended jazz-and-what-not series, while downstairs there is a billiards table, juke-box, photo booth and lots of mirrors for admiring the crowd of mostly hetero singles. There's standing room only from Thursday to Saturday nights. Definitely in the 'upscale dive' category.

The 500 Club

500 Guerrero Street, at 17th Street (861 2500). Bus 22, 26. **Open** 2pm-2am Mon-Fri; noon-2am Sat, Sun. **No credit cards.**
There seem to be few reasons to recommend the 500 Club to a tourist, with its cramped billiards table (there's a short cue for certain shots against the wall), disillusioned grunge kids and career alcoholics – unless you're a grunge kid or alcoholic yourself, or you want to go somewhere sure to be tourist-free. Actually, there are other reasons to like this low-scale dive, including its pinball machines and, of course, the Giant Martini in the Sky – one of the most impressive electric and neon signs anywhere in the free world.

Garden Court

Sheraton Palace Hotel, 639 Market Street, at New Montgomery Street (392 8600). Muni Metro F, J, K, L, M, N/BART Montgomery Street. **Breakfast served** 6.30am-11am, **lunch served** 11.30am-2pm, daily.

Dinner served 6-10pm Tue-Sat. **Credit** AmEx, DC, MC, V.
Those wishing to feel like royalty, or merely tourists at a time when only the wealthiest could afford leisure travel, will want to sip a cocktail here, in the grandest Art Deco bar in town. Opulent gold leaf climbs the walls like vines. A vintage clock, straight out of the movies (imagine a tearful train station goodbye), reminds you how long you've been drinking. And, the clincher: no one will think you look silly in a bow tie. *See also chapter* **Architecture**.

Harry's on Fillmore

2020 Fillmore Street, between California and Pine Streets (921 1000). Bus 1, 3, 22. **Open** 3.30pm-2am daily. **Credit** AmEx, MC, V.
A classic bar in any dog's town, Harry's on Fillmore could easily fit in the lobby of a five-star hotel in Chicago. Ornate but not overdone, it draws a well-to-do crowd but doesn't shun the less upwardly mobile. It is also a classic San Francisco bar because of its history (it has opened and closed several times under circumstances which have brought previous owners to the Justice Department), and because it is essentially a neighbourhood bar that attracts patrons from other neighbourhoods.

Hotel Utah

500 Fourth Street, at Bryant Street (421 8308). Bus 30, 45. **Open** 11.30am-2am Mon-Fri; 6pm-2am Sat, Sun. **Credit** MC, V.
Instead of class, the Utah has charm; instead of star-gazers, pranksters. With one long front room separated from a split-level back room, the Utah doubles as a hideout and a venue for local bands. The divided rooms allow you to immerse

Spec's, *for literary drunks. See page 129.*

yourself in the music at the back or carry on a conversation at the front. If the pace is slow, you may want to see about operating the alcohol-fuelled steam locomotive kept behind the bar.

Green's Sports Bar
2239 Polk Street, between Vallejo and Green Streets (775 4287). Bus 19, 41, 45. **Open** 3pm-2am Mon-Fri; 10am-2am Sat, Sun. **No credit cards.**
With a big-screen television for an audience of a dozen or more as well as TVs in every field of vision throughout, you can't possibly miss the action in this archetypal sports bar. (The sports page from the *San Francisco Chronicle* is even tacked up over the urinals). During big games, the joint becomes a virtual bleachers section, the thrill of victory and agony of defeat registered loud enough to be heard by passers-by on the street.

Latin American Club
3286 22nd Street, at between Mission and Valencia Streets (647 2732). Bus 26. **Open** 6pm-2am Mon-Thur; 5pm-2am Fri; 4pm-2am Sat, Sun. **No credit cards.**
Dig the 'installation' in the loft above the door: the word sin in red flashing lights and a papier-mâché mummy that always looks one gust of wind short of becoming confetti. More a saloon than a dive, the Latin American Club could easily be called the Gringo American Club, based on its clientele. The management has a come-as-you-are attitude (one of the neighbourhood's most notorious crazies, the enigmatic Red Man, is often spotted here). There's a pool table, several draught beers and work by local artists on the walls.

The Lone Palm
3394 22nd Street, at Guerrero Street (648 0109). Bus 26. **Open** 6pm-2am daily. **No credit cards.**
The epitome of an upscale dive, the Lone Palm's interior

suggests a bar sandwiched between the sound stages of *Miami Vice* and *Twin Peaks*. With a piano (sometimes accompanied by trumpet or crooner Mr Lucky), the Palm borders on a 'scene' on some nights, but regresses to a comfortable corner bar the rest of the time. It's across the street from Cafe Babar (*see p123*).

Mad Dog in the Fog
530 Haight Street, between Fillmore and Steiner Streets (626 7279). Bus 6, 7, 22. **Open** 11am-2am Mon-Fri; 9am-2am Sat, Sun. **No credit cards.**
Imagine a pub from Newcastle upon Tyne spun into the sky like Dorothy's farmhouse in *The Wizard of Oz* and landing in the Lower Haight – and you'll have an idea of what's in store at the Mad Dog in the Fog. Even the patio looks as if it just fell into place. Perfect for homesick Geordies, but with enough local flavour to keep it unique.

Mick's Lounge
2513 Van Ness Avenue, between Union and Filbert Streets (928 0404). Bus 41, 45. **Open** 5pm-2am Mon-Sat; 6pm-2am Sun. **Credit** AmEx, MC, V.
Mick's is a tough call: at the weekend it can become an unbearable frat house party, with everyone sweating and drinking from plastic cups (when the pint glasses can't be washed fast enough), and cover bands that encourage drunken sing-a-longs. But it does book some decent musical acts and there's no question that the lonely traveller might find company for the night here.

Miss Pearl's Jam House
601 Eddy Street, between Polk and Larkin Streets (775 5267). Bus 19, 31. **Open** 6pm-11pm Mon, Tue, Fri; 6pm-10pm Thur, Fri; 11.30am-9.30pm Sun. **Credit** AmEx, DC, MC, V.
A Caribbean restaurant that condones fully-clothed dips in the swimming pool (it's part of a motel), Miss Pearl's is a concept that works. The bar room, known to spontaneously transform into a reggae dance floor, is essentially a dark lobby to the restaurant, but is still a worthwhile stop for drinks only.

Noc Noc
557 Haight Street, between Fillmore and Steiner Streets (861 5811). Bus 6, 7, 66, 71. **Open** 5pm-2am daily. **No credit cards.**
Something about this place says hair boutique, or maybe it's just that the interior looks like the backdrop to a fashion spread in *The Face*. The Noc Noc is a place to sit on pillows and drink and talk with some intimate (or soon-to-be-intimate) acquaintance. It has stools and a couple of tables for those not inclined to pillow talk, but if you're allergic to kitsch, avoid this place.

The Plough & Stars
116 Clement Street, at Third Avenue (751 1122). Bus 2. **Open** 4pm-2am Mon; 2pm-2am Tue-Thur; noon-2am Fri-Sun. **Credit** (minimum $15) MC, V.
Perhaps the most suitable Irish bar for out-of-towners, the Plough & Stars is by no means the only Irish bar in town. Irish sports fans should check out **Pat O'Shea's Mad Hatter** (3848 Geary Boulevard, 752 3148); for Irish politicos there's **Ireland's 32's** (3920 Geary Boulevard, 386 6173); the **Dovre Club** (3541 18th Street, 552 0074) is the place to get involved in San Francisco mayoral politics, and **The Dubliner** (3838 24th Street, 826 2279) is patronised by a nice mix of middle-class artisans and professionals from nearby Noe Valley. But the Plough & Stars does the trick. They keep the dartboards in fine condition, the felt on the billiards table smooth, the Guinness fresh and the humour's on the house.

Rat & Raven
4054 24th Street, between Castro and Noe Streets (285 0674). Bus 24, 48. **Open** noon-2am daily. **No credit cards.**

A sprawling local pub/saloon in Noe Valley, the Rat & Raven attracts a multi-generational crowd and boasts one of the city's better, funkier patios. Long, high tables make for communal drinking and there's a pool table at the rear and a dartboard, although it is perilously close to the door of the men's toilets.

Redwood Room

Four Seasons Clift Hotel, 495 Geary Street, at Taylor Street (775 4700). Bus 2, 3, 4, 38. **Open** 11am-midnight Mon-Thur, Sun; 11am-1.30am Fri, Sat. **Credit** AmEx, DC, MC, V.

MTV, the Internet, and Calvin Klein ads are all unheard of in the nostalgic Redwood Room. Drinks may be pricey, but check out the Aztec chandeliers, the polished, Art Deco wood panelling and mantelpieces (all made from one giant redwood tree) and the Klimt prints. Set inside the well-known Clift Hotel, the Redwood Room is most certainly a 'room'.

Brewpubs

Since the beginning of the 1990s, brewpubs have come into their own in San Francisco and beer itself has evolved in the collective imagination from being the drink for barbecues and football fans to a gourmet beverage enjoyed by all. In retrospect, it makes perfect sense, since San Francisco bars have always boasted their democratic sensibility – as places where corporate execs in grey suits, bike messengers in cut-offs and New Age freaks mumbling their mantras ('I drink it for the Vitamin B, man') all sit side-by-side at the bar and opine on whatever.

Anchor Steam Brewing Company

1705 Mariposa Street, at De Haro Street (863 8350). Bus 19, 22. **Open** *by appointment only* 9am-5pm Mon-Fri.

Although it discourages tourists, San Francisco's famous brewery (which celebrates its centennial in 1996) offers free tours of its brewing facilities – with a tasting afterwards for home brewers and beer professionals. To join a tour, call at least two weeks in advance for a reservation and make sure you tell them you have an interest in brewing, not just drinking.

Gordon Biersch

2 Harrison Street, at Steuart Street and the Embarcadero (243 8246). Bus 1, 32, 41. **Open** 11am-11.45pm Mon, Tue, Sun; 11am-12.30am Wed, Thur; 11am-2am Fri, Sat. **Credit** AmEx, DC, MC, V.

Gordon Biersch was the last of the big three brewpubs to open in San Francisco, but quickly established itself as the top dog, serving the city's best lager as well as four-star dinners in the restaurant upstairs. Being top dog in San Francisco is never easy, though, since the locals are generally ambivalent about commercial success. Consequently – although the rumours about opiates in the beer turned out not to be true and the hype about Gordon Biersch as a yuppie breeding ground has died out – the cold, minimalist structure, Bay views and prices (about $1 more per beer than the competition) give it an élitist atmosphere.

Jupiter

2181 Shattuck Avenue, Berkeley (1-510 843 8277). BART Berkeley. **Open** 11.30am-midnight Mon-Fri; noon-1am Sat, Sun. **Credit** MC, V.

A draught bar as well as a brewpub, the Jupiter's biggest draw is not its own beer, but the beer garden at the back, the mezzanine inside, the pizza and the egalitarian atmosphere. Bands play in the back in the summer. If you're staying in the city, it's a convenient stop on the way to or from Berkeley campus or Telegraph Avenue.

Twenty Tank Brewery.

Marin Brewing Company

1809 Larkspur Landing, Larkspur (332 6600). Golden Gate Transit Ferry to Larkspur. **Open** 11.30am-12.30pm daily. **Credit** AmEx, MC, V.

Located in what may be the world's most civilised shopping centre, the Marin Brewing Company is a family-friendly place, with burgers, pizza, veggie food and a patio. A brewpub in a shopping centre may sound awful, but it's a beautiful ferry ride from the city, and the place wins medals by the bucketful for the beers (including the famous Bluebeery Ale). Surfer dudes, mountain biking babes and seen-it-all-before Marinites keep the bar real.

San Francisco Brewing Company

155 Columbus Avenue, at Pacific Avenue (434 3344). Bus 12, 15, 41, 83. **Open** 11.30am-1am Mon-Fri; noon-1.30am Sat, Sun. **Credit** AmEx, MC, V.

Of the three brewpubs in the city, the quality of the San Francisco Brewing Company's beer varies the most – which is a shame because the place is a treasure. Restored to turn-of-the-century specs, the woodwork is stunning: ornate and brushed with air from a vintage ceiling fan that runs the length of the room. There's live music on some nights and great french fries every night.

Twenty Tank Brewery

316 11th Street, between Harrison and Folsom Streets (255 9455). Bus 12, 42. **Open** 11.30am-1.30am daily. **Credit** MC, V.

A landmark among the many nightlife landmarks at 11th and Folsom Streets, the Twenty Tank is the kind of place that feels like home after one visit. Stocked with more beers than the other two city brewpubs, the Twenty Tank has a decent juke-box, shuffleboard, big tables for large parties, a massive upstairs area, sandwiches and table service during dinner hours. Don't miss the selection of finger foods (animal crackers and pickled eggs).

The Rite Spot

2099 Folsom Street, at 17th Street (552 6066). Bus 12, 33. **Open** 4pm-2am Mon-Thur; 2pm-2am Fri; 7pm-2am Sat, Sun. **No credit cards.**

Situated in one of the least attractive blocks of San Francisco, the Rite Spot sits on a corner opposite a funeral parlour. Inside the bar, however, one would never suspect that the dearly departed are being cremated across the way, especially not with the miniature candles and flowers, the tablecloths and the pianist tickling the ivories. Featuring tasty bar food and acerbic bartenders, this is an upscale dive.

Spec's

12 Jack Kerouac Alley at Broadway (421 4112). Bus 15, 41, 83. **Open** 4.30pm-2am Mon-Fri; 5pm-2am Sat, Sun. **No credit cards.**

From time to time, William Saroyan's *The Time of Your Life* gets staged inside Spec's, and aptly so. It is a quintessential San Francisco play and Spec's is a quintessential San Francisco bar. Here the bohos still bend elbows with society, call each other names and find cause to laugh. Order up some bread and cheese, a pint or a cocktail, sit back and soak in the lore. Listen, in particular, for echoes of the Beats. *See also chapter* **Literary San Francisco.**

Tonga Room

The Fairmont, 950 Mason Street, at California Street (772 5000). Powell-Hyde, Powell-Mason or California cable car. **Open** 5-10pm Mon-Thur, Sun; 6-11pm Fri, Sat. **Credit** AmEx, DC, MC, V.

From time to time lightning flashes from behind the *faux* cottage walls and palm fronds, thunder rumbles from the speakers and it begins to rain (from sprinklers, over a pool in the centre of the room). The Tonga Room couldn't be cheesier: a kitsch bar to the nth degree. There's usually a band,

Tosca Cafe – *another literary landmark.*

He drank in the bar and slept in the alley.

floating on an island in the pool, and plenty of tropical/nautical detail, should you need conversation starters. Expect a little gasp when the bill comes.

Tosca Cafe

242 Columbus Avenue, between Broadway and Pacific Avenue (986 9651). Bus 15, 41, 83. **Open** 5pm-1.45am daily. **No credit cards.**

Some time ago Tosca crossed over in the imagination from being the place that San Francisco society visits, to the place that tourists visit to see San Francisco society. Now it seems to have reached a kind of equilibrium. It's true that Francis Ford Coppola, whose offices are across the street, keeps a stash of wine here. And this is indeed the place filmgoers glimpsed in *Basic Instinct*. But – with opera on the juke-box, booths, dim lighting, black-tie service and the essential cappuccino – the celebs are hardly necessary. Tosca has retained that rarest of qualities at the close of the century: class. *See also chapter* **Literary San Francisco.**

Union Ale House

1980 Union Street at Buchanan Street (721 0300). Bus 41. **Open** 3.30pm-1.30am Mon-Fri; 11.30am-1.30am Sat, Sun. **Credit** MC, V.

If a place chock full of American jocks and young women looking for husbands sounds dreadful, avoid the Ale House, aka 'Male House'. If, however, a bit of frat house fun is what you're in the mood for, you've found your haunt. Jammed at the weekend, the Ale House can be (thankfully) less of a party and more of a hangout earlier in the week.

Vesuvio's Café

255 Columbus Avenue, between Broadway and Pacific Avenue (362 3370). Bus 15, 41, 83. **Open** 6pm-2am daily. **No credit cards.**

The alley that separates Vesuvio's from the City Lights Bookstore is now named after Jack Kerouac, appropriately enough, since it was one his favourite places to vomit. A notorious red wine drunk, Kerouac was notorious at Vesuvio's – and once inside you'll see why he liked it so much. It's kitsch, but it's pre-1970s kitsch so it isn't too tacky – it could even be called bohemian. A mezzanine has seats above the alley, chess is played in the seats by the door, and there's plenty of cheap red wine, of course.

Zeitgeist

199 Valencia Street, at Duboce Avenue (255 7505). Bus 26. **Open** noon-2am daily. **Credit** AmEx, MC, V.

A few pints at the Zeitgeist can leave one certain that the place has shifted since you entered, such is the ersatz floorplan and deck at the back resting in the eaves of a freeway. The Zeitgeist is a biker bar, but will tolerate non-biking punk rockers, unpretentious artists and cyclists – especially bike couriers, who are a regular part of the Happy Hour crowd. Beer is served by the pint, quart and pitcher.

Fun for all the family at **Caffè Trieste**. *See page 132.*

Cafés

Recommending a café is no easy task in San Francisco. For a start there are the chains: **Peet's Coffee & Tea** and the **Spinelli Coffee Company**, the local favourites and rivals to the national interloper **Starbucks**, as well as downtown commuter coffee shops like **Oh La! La!** and **Pasqua**. These five purveyors of fine coffee alone account for more than 100 outlets in the city (consult the Yellow Pages to find your nearest branch). Then there are at least 150 independent cafés whose names begin with the word 'café' and as many or more that end their name with it. Most locals have their favourites within walking distance. What follows, then, is not an attempt to be comprehensive, but a select list of cafés worth seeking out. For $10.95, true coffee lovers can purchase *Café San Francisco* by James M Forbes, an exhaustive survey of local coffee houses (available at Spinelli locations, among others).

Ace Café
1539 Folsom Street, between 11th and 12th Streets (621 4752). Muni Metro F, J, K, L, M, N/9, 12, 42 bus. **Open** 5.30pm-2am Tue-Sat. **Credit** AmEx, DC, MC, V.
Close to a host of nightspots, the Ace Cafe is a casual storefront bar/restaurant that feels slightly more like a bar than a bistro. The food is Southwestern and Latin. If you go for the live music (jazz, rockabilly), don't expect to have a deep conversation; although efforts have been made to soften the interior, the volume can still leave you shell-shocked.

Art Institute Cafe
800 Chestnut Street, at Jones Street (749 4567). Bus 41. **Open** *May-Sept* 9am-9pm Mon-Sat. **No credit cards.**

The advantages of this place are multiple: a view of the Bay; shows of students' work-in-progress; the Diego Rivera mural on the way in – and it's rarely busy. Inexpensive, but not especially fancy or filling meals (intended for the students), are served, as is coffee and art talk. The only catch: it's only open during the school year.

Café Bastille
22 Belden Alley, between Montgomery and Kearny, Pine and Bush Streets (986 5673). Bus 2, 3, 4, 15. **Open** 11am-10.30pm Mon-Sat. **Credit** AmEx, MC, V.
Francophiles and Frogs congregate here, in an alley near the city's more prestigious advertising firms. Light lunches (salads and sandwiches) are served in a self-consciously European fashion, and there are several tables outside in the alley. The café also throws an annual fête on Bastille Day (14 July) and entertains with jazz from Thursday to Saturday evenings.

Café Capriccio
701A Market Street, at Third Street (243 8252). BART Montgomery Street/Muni Metro F, J, K, L, M, N. **Open** 7am-7pm Mon-Fri; 9am-6pm Sat. **No credit cards.**
What Café Bastille is to homesick French travellers and ex-pats, Café Capriccio is to Italians and Mediterranean *aficionados*. Stylish but small, it can get hectic at lunch-time, and with good reason – the sandwiches are fresh and inventive. Great lattes and cappuccinos, too.

Cafe Flore
2298 Market Street, at Noe Street (621 8579). Muni Metro K, L, M/22, 37 bus. **Open** 7.30am-11.30pm Mon-Thur, Sun; 7.30am-midnight Fri, Sat. **No credit cards.**
'Cafe hair-do' to many locals, Flore is quite the scene. Almost always packed (especially the comfortable patio), it is a place

Cruise the Castro from the comfort of the terrace at **Cafe Flore.**

to make lots of eye contact, show off your new honey or simply pen a postcard amid the beautiful people. A Castro landmark, it's not the place for the homophobic – or maybe it is, because you won't stay homophobic for long.

Café la Boheme
3318 24th Street, at Mission Street (285 4122). BART 24th Street. **Open** 5am-11pm Mon-Fri; 6am-11pm Sat; 7am-11pm Sun. **No credit cards.**
For better or worse, La Boheme feels like an all-ages youth hostel. Located across the street from the BART station and scant feet from one of the city's true crossroads, La Boheme sees its share of riff-raff and down-and-outs. Undeterred, poets, musicians and students come for a bagel or tea and stay for hours.

Caffè Centro
102 South Park, between Bryant and Brannan, Second and Third Streets (882 1500). Bus 30, 45, 76. **Open** 7.30am-7.30pm Mon-Fri; 9am-5.30pm Sat. **No credit cards.**
Serving the multimedia élite their caffeine and tuna sandwiches, Caffe Centro is the place most often photographed to represent the epicentre of New Media. It offers excellent pastries, espresso and a window for take-away orders, which is used by those who prefer to sit on the lawn of South Park not 20 yards away.

*The **Steps of Rome**. See page 133.*

Caffe Greco
423 Columbus Avenue, between Green and Vallejo Streets (397 6261). Bus 15, 30, 41, 45. **Open** 7am-midnight daily. **No credit cards.**
In a district brimming with sidewalk cafes, Greco stands out. With large sliding windows opening onto Columbus Avenue, it doesn't have the singles scene of the Steps of Rome, the history of Caffe Trieste or the oven-bistro cosiness of Mario's (*see below* for all three), but it does serve what is arguably the town's best cappuccino and tiramisu.

Caffè Trieste
601 Vallejo Street, at Grant Avenue (392 6739). Bus 15, 30, 41, 45. **Open** 6.30am-11.30pm Mon-Thur, Sun; 6.30am-12.30am Fri, Sat. **No credit cards.**
How to describe Trieste without hyperbole? Unchanged since 1956 and still owned by the same family (the Giottas), it has seen many of San Francisco's most famous literary and philosophical sons through a hangover, been written up for its opera nights (rare nowadays) – but it's mainly known for its atmosphere, which makes it almost impossible not to make friends.

Enrico's
504 Broadway, at Kearny Street (982 6223). Bus 12, 15, 83 9AX, 9BX. **Open** noon-1.30am daily. **Credit** AmEx, MC, V.
Enrico's no longer belongs to Enrico, but he has endorsed the new owners who have done a splendid job of remodelling this sidewalk bistro/restaurant and historic gathering place of bohemians, musicians and comedians. Dinners here are sophisticated occasions matched with an excellent (if slightly over-priced) wine list. Modest cabaret and jazz acts keep the place lively.

Horseshoe Coffee House
566 Haight Street, between Fillmore and Steiner Streets (626 8852). Muni Metro N/6, 7, 22, 66, 71 bus. **Open** 7am-12.30am daily. **No credit cards.**
If you want to see slackers in action (or inaction), this is the place to come. A den that attracts a few aloof jazz cats but mainly twentysomething artists, rockers, anarchists, hitchhikers and squatters, the Horseshoe will make you feel old as it fills with skate rats and jail bait when school's out. It has bulletin boards, free literature and club information, and coffee as strong as turpentine served in 16oz pint glasses.

On a clear day you can see forever

Several high-rise buildings in San Francisco have roof-top areas for views and repose, including the 24-hour sky garden at the **Fairmont Hotel** (950 Mason Street, at California Street).The garden atop **One Market Plaza** (1 Market Street) has circular lawns, stone benches and a knock-out view of the San Francisco-Oakland Bay Bridge, and is open 8am-5pm, Mon-Fri. But if you want a libation in hand as you gaze out across the city (and who can blame you?), try one of the bars below.

Top of the Mark
Mark Hopkins Inter-Continental Hotel, 1 Nob Hill, at California and Mason Streets (392 3434). Cable car California. **Open** 4pm-12.30am Mon-Thur, Sun; 4pm-1.30am Fri, Sat. **Credit** AmEx, MC, V.

Set on the top of Nob Hill, this landmark building was originally owned by San Francisco financier Hopkins, burnt down in the Great Fire of 1906 and was rebuilt in the 1920s. The Art Deco restaurant and bar on the 19th floor offers spectacular views and on foggy days you feel as if you're flying above the clouds.

View Lounge
Marriott Hotel, 55 Fourth Street, between Market and Mission Streets (896 1600). Bus 30, 45, 76. **Open** 11.30am-1.30am daily. **Credit** AmEx, MC, V.
Likened to a juke-box and described by *New York Times* architecture critic Paul Goldberger as 'vulgar', the Marriott boasts a top-floor bar with somewhat generic furniture and snacks but a breathtaking panorama of SoMa, downtown San Francisco and the East Bay. Dusk is particularly brilliant here, when office windows are set ablaze by the fading sun, electric lights start winking and billboards begin to glow.

*It's slacker city at the **Horseshoe Coffee House**. See page 132.*

Josie's Juice Bar and Cabaret
3583 16th Street, at Market (861 7933). Muni Metro K, L, M/8, 22, 37 bus. **Open** *9am-7.45pm Mon, Wed-Sun; 9am-6pm Tue.* **No credit cards**.
A non-alcoholic gathering place for cutting edge performance by gay friends and lovers or the health conscious of any sexual proclivity. A patio at the back has a dozen or so tables and there's seating inside during the day, when the stage is not being used. *See also chapters* **Theatre & Dance** *and* **Gay & Lesbian San Francisco**.

Le Petit Cafe
2164 Larkin Street, at Green Street (776 5356). Bus 19, 45. **Open** *8am-9.30pm Mon-Fri; 8.30am-3pm Sat, Sun.* **Credit** *AmEx, MC, V.*
Some find the cosy, refined quality of Le Petit Cafe constrained, but they're probably inverted snobs and would prefer to drink from dirty coffee mugs. With classical music on the sound system, books on the shelves and delectable pastries, Le Petit Cafe, in the centre of the Russian Hill residential district, is for those who appreciate the finer things in life.

Mario's Bohemian Cigar Store
566 Columbus Avenue, at Union Street (362 0536). Bus 15, 30, 39, 41, 45. **Open** *10am-midnight Mon-Sat; 10am-11pm Sun.* **No credit cards**.
A likeable bistro in North Beach that serves delicious focaccia sandwiches with meatballs, chicken or breaded eggplant. It's a great place for a beer with a hippie entrepreneur, a cappuccino with a conspiracy theorist or Blood of the Bull alone with your diary. There are no cigars for sale, by the way.

Savoy Tivoli
1434 Grant Avenue, between Union and Green Streets (362 7023). Bus 15, 30, 39, 41, 45. **Open** *5pm-2am Tue-Thur; 3pm-2am Fri, Sat.* **No credit cards**.
Nearly every single twentysomething goes through a brief Savoy Tivoli phase when they first hit town – it's the place to find a date, drink imported beers, shoot pool and be grateful to be in a continental, open air café. However, be warned that the allure wears off quickly. At any rate, if you can't meet someone new here, you're not trying hard enough.

Slow Club
2501 Mariposa Street, at Hampshire Street (241 9390). Bus 9, 33. **Open** *7am-4pm Mon; 7am-11pm Tue-Sat.* **Credit** *MC, V.*
Off the beaten track, except for journalists at KQED, the local public broadcast network, and the *Bay Guardian* newspaper, the Slow Club is a simple, clean and tasty luncheon spot by day and something of a bistro/speakeasy after dark. An excellent place for a part-business/part-pleasure meal and conversation.

Steps of Rome
348 Columbus Avenue, between Grant and Vallejo Streets (397 0435). Bus 15, 41, 45, 83, 9X, 9AX, 9BX. **Open** *8.30am-3pm Mon-Fri; 8.30am-2pm Sat, Sun.* **No credit cards**.
A favourite dessert spot in North Beach, the Steps of Rome succeeds in providing the bustle and glamour that convinces people that they are, in fact, painting the town. Eye-level mirrors make an art of furtive glances, the espresso drinks are deftly prepared and the outside seating is perfect for people-watching and heckling.

Zuni Café
1658 Market Street, at between Franklin and Gough Streets (552 2522). Muni Metro F, J, K, L, M, N/6, 7, 8, 26, 66, 71 bus. **Open** *7.30am-midnight Tue-Sat; 7.30am-11.30pm Sun.* **Credit** *AmEx, MC, V.*
No one wishing to see Californians-on-the-make in their element can afford to miss the Zuni, a café that could succeed in LA but is tolerable because it's not there. The Zuni serves food round the clock, from breakfast to full course meals (Mediterranean with a Californian slant), with a bar menu and a thriving late-night martini scene in between. Through the many square-yards of glass facing Market Street – or sitting at one of the tables outside – you can watch the oysters being shucked and gawk at passers-by.

Shopping & Services

Shopping & Services by Area

Downtown

Architects and Heroes p151; Arthur Beren Shoes p147; Bang & Olufsen p155; BASS p155; Borders Books and Music p140; Britex Fabrics p155; Bruno Magli p147; The Coach Store p147; Compositions p150; Crate & Barrel p153; Diana Slavin p143; Di Lelio's p153; Discount Camera p141; Duty-free Shops p142; Emporio Armani p143; Emporium p137; Fox's Photo 1-Hour Lab p142; The Gap p143; Gump's p137; Lang p153; Loehmann's p145; MAC p143; Macy's p139; Maraolo p145; Mark Cross p147; Métier p143; Neiman Marcus p139; Nordstrom p139; North Beach Leather p145; Opals & Gems of Australis p153; Pendleton p139; Podesta Baldocchi p148; Quantity Postcards p150; Saks Fifth Avenue p139; 77 Maiden Lane p151; Spa Nordstrom p152; Tannery West p147; Tillman Place Bookshop p140; TIX Bay Area p155; TSE Cashmere p145; 22 Steps p148; Virgin Megastore p154; Vivon p145; Wilkes Bashford p145.

Civic Center

A Clean, Well-Lighted Place for Books p140; Sierra Club Bookstore; 141.

Chinatown & North Beach

Chinatown & North Beach

Canton Bazaar p139; City Lights p140; Ed Hardy's Tattoo City p152; Graffeo Coffee Roasting Company; Lyle Tuttle Tattooing p153; Molinari Delicatessen p149; Naomi's Antiques to Go p153; North Beach Pizza pp149; Quetzal Weavers p139; SF Rock Posters & Collectibles p155; Stella Pastry & Caffe p149; Ten Ren Tea Company p150; Tower Records p154.

Nob Hill & Russian Hill

American Rag p147; Dine One One p149; Fields Book Store p140; Johnson Leather Corp p147; Some Like it Hot, A Fiery Food Emporium p149; Tibet Shop p140.

SoMa & the Mission

SoMa

Adolph Gasser p141; Balloon Lady p150; The Body Shop p151; Brainwash p153; Burlington Coat Factory p145; Cake Gallery p149; International Electronics p142; Isda and Company Outlet p145; The Luggage Center p147; Martha Egan p151; New West p145; Pink Tarantula p151; Real Guitars p155; Shoe Pavilion p145; Site for Sore Eyes p154; Six Sixty Factory Outlets p145; Trader Joe's p149; The Wine Club p149.

The Mission

Botanica Yoruba p154; Casa Lucas Market p149; Dianda Italian American Pastry p149; Modern Times Bookstore p140; Metronome p142; Old Wives' Tales p140; Osento p150; Ritmo Latino p154.

The Haight & the Castro

The Haight-Asbury

Ambiance p143; Anubis Warpus p152; Body Manipulations p152; The Booksmith p140; Buffalo Exchange p147; Daljeets p148; Elite Shoe Repair p148;

Great Expectations p140; Haight-Ashbury Music Center; Haight-Asbury T-shirts p155; Mascara Club p139; Naked Eye News and Video p155; Pipe Dreams p155; Reckless Records p154; Star Classics p154; Tassajara Bread Bakery p149; Used Rubber USA p142; La Victoria p149; Wasteland p147.

The Castro & Noe Valley

Centrium Furnishings p153; Cotton Basics p143; A Different Light p140; Gauntlet p152; Global Exchange Third World Craft Center p139; Ixia p148; Image Leather p155; The Jerusalem p153; Joshua Simon p143; Na Na p145; Peek-A-Boutique p147; Rolo p145; Southwest Tradewinds p140; Star Magic Space Age Gifts p155; Streetlight Records p154.

The Waterfront

The Anchorage p138; Boudin Sourdough Bakery & Café p148; The Cannery p138; Cost Plus Imports p150; Ghirardelli Square p138; Ghirardelli Craft Gallery p139; Ferry Plaza Farmers' Market p146; Meaders Cleaners p153; Just Desserts p149; Pappas at the Plaza p148; Victoria's Secret p147.

The Marina & Union Street

Brew City p149; City Optix p154; CP Shades p143; Enchanted Crystal p154; Greenwich Yarn p155; Images of the North p139; Kenneth Cole p148; MAC on Union p151; Mudpie p147; The Painter's Place p154; A Touch of Asia p140; Zuni Pueblo p140.

The Central Neighbourhoods

Pacific Heights

Betsey Johnson p143; Fillamento p153; Thirdhand Store p147; Virginia Breier p150; Zoë p145.

Japantown & the Western Addition

Asakichi p139; Kabuki Hot Springs p150; Marcus Books p140; Nichi Bei Bussan p139.

Hayes Valley

The African Outlet p139; Bella Donna p143; Bulo p147; Coulars Boutique p143; de Vera p150; Gimme Shoes p148; Nomads p145; Worldware p142; Zeitgeist p153; Zonal p140.

Golden Gate Park & the West

Richmond

Family Sauna p151; Green Apple Books p140; Haig's Delicacies p149; Locust Cleaners p153; Vinh Khang Herbs & Gensengs p150.

Sunset

Le Video p155.

Further Afield

Claremont Resort and Spa p151; Drum World p154; Fry's Electronics p141; Green Gulch p151; Tail of the Yak Trading Company p150; Rasputin's p155; Whole Earth Electronics p142.

Shopping & Services

A shopaholic's paradise, 'Baghdad by the Bay' has got the lot, from big name department stores and waterfront shopping centres, to one-off boutiques. Enjoy.

San Francisco is a unique amalgam of diverse influences, so shopping in the city has a distinct flavour all its own. The mix of Japanese, Chinese, Mexican, South-east Asian, Pacific Islander and Native American that meets in the relatively small confines of 'Baghdad-by-the-Bay', results in an eclectic assortment of relics from all these cultures, as well as a lively commitment to the quirky idiosyncrasies of extreme individual eccentricity.

SHOPPING AREAS

Although San Francisco has its fair share of department stores and malls filled with the chain-stores that are fast eliminating regional differences throughout the US, the most rewarding shopping is found among the quirky one-off boutiques unique to each neighbourhood.

Hayes Valley, a scant three blocks of Hayes Street between Laguna and Civic Center, is the most interesting and forward-looking shopping area at the moment. Each store has such a different ambience that going from place to place makes the senses reel. **Union Square** is for the conservative, the tried-and-true and top-of-the-line, but you might find an up-and-coming local designer's wares hidden away on Claude Lane, or a shoe shop that looks as if it should be in Hayes Valley.

The historic corner of Haight and Ashbury Streets now sports a giant Gap and a Ben and Jerry's ice-cream branch, but **Haight Street** still lives up to its past with plenty of tie-dye emporiums and a wide variety of vintage clothing and body art shops (*see chapter* **San Francisco by Neighbourhood** for more on these and the surrounding areas).

Bookshops are in every neighbourhood, but the highest concentration of both new and second-hand books is on Valencia Street in the Mission district, where, just a few blocks to the east you can find Mexican and Central American arts and goods. You can find Japanese language books and periodicals in the **Japan Center**, along with serene shops specialising in incense and miniature teapots for the tea ceremony. Medicinal herbs,

export porcelain, silks, pearls and jade abound in **Chinatown**, among restaurants, food shops and souvenir shops crowded with tourists.

Italian-American **North Beach** has the best pasta and cappuccino, but walk along **Grant Avenue** to discover unique shops with wild collections of postcards and beads. And so it continues, from elegant goods of every description on **Union Street** (not to be confused with Union Square), trendy urban fashion and furniture in the Castro, and kidswear and less expensive imported goods in low-key Noe Valley, to mural art and Mexican culture in the **Mission**.

TAX & DUTY

Most shops will accept travellers' cheques, but remember that label prices are not the full price; you will have to add California sales tax of eight and a half per cent to everything you buy. British travellers are permitted to bring goods for personal use worth £136 through UK Customs, duty-free. Over that amount, duty and VAT will be added upon your return home; note that if you bring in an item worth more than £136 pounds, you will have to pay charges on the full value, not just its value over £136. If you would like to know the rates of duty in advance, phone the **US Department of Commerce** on 1-202 482 2905/2920.

Department Stores

Emporium

835 Market Street, between Fourth and Fifth Streets (764 2222). BART Powell Street/Muni Metro F, J, K, L, M, N/6, 7, 27, 31, 66, 71 bus/Powell-Mason, Powell-Hyde cable car. **Open** 9.30am-8pm Mon-Sat; 11am-8pm Sun. **Credit** AmEx, MC, V.
Lower-priced and slightly lacklustre compared to its competitors, Emporium is a serviceable all-purpose department store. Stocks good men's and boys' sportswear.

Gump's

135 Post Street, between Grant Avenue and Kearny Street (984 9439). BART Montgomery Street/Muni Metro F, J, K, L, M, N/2, 3, 4, 15 bus. **Open** 10am-6pm Mon-Wed, Fri; 10am-7pm Thur; 10am-6pm Sat. **Credit** AmEx, MC, V.

Shopping centres

Walk into a mall in any major American city and you'll see a combination of the same standard chain retailers over and over: brands such as **Ann Taylor** (tailored business clothes); **The Limited** and **Express** (stylish sportswear); **Victoria's Secret** (lingerie); **J Crew** (classic unisex sportswear); **Crabtree & Evelyn** (English toiletries); **The Body Shop** (natural cosmetics and beauty products), and so on. San Francisco is no exception. Well-known shopping centres – the **Embarcadero Center**, the **San Francisco Shopping Center**, **Stonestown Galleria**, **Crocker Galleria** – house European and American designers and the standard mix of brands, blended with individually owned and operated shops and a nice assortment of restaurants, fast food joints and cafés.

If you want to visit a typical American mall, start with the **San Francisco Shopping Center** at Market and Fifth Streets (495 5656); its vertical layout makes it more interesting than most, and its anchor stores, **Nordstrom** and **Emporium**, are more or less locally-based. But unless you have a specific objective in mind, one shopping centre is pretty much like the next.

The exception to this rule are the outdoor shopping complexes along San Francisco's waterfront and **Fisherman's Wharf**. This is where the city dresses itself up for the tourist trade, and where its merchants compete fiercely for the visitors' patronage. These areas have plenty of interesting shops and sights but, be warned, they can be tourist-packed nightmares.

The great advantage of **Pier 39** (at Beach and Embarcadero Streets, 981 8030) is the pack of noisy seals that lies about on the docks and swim close by in the water. Wonderful views of the Bay are a bonus to shopping in all these spots, as is the chance to sample a crab cocktail and a hunk of sourdough bread as you stroll.

Ghirardelli Square (900 North Point, between Larkin, Polk and Beach Streets, 775 5500) features the still-functioning Ghirardelli Chocolate Factory (771 4903), where you can watch the chocolate being made and buy some for consumption. A variety of shops occupy the several levels of the square, including a Native American art and jewellery shop, The White Buffalo Gallery (931 0665); an elegant shop specialising in pearls, Pearl of Orient (441 2288); and The Outlaw (563 8986), which carries Harley Davidson merchandise and T-shirts. The fountain with the nursing mermaids is a nice place to sit and enjoy the view.

The Cannery (2801 Leavenworth Street, between Beach and Jefferson Streets, 771 3112), former site of the Del Monte fruit-canning factory, has a large open space that's usually occupied by street musicians. Its upper levels are a rabbit warren of shops, with the odd, the unusual and the downright weird predominating. Russian Treasure (346 1104) has nesting dolls, lacquered boxes and shawls. The Kachina Gallery (441 2636) has a good selection of the carved dolls representing sacred figures of Hopi Indian religious life. But for the quintessential San Francisco experience, stop in at Psychic Reality (202 8860) and have a photograph taken of your aura, a bargain at only $15.

The Anchorage (next door at 2800 Leavenworth Street, between Beach and Jefferson Streets, 775 6000) also has some interesting shops. The Rubber Stamp Image (921 1828) carries nothing but rubber stamps and inkpads; The Endangered Species Store (346 7663) stocks everything pertaining to our vanishing wildlife and a decent assortment of environmental CDs and tapes. It's an essential tradition, when the fog rolls in and you're freezing in your shorts, to duck into the Buena Vista Café nearby (474 5044) for a bracing cup of strong Irish coffee.

Load up at **Ghirardelli Square**.

The treasure chest of Old San Francisco, presided over by a large golden Buddha on the ground floor. Gump's advertises its wares as 'The Rare. The Unique. The Imaginative'. It sells precious Oriental wares and pearls, pearls, pearls.

Macy's
Union Square (397 3333). BART Montgomery Street/ Muni Metro F, J, K, L, M, N/2, 3, 4, 38, 45 bus/Powell-Mason, Powell-Hyde cable car. **Open** 10am-8pm Mon-Fri; 9am-9pm Sat; 11am-7pm Sun. **Credit** AmEx, MC, V.
Having taken over the former I Magnin building, Macy's now reigns as the giant of Union Square. It has everything under the sun, under several roofs, with prices from moderate to high. It has an excellent menswear department.

Neiman Marcus
150 Stockton Street, at Geary Street (362 3900). BART Montgomery Street/Muni Metro F, J, K, L, M, N/2, 3, 4, 38, 45, 76 bus/Powell-Mason, Powell-Hyde cable car. **Open** 10am-8pm Mon, Thur, Fri; 10am-6pm Tue, Wed; 10am-7pm Sat; noon-6pm Sun. **Credit** AmEx.
Sometimes parodied as 'Needless Markup' by its detractors, the Dallas-based chain offers top-of-the-line designer clothing and a particularly well-stocked cosmetics department, including Chanel and the new Trish McEvoy line.

Nordstrom
San Francisco Shopping Center, 865 Market Street, at Fifth Street (243 8500). BART Powell Street/Muni Metro F, J, K, L, M, N/6, 7, 27, 31, 66, 71 bus/Powell-Mason, Powell-Hyde cable car. **Open** 9.30am-9pm Mon-Sat; 10am-7pm Sun. **Credit** AmEx, MC, V.
From its perch atop the SF Center, Nordstrom continues to grow in popularity, not least because of its extremely helpful customer service. Sensible business clothing and a large shoe department are its stock in trade and it's also known for live piano music from a baby grand in each of its stores. There are good women's leather jackets. The Personal Touch service offers a customised fashion service; ring for an appointment.

Saks Fifth Avenue
384 Post Street, at Union Square (986 4300). BART Montgomery Street/Muni Metro F, J, K, L, M, N/2, 3, 4, 38, 45, 76 bus/Powell-Mason, Powell-Hyde cable car. **Open** 10am-6.30pm Mon-Wed; 10am-8pm Thur, Fri; 10am-7pm Sat; noon-6pm Sun. **Credit** AmEx, JCB, MC, V.
A small branch of the New York store. It stocks more conservative designer clothing than Neiman Marcus, but has a good lingerie department with knowledgeable salespeople.

Antique Repairing & Restoring

Butterfield & Butterfield
220 San Bruno Avenue, at 16th Street (861 7500 ext 337). Bus 22, 53. **Open** 8.30am-5pm Mon-Fri. **No credit cards.**
A San Francisco institution since 1865, B&B appraises all collectables, but is better known for its year-round auctions of furniture, art, antiques, silver, rugs, jewellery and wine.

Arts & Crafts

The African Outlet
524 Octavia Street, between Hayes and Grove Streets (864 3576). Bus 21. **Open** 10am-7pm Mon-Sat; noon-6pm Sun. **Credit** AmEx, MC, V.
Sells everything African, from carvings to *objets d'art.*

Asakichi
Japan Center, 1730 Geary Boulevard, between Webster and Fillmore Streets (921 3821). Bus 2, 3, 4, 22, 38. **Open** 11am-6pm Mon, Tue; 10am-6pm Wed-Sun. **Credit** AmEx, MC, V.

There are three shops in the Japan Center, one devoted entirely to incense, one to full-size and miniature teapots and one to furniture.

Canton Bazaar
616 Grant Avenue, between California and Sacramento Streets (362 5750). Bus 1, 15/California cable car. **Open** 10am-10pm daily. **Credit** AmEx, MC, V.
Cloisonné enamelwork, carved jade, rose Canton chinaware, hand embroidery, jewellery and antiques are all imported from mainland China and sold here.

Ghirardelli Craft Gallery
900 North Point Street (441 0780). Bus 30X, 60. **Open** 10am-6pm Mon-Wed, Fri, Sat, Sun; 10am-9pm Thur. **Credit** AmEx, MC, V.
You can buy the type of pan-American crafts you lusted after at the Craft and Folk Art Museum in Fort Mason here.

Global Exchange Third World Craft Center
3900 24th Street, at Sanchez Street (648 8068). Bus 48. **Open** 10.30am-6.30pm daily. **Credit** AmEx, MC, V.
Imported crafts from Mexico and Guatemala include woven, embroidered and crocheted shoulder bags; potholders; tiny gifts for children; *retablo* paintings on tin and animal hides; and carved fantastic creatures from Oaxaca. There are some nice Tibetan necklaces and other gifts as well. Profits from your purchase may go to support a crafts co-operative in a small village.

Images of the North
1782 Union Street, at Octavia and Gough Streets (673 1273). Bus 41, 45. **Open** 11am-5.30pm Mon-Sat; noon-4pm Sun. **Credit** AmEx, MC, V.
Images specialises in sculpture and carvings of the Eskimo and Northwest Coast American Indians. Beautiful jewellery.

Mascara Club
1408 Haight Street, at Masonic Avenue (863 2837). Bus 6, 7, 43, 66, 71. **Open** 11am-6pm daily. **Credit** AmEx, MC, V.
This Mexican folk art store sells colourful oilcloth at $4.50 per foot, along with enough images of Jesus and the Virgin of Guadaloupe to keep collectors happy for years. There are also Frida Kahlo paper dolls, tin toys, plenty of $5 items and a shrine maker's kit for only $17. It's worth a trip to the Haight just to see this place.

Nichi Bei Bussan
1715 Buchanan Mall, at Post and Sutter Streets (346 2117). Bus 2, 3, 4. **Open** 10am-5.30pm Mon-Fri; 10am-5pm Sat; noon-5pm Sun (summer only). **Credit** AmEx, MC, V.
Where to find fluffy quilts covered with colourful Japanese fabrics, kimonos, tatami lamps, and many small and interesting trinkets.

Pendleton
464 Sutter Street, at Powell Street (788 6383). Bus 2, 3, 4, 76/Powell-Mason, Powell-Hyde cable car. **Open** 9am-6pm Mon-Sat. **Credit** AmEx, MC, V.
For years the well-known American woollens factory has produced the strikingly beautiful blankets favoured by American Indians. Some blankets are numbered and collectable, some are made into clothing (you pay around $300 for a coat).

Quetzal Weavers
754 Columbus Avenue, between Filbert and Greenwich Streets (392 9205). Bus 30/Powell-Mason cable car. **Open** 10am-7pm Mon-Sat; 11am-7pm Sun. **Credit** MC, V.
Sells items made from cloth woven in two Mayan villages in Guatemala. There's a small but well-chosen selection.

Southwest Tradewinds

Corner of Sanchez and 18th Streets (255 9602). BART Castro/Muni Metro F, K, L, M/8, 33, 35 bus. **Open** noon-6pm Tue-Sun. **Credit** AmEx, MC, V.
Native American jewellery and pottery, Himalayan antiques, rugs, clothing and exotic cacti.

Tibet Shop

1807 Polk Street, at Washington Street (982 0326). Bus 19, 27. **Open** 10am-6pm Mon-Sat; 1-5pm Sun. **Credit** AmEx, MC, V.
Bells, incense, singing bowls, carved skulls, prayer beads; lapis lazuli, turquoise, silver and coral necklaces; clothing and crafts of Tibet, including everything you need for the practice of Tibetan Buddhism can be found here. The shop is run by a disciple of the Dalai Lama.

A Touch of Asia

1784 Union Street, at Gough Street (474 3115). Bus 41, 45. **Open** 11am-5pm Mon-Sat; noon-5pm Sun. **Credit** AmEx, MC, V.
Specialises in Kyoto *tansus* chests, moderately priced. Some antique, some reproduction.

Zonal

568 Hayes Street, at Laguna Street (255 9307). Bus 21. **Open** 11am-7pm Tue-Sat; 11am-5pm Sun. **Credit** AmEx, MC, V.
Found objects, architectural details, furniture and more – everything looking as though it was dug up from being buried for years, but possessed of a haunting beauty.

Zuni Pueblo

1749 Union Street, at Gough Street (567 0941). Bus 41, 45. **Open** 11am-7pm Mon-Sat; noon-5pm Sun. **Credit** AmEx, MC, V.
Native American goods from the Southwest, especially carved fetishes and pottery, are sold in this tribally-owned gallery.

Bookshops

San Francisco is a great literary town, a joy for both writers and readers who have made it their home. Almost every neighbourhood has its own bookshop, and there are many shops that specialise in a certain subject or type of volume. However, sadly, the survival of small, independent bookshops in the Bay Area – as elsewhere – is under threat from the giant chains, to whom publishers offer astronomical discounts.

A Different Light

489 Castro Street, at 18th Street (431 0891). Muni Metro F, K, L, M/8, 33, 35 bus. **Open** 10am-midnight daily. **Credit** AmEx, MC, V.
A thorough selection of books by and about gays and lesbians.

The Booksmith

1644 Haight Street, between Clayton and Cole Streets (863 8688). Bus 6, 7, 43, 66, 71. **Open** 10am-9pm Mon-Sat; 10am-6pm Sun. **Credit** AmEx, MC, V.
A good, all-purpose bookstore in the Haight.

Borders Books and Music

Union Square, at corner of Powell and Post Streets (399 1633). BART Powell Street/Muni Metro F, J, K, L, M, N/2, 3, 4, 76 bus/Powell-Mason, Powell-Hyde cable car. **Open** 9am-11pm Mon-Wed; 9am-midnight Thur-Sat; 10am-9pm Sun. **Credit** AmEx, MC, V.

Situated downtown and open late, this giant has much to recommend it. There's a good café to hang out in and a huge selection of magazines. Like its fellow chainstores, it discounts the bestsellers.

City Lights

261 Columbus Avenue, between Broadway and Pacific Avenue (362 8193). Bus, 15, 41, 83. **Open** 10am-midnight daily. **Credit** AmEx, MC, V.
Founded by poet Lawrence Ferlinghetti, this historic bookshop is one of the places where the Beat movement began. The stock is strong on literature, and it's still a great spot for reading or writing poetry. *See also chapter* **Literary San Francisco**.

A Clean Well-Lighted Place for Books

Opera Plaza, 601 Van Ness Avenue, at Golden Gate Avenue (441 6670). Bus 42, 47, 49. **Open** 10am-11pm Mon-Fri, Sun; 10am-midnight Sat. **Credit** AmEx, MC, V.
This centrally located, general interest bookstore hosts frequent and wildly popular readings and author events.

Fields Book Store

1419 Polk Street, between Pine and California Streets (673 2027). Bus 19. **Open** 11am-9pm Tue-Sat. **Credit** MC, V.
Fields specialises in books on metaphysics and spirituality.

Great Expectations

1512 Haight Street, at Ashbury Street (863 5515). Bus 6, 7, 43, 66, 71. **Open** 10am-8pm daily. **Credit** AmEx, MC, V.
Where to find hip reading material, underground comics, rockstar biographies, and cult classics such as Charles Bukowski's *Love is a Dog from Hell*. Stocks as many T-shirts as books.

Green Apple Books

506 Clement Street, at Sixth Avenue (387 2272). Bus 38, 44. **Open** 9.30am-11pm Mon-Thur, Sun; 9.30am-midnight Fri, Sat. **Credit** MC, V.
San Franciscans are great believers in 'good vibes', and this store has the some of the best. A wonderful mix of new and second-hand books, with helpful staff, it's a shop full of soul in a neighbourhood of great ethnic restaurants. Highly recommended for the dedicated browser.

Marcus Book Stores

712 Fillmore Street, between Post and Sutter Streets (346 4222). Bus 2, 3, 4, 22. **Open** 10am-7pm Mon-Sat; noon-5pm Sun. **Credit** MC, V.
Specialises in books by African and African-American writers and on topics of interest to African-American readers.

Modern Times Bookstore

888 Valencia Street, between 19th and 20th Streets (282 9246). Bus 26. **Open** 11am-8pm Mon-Thur; 11am-9pm Fri, Sat; 11am-6pm Sun. **Credit** AmEx, MC, V.
Originally a source for left-leaning political tracts, Modern Times is now a community centre for the Mission district. It sells new and used books, and is excellent browsing territory.

Old Wives' Tales

1009 Valencia Street, at 21st Street (821 4675). Bus 26. **Open** 11am-7pm Mon-Sat; 11am-6pm Sun. **Credit** AmEx, MC, V.
Books by and about women. Feminist books, gifts and music.

Tillman Place Bookshop

8 Tillman Place, off Grant Avenue, between Post and Sutter Streets (392 4668). Bus 2, 3, 4, 76. **Open** 9.30am-5.30pm Mon-Sat. **Credit** AmEx, MC, V.
If you're footsore and weary in Union Square, stop in at this charming spot for a good book to read at a nearby café.

The **City Lights** bookshop, where the Beats began.

Sierra Club Bookstore

730 Polk Street, between Eddy and Ellis Streets (923 5600). Bus 31/Powell-Hyde, Powell-Mason cable car. **Open** 10am-5.30pm Mon-Fri; 10am-5pm Sat. **Credit** MC, V.
A good range of books about the environment and ecological resources, plus a complete selection of hiking trails and maps.

Cameras & Electronics

One advantage of shopping for electronics in the Bay Area is the geographical proximity of Silicon Valley, which means that new computer technologies are available here three or four months before they're seen in other parts of the world. The other advantage is that laptop or notebook computers often cost half European prices.

According to local retailers, tourists' favourite buys include portable computers and camcorders, along with such small electronic items as portable CD players. It's essential you make sure that your item will work in the country in which you want to use it. TVs in America and Japan use the NTSC system while the UK and most of Europe uses the PAL system; consequently, American TVs, VCRs, camcorders, laser disks and videotapes will not work in the UK, unless you happen to have an NTSC-compatible VCR.

However, the American-made cartridge-based video games (such as Super Nintendo) are playable, provided you have a converter. Also check that the item has a built-in voltage selector; transformers and voltage converters are available but are bulky and fairly costly.

It is always good policy to deal with reputable merchants. Many stores downtown that advertise cheap cameras and electronics are somewhat unscrupulous and fly-by-night. If a deal seems too good to be true, it probably is. *See page 137* for a note on duty.

Adolph Gasser

181 Second Street, between Mission and Howard Streets (495 3852). Bus 12, 14, 26, 76. **Open** 9am-6pm Mon-Sat. **Credit** AmEx, MC, V.
This complete photographic store, justly famous all over the Pacific Rim, has SLR cameras by Canon and Nikon at prices that are 50% to 100% cheaper than the UK; all sorts of lenses; point-and-shoot cameras; and, according to one staff member, 'every kind of photographic doohickey you can imagine'. If you're looking for a camcorder, however, read on.

Discount Camera

33 Kearny Street, between Post and Market Streets (392 1100). BART Montgomery Street/Muni Metro F, J, K, L, M, N/2, 3, 4, 7, 8, 9, 15 bus. **Open** 8.30am-6.30pm Mon-Sat; 9.30am-6pm Sun. **Credit** AmEx, MC, V.
Concierges at all the major downtown hotels direct their guests here in the hope that they'll avoid the unscrupulous tourist traps that dot Powell Street by the cable car turn-around. It carries a full line of all major brands, but, most importantly, stocks the PAL system camcorders that British visitors need.

Fry's Electronics

340 Portage Avenue, Palo Alto (496 6000). CalTrain to California Avenue, walk to Park Boulevard, turn left to Portage Avenue. **Open** 8am-9pm Mon-Fri; 9am-9pm Sat; 9am-7pm Sun. **Credit** MC, V.
Located outside the city, in Palo Alto, home of Stamford University, Fry's sells computers for export and will ship outside the US.

International Electronics

1161/3 Mission Streets, between Seventh and Eighth Streets (626 6382). BART Civic Center/Muni Metro F, J, K, L, M, N/19, 26 bus. **Open** 9am-6pm Mon-Sat. **Credit** MC, V.

Sells Walkmans, portable CD players, mini-stereos that work in the UK and voltage converters and transformers for computers: a transformer for a laptop will cost $49-$59, for a desktop $89-$139. The shop also specialises in kitchen appliances.

Whole Earth Access

401 Bayshore Boulevard, between Oakdale and Courtland Streets (285 5244). Bus 9, 23, 24. **Open** 10am-7pm Mon-Fri; 10am-6pm Sat, Sun. **Credit** MC, V.

The computer department is small, but the sales and technical support people are well versed in what's currently available and can order almost any model you desire, although not all will be equipped with universal voltage. Whole Earth doesn't ship outside the US.

Film Processing

There are hundreds of one-hour photo shops that count on you to part with big bucks for instant developing, but if you're not impatient, the best bargains are at **Safeway** supermarkets and **Walgreens** drugstores, which offer over-night processing at amazingly low rates. You can choose large or small and single or double prints. Make the daily deadline (around 1pm) to guarantee next-day service. Check the Yellow Pages for branches.

Fox Photo 1-Hour Labs

455 Powell Street, between Sutter and Post Streets (421 8033). BART Powell Street/Muni Metro F, J, K, L, M, N/30, 45 bus/Powell-Hyde, Powell-Mason cable car. **Open** 8am-7pm Mon-Fri; 9am-5pm Sat; 10am-4pm Sun. **Credit** AmEx, MC, V.

Chain offering one-hour service on all C41 colour print film and same-day turnaround on E-6 slide processing, enlargements and other services. Cameras and photo frames are also sold, but are not too cheap. Check the Yellow Pages for branches.

Dance Instruction

For salsa and latin lessons, try Caesar's Latin Palace (*see chapter* **Clubs**); and for western dancing, go to **Rawhide II** (*see chapter* **Gay & Lesbian San Francisco**).

Metronome

1830 17th Street, at DeHaro Street (252 9000). Bus 19, 22. **Open** *office* 1-9pm. **Credit** MC, V.

Nallroom, swing, Latin, nightclub and salsa dance classes for individuals and groups. Ask about weekend dance parties.

Duty-free

Duty-free Shops

88 Grant Avenue, at Geary Street (296 3620). BART Powell Street/Muni Metro F, J, K, L, M, N/30, 38, 45 bus. **Open** 9am-9.30pm daily. **Credit** AmEx, MC, V.

Duty-free shops carry cosmetics, perfume, clothing, liquor, tobacco, food, some small electronic items and a tiny selection of cameras. At the airport branch, you will have to show your airline ticket to the sales staff; at the downtown store, they will check your ticket and give you a shopping pass. Whatever items you purchase will be waiting for you at the boarding gate of your return flight home.

Branch: San Francisco International Airport (827 8700).

Eco-correct

Used Rubber USA

597 Haight Street at Steiner Street (626 7855). Bus 6, 7, 66, 71. **Open** noon-6pm Mon, Wed-Sun. **Credit** MC, V.

Sells clothing made from recycled rubber, as well as products and clothing made from hemp.

Worldware

336 Hayes Street, between Franklin and Gough Streets (487 9030). Bus 21. **Open** 11am-6pm Tue-Fri; noon-5pm Sat, Sun. **Credit** AmEx, MC, V.

Eco-friendly clothing, bedding, cosmetics and babyclothes.

Fashion on the cheap

Definitely worth the trip out of town are the **Factory Outlets** located in Gilroy, about an hour and a quarter south of San Francisco on Highway 101; exit at the first Leavesley Road exit and turn left under the freeway. Getting there by public transport is possible but complicated and may involve an overnight stay; the easiest method is to catch a Greyhound bus (1-800 231 2222) from Transbay Terminal to Gilroy Terminal (nine buses per day; $15 one-way), then take Country Transit bus 68 to Sixth and Hanna Streets, then bus 17 to Arroyo Circle, where the outlet stores are.

There are 57 manufacturers' and designers' outlets divided into three separate sections, each with its own café. Discounts range from 20-70 per cent; in general, expect to get twice the amount of goods you would for a comparable amount of money in a department store.

The outlets vary wildly in quality. For example the **Liz Claiborne** outlet has out-of-date merchandise at minimal discounts, but the **Carole Little** and **Jones New York** outlets are terrific. **Osh Kosh** overalls for adults and children sell for around half-price, and the **Esprit** outlet is about evenly divided between adult and childrenswear. At **J Crew's** large store the discounts aren't great, but the selection is; the sales staff are helpful and the shop airy and comfortable.

Shoe manufacturers include **Timberland**, **Bass**, **Nike**, **Reebok** and **Fila**. There are also good deals to be had on sleepwear and underwear, and some on silverplate and crystal. Go on a week-day; wear comfy shoes and allow plenty of time.

The elegant **Wilkes Bashford**. *See page 145.*

Fashion

For a clothing size conversion chart, *see chapter* **Survival**. For more fashion, *see also page 137* **Department Stores**.

Ambiance
1458 Haight Street, between Ashbury and Masonic Streets (552 5095). Bus 6, 7, 66, 71. **Open** 10am-8pm Mon-Fri; 10am-7pm Sat, Sun. **Credit** AmEx, MC, V.
Sells an enormous selection of dresses, with all the appropriate accessories in a blend of vintage and modern versions: hats, bags and jewellery. There's a good mix of sizes and styles.

Bella Donna
539 Hayes Street, between Laguna and Octavia Streets (861 7182). Bus 21. **Open** 11am-7pm daily. **Credit** AmEx, MC, V.
Contemporary, hand-made clothing for the Bay Area. Straw hats by Laurel Fenenga complement linen garden party dresses. There are hand-dyed cotton stockings, antique buttons, hand-knit women's sweaters and a nice bridal department, too.

Betsey Johnson
2031 Fillmore Street, between California and Pine Streets (567 2726). Bus 3, 22. **Open** 11am-7pm Mon-Sat; noon-6pm Sun. **Credit** AmEx, MC, V.
What Mary Quant was to England, Betsey Johnson was – and is – to America. Young, clingy, pretty and outrageous clothes for women.

Cotton Basics
1301 Castro Street, 24th Street (550 8646). Bus 24. **Open** 10am-7pm Mon-Sat; 11am-6pm Sun. **Credit** AmEx, MC, V.
Simply made but fashionable, comfortable, clothing for women. All cotton, of course.

Coulars Boutique
327 Hayes Street, between Franklin and Gough Streets (255 2925). Bus 21. **Open** 11am-7pm Mon-Sat. **Credit** AmEx, MC, V.

The owner of this tiny shop has managed to assemble an exquisite selection of women's dresses, including flouncy 'romantic' styles from Marrika Nakk, a Los Angeles designer favoured by many actresses.

CP Shades
1861 Union Street, between Laguna and Octavia Streets (292 3588). Bus 41, 45. **Open** 11am-7pm Mon-Sat; 11am-6pm Sun. **Credit** AmEx, MC, V.
Half San Francisco seems to wear these loose, comfortable, colourful, washable and co-ordinated separates by a local designer.

Diana Slavin
3 Claude Lane, off Bush Street at Kearny Street (677 9939). Bus 2, 3, 4, 15, 76. **Open** 11am-6pm Tue-Fri; noon-5pm Sun. **Credit** AmEx, MC, V.
Sells beautifully cut and tailored womenswear by a much respected local designer.

Emporio Armani
1 Grant Avenue, at Market Street (677 9400/café 677 9010). BART Montgomery/Muni Metro F, J, K, L, M, N. **Open** 10am-7pm Mon-Fri; 10am-6pm Sat; noon-6pm Sun. **Credit** AmEx, MC, V.
Top of the line androgynous clothing for men and women by America's designer of choice. Stop into the café for an upmarket cappuccino experience.

The Gap
890 Market Street, at Powell Street (788 5909). BART Powell Street/Muni Metro J, K, L, M, N/6, 7, 8, 9, 21, 30, 45, 66 bus/Powell-Mason, Powell-Hyde cable car. **Open** 9.30am-8pm Mon-Sat; 10am-6pm Sun. **Credit** AmEx, MC, V.
The ubiquitous retailer of American style on the cheap. Jeans, T-shirts, sweaters, all-purpose sportswear all come at moderate prices. Check the Yellow Pages for your nearest branch.

Joshua Simon
3915 24th Street, at Sanchez Street (821 1068). Muni Metro J/48 bus. **Open** 10.30am-6.30pm Mon-Fri; 10am-6.30pm Sat; 11am-6pm Sun. **Credit** AmEx, MC, V.
Loose-fitting women's clothing in natural fibres; a large selection of Flax and Angelheart linen separates; many styles by Bluefish, a women-owned line of block-printed cottons in muted colours from New Mexico.

MAC
5 Claude Lane, off Bush Street at Kearny Street (837 0615). Bus, 2, 3, 4, 15, 76. **Open** 11am-7pm Mon-Sat; noon-5pm Sun. **Credit** AmEx, MC, V.
Trendy menswear and shoes, including Hush Puppies in lime green, grape purple and vivid puce suede.

Martha Egan
1127 Folsom Street, between Seventh and Eighth Streets (252 1072). Bus 12. **Open** 10am-4pm Mon, Tue, Sat; 10am-6pm Wed, Thur, Fri. **Credit** AmEx, MC, V.
This up-and-coming designer has her own studio and shop in SoMa, among the clubs. Women's blouses, dresses and jackets, with vintage styling in contemporary cuts, are all decorated with unique, sometimes handcut buttons. Prices are moderate.

Métier
50 Maiden Lane, between Grant Avenue and Kearny Street (989 5395). BART Montgomery Street/Muni Metro F, J, K, L, M, N/2, 3, 4, 30, 45, 76 bus. **Open** 10.30am-6.30pm Mon-Sat; noon-5pm Sun. **Credit** AmEx, MC, V.
Women's clothing in luxurious fabrics by Peter Cohen, Harriet Selwyn, Lat Naylor and others.

TOWER OUTLET
PLANET EARTH'S ENTERTAINMENT
INSTITUTE OF CHEAPOLOGY...
UNLEASHES A UNIVERSAL EXPLOSION OF BARGAINS
AN INFINITE COLLECTION
OF MASSIVELY DISCOUNTED...
CDs • BOOKS • CASSETTES • FRAMED ART
VIDEOS • BLANK TAPE • VIDEO GAMES
T-SHIRTS • ACCESSORIES
AMASSED FROM TOWER RECORDS VIDEO & BOOK STORES ALL OVER THE GLOBE.
DEFY THE GRAVITATIONAL PULL ON YOUR POCKET & EXTEND YOUR GLOBAL REACH!
TOWER OUTLET
660 3RD & TOWNSEND SAN FRANCISCO TEL: (415) 957 9660

Na Na

2276 Market Street, at Noe Street (861 6262). Muni Metro F, K, L, M/8, 37 bus. **Open** 11am-8pm Mon-Thur; 11am-8.30pm Fri, Sat; 11am-7pm Sun. **Credit** AmEx, MC, V.
Up to the minute city shoes, fashion and accessories for men and women who are actually twentysomething, or at least want to look that way.

New West

426 Brannan Street, between Third and Fourth Streets (882 4929). Bus 15, 30, 45. **Open** 10am-5pm Mon-Sat; noon-5pm Sun. **Credit** V.
If you can't afford Armani, but you like the look, this designer's sale house is the place to stop. It's in the SoMa outlet district, within walking distance of other outlets.

Nomads

556 Hayes Lane, between Laguna and Octavia Streets (864 5692). Bus 21. **Open** 11am-6pm Mon; 11am-7pm Tue-Sat; 11am-5pm Sun. **Credit** AmEx, MC, V.
Contemporary menswear in natural fabrics.

Rolo

450 Castro Street, between Market and 18th Streets (626 7171). Muni Metro F, K, L, M/35, 37 bus. **Open** 10am-9pm Mon-Sat; 10.30-7.30pm Sun. **Credit** AmEx, JCB, MC, V.
Trendy, high quality urban menswear. Check the Yellow Pages for your nearest branch.
Branches: 2351 Market Street (431 4545); 1301 Howard Street (861 1999).

TSE Cashmere

171 Post Street, between Grant Avenue and Kearny Street (391 1112). BART Montgomery Street/Muni Metro F, J, K, L, M, N/2, 3, 4, 15, 76 bus. **Open** 10am-6pm Mon-Sat. **Credit** AmEx, JCB, MC, V.
With its own farm in Mongolia and own designers and manufacturers, this outfit produces consistently wearable and elegant cashmere knits.

Wilkes Bashford

375 Sutter Street, at Stockton Street (986 4380). Bus 2, 3, 4, 76/Powell-Hyde, Powell-Mason cable car. **Open** 10am-6pm Mon-Wed, Fri, Sat; 10am-8pm Thur. **Credit** AmEx, MC, V.
Haberdasher to the stars, Wilkes Bashford has long been a fixture of the local scene. Bashford sells the best of everything, especially for men: suits, coats, evening wear, cashmere sweaters, all from top designers. A small but exquisitely chosen women's section completes the store. If you're in town on a budget, don't even think about coming here.

Zoë

2400 Fillmore Street, at Washington Street (929 0441). Bus 12, 22, 24. **Open** 11am-7pm Mon-Sat; noon-5pm Sun. **Credit** AmEx, MC, V.
Top class womenswear including vintage-look suits and blouses by Zelda and Margaret O'Leary sweaters.

Discount Fashion

There are several fashion discount outlets based in SoMa, around Third and Townsend Streets. Stop in at the **Six Sixty Factory Outlets Center** (660 Third Street, 227 0464), check out the shops and pick up a map of Market Outlets map. Within a four-block radius to the west and north, there are dozens of small outlet shops catering to every taste imaginable. When you get tired, you can stop off at the **South Park Café** for refreshments (on

Virginia Breier, *for folk art. See page 150.*

South Park, off Third Street), and then continue on to the **Burlington Coat Factory** and **Shoe Pavilion** (the best selection of discounted shoes within miles), which are both at Sixth and Howard Streets. *See also page 142.*

Loehmann's

222 Sutter Street, at Kearny Street (982 3215). BART Montgomery Street/Muni Metro F, J, K, L, M, N/2, 3, 4, 15, 76 bus. **Open** 8am-8pm Mon-Fri; 11am-7pm Sat; 11am-6pm Sun. **Credit** MC, V.
New York women who never, ever pay full price swear by this designer discount department store.

Isda and Company Outlet

29 South Park, between Second, Third, Bryant and Brannon Streets (247 0930 ext 110). Bus 15, 30, 76. **Open** 10am-5.30pm Mon-Sat. **Credit** MC, V.
Spare, simple, small-scale designs, discounted by as much as 70%.

Maraolo

404 Sutter Street, at Stockton Street (781 0895). Bus 2, 3, 4, 30, 45, 76. **Open** 10am-6pm Mon-Sat. **Credit** AmEx, DC, MC, V.
Discounts on designer shoes, including 50% off all DKNY styles. Men and women.

Vivon

424 Sutter Street, between Stockton and Powell Streets (781 2666). Bus 2, 3, 4, 30, 45, 76/Powell-Mason, Powell-Hyde cable car. **Open** 10am-7pm Mon-Sat; noon-5pm Sun. **Credit** AmEx, DC, JCB, MC, V.
Imported menswear at wholesale prices. Multicoloured Coogi sweaters, in computer-generated designs, are roughly half-price, at around $150.

Green scene

It's always fun to take visitors to a supermarket and watch their mouths drop open at the sight of the heavenly California produce sections. But the farmers' markets of the Bay Area go one better. A feast for the senses as well as the palate, with free samples and an interesting mix of fellow shoppers, they are a weekend ritual for locals.

Apart from the Ferry Plaza market, there are two other farmers' markets in the city: one in Bernal Heights at 100 Allemany Boulevard near Crescent Avenue and Putnam Street (647 9423), which operates from dawn to dusk on Saturdays, and the other, called 'Heart of the City', which is based at the UN Plaza on Seventh and Market Streets (558 9455) and operates on Wednesday and Sunday mornings.

Across the Bay Bridge, East Bay cities Oakland, Berkeley and Alameda have farmers' markets almost every day of the week. Three year-round markets in Berkeley are sponsored by the Ecology Center (phone 1-510 548 3333 for the current locations, days and times). The Tuesday afternoon market at Derby Street and

Martin Luther King Jr. Way (2-7pm), is known for its organic produce and is extremely lively and popular. If you go, watch out for the June Taylor Baking Company's hand-made marmalades and jams, which, like the farmers' markets themselves, are not to be missed.

Ferry Plaza Farmers' Market

Ferry Plaza, The Embarcadero, at Market Street (981 3004). BART Embarcadero/Muni Metro F, J, K, L, M, N/6, 7, 8, 9, 14, 21, 66. **Open** 8am-1.30pm Sat. **No credit cards.**

This is San Francisco's largest and probably best attended market. Local restaurants have booths with classes and lectures, as well as samples of the chefs' best works, and you can buy everything from a loaf of Acme bread to a clutch of tiny quail's eggs. Goat cheeses, home-made salsas, smoked salmon, fish from Monterey Bay, game birds, free range eggs, orchids, cut flowers, wild mushrooms (shiitakes, portabellas, chanterelles, morels, oyster mushrooms and porcini, depending on the season), make this market a foodie's dream come true. Locally grown produce, much of it organic, might include purple potatoes and white peaches, rainbow bell peppers, exotic salad greens like mizuma and arugula, and anything anyone can think of to grow. The market operates on a Saturday morning (and on Tuesdays during the summer) and it's best to go early to beat the crowds.

Vintage & Second-hand Clothes

The best place to look is Haight Street, where every second shop seems to specialise in bizarre and colourful garments from yesteryear.

American Rag

1305 Van Ness Avenue, between Bush and Sutter Streets (474 5214). Bus 47, 49, 76. **Open** 10am-9pm Mon-Wed; 10am-10.30pm Thur-Sat; noon-7pm Sun. **Credit** AmEx, MC, V.

Vintage clothing in excellent condition and taste. Lots of new fashion made of denim. Unisex and ultra hip.

Buffalo Exchange

1555 Haight Street, between Clayton and Ashbury Streets (431 7733). Bus 6, 7, 43, 66, 71. **Open** 11am-7pm Mon-Sat; noon-6pm Sun. **Credit** AmEx, MC, V.

Well-known second-hand recyclers in the middle of Haight. **Branches**: 1800 Polk Street, at Washington Street (346 5726); 2512 Telegraph Avenue, at Dwight Way, Berkeley (1-510 644 9202).

Thirdhand Store

1839 Divisadero Street, between Bush and Pine Streets (567 7332). Bus 2, 4, 24. **Open** noon-6pm Mon-Sat. **Credit** AmEx, MC, V.

When hippies started pulling bedspreads and curtains out of their attics in the 1960s and wearing them to dances, the Thirdhand Store was born. It's still a great place for wearable, affordable treasures, with an especially nice bridal section.

Wasteland

1660 Haight Street, at Belvedere Street (863 3150). Bus 6, 7, 66, 43, 71. **Open** 11am-7pm daily. **Credit** AmEx, MC, V.

Trendy and outrageous second-hand clothing.

Children's Clothes

See also page 137 **Department Stores** *and page 143* **Fashion**: **The Gap**.

Mudpie

1694 Union Street, at Gough Street (771 9262). Bus 41, 45. **Open** 10am-6pm Mon-Sat; 11am-5pm Sun. **Credit** AmEx, MC, V.

An utterly charming shop for clothes and toys, full of unique, hand-made and pricey gifts for privileged tots.

Peek-A-Boutique

1306 Castro Street, at 24th Street (641 6192). Bus 24, 48. **Open** 10.30am-6pm Mon-Sat; noon-5pm Sun. **Credit** MC, V.

The place to come for second-hand children's clothing.

Fashion Accessories
Leather Goods & Luggage

The Coach Store

190 Post Street, at Grant Avenue (392 1772). BART Montgomery Street/Muni Metro F, J, K, L, M, N/2, 3, 4 bus. **Open** 9.30am-7pm Mon-Fri; 9.30am-6pm Sat; noon-5pm Sun. **Credit** AmEx, JCB, MC, V.

The place to buy those Coach handbags worn by all-American legends in the endless advertising campaign.

Johnson Leather Corp

1833 Polk Street, between Jackson and Washington Streets (775 7392). Bus 12, 30, 47, 49. **Open** 10.30am-6.30pm Mon-Sat; noon-5pm, Sun. **Credit** AmEx, JCB, MC, V.

Both a factory and a shop, which means you can get good buys on lambskin unisex jackets and have your alterations done while you wait.

Mark Cross

170 Post Street, between Grant Avenue and Kearny Street (391 7770). BART Montgomery Street/Muni Metro F, J, K, L, M, N/2, 3, 4 bus. **Open** 10am-6pm Mon-Sat; noon-5pm Sun. **Credit** AmEx, JCB, MC, V.

Small items of expensive Italian leather.

North Beach Leather

190 Geary Street, at Stockton Street (362 8300). BART Montgomery, Powell Streets/Muni Metro F, J, K, L, M, N/2, 3, 4, 30, 38, 45 bus. **Open** 10am-7pm Mon-Sat; noon-5pm Sun. **Credit** AmEx, MC, V.

The walls are covered with photos of celebrities wearing multicoloured jackets and tight-fitting dresses in NBL's signature styles.

Tannery West

San Francisco Shopping Center (227 0140). BART Powell Street/Muni Metro F, J, K, L, M, N/7, 8, 66 bus. **Open** 9.30am-8pm Mon-Sat; 11am-6pm Sun. **Credit** AmEx, MC, V.

Leather here comes in fancy beaded and fringed styles. The classic black motorcycle jacket, in better than usual quality, goes for $150-$200.

Lingerie

See also page 137.

Victoria's Secret

1 Embarcadero Center, at Sacramento and Drumm Streets (433 9473). BART Embarcadero/Muni Metro F, J, K, L, M, N/1, 41, 42 bus. **Open** 10am-7pm Mon-Fri; 10am-5pm Sat; noon-5pm Sun. **Credit** AmEx, MC, V.

The standard mall chain has nosed out everyone else in this area; their soft porn catalogues haven't hurt sales, either.

Luggage Repair

The Luggage Center

828 Mission Street, between Fourth and Fifth Streets (543 3771). BART Powell Street/Muni Metro F, J, K, L, M, N/14, 26, 45 bus. **Open** 9.30am-6pm Mon-Sat; 11.30am-5pm Sun. **Credit** AmEx, MC, V.

Luggage professionals will either repair your busted bag or guarantee you the lowest price on a new one.

Shoes

Arthur Beren Shoes

222 Stockton Street, at Maiden Lane (397 8900). Bus 30, 45/Powell-Mason, Powell-Hyde cable car. **Open** 9.30am-6.30pm Mon-Wed; 9.30am-7pm Thur, Fri; 9.30am-6pm Sat. **Credit** AmEx, JCB, MC, V.

Classic, high quality footwear, specialising in Cole-Haan and comfortable Arche shoes from France.

Bulo

437A Hayes Street, at Gough Street (864 3244). Bus 21. **Open** 11am-6pm Mon-Sat; noon-5pm Sun. **Credit** AmEx, MC, V.

Imported Italian shoes in the latest styles.

Bruno Magli

285 Geary Street, at Powell Street (421 0356). Bus 2, 3, 4, 38, 76/Powell-Mason, Powell-Hyde cable car. **Open** 9.30am-6.30pm Mon-Wed; 9.30am-7pm Thur, Fri; 9.30am-6pm Sat; 11.30am-5.30pm Sun. **Credit** AmEx, DC, JCB, MC, V.

Follow in OJ's footsteps with these élite Italian men's shoes.

Daljeets

1744 Haight Street, at Cole Street (752 5610). Muni Metro L/7, 33, 37, 43 bus. **Open** 11am-7pm daily. **Credit** AmEx, MC, V.

Doc Marten's, the basic British shoe for many a city outfit, have inspired American designers no end. This is where to find 'em.

Gimme Shoes

416 Hayes Street, at Gough Street (864 0691). Bus 21. **Open** 11am-6pm Mon-Sat; noon-5pm Sun. **Credit** AmEx, MC, V.

European designer shoes for men and women. Also stockists of hard-to-find trainers by Adidas and other elusive manufacturers.

Kenneth Cole

2078 Union Street, at Webster Street (346 2161). Bus 41, 45. **Open** 10am-8pm Mon-Sat; 11am-6pm Sun. **Credit** AmEx, MC, V.

Black, black and more black. Also backpacks and boots (in black).

22 Steps

280 Sutter Street, at Grant Avenue (398 7797). Bus 2, 3, 4, 76. **Open** 10am-6pm Mon-Sat. **Credit** AmEx, MC, V.

The hippest, most up-to-date styles for both men and women, in a wild environment that defies description.

Shoe Repair

Elite Shoe Repair

1614 Haight Street, at Clayton Street (863 3260). Bus 6, 7, 66, 71. **Open** 9.30am-6pm Mon-Sat. **No credit cards.**

This Haight-Ashbury establishment comes highly recommended by shoe gurus at the trendy Bulo shoe shop (*see above*).

Florists

Ixia

2331 Market Street, between Castro and Noe Streets (431 3134). Muni Metro F, K, L, M, N/8, 37, 35 bus. **Open** 9am-6.30pm Mon-Fri; 11am-6pm Sat. **Credit** AmEx, MC, V.

You should at least window shop at this Castro shop – the likes of the living plant and flower sculptures have never been seen. The window displays are changed weekly.

Pappas at the Plaza

1255 Battery Street, at Filbert Street (434 1313). Bus 39, 42. **Open** 8.30am-5.30pm Mon-Fri. **Credit** AmEx, MC, V.

This tiny shop magically builds bouquets into structural masterpieces. While the flowers are sure to dazzle the recipient, they may also stun your wallet.

Podesta Baldocchi

475 Sansome Street, at Clay Street (288 1300). Bus 1, 30X, 42. **Open** 7am-6pm Mon-Fri. **Credit** AmEx, DC, MC, V.

Everyone's favourite local source for floral arrangements and live plants. With 130 years in business under its belt, you can expect exceptional arrangements. Pricey but worth it.

Food & Drink

Bakeries

Boudin Sourdough Bakery & Café

2890 Taylor Street, at Jefferson Street (776 1849). Bus 32, 39/Powell-Mason cable car. **Open** 7.30am-8pm daily. **Credit** AmEx, MC, V.

Stop in for a fresh loaf of San Francisco's famous sourdough bread. Boudin will deliver all over the world: check the Yellow Pages for the branch nearest to you.

Become a dedicated follower of fashion at **Arthur Beren Shoes**. *See page 147.*

Cake Gallery
*2909 Ninth Street at Folsom Street (861 2253). Bus 9,
12.* **Open** 9am-6pm Mon-Sat. **Credit** AmEx, MC, V.
San Francisco's eclectic artistic community is personified
here by cake decorators who recreate a traditional dessert as
anything from a panda bear to an enormous chocolate penis.
If you are looking for an unusual cake, talk to the folks here.
There's nothing they can't do with their custom shaped and
designed edible masterpieces.

Dianda Italian American Pastry
*2883 Mission Street, at 24th Street (647 5469). BART
24th Street/14, 48, 49 bus.* **Open** 5am-5pm daily. **No
credit cards.**
Delight your taste buds with cream-filled Italian cakes and
pastries. Eat in or take away.

Just Desserts
*3 Embarcadero, between Sacramento and Davies Streets
(421 1609). BART Embarcadero/Muni Metro F, J, K, L,
M, N/32 bus.* **Open** 7am-7pm Mon-Fri; 10am-5pm Sat;
noon-5pm Sun. **Credit** MC, V.
A good bet for last-minute birthday cakes, this bakery and
café makes some of the best chocolate gateaux and poppy-
seed cakes in town. Check the Yellow Pages for your nearest
branch.

La Victoria
*2937 Alabama Street, at 24th Street (550 9292). Bus 12,
27, 48.* **Open** 7am-10pm daily. **No credit cards.**
A real Mexican bakery in the heart of the Mission district.

Stella Pastry & Caffe
*446 Columbus Avenue, between Green and Vallejo
Streets (986 2914). Bus 15, 41.* **Open** 7.30am-8pm Mon-
Thur, Sun; 7.30am-midnight Fri, Sat. **No credit cards.**
Famous for its St Honoré cake, a gooey rum-soaked delight.

Tassajara Bread Bakery
*1000 Cole Street, at Parnassus Avenue (664 8947).
Muni Metro J/6, 37, 43 bus.* **Open** 7am-10pm Mon-Sat;
8am-10pm Sun. **Credit** MC, V.
This neighbourhood favourite continues to bake the freshest breads, cakes and pastries. It was recently taken over by
Just Desserts (*see above*).

Beer & Wine

Brew City
*2198 Filbert Street, at Fillmore Street (929 2255). Bus
22, 41, 45.* **Open** 11am-6pm Mon, Sun; 11am-10pm Tue-
Sat. **Credit** AmEx, MC, V.
Follow dozens of recipes and brew yourself silly at San
Francisco's first and best public brewing facility.

Trader Joe's
*555 Ninth Street, between Bryant and Brannan Streets
(863 1292). Bus 19, 27, 42.* **Open** 9am-9pm daily.
Credit AmEx, MC, V.
This upmarket wine, beer and gourmet and health food
grocery store is part of a chain that is beginning to define
California's consumer culture. You'll find delicious organic
goods, healthy fast food, and the least expensive but best
tasting selection of wine and beer in the city.

The Wine Club
*953 Harrison Street, between Eighth and Ninth Streets
(512 9086). Bus 19, 37, 42.* **Open** 9am-7pm Mon-Sat;
11am-6pm Sun. **Credit** MC, V.
While you can sample great varietals in almost every restaurant in town, you will undoubtedly want to pick up a few
bottles of California's best to take on a picnic or back home.
The Wine Club offers some of the greatest bargains around,
with prices ranging from $3.99 to $1,100 per bottle. Don't be

intimidated if you're not a connoisseur – the club's knowledgeable staff will guide you through the 1,200 options to
the right wine for your tastes. Since they only mark-up
wholesale prices by 6-12%, you'll get better deals here than
you will at the wineries.

Gourmet Groceries

Casa Lucas Market
*2934 24th Street, between Alabama and Florida Streets
(826 4334). BART 24th Street/48, 67 bus.* **Open** 7am-
7.30pm daily. **No credit cards.**
Produce, groceries and spices used in Mexican cooking, with
imported Latin tinned goods and numerous types of chilli
pepper.

Haig's Delicacies
*642 Clement Street, at Eighth Avenue (752 6283). Bus 2,
4, 38.* **Open** 9.30am-6.30pm Mon-Fri; 9am-6pm Sat.
Credit MC, V.
British food, Middle Eastern goods, Indian spices and all
manner of exotic flavourings.

Molinari Delicatessen
*373 Columbus Avenue, at Vallejo Street (421 2337). Bus
15, 41.* **Open** 8am-6pm Mon-Fri; 7.30am-5.30pm Sat. **No
credit cards.**
Molinari was dishing out home-made pasta and *pesto alla
genovese* long before yuppies ever heard of the stuff, and it's
still going strong.

Real Foods
*2164 Polk Street, at Vallejo Street (775 2805). Bus 27,
42, 47, 49, 76 bus.* **Open** 8am-8pm daily. **Credit** MC, V.
Strong on prepared dishes – from casseroles to puddings –
this gourmet deli is ideal for stocking up for a picnic.
Branch: 2929 24th Street, between Sanchez and Noe (282
9500).

Some Like it Hot, A Fiery Food Emporium
*3208 Hyde Street, between Chestnut and Lombard
Streets (441 7468). Bus 30, 42/Powell-Hyde cable car.*
Open 11am-6pm daily. **Credit** MC, V.
As the name suggests, they stock over 350 types of spicy
sauce here: salsas, barbecues, bottled hot sauces from around
the world, chutneys, mustards, and every conceivable product that a chilli pepper can flavour.

Food Delivery

Many of the smaller restaurants in the city offer
free delivery services (although a tip of 15 per cent
is customary), so they are worth watching out for
on your travels. *See also chapter* **Restaurants**.

Dine One One
*2075 Van Ness Avenue, at Pacific Avenue (928 3278).
Bus 12, 42, 47, 49, 83.* **Open** 9am-11pm daily. **Credit**
AmEx, MC, V.
This restaurant delivery service brings dishes
from more than 75 restaurants to your doorstep. Open daily
for lunch and dinner, serving any silver-walleted soul within the city limits.

North Beach Pizza
1499 Grant Avenue, at Union Street (433 2444). Bus 39.
Open 11am-midnight Mon-Thur; 11am-3am Fri, Sat;
noon-midnight Sun. **Credit** AmEx, MC, V.
Some argue that it's overrated, but a huge and loyal crowd
of San Franciscans order only from this pizza parlour.
There's a take away and delivery service and five city-wide
locations; ring for details of the one nearest you.

Waiters on Wheels
425 Divisadero Street, at Oak Street (252 1470). Bus 6, 7, 66, 71. **Open** 11am-11pm daily. **Credit** AmEx, MC, V.
Like Dine One One, this service delivers restaurant fare to your home – for a price.

Tea & Coffee
Caffè Trieste sells coffee beans blended and roasted to your specification, as well as coffee-making equipment (*see chapter* **Bars & Cafés**); so do the chains **Peet's Coffee & Tea** and the **Spinelli Coffee Company** (check the Yellow Pages for your nearest branch).

Ten Ren Tea Company of San Francisco
949 Grant Avenue, between Washington and Jackson Streets (362 0656). Bus 1, 15, 31, 45/California cable car. **Open** 9am-9pm daily. **Credit** AmEx, MC, V.
This charming shop stocks around 40 different types of Chinese tea, from the leaves recommended for an ordinary cuppa, to the expensive infusions kept for special occasions, like patching up a quarrel with your neighbour. Taste before you buy.

Graffeo Coffee Roasting Company
735 Columbus Avenue, at Filbert Street (986 2429/ 1-800 222 6250). Bus 15, 30, 41/Powell-Mason cable car. **Open** 9am-6pm Mon-Fri; 9am-5pm Sat.* **Credit** MC, V.
A long-standing North Beach shop.

Gifts & Stationery
See also **Arts & Crafts** *above.*

The Balloon Lady
1263 Howard Street, between Eighth and Ninth Streets (864 3737). Bus 12, 19, 47. **Open** 8.30am-5.30pm Mon-Sat; 10am-2pm Sun. **Credit** AmEx, MC, V.
Amazingly creative balloon bouquets and structures are created out of 100 per cent biodegradable latex. Balloons can be delivered for any occasion. Prices range from $29.95-$59.95, with delivery by a tuxedo-clad man.

Cost Plus Imports
2552 Taylor Street, at North Point Street (928 6200). Bus 39, 42. **Open** 9am-9pm daily. **Credit** MC, V.
With a constantly changing mix of over 20,000 products from more than 40 countries – including exotic collectables such as statues and masks, dinner and glassware, gourmet foodstuffs, clothing and accessories, baskets and kitchenware – Cost Plus is a San Francisco landmark. A great place to buy unusual and inexpensive gifts, especially small ones.

Quantity Postcards
1441 Grant Avenue, between Union and Green Streets (986 8866). Bus 15, 30, 39, 41. **Open** 11am-11pm Mon-Thur, Sun; 11am-12.30am, Fri, Sat. **No credit cards.**
An incredible selection of new and vintage postcards, including quaint Victorian flowery tributes and domestic scenes from the 1950s, as well as tinted landscapes of far-away places. Also a good selection of Frank Kozik's music posters.

Tail of the Yak Trading Company
2632 Ashby Avenue at College Avenue, Berkeley (1-510 841 9891). BART Rockridge. **Open** 11am-5.30pm Mon-Sat. **Credit** MC, V.
Antique jewellery from Europe and Mexico, French ribbons,

fabulous paper knick-knacks, religious memorabilia, post-cards, in a beautiful and unique shop. Worth the trip to Berkeley.

Virginia Breier
3091 Sacramento Street, at Baker Street (929 7173). Bus 1, 3. **Open** 11am-6pm Mon-Sat; noon-5pm Sun. **Credit** MC, V.
A folk art gallery, specialising in the works of local artists. A good place for one-of-a-kind gifts. *See also chapter* **Museums & Galleries**.

Glass

Compositions
317 Sutter Street, between Grant Avenue and Stockton Street (693 9111). Bus 2, 3, 4, 30, 45, 76. **Open** 10am-6pm Mon-Sat. **Credit** AmEx, DC, MC, V.
A gallery of blown glass art.

de Vera
384 Hayes Street at Gough Street (861 8480). Muni Metro J, K, L, M, N/21 42 47, 49 bus. **Open** noon-6pm Tue-Sat. **Credit** AmEx, MC, V.
Federico de Vera sells contemporary, 1950s and 1960s Italian and Swedish glass from this Hayes Valley shop.
Branch: 334 Gough Street, at Hayes Street (558 8865).

Health & Beauty
Bath Houses

Kabuki Hot Springs
Japan Center, 1750 Geary Boulevard, at Fillmore Street (922 6002). Bus 22, 38. **Open** 10am-10pm Mon-Fri; 9am-10pm Sat, Sun. **Admission** day pass without massage $10; day pass with 25-minute massage $35; baths, steam and 55-minute massage $60. **Credit** AmEx, MC, V.
A traditional Japanese bath house, complete with deep ceramic communal tubs, a steam room, sit-down showers, saunas and even a restful tatami room. Massages are given between 2pm and 9.30pm on weekdays, 10am-9.30pm weekends, and are by appointment only. Women-only days are on Wednesday, Friday and Sunday; it's men-only the rest of the week. Spend an hour here and you'll come out feeling like a champ.

Osento
955 Valencia Street, at 21st Street (282 6333). Muni Metro J/14, 26, 49 bus. **Open** 1pm-1am daily; last admission midnight. **Admission** $7-$11. **No credit cards.**
A bath house for women only. Walk in to the peaceful surroundings, leave your clothes in a locker, shower off and relax in the whirlpool. Take a dip in the cold plunge, and then choose between the wet and dry saunas. An outdoor deck offers the chance to cool down or enjoy the weather on a sunny day. Massages are available by appointment.

Chinese Herbalist

Vinh Khang Herbs & Gensengs
512 Clement Street, between Sixth and Seventh Avenues (752 8336). Bus 2, 44. **Open** 9.30am-7pm daily. **No credit cards.**
Chinese herbalism is one of the hottest trends in alternative medicine and this shop is open seven days a week to cater for the city's ills. Inspect the splendid array of roots and remedies as the herbal specialists mix up a customised concoction of ancient remedies to cure what ails you.

Cosmetics & Beauty Products

The Body Shop
865 Market Street, between Fourth and Fifth Streets (281 3760). BART Powell Street/Muni Metro F, J, K, L, M, N/8 bus. **Open** *9.30am-8.30pm Mon-Sat; 11am-6pm Sun.* **Credit** *AmEx, DC, MC, V.*
The Californians' love affair with pampering themselves has definitely been a blessing to the Body Shop – out of almost 250 stores nationwide, you'll find at least 40 in the Golden State offering skin and hair care products that smell so good, you might be tempted to taste them (don't). Aside from the scented slew of moisturising creams, soaps, and scrubs, the company's would-be eco principles keep them in the public's favour.
Branches: 2106 Chestnut, between Pierce and Steiner Streets (202 0112); 215 California Street, in the Embarcadero Center, (397 7455); 506 Castro Street, at 18th Street (431 8860).

MAC on Union
1833 Union Street, between Laguna and Octavia Streets (771 6113). BART Montgomery Street/Muni Metro F, J, K, L, M, N/2, 3, 4, 38, 45, 76 bus/Powell-Mason, Powell-Hyde cable car. **Open** *noon-7pm Mon-Sat; noon-6pm Sun.* **Credit** *AmEx, MC, V.*
This gigantic, well-lit shop carries natural look cosmetics formerly available only in the top department stores.

Hair Salons

Architects and Heroes
580 Bush Street, between Grant Avenue and Stockton Street (391 8833). Bus 2, 3, 4, 15, 76. **Open** *9am-6pm Tue-Sat.* **Credit** *MC, V.*
There are plenty of $10 cuts available at small hairdressers throughout the city, but if you want a hair experience, book in advance for a cut with one of this salon's professionals. The pre-cut shampoo is more like a luxurious head massage (and will probably lull you to sleep). If you don't have lots of cash, ask if any trainees are available for cuts or colouring; even the novices here are top-notch.

Pink Tarantula
71 Langton Street, between Seventh and Eighth Streets (626 3636). Bus 12, 14, 27, 42. **Open** *9.30am-7pm Tue-Sat.* **No credit cards.**
Don't let the name fool you. The only black hairy thing moving around in this SoMa salon is the long mane of the owner and stylist called Carmel. You will encounter a few arachnid trinkets, but the real eye-catcher is the salon's décor – a mishmash of toy trolls and ceramic deco-style fish, amidst an airbrushed Day-Glo world of flying creatures and slack-jawed aliens. Carmel and her group of in-the-know hair designers will do virtually anything – from extensions and colour to

Get in line at **Architects and Heroes**.

retro hair ensembles. You won't leave looking like a punk rocker unless you want to. Best of all (and most uncommon), it's reasonably priced.

Manicures & Pedicures

As in most big cities, there are hundreds of small boutiques in San Francisco offering manicures, pedicures and waxes (consult the Yellow Pages for a full list). Expect to pay $8-$12 for a manicure and $10-$15 for a pedicure. Salon prices are substantially higher, but if it's pampering you're after, they're your best bet.

77 Maiden Lane
Second Floor, 77 Maiden Lane, between Grant Avenue and Kearny Street (391 7777). Bus 12, 15, 30, 30X, 41, 45. **Open** *9am-7pm Mon-Sat; 11am-4pm Sun.* **Credit** *MC, V.*
If you've got $40 to spare, treat yourself to the hour-long heavenly pedicure here and you'll have a new spring in your step. Recently renovated and expanded, this full-service salon runs the pampering gamut, including massage, makeovers, hair styling and facials. It's not the cheapest place in town, but the services come highly recommended.

Spas, Saunas & Retreats

There are a number of health and fitness centres in San Francisco itself, but if you want a relaxing escape from the city, head for the mud baths, mineral spas and massages in the historic small town of Calistoga in the Wine Country. Recommended spas are **Dr Wilkinson's Hot Springs** (1-707 942 4102) and **Calistoga Spa Hot Springs** (1-707 942 6269). A little further north of Calistoga is **Harbin Hot Springs** (1-707 987 2477), near Middletown in Lake County. *See also chapter* **Trips Out of Town**.

Claremont Resort and Spa
Ashby and Domingo Avenues, Oakland (1-510 843 3000). BART Rockridge, then bus 65. **Open** *for telephone enquiries* 24-hours daily. **Rates** $165-$700 depending on room and services. **Credit** AmEx, MC, V.
If you want a spa retreat but don't want a long drive or the high prices of Wine Country getaways, head to this East Bay haven. In summer, when the city is blanketed in fog, the Claremont basks in sunshine and visitors soak up the rays alongside the enormous outdoor pool. Services include mud body wraps, glycolic acid treatments, waxing, a hair salon, tennis, swimming and fitness programmes.

Family Sauna
2308 Clement Street, at 24th Avenue (221-2208). Bus 2, 29, 38. **Open** *noon-10pm daily.* **Credit** *MC, V.*
Everyone has good things to say about this very mellow neighbourhood retreat offering dry-heat Finnish saunas, two therapeutic whirlpool spas (the redwood tub retains heat better but the fibreglass option has more leg room), massage, facials, and waxing. Unlike most of the city's spas, there's no pretension here (and subsequently cheaper prices), only a casual, clean, and comfortable environment where all types of San Franciscans come to cleanse their body and mind in a private hot tub (fitting up to 3 people).

Green Gulch
Green Gulch Farm, 1601 Shoreline Highway, Sausalito (383 3134). Golden Gate Transit bus 4 to Tam Junction, then cab. **Open** *office 9am-4pm daily.* **Rates** *Single* small room $55-$105; large room $70-$120. **No credit cards.**

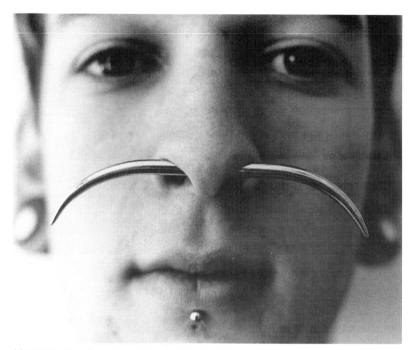

It's never easy, plugging into the zeitgeist. *Look sharp at* **Body Manipulations**.

A short drive across the Golden Gate and a few winding roads later, you'll find yourself at this deservedly popular Buddhist getaway. Whether you want to meditate, hike or just mellow out, the tranquillity and reasonable prices can't be beaten.

Spa Nordstrom

San Francisco Shopping Center, 865 Market Street, at Fifth Street (978 5102). BART Powell Street/Muni Metro F, J, K, L, M, N/6, 7, 27, 31, 66, 71 bus/Powell-Mason, Powell-Hyde cable car. **Open** 9am-7pm Mon-Sat; 10.15am-5.45pm Sun. **Credit** AmEx, MC, V.

When you're struggling for air in the middle of hundreds of shoppers at this downtown shopping centre, you'd never know that rejuvenation is just a few floors away. But the minute you collapse through the door of this spa, you leave the hectic retail pace behind you. Soak your shopping-tired feet in a warm tub before going to a private room to indulge in one of many restorative services, ranging from aromatherapy, massage and skin care spa packages, to an eyebrow or bikini wax. Save the manicure for the small – and cheaper – independents.

Tattooing & Body Piercing

What the hell. You're in San Francisco.

Anubis Warpus

1525 Haight Street, at Ashbury Street (431 2218). Bus 6, 7, 43, 66, 71. **Open** 11am-8pm Mon-Thur; noon-9pm Fri-Sun. **Credit** AmEx, MC, V.

Tattooing, body piercing, body art jewellery, Manic Panic hair dyes and make-up.

Body Manipulations

254 Fillmore Street, at Haight Street (621 0408). Bus 6, 7, 22, 66, 71. **Open** noon-6.30pm daily. **Credit** MC, V.

A typically Haight Street service, specialising in custom body piercing, scarring, branding, tattooing and just about anything else that can be done to the human body. Although it may sound like a back-alley business, the shop's owners take their profession very seriously – the white-washed office is painfully sanitary and a professional medical consultant is on hand.

Ed Hardy's Tattoo City

722 Columbus Avenue, between Filbert and Greenwich Streets (433 9437). Bus 15, 39. **Open** noon-8pm Mon-Sat; noon-7pm Sun. **Credit** MC, V.

A feast for the *aficionado* offering some of the most spectacular designs in the city; it's all in the eye of the beholder after all.

Gauntlet

2377 Market Street, at Castro Street (431 3133). Muni Metro F, K, L, M/8, 24 bus. **Open** 2-7pm Mon-Wed, Fri, Sat; noon-9pm Thur; noon-6pm Sun. **Credit** AmEx, MC, V.

It seems tattooing is almost passé now that body piercing, the latest in corporal decoration, has gone mainstream. But it's not new fashion to these experts who have been piercing everything from noses to labia for over 20 years. The possibilities and types of body jewellery you can acquire here goes far beyond a measly nose or navel ring. But if you're into it, this is the place to get yourself a new hole or two. This branch is located in the heart of the Castro – there are others in Los Angeles, New York, Paris, and Chicago.

Lyle Tuttle Tattooing

841 Columbus Avenue, at Greenwich Street (775 4991). Bus 15, 30/Powell-Mason cable car. **Open** noon-9pm Mon-Thur; noon-10pm Fri, Sat; noon-8pm Sun. **Credit** AmEx, MC, V.

Lyle Tuttle is one of the most respected tattoo artists in the world, and for those in the know, this parlour is an essential stop-off point. It's best to make an appointment in advance.

Household

Also worth checking out is the ancient, chaotic but well-stocked hardware store, **Workingman's Headquarters** at 2817 Mission Street near 24th Street (282 2403).

Centrium Furnishings

2166 Market Street, between Church and Sanchez Streets (863 4195). Muni Metro F, J, K, L, M. **Open** noon-6pm Tue-Sat; 1-5pm Sun. **Credit** AmEx, MC, V.

Furniture, lighting and decorative arts from the 1930s to the 1970s.

Crate & Barrel

125 Grant Avenue, at Geary Street (986 4000). Bus 2, 3, 4, 38, 76. **Open** 10am-7pm Mon-Fri; 10am-6pm Sat; 11am-5pm Sun. **Credit** AmEx, MC, V.

Simple, clean-lined functional designs for the home.

Fillamento

2185 Fillmore Street, at Sacramento Street (931 2224). Bus 1, 3, 22. **Open** 10am-7pm Mon-Fri; 10am-6pm Sat, Sun. **Credit** AmEx, MC, V.

Elegant dishes, glassware, lamps, home furnishings and a few nice things to wear, such as silk pajamas in their own travelling case. It's not unusual to see visitors from other cities – like LA – return home with shopping bags full of goodies from this store.

Naomi's Antiques to Go

1817 Polk Street, between Washington and Jackson Streets (775 1207). Bus 12, 19, 27. **Open** 11am-6pm Tue-Sat. **Credit** MC, V.

Classic American dinner ware and collectable pottery.

Jewellery & Watches

See also page 137 **Department Stores** *and page 147* **Fashion Accessories**.

Di Lelio's

San Francisco Shopping Center, 865 Market Street, at Fifth Street (243 9784). BART Powell Street/Muni Metro F, J, K, L, M, N/6, 7, 8, 9, 21, 27, 31, 66 bus. **Open** 9.30am-8pm Mon-Sat; 11am-6pm Sun. **Credit** AmEx, MC, V.

Antique jewellery and *objets d'art*.

The Jerusalem Shop

531 Castro Street, between 18th and 19th Streets (626 7906). Bus 24. **Open** 10am-8.30pm Mon-Thur; 10am-9pm Fri, Sat; 10am-6pm Sun. **Credit** AmEx, MC, V.

This little women's clothing and jewellery shop has been lauded as the best in town for handcrafted jewellery. The selection is wide ranging, with an emphasis on silver and semi-precious stones.

Lang

323 Sutter Street, between Stockton Street and Grant Avenue (982 2213). BART Montgomery Street/Muni

Fillamento, *for the relaxed shopper.*

Metro F, J, K, L, M, N/2, 3, 4, 76 bus. **Open** 10am-5pm Mon-Sat. **Credit** AmEx, DC, JCB, MC, V.

Stocks an extensive selection of antique and estate jewellery and lots of old silver.

Opals & Gems of Australia

San Francisco Shopping Center, 865 Market Street, at Fifth Street (543 3160). BART Powell Street/Muni Metro F, J, K, L, M, N/6, 7, 8, 9, 21, 27, 31, 66 bus. **Open** 9.30am-6pm Mon-Wed; 9.30am-8pm Thur-Sat; 11am-6pm Sun. **Credit** AmEx, DC, MC, V.

A glittering array of jewellery, from the fiery to the pale. Some inexpensive gifts.

Zeitgeist

437B Hayes Street at Gough Street (864 0185). BART Van Ness/Muni Metro F, J, K, L, M, N. **Open** noon-6pm Tue-Sat. **Credit** MC, V.

The place to come for second-hand watches, including Philippe Patek and Rolex.

Laundrettes & Dry Cleaners

Brainwash

1122 Folsom Street, between Seventh and Eighth Streets (café 861 3663/laundromat 431 9274). Bus 12, 27, 42. **Open** 7.30am-11pm Mon-Thur, Sun; 7.30am-1am Fri, Sat. **Credit** AmEx, MC, V.

San Francisco's first and only café/cabaret/laundromat was established in 1989 and has been a trendy neighbourhood gathering spot ever since. Rock out with the latest CDs and live music at the weekend, and indulge in an espresso, a glass of wine or some pasta while you throw your clothes into a machine or have them dry cleaned. For the frequent cabaret performances and experimental shows, *see* **Above Brainwash** *in chapter* **Theatre & Dance**.

Locust Cleaners

3585 Sacramento Street, between Locust and Laurel Streets (346 9271). Bus 1, 3, 4. **Open** 7.30am-6pm Mon-Fri; 8.30am-5pm Sat. **No credit cards.**

Locust may not be as convenient (or as cheap) as the downtown one-day cleaning operations, but if you want quality alterations, then bring your garments here.

Meaders Cleaners

1475 Sansome Street, at Lombard Street (781 8200). Bus 42. **Open** 7am-7pm Mon-Fri; 8.30am-5pm Sat. **Credit** MC, V.

In the washing and scrubbing business since 1912, Meaders Cleaners offers a reliable dry cleaning and cleaning service from four different locations in the city. Phone for your nearest branch.

Religion, New Age & Magic

Botanica Yoruba
998 Valencia Street, at 21st Street (826 4967). BART 24th Street/14, 26, 49 bus. **Open** 10am-6pm Mon-Fri; 10am-6.30pm Sat; noon-5pm Sun. **No credit cards.**
Candles, potions, powders, oils, herbs, statues of saints – everything you need for the practice of Santeria, the African-Cuban religion practiced in some Latin countries.

The Enchanted Crystal
1895 Union Street, at Laguna Street (885 1335). Bus 41, 45. **Open** 10am-6pm Mon-Sat; noon-5pm Sun. **Credit** AmEx, JCB, MC, V.
Crystals of every description: geodes, pendants, jewels. Lots of little fairies and magical things.

Opticians

City Optix
2154 Chestnut Street, between Pierce and Steiner Streets (921 1188). Bus 22, 28, 43, 76. **Open** 10am-6pm Mon-Wed, Sat; 10am-8pm Thur; noon-6pm Sun. **Credit** MC, V.
Sometimes shopping for new frames in this comprehensive store can feel like a group project – customers advise each other on their look and the staff are helpful. You might come out a new person.

Site for Sore Eyes
901 Market Street, at Fifth Street (495 2020). Bus 6, 7, 8, 9, 21, 27, 66. **Open** 9am-6.30pm Mon-Sat; 11am-5pm Sun. **Credit** AmEx, MC, V.
Contact lenses or glasses, sunglasses and special orders. There are over 3,000 frames in stock.

Pumpkin seeks Honeybunny

For a real insight into what's going on in the Bay Area, pick up a free copy of the *Bay Guardian* from a newsstand (located on nearly every street corner), turn to the Personals at the back and indulge in some racy entertainment. 'The Bay Area's #1 Choice for Romance' is where to read about the 'Tough Hairy Muscle' in search of a 'similarly tough, hairy buddy', the 'Uppity Woman interested in meeting a lesbian woman comfortable with her sexuality' or even the 'pro-absurdity goth bookworm' sought by one whom the Pope asks for pointers on celibacy. If you're feeling adventurous or bored, you might want to reply to an ad that grabs you: if nothing else, you'll probably get a great tour guide out of the deal. Phone responses are charged at $1.89 per minute. If, on the other hand you just want to get on-line, obtain a fast divorce or kick your coke habit, turn to the back page bulletin board.

Picture Framing

The Painter's Place
355 Hayes Street, between Franklin and Gough Streets (431 9827). Muni Metro F, J, K, L, M, N/21, 42, 47, 49 bus. **Open** 10am-4pm Mon, Sat; 10am-6pm Tue-Fri. **Credit** AmEx, MC, V.
The place to visit when you just can't wait to get your favourite print or artwork behind glass.

Records, Tapes & CDs

Ritmo Latino
241 Mission Street, at 20th Street (824 8556). BART 24th Street/15, 49 bus. **Open** 10am-9.30pm Mon-Thur, Sun; 10am-midnight Fri, Sat. **Credit** AmEx, DC, JCB, MC, V.
Got a yen for some salsa dancing? This is the spot for Latin music.

Reckless Records
1401 Haight Street, at Masonic Street (431 3434). Muni Metro L/37 bus. **Open** 10am-10pm Mon-Sat; 10am-9pm Sun. **Credit** MC, V.
Secondhand CDs, vinyl and tapes: indie, hip hop and soul.

Rasputin's
2401 Telegraph Avenue, at Channing Street, Berkeley (1-510 848 9004). BART Berkeley. **Open** 10am-11pm daily. **Credit** AmEx, DC, JCB, MC, V.
A vast and cavernous space full of new and second-hand records, tapes and CDs, including many imported labels.

Star Classics
1401 Haight Street, at Masonic Street (552 1110). Bus 6, 7, 66, 71, 43, 48. **Open** 10am-10pm Mon-Sat; 10am-9pm Sun. **Credit** AmEx, DC, JCB, MC, V.
The classical music specialists. *See chapter* **Music: Classical & Opera** for more classical music shops.

Streetlight Records
3979 24th Street, between Sanchez and Noe Streets (282 3550). Bus 48. **Open** 10am-10pm Mon-Sat; 10.30am-8.30pm Sun. **Credit** AmEx, MC, V.
For the used and the rare. Moneyback guaranteed.
Branch: 2350 Market Street, Castro Street (282 8000).

Tower Records
Columbus Avenue, at Bay Street (885 0500). Bus 15, 41/Powell-Mason cable car. **Open** 9am-midnight daily. **Credit** AmEx, MC, V.
The giant music store on Columbus Avenue is still the locals' favourite spot for browsing and buying, and it's open late.
Branch: 2280 Market Street, between Noe and 16th Streets (621 0588).

Virgin Megastore
2 Stockton Street, at Market Street (397 4525). BART Powell Street/Muni Metro F, J, K, L, M, N/6, 7, 8, 9, 21, 30, 45, 66. **Open** 8am-11pm Mon-Thur; 8am-midnight, Fri; 9am-11pm Sun. **Credit** AmEx, MC, V.
The largest music and entertainment store in North America – at least until the much-trumpeted New York branch opens in Times Square.

Musical Instruments

Drum World
5016 Mission Street, at Geneva Street (334 7559). Bus 9AX, 14, 15, 29, 52. **Open** 10am-7pm Mon-Fri; 10am-6pm Sat. **Credit** AmEx, MC, V.
Zildjian cymbals and small percussion instruments.

Haight-Ashbury Music Center

1540 Haight Street, at Ashbury Street (863 7327). Bus 6, 7, 43, 66, 71. **Open** *11am-7pm Mon-Fri; 10am-6pm Sat; noon-6pm Sun.* **Credit** *AmEx, MC, V.*

A stop-off point for musicians of all sorts, but a particular favourite with local and out-of-town rock and rollers. The shop sells new and second-hand instruments, sheet music, amps and posts notice about bands looking for new members.

Real Guitars

15 Lafayette Street, off Mission Street (552 3310). BART Van Ness Avenue/Muni Metro J, K, L, M, N/9, 42, 47 bus. **Open** *11am-6pm Mon-Sat.* **Credit** *MC, V.*

Sells used and vintage guitars, including Martin, Gibson and Gretsch.

Stereo Equipment

Bang & Olufsen

345 Powell Street, at Post Street (274 3320). Bus 2, 3, 4, 76/Powell-Mason, Powell-Hyde cable car. **Open** *10am-7pm Mon-Wed, Sun; 10am-8pm Thur-Sat.* **Credit** *AmEx, DC, JCB, MC, V.*

State-of-the-art stereo and audio equipment by appointment to Danish royalty.

Smoking

Pipe Dreams

1736 Haight Street, at Masonic Street (431 3553). Bus 6, 7, 43, 66, 71. **Open** *10am-7.50pm Mon-Sat; 11am-6.50pm Sun.* **Credit** *MC, V.*

This Haight shop will take you back in time to when the area was known as the 'Hashbury'. It offers the full monte in smoking paraphernalia, T-shirts and psychedelic sundries. Don't ask for a 'bong' but for a water pipe, and remember that the shop can only sell to those who intend, or at least seem to intend, to use their products with legal substances.

Speciality Shops

Britex Fabrics

146 Geary Street, at Stockton Street (392 2910). Bus 30, 38, 45/Powell-Mason, Powell-Hyde cable car. **Open** *9.30am-6pm Mon-Wed, Fri, Sat; 9.30am-8pm Thur.* **Credit** *AmEx, MC, V.*

Four floors of fashion and home textiles, including an awesome collection of buttons.

Greenwich Yarn

2073 Greenwich Street, between Webster and Buchanan Streets (567 2535). Bus 22, 41, 45. **Open** *10am-6pm Mon, Tue, Thur-Sat; 1pm-5pm Sun.* **Credit** *MC, V.*

Travelling knitters take note of this well-stocked shop full of patterns, yarn and helpful advice.

Haight-Ashbury T-shirts

1500 Haight Street, at Ashbury Street (863 4639). Bus 6, 7, 43, 66, 71. **Open** *10am-8pm daily.* **Credit** *AmEx, MC, V.*

Everything you ever dreamed of in a music scene, hip cartoon or rock show commemorative shirt.

SF Rock Posters & Collectibles

1851 Powell Street, between Green and Filbert Streets (956 6749). Bus 15, 39. **Open** *10am-6pm Mon-Sat.* **Credit** *MC, V.*

Handbills, tickets, original art and posters galore.

Sex Accessories

See also **Good Vibrations** *and* **Stormy Leather,** *in chapters* **Women's San Francisco** *and* **Gay & Lesbian San Francisco**.

Image Leather

2199 Market Street, at Sanchez Street (621 7551). Muni Metro F, J, K, L, M/8, 22 bus. **Open** *9am-10pm Mon-Sat; 11am-7pm Sun.* **Credit** *AmEx, DC, MC, V.*

Whips, chains, harnesses, nipple rings, corsets, masks and all that kinky jazz.

Sports Equipment

See chapter **Sport & Fitness**.

Ticket Agencies

TIX Bay Area

Union Square, on Stockton Street (433 7827). BART Powell Street/Muni Metro F, J, K, L, M, N/2, 3, 4, 30, 45, 76 bus/Powell-Hyde, Powell-Mason cable car. **Open** *11am-6pm Tue-Thur; 11am-7pm Fri, Sat.* **Credit** *MC, V* (full-price tickets only).

TIX Bay Area is San Francisco's only outlet for half-price tickets on selected theatre, dance, opera and performance events. Standard price tickets are available, too. You pay a service charge.

BASS

(1-510 762 2277/1-800 225 2277 outside California). **Open** *8.30am-9pm Mon-Sat; 9.30am-9pm Sun.* **Credit** *AmEx, MC, V.*

If you need a ticket, the Bay Area Seating Service can probably sell it to you, either over the phone (be armed with your credit card) or at one of its many of their outlets throughout the city. Check the phone book for your nearest outlet.

Toys

See also **Arts & Crafts** *and* **Gifts & Stationery** *above.* For the toy shop **FAO Schwartz**, *see chapter* **Children**.

Star Magic Space Age Gifts

4026 24th Street, at Castro Street (641 8626). Bus 24, 48. **Open** *10am-8pm Mon-Thur; 10am-9pm Fri, Sat; 11am-7pm Sun.* **Credit** *AmEx, MC, V.*

Toys for grownups as well as children: New Age and Space Age combined.

Video Rental

Le Video

1239 Ninth Avenue, between Lincoln Way and Irving Street (566 3606). Muni Metro N/44, 71 bus. **Open** *10am-11pm daily.* **Credit** *AmEx, MC, V.*

If it's on video, you'll find it here. Peruse more than 31,000 titles ranging from good ol' American pop films to New Age, cult or Japanese animation.

Naked Eye News and Video

533 Haight Street, between Fillmore and Steiner Streets (864 2985). Bus 6, 7, 22, 66, 71. **Open** *10am-10pm Mon-Thur; 10am-11pm Fri, Sat; 11am-10pm Sun.* **Credit** *AmEx, MC, V.*

Alternative media, trading cards and cult videos.

Museums & Galleries

Museums & Galleries

The opening of SFMOMA should revive the city's marginal art scene; or, at least, that's the plan.

There is no doubt that 1995 will long be considered a watershed for Bay Area museums, beginning with the opening of the San Francisco Museum of Modern Art (SFMOMA) and winding up with the long-anticipated re-opening of the California Palace of the Legion of Honor, which had been closed for three years for renovation.

The MH de Young Memorial Museum and the Legion of Honor, now joined under the aegis of the Fine Arts Museums of San Francisco, were once arch rivals. The concepts for both derived from international expositions: the de Young out of the California Midwinter International Exposition in 1894, and the Legion from the 1915 Panama-Pacific Exposition. The de Young is named after the same family that launched the *San Francisco Chronicle* and began life as a depository for art and artefacts from the 1894 fair, while the Legion was founded by another well-known city name, Alma de Bretteville Spreckels, and was envisioned from the very start as a fine arts museum.

Though San Francisco most definitely lacks the major collections found elsewhere and has never been a leader in mounting avant-garde exhibitions (rather following in the steps of curators in other cities) numerous other museums opened in the wake of the Legion and the de Young, most notably the Asian Art Museum and the university museums, but also museums of science, history – both natural and cultural – as well as the special interest museums that often offer more kitsch than culture.

GALLERIES GALORE

The opening of SFMOMA put the city's commercial art scene in the spotlight once again; curators and collectors have gravitated to the city, and the ripple effects are likely to be long-lasting. Considering the city's small size – only 46 square miles – there is a plethora of private art galleries. In general, the majority of older, more mainstream galleries are located downtown, north of Market Street. To make art touring even easier, many are clustered in a single building. Alternative spaces, especially those that favour installations and cutting-edge work, are more prevalent in SoMa. The construction of SFMOMA has helped blur the lines, however, since it is located just two blocks south of Market Street, within easy walking distance of the business districts and upmarket shops, yet only a block or so from the more avant-garde galleries.

Bay Area figurative art continues to flourish and local artists like Wayne Thiebaud have withstood the ravages of time and economics. By most accounts, however, the booming art scene of the early 1980s has faded to a dull roar, and the overpricing of collectable art has been corrected. Relatively few established galleries failed during the economic downturn, but several gallery owners have cited the effect of the poor Japanese economy on California's artistic community. Nonetheless, the California art market has remained more stable than that in other major American cities such as New York and Los Angeles.

You can pick up a copy of the *San Francisco Gallery Guide* at any of the art galleries listed below – it contains a map and the addresses of dozens of places to visit in the city.

Don't miss

Ansel Adams Center for Photography
All the big names in photography.
Asian Art Museum
The biggest collection in the Western World.
California Palace of the Legion of Honor
European and ancient art in spectacular surroundings.
Capp Street Project
Probably the most progressive space in town.
Exploratorium
Who said science was boring?
Musée Mécanique
Fabulous mechanical gizmos and a cliff-edge setting.
SFMOMA
For the building, if not the collection.

The **Asian Art Museum** *houses a vast collection from more than 40 different countries.*

Museums

Major Museums

Asian Art Museum
Music Concourse, Golden Gate Park (668 8921). Bus 44.
Open 10am-5.45pm Tue, Thur-Sun; 10am-8.45pm Wed.
Admission $5 adults; $3 students, senior citizens; $2 12-17s; free under-12s; free first Wed of the month. **Credit** MC, V.
Adjacent to the de Young, 'the Asian' makes the most of San Francisco's enviable position on the Pacific Rim. The Avery Brundage Collection here is considered the biggest and best of its kind in the Western world, so large that only a fraction of its holdings is on display at any given time. These exhibits put European history in perspective: some Chinese pieces date from 70 centuries ago. There are jade pieces, bronzes, ceramics, fans, albums, scrolls – all in the first floor galleries devoted to Chinese and Korean art. Works from 40 other countries – including India, Tibet, Southeast Asia, Japan and Middle Eastern nations – are displayed upstairs. There are plans to relocate the museum to the Civic Center building vacated by the Main Library sometime during the next few years.

California Academy of Sciences
Music Concourse, Golden Gate Park (750 7365/24-hour recorded information 750 7145/Morrison Planetarium 750 7141). Bus 44. **Open** 10am-5pm daily. **Admission** $7 adults; $4 12-17s; $1.50 6-11s; free under-6s. **Credit** AmEx, MC, V.
This science museum, which faces the MH de Young Memorial Museum, is a perennial favourite for locals as well as out-of-towners. More than 1.5 million visitors come here each year to see the exhibits mounted by the oldest scientific institution in the western US. The big attraction is the Steinhart Aquarium, a spectacular facility boasting the most diverse collection of fish in the world, as well as reptiles and amphibians. The penguins, seals and dolphins are irresistible, and it would be easy to spend a day investigating just marine life, including the hands-on Touch Tidepool and the Fish Roundabout, where fast-swimming ocean fish move

in circles around a viewing area. But there's much more, including a simulated earthquake exhibit that literally moves you and a brilliant display of the flora and fauna of California's numerous climates and terrains. The Academy also has a permanent exhibit of works by cartoonist/science freak Gary Larson. Also within the complex is the Morrison Planetarium, presenting educational and amusing sky shows as well as laser light and music spectaculars.

California Palace of the Legion of Honor
Lincoln Park, at Legion of Honor Drive (750 3600). Bus 18, 38. **Open** 10am-5pm Wed-Sun. **Admission** $5 adults; $3 children. **Credit** MC, V.
San Francisco's prettiest museum site re-opened in the autumn of 1995 after a three-year hiatus for renovation (including seismic upgrades) and interior expansion. Located in a wooded spot near the Pacific, the Legion's historic Neo-Classical façade has not been altered. A cast of Rodin's 'Le Penseur' still dominates the entrance, which has now been enhanced by a glass pyramid. The Legion's famed collections include more than 87,000 paintings, sculptures, decorative arts, works on paper, tapestries and other objects, spanning 4,000 years. The entry level is now dedicated to the permanent collection; an expanded garden level houses temporary exhibition galleries, as well as the **Achenbach Foundation for Graphic Arts** and the **Bowles Porcelain Gallery** and study centre. The Fine Arts Museums of San Francisco has redistributed its holdings, concentrating the art of the Americas at the MH de Young Memorial Museum (*see p160*), and the European and ancient art collections here.

Center for the Arts at Yerba Buena Gardens
701 Mission Street, at Third Street (978 2787). BART Powell Street/Muni Metro F, J, K, L, M, N/15, 30, 45, 76 bus. **Open** 11am-6pm Tue-Sun; 11am-8pm first Thur of the month. **Admission** $5 adults; $2 students, senior citizens; free first Thur of the month. **Credit** AmEx, MC, V.
Opened in 1993, the ambitious Yerba Buena Gardens project overcame controversy, criticism and three decades of

Part of Fumihiko Maki's futuristic **Center for the Arts at Yerba Buena Gardens**. *See page 159.*

intra-city bickering and now provides one of the most appreciated greenswards in the city. The centrepiece is the Center for the Arts, which includes galleries, a small (96-seater) theatre for film and video, the Forum for performances and a café. First-time visitors may be a bit confused when trying to find the exhibition galleries, which are housed in a futuristic-looking building designed by top Japanese architect Fumihiko Maki. In lieu of a permanent collection, the centre serves as an outlet for new artists (or even unlikely ones, such as prisoners at San Quentin) working in a variety of media.

Exploratorium

3601 Lyon Street, between Jefferson and Bay Streets (563 7337/24-hour recorded information 561 0360/ Tactile Dome 561 0362). Bus 22, 28, 29, 30, 43. **Open** *summer* 10am-6pm Tue-Sun; 10am-9.30pm Wed; *winter* 10am-5pm Tue-Sun; 10am-9.30pm Wed. **Admission** $9 adults; $7 students, senior citizens; $5 disabled, 6-17s; $2.50 3-5s; free under-3s; free first Wed of the month. **Credit** MC, V.

Meteorological events such as tornadoes are difficult for children to grasp – unless they create their own at the Exploratorium. Even adults become childlike in this wonderful cavernous space, where curiosity is the name of the game. Conceived by physicist Frank Oppenheimer and opened in 1969, the museum reveals the secrets of heat, light, electricity, electronics, temperature, touch, vision, waves, patterns, motion, language and colour through clever, mostly hands-on exhibits. While much of the space resembles a post-Space Age video arcade, there are also more passive displays. A series of charts on the history of language, for example, traces hundreds of languages according to their family trees, while simple exhibits impart theories on balance, perspective and other concepts that kids often grasp quicker than adults. There's also a library where you can search for explanations the old-fashioned way. The Exploratorium offers a smorgasbord of seminars and weekends devoted to such offbeat topics as bubble blowing. To a background cacophony of blinking lights, whizzing machines and 'oohs' and 'ahhs', you can grab a decent bite at the Angel's Café right on the spot, or pick up an espresso or Spanish *churros* as you go along. There's also a great gift shop filled with scientific toys and educational baubles.

MH de Young Memorial Museum

Music Concourse, Golden Gate Park (863 3300). Bus 44. **Open** 10am-5.45pm Tue, Thur-Sun; 10am-8.45pm Wed. **Admission** $5 adults; $3 senior citizens; $2 12-17s; free first Wed of the month. **Credit** MC, V.

The recent re-organisation of the Fine Arts Museums of San Francisco has tightened the focus both here and at the California Palace of the Legion of Honor (*above*). Now the de Young, as it's known, houses the art of the Americas. The collections, which date from Colonial times to the present, include sculpture, paintings, textiles and decorative arts. American masters such as Thomas Eakins, John Singer Sargent and George Caleb Bingham are included, as well as works by contemporary Bay Area artists. The de Young also hosts travelling blockbusters such as the exhibitions on King Tut, Tiffany and Teotihuacan. The indoor/outdoor café has decent food, and the gift shop is excellent.

Specialist Museums

African-American Historical & Cultural Society

Building C, Fort Mason Center, at Buchanan Street and Marina Boulevard (441 0640). **Open** 11am-5pm Tue-Sun; 11am-7pm first Wed of the month. **Admission** $3 adults, students, senior citizens; $2 under-12s; free first Wed of the month. **Credit** AmEx, MC, V.

One of two facilities managed by the society (the other, with a library and listening room for historical tapes, is on Fulton Street), this museum/gallery features a permanent collection and changing exhibitions. The archival materials relate to African-American life and culture from the nineteenth century to the present day, including photographs and related items that shed light on little known aspects of American history, while the gallery's emphasis is on new and master artists of African descent. The gift shop sells African and African-American arts and crafts.

Cable Car Barn Museum

1201 Mason Street, at Washington Street (474 1887). Cable car Powell-Mason, Powell-Hyde. **Open** 10am-6pm daily. **Admission** free.

The single sound most often associated with San Francisco is the clanging of the cable cars, the city's mobile landmarks. Supposedly inspired by a disastrous carriage crash, the Scotsman Andrew Hallidie introduced cable cars to this hilly town more than 120 years ago. The best way to study them is, of course, to take a ride, though only three lines operate nowadays. The second best way is to tour the Cable Car Barn, where an underground excavation area allows visitors to see the system in operation and to understand how the cables, wheels and engines keep everything moving. Vintage cable cars, associated artefacts and a short film round out the exhibits.

Cartoon Art Museum

814 Mission Street, between Fourth and Fifth Streets (227 8666/recorded information 546 3922). BART Powell Street/Muni Metro F, J, K, L, M, N/14, 15, 26, 27, 30, 45, 76 bus. **Admission** $3.50 adults; $2.50 students, senior citizens; $1.50 children; free under-5s. **Open** 11am-5pm Wed-Fri; 10am-5pm Sat; 1pm-5pm Sun. **Credit** MC, V

Finally settled in 1995 in what are hopefully permanent quarters, the Cartoon Art Museum consists of four rooms of exceedingly well arranged exhibits relating to the art of the cartoon. The sources are myriad – individual artists, comic books, *The New Yorker* – and add up to an informative lesson on this original art form for its artistic, cultural and historic merits. Currently the only museum west of the Mississippi dedicated to the preservation, collection and exhibition of original cartoon art, it is home to a 10,000-piece collection ranging from the late 1700s to the present. The 558sq m/6,000sq ft space also includes a children's museum, an interactive CD-ROM gallery and a nifty gift shop with books, comics, cards and related paraphernalia.

Chinese Historical Society Museum

650 Commercial Street, between Montgomery and Kearny Streets (391 1188). Bus 1, 15/California cable car. **Open** noon-4pm Tue-Sat. **Admission** free.

You get a little bonus at this subterranean space – its location and ambiance are pure Old Chinatown – which is appropriate considering the scope of its holdings. Bilingual displays trace the presence and contributions of the Chinese in California, from the frontier years to the Gold Rush, the building of the railroads (which would have taken another 100 years were it not for low-paid Chinese labour) and the days of opium dens on the old Barbary Coast. The lovingly kept exhibits include a small Chinese Buddhist altar dating from 1880; a 4 metre/14ft Californian sampan for fishing, and a Chinese dragon head made in 1911 for use in ceremonies and parades, one of the first to incorporate lights. Like the Wells Fargo museum (*see p162*), this is a must for unravelling California's complex tapestry of history.

Jewish Community Museum

121 Steuart Street, between Mission and Howard Streets (543 8880). BART Embarcadero/Muni Metro F, J, K, L, M, N/1, 14, 30X, 32 bus. **Open** noon-6pm Mon-Wed; noon-8pm Thur; 11am-6pm Sun. **Admission** $3 adults; $1.50 children, students; senior citizens; free under-5s. **Credit** MC, V.

One of the most diverse cities in the country, ethnically as well as religiously, San Francisco now has its own museum devoted to linking the Jewish community with the community at large, through exhibitions and educational programmes. More a gallery than a stodgy museum, the 12 year-old Jewish Museum shows works by established artists and students. To its credit, many of them are political and controversial in nature.

Levi Strauss Museum

250 Valencia Street, between 14th Street and Duboce Avenue (565 9159). Bus 26. **Open** *tours only* 10.30am, 1pm Wed. **Admission** free.

Of all the inventions emanating from the West Coast,

perhaps the most lasting and certainly the most ubiquitous is blue jeans. The history of this all-American icon is displayed at this museum, housed in a 1906 commercial Victorian structure. It all started during the Gold Rush, when a young German immigrant named Levi Strauss fashioned a pair of trousers from the heavyweight canvas normally used for gold miners' tents. When Strauss began importing a similar fabric in blue from Nîmes in France, the trousers were called 'denims'. When Hollywood dressed stars from Gary Cooper to James Dean in jeans, the stage was set for middle America to follow suit. The walking tour includes a video and a visit to the factory's cutting and sewing rooms. Book in advance.

Mexican Museum

Building D, Fort Mason Center, at Laguna Street and Marina Boulevard (441 0404). Bus 28. **Open** noon-5pm Wed-Sun; noon-7pm first Wed of the month. **Admission** $3 adults; $2 children, students, senior citizens; free under-10s. **Credit** (shop only) AmEx, MC, V.

The first museum in the US dedicated to the work of Mexican and other Latino artists is currently ensconced in rather limited quarters, but is expected to relocate to a new building in SoMa, across the road from Yerba Buena Gardens in 1998. Over the years, the curators have acquired some 9,000 objects reflecting a spectrum of Mexican art ranging from traditional to experimental, decorative to functional, ancient to contemporary. It holds its own shows on such subjects as Mexican surrealism, and also mounts travelling exhibits, which have included a major Frida Kahlo retrospective. Without this museum, works by many contemporary Mexican, Mexican-American and Chicano artists would not get the exposure they deserve. There is also a sizeable gift shop.

Musée Mécanique

Cliff House, 1090 Point Lobos Avenue, at the Great Highway (386 1170). Bus 18, 38. **Open** 10am-8pm daily. **Admission** free.

Make sure you pack a pocketful of quarters when you visit this wonderful cliffside museum – actually an arcade housing a few dozen old-fashioned mechanical gizmos ranging from Laughing Sal to fortune-telling machines. Many of the dioramas are remarkable in the number of moving parts that are activated when you drop in a coin. Toothpick Fantasy is an intricate miniature of a circus, with a train, ferris wheel, rollercoaster and other rides – all made of toothpicks by inmates at San Quentin prison. There's a French guillotine and, to be fair, an 'English execution', as well as belly dancers and X-rated peep shows that seem charmingly innocent. Best of all is the Unbelievable Mechanical Farm, with 150 moving objects and figures. Check out the Camera Obscura, a replica of Leonardo da Vinci's invention, which 'films' the world outside and projects it onto a giant parabolic screen.

Museo Italo-Americano

Building C, Fort Mason Center, at Buchanan Street and Marina Boulevard (673 2200). Bus 28. **Open** noon-5pm Wed-Sun; noon-7pm first Wed of the month. **Admission** $2 adults; $1 children, students, senior citizens; free under-12s; free first Wed of the month. **Credit** (shop only) MC, V.

One of three ethnic museums housed in rather unprepossessing quarters in the Fort Mason complex, the Museo Italo-Americano functions as a gallery and a sort of community centre, offering classes in Italian language, art, architecture and related subjects. Along with a few historical exhibits the museum shows works by Italian and Italian-American artists. It also has a nice little gift shop.

National Maritime Museum

Jefferson Street, at Polk Street (929 0202). Bus 30, 42/Powell-Hyde cable car. **Open** 10am-5pm daily. **Admission** $2. **No credit cards.**

Find out all you need to know about those travelling landmarks at the **Cable Car Barn Museum**. *See page 160.*

San Francisco's waterfront is not quite as bustling as it once was, but there are still worthwhile sites, including this museum, which documents maritime history with the aid of photographs and ship models, including miniatures of passenger liners and US Navy ships. Located in a classic 1930s building, typical of both Art Deco and the Public Works of Art Project, the museum also offers some interactive exhibits that children will enjoy. The museum is a block away from the Ghirardelli Square shopping centre.

Performing Arts Library and Museum
399 Grove Street, at Gough Street (255 4800). Bus 21, 42, 47, 49. **Open** *10am-5pm Tue-Fri; noon-4pm Sat.* **Admission** *free.*
With exhibitions relating to the performing arts, be it a puppet show or an opera, this museum is worth a visit if you're in the Civic Center neighbourhood. Of most interest to fine arts scholars is the prodigious amount of resource material. Thousands of books on design, fashion, music, theatre, opera and other art forms (including circus and mime performances) provide the backbone, augmented by video tapes, newspaper clippings and even *Harpers Bazaar* magazines going back to the 1850s. The focus is on local arts groups, but if the Ballet Russe, for example, performed in San Francisco, you'll probably find a review of the production here.

Tattoo Museum
841 Columbus Avenue, at Lombard Street (775 4991). Bus 30. **Open** *noon-9pm Mon-Thur; noon-10pm Fri, Sat; noon-8pm Sun.* **Admission** *free.*
Trust quirky San Francisco to have a museum in a tattoo parlour. Master tattoo artist Lyle Tuttle has gathered what may be the world's largest assortment of tattoo paraphernalia – designs, newspaper articles, photographs and even old equipment such as a set of hand needles. The revival of the art of tattooing in the Western world supposedly happened after the English privateer William Dampier returned from the South Pacific to shock and titillate London with the sight of Giolo, a native 'painted prince' (pictured in the museum). If you're thinking of having a tattoo done, you're in good company: Tuttle decorated both Joan Baez and Janis Joplin. If you just want to watch, all you have to do is ask.

Wells Fargo History Room
420 Montgomery Street, at California Street (396 2619). Bus 15, 41/California cable car. **Open** *9am-5pm Mon-Fri.* **Admission** *free.*
Cinema has often depicted the days of the Wild West in terms of stagecoach robberies, certainly one of the more dramatic images of the day. Seeing a century-old coach close up, however, one is most impressed with how fragile it looks. The bright red one in the front window at the spacious ground-floor Wells Fargo museum would have held as many as 18 people, although it's difficult to imagine them all fitting in. This and other exhibits managed by the Wells Fargo bank, which is still synonymous with old California, are so wonderful that they overshadow the displays that seek to tout the bank, although the histories are inextricably linked. Pony Express memorabilia and a first-rate relief map created in the 1940s illustrate the routes and the risks run by the banks in the old days before Federal Express came to the rescue. In one corner, an old telegraph machine lets visitors try their hand at tapping out a message. Most impressive is the elaborate leather, brass and iron harness once used to control a 'six-up' stage coach; driving six horses along rocky roads and perilous cliffsides must have been harder than manoeuvring an 18-wheeler rig today. In all, the museum paints an expansive and exciting picture of the Old West.

Further Afield

For details of the Bay Area Discovery Museum, a paradise for kids, *see chapter* **Children**.

Bay Model Visitors Center
2100 Bridgeway Avenue, Sausalito (332 3871). Golden Gate Transit 10/ferry from Ferry Building or Pier 43$\frac{1}{2}$. **Open** *Apr-Sep 9am-4pm Tue-Fri; 10am-6pm Sat, Sun; Oct-Mar 9am-4pm Tue-Sat.* **Admission** *free.*
A 15-acre model of the Bay established by the US Army Corps of Engineers shows how navigation, recreation and ecology all interact in this complex water system. Best of all, walkways are strung all over so that visitors can, figuratively at least, walk on water. When the model is in operation,

SFMOMA

In January 1995 the citizens of San Francisco finally feasted their eyes on the $62 million modern art museum built to showcase the bulging collection formerly cramped into the Veteran's Building in the Civic Center. Designed by Swiss architect Mario Botta, the 20,925-square metre/225,000-square foot edifice is the largest new American art museum of the decade and the second largest single structure in the United States devoted to modern art. To appreciate the scope of this undertaking – and to understand San Francisco's commitment to the arts – it helps to know that pledges of some $90 million (more than the $85 million sought to build and endow the museum) came almost entirely from private donations.

SFMOMA opened to enthusiastic approval, as much for its Modernist design as for its improvement over its predecessor. Approached from the west in particular, it looms above Yerba Buena Gardens, revealing itself in segments. The façade is stepped-back brick and stone, distinguished by a cylinder that soars from the roof, finished in alternating black and white stone, and topped with a radial pattern of the same contrasting materials. Although it will probably eventually be flanked by high-rise towers, it was instantly heralded as a new architectural landmark.

The new building contains 4,650 square metres/50,000 square feet of gallery space, nearly double the previous footage, with additional room for educational, administrative and other facilities. The permanent collection of over 15,000 works is international in scope, and includes some 4,700 paintings, sculptures and works on paper; 9,000 photographs; 1,500 architectural drawings, models and design objects; and a growing collection of works related to the media arts.

Californian, American and international artists are represented in the painting and sculpture collection, which is distinguished by major paintings by Clyfford Still, Jackson Pollock, Philip Guston and others working in American Abstract Expressionism. The collection is also strong on Fauvism (notably the works of Henri Matisse), German Expressionism, Latin American painting, works by Paul Klee, and contemporary work.

Alfred Stieglitz, Ansel Adams, Edward Weston, the German avant-garde artists of the 1920s and the European Surrealists of the 1930s are represented in the photography collection.

A diverse range of design objects and architectural drawings and models by figures linked with the West Coast and the Pacific Rim – Bernard Maybeck, Frank Gehry, Shiro Kuramata, Timothy Pflueger and William Turnbull – are highlights of the architecture and design collection.

On the ground floor, a svelte café and a greatly expanded bookshop provide rest stops for the weary art viewer. As in the old quarters, a lot of stair climbing is required (there are lifts, but they are slow) to reach the fifth floor galleries. In addition to the art, don't miss the spectacular catwalk at the top, just beneath a giant skylight.

The collection still cannot all be displayed at one time, however, and there are moments of disjointedness. What's more, although there is a feeling of vast interior space, the virtual lack of windows can be unsettling, and the collection does not always seem to be displayed to its best advantage. Many visitors leave feeling that the wrapping promised more than the present delivers.

San Francisco Museum of Modern Art

151 Third Street, between Mission and Howard Streets (357 4000). BART Montgomery/Muni Metro F, J, K, L, M, N/12, 30, 45, 76 bus. **Open** 11am-6pm Tue, Wed, Fri-Sun; 11am-9pm Thur. **Admission** $7 adults; $3.50 13-18s, students, senior citizens; free under-13s. **Credit** (café and bookstore only) AmEx, MC, V.

a lunar day is simulated in under 15 minutes, complete with tidal action. Hands-on exhibits include video games and an introduction to indigenous birds and fish, and there are videos on the Corps' work in hydro-electric power, flood control and construction.

Oakland Museum of California

1000 Oak Street, at 10th Street, Oakland (1-510 238 3401). BART Lake Merritt. **Open** 10am-5pm Wed-Sat; noon-7pm Sun. **Admission** $5 adults; $3 children, students, senior citizens; free under-5s; free 4pm-7pm Sun. **No credit cards**.

The only museum in California devoted exclusively to the art, history and environment of the state, the Oakland Museum was established in 1969. The Gallery of California Art displays paintings, sculpture, prints, illustrations, photographs and decorative arts by Californian artists, or by artists addressing related themes and subjects. Exhibited in some 2,790sq m/30,000sq ft of space, the collection includes sketches by early explorers; genre pictures from the Gold Rush; massive panoramic landscapes; Bay Area figurative, Pop and Funk works. The Natural Sciences displays are devoted to the variegated Californian landscape and the Cowell Hall of California History has furniture, machines, tools, costumes, craftwork, clothing, decorations and vehicles prominent in the state's development.

University Art Museum

2626 Bancroft Way, between Bowditch and College Streets (1-510 642 0808). BART Berkeley. **Open** 11am-5pm Wed-Sun. **Admission** $6 adults; $4 children, students, disabled. **No credit cards**.

It was modernist printer Hans Hofmann who provided the impetus for an art museum on the UC Berkeley campus. Opened in 1970, the exhibition space is dramatic, arranged in terraces enabling visitors to see the works from various vantage points. The collection's strength is in twentieth-century painting, sculpture, photography and conceptual art, as well as Asian art. Ten galleries and a bookstore occupy the upper level, while the Sculpture Garden and café share the lower level with the Pacific Film Archive, one of the country's most comprehensive academic film programmes. The PFA screens some 650 films and videos a year, and has a collection of 7,000 titles, including Soviet, American avant-garde and Japanese cinema (*see also* chapter **Film**).

Galleries

Open Studios

For four weekends during each October, more than 600 San Francisco artists open their studios to the public from 11am to 6pm. For 24-hour information about where to go and how to get a map, phone 861 9838.

Campbell/Thiebaud

645 Chestnut Street, at Columbus Avenue (441 8680). Bus 30/Powell-Mason cable car. **Open** 11am-5pm Tue-Fri; noon-4pm Sat. **No credit cards**.

Located on a quiet residential street in North Beach, this is a joint venture between Charles Campbell, long-time gallery owner, and Paul Thiebaud, son of acclaimed local artist Wayne Thiebaud. Some of the latter's paintings hang in this two-storey gallery, along with work by many other Bay Area figurative artists. Most of the names on display are well-known: Frank Auerbach, Robert Kulicke, Fairfield Porter, Willem de Kooning, August Gay, Bay Area painter and sculptor Manuel Neri, and painter Frank Lobdell, who taught at the San Francisco Art Institute and Stanford.

Capp Street Project

525 Second Street, between Bryant and Brannan Streets (495 7101). Bus 15, 42. **Open** noon-6pm Tue-Sat. **No credit cards**.

Many local artists agree that this is one of the more progressive spaces in town. The non profit-making Capp Street Project mounts site-specific installations, and also offers a three-month residency programme whereby artists can live and work on large-scale installation pieces for the gallery. Admission is free but donations are welcome.

The sculpture garden is one of the highlights of the **University Art Museum** *in Berkeley.*

Don Soker Gallery

251 Post Street, between Grant Avenue and Stockton Street (291 0966). BART Montgomery Street/Muni Metro F, J, K, L, M, N/2, 3, 4, 30, 45, 76 bus. **Open** 11am-5pm Tue-Sat. **No credit cards.**

Though no longer based in the cheaper, hipper SoMa district, where his premises were destroyed during the earthquake, Don Soker still specialises in minimalist, abstract work, which means a lot of Japanese works on paper. The gallery also has etchings by Theodora Varnay-Jones, who recently studied in Japan, and works by other local artists such as Peter Boyer, Susan Parker, Roland Castellon (ex-curator of SFMOMA) and Yutaka Yoshinaga.

Dorothy Weiss

256 Sutter Street, between Grant Avenue and Kearny Street (397 3611). Bus 2, 3, 4, 30, 45, 76. **Open** 11am-5pm Tue-Sat. **No credit cards.**

This upper-floor gallery can be described simply: dynamite contemporary ceramics.

Gallery Paule Anglim

14 Geary Street, between Grant Avenue and Kearny Street (433 2710). BART Montgomery Street/Muni Metro F, J, K, L, M, N/2, 3, 4, 15, 38, 76 bus. **Open** 11am-5.30pm Tue-Sat. **No credit cards.**

Situated between the chic shopping streets of Union Square and the alternative spaces south of Market Street, this gallery is on the cusp in more ways than one. Paule Anglim is known for exhibiting Bay Area and international artists in a variety of media – both established as well as cutting-edge talent. Two young sculptors discovered by the gallery – Melissa Pokorny and Michelle Rollman – are now being shown in minor museums. Some of the exhibits are controversial, but this gallery is one of only three in the city to claim membership of the prestigious Art Dealers Association of America (the others being John Berggruen and Fraenkel).

Galeria de la Raza

2857 24th Street, at Bryant Street (826 8009). Bus 27, 48. **Open** noon-6pm Tue-Sat. **Credit** AmEx, MC, V.

An unpretentious corner shopfront is the setting for up to six exhibitions a year of Latin American artists new to the US. Galeria de la Raza devotes all its space, and time, to artists from Mexico, El Salvador and other Latin American countries. La Raza's adjacent shop, Studio 24, sells handcrafts, books and children's toys from these same countries. Donations are welcome.

John Berggruen Gallery

228 Grant Avenue, between Post and Sutter Streets (781 4629). BART Montgomery Street/Muni Metro F, J, K, L, M, N/2, 3, 4, 76 bus. **Open** 9.30am-5.30pm Mon-Fri; 10.30am-5pm Sat. **Credit** MC, V.

This blue-chip gallery celebrated its 25th anniversary in 1995, and its openings are a routine stop for socialites as well as collectors of more modest means. Occupying two floors in a narrow Grant Avenue building in the heart of the gallery district, John Berggruen is known for major artists; recent acquisitions include work by Henri Matisse, Alberto Giacometti, Nathan Oliveira, Mark Tansey, William Bailey, painter and ceramicist Squeak Carnwath and Saul Steinberg.

Limn Studio Furniture & Art

457 Pacific Avenue, between Sansome and Montgomery Streets (397 7474). Bus 12, 42, 83. **Open** 9.30am-5.30pm Tue-Fri; 11am-5.30pm Sat. **Credit** AmEx, MC, V.

The line between form and function is intentionally blurred in many of the intriguing pieces of furniture on display at this cross between a gallery and a showroom. Limn has a strong presence in this niche; many of the artists and craftspeople represented here are shown in various special exhibits, such as Brian Russell, known for tables and candelabra utilising forged steel or copper; Stephen Tiffany, who does mostly lighting fixtures; Alan Sklansky, who makes cabinetry, bookcases and chairs in wood and metal; and Michael Albrecht, famous for his maplewood armoires in a contemporary design.

Meyerovich Gallery

251 Post Street, between Grant Avenue and Stockton Street (421 7171). BART Montgomery Street/Muni Metro F, J, K, L, M, N/2, 3, 4, 30, 45, 76 bus. **Open** 10am-5.30pm Mon-Fri; 11am-5pm Sat. **Credit** AmEx, MC, V.

Although it has been several years since Grisha Bruskin's painting *Fundamental Lexicon* sold for nearly half a million dollars at the Sotheby's auction in Moscow, ripples of excitement are still being felt at this elegant little gallery which has been representing him for some time. The Russian-Jewish painter-turned-sculptor moved from the edge of respectability to the pinnacle of fame. The gallery also has works by Chagall, Keith Haring, David Hockney, Roy Lichtenstein, Matisse, Miró, Picasso, Frank Stella and Warhol.

New Langton Arts

1246 Folsom Street, between Eighth and Ninth Streets (626 5416). Bus 12, 19, 27, 42. **Open** noon-5pm Wed-Sat. **No credit cards.**

In the forefront of the alternative art spaces, this second-floor loft is as unprepossessing as some of its SoMa neighbourhood, at least from the outside. The choice of exhibitions is eclectic, to say the least, but the gallery is best known for its installations and performance pieces. It hosts an annual autumn showcase, the Bay Area Awards show, presenting top regional talent in literature, media arts, music, performance and the visual arts, and as the NEA regional grant-making site for northern California, act as an unofficial cultural centre for many different artists.

Olga Dollar Gallery

210 Post Street, at Grant Avenue (398 2297). BART Montgomery/Muni Metro F, J, K, L, M, N/2, 3, 4, 76 bus. **Open** 10.30am-5.30pm Tue-Sat. **No credit cards.**

Formerly the Allport Gallery and known for its prints, the gallery has shifted emphasis to contemporary and emerging Californian artists – the stranger the better. If hyper-realism appeals to you, this is the place to look for it. Also here are works by Troy Dalton, Stephen Braun, Patricia Ancona and Seiji Kunishima as well as two young female artists, Francesca Sundsten and Chicako Okada.

Virginia Breier

3091 Sacramento Street, at Baker Street (929 7173). Bus 1, 3. **Open** 11am-6pm Mon-Sat; noon-5pm Sun. **Credit** MC, V.

Always a pleasure to visit, this gallery specialises in sculpture, wall hangings, furniture and other three-dimensional pieces that defy categorisation. Metal sculptures by William Allen reflect his background as a professional zoologist; his over-scale insects, for instance, feature incredible anatomical detail. Patricia Sannit, Paul di Pasqua, Stan Peterson and many other artists represented here have day jobs as professors in northern California, but this is no one-size-fits-all collection. How do you categorise a massive wall installation comprised of dozens of neon fish that can be set to flash by computer? No wonder a local rag recently dubbed Breier the 'high priestess of American crafts'.

Vorpal Gallery

393 Grove Street, near Gough Street (397 9200). Bus 21, 42, 47, 49. **Open** 11am-6pm Tue-Sat. **Credit** MC, V.

Located in a turn-of-the-century building replete with high ceilings, hardwood floors and white brick walls, Vorpal bills itself as an eclectic gallery. Among the better-known contemporary artists here is Yoyo Hamaguchi, but Latin American artists also have a presence and the gallery carries

Off the beaten track, but worth the detour: the **San Francisco Art Institute Galleries**.

prints by Escher, Picasso, Rembrandt and the Belgian pre-Expressionist James Ensor. Vorpal mounts half a dozen special exhibitions each year.

Photography Galleries

Ansel Adams Center for Photography

250 Fourth Street, between Folsom and Howard Streets (495 7000). Bus 12, 30, 45, 76. **Open** 11am-5pm Tue-Sun; 11am-8pm first Thur of the month. **Admission** $4 adults; $3 students; $2 senior citizens, 12-18s; free under-12s; free first Thur of the month. **Credit** AmEx, MC, V.

In 1989, 22 years after Ansel Adams founded the Friends of Photography with other prominent photographers, the group relocated headquarters from Carmel to the area around Yerba Buena Gardens. Of the centre's five galleries, one is devoted to exploring and preserving Adams' photographic legacy; the rest showcase contemporary and historical photography, such as the Nagasaki exhibition held on the 50th anniversary of its bombing. Students of photography should take a look at the outstanding selection of books in the shop.

Fraenkel Gallery

49 Geary Street, at Kearny Street (981 2661). BART Montgomery Street/Muni Metro F, J, K, L, M, N/7, 8, 38, 71 bus. **Open** 10.30am-5.30pm Tue-Fri; 11am-5pm Sat. **No credit cards**.

Walking around the exhibition rooms at the Fraenkel Gallery – housed in a building packed with commercial galleries – one starts to wonder if there is any major twentieth-century photographer not on view. As it turns out, there are a few gaps in the collection, but photographers represented include Robert Mapplethorpe, Henri Cartier-Bresson, Irving Penn, Diane Arbus, Helen Levitt, Garry Winogrand, Richard Misrach, Edward Weston, Walker Evans, Paul Strand, Alfred Stieglitz, Edward Steichen and Chuck Gibson, as well as photos by Carleton E Watkins and Edward Muybridge.

Michael Shapiro

250 Sutter Street, between Grant Avenue and Kearny Street (398 6655). BART Montgomery Street/Muni Metro F, J, K, L, M, N/2, 3, 4, 15, 30, 45, 76 bus. **Open** 11am-5.30pm Tue-Sat. **Credit** MC, V.

A relatively small gallery, Michael Shapiro is devoted exclusively to twentieth-century photography. The gallery represents Steven Brock, Kenro Izu, Margaretta Mitchell, George Tice, Masao Yamamoto and others; works by Ruth Bernhard, Margaret Bourke-White, Henri Cartier-Bresson, Imogen Cunningham and Edward Weston are also available.

San Francisco Art Institute Galleries

800 Chestnut Street, at Jones Street (774 7020). Cable car Powell-Hyde. **Open** 8am-5pm Mon-Wed, Fri, Sat; 8am-8pm Thur. **No credit cards**.

The Art Institute may seem a detour from the cluster of galleries downtown and south of Market Street. But a trip here is worth it for several reasons: if you take the Powell-Hyde cable car to Chestnut and walk two blocks (over a hill) to Jones, you can take in one of the most breathtaking (and off-the-beaten-track) views of San Francisco. There are three galleries. In one you have the rare chance to see an original Diego Rivera mural, in the next a solid collection of contemporary art, and in the third work is on display and on sale by the talented students at the Institute.

Vision Gallery

1155 Mission Street, between Seventh and Eighth Streets (621 2107/2118). BART Civic Center/Muni Metro F, J, K, L, M, N/14, 19, 36 bus. **Open** 9am-6pm Mon-Sat. **Credit** AmEx, MC, V.

One of the largest photography galleries in the US, this has four main rooms with space for in-depth exhibitions of contemporary and vintage work. The Vintage Room is set aside for rare or unusual works by well-known twentieth-century photographers. Vision Editions, started here in 1992, publishes and distributes photographs in single editions, and portfolios by the likes of Paul Caponigro, whose illustrious career began in 1951 and most recently led him to photograph ancient ruins in Ireland.

Public Art

Public art is on plain view throughout the city, not only in the museums but in hotel lobbies, on street corners and even at bus stops. San Francisco's investment in the arts allocates up to two per cent of the cost of new public buildings for public art. The San Francisco Art Commission, at 25 Van Ness Avenue, Suite 240 (252 2590) publishes a brochure of many of these works, which describes several walking tours, particularly along the waterfront and south of Market Street. Many works have been set in what might seem unlikely places – a jail, a children's recreation centre in an at-risk neighbourhood and in a mental health institution.

The **Moscone Convention Center** is a good bet in rainy weather, with works by Hung Lui, Viola Frey, Paul Wonner, Gustavo Rivera, Stephen De Staebler (a slender bronze figure entitled 'Man with Flame', in the pedestrian mall near the garage), Jim Dine and Dan Rice.

Temporary works in all disciplines are found along **Market Street** courtesy of the Art in Transit Program, which borrows works from private spaces and exhibits them along that heavily travelled thoroughfare. The poster series on bus shelters between the Castro and the Embarcadero, expresses the hopes and frustrations of immigrants from 12 different countries. Another established locale for art in transit is the **San Francisco International Airport**, where changing art exhibits are mounted in all the terminals. Almost all the shows are clever, the best ones being three-dimensional, on topics ranging from transportation to violins.

As for specific artists, you can find a sensuous Benny Bufano sculpture on the lobby level of the **Alcoa Building** (in the Maritime Plaza on Battery Street) in the Financial district. Jean Dubuffet's splendid *Rag Lady* sculpture (*pictured*) is outside the **Hyatt Regency** (5 Embarcadero Center). Diego Rivera murals are located at the **San Francisco Art Institute** (800 Chestnut Street), the **Pacific Coast Stock Exchange** (301 Pine Street) and at **City College** (50 Phelan Avenue).

The **Coit Tower** is home to some of the finest 1930s' murals in the US: painted by 25 master artists (and 19 assistants) they cover nearly 4,000 square feet of wall space. The colours and the forms were inspired by Diego Rivera, who lived in the city during that period.

The **Precita Eyes Mural Art Center** (348 Precita Avenue, 285 2287) conducts free guided tours of the fabulously colourful murals to be found in the Mission district – particularly around the eight blocks bounded by 14th, Army, Mission and York Streets. Tours run every Saturday at 1.30pm, and the centre also sells a map (*see also chapters* **Sightseeing** *and* **San Francisco by Neighbourhood**).

In true San Francisco tradition, the **Ritz-Carlton** hotel displays a museum-quality collection of eighteenth- and nineteenth-century European and American art and antiques. True to the collection's theme – San Francisco's position as an international gateway – the most notable oil is Henry Scott's impressive painting from the early 1900s, *The Pericles and Benjamin F Packard Entering San Francisco Harbour*. Other works include signed oil paintings by John James Hill, Thomas Luny, Abraham Solomon, Alfred A Glendenning, Deryk Foster and Edwin Roberts.

Eating & Drinking

Film

Music

Nightlife

Art

Sport

Theatre

Shopping

Comedy

Your passport to London

TimeOut

At newsagents every Wednesday

Arts & Entertainment

Literary San Francisco

Generations of restless writers have been drawn to San Francisco, leaving behind them a rich and off-beat literary heritage and a thriving poetry-slam scene.

San Francisco has always been a mecca for adventurers and runaways – and writers. Mark Twain and Bret Harte came to report the weirdness during the Gold Rush; Tom Wolfe came to see the hippies a hundred years later. Jack Kerouac was in and out between 1947 and 1955, and Ken Kesey invented the counterculture in and around San Francisco. Today's sexual-frontier bohemians can be found in the Mission and the Lower Haight. Restless Americans come to San Francisco when they can't stand where they are.

FROM TOM SAWYER TO MCTEAGUE

Mark Twain worked here in the 1860s as a journalist and a budding fiction writer, constructing his literary persona and finally leaving for New York when *The Celebrated Jumping Frog of Calaveras County* hit the big time in 1867. Like most San Francisco writers Twain came here to create himself and went East when he was ready. He's supposed to have taken the name Tom Sawyer from a man who owned a bar on Montgomery Street. Twain, **Harte** and **Ambrose Bierce** built on a foundation of journalistic irony and muckraking to give the West an independent literary culture in the 1860s and 1870s – something that didn't happen again until after World War II.

Robert Louis Stevenson came here in 1879, chasing the strong-willed (but already married) Fanny Osbourne. He lived at 868 Bush Street while she was in Oakland waiting for her divorce to come through. Eventually he collapsed from tuberculosis and she scooped him up. He wrote about San Francisco in *The Wrecker*, and about their honeymoon at the top of the Napa Valley in *The Silverado Squatters*. His house is in Saint Helena, (the Silverado Museum at Library Lane, St Helena, Napa County, 1-707 963 3757), and the Stevenson State Park is nearby.

Jack London, one of San Francisco's few native sons to make it as a writer, was born at Third and Brannan Streets, the illegitimate son of a wandering astrologer and a medium. He survived all manner of child labour and worked himself up to oyster pirate on the Bay by the age of 16. Then he went to Berkeley, but found it dull and headed north for the Yukon gold rush. He is the Bay Area's only world-class novelist and the first great American writer of proletarian origins. London became famous with *The Call of the Wild* and *The Sea Wolf* and spent his later years in the somewhat fascistically-named Wolf House in Glen Ellen in the Sonoma Valley, north of San Francisco. The rebuilt Wolf House is worth a visit, if only to get a chilling sense of the connection between turn-of-the-century American Nietzscheanism and the creepier romance of the Nazis. The Jack London Museum, Wolf House and the writer's grave are all in the Jack London State Historic Park in Glen Ellen (1-707 938 5216).

Most Jack London sites are in Oakland, where he was raised, as was **Gertrude Stein**, who said, somewhat unfairly, that there was no 'there' there. **Alice B Toklas**, on the other hand, was born on O'Farrell Street and raised at 2300 California in the Jewish haute bourgeoisie. She wrote about it and about the 1906 earthquake in her autobiography *What is Remembered*. 'My father was apparently asleep,' Toklas wrote about the earthquake. 'Do get up, I said to him. The city is on fire. That, said he with his usual calm, will give us a black eye in the East'. Jack London wrote a more dramatic account for the *Argonaut*. Both are published in *San Francisco Stories*, edited by John Miller (Chronicle Books, 1990).

Frank Norris, London's contemporary, represents the left-wing version of the turn-of-the-century mixture of romanticism and naturalism. Norris was one of the first American disciples of Zola and a forerunner of the progressive era; his most famous novel is *The Octopus*, about the railroad barons, but *McTeague*, set on Polk Gulch where Norris grew up, was made into the silent movie *Greed*, by Eric von Stroheim.

THE CITY OF SAM SPADE

Dashiell Hammett was the writer of the booming, post-World War I, post-earthquake downtown.

Herb Caen, longtime city columnist for the *San Francisco Chronicle*, described the city as follows: 'The Hall of Justice was dirty and reeked of evil. The criminal lawyers were young and hungry and used every shyster trick... The City Hall, the DA and the cops ran the town as though they owned it, and they did'. This is the 'hard-boiled' view of the world, and it was Hammett who invented it.

Hammett came to San Francisco in 1921, at the tail end of his career as a Pinkerton operative. Beginning in 1923, *Black Mask* published 11 of Hammett's 'Continental Op' stories, set in San Francisco and written while the tubercular Hammett was living at 620 Eddy Street. In 1926 he went to work for the Albert Samuels jewellery company at 985 Market (the Samuels clock is still standing). Shortly afterwards he was found collapsed in a pool of blood. He went on full disability pay, shipped his family to the country and became a full-time writer. Living at 891 Post Street, he wrote the sequence of novels which established the crime story as *the* American genre: *Red Harvest* and *The Dain Curse* (1929), *The Maltese Falcon* (1930), and *The Glass Key* (1931).

The Maltese Falcon sent Hammett to Hollywood. He wrote *The Thin Man*, and a string of awful movie sequels and was saved from drinking himself to death by World War II. Considered an un-person in the 1950s because he had been a Communist, he went to jail and disappeared until Lillian Helman rehabilitated him. America is still uncomfortable with Hammett, which may be why his plaque, on Burritt Street off Bush, written by **Warren Hinkle**, commemorates Sam Spade, not his creator. 'On approximately this spot,' it savs, 'Miles Archer, partner of Sam Spade, was done in by Brigid O'Shaughnessy'.

Hinkle, a San Francisco journalist in the Ambrose Bierce tradition, famous for bankrupting more magazines than any other editor in history, published a Dashiell Hammett issue of his magazine *City* in 1975. It lists every known Hammett and Sam Spade location and is required reading for enthusiasts. Hammett's and Spade's intertwined journeys are also detailed in Don Herron's *Literary Guide to San Francisco* (City Lights, 1985). John's Grill, which appeared in *The Maltese Falcon*, at 63 Ellis Street is another shrine for Hammett fans (986 0069).

THE BEAT GENERATION

The leading figure of post-World War II literary San Francisco was **Kenneth Rexroth**, an irascible literary pacifist and orientalist whose salon at

---

Spoken word

Bohemia itself, in its current post-modern incarnation, is mostly down in the Mission, where the sun is warm and the rent is cheap. It's booming. The spoken-word and poetry-slam scene within half a mile of 16th and Valencia Streets has more literary energy than anything since the great days of North Beach. Peter Plate, a local novelist, describes the scene as 'a crossover: spoken word using rock 'n' roll media, sensibilities, technology, equipment.'

Recommended venues include **Above Paradise** (1501 Folsom, 861 6906) where Sunday nights are probably the most inclusive – politically and socially – and most accomplished gathering in the city. Monday nights at the **Chameleon** (853 Valencia, 821 1891) are rowdy, with poets and hecklers behaving in ways that the term 'poetry reading' doesn't quite describe. **Red Dora's Bearded Lady Café** (485 14th Street; 626 2805) often becomes a performance space at the weekend, where up to eight readers – mostly women – perform to a packed house. **A Different**

Light Bookstore (489 Castro, 431 0891) is 'where gay identity politics meets pop culture', and **Club Coco** (139 Eighth Street, 626 2337) bills an up-and-coming lesbian series, Sister Spit, on Sunday nights. **Jammin' Java** (701 Cole Street, 668 5282) has a low-key open-mike night on Wednesdays, when poets and storytellers stand in the middle of the room and testify. Another venue to watch out for is **Intersection for the Arts** (446 Valencia, 626 2787) which attracts writers sponsored by the NEA (National Endowment for the Arts) at the extreme end of the avant-garde.

Events with featured readers are listed in *Poetry Flash*, a free newspaper found in most bookshops, and in the *Bay Guardian* and *SF Weekly*. Big-name authors on reading tours appear at **A Clean Well-Lighted Place for Books** (441 6670), **The Booksmith** (863 8688) and **Modern Times Bookstore** (282 9246) – *see chapter* **Shopping & Services** for listings.

250 Scott Street was the centre of the post-war poetry renaissance. However, Rexroth's main contribution to San Francisco literary history, much to his own disgust, was as godfather to the Beats. It was Rexroth who presided over the famous reading at the old Six Gallery on Fillmore Street at which **Allen Ginsberg** read the first part of *Howl*, with **Jack Kerouac** chanting 'Go! Go! Go!'

Kerouac came to the city in 1947, at the end of the cross-country trip that was to make him famous a decade later with the publication of *On the Road*. Because Neal Cassady was in San Francisco, the city became the western terminus of Kerouac's restless cross-country swings. He cut the original teletype-roll manuscript of *On the Road* into paragraphs in Cassady's house on Russian Hill in 1952. *San Francisco Blues* was written in the Cameo Hotel in what was then skid row on Third Street. *The Subterraneans*, written in 1953, is set in North Beach but is actually a New York story transposed to protect the characters. The old Third Street that was Kerouac's spiritual home was bulldozed to make way for the Moscone Center, but skid row itself just moved west to Sixth Street.

Meanwhile, Ginsberg had come to San Francisco to 'find the Whitman self-reliance to indulge a celebration of self,' as he put it. Ginsberg decided it was OK to be homosexual, met Peter Orlovsky, moved into the Hotel Wentley at 1214 Polk Street, and began writing a poem that would turn out to be *Howl*. The central image of *Howl* is the Moloch-face of the Drake Hotel on Powell Street as observed by Ginsberg on peyote. There is a fine picture of Ginsberg and the Moloch-faced hotel in Lawrence Ferlinghetti and Nancy Peters' *Literary San Francisco* (City Lights, 1980). 'So here comes Snyder with a bottle of wine,' Kerouac wrote, 'and here comes Whalen, and here comes what's-his-name... Rexroth and everybody... and we had the Poetry Renaissance of San Francisco.'

At the Six Gallery, on 13 October 1955, Rexroth was the MC, the other poets were Ginsberg, Gary Snyder, Philip Whalen, Michael McClure, and Philip Lamantia – and everybody was blown away. **Ferlinghetti**, owner of City Lights Bookstore, wrote to Ginsberg: 'I greet you at the beginning of a great career. Where's the manuscript?' The subsequent obscenity trial of *Howl* catapulted the Beats to public attention and opened the way for the breakdown of the obscenity laws in the 1960s.

The Beat scene was centred around North Beach – the Coexistence Bagel Store at Grant Avenue and Green Street, the Cellar on Green, the Coffee Gallery and the Place on Upper Grant (the Place was home of the blabbermouth nights, ancestors of today's poetry-slams). Perhaps the best reminder today is Gino and Carlo's bar at 548 Green Street (421 0896). Vesuvio's Café (255 Columbus Avenue, 362 3370) is where Kerouac drank away his chance of meeting Henry Miller,

and is across what's now called Jack Kerouac Alley from the City Lights Bookstore (261 Columbus), still the best literary bookshop in San Francisco.

Opposite City Lights are two other bars associated with the Beats: Spec's (421 4112) at 12 Jack Kerouac Alley and Tosca at 242 Columbus Avenue (391 1244). There are ghosts of the Beats all around North Beach and there is a coffee house revival going on at the moment, but the scene itself died a generation ago when the Grey Line tour buses began bringing tourists down Broadway to look at the beatniks.

FROM THE HASHBURY TO BARBARY LANE

The Haight-Ashbury scene doesn't seem to have left much of a literary monument, perhaps because, as **Tom Wolfe** said, if you can remember it you weren't really there. **Ken Kesey** and the reborn **Neal Cassady** began their trips festivals at the Longshoreman's Hall on Fisherman's Wharf, and the scene moved through the Avalon Ballroom on Polk Street and the Fillmore, off Fillmore Street on Geary, as well as the Haight itself. Wolfe's *Electric Kool-Aid Acid Test* is the best account, along with Emmet Grogan's memoir of the Diggers, *Ringolevio*. Kesey and Robert Stone, who was around the scene and wrote about its psychic fallout of the era in *Dog Soldiers*, were both products of Wallace Stegner's writing programme at Stanford. Stegner, a crusty Western gentleman of an older school, must have been horrified to see what his literary children were like.

The Castro hasn't really produced its literary testament yet either, perhaps because the awful events that brought the wide-open Castro of the early 1980s to a crashing halt are still going on. **Randy Shilts** gave a somewhat melodramatic account of the coming of Aids in *And The Band Played On* and also wrote the biography of Harvey Milk. **Frances Fitzgerald** gives a cooler view in *Cities on a Hill*. **Armistead Maupin's** charming and dippy 'Tales of the City' series is in fact set in Macondray Lane on Russian Hill, a not particularly gay venue.

The writing tradition remains strong in San Francisco, however, as writers continue to settle in and write about the city. Literary readings and author signings are still a popular SF pastime. The Bay Area of the 1990s enjoys a strong multicultural feminist presence, and authors including **Amy Tan** (whose *Joy Luck Club* is set in Chinatown), **Alice Walker** (who wrote the *Color Purple* in her Alamo Square Victorian), **Dorothy Allison** (who won the 1994 National Book Award for her coming of age novel, *Bastard Out of Carolina*), Isabel Allende, Terry McMillan and Anne Lamott all regularly sell out the city's largest auditoriums for their reading and speaking engagements. *See also page 258* **Further Reading**.

Media

Where to catch up on world news, watch the latest soap or surf the wilder shores of the Internet.

Mass media may not be as pronounced in the lives of San Franciscans as it is, say, for New Yorkers, but media is no less essential to Left Coasters. In fact, there is arguably no other place where mass media is so essential to the collective psyche. In the San Francisco Bay Area, media is directly related to self-esteem. Its coverage functions not only to report and reflect what's going on, but to confirm the local audience's belief that theirs are the zaniest, most trend-setting, most exceptional lives ever, and there is no place else they ought to be.

Newspapers & Magazines

For information on specialist business publications, *see chapter* **Business**.

Dailies

San Francisco Chronicle

The *Chron* (50¢) is the region's largest circulation paper and complaining about how bad it is has become something of a cliché. But the paper thrives in the suburbs, where its emphasis on 'quality of life' over hard news and business is welcome. The paper also contains the daily (Mon-Fri) gossip column of the city's most-read scribe, Herb Caen. Now in his eighties, Caen remains lucid, often amusing, and, most importantly, no one has yet proved themselves more deft at playing to the city's civic ego.

San Francisco Examiner

No doubt the *Chronicle* would be better if it had some real competition, but the *Examiner* (25¢), the other daily paper, has a joint operating agreement with the *Chronicle* that has consigned the *Examiner* to the afternoon, where it has wilted and become a financial liability to both partners. In 1995, perpetual rumours of the *Examiner*'s impending demise reached

Wave hello to the San Francisco Chronicle.

a new high, and the city has been waiting for an announcement to that effect with each pasing day. Article for article, the *Ex* may be better written, but, like the *Chron*, most of its non-local news coverage comes from wire services or reprints from the *New York Times* or *Los Angeles Times*. Its arts coverage, however, commands nationwide respect.

Sunday Examiner/Chronicle

On Sundays, the *Chron* combines with the *Examiner* to produce the fat Sunday *Examiner/Chronicle* ($1.50). It contains a 'Datebook' supplement, or what locals call the 'pink section' – a tabloid entertainment and arts section published on pink paper which has listings, concert reviews, capsule movie reviews and such like. For visitors, this is probably the single most valuable section of any newspaper.

Other Daily Papers

Even though you're in San Francisco, the national editions of the *New York Times* ($1) or *Los Angeles Times* ($1) are your best bet for good news reporting. The *Wall Street Journal* ($1) has an excellent news brief on the front page and some of the best feature writing in the country, but its Op-Ed page is dominated by reactionary and ultimately tiresome conservatives who blame the country's ills on the 1960s. There's also *USA Today* (50¢), which is often handed out free in hotels, though its best feature is its colour weather map.

Weeklies

San Francisco Bay Guardian

Some pundits have suggested that most Americans only pay attention to public affairs once a week, and this would seem consistent with the growth of San Francisco's two weeklies, the *San Francisco Bay Guardian* and the *SF Weekly*. Both are free and found in boxes, cafés and corner shops throughout the city. Independently owned, the *Bay Guardian* is an earnest, 88-page tabloid that thinks of itself as 'alternative' even though it has come to reflect, more or less, mainstream San Francisco. Although reputed for its challenges to big business, it also has an extensive dining and events section, complete with recommended activities and a 'movie clock', as well as the best-read column after Herb Caen: 'Ask Isadora', a no-holds-barred sex advice column.

SF Weekly

Recently purchased by a corporation which owns several, identical-looking papers each in a different US city, the *SF Weekly* has become stronger in its news and more acerbic and glib in its take on local life. Still, it has an easy-to-read listings section and a bit more humour than the *Bay Guardian*. Best for its cultural coverage.

Gay & Lesbian Papers

There is a host of free papers targeted at gay and lesbian readers, including the *Bay Times* (a tabloid), *BAR* (Bay Area Reporter), *San Francisco Frontiers* and *Icon*. Available from coffee shops and bookstores in the Castro and New Bohemia (the Mission), almost all carry listings of events for gay audiences as well as social and political commentary. Other queer publications produced in San Francisco include *Deneuve* for lesbians and the X-rated *Taste of Latex*.

Monthlies

In San Francisco, magazines are like screenplays in Los Angeles – everyone's working on one. Some of them actually make it to production and even make a splash, like *Wired* and, before it, *Mondo 2000*, now sadly defunct. At the time of writing, a number of new magazines were enduring precariously. They include *Might* ($3.95), a publication of satire and resources for young people; *Juxtapoz* ($3.95), a lowbrow 'art through chaos' journal; *Factsheet Five* ($3.95), which reviews all the desktop/xerox 'zines; and *Surface* ($3.95), an *Interview* wannabe fashion magazine.

San Francisco Focus

San Francisco lacks a magazine along the lines of the weekly *New Yorker* ($2.50), which, in addition to local listings, regularly publishes stories in the national interest. There is the monthly *San Francisco Focus* ($2.95). Published by KQED, the largest public broadcasting station in the Bay Area, it is sent to KQED subscribers and is also available at some newsstands and grocers. It has interviews with regional personalities and reportage on such northern California issues as the environment; it also has a 'Hot Tickets' page of recommended events for the month.

SF Live & Monthly Arts Calendar

Useful if you already have an idea of what you're looking for, these two freebie newspapers can be found in boxes at downtown bus stops, cafés and in the lobbies of some cinemas.

Wired

Entering its fourth year, *Wired* represents the most visible magazine success from San Francisco since *Rolling Stone*. To those who don't play video games or imagine that working with computers ushers them into a new reality, *Wired* can prove bewildering, but its journalism is first-rate and there is no better emblem of the digital revolution.

Foreign-language Publications

At a conservative estimate, San Francisco has more than 70 resident nationalities, and almost all of them have an own-language paper serving their respective community's local needs and desire for news from 'home'. *The Tenderloin Times*, for instance, is published in Cambodian, Vietnamese, Cantonese and English for those mid-town district folk. On Valencia Street, in the predominantly Latin-American Mission district, the following bookshops sell Spanish language newspapers and *libros en Español*: **Modern Times Bookstore** (888 Valencia; 282 9246), **Dog Eared Books**, (1173 Valencia; 282 1901), and **Books On Wings** (La Casa del Libros, 973 Valencia; 285 1145). On the same street you can also find the **Arabic Book Center** (791 Valencia; 864 1585). An ex-pat Filipino, who runs the *Examiner* kiosk near the Hyatt Regency hotel on Market Street, keeps abreast of events on the Pacific Islands. Chinatown is also the place for news from Asia, and **Books On Japan** (1581 Webster Street in Japantown; 567 7625) stocks Japanese language publications. Italians can pick up the latest installment of *Diabolik* at **Cavalli Italian Bookstore** (1441 Stockton; 421 4219); and the **European Book Company** (925 Larkin; 474 0626) stocks various European language publications.

Outlets

As far as newsstands go, San Francisco is a town long on specialists and short on generalists. Still, there are a few locations that endeavour to give readers a single destination for all their periodical needs. The very well-read **Harold's**

Harold's International Newsstand.

International Newsstand at 524 Geary Boulevard, between Jones and Taylor Streets (441 2665) offers as complete a selection as you'll find in the city; **Farley's** at 1315 18th Street, between Texas and Missouri Streets (648 1545) is a decent café with magazines; and **Juicy News** at 2453 Fillmore Street, between Jackson and Washington Streets (441 3051), is a deceptively small shop given the number of titles it carries.

Those on the hunt for art and poetry publications should try **City Lights Bookstore** (*see chapter* **Shopping & Services**). Co-founded by Lawrence Ferlinghetti and made famous by the Beats he published, City Lights has an eclectic magazine rack that emphasises creative energies.

Collectors will want to visit **the Magazine** at 920 Larkin Street, between Geary Boulevard and Post Street (441 7737), a store of vintage publications. Those wishing to see first hand what the buzz about 'zines (self-published, desktop publications usually written with a very personal perspective) is all about are advised to visit **Naked Eye News & Video**, or, for an excellent selection of gay and lesbian 'zines, try **A Different Light** (*see chapter* **Shopping & Services** for both).

Tower Records at Market and Noe Streets (621 0588) and Columbus and Bay Avenues (885 0500) can be counted on for the latest pop culture and music rags. Homesick Europeans needn't miss a beat at **Le Café de la Presse** (inside the Triton Hotel at 352 Grant Avenue and Bush Street; 398 2680), an ultra-modern Parisian-style café, which has all the major European dailies and glossies.

The region's best newsstand, however, is not in San Francisco, but in Oakland. At the 12th Street BART Station, **De Lauer Super Newsstand** (1310 Broadway, Oakland; 1-510 451 6157) is open 24-hours a day and is almost always busy.

Television

If you have never seen North American TV, then you might want to watch a few hours. If, however, you have experienced this particular pleasure before, don't expect San Francisco broadcasters to provide anything new. For those unaccustomed to TV in the US, be prepared for a blaring deluge of advertisements and a surprising lack of resistance to it from regular viewers. The fact, for instance, that programming is driven by advertising has moved from the evident to the obvious, the result being that few give this troubling relationship a second thought. What's more, many of television's greatest talents are employed part- or full-time by advertisers to direct or star in their spots. Consequently, for pure entertainment value, advertisements often outshine the programming.

The best printed resource for what's on the air remains the *TV Guide* (99¢). Daily newspapers have 24-hour TV listings, and a stapled catalogue for the week is included in the Sunday *Examiner/Chronicle*.

The Networks

The San Francisco Bay Area has affiliates of all three major networks: **ABC** (local station is KGO, found on channel 7), **NBC** (KRON, channel 4) and **CBS** (KPIX, channel 5). The long-lasting independent station, KTVU (channel 2) is now part of the **Fox TV** network.

Reflecting their dependence on advertising, there is little difference, politically or ideologically, between these four networks – their primary concern is the size of their audience, not any social tendency within it. Their daily fare is almost identical, with variations on a theme. The morning brings chatty news reports – *Today* on NBC, *This Morning* on CBS, *Good Morning America* on ABC – plus exercise programmes and *Sesame Street* for the kids. Mid-morning, the confessional and celebrity-driven talk shows begin (for example, *Donahue* and *Maury Povich* on NBC and *Geraldo* on CBS), yielding to soap operas at midday. After lunch, the soaps wrap up and it's back to more talk shows, including the *Oprah Winfrey Show* (KGO, channel 7, 3pm Mon-Fri). As early as 4pm you can catch national network news taped on the East Coast or broadcast live from its 7pm slot in New York and Washington.

Early evenings are dominated by news programmes, game shows and re-runs of sitcoms. Melodramas and movies edited for commercial breaks dominate 'Prime Time' and then it's onto the late-night talk shows where celebrity hosts (David Letterman on CBS at 11pm; Jay Leno on NBC at 11.35pm) interview stars, introduce hit-making bands and work for laughs.

CNN and a local independent station, **KOFY** (channel 20), broadcast news. Weekly highlights on the networks include *60 Minutes* (CBS, Sundays at 7pm) and the ever-popular *Saturday Night Live* (NBC, Saturdays at 12.30am). Most stations run programming around the clock, so insomniacs with a TV are never without distraction in America.

Cable TV

To improve their choice of small screen entertainment, most people in the Bay Area pay monthly fees for cable TV (and most hotels worth their nightly rates offer cable as a standard feature). In addition to the 24-hour music videos of **MTV** (on cable channel 48) and round-the-clock sport on **ESPN** (cable 34), cable provides access to a number of stations that specialise in news (**CNN**, cable 42), classic movies (**AMC**, cable 34; the **Movie Channel**, cable 1) or recently released movies (**HBO**, cable 8). Furthermore, some hit movies and sporting events (usually boxing matches) are available on a pay-as-you-view basis. Some sports bars will pay these fees to attract customers. For Public Access television, check out **Bay TV** (cable 35), a station dedicated to local issues, with mixed results so far.

Public TV

The alternative to the relentless advertising of commercial stations is **PBS**, the Public Broadcasting Service, which has stations in San Francisco (**KQED**, found on cable 9), San Jose (**KTEH**, channel 54, cable 19) and San Mateo (**KCSM**, channel 60, cable 21). These stations receive a subsidy from the federal government (currently being contested) and solicit funds from viewers.

Criticised for being short on local programming, KQED has an unenviable reputation as one of the fattest of the subsidised stations, with much of the money going into fat cats' salaries. It broadcasts the *MacNeil/Lehrer NewsHour* every weekday at 6pm. Although an improvement on the advertised news of the three big networks, the *NewsHour* still goes for the reassuring patrician model of news delivery.

While PBS may be a respite from the advertised life, it trades off its 'prestige' reputation a touch too smugly. This is fine for homesick Brits pining for 'quality' TV or re-runs of ancient British sitcoms, but hardly the authentic American TV experience. More in tune with American grazing habits is *Talk Soup*, on C-Net (*see below* **Web-sites and On-line Locations**) which provides a weekly digest of the best of the talk shows.

Radio

San Francisco has a vibrant radio market, in part because radio signals manage to unite listeners separated by steep hills and bodies of water. Unfortunately for music lovers, however, where the tendency ten, or even five, years ago was to boast 'less talk, more music', the reverse is true today. And even in the San Francisco area, most of the talk jocks tend to be reactionary right-wingers set on finding someone to blame for the decline of Western Civilisation.

News & Talk

If there's still a fine distinction to be made between commercial and alternative radio, few stations make any attempt at an equal balance between talk and music, and for the latest news **KGO** (810 AM), **KQED** (88.5 FM) and **KPFA** (94.1 FM) are your best bets. Once the radical voice of the Bay Area, KPFA is now retuning to give KQED a run for its money. It features ex-governor Jerry Brown's national talk show *We the People* **KCBS** (740 AM) and has proved itself indispensable during emergencies, such as the 1989 earthquake.

KSFO (740 AM), meanwhile, boasts the aforementioned reactionary talk radio programmes in the morning and also broadcasts Oakland A's baseball games. **KNBR** (680 AM) is the city's leader for sports talk, the perfect place to tune in if you want proof that Americans are, in fact, very well-informed and skilled in debate – as long as the subject is sport.

Classical

KDFC (102.1 FM, 1220 AM), advertised as 'your radio concert hall', used to be a bit on the stuffy side, but that profile has been shattered by its new hyperactive ads, which would turn off many a music lover if there were a serious alternative to its standard repertoire programming. **KKHI** (100.7 FM) has a popular Morning Concert at 10am and an Afternoon Concert at 3pm.

Jazz

The Bay Area lost **KJAZ** radio station in 1995. A venerable source of jazz for decades, it is survived by the far more adventurous **KCSM** (97.7 FM), a public radio station broadcast from a college in San Mateo. **KKSF** (103.7 FM) is where jazz meets New Age. Although they play many talented artists, hour after hour, it can sometimes sound like muzak for the 1990s.

Dance & Hip Hop

Rarely can one find more energy than on **KMEL** (106 FM), the Bay Area's station for pop and hip hop. **WILD 107** (107.7 FM) is something of a contender and definitely gets partygoers in the mood on weekend nights, but for the latest in urban sounds, **KMEL** gets it. KMEL also hosts *Street Soldiers*, a model call-in talk show for gang members to vent their troubles and get advice.

Rock & Pop

KFOG (104.5 FM) may have the most loyal following on the West Coast. These adoring masses even have a name: Fog Heads. KFOG describes its programming as 'quality rock', and it does provide an above average mix of classic rock with

new material, much of it local. **KITS** (Live 105 FM) is the kiddie rock station, with oldies for twentysomethings thrown in for good measure.

One of the most obnoxious, *ergo* most popular, morning show hosts is Alex Bennett on KITS. Bennett regularly interviews comedians who have local gigs. **KOME** (98.5 FM) has staked out the newest and youngest rock/pop territory and is a hit with teenagers.

College Radio

Those in search of more eclectic and experimental listening should try **UC-Berkeley** (90.7 FM), **KUSF** (90.3 FM) and **KPOO** (89.5 FM). Though affiliated with colleges, many of those involved with the stations are professionals looking for an outlet for their less commercial interests.

Web Sites and On-line Locations

Away from the broadcast and print media, the Internet offers a whole new range of interesting information sites. A print link-up provides a useful port of entry. Anyone with a computer, modem

Multimedia Gulch

'Like Pac-Men chasing blinking ghosts, hundreds are pursuing the multimedia dream – the adrenalin rush apparently worth the risk of losing it all.' (*Los Angeles Times*, 30 September 1994).

Despite prophecies that computers and telecommunications technologies will decentralise business, enabling individuals hundreds or thousands of miles apart to collaborate as if they were in the same room, the most visible, computer-driven industry of all, multimedia, remains, for now, centrally located. It resides in 'Multimedia Gulch' – the area in the SoMa district surrounding South Park – and has many convinced that San Francisco will be a seat of media power for years to come, just as New York has publishing and Los Angeles the movies.

And yet, to the casual visitor, such claims might seem delusional, another occasion to apply Gertrude Stein's remark that 'there is no there, there'. For one thing, not only are the warehouses in SoMa largely unmarked, but if you went by the topography, Multimedia Gulch would be more appropriately known as the Slope, or, perhaps, Steppe.

'The Multimedia Gulch is really a sensibility more than a location,' says Victoria Dawson, a multimedia designer/producer at Macromedia and the editorial director of *City Culture*, a guide to SoMa venues. 'Being in a specific place isn't what makes you a part of it. It's just being involved with those doing it.' Jonathan E, who generates a Gulch Gossip column for *Micro Times*, a local computer magazine, agrees. 'It's more a state of mind. It's

representative. Like the way Madison Avenue stands for all of advertising.'

Yet there are more concrete reasons why Multimedia Gulch took root in San Francisco, the proximity of Silicon Valley's hardware manufacturing centre and software development sites being just one of them. Early development of digital video took place in the city, and it also contains many studios specialising in world

*Get wired at the **Icon Byte & Grill**.*

and dial-up software can ring the *Bay Guardian* at 487 5700 to download the software that operates the paper's free on-line service. Additionally the service allows you to send and receive email from the Internet. The *San Francisco Chronicle* and *San Francisco Examiner* share an on-line link, called the **SF Gate** (http://www.sfgate.com).

Standing for Whole Earth 'Lectronic Link, **the Well** (http://www.well.com) was founded on April Fools Day, 1984 and was one of the first virtual communities to attract public use. It is an ideal source of information for exploring 'overground' San Francisco.

C-net (http://www.cnet.com) is an indispensable source for what's happening in computers and multimedia. It combines a computer network, the largest original content on the World Wide Web and the television series **C/net Central**, the latter boasting that it's the world's first on-air and on-line showcase for computers, multimedia and digital technologies. It reaches more than 60 million techno enthusiasts. C/net Central airs on the USA Network on Saturdays at 9.30am, Sundays at 6.30am and Mondays at 1am. It can be picked up on the Sci-Fi Channel on Sundays at 7.30am, 7.30pm, and 11.30pm. The show also runs on the local KPIX 5 on Saturdays at 5pm.

Useful travel and hotel information can be looked up at the **San Francisco Hotel Reservations** (http://www.hotelres.com/) and **Bay Area Transit Information** (http://server. berkeley.edu/Transit/index.html). And for that full psychedelic rock poster experience call up the **Rock & Roll Digital Gallery** (http://www. hooked.net/julianne/index.html).

For a list of useful websites covering San Francisco and the Bay Area, *see page 9* **Essential Information**.

---

class production of film, sound and prints. Last but not least, many of the professionals best suited to multimedia activity want to live and work here.

The Bay Area is home to a large number of firms developing various forms of multimedia, even if they insist that their 'experiential' or 'interactive entertainment' technology is somehow distinct from multimedia. In addition to hardware providers like Apple, software developers like Macromedia, Xaos, Ibis Software and Autodesk, and major multimedia publishers like Broderbund, Lucas Arts, Electronic Arts, Spectrum Holobyte, Time-Warner Interactive, Mondo Media and PF Magic, there are a number of smaller fries like Ion and Pop Rocket, as well as hotshots in established mediums, such as film company Colossal Pictures, which has launched its own New Media division.

Even so, as with any 'scene', the most visible habitués of Multimedia Gulch, the ones modelling the *haute* grungewear and sipping Pellegrino water, are the glommers-on, the wannabes, the people who call themselves 'virtual architects' or 'interactive directors'. The folks who really are busy producing multimedia, meanwhile, are generally in front of their computers 14 to 15 hours a day, six to seven days a week, and if they're spotted at an outdoor café, it's probably because their doctor or therapist told them to get at least 30 minutes of sun each day.

Multimedia is best defined as the computer-based integration of visual and audio content, stored in formats like CDs or displayed and manipulated on-line. Though this is not such a difficult concept, it can prove otherwise. For example, to some this simply means video games which, after all, combine audio and visuals. To others, multimedia is the kiosk in the airport with pleasant colour-coded instructions. Or multimedia means virtual reality – something like space-age surgery conducted with VR goggles and gloves. It is, of course a combination of all of these, depending on who you talk to. The confusion comes from those eager to mark out their own territories by talking down the competition as 'less serious' multimedia. So video games get translated into 'interactive entertainment', and so on.

At street level, the cyber café trend that provided the visual evidence of San Francisco's multimedia capital status peaked a while ago. As most people are connected at home or work nowadays, cafés provide terminals with Internet access more as a matter of course than as a major selling point. **Cafe Babar** (*see chapter* **Bars & Cafés**), the **Icon Byte & Grill** (299 Ninth Street, at Folsom; 861 2983) and **Mad Magda's Russian Tea Room**, (579 Hayes Street; 864 7654) all have terminals for customers' use and are handy stop-offs for visitors wanting to get on-line.

However, if you want to venture into the next millennium, you can visit **Cybermind** in the Embarcadero Center (693 0348): don a virtual reality helmet, leave your body behind and cruise through cyberspace.

Clubs

Dancing queens, soul survivors, and jazz cats can bop till they drop with our guide to club culture.

Just what makes one venue a club and another merely a bar with music is never all that clear, especially in San Francisco, where there are only a handful of full-time, full-scale dance clubs. Suffice it to say that the listings that appear here are those places that encourage and emphasise the politics of dancing, as opposed to politics over a beer. They draw crowds who, as often as not, spend some time cultivating a look or pose for the evening; venues where it pays to know what's on the calendar for the evening or else face fashion-conscious agoraphobia; venues where you may well leave in a sweat or a stupor.

Although many dance clubs stay open well past last orders, by law they cannot serve alcohol from 2am-6am. They also cannot serve alcohol to anyone under 21. Nevertheless, some clubs, including **DV8** (*see below*) and **Komotion** (*see chapter* **Music: Rock, Roots & Jazz**), are open to those aged 18 and under, or 'all ages', with blacklight reflective hand stamps to determine who can and can't drink booze. If you are under 21, check in advance whether you can get into a club.

Admission prices for the clubs listed below vary, depending on the night, but are usually between $5 and $10.

INFORMATION

For club information on the fly, try the recorded Be-At Line (626 4087), which has daily details of where to be and when (phone after 2pm or you'll get the previous night's information). Also try one of the number of low-budget magazines with club listings and gossip that proliferate in cafés, bars and kiosks around the city. For gay and lesbian clubs, *Odyssey* is fairly reliable and fun (*see chapter* **Gay & Lesbian San Francisco**). There's also a high gloss mag,**Surface* ($3.95), which is making a run at being the style bible for San Francisco nightlifers (it looks and reads the way *Interview* or *The Face* would if they were produced in the city).

TRANSPORT

The Muni Metro Owl Service operates on the L & N lines from 12.30am until 5.30am. All other lines stop at 12.30am, and the major routes are covered instead by Owl Service buses, which run from 1am until 5am. BART runs roughly until midnight, although it's always best to check the time of the last train to your destination. *See chapter* **Getting Around** for a list of taxi companies.

One-offs

Many of the most interesting clubs are produced on a freelance basis by professional club promoters and move through the city quickly, like raves, the popularity of which peaked in less than a year. Still, there are a finite number of venues with enough square footage for a real dance party, and if you know where they are, you can usually find the latest thing. Some notorious shelters for roving clubs include **174 King Street** (974 1719) and **177 Townsend Street** (974 1156), which are in the same building but have different entrances; **525 Harrison Street** (543 1300), home to the Sound Factory on Friday nights; **278 11th Street** (621 3859), formerly the Oasis; and **650 Howard Street** (896 1950). Check the newspapers and scan café bulletin boards and literature piles in SoMa, the Mission, the Castro and the Haight for one-night club happenings. If you like the sensibility of the flyer, chances are you'll enjoy the club.

Ballroom/Latin

Bahia Cabana Restaurant and Club

1600 Market Street, at Franklin Street (626 3306). BART Van Ness/Muni Metro F, J, K, L, M, N. **Open** *restaurant* lunch served 11am-2pm Mon-Sat; dinner served 5-10pm daily; *club* 8.30pm-2am Tue-Sat.
There's salsa and samba most nights of the week plus lambada classes on Saturdays and African music on Fridays. Phone for the latest schedule of events.

Cesar's Latin Palace

3140 Mission Street, at Army Street (648 6611). Muni Metro J. **Open** phone for schedule.
The place to catch a big brass salsa band: look out for Tito Puente. With room for 1,000, Cesar's is indeed palatial.

One of SoMa's stalwarts: the many faces of the **DNA Lounge.** *See page 180.*

Third Wave Dance Studio

3316 24th Street, at Mission Street (282 4020). BART 24th Street/Muni Metro L/14, 67 bus. **Open** phone for schedule.

On Wednesday and Sunday nights, this dance studio hosts the Bare Foot Boogie, with the musical selection including classical, samba and hip hop. There are other dance classes throughout the week.

Dance

Babylon

2260 Van Ness Avenue, at Vallejo Street (567 1222). Bus 30X, 42, 47, 49, 76. **Open** 7pm-2am Tue-Sat.

Further north than most night spots and located on the busy three-lane artery that is Van Ness Avenue, Babylon can be a bit pretentious, turning out the Euro-philes (or Euro-trash, if you are feeling less forgiving). The interior, however, has rich colours and textures and, with the right company, it can feel less like a deliberate money-clip and Versace scene and more like a restaurant that erupted into a dance party. Dress code on Saturdays.

Club 181

181 Eddy Street, at Taylor Street (673 8181). BART Powell Street/Muni Metro F, J, K, L, M, N/27, 31 bus. **Open** 9pm-2am Wed, Sun; 9pm-2am Fri, Sat.

Night owls

San Francisco has a notorious shortage of after-hours clubs and cafés, although a recent effort has been made to remedy this by the diner **It's Tops** (1801 Market Street, 431 6395). Otherwise, there's always **Mel's Drive In** (3355 Geary Street, at Parker Street; 387 2244, and 2165 Lombard Street; 921 3039); **Denny's** (1700 Post Street; 563 1400), and the ugly cafeteria known as **Sparky's** (246 Church Street; 626 8666), which is usually full of other dance-tired, strung-out night hawks and cabbies and, like the others is open 24-hours a day.

If you're determined to shop till you drop, there are a few late-night possibilities, including the famous North Beach bookstore **City Lights** (open until midnight daily); **Borders Books and Music** in Union Square (open until midnight Thur-Sat); **A Clean Well-Lighted Place for Books** (open until midnight Sat); **Tower Records** (open until midnight daily); **Virgin Records** (open until midnight Fri and Sat). And if you want to soak in a hot tub until the small hours, **Osento** women's bath house is open until 1am Fri, Sat (last admission midnight); or you could give your clothes the same treatment at Brainwash, the café-cabaret-cum-laundrette. For more details of all of these, *see* chapter **Shopping & Services**.

Club 181's moment as the lounge and dance floor for the beautiful people may have elapsed, but stylish, mostly straight singles gather here to shoot pool, make alluring eye contact and dance to hip hop and soul flavours. Located in the Tenderloin, one of the city's sketchier districts, it's best to take a cab here. A single wave of dinners is served early in the evening. Then the tables and candelabras are removed to make room for dancing.

Covered Wagon

911 Folsom Street, at Fifth Street (974 1585). Bus 12, 27. **Open** 4.30pm-2am Mon-Fri; 8pm-2am Sat; 9pm-2am Sun.

Two rooms and a bar that can get to feel cramped, the CW Saloon (as it's more commonly known), is no place to go if you can't stand to sweat. The interior and live music run toward grunge, and there's a different club each night of the week. On Saturdays it's 'Muffdive – a Dive for Dykes'; the rest of the week draws a mixed, youngish crowd, and plenty of bike messengers.

DNA Lounge

375 11th Street, at Harrison Street (626 1409). Bus 9, 19, 42. **Open** 9am-2am Tue-Thur; 9pm-4am Fri, Sat.

The DNA feels a bit like a dungeon inside, as though you hadn't walked in but fallen through a trap door. A main stage (open for show-offs when there isn't a band) is flanked by stairs that lead to a mezzanine with corner booths for drinking and necking. DJs spin music between (or instead of) sets of live music. A solid, if not especially inspired choice for a night's entertainment.

DV8

55 Natoma Street (957 1730). BART Civic Center/Muni Metro F, J, K, L, M, N. **Open** 10pm-5am Fri, Sat.

DV8 is the superstore of dance clubs and always packed at the weekends, but usually not with locals. A date destination for the evening, DV8 has three floors, lots of twirling lamps, disco balls and strobes and as many as four DJs at a time. A back exit/entrance leads to the Caribbean Zone (*see chapter* **Bars & Cafés**) and there is usually a medium to high level of glam: limos out front, dressed-to-kill human dance machines, go-go dancers to show you how it's done. Expect to queue.

El Rio

3158 Mission Street, at Cesar Chavez Street (282 3325). Bus 12, 14, 27, 49. **Open** 3pm-midnight Mon; 3pm-2am Tue-Sun.

The sign reads 'El Rio: Your Dive' and it's true. But El Rio draws one of the most friendly, eclectic and relaxed crowds in the city. Friday night happy hour features free fresh shucked oysters, Club NZinga the same evening has wide-ranging world beat music, and Sunday afternoon in the garden is a city favourite – live Latin music and dancing: you never know who will ask you to dance next.

Harry Denton's

161 Steuart Street, at Embarcadero (882 1333). BART Embarcadero/Muni Metro J, K, L, M, N/2, 7, 8, 9, 14, 21, 31, 66, 72 bus. **Open** 9pm-7am Mon-Fri; 9pm-8am Sat, Sun.

Ostentatious and pretentious Harry Denton's has a dress code and a two-figure admission charge on weekends. For this, you can dance with mostly straight, middle-aged singles to a cover band (Motown faves) and squeeze through the crowd to the back dance floor, where the waterfront is visible. It can be nightmarish, but, as most cabbies will tell you, if you can't get laid at Harry Denton's, you can't get laid.

Nikki's BBQ

460 Haight Street, between Webster and Fillmore Streets (621 6508). Bus 6, 6, 22, 66, 71. **Open** 9pm-2am daily.

Nikki's is an intimate space, and although no one will hold it against you that you're a tourist, they'd just as soon you didn't tell all your travelling friends about it – it gets full enough as it is. The club is located on a block of Haight Street that sees its share of trouble, but the folks at Nikki's are mostly looking to dance their troubles away. The musical selection is fluid – lots of soul, funk, hip hop, bass – and the crowd is generally straight.

Ten 15

1015 Folsom Street, between Sixth and Seventh Streets (431 0700). Bus 12, 14X, 27, 42. **Open** 10pm-2am Tue, Wed, Fri, Sat.
Like the DNA lounge, the 1015 is always a safe bet for several hours of dancing. With three rooms, each with its own vibe, you can move through space and time without changing venues. The 1015 also has a speakeasy downstairs where jazz power trios often provide a cool-down groove or where you might stumble on a record or magazine release party. It's further east on Folsom Street than the more pedestrian-friendly club-land around 11th Street, so you'll probably want to flag down a cab.

Sound Factory

525 Harrison Street, at First Street (543 1300). Bus 42, 76. **Open** 9.30pm-7am Fri; 9.30pm-4am Sat.
In a cavernous warehouse space, the Sound Factory boasts two floors, multiple rooms and is known to attract late waves of new, mostly young party-goers coming in after they finish their jobs waiting tables or cocktailing. Like its twin in New York, the Sound Factory is as close to an institution as one can get for a dance club. Plenty of house, funk, the latest imports and pop. Admission is free until 10pm.

Transmission Productions

1501 Folsom Street, at 11th Street (861 6906/621 7923). Bus 9, 12, 42. **Open** 3pm-2am daily.
This space has potential but hasn't really found its mark of distinction yet. At the time of writing, it was portraying itself as a nightclub/theatre where displays of mixed media and tech-heavy artwork mix with breaks from dance beats or ambient music. Constantly changing, projected visuals add to the suggestion of something out of science fiction, but play out more like multimedia – if multimedia could be played from an old vinyl LP. It's next door to the Paradise Lounge (*see chapter* **Music: Rock, Roots & Jazz**).

Trocadero Transfer

520 Fourth Street, at Bryant Street (995 4600). Bus 9X, 9AX, 9BX, 27, 30, 42, 45, 76. **Open** 9pm-2am Mon, Wed, Fri; from 9.30pm-2am Sat.
Home to the longest running (and only weekly) S&M fetish club – Bondage-a-Go-Go, on Wednesday nights and a big GothRock scene – the Troc has something going at least five nights a week, and it's almost always pushing the envelope of social decorum. Expect a crowd of wealthy participant-observers investigating the fringe and some hardcore leather and modern primitives.

Gay & Lesbian Clubs

There are predominantly straight clubs as opposed to gay and lesbian clubs, but given both the visibility of gayness in San Francisco and the presence of at least a few highly evolved heterosexuals, there's a fair amount of poly-sexual mixing. Try the **End-up** – which feels like a party at someone's flat, and where the risqué family atmosphere is at its best on Sundays, which is one long hangout and vibrating cure for whatever ails you; or the **Stud**, a gay and lesbian bar with a dance floor which never seems to have evolved out of the 1970s. For more information on these and other gay clubs, *see* chapter **Gay & Lesbian San Francisco**.

Comedy Clubs

An alternative to the nightclub scene is comedy clubs, where you can sip drinks and dare stand-up comedians to make you laugh. San Francisco has been the starting point – or at least a stop along the way – for many of the most prominent comedians in the US, notably film stars Whoopi Goldberg and Robin Williams, and television sitcom stars Ellen DeGeneres and Margaret Cho. The winner of the annual SF International Comedy Competition can be the comedian to watch in the coming year. For comedy nightlife try **Cobb's Comedy Club** (563 5157) at Fisherman's Wharf; **The Improv** (441 7787) near Union Square; **Morty's** (986 6678) in North Beach; and the **Punch Line** (397 7573); also, don't miss **Josie's Cabaret and Juice Bar** (861 7933) for Monday night 'open mike' comedy (*see chapters* **Theatre & Dance** *and* **Gay & Lesbian San Francisco**).

Supper Clubs

Supper clubs are an idea whose time has come again in San Francisco, remodelling Jazz Age dining clubs with plenty of 1990s' motifs – international tapas to eat; hip hop/jazz improvisation; deep sofas and/or minimalist furniture warmly lit and buffered with more shades of grey than Woody Allen's *Manhattan*. In short, this everything-old-is-new-again trend means venues which combine fine dining and live music, treating the music not as a concert but as part of an engaging backdrop – in other words, jazz as context.

Coconut Grove

1415 Van Ness Avenue, between Pine and Bush Streets (776 1616). Bus 2, 3, 4, 19, 42, 47, 49. **Open** 5pm-2.30am daily. **Admission** $7-$25. **Credit** AmEx, MC, V.
The Coconut Grove secured its reputation by having Tom Jones on its opening night bill. *Sans* Jones, it is still notable for its lobster Thermidor with black truffle risotto. Dinner seating is staggered for the two nightly shows (at 7pm and 10.30pm) and those eating dinner must conform to a dress code (men, carry a tie in your jacket and women, don't wear jeans). As for the shows, they're big name Tahoe and Vegas acts: Kris Kristofferson, Debbie Reynolds, Nancy Wilson. The problem is, the interior is a bit too Vegas as well – Casino cheesy. The CG is not a place for those on a tight budget.

Eichelberger's

2742 17th Street, between Bryant and Harrison Streets (863 4177). Bus 22, 27, 33, 53. **Open** 4-11pm Tue-Thur; 4pm-1am Fri, Sat. **Admission** free. **Credit** AmEx, MC, V.
Named after Ethyl Eichelberger – a performance artist – and owned and bartended by two survivors of experimental theatre, the spirit of this place is nothing if not zany. Hosting modest cabaret acts, leatherwear contests and drag nights, Eichelberger's is an upstairs/downstairs sort of place, with a full service dining room above (complete with beautiful, elaborate candelabras) and a bar room below. Although the food is good (yes, they do serve an Eichel Burger), the chefs have concentrated more on the bar scene than on forging a new culinary paradigm. Combined with a night at Theater Artaud (in a warehouse across the street, *see chapter* **Theatre & Dance**), Eichelberger's offers a true San Francisco experience.

330 Ritch: *if you can't find it, you ain't hip.*

Eleven

*374 11th Street, between Harrison and Folsom Streets
(431 3337). Bus 9, 27, 42.* **Open** 5.30pm-1.30am Mon-
Sat. **Admission** $5 after 9.30pm Wed-Sat (unless dining).
Credit AmEx, MC, V.

Formerly Undici (before the name was translated from the
Italian), Eleven's owner Tim Dale evidently took note of the
crowds who were turning out for the jazz acts at his previous venue, the Up & Down Club (*below*), and began offering
jazz nightly in the loft above the bar here. It was a wise move,
as the music transforms a room that can feel more like a
gallery space than a restaurant into a warmer, inviting scene.
The cuisine is Italian, the service super-great when you can
get it.

Harry Denton's Starlite Room

*Sir Francis Drake Hotel, 450 Powell Street, between Post
and Sutter Streets (395 8595). Bus 2, 3, 4, 30, 45, 76/
Powell-Mason, Powell-Hyde cable car.* **Open** 4.30pm-
12.30am Mon; 4.30pm-1.30am Tue-Sat. **Admission** after
8pm $6 Wed; $8 Thur; $12 Fri, Sat. **Credit** AmEx, MC, V.

Harry Denton is famous in San Francisco as a man who
makes his bars a non-stop party (for the press night here he
dropped his trousers, a moment broadcast on local TV).
Denton's favourite drink is Chartreuse and if he takes a liking
to you, you may discover first-hand that it's not easy being
green. Denton and his places are a love 'em and leave 'em
affair. This one has a stunning 21st-floor view over Union
Square, lots of mirrors for askance eye contact, floral carpets
and booths filled with social and financial climbers. The
music, meanwhile, is less innovative jazz, more R&B covers:
don't come to the Starlite if you can't stand 'Mustang Sally'.

Julie Ring's Heart and Soul

*1695 Polk Street, at Clay Street (673 7100). Bus 1, 19,
42, 47, 49, 76.* **Open** 8pm-2am Mon, Sun; 5pm-2am Tue-
Fri; 6pm-2am Sat. **Admission** $4-$10 Tue-Sat. **Credit**
AmEx, MC, V.

Evenings begin with a gentle tinkling of the ivories (5.30-
8pm) followed by the main event at 8.30pm. The tunes tend

to be less hectic than at the Up & Down Club or 330 Ritch
(*see below*), Julie insisting on swing era and blues material,
but the crowd tends to get involved with the band person-
ally. The interior is warm and comfortable, boasts a modest
mezzanine and stylish curtain 'bulbs' over the ceiling lights.
The cuisine is Californian with a touch of French Creole and
they stock a fine collection of whisky. For a crowd, go at the
weekend; to talk all night without feeling rushed, grab a table
upstairs early in the week.

330 Ritch

*330 Ritch Street, between Third and Fourth Streets (541
9574). Bus 15, 30, 42, 45, 76.* **Open** 11am-3pm, 4pm-
2am Tue, Wed; 11am-2am Thur-Sat. **Admission** $5-$8.
Credit AmEx, MC, V.

One of the strengths of 330 Ritch is that it stays open later
than the rest (not that it isn't good for a visit earlier in the
evening). And that's no small deal in this town. It epitomis-
es the nouveau supper club scene: jam sessions-in-progress;
recessed lighting in the rafters; international cuisine; a regular Colours of Benetton mix of folks in the house – but with
better fashion sense. The service is enthusiastic, and the only
drawback is finding the place (then again, if you can't find
it, you ain't hip).

Up & Down Club

*1151 Folsom Street, between Seventh and Eighth Streets
(626 2388). Bus 12, 19.* **Open** 8pm-2am Mon-Thur;
7.30pm-2am Fri, Sat. **Admission** $5. **Credit** AmEx,
MC, V.

As one of the centres of the jazz renaissance in San
Francisco, the Up & Down has built up a reputation for
quality tunes, hosting original bands with a sound that can
hold your full attention. The upstairs offers another groove
(often house music), so that you can sample two scenes for
the price of one. It gets crowded and can get claustrophobic. Model Christy Turlington is a co-owner and has been
known to appear for fundraisers and special occasions. The
kitchen serves nouveau North American cuisine early in
the evening.

Film

San Francisco has enough retro movie houses, avant-garde film festivals and familiar locations to satisfy even the most jaded film buff.

San Francisco is best known for its prolific and award-winning avant-garde and documentary film makers. Terry Zwiegoff, who made 1994's successful *Crumb*, Rob Epstein and Jeffrey Friedman who won an academy award for both *The Life and Times of Harvey Milk* and *Common Threads* (the story of the Names Project AIDS quilt) are among the city's better known film makers in that genre.

The city is also a favourite location, and several mainstream directors have settled in the Bay Area (notably Francis Ford Coppola and George Lucas, whose Marin-based LucasFilm studio is noted for its special effects abilities). It's said that San Francisco has more film-makers per capita than any other city in the world – except for one small town in Kentucky that is home to a film making foundation.

San Francisco State University, Stanford University, the San Francisco Art Institute and even City College have thriving film making programmes, each encouraging and developing new and established film and video artists (*see chapter* **Students**). In addition, two San Francisco institutions – the Film Arts Foundation and the Bay Area Video Action Coalition – provide services and continuing education and networking for film-makers in the area, and the San Francisco Cinemateque provides a prime venue for avant-garde screenings. Where local programming is featured, keep an eye open for international notables Bruce Conner, Trinh T Minh-ha, Larry Jordan and Lynn Hershman.

THE CINEMAS

San Franciscans also have a sizeable appetite for foreign and art house fare and the city contains more than a few theatres that specialise in screening those films. The Landmark theatre chain is one and includes the **Lumière** (1572 California Street, between Polk and Larkin Streets; 885 3200), the **Bridge** (3010 Geary Boulevard, at Blake Street; 751 3212), the **Opera Plaza** (601 Van Ness Avenue, between Turk Street and Golden Gate Avenue; 771 0102), the **Gateway** (215 Jackson Street, between Battery and Front Streets; 421 3353), and the **Embarcadero Center Cinema** (352 0810). Landmark cinemas will often pick up audience favourites from one of the frequent San Francisco film festivals.

Pop into the **Roxie** *for classic revivals.*

Many of the city's mainstream movie houses are well-appointed, with comfortable seating and state-of-the-art sound systems. Notable among them are the **Kabuki 8 Cinema** (1181 Post Street, at Fillmore Street; 931 9088), the **Galaxy** (1285 Sutter Street, at Van Ness Avenue; 474 8700), the **Regency** (1320 Van Ness Avenue, at Sutter Street; 885 6773), the **UA Coronet** (752 4400/03; don't worry if you see a queue snaking through the car park – more people can fit in this cinema than you'd have thought possible) and the **UA Emery Bay** just across the Bay Bridge in Emeryville (510-420 0107).

It's also always worth checking festival programming when you're in town, since you might be able to catch a talk by a director or several of the actors before or after a show. And if you're after a film-going 'experience', head straight for one of the old movie palaces, like the **Regency** (*see above*), or the **Castro Theater** (*see below*), where the mighty Wurlitzer organ entertains the audience before the show at the weekend.

TICKETS & INFORMATION

Check the newspapers for listings and film times at all of the theatres (the *San Francisco Examiner* and the *East Bay Express* have the best reviews), and expect opening nights to be as popular as they are elsewhere. Advance tickets for some of the festivals and most of the cinemas are available by credit card on 777 3456 (there's a $1 service charge per ticket). Otherwise you should get tickets from the festival organisers and the cinema box offices.

Film Festivals

That San Franciscans appreciate film is obvious from looking at the city's film calendar. Almost every month of the year there's a film festival taking place, many of them drawing film-makers from around the world. The work of local film and video artists also features prominently in every San Francisco festival, and depending on the event, work can vary from extremely high quality to dire. In addition to the festivals listed here, check the festival calendar once you're in town, by phoning the **San Francisco Film and Video Arts Commission** (554 6244).

Bay Area Women's Film Festival

Information (554 6244). **Date** March, at the UC Theater, Berkeley.
Programmers at this young festival aim to introduce the work of first-time women directors, show new work by experienced directors and help to build an international women's film-making community. The festival has included retrospectives: in 1993 for example, one thread of the programme screened most of the films, short and full-length, directed by Academy Award winning Kiwi director Jane Campion.

Black Filmworks Festival of Film and Video

Information (554 6244). **Date** April, at the Paramount, Laney College, the Oakland Museum in Oakland, and the UA Emery Bay in Emeryville.
Presented by the Black Film-makers Hall of Fame, this fest features films by, for and about the African and African American experience. The 1995 festival included a tribute to the late Marlon Riggs, whose groundbreaking experimental documentary *Tongues Untied,* exploring the experiences of African American gay men, became a conservative US congressional argument for cutting off funding to the Public Broadcasting Service.

!Festival Cine Latino!

Information (554 6244). **Date** September, at Yerba Buena Gardens and the Victoria Theater, 2961 16th Street, at Mission Street.
Although it's relatively young in comparison to some other Bay Area festivals, Cine Accion's festival has quickly come into its own as the premier showcase for films from South and Central America, Mexico and those by US Latino film-makers – films that are surprisingly under distributed in the US. The festival includes films, videos and appearances by the film-makers.

Film Arts Foundation Festival

Second Floor, 346 Ninth Street, at Folsom Street (552 8760). Bus 12, 19, 27, 42. **Date** first week of November at the Castro Theater, the Roxie and the UC Theater, Berkeley.
The festival provides the essential venue for a real snapshot of film-making in Northern California. All programming is drawn from Bay Area independent work, and features documentary, experimental and traditional narrative work.

Jewish Film Festival

Information (1-510 548 0556). **Date** late July-early August, at the Castro Theatre and the UC Theater.
This festival is intended to showcase contemporary films from around the world on Jewish subjects and to strengthen awareness of Jewish secular culture. Most of the programming is contemporary, but does include some retrospective and archival work. Information is available on the World Wide Web at http://www.well.com/user/ari/jff/

Mill Valley Film Festival and Videofest

Information (554 6244). **Date** October, at the Sequoia Twin Theaters and the Masonic Hall, both in Mill Valley.
American and international independent films and videos are the focus of this Marin County festival, which is coming up to its 20th year. The festival screens dozens of feature films, and also includes a six-day 'Videofest', interactive media exhibitions, seminars, special events and children's programmes.

National Educational Media Network

Information (554 6244). **Date** May, at the Paramount Theater, 2025 Broadway, between 20th and 21st Streets, Oakland.
One of the most highly regarded organisations for the Bay Area's extended community of documentary makers. Formerly called the National Educational Film & Video Festival, festival week for the NEMN screens 30 award winning documentary films chosen from upwards of 1,000 entries. Daytime events include seminars and workshops.

SF International Asian-American Film Festival

Information (554 6244). **Date** March, at the Kabuki 8 Cinema and the Castro Theater.
The festival features film by and/or about Asian Pacific people, their culture and experience. Recent hits have included a sneak preview of *The Wedding Banquet,* and Steven Okasaki's award winning *Days of Waiting,* about the imprisonment of Japanese Americans during World War II. An eight-day event, the festival draws huge audiences.

SF International Film Festival

Information (931 3456/929 5000). Kabuki 8 Cinema, and other cinemas around town. **Date** mid April-early May.
Produced by the San Francisco Film Society, this event galvanises the city (over 65,000 tickets were sold at a recent festival). Over the course of a few weeks, the society presents multiple screenings of over 200 films and videos, from dozens of countries and in dozens of languages, and it's usually hard to find a loser in the bunch. Most films are screened at the Kabuki 8 Cinema in Japantown, with related screenings at other venues around town. Tickets go on sale, in advance, at the Kabuki a few weeks before the festival opens.

SF International Lesbian & Gay Film Festival

Information (703 8650). **Date** last two weeks of June; ends with Freedom Day parade.
Opening night at the Lesbian and Gay Film Festival has become the kickoff for San Francisco's month-long celebration of Gay Pride. Recent years have seen a rise in gay-themed films produced in Hollywood and the festival will often première such mainstream fare. Other festival programming runs the gamut from high quality independent shorts and full length features, to avant-garde film with

Celluloid city

From Erich von Stroheim's adaptation of *McTeague* into the 1923 mammoth silent *Greed*, to the foggy drama starring Humphrey Bogart and Lauren Bacall, *Dark Passage* (1947), Alfred Hitchcock's *Vertigo* (1958, *right*), or MTV's ultra-contemporary *Real World*, San Francisco's photogenic setting, views and distinctive architecture have appeared in countless films.

It's hard to pinpoint specific locations because almost every time you reach the crest of a hill the surrounding vista looks like a movie backdrop. But a few locations may resonate with the film buff: Lauren Bacall's sophisticated apartment from *Dark Passage* is at 1360 Montgomery, tucked off a winding downhill stairway leading towards the Bay from the Coit Tower. The Tower itself was used as lucky Rita Hayworth's mansion in *Pal Joey* (1957).

The Bank of America building at 555 California is another familiar spot, first seen in less than happy circumstances in the 1970s disaster flick *The Towering Inferno* (1974), and later masquerading as an apartment building in *Sister Act II* (1993) starring Whoopi Goldberg.

The Golden Gate Bridge, of course, is probably one of the most photographed spans in the world, but was perhaps most recently seen as a suitably foggy backdrop to Neil Jordan's *Interview With a Vampire* (1994), the film in which Christian Slater interviews Brad Pitt in the beautiful space at 1000 Market Street at

Sixth Street. San Franciscans noticed something unreal about that scene straight away – Christian Slater's character managed the impossible feat of parking right outside the apartment.

And the list goes on: a plaque in Burritt Street off Bush commemorates the spot where Miles Archer, partner of Sam Spade (Humphrey Bogart), was done in by Brigid O'Shaughnessy in John Huston's version of Dashiell Hammett's *Maltese Falcon* (1941). Orson Welles and the *Lady from Shanghai*, Rita Hayworth, stroll through the Steinhart Acquarium (1949); Steve McQueen takes part in the mother of all car chases in *Bullitt* (1968); Clint Eastwood's *Dirty Harry* tracks his man across town, from North Beach to the top of Mount Davidson (1971); and a bewigged Captain Kirk and his ageing crew drop into Golden Gate Park in *Voyage Home: Star Trek IV* (1986).

---

a queer sensibility, to high and low quality shorts from new and old film-makers alike. Sponsored by Frameline, the event is the world's oldest and largest of its kind. Screenings are principally at the Castro Theater (*see below*) and the Victoria Theater (2961 16th Street, at Mission Street; 863 7576); a programme is available a month in advance from bookshops and cafés and in the *Bay Guardian*.

Spike and Mike's Festival of Animation
Information (567 6642). **Date** April and November, at the Palace of Fine Arts, Bay and Lyon Street.
The Animation Fest, as it's known, is not a film festival in the traditional sense. The 90-minute programme is compiled each year to include top animation shorts from around the world and often includes the year's Academy Award-winners and nominees. The regular programme, which plays twice nightly while it's in town, is suitable for all ages. The 'Sick and Twisted' midnight showing is not.

Classic, New & Experimental

Alliance Française
1345 Bush Street, between Polk and Larkin Streets (775 7755). Bus 2, 3, 4, 19, 76. **Admission** free members; $2-$3 non-members. **No credit cards.**
Mostly contemporary French films, once a week on Tuesdays.

Artists Television Access
992 Valencia Street, at 21st Street (824 3890). BART 24th Street/14, 26, 49 bus. **Open** 10am-10pm daily. **Admission** around $5. **No credit cards.**
Artists Television Access often has experimental and unusual programming, usually from Thursday to Saturday. Look out for the Short Attention Span Film & Video Festival in September – a programme of *very* short shorts (each offering is under two minutes).

Center for the Arts at Yerba Buena Gardens
701 Mission Street, at Third Street (978 2787). BART Powell Street/Muni Metro F, J, K, L, M, N/15, 30, 45, 76 bus. **Admission** varies. **Credit** AmEx, MC, V.
Located on the second floor of the arts building, the Yerba Buena media screening room is often used for contemporary and experimental offerings connected with the exhibits in the Center's galleries.

Film Arts Foundation
346 Ninth Street, at Folsom Street (552 8760). BART Civic Center/Muni Metro F, J, K, L, M, N/12, 19, 42 bus. **Admission** varies.
The Foundation screens works-in-progress (there's no regular schedule) and hosts lectures and classes by and for film-makers.

The **Red Vic** is an insanely relaxed movie house.

Goethe Institute
530 Bush Street, between Stockton Street and Grant Avenue (391 0370). Bus 30, 45. **Admission** free.
Both contemporary and classic German films are screened at the Institute, usually on Tuesdays and Thursdays.

Instituto Italiano di Cultura
425 Bush Street, between Keary Street and Grant Avenue (788 7142). Bus 30, 45. **Admission** free.
Shows both contemporary and classic Italian films. Screening are usually on Tuesdays.

Pacific Film Archive
University Art Museum, 2626 Bancroft Way, between Bowditch and College Streets, Berkeley (1-510 642 5249/0808). BART Berkeley. **Admission** varies.
Located in the same complex as the University Art Museum, the Pacific Film Archive keeps the reels rolling almost every evening with classic films, and a serious program of Bay Area-based independent documentaries or avant-garde work.

San Francisco Cinematheque
Information (558 8129). Thursday night screenings at Centre for the Arts at Yerba Buena Gardens; Sunday night screenings at San Francisco Art Institute, 800 Chestnut Street, at Jones Street. BART Montgomery Street/Muni Metro F, J, K, L, M, N/30 bus. **Admission** $6. **No credit cards**.
The Cinemateque is the centre for avant-garde film in the Bay Area. It's a place to gather information and inspiration and to see experimental programming.

San Francisco Museum of Modern Art
151 Third Street, between Mission and Howard Streets (357 4000). BART Montgomery/Muni Metro F, J, K, L, M, N/12, 30, 45, 76 bus. **Admission** varies.
The small screening rooms in the basement of SOMA are often used in conjuncton with arts conferences in the city, and for films connected with museum exhibits.

Repertory

Castro Theater
429 Castro Street, off Market Street (621 6120). Muni Metro F, K, L, M/8, 24, 33, 35, 37 bus. **Admission** $6. **No credit cards**.
Go on a weekend night for the full experience. The popcorn-munching audience is entertained before the screening by an organist playing 'San Francisco Open Your Golden Gate' on a Wurlitzer; there are lushly painted murals on the domed deco ceilings, and the film might be anything from an old Bette Davis picture where everyone knows (and recites) the best lines, or a world première by an independent queer film-maker.

The Paramount
2025 Broadway, between 20th and 21st Streets, Oakland (1-510 465 6400). BART 19th Street. **Admission** from $5. **Credit** MC, V.
A wonderful, cavernous theatre in which to see a rep film.

The Red Vic
1727 Haight Street, at Cole Street (668 3994). Bus 6, 7, 43, 61, 77. **Admission** $4.50-$5.50. **No credit cards**.
Where else can you sprawl on an old sofa in the heart of the Haight, eat popcorn out of wooden bowls, and watch 1970s revivals or a current funky flick with a wildly eclectic crowd?

The Roxie
3117 16th Street, at Valencia Street (863 1087). BART 16th Street/22, 26, 53 bus. **Admission** $6 adults; $3 senior citizens. **No credit cards**.
Revivals of film noir classics, Fassbinder festivals and horror movies. It isn't very comfortable and the sound system is second-rate, but go for the atmosphere.

The UC Theater
2036 University Avenue, at Shattuck Avenue, Berkeley (1-510 843 6267). BART Berkeley. **Admission** $4-$6.50. **No credit cards**.
The Rocky Horror Picture Show every Sat, during term-time.

Music: Classical & Opera

Gay male voice choirs, operas about earthquakes and a healthy interest in the avant-garde: San Francisco's music scene is thriving.

San Francisco's finest: the male voice Canticleer.

San Francisco's reputation for classical music – especially contemporary music, early music and opera – has always been high, and today there is more going on here than in any other city on the West Coast. Though the War Memorial Opera House is under renovation and so out of action, the Davies Symphony Hall, Civic Auditorium and Herbst Theater next door to it combine to form a monumental civic complex for all downtown musical events, attracting audiences in ever-increasing numbers. This is where the San Francisco Symphony Orchestra is based, whose season runs between September and May. The multi-million dollar arts complex at Yerba Buena Gardens has also begun hosting musical events, in an attempt, in its own unconventional, low-budget way, to become the Lincoln Center of the West.

NEW MUSIC

True to its counter-culture roots, San Francisco continues to encourage musical adventure, and is the base for many small, experimental musical outfits, like the globe-trotting Kronos Quartet or the internationally acclaimed *a capella* choir Chanticleer, as well as countless choirs, from the SF Bach Choir, to the SF Gay Men's Chorus. Some of these groups are keen to commission new works by young composers, and the result can be anything from a new opera about the earthquake by *Nixon in China* composer John Adams (called *I Was Looking At The Ceiling...And Then I Saw The Sky*), to Lou Harrison's compositions for gamelan, played on homemade instruments.

To the great annoyance of the smaller musical outfits, however, it is the three major companies – the San Francisco Symphony, the Opera and the Ballet – that continue to get the lion's share of city grants for the arts, although with the pending demise of the National Endowment for the Arts they stand to lose their federal funds. However they are all lucky enough to have an art-conscious array of wealthy benefactors, sponsors and 'angels' to top up their funds.

OPERA BUFFS

Above all, San Francisco has always been an opera town. The San Francisco Opera attracts frequent visits from big names like Placido Domingo and Luciano Pavarotti, Jessye Norman and Cecilia Bartoli. The opening Gala night, always held on the first Friday after Labor Day, is a glittering event attended by everyone from the Mayor to the latest reigning football champion, and the sweltering heat never deters elderly socialites from dusting off their furs. Free **Opera in the Park** follows the Gala on the first Sunday after Labor Day, and features the singers of the season in arias and duets performed in Golden Gate Park.

INFORMATION

To find out what's on when you're in town, check the Datebook section of the *San Francisco Chronicle* or the Style section of the *San Francisco Examiner*. The 'pink pages' of the combined Sunday *Chronicle/ Examiner* and the free *San Francisco Bay Guardian* or *SF Weekly* also have music listings.

TICKETS

Where possible, buy tickets from the box offices of the major venues, and you won't have to pay the mark-up charged by **BASS**. Cut price tickets are available each day at the **Tix Bay Area** kiosk in Union Square (*see chapter* **Shopping & Services** *and* **Theatre & Dance**).

On air

Local classical music stations include **KDFC** (102.1 FM, 1220 AM), which broadcasts the Metropolitan Opera productions live from New York on Saturdays during the season, starting at 10am; **KKHI** (100.7 FM) broadcasts a morning and afternoon concert; while **KALW** (91.7 FM) covers the popular classics and musicals.

Music Shops

No slouch in any musical department, the city has a good selection of shops where you can buy music, recorded or published. At **Byron Hoyt** (431 8055), a venerable sheet music and instrument shop at the top of Lion House at 2525 16th Street, there is a stunning view, solicitous and knowledgeable assistants, and copies of every possible score you could ever want, from Bach to Irving Berlin. It's also a good place for finding out information about musical events in the city. **Velvet Ear Music**, at 2075 Market Street at Church Street (864 5806), also stocks music and has information about concerts and music clubs. Of all the CD and tape stores in town, the **Tower Outlet** at 660 Third Street, between Townsend and Brannan Streets (957 9660) is a lucky dip of great bargains, while the **Wherehouse** at 165 Kearney has a wide range of opera recordings upstairs. **Star Classics** (425 Hayes Street; 552 1110) is a wonderful small shop devoted entirely to classical CDs and tapes. The huge new **Virgin Megastore** (2 Stockton Street, at Market Street, 397 4525) also has a cheap selection of classical CDs. The **Opera House Gift Shop** in the opera house itself (565 6414), stocks boxed opera sets and other musical paraphernalia, though at the time of writing it was temporarily closed for renovation.

Civic Center Venues

Louise M Davies Symphony Hall

Corner of Grove Street and Van Ness Avenue (431 5400). BART Civic Center/Muni Metro F, J, K, L, M, N. **Open** *box office 10am-6pm Mon-Fri; noon-6pm Sun.*
A circular, multi-tiered, glittering glass doughnut with good sightlines, the home base of the **San Francisco Symphony Orchestra** opened in 1980 but was recently renovated, and now flaunts expensively improved, hear-every-pin-drop acoustics. Even from the top row of the back balcony you can hear everything and see it all too. Tickets start at $20, though there are concessions for the old, young and students, and other occasional discounts. The recent arrival of Californian-born conductor Michael Tilson Thomas, hot from the London Symphony Orchestra, is likely to bring a much-needed blast of renewal to the Symphony's hitherto rather tired repertoire. A former protégé of Leonard Bernstein, Tilson Thomas has pledged to make American twentieth-century music his special focus, starting with the annual American Music Festival in June 1996. He commissioned 'MTT Parade' from local veteran composer Lou Harrison to launch his new season: a promising sign of things to come.

Bill Graham Civic Auditorium

99 Grove Street, between Polk and Larkin Streets (974 4000/267 6400). Muni Metro F, J, K, L, M, N/BART Civic Center.
San Francisco Opera was born in the barn-like, broad-staged Civic Auditorium on 26 September 1923, when an adventurous young Neapolitan called Gaetano Merola took the podium to conduct *La Bohème* starring Queena Mario as Mimi, Giovanni Martinelli as Rudolfo and local girl Anna Young as Musetta. Built for the 1915 Panama-Pacific Exposition, this Italian Renaissance-style four-storey building is part of the Civic Center complex and a close neighbour

of Symphony Hall (*p188*), and the Opera House (*below*). Over 5,000 people paid $4 a seat here for the opening night, but the hall had such an ill-suited stage that eventually Merola and his supporters opened their own Opera House across Van Ness Avenue. Ironically, the Opera is temporarily back at the Civic Auditorium, which was rededicated in 1992 to the rock impresario who put on over 100 gigs here. The 'barn' has been expensively refurbished to handle productions until renovation on the Opera House is completed in 1997. The season opens during the first week after Labor Day, and house seats cost from $55 to $375, though subscription tick-

ets often cost under $30. Standing-room tickets are available before the performance for $8. (Local opera buffs volunteer to become unpaid ushers, seeing everything free in return for carrying a torch to lead patrons to safety in the next quake).

War Memorial Opera House
301 Van Ness Avenue, at Grove Street (864 3330/865 2000). Muni Metro F, J, K, L, M, N/BART Civic Center. **Closed for renovation**.
Lately, the imposing Opera House has been wearing a 'hair net' as a precaution against cracks in the gilt ceiling which

Open air concerts

As well as the annual **Opera in the Park** series in Golden Gate Park, the **Stern Grove Midsummer Music Festival** (252 6252, *pictured*) offers free open-air symphony orchestra, ballet and opera performances every Sunday for three months during the summer. The festival – which has just completed its 58th season – is named after Levi Strauss' son Sigmund Stern, who spent the fortune his father earned making jeans on turning this tree-shaded amphitheatre into 'nature's music box'. Unlike Glyndebourne, it requires neither a ball-gown to attend, nor the shirt off your back to buy tickets. 'The Grove' has picnic tables, barbecues and portaloos; all you have to do is arrive early (well before 2pm, when the performance starts) and bring a sweater with your picnic in case of fog. (Watch out for the gophers, who like to make off with your food, pens, car keys and even your socks.)

What was formerly the parade ground at the Presidio barracks has recently been given a new lease of life as an open air venue, starting with the San Francisco Symphony's **Pops Concert** in the summer of 1995, which drew appreciative crowds in the hot sunshine (phone 431 5400 or the Visitor's Information Center for more information).

Also worth keeping an eye out for are impromptu performances by **Brown Bag Opera** (check the daily paper for details). This marauding troop of opera students and graduates alight in the city centre and sing arias and duets to the accompaniment of a piano on wheels; the plaza behind Sharper Image at Sansome and Market Streets on Friday lunchtimes is one of their spots, as is the Crocker Galleria on Post Street.

appeared during the 1989 earthquake, and it has closed for a $80.5 million renovation, which will include the retrofitting of backstage facilities, dining and bar areas, and rehearsal rooms. The auditorium will retain its exquisite acoustics, best appreciated from the back of the uppermost circle (some even believe in lying on the floor to listen). San Francisco's Opera House was among the first in the world to introduce 'supertitles', the simultaneous translation above the proscenium that was so resisted elsewhere. The Opera House is due to re-open for its 75th anniversary season in September 1997, and meanwhile the company is making use of the **Orpheum Theatre** (*see chapter* **Theatre & Dance**) and the **Bill Graham Civic Auditorium** (*above*), both of which have been upgraded for this purpose. One of three productions that will be presented at the Orpheum during the 1996/1997 season will be a new opera based on the life of Harvey Milk by Stewart Wallace and Michael Korie. For advance information about the Opera, phone the **San Francisco Opera Association** (864 3330).

Other Venues

Center for the Arts at Yerba Buena Gardens

701 Mission Street, at Third Street (978 2787). BART Powell Street/Muni Metro F, J, K, L, M, N/15, 30, 45, 76 bus.
Yerba Buena has the city's most graceful middle-sized theatre, which so far has been used mostly for a brilliantly conceived avant-garde music programme, with an emphasis on San Francisco-based artists. *See also chapter* **Theatre & Dance**.

Herbst Theater

401 Van Ness Avenue, at McAllister Street (621 6600/ticket information 392 4400). Muni Metro F, J, K, L, M, N/BART Civic Center.
The Art Deco Herbst Auditorium is used by the Kronos Quartet, when they are not performing at **Theater Artaud** (*see chapter* **Theatre & Dance**). It's a good size for solo recitals, talks and seminars, and small-scale dance and ballet performances, though the acoustics are atrocious at the back. Under the same roof is the **Green Room**, used by chamber ensembles and quartet recitals. The **San Francisco Chamber Symphony** is based here.

Palace of the Legion of Honor

Florence Gould Auditorium, Lincoln Park at Clement Street and 33rd Avenue (750 3600). Bus 18, 38.
Now re-opened after seismic upgrading, this gloriously sited building near Land's End is making a comeback as a venue for Sunday organ and chamber concerts.

San Francisco Conservatory of Music

1201 Ortega Street, at 19th Avenue (759 3475). Bus 28. 28L.
As the cradle for local singers and musicians, this has a loyal following, who come for recitals by the **San Francisco Sinfonietta**, as well as other concerts by music students, (usually free).

Churches & Temples

Recitals and concerts – often free – are performed in many of San Francisco's churches. They include the **Old First Church** at 1751 Sacramento Street (474 1608, where Chanticleer often performs), the **Unitarian Church** on Franklin Street, and **Grace Cathedral** (*see chapter* **Sightseeing**). The **Temple Emanu-El** (2 Lake Street, near Arguello Boulevard; 751 2535), hosts the talented

Pocket Opera chamber company and regular concerts by the San Francisco Chamber Orchestra, and the **Noe Valley Ministry** puts on a diverse array of concerts from baroque music to Philip Glass or John Cage (1021 Sanchez Street at 23rd Street; 282 2317).

In addition, **Old St Mary's Cathedral** is a regular venue for piano and quartet recitals, and has a Tuesday Noontime Concert Series (982 6666); **St Mary's Cathedral** is a great venue for organ recitals or performances by the San Francisco Bach Choir, and the **Mission Dolores Basilica** also sees performances by Canticleer, among others. *See chapter* **Sightseeing** for listings.

Further Afield

The East Bay's annual music season, based in the **Zellerbach Hall** on the US Berkeley campus (1-510 841 2800/642 9988) is now over 25 years old and attracts a roster of distinguished stars under the direction of conductor Kent Nagano. **Berkeley Opera** also puts on about three productions a year here (1-510 524 5256).

Other musical venues to watch include the **First Congregational Church** in Berkeley (1-510 848 3696), and the **Mormon Temple Auditorium** in Oakland (1-510 444 5767) where the Oakland Symphony and Chorus regularly perform. Travelling even further afield, the **Mountain View Center for the Performing Arts** in Mountain View's Civic Center complex (254 1700/903 6000) is an ultramodern and facility-laden venue for concerts.

Festivals

Check the Visitor Information Center's 24-hour information line for details on what's on while you're in town (837 6191). Events to watch out for include the annual **Midsummer Mozart Festival** (626 3544), which celebrated its 21st birthday in 1994 under director George Cleve, with concerts at Berkeley's Congregational Church and in the Davies Symphony Hall. The more experimental **High Tides Music Festival** concentrates on music written for new instruments, while the **Early Music Society** has an annual concert series that concentrates on chamber music played on original instruments; the **Philharmonic Baroque Orchestra** has an annual baroque series, and there's also an excellent annual **Contemporary Music Festival**.

Over the Golden Gate Bridge, the **West Marin Music Festival** concentrates on early and baroque music, 'loud band' and secular music, and takes place at St Columba's off Sir Francis Drake Boulevard in Inverness, a delightful village near Point Reyes, and less than an hour by car north of the city.

Music: Rock, Roots & Jazz

From hardcore blues to trad jazz, the Bay Area offers an eclectic mix of music, as befits its multicultural background.

Call it New Jazz, Young Jazz, or Jazz Hip Hop, but whatever you call it, get the 4-1-1 while you're in town and check out San Francisco's jazz clubs. Influenced by a strong history of blues musicians in the Bay Area, and the funky proximity of the hip hop scene in Oakland, young jazz musicians are playing up a storm in San Francisco nightclubs and music lovers are turning out in droves to hear them play.

Bands to watch out for include Alphabet Soup and the Broun Fellinis who play regularly at nightspots like the **Cafe Du Nord** and the **Up & Down Club** (*see chapter* **Clubs**), and the Charlie Hunter Trio, regulars at the **Elbo Room** (*see chapter* **Bars & Cafés**), who've just released their first major label CD. Musicians are making their living from their live performances rather than recordings for the most part, but the door charges at the jazz clubs are still low, and an evening at the sultry, dimly lit venues packed with multi-racial crowds lets you know you're in a thriving cosmopolitan city.

Although the Haight-Ashbury music scene that exploded onto the national consciousness in the late 1960s and early 1970s seemed to let out its final gasp with the death of Grateful Dead lead guitarist Jerry Garcia in the summer of 1995, the rockers that put down their roots in the Summer of Love have had a profound impact on the city's music scene. Janis Joplin, Jimi Hendrix and Jefferson Airplane all played the **Fillmore Auditorium**, which closed for a time and then reopened in 1993 to re-establish itself as one of the prime venues for live music. And the city's major concert producers, Bill Graham's company, began by producing Grateful Dead shows – now they produce just about everything that comes to town.

Perhaps because the ghosts of so many rock 'n' roll greats haunt the city, today's musicians have, with a few exceptions such as the popular Counting Crows, stayed away from traditional rock 'n' roll. In addition to the new jazz sensation, San Francisco has emerged as a centre for a new form of punk/thrash, designated as queercore. For those who like the thrasher style, **Bottom of the Hill** is the venue to watch. The little club in Potrero Hill often features the all-female or female-led alternative bands that dominate queercore.

San Francisco is also the home to OutPunk Records, the label for many queercore bands. And though the rap and hip hop scene that earned 'Oaktown' its reputation may have begun to ebb when MC Hammer, who began selling his own rap CDs out of the boot of his car near Lake Merritt, crossed over to mainstream pop, it's by no means defunct. Keep an eye out for hip hop shows in Oakland, and for the hip hop influence on today's jazz musicians.

Testament to both the city's Latino population and its cosmopolitan aspirations, Latin music also remains vibrant. You can find traditional forms such as flamenco (at **Cesar's Latin Palace**), salsa and Brazilian-inspired dances (at the **Bahia Cabana**, *see chapter* **Clubs** *for both*), as well as emergent vibes like the bi-lingual and Spanish-only rock bands known collectively as Los Rockeros (at the **Berkeley Square**).

As in all other areas of the city's arts and culture, San Francisco is also home to experimental and avant-garde musicians making a name for themselves around the world. Look for electronic, synthesiser and computerised music from groups like Splatter Trio, or musicians Mia Masaoka or Bob Ostertag, who sometimes play tiny venues like **New Langton Arts** (*see chapter* **Theatre & Dance**), or the larger and sometimes experimental **Great American Music Hall**. Also look out for the Club Foot Orchestra, a large experimental orchestra that sometimes plays original scores to accompany silent films at the Castro Theater.

INFORMATION

For the most up-to-date information, pick up the *San Francisco Bay Guardian* (which is free on Wednesdays), or one of many free papers devoted to the music scene, including the bi-weekly *BAM* and *Sound Check*. If your interest is more along the lines of bands featured in *Rolling Stone*, don't worry: San Francisco is on the itinerary of all the national and international tours by bands currently in the

Rock and roll down to the **Bottom of the Hill** *see page 193.*

pop charts. Such shows tend to take place at one of the larger venues: check the ads in the Datebook section of the combined Sunday *Examiner/Chronicle*. Also keep an eye out for handouts and posters.

For details of the city's annual jazz and blues festivals and the jazz-orientated Fillmore street fair, *see chapter* **San Francisco by Season**. For other live music venues, *see chapters* **Clubs**, **Gay & Lesbian San Francisco** *and* **Bars & Cafés**. *See chapter* **Shopping & Services** for record and CD shops.

TICKETS

As a rule, going direct to a venue is the best approach for buying tickets, but in some cases, especially at the larger venues, it may be easier to swallow the surcharge and get your seats by credit card from **BASS** (*see chapter* **Shopping & Services**). For the smaller venues, phone the club and listen to their recorded message, which will typically give up-to-date information on where and when tickets go on sale – if they are sold in advance. Many small clubs just collect a door charge or insist on a drink minimum.

Major Venues

Cow Palace

Geneva Avenue, at Santos Street, Daly City (469 6065). Bus 9, 9X, 9AX, 9BX, 15/CalTrain Bayshore, then bus 15. **Open** *office 10am-5.45pm Mon-Sat.* **Admission** depends on event. **Credit** AmEx, MC, V.
The most revealing fact about the Cow Palace, is that it is used for many other events besides music, including monster

truck derbies, International Hockey League games and even livestock auctions and rodeos. Not an intimate space for music, concerts here are little better than stadium shows, but the parking lot is big, with plenty of room for pre-show tailgate parties. Book through BASS.

Fillmore Auditorium

1805 Geary Boulevard, at Fillmore Street (346 6000/24-hour hotline 346 0600). Bus 22, 38. **Open** *box office 2 hrs before show.* **Admission** depends on event. **Credit** AmEx, MC, V.
Closed for five years after the 1989 earthquake, the Fillmore is a classic – a dance hall with a ballroom and mezzanine upstairs, a carpeted lounge, and its own traditions, such as a pail of apples by the front entrance. One of the true institutions of the 1960s, it was here that Bill Graham began building his music empire, giving psychedelic rock to San Francisco and the world. And it's still a great venue for live tunes, with plenty of room to shake it or to stand back and soak in the vibes. Book well in advance through BASS.

Great American Music Hall

859 O'Farrell Street, between Polk and Larkin Streets (885 0750). Bus 19, 38, 42, 47, 49. **Open** *office 10am-4pm Mon, Sun; noon-6pm Tue-Sat.* **Admission** $6-$20. **Credit** MC, V.
One of the oldest theatres still in operation, the Great American Music Hall presents an eclectic, virtuoso-studded play list, including stand-up comedy and local and touring musicians in equal measure. The interior is old world (for San Francisco) and welcoming, with tables to hold your delivered beer.

Greek Theater

Piedmont Avenue and Gayley Road, Berkeley (1-510 642 0527/9988). BART Berkeley, then bus 52 or walk. **Open** *office May-Sept 10am-5.30pm Mon-Fri; 10am-2pm Sat, Sun.* **Admission** depends on event. **Credit** MC, V.
The Greek Theater is an open-air, stone amphitheatre with a lawn at the rear serving as the cheap seats. When the Greek is packed for a pop show, it can be a bit hectic, but most of

the crowd comes for love of the music, not the scene. Touring pop and jazz acts usually gig at the Greek, offering shows that, with luck, defy the 'adult contemporary' radio format they often qualify as on the airwaves.

Oakland-Alameda County Coliseum Complex

700 Coliseum Way, Oakland (1-510 639 7700). BART Coliseum. **Open** *office* 9am-5pm Mon-Sat. **Admission** depends on event. **Credit** AmEx, MC, V.

Home to the Golden State Warriors basketball team, the Oakland Coliseum (as it is most often called) is an indoor sports arena first and concert hall second – which may be all you need to know. It seats 15,000 or so and the last of the super-groups – U2, REM, Pearl Jam – sell out massively unatmospheric shows here. If you're buying tickets in advance, have a look at a seating chart or you might end up behind the bandstand. There are no phone sales, so book through BASS.

Shoreline Amphitheater

1 Amphitheater Parkway, Mountain View (967 4040). CalTrain Mountain View, then cab/drive south on Highway 101 to Mountain View, take Rentsporff Avenue, then Amphitheater Parkway. **Open** *box office* 10am-6pm Mon-Fri; 10am-2pm Sun. **Admission** depends on event. **Credit** MC, V.

The Shoreline is built on top of a garbage dump, so when it first opened there were some unexpected hazards – tyres popping up out of the lawn, escaping gases that turned a lit joint into a fireball – or so went the rumours, anyway. A perfectly pleasant place to see a show, the Shoreline has reserved seating near the stage and a groomed lawn for the rest. It can handle large and unruly crowds, such as those that partied at Lollapolooza the last few summers. Getting back to the city in the evening by public transport is difficult, so you'll probably need to drive.

Warfield

982 Market Street, between Fifth and Sixth Streets (775 7722). BART Powell Street/Muni Metro F, J, K, L, M, N/7, 8, 27, 31, 66, 71 bus. **Open** *box office* 2 hrs before show. **Admission** depends on event. **Credit** V.

A favourite venue for rock fans, the Warfield was built in 1922 and has an ornate interior, rows of seats and some VIP booths at the back where cocktails are swiftly delivered to the big tippers. With its high ceiling and balcony, the Warfield feels like a box cavern and fills easily with a decent sound. High-energy acts here often prove the most memorable of a concert-goer's career. Book in advance through BASS.

Rock/R&B

Berkeley Square

1333 University Avenue, near Sacramento Street, Berkeley (1-510 841 6555). BART North Berkeley. **Open** 9.30am-2am Tue-Sun. **Admission** $3-$12. **No credit cards.**

Home to Rock en Español on Sundays and other burgeoning local talent from Tuesday to Saturday, the Berkeley Square can hold 450, but has the intimacy of a mosh pit.

Blake's

2367 Telegraph Avenue, at Durant Avenue, Berkeley (1-510 848 0886). BART Berkeley, then bus 51, 64 or walk. **Open** 11am-1pm Mon-Sat; 11am-10pm Sun. **Admission** $2-$8; free Sun. **Credit** AmEx, MC, V.

Over 50 years old, Blake's remains a Berkeley institution, but its musical fare has changed considerably over the last few years from traditional blues to modern rock, acid jazz, with acoustic sets one night a week. A DJ stands in for live music on Tuesday and Wednesdays.

Blues

2125 Lombard Street, at Fillmore Street (771 2583). Bus 22, 28, 43, 76. **Open** 8pm-1.30am daily. **Admission** $5. **Credit** MC, V.

Blues books the kind of hard-driving blues that can leave you feeling whiplashed. Another club, Biscuit and Blues (410 Mason Street, 292 2583), books a similar brand of music, is closer to Union Square and, therefore, the hotels and tourists – but Blues will find you hanging with the locals, especially on Sunday nights when they'll often have some New Orleans zydeco on the bill.

Bottom of the Hill

1233 17th Street, at Missouri Street (621 4455). Bus 22, 53. **Open** 5.30pm-1am Tue-Thur, Sun; 5.30pm-2am Fri, Sat. **Admission** $3-$8. **Credit** V.

A favourite of local musicians and their fans, Bottom of the Hill occupies the first floor of an old Victorian at the foot of Potrero Hill and sports one of the best neon signs ever above its front door. The main room can get a bit cramped, but there's a small patio at the back for cooling off – anyway, sweating and a ringing in the ears are all part of the experience.

Jack's Bar

1601 Fillmore Street, at Geary Boulevard (567 3227). Bus 2, 3, 4, 22, 38. **Open** 4pm-2am Mon-Thur; 2pm-2am Fri-Sun. **Admission** $5. **No credit cards.**

Jack's Bar is located on one of the city's busier corners and sees its fair share of traffic, inside and out. A blues bar where denim is the closest thing to a dress code, Jack's has been legendary over the years for the acts it books, serving as the B-side to the Fillmore Auditorium, located across Geary Boulevard. Jack's is also a good call for beer drinkers, with several dozen beers on tap.

Komotion

2779 16th Street, at South Van Ness Avenue (861 6423). BART 16th Street/22, 49, 53 bus. **Open** phone for schedule. **Admission** depends on event. **No credit cards.**

Komotion's not for everyone; in fact, it's not for most people. It is something of a performance laboratory; in the past few years the club hosted noisy punk rock and several other deconstructed sounds. If you're allergic to youth, don't attend. When not interrupted by the authorities, Komotion shows tend to be memorable, a peek into, if not the future, then some parallel 'underground' universe.

Paradise Lounge

1501 Folsom Street, at 11th Street (861 6906). Bus 9, 12, 42. **Open** 3pm-2am daily. **Admission** from $3. **Credit** MC, V.

The Paradise Lounge is something of a superstore nightclub, with as many as three stages active concurrently or in series during the course of an evening – although it's more intimate than it sounds. With a few regulars (such as the Bud E Luv act, a parody of a Vegas lounge crooner) and poetry slams on Sundays, the Paradise has a bit of something for everyone – and plenty of heart-pounding tunes. The pool tables and drink specials may not be your idea of paradise, but it's a safe bet you'll find something to like. The upstairs lounge, known as **Above Paradise**, is reserved for acoustic and folk music or spoken word events. You have to be 21 or older to get in: bring photo ID. *See also chapter* **Literary San Francisco**.

Purple Onion

140 Columbus Avenue, at Broadway (398 8415). Bus 15, 30, 41, 45. **Open** phone for schedule. **Admission** depends on event. **No credit cards.**

The Purple Onion, located where North Beach slips into downtown, has had its ups and downs, but currently attracts a regular crowd to its shows of psychedelic and surf rock, played by such bands as the Ultras and Mermen.

Slim's

*333 11th Street, between Folsom and Harrison Streets
(621 3330). Bus 9, 42.* **Open** 8pm-1am most days; phone
to check. **Admission** $5-$25. **Credit** AmEx, MC, V.
Slim's has one of the best booking agents in the business,
attracting big names for limited, more intimate engagements as well as a variety of artists to ensure that the
crowd is ethnically mixed and multi-generational. The
sightlines are somewhat compromised by some floor-to-
ceiling pillars in the centre of the room, but, since music is
often best heard and not seen, it's a minor drawback. You'll
feel comfortable here whether you're in the clothes you
wore at the business convention or the outfit you save for
painting the town.

The Saloon

*1232 Grant Street, at Vallejo Street and Columbus
Avenue (989 7666). Bus 15, 30, 41, 45.* **Open** noon-2am
daily. **Admission** $3-$6 Fri, Sat. **No credit cards.**
A blue-collar bar that showcases many of the city's best local
blues acts, the Saloon is a low-rent joint, a piece of North
Beach that pre-dates the upmarket eateries and hints at a
district that Tom Wolfe aptly described as 'slums with a
view'. The interior is lit up like a pinball machine and blues
will quickly strike you as the only possible soundtrack.

Roots & Reggae

Ashkenaz

*1317 San Pablo Avenue, at Gilman Street, Berkeley (1-
510 525 5054). BART El Cerrito Plaza, then bus 72, 73.*
Open 8-11.30pm Tue, Wed; 8.30pm-12.30am Thur; 9pm-
1.30am Fri, Sat. **Admission** $5-$8. **No credit cards.**
Ashkenaz is non-institutionalised multiculturalism in action.
Booking 'world beat', Afro-Cuban and reggae acts, and with
timber rafters, it's like a Jamaican mountain lodge. Get
sweaty on the dance floor with students, travellers and free-
thinking locals and then cool off with a Red Stripe.

Sweetwater

*153 Throckmorton Street, at Miller Street, Mill Valley
(388 2820). Bus Golden Gate Transit 10.* **Open** 12.30pm-
1am daily. **Admission** $4-$25. **No credit cards.**
The Sweetwater is a cool, woodsy bar in downtown Mill
Valley, a suburb in the lap of Mount Tamalpais. It might be
just another local tavern were it not for the talented folk and
blues musicians who call Mill Valley home – and their
friends. Of course, it's not every night that Carlos Santana
sits in with blues giant John Lee Hooker or Van Morrison
scats or Huey Lewis rocks the house, but you get the general idea.

Jazz

See also **Supper Clubs** *in chapter* **Clubs.**

Addarash Lounge

*Ramada Inn, 920 University Avenue, at Eighth Street,
Berkeley (1-510 849 4447). BART Berkeley, then bus 51.*
Open 4pm-1am daily. **Admission** free weekdays; varies
at weekends. **Credit** AmEx, MC, V.
The Addarash is not where you'd think of looking for local
flavour, since it's inside a motor lodge, but the music here is
for those who place music above yuppified or dive bar ambience. On Saturdays, a jam session of several ex-pat Africans
provides a foundation for touring vocalists and other
soloists.

Bimbo's 365 Club

*1025 Columbus Avenue, at Chestnut Street (474 0365).
Bus 30.* **Open** phone for schedule. **Admission** depends
on event. **No credit cards.**

Only open when it's hosting a show, Bimbo's 365 Club is the
perfect place to indulge in a time-travel delusion: just set your
clock for the 1940s. With a ballroom-sized dance floor, main
stage and separate cocktail lounge, bands with a full, rich
sound (big bands, reggae and so on) do best here. Book in
advance through BASS.

Cafe Du Nord

*2170 Market Street, between Church and Sanchez Streets
(861 5016). Muni Metro F, K, L, M/8, 22, 37 bus.* **Open**
3.30pm-2am daily. **Admission** $2-$5. **Credit** AmEx,
MC, V.
Du Nord offers something different every night of the week,
(including salsa lessons on Tuesdays). Regulars Lavay
Smith and the Red Hot Skillet Lickers keep the spirit of
Bessie Smith alive, and the club has also been one of the stop-
overs for the hip hop acid-whatever-you-call-it-jazz that has
flourished in the 1990s. Every once in a while, too, they book
a legend. *See also* chapter **Bars & Cafés.**

Kimball's East

*5800 Shellmound Street, at Christie Street, Emeryville (1-
510 658 2555). BART Ashby, then 7 bus.* **Open** *office*
11am-6pm Mon, Tue; 10am-10pm Wed-Sun. **Admission**
average $20. **Credit** MC, V.
Odd as it may seem, Kimball's East (in the East Bay) has
become more renowned in its time than the original
Kimball's in San Francisco (300 Grove Street, 861 5555)
even though the latter has been making something of a
comeback recently. The reason for this upsurge is that
Kimball's floorplan recommends it as a nightclub for
dancing and moving around, whereas Kimball's East
gives the audience a more close-up and personal experience with the musicians, many of whom are at the peak
of their careers.

Rassela's

*2801 California Street, at Divisadero Street (567 5010).
Bus 12, 24.* **Open** 8pm-midnight Mon-Thur, Sun; 9pm-
1am Fri, Sat. **Admission** two drink minimum. **Credit**
AmEx, MC, V.
Rassela's boasts a perfectly fine sounding band of studio
musicians who jam, but don't swing so wildly as to cause
anyone to forget the flavour of the Ethiopian food they're
having for dinner. The club also regularly books big names
in jazz.

Schooner Tavern

*26th and Valencia Streets (285 4169). BART 24th
Street/26 bus.* **Open** 2pm-2am Mon-Fri; 10am-2am Sat,
Sun. **Admission** free. **No credit cards.**
With three dartboards on two walls (which can seem like
four after a few), the Schooner, make no mistake, is a corner
dive, and in a part of town where you don't want to stumble
around drunk and lost. But the Sunday night jam of true
Frisco jazz is well worth the trip. Vince Wallis plays an
enchanting saxophone and the tunes suggest nothing so
much as a flashback montage of all the laughs and disap-
pointments found at the edge of the continent.

Yoshi's

*6030 Claremont Street, at College Avenue, Oakland
(1-510 652 9200). BART Rockridge, then bus 64
or walk.* **Open** *restaurant* 5.30pm-10pm daily; *club*
5.30pm-12.30am daily. **Admission** $8-$20. **Credit**
AmEx, MC, V.
It doesn't get much sweeter than Yoshi's, the Bay Area's
number one jazz club/sushi restaurant. It has the kind of
refined setting that makes just being there a splendid occasion. With a separate dining room that does a good business
on the strength of its kitchen, Yoshi's books the hottest travelling talent every week and plays host to some of the best
local musicians as well. Shows are often booked out, so phone
first to check availability.

Sport & Fitness

Whatever your sporting fix – from rollerblading to whale watching – you can watch it, play it or learn it somewhere here.

Spectator Sports

Don't be misled. Though big-money spectator sports like baseball, football or ice hockey might not seem to have a place in the 'alternative' lifestyles of San Francisco, the Bay Area teems with sports fans. In fact, many fans revel in sport as if it were a guilty pleasure left over from the era before their Californian enlightenment. Moreover, Bay Area denizens often celebrate aspects of the game that make other fans nervous, such as the homo-erotic undertones of football – with its touchdowns, end zones, wide receivers and tight ends.

Of course, it doesn't hurt the enthusiasm of local fans that the San Francisco Forty-Niners (NFL football), have, in the last decade or so, proved to be one of the most polished and successful teams in North America. Winners of five Super Bowl championships in 14 seasons, the gold and red colours of the 'Niners' hang in gas stations, convenience stores, bars and even upmarket boutiques.

Information

The 'Sporting Green' section of the *San Francisco Chronicle* (50¢), is a good place to start. It has a calendar with each of the pro team engagements as well as details of broadcasts. The Chron and the *San Francisco Examiner* both maintain a free sports information line (808 5000) as does NewsCenter 4, KRON-TV (837 5000 ext 4444). 'Sports talk' radio remains popular but is not an efficient source of information. KNBR (680 AM) can be counted on for anticipation, second guessing, hyperbole and the occasional bit of practical advice. Reflecting the nation's passion for sport, newsstands are swamped with weekly and monthly publications; *Sports Illustrated* ($2.95) remains one of America's best written magazines. For special events or printed schedules, visit the San Francisco Visitor Information Center (*see chapter* **Essential Information**).

Tickets

The sanest and thriftiest place to go for tickets is the box office of the team you want to see. This direct approach may save effort and, even if you do end up going to a ticket service or broker, will at least give you a better idea of prices. If you get referred to **BASS Tickets** (1-510 762 2277), which has several offices, desks in Tower Records and a telephone switchboard, expect to pay a service fee of $2.75 or more, especially for tickets charged to a credit card.

Ticket Brokers

Money may not buy you love, but it can, on occasion, buy a seat at a sold-out game. Find ticket brokers in the Yellow Pages under Ticket Sales – Entertainment & Sports. Ticket brokers buy and sell tickets, so if you're stuck with a valuable ticket you can't use you could sell it for some quick cash. You could check with the **St Francis Theater Ticket Service** (362 3500) inside the Westin St Francis on Union Square. Better for sports, however, are **Mr Ticket** (292 7328/1-800

For **Rollerblading**, *see page 199.*

424 7328 from outside the Bay Area), **Entertainment Ticketfinder** (756 1414) or **Premier Tickets** (346 7222).

Scalpers (Touts)

This ought to be a last resort, although sometimes going to the stadium without a ticket and seeing what happens can add adventure to an evening out. There are risks, of course, including buying a fake ticket, getting a ticket for the next evening's game or ending up with a seat in the third deck where you need binoculars to see the action. Needless to say, plan to pay scalpers in cash.

Auto Racing

Sears Point Raceway

At the intersection of State Highways 37 and 121, Sonoma (1-707 938 8448). US101 north to SR37 exit, then 10 miles to SR121. **Admission** $5-$35. **Credit** MC, V.
Sears Point hosts just about every kind of motorised race on land, from nostalgic cars to monster truck derbies. It's one loud slice of Americana.
Disabled: access; toilets.

Baseball

The Bay Area sports two baseball teams, one in each league of 'the Majors'. As with many West Coast teams, the Giants and A's have a history in New York and Philadelphia prior to their years here, but plenty of local lore as well. The A's won three World Series in a row in the 1970s; the Giants in the 1990s have Barry Bonds, three-times-winner of the Most Valuable Player award. The two teams were about to play Game One of the World Series in 1989 when they were rudely interrupted by the Loma Prieta earthquake. The season runs from April to October and tickets are usually available at the ballpark the day of the game.

Oakland A's

Oakland-Alameda County Coliseum Complex (A's 1-510 638 0500/Coliseum 1-510 639 7700). BART Coliseum. **Open** *A's office* 9am-6pm Mon-Fri; 10am-4pm Sat. **Admission** $4.50-$17.50.
Disabled: access; toilets.

San Francisco Giants

Candlestick Park, Giants Drive, at Gilman Avenue (467 8000). Special event Muni bus 47X at Van Ness Avenue and Market Street, 28X at Funston and California Streets. **Open** *8.30am-5.30pm Mon-Fri; from 8.30pm on game days.* **Admission** *$5.50-$20.*
Except on the sunniest of afternoons, bring a warm jacket or you may find yourself a wind-whipped icicle.
Disabled: access; toilets.

Basketball

From fast, trash-talking games in the panhandle of Golden Gate Park to college and professional squads, if you want to watch (or play) roundball while in town, you shouldn't have a problem. The Warriors represent the Bay Area in the National Basketball Association (NBA) and play from November to May. The women of the Stanford (University) Cardinal are the pride of northern California and regular contenders for the collegiate championship.

Golden State Warriors

Oakland-Alameda County Coliseum Complex (Warriors 1-510 382 2305/Coliseum 1-510 639 7700). BART Coliseum. **Open** *8.30am-5.30pm Mon-Fri.* **Admission** *$9.75-$60.*
Disabled: access; toilets.

Stanford Cardinal

Maples Pavilion, Palo Alto (1-723 1021/1-800 232 8225). CalTrain to Palo Alto. **Open** *9am-4pm Mon-Fri.* **Admission** *$7-$35.*
The college basketball season runs from November to March.
Disabled: access; toilets.

Football

Autumn Sundays in the Bay Area could leave one convinced that football is the new religion. The Raiders' return to Oakland (for the 1995-96 season) brought the league's most notorious winners of yesteryear back into the fold while the Forty-Niners continue as the National Football League's élite. The season runs from September to January. Also popular are the Bears from the University of California; the annual contest between Cal and Stanford is known simply as 'The Big Game'. Getting tickets to football games is almost impossible.

Oakland Raiders

Oakland-Alameda County Coliseum Complex (1-510 639 7700). BART Coliseum. **Open** *9am-5pm Mon-Sat.*
Admission *from $50.*
Disabled: access; toilets.

San Francisco Forty-Niners

Candlestick Park, Giants Drive, at Gilman Avenue (468 2249). Special event Muni bus: 47X at Van Ness Avenue and Market Street, 28X at Funston and California Streets. **Open** *9am-5pm Mon-Fri (and weekend if game is on).* **Admission** *$39.75.*
All tickets sold by phone by BASS (1-510 762 2277) from the second-to-last week in July.
Disabled: access; toilets.

University of California, Berkeley

California Memorial Stadium, Piedmont Avenue, at Bancroft Way, UC Berkeley (1-800 462 3277). BART Berkeley, then campus shuttle to stadium. **Open** *8.30am-4.30pm Mon-Fri.* **Admission** *$12-$20.*
College football games are played on Saturdays from September to November, as opposed to the pros who play on Sundays from September to January.
Disabled: access; toilets.

Horse Racing

Bay Meadows Racecourse

2600 S Delaware Street, San Mateo (574 7223). CalTrain to Bay Meadows or Hillsdale. **Open** *phone for details.* **Admission** *$3-$15.* **Credit** *AmEx, MC, V.*
Disabled: access; toilets.

Ice Hockey

Spectacularly fast-paced and, despite the National Hockey League's efforts, still known for its violence, ice hockey has found surprisingly broad support in the Bay Area. New to the NHL, the San Jose Sharks may not be the most accomplished team on the ice, but they sure are one of the leading merchandisers, their teal and black colours worn all over. Sharks games come complete with music from *Jaws* and a signature cheer, the 'Shark bite'. The season runs from October to May.

San Jose Sharks

San Jose Arena, at W Santa Clara and Autumn Streets (tickets 1-800 888 2736/arena 1-408 287 9200). CalTrain to San Jose. **Open** *9.30am-5.30pm Mon-Fri; 9.30am-1pm Sat.* **Admission** *$15-$73.*
Disabled: access; toilets.

Active Sports

To claim that many prefer life in the San Francisco Bay Area because of its easy access to outdoor pleasures and adventures is an understatement along the lines of 'San Francisco sees its share of fog'. Participatory sports – the zanier the better – and healing arts – the more arcane the better – come with the territory.

When hiring equipment, photo ID or a credit card is usually necessary as a deposit.

General Information

As with spectator sports, the *San Francisco Chronicle* has listings and information on outdoor activities. On Thursdays it publishes an Outdoors mini-section within the daily Sporting Green section. Also useful is *CitySports*, a free magazine available in the lobby of most gyms. Also try Cal Adventures (1-510 642 4000), which offers everything from rentals on water sports equipment to beginners' lessons and weekend skiing trips.

Boating

Capt Case Powerboat & Waterbike Rental

W10 Schoonemaker Point Marina, Libertyship Way, Sausalito (331 0444). Bus Golden Gate Transit 10, 50. **Open** *10am-6pm daily.* **Rates** *$50-$90 per hour.* **Credit** *AmEx, MC, V.*
Located opposite a café on a remodelled section of the Sausalito waterfront, Capt Case is the only one who can get you on the San Francisco Bay proper in a powerboat. The boats are Boston Whalers with outboards and require some experience. Capt Case also has human-powered water bikes that spider along at 5-10mph.

A Day on the Bay

San Francisco Marina, Gate 10, Marina Boulevard at Buchanan Street (922 0227). Bus 26. **Open** *8am-10pm daily.* **No credit cards.**
The oldest boat charter service in San Francisco operates out of the Marina for trips around the Bay. Caters for one to 30 passengers; prices range from $30-$350.

Stow Lake Boathouse

Stow Lake, Golden Gate Park (752 0347). Bus 5, 28, 29, 71. **Open** 9am-5pm daily. **No credit cards.**
On a clear day, pack a picnic, grab some company and head to Stow Lake in Golden Gate Park, where you can rent a paddleboat, rowing boat or motorboat.

Bowling

Park Bowl

1855 Haight Street (752 2366). Bus 6, 7, 33, 66, 71. **Open** 10am-midnight Mon-Thur; 10am-2am Fri, Sat; midnight Sun. **Rates** $1 shoe rental; $1.75 per game until 5pm; $2.35 per person per game after 5pm. **Credit** MC, V.
Park Bowl is as much a party as it is a bowling alley. On Friday and Saturday nights, 'Rock 'n' Bowl' features a DJ and several video screens. Not for the demure.

Camping

Dave Sullivan's Sport Shop

5323 Geary Boulevard, between 17th and 18th Avenues (751 7070). Bus 38, 38AX, 38BX. **Open** 8.30am-8pm Mon-Fri; 8.30am-6pm Sat; 9am-5pm Sun. **Credit** AmEx, MC, V.
A San Francisco institution: friendly, helpful service and great deals on camping and ski equipment rentals.

G & M Sales

1667 Market Street, at Gough Street (863 2855). Muni Metro F, J, K, L, M, N/6, 7, 8, 66, 71 bus. **Open** 9.30am-6pm Mon-Fri; 9am-5pm Sat; 11am-4pm Sun. **Credit** AmEx, MC, V.
A cornucopia of sporting paraphernalia for every rigorous outing you can think off, including backpacking, skiing and fishing equipment.

Cycling

Just about anywhere you want to go in San Francisco you can go by bicycle. Day trips over the Golden Gate Bridge to Marin or to Tilden Park in Oakland offer an excellent combination of exercise and sightseeing. Cycle route maps ($2.95) are available in most bike shops, and if you plan on seeing the Bay Area by bike, pick up Ray Hosler's *Bay Area Bike Rides* ($10.95). Legend has it that mountain biking originated on the slopes of Mount Tamalpais, an hour (by bike) north of San Francisco. For specific trail information, call the Golden Gate National Recreation Area Visitor Center (331 1540) or the Pan Toll Ranger Station (388 2070).

Most local buses and trains have bowed to bike activists. BART (1-510 464 7133) requires a pass ($3) and bans travel during commuter hours. CalTrain (1-800 660 4287/495 4546) has limited bike space on a first-come-first-served basis. AC Transit (1-510 839 2882) charges $1 and only allows bikes at off-peak hours except on the T bus when they are permitted any time, free of charge. The best way to travel on public transport with a bike is by ferry.

Karim's Cyclery

2801 Telegraph Avenue, Berkeley (1-510 841 2181). BART Ashby. **Open** 11am-6pm Mon-Sat; noon-5pm Sun. **Rates** $12 per day; $20 overnight. **Credit** MC, V.
Karim has a variety of bikes for hire, including mountain, road and crossrigs. For those wishing to improvise their own decathlon, they also hire rollerblades.

Waller's Sports

1749 Waller Street at Stanyan Street (752 8383). Muni Metro N/6, 7, 33, 66, 71 bus. **Open** 10am-6pm daily. **Rates** $5 per hour; $25 per day; $30 overnight. **Credit** MC, V.
Conveniently located on the corner of Golden Gate Park.

Wheel Escapes

30 Libertyship Way, Sausalito (332 0218). Bus Golden Gate Transit 10, 50/Sausalito Ferry. **Open** 10am-6pm Mon,Wed-Fri; 9am-7pm Sat, Sun. **Rates** $5 per hour; $21 per day. **Credit** AmEx, MC, V.
Serious mountain bikes (with suspension forks) cost extra: $8 per hour or $35 per day.

Fitness Classes

To join an aerobics class check the schedule and facilities of the gym nearest to where you're staying. Just as San Franciscans have their corner cafés and bars, they have their corner gyms – boutique-sized studios abound in the neighbourhoods. The Embarcadero Y (*see below* **YMCAs**) runs over 80 fitness classes a week.

24 Hour Nautilus Fitness Center

1335 Sutter Street (776 2200). Bus 2, 3, 4, 38, 42, 47, 49. **Open** 24-hours daily. **Rates** day use $15. **Credit** AmEx, MC, V.
Not exceptionally personal, 24 Hour Nautilus gets the job done – and it's ready when you are. Most fitness classes are held around the workday schedule so the best times to drop in are early morning, lunch hour or early evening.
Branches: 100 California Street (434 5080); 350 Bay Street (395 9595).

Golf Courses

Harding Park & Golf Course

Harding Road and Skyline Boulevard (664 4690). Bus 18, 88. **Open** 6.30am-7pm daily. **Rates** *18 holes* $26 Mon-Fri; $31 Sat, Sun; *9 holes* $9 daily. **No credit cards.**
City-owned and operated, the Harding Golf Course lies by Lake Merced and has a shop and a small bar/café.

Lincoln Park Golf Course

34th Avenue and Clement Street (221 9911). Bus 2, 18, 38. **Open** sunrise to sunset. **Rates** $23-$9 Mon-Fri; $27-$10 Sat, Sun. **Credit** AmEx, MC, V.
One of the most photographed courses in the States, with the famous 17th hole view of the Golden Gate Bridge. Prices drop as the light fades. There's also a practice area, putting green, rental shop, pro shop, bar and refreshments.

Tilden Park Golf Course

Grizzly Peak and Shasta Road, Berkeley (1-510 848 7373). BART Berkeley, then 65 or 67 bus to Grizzly Peak, then short walk. **Open** 6am-dusk. **Rates** *18 holes* $18 Mon-Fri; $25 Sat, Sun. **Credit** MC, V.
The only problem with Tilden Park Golf Course is that you really need a car to get there.

Golf Instruction

Driving Obsession

Suite 402, 310 Grant Avenue, between Bush and Sutter Streets (397 4653). BART Montgomery Street/Muni Metro F, J, K, L, M, N/15, 30, 45 bus. **Open** 9am-6pm Mon-Sat. **Credit** AmEx, JCB, MC, V.
Individual and group golf instruction using computers and digital video analysis. Initial one-hour lesson and evaluation costs $110.

Hiking

Hiking trails with rewarding views or paths that lead through redwood groves to the ocean await you just 30 minutes from downtown San Francisco. For a short, introductory hike, try the **Morning Sun Trail** which climbs from a parking lot at the Spencer Avenue exit off US101 north, just above the Golden Gate Bridge. You can look east over the Bay, Angel Island and the urban sprawl or west to the Pacific. A good day hike, a little further into Marin County, is the **Dipsea Trail**, which leads from Mill Valley to Stinson Beach. Reach Mill Valley on Golden Gate Transit bus 10. The **Bootjack Trail**, which leads to the summit of Mount Tamalpais, is also popular. Get trail information for Mount Tam from the Pan Toll Ranger Station (388 2070).

Horse Riding

Horse riding in San Francisco – unless you're a mounted police officer – is mostly limited to Golden Gate Park. Within a 30- to 75-minute drive, however, the options open up. Stables which hire horses and lead tours include Sea Horse & Friendly Acres Ranches (726 2362), near Half Moon Bay, or Chanslor Guest Ranch & Stables (1-707 875 2721), next to Bodega Bay.

Golden Gate Park Stables

John F Kennedy Drive at 36th Avenue (668 7360). Bus 5. **Open** 9am-5pm Tue-Sun. **Rates** $35 private lesson; $20 trail ride. **No credit cards.**
Golden Gate Park Stables offers everything from pony rides for small kids to advanced equestrian courses for experienced cowboys and girls.

Indoor Rock Climbing

Mission Cliffs

2295 Harrison Street, at 19th Street (550 0515). Bus 12, 22, 33. **Open** 11am-10pm Mon-Fri; 10am-6pm Sat, Sun. **Rates** $12-$27.
To enter Mission Cliffs is to enter a 3,800sq m/12,000sq ft kingdom that melts the boundary of 'urban' and 'wilderness' and distills it into a highly-polished jungle gym.

Inline Hockey

Street hockey has made a comeback with rollerblades, and a number of San Franciscans are rushing to place their knees and ankles in harm's (and fun's) way. You can often join in a game at the playground on the corner of Scott and North Point Streets. Rentals at Achilles' Wheels (*see below* **Rollerblading**) include pads and a free lesson. Serious players will want to go to the Bladium, where any level of play is possible, morning, noon and night.

Bladium

1050 Third Street, at Berry Street (442 5060). Bus 15, 30, 42, 45. **Open** 8am-noon daily. **Rate** $5 per person during 'open session'. **Credit** MC, V.
An inline skating rink, Bladium houses several hockey leagues, a licensed juice bar, pro shop and rents all the gear you need for a drop-in game. A midnight league runs on Wed and Thur (midnight-2am) and pick-up games happen on weekday afternoons.

Kayaking

Rarely seen outside the Olympics or French action-adventure television, kayaking is an almost religious experience to its devotees. The San Francisco Bay Area, with its tides, islands and deltas, offers kayakers plenty of excitement and convincing proof that there are few better ways to exorcise anxiety than shooting the Raccoon Straits.

California Canoe & Kayak

409 Water Street, on Jack London Square at Franklin Street, Oakland (1-510 893 7833). BART 12th Street. **Open** 10am-8pm Mon-Sat; 9am-6.30pm Sun. **Rates** *basic package* $15 for 4 hours. **Credit** AmEx, MC, V.

Branch out with some tai chi in the park.

A quality shop for hiring and buying kayaks and sea-going gear. Lessons and day outings are available on the nearby Oakland Estuary.

Escape Artist Tours

(726 7626/1-800 728 1384). **Open** 9am-9pm Mon-Sat. **Credit** MC, V.
Looking for something unusual to do? This service arranges adventures for groups and individuals ranging from kayaking on the Bay to flying air-combat planes.

Sea Trek

Schoonemaker Point Marina, Libertyship Way, Sausalito (488 1000/332 4465). Bus Golden Gate Transit 10, 50. **Open** 9.30am-5.30pm Mon-Fri; on the 'beach' *during season* 9am-5pm Tue-Sun; *winter* 9am-5pm Sat, Sun. **Rates** beginners' class $80. **Credit** MC, V.
Sea Trek has grown into something of an institution. It runs summer camps and trips for kids, books expeditions to Alaska and Baja and joins forces with environmentalists to preserve waterways as well as offering beginners several opportunities to explore the Bay, from guided tours and lessons to moonlight paddles.

Paragliding

Easier to learn than most flying methods, paragliding offers the chance to fly for minutes to hours with less than a day's instruction. Not to be confused with parasailing, paragliding involves no boat. The paraglider itself weighs only 10lbs and can do just about anything a hang-glider can do, except turn upside-down.

Air Time of San Francisco

3620 Wawona Street, at 47th Avenue (759 1177). Muni Metro L. **Open** 11am-6pm Mon, Wed-Fri; 10am-4pm Sat. **Rates** $150-$160. **Credit** MC, V.
You couldn't ask for a better place to learn to paraglide or to take the five-day course to get Class 1 certification.

Pool & Billards

Pool tables are as common to bars as sofas are to living rooms. But if you want to go to a place where pool is all they do, you can.

Chalkers

1 Rincon Center, at Spear and Mission Streets (512 0450). BART Embarcadero/14 bus. **Open** 11.30am-2am Mon-Fri; 2pm-2am Sat; 2pm-midnight Sun. **Rates** $2-$7 per hour. **Credit** AmEx, M, V.

With 30 cherrywood tables, a bar and restaurant, Chalkers occasionally invites trick-shot experts and pros to dazzle the lunch crowd. Families are allowed from 2pm to 7pm, at the weekend. If you prefer it busy, Friday is your night, when the after-work crowd stops in for happy hour.

Racquetball

The Embarcadero YMCA also has two courts (*see below* **YMCAs**).

Telegraph Hill Club

1850 Kearny Street, between Bay and Chestnut Streets (982 4700). Bus 42. **Open** 5.30am-11pm Mon-Fri; 8am-8pm Sat. **Rates** day pass $15. **No credit cards**.

This club has a dozen courts, some of which get converted into aerobic studios at rush hour; phone first to make sure one is available. Ask for directions, since the entrance is hidden away in the maze-like streets of Telegraph Hill.

Rollerblading (Inline Skating)

Formerly only for die-hard outdoor enthusiasts, rollerblading is now making the crossover to the mainstream. And, given the speeds reached and the widely varying degrees of mastery, the skish-skish sound of a rollerblader makes more than a few pedestrians skittish. For the novice or veteran, rollerblading in Golden Gate Park is hard to top, with the beach at one end and plenty of sunny meadows and shady benches. A mix of rollerblading and break dancing provides entertainment near the De Young Museum on John F Kennedy Drive.

Achilles' Wheels

2271 Chestnut Street, at Scott Street (567 8400). Bus 22, 30. **Open** 10am-8pm Mon-Fri; 8am-8pm Sat, Sun. **Rates** $5.50 per hour; $19 for 24 hours. **Credit** AmEx, MC, V.

Check out the young, single and beautiful on nearby Marina Green, on rental skates from this shop, which also specialises in the latest snowboards and skate-rat attire.

Golden Gate Park Skate and Bike

3038 Fulton Street, at Sixth Avenue (668 1117). Bus 5, 21, 44. **Open** 10am-6pm Mon-Sat; 10am-7pm Sun. **Credit** MC, V.

Spending the day in the park? Stop here for bicycles, roller skates, in-line skates and safety gear.

Nuvo

3108C Fillmore Street, between Filbert and Pixley Streets (771 6886). Bus 1, 2, 3, 4, 22. **Open** 11am-7pm Mon, Tue, Thur; 10am-6.30pm Wed; 10am-7pm Fri; 9am-7pm Sat; 9am-6pm Sun. **Rates** *Mon-Fri* $7 per hour, $10 for two hours, $15 for 24 hours; *Sat, Sun* $7 per hour, $20 for 24 hours. **Credit** AmEx, MC, V.

Fees include protective gear (knee and elbow pads, helmet).

Skates on Haight (SOH)

1818 Haight Street, at Stanyan Street (752 8375). Bus 6, 7, 71. **Open** 11.30am-6.30pm Mon, Wed-Fri; 10am-6pm Sat, Sun. **Rates** $7 per hour. **Credit** AmEx, MC, V.

Rent or buy in-line skates, roller skates or snowboards at this outlet responsible for inspiring the world-wide skateboard craze back in the 1970s.

Rowing

Rowing of all kinds can be had in the Bay Area, from single sculls to whale boat racing. For sweep rowing, call the Lake Merritt Rowing Club (1-510 273 9041). Scullers may want to have a go on the San Francisco Bay itself; call Open Water Rowing (332 1091).

Running

Many locals will tell you the best place to run, bike and rollerblade are the same – Golden Gate Park – but there's some disagreement on this. One of the most stunning places for a jog is the Marina Green (bus 22). A track encircles the esplanade itself, but a trail extends all the way to Fort Point, just before the Golden Gate Bridge.

Sailing

If you sail a lot, chances are you'll find a mate, captain or boat you know in one of the several marinas around the Bay. If you want to learn, Cal Adventures is an excellent first resource.

Cal Adventures

UC Aquatic Center, Berkeley Marina (1-510 642 4000). BART Berkeley, then 51 bus. **Open** 10am-6pm Mon-Thur; 10am-7pm Fri. **Rates** $35-$95. **Credit** MC, V.

Cal Adventures hires out Coronado 15-footers for sporty sailing on the South Sailing Basin. To lease one without recognised certification you must spend $35 to sail with an instructor who will confirm your ability.

Scuba Diving

Cal Dive & Travel

1750 Sixth Street, Berkeley (1-510 524 3248). BART North Berkeley. **Open** 10am-6pm Mon-Fri; 10am-2pm Sat. **Rates** equipment $60-$70; beginner's courses from $250. **Credit** AmEx, MC, V.

Beginners' classes are held four blocks from the shop in a swimming pool. When you're ready they arrange and book trips down to Monterey.

Skateboarding

No one needs to tell a skate rat where to go. If you're one, you'll find Justin Herman Plaza, a Safeway parking lot or the earthquake-damaged freeway ramps and be on your way. For new attire or rigs skating has gone upscale at the **Deluxe Store**, 1831 Market Street (626 5588).

Skiing/Snowboarding

The ambitious sometimes make a day trip to the Sierra for skiing, but it's best to give yourself at least a weekend. Leading ski resorts include **Alpine Meadows** (1-916 581 8374), **Heavenly** (1-916 541 7544), **Kirkwood** (1-209 258 3000), **Northstar-at-Tahoe** (1-916 562 1330) and **Squaw Valley** (1-916 583 6955). **Mogul Ski Club** (456 1000) can hook you up with other skiers and provide the latest snow information. During the season (usually end of Nov-early Apr), most ski shops will have calendars of events and ads for package deals. Cross-country skiers will want to try **Cal Adventures** (*see above* **Sailing**).

Squash

Bay Club

150 Greenwich Street (433 2200). Bus 42/Bay Club shuttle from Embarcadero BART. **Open** 5.30am-11pm Mon-Fri; 7am-9pm Sat, Sun. **Rates** $10-$15. **No credit cards**.

Take a board into the Bay.

Without turning away business, the Bay Club does try to make its well-to-do members feel exclusive. As such, they insist drop-in players either come with a member or demonstrate that they are a member of a squash gym, club or organisation.

Swimming

For Olympic-sized pools, try Embarcadero YMCA (*see below* **YMCAs**) or the Bay Club (*see above* **Squash**).

Tennis

Indoor tennis in San Francisco is almost exclusively a members-only affair, but much of the best play is outdoors anyway. **Golden Gate Park** has several courts (at the Stanyan Street entrance) and **Dolores Park** in the Mission district is always busy. Both are open from sunrise to sunset, and are free.

Volleyball

More popular in southern California, where beach volleyball has become a televised and well-attended spectator sport, volleyball is also played in San Francisco. Experienced players can look up the SF Volleyball Association (931 6385) which organises leagues. Otherwise, look for pick-up action at the north end of Marina Green on weekend mornings or in People's Park, Berkeley (Telegraph Avenue, between Haste and Dwight Way), where the sand volleyball courts were once decried as a fascist plot to decamp the homeless.

Whale Watching

Whale watching can be as easy as taking a pair of binoculars to the shore and having a look. One recommended shore location is the tip of Point Reyes, an hour's drive north of San Francisco. For more land-locked views of passing whales, pick up *The Delicate Art of Whale Watching* ($10) in the Sierra Club Bookstore, 730 Polk Street (923 5600).

Oceanic Society Expeditions
Fort Mason Center (474 3385). Bus 22, 28, 42, 47, 49. Open 9am-5pm Mon-Fri. Rates $29-$58. Credit AmEx, MC, V.
Trips are a cut above most tourist excursions because the staff are experts in natural history and marine life. The full-day trip heads 26 miles west of the Golden Gate to the Farallon Islands, home of the largest sea bird rookery in the contiguous US; along the way, guides lead the search for humpback and gray whales, seals and sea lions.

Windsurfing (Sailboarding)

The San Francisco Bay Area boasts no less than 32 launch sites for windsurfing, including Coyote Point, Candlestick and Crissy Field – the latter has been the site of several international competitions, among them windsurfing's World Cup.

SF School of Windsurfing
1 Harding Road, Lake Merced (753 3235). Muni Metro M, then bus 18/18, 23, 29 bus. Open 9am-noon daily. Rates two-day beginner's course $95. Credit MC, V.
Offers lessons at all levels; equipment is provided. The school also rents gear on Candlestick Beach near Candlestick Park.

City Front Sailboards
2936 Lyon Street, between Lombard and Greenwich Streets (929 7873). Bus 28, 30, 41, 43. 45. Open 10am-6pm daily. Rates complete sailing rig $45. Credit AmEx, MC, V.
City Front is the 'pro' shop, the place to go if you're already good and have brought along your wet suit and harness.

YMCAs

Embarcadero YMCA
169 Steuart Street, at Mission Street (957 9622). BART Embarcadero/Muni Metro F, J, K, L, M, N/2, 7, 8, 9, 14, 21, 31 bus. Open 5.30am-10pm Mon-Fri; 8am-8pm Sat; 9am-6pm Sun. Rates day pass $12. Credit M, V.
A new facility, the Embarcadero Y serves downtown SF from a waterfront location. A day pass covers any one of 80 weekly aerobics classes, free weights, Cybex and Nautilus machines, racquetball and basketball courts and 25m pool.

Yoga

Also try the Yoga Society of San Francisco (285 5537).

Yoga College of India
Second Floor, 910 Columbus Avenue, at Lombard Street (346 5400). Bus 15, 39, 41/Powell-Mason cable car. Open classes for visitors 9am, 4.30pm, 6pm Mon-Fri; 9am Sat, Sun. Rates $10 per class. No credit cards.
First-time guests can have a second class free. Bring a towel.

Surf's up

Conditions in the Bay Area are punishing enough to make most surf dudes head south for the kinder waters near Santa Cruz. However, despite the freezing water temperatures and rip-roaring currents, there are several beaches where you can take the waves. Beginners should avoid **Ocean Beach**, where the current is strong and waves can reach 25 or 30 feet (7.6-9 metres) in the winter; **Fort Point** is a better bet, though the current is still strong here. **Stinson Beach**, north over the Golden Gate Bridge on Highway 1, is another good spot for beginners, and the water rarely gets crowded. Wetsuits (and a hardy constitution) are essential all year round. For information on day-to-day conditions and where to hire equipment, try the following: **Wise Surfboards** (recorded information 665 9473/shop 665 7745); **Live Water** (868 0333); or **Sunlight Surfshop** (recorded information 359 0353/shop 359 5471).

Theatre & Dance

It may lack the pazazz of New York or LA, but Bay Area theatre still manages to keep audiences amused with anything from Broadway smashes to virtual theatre.

The San Francisco Ballet performs in the great outdoors at Stern Grove.

Although the Bay Area theatre and dance scene doesn't have the depth and flash of New York or Los Angeles, San Francisco's tolerance for the experimental and the weird makes it possible to see truly original work here (for better and for worse). Experimentation is encouraged, even savoured, and cutting-edge work isn't instantly sucked up, commercially packaged and hyped the way it is in NY and LA.

Offbeat performers are allowed the space to hone their creative vision: Whoopi Goldberg and Robin Williams both cut their teeth in stand up comedy in San Francisco. Socially conscious artists also thrive: Tony Kushner, the Pulitzer Prize-winning playwright of the New York Broadway smash *Angels in America*, developed the play and premièred it, in progress, at San Francisco's Eureka Theater. And there's also room for lunatic fringe performers like Mark Pauline, formerly of the rogue robot and munitions makers Survival Research Laboratories, to blow themselves apart in the name of art. Other nationally known playwrights and

performers such as Anna Deavere Smith and Eric Bogosian, of *Talk Radio* fame, have also recharged their cultural batteries in the city.

Gender-bending and culturally and ethnically specific theatre performances are stronger here than elsewhere in the US, as befits the Bay Area's radical, multicultural artistic and political traditions. And Silicon Valley's hackers and inventors have also had an impact. Holograms are deployed alongside actors, and the alternation of computer muzak and live musicians further break down the barriers separating virtual and theatrical reality.

Diehard traditionalists are also catered for. Visiting companies bring successful Broadway shows to theatres like the Golden Gate, Curran and Orpheum. Smaller repertory companies like the Lamplighters may specialise in Gilbert and Sullivan. About 14 per cent of the city's sky-high hotel tax goes to the arts, so get your money's worth and enjoy them while you're here.

If you want to plan ahead, the Datebook section of the combined Sunday *Examiner/Chronicle*, the free weeklies, and *SF Arts Monthly* carry up-to-date reviews and listings. The opening hours listed below are for the box office unless otherwise stated. Prices range from as little as $5 for an experimental show to $50 or more for a Broadway extravaganza.

TICKETS

The theatres' own box offices are usually the cheapest bet for tickets (phone ahead for opening times, but bear in mind that there's often a fee for telephone bookings). **TIX Bay Area**, the small kiosk on the Stockton Street side of Union Square (433 7827), sells half-price tickets for theatre, dance and opera events on the day of the show (cash only). TIX also sells full-price tickets in advance (for which you can pay by credit card). Ticket brokers **BASS** (1-510 762 2277/1-800 225 2277 from outside California) has outlets all over the city, but expect to pay a hefty surcharge; you can also try **St Francis Theater Ticket Service** (262 3500), **Mr Ticket** (292 7328/1-800 424 7328) or **City Box Office** (392 4400).

Mainstream

Three beautifully restored theatres bring Broadway and other large-scale commercial productions to the City for a 'Best of Broadway' series. They share an information line for box office hours and ticket information.

Curran Theater

445 Geary Street, between Mason and Taylor Streets (474 3800). BART Powell Street/Muni Metro F, J, K, L, M, N/27, 38 bus/Powell-Mason, Powell-Hyde cable car. **Open** 10am-6pm Mon; 10am-8.30pm Tue-Sat; noon-4pm Sun. **Credit** AmEx, MC, V.

Golden Gate Theater

1 Taylor Street, between Sixth and Market Streets (474 3800/441 0919). BART Civic Center/Muni Metro F, J, K, L, M, N/5, 8, 27 bus. **Open** 10am-6pm Mon; 10am-8.30pm Tue-Sat; noon-4pm Sun. **Credit** AmEx, MC, V.

Orpheum

1192 Market Street, at Hyde Streets (474 3800). BART Civic Center/Muni Metro F, J, K, L, M, N/5, 8, 27 bus. **Open** 10am-6pm Mon; 10am-8.30pm Tue-Sat; noon-4pm Sun. **Credit** AmEx, MC, V.

Regional Theatres

The Bay Area's two largest and best established theatre companies mount a full season of shows each year.

American Conservatory Theater (ACT)

Geary Theater, 415 Geary Street, between Mason and Taylor Streets; box office at 405 Geary Street (749 2228). BART Powell Street/Muni Metro F, J, K, L, M, N/27, 38 bus/Powell-Mason, Powell-Hyde cable car. **Open** noon-6pm Mon, Sun; noon-8pm Tue-Sat. **Credit** AmEx, MC, V.
Theater ACT mounts traditional and contemporary shows (recent productions have included Chekov's *Uncle Vanya* and

Tony Kushner's *Angels in America*). Since the 1989 earthquake, the company has led a nomadic existence, but at the time of writing, it was poised to resume residency at the beautiful, restored (and quake-proofed) Geary Theater.

Berkeley Repertory

2025 Addison Street, between Shattuck Avenue and Milvia Street (1-510 845 4700). BART Berkeley. **Open** noon-7pm daily. **Credit** MC, V.
This East Bay company divides productions between its main stage, where it presents five plays a year, and a 'Parallel Season' of experimental and developing work. The productions often reflect the diverse communities and traditions of the Bay Area and California as a whole, making it a great place to catch innovative and insightful work. Half-price tickets are available from the box office on the day of each performance.

Midsize Theatres

Some of the smaller theatre companies in the Bay Area are often the most interesting. The Magic, the Asian American, Theater 'Rhino' and the Lorraine Hansberry all mount original productions, often by local artists. And although Theater Artaud doesn't have a company in residence, this unique theatre-in-a-warehouse is the place to find cutting-edge national and international performances.

Asian American Theater

403 Arguello Boulevard, at Clement Street (751 2600). Bus 2, 33. **Open** July-June, half-hour before show. **No credit cards.**
The 135-seat main stage often showcases high quality new work by Asian and Pacific Islander Americans. Downstairs offers sneak previews of developing works.

Eureka Theater Company

(243 9895). **Open** 1-5pm Mon-Fri. **No credit cards.**
1996 is the comeback season for the cutting-edge Eureka Theater Company, best known for helping Tony Kushner develop the Pulitzer prize-winning and Emmy-laden *Angels in America*. Despite its reputation for innovation, the company was forced by financial constraints to close for a while, but at the time of writing was about to take up residence in a state-of-the-art South of Market space, promising to revive its tradition of encouraging new talent. Phone the number listed above for details and the location of the company's next production.

Lorraine Hansberry Theater

500 Sutter Street, between Mason and Powell Streets (288 0320). Bus 2, 3, 4, 30, 45, 76/Powell-Mason, Powell-Hyde cable car. **Open** 11am-5pm Mon-Fri. **No credit cards.**
The Lorraine Hansberry presents plays by America's foremost black playwrights, such as Pulitzer prize-winners Charles Fuller and August Wilson. It also stages adaptations of works by Alice Walker and Toni Morrison, among others.

Magic Theater

Building D, Fort Mason Center, at Laguna and Buchanan Streets (441 8822/441 8001 info). Bus 28. **Open** just before show. **Credit** AmEx, MC, V.
The Magic Theater has been dedicated to developing new plays for more than 25 years, many of them responding to topical political and social events. For a time, the theatre premièred a new work by Sam Shepard every year; today, regulars include San Francisco playwright Claire Chafee.

Theater Artaud

2800 Mariposa Street, between Florida and Alabama Streets; box office at 450 Florida Street, at 17th Street (621 7797/647 2200). Bus 27, 33, 53. **Open** 2-6pm Tue, Wed; 2-8pm Thur-Sun. **Credit** MC, V.

Theater Artaud stages high quality avant-garde theatre, music and dance performances from around the world, the US – and even San Francisco. It's almost worth seeing for the space alone, which is built into a renovated warehouse. Every summer the theatre sponsors a weekend-long performance marathon, featuring dozens of artists working round the clock.

Theater Rhinoceros

2926 16th Street, at South Van Ness Avenue (861 5079). BART 16th Street/14, 22, 33, 49, 53 bus. **Open** 1pm until show starts Tue-Sun. **Credit** MC, V.

Theater Rhino presents work by lesbian and gay playwrights and performers to a mostly gay audience on both its main and studio stages. Mainstage work is mostly traditional, mainstream even, while the studio presents more experimental material. *See also chapter* **Gay & Lesbian San Francisco**.

Smaller Spaces

There are dozens of smaller theatres and performance spaces dotting San Francisco and the Bay Area. Some feature long-running performances with proven commercial appeal: check the **Cable Car Theater** (956 8497), **Mason Street Theater** (982 5463), **Theater on the Square** (433 9500), and **Marine's Memorial** (771 6900), among others. Space for local experimental work and festival programming is provided by the **Bayfront** and **Cowell Theaters** (both at Fort Mason, 979 3010), **Brava! for Women in the Arts** (641 7657), and **Josie's Juice Bar and Cabaret** has done plenty to develop queer performance in the area (*see chapter* **Gay & Lesbian San Francisco**). The handful of theatres listed below all have interesting reputations.

Climate Theater

252 Ninth Street, between Folsom and Howard Streets (978 2345). BART Civic Center/Muni Metro F, J, K, L, M, N/5, 8, 27 bus. **Open** phone for details. **Credit** MC, V.

Home to the acclaimed Solo Mio Festival (*see chapter* **San Francisco by Season**), the Climate nurtures new work by solo performers who have gone on to achieve wider acclaim. It also produces the annual Festival Fantochio, a fantastical puppet event that is definitely not for children only.

Exit Theater

156 Eddy Street, between Mason and Taylor Streets (673 3847). BART Powell Street/Muni Metro F, J, K, L, M, N/27, 31 bus. **Open** half-hour before show. **No credit cards.**

The small Exit organises the annual San Francisco Fringe Festival, and otherwise offers a variety of works, from one-act plays to adaptations of the likes of Edward Albee.

450 Geary Studio Theater

450 Geary Street, between Mason and Taylor Streets (673 1172). Cable car Powell-Hyde or Powell-Mason. **Open** phone for details. **Credit** MC, V.

Much like the Exit Theater (*above*), 450 Geary is a small space devoted to new work, including children's plays, and some solo performances.

Stage Door Theater

420 Mason Street, at Geary Street (749 2228/834-3200). Bus 2, 3, 4, 38L, 76. **Open** phone for details. **Credit** AmEx, MC, V.

The Stage Door offered shelter to ACT during its homeless years following the earthquake (*see p202*). Now ACT has been rehoused, its own future is in doubt. But for the time being, it is staging secondary ACT offerings and new works in development.

Experimental & Performance Art

By its very nature, experimental and performance art is a hit and miss affair. But the Bay Area has produced more than its fair share of underground hits. Indeed, the city's theatrical reputation is fired by the raw creative energies generated in its alternative performance spaces.

Above Brainwash

1122 Folsom Street, between Seventh and Eighth Streets (café 861 3663/laundromat 431 9274). Bus 12, 27, 42. **Open** 7.30am-11pm Mon-Thur, Sun; 7.30am-1am Fri, Sat; performances Fri, Sat. **Admission** free. **Credit** AmEx, MC, V.

Located, appropriately enough, above the laundromat/café Brainwash, this small space is a favourite hangout for South of Market hipsters. Throw your laundry in a washer, catch a short play, and run downstairs in time for the dryer (*see also chapter* **Shopping & Services**).

Intersection for the Arts

446 Valencia Street, between 15th and 16th Streets (626 3311/2787). BART 16th Street/Muni Metro F, J, K, L, M, N. **Open** phone for details. **No credit cards.**

An alternative arts centre mixing theatre with poetry and prose readings, community-minded art shows, and avant-garde music.

The Marsh

1062 Valencia Street, at 22nd Street (641 0235). BART 24th Street/26 bus. **Open** phone for details. **No credit cards.**

A breeding ground for new performance, The Marsh offers select playwrights and performers an open stage to try out whatever they like. It features mostly solo work, with an occasional ensemble piece thrown in.

New Langton Arts

1246 Folsom Street, between Eighth and Ninth Streets (626 5416). Bus 12, 19, 27, 42. **Open** 10am-6pm Mon-Fri. **Credit** MC, V.

The centre makes space in its programme of experimental art shows for original presentations by regional arts grants winners. Expect political and social commentary, gender-bending art and performance.

The Lab

2948 16th Street, between Capp Street and South Van Ness Avenue (864 8855). BART 16th Street/33, 53 bus. **Open** phone for details. **No credit cards.**

An experimental gallery for performance artists and visual art.

LunaSea

Room 216C, 2940 16th Street, between Capp Street and South Van Ness Avenue (863 2989). BART 16th Street/33, 53 bus. **Open** *performances start 8pm.* **No credit cards.**

Mostly queer and cutting edge women's arts centre for spoken word, performance art, dance and music (*see chapter* **Gay & Lesbian San Francisco**).

In a Class of Their Own

Beach Blanket Babylon

Club Fugazi, 678 Green Street, between Columbus Avenue and Powell Street (421 4222). Bus 15, 30, 41, 45. **Open** 10am-7.30pm Mon-Thur; 10am-6pm Fri, Sat; noon-7.30pm Sun. **Credit** MC, V.

This long-running musical revue features a constantly changing array of characters drawn from American popular culture and the politics of the day. The slapstick humour places heavy emphasis on the formulaic and the visual. Even so, it's a San Francisco original.

George Coates Performance Works

110 McAllister Street, at Leavenworth Street (863 4130). BART Civic Center/Muni Metro F, J, K, L, M, N/5 bus. **Open** 11am-9pm Mon-Fri. **Credit** AmEx, V.

Techno wizard George Coates is a pioneer in 'virtual' theatre, working actors and musicians into dazzling computer-generated environments. Operating out of a pseudo-gothic chapel over whose walls and ceilings 'float' images of everything from the wilderness to Chartres Cathedral to outer space, Coates creates a theatrical *son et lumière*. KQED radio's live Saturday morning arts show is broadcast from the church.

Festivals

San Francisco's theatre festivals offer something for everyone. Look out for free events like the Golden Gate favourite, **Shakespeare in the Park** and the **California Shakespeare Festival** (both in September), and Sundays in Stern Grove (June-August) where the city's finest – including the San Francisco Opera and Ballet – stage productions for Sunday afternoon picnickers. The **Solo Mio Festival** includes a feisty series of high-quality solo performances and is a high point of Bay Area theatre, as is the annual **Mime Troupe in the Park**, when the San Francisco Mime Troupe performs its unique combination of humour and hard-hitting politics at various park locations around the Bay Area. For more details on these events, *see chapter* **San Francisco by Season**. And finally, at the tenday **Annual San Francisco Fringe Festival** (837 6191) in September, you can expect anything from Oscar Wilde performances to Betty Grable impersonations from local and visiting companies in various venues around town.

Dance

A number of dance companies thrive in San Francisco, among them the **Margaret Jenkins Dance Company**, which celebrated 20 years of modern dance in 1994, **Lines Dance Company**, **Contraband** and Oakland's **Dance Brigade** (which produces *The Revolutionary Nutcracker Sweetie* each year as an alternative holiday season offering to the traditional Nutcracker ballet). However, SF's companies are in heavy demand around the world, so catch them in the Bay Area if you can. Watch out also for the black choreographers' series at the Theater Artaud (*see page 203*).

Bay Area Dance Series

Delaney College, 900 Fallon Street, at Ninth Street, Oakland (1-510 464 3234). BART Lake Merritt.

This summer dance season in Oakland is the best place to see experimental work from local and touring groups. Look our especially for Contraband and Butoh groups like Ilarupin-Ila Theater.

Cal Performances

Zellerbach Hall, UC Berkeley campus (1-510 642 9988). BART Berkeley. **Open** 10am-5.30pm Mon-Fri; 10am-2pm Sat, Sun. **Credit** MC, V.

Hosted in conjunction with UC Berkeley at Zellerbach Hall on campus, this series draws the best national dance companies, from Bill T Jones/Arnie Zane and Merce Cunningham to Trisha Brown and June Watanabe, as well as traditional companies from countries such as Indonesia, Senegal and Cambodia, and the odd local company like Margaret Jenkins.

Center for the Arts at Yerba Buena Gardens

701 Mission Street, at Third Street (978 2787). BART Powell Street/Muni Metro F, J, K, L, M, N/15, 30, 45, 76 bus. **Open** 11am-6pm Tue-Sun; 11am-8pm first Thur of the month. **Credit** AmEx, MC, V.

The beautiful state-of-the-art theatre at the city's newest arts complex presents theatre, dance and music performances, with an emphasis on San Francisco-based artists. Its mission is to encourage experimentation and debate. Performances are drawn from the various ethnic communities that make up the Bay Area's population.

Dancers Group/Footwork

3221 22nd Street, at Mission Street (information 824 5044). BART 24th Street/14, 67 bus.

Look for the annual Edge Festival in February and March, the Improvisational Dance Festival in June, and occasional residencies by dance troupes like Asian American Dance Performances.

New Performance Gallery

3153 17th Street, between South Van Ness Avenue and Folsom Street (863 9834). BART 16th Street/33 bus. **Open** phone for details. **No credit cards**.

Like Footwork, this larger space showcases the work of mostly local dancers and helps develop innovative modern dance performances.

San Francisco Ballet

War Memorial Opera House, 301 Van Ness Avenue, at Grove Street (865 2000/864 3330). Muni Metro F, J, K, L, M, N/BART Civic Center. **Open** 10am-4pm Mon-Fri. **Credit** AmEx, MC, V.

The San Francisco Ballet is America's oldest professional ballet company (founded in 1933). Following its traditional seasonal opening with the *Nutcracker Suite*, it features other works choreographed by George Ballanchine and Jerome Robbins, and its artistic director Helgi Tomasson among others. One of its most successful recent shows was *Billboards*, an uncharacteristically modern ballet with a score by the artist formerly known as Prince. Until the renovation at the War Memorial Opera House is completed, the company will be performing at the Palace of Fine Arts, the Yerba Buena Gardens complex, and the Zellerbach Hall in Berkeley. Phone the number above for more details.

SF Performances

Suite 710, 500 Sutter Street, between Mason and Powell Streets (information 398 6449). Bus 2, 3, 4, 30, 45, 76/Powell-Mason, Powell-Hyde cable car.

The season runs at five venues from September to May and, much like Cal Performances (*above*), the series brings national and international performers to the Bay Area.

In Focus

Business

Need to send a fax at 2am, or catch up with the latest trade figures? Don't worry: doing business is a pleasure in Silicon City.

Every year 14 million people from around the United States and the world cross picturesque bridges or land at busy airports to visit San Francisco. They take tours of that famous former prison, cruise down that crooked street and ride up and down on those clanging cable cars. Increasingly, a significant number of these visitors are also squeezing business seminars, hard-nosed trade negotiations and legal depositions into their visits.

With an increasingly global marketplace requiring managers and professionals to do business anywhere, anytime – and because people need to be more creative with their leisure time and money – many travellers are combining business with pleasure. For this growing class of travellers, San Francisco is an ideal city. There are, arguably, only one or two other cities in the US that can match its simultaneous qualifications as a world-class holiday and business destination.

It is therefore no surprise that San Francisco's business meeting and convention industry is the envy of the country. Its meeting venues – led by the massive (and soon-to-be-expanded) Moscone Convention Center, which straddles the city's bustling financial and arts districts – are almost completely booked for years in advance.

Keystone events such as the annual MacWorld Technology Conference and the Windows Solutions meetings attract more than 100,000 techno-business tourists. Overall, conventions annually draw 1.2 million participants. No wonder then, that San Francisco's 30,500 hotel rooms are often sold out on peak holiday and convention weekends, and that the city's average hotel occupancy rate hovers around 72 per cent in the summer, higher than the national average.

Based on a 1993 survey, city Visitor and Convention Bureau officials say that seven million of San Francisco's yearly visitors perform at least a day or two for their bosses back home. Of that number, roughly 5.5 million are in town primarily for business meetings or conventions.

BAY AREA INDUSTRIES

The city and its greater Bay Area zone of influence are home to several of the country's biggest companies. The region's list of resident big businesses features companies in each of the current, high-performance business sectors – industries such as telecommunications (Airtouch Communications,

Pacific Telesis); finance (Bank of America, Wells Fargo Bank, Charles Schwab & Co); bio-medical technology (Genentech); law (Pilsbury, Madison and Sutro, and Morrison, Foerster); shipping (American Pacific Lines); and clothes manufacturing (Levi Strauss, The Gap, Esprit).

High technology is also, of course, big business here. Silicon Valley, the name given to the stretch of the Bay Area from south of San Jose to Redwood City, is where the first working models of personal computers were developed some 25 years ago. Apple Computers, Sun Microsystems, Hewlett Packard, Intel and Advanced Micro Devices are all based in Silicon Valley. What's more, the city's revived South Park area has been nicknamed Multimedia Gulch because of the ever-growing number of small and profitable companies that have fused computers, graphics, information and art (*see chapter* **Media** for more on this).

Wells Fargo: *as safe as houses.*

Doing Business in San Francisco

While most business visitors will have a host company that can meet their on-the-road clerical, communications, information and technological requirements, many may still find themselves in need of additional business support in order to meet unusual international deadlines. When it's 8am in London, it's midnight in San Francisco – yet a lawyer or trade negotiator may still need to send terms of a proposed deal or notes from a conference back to the home office. Where's the executive going to find help at that hour? And, where might the solo business traveller go for help when he or she is without a guest office to use? Here are some suggestions that might ease the problem.

Convention Centres

Moscone Convention Center

Howard Street, between Third and Fourth Streets (974 4000). Bus 15, 30, 45, 76.
The centrepiece of the Yerba Buena Gardens complex, this 1.2 million sq ft exhibition centre nearly doubled its original working space after Moscone North was completed in 1992. Named after assassinated mayor George Moscone, it is the city's premier convention complex, hosting a number of international trade fairs. The **SF Hilton and Towers** (771 1400) is the city's largest hotel convention space, with the **Marriott** (896 1600) close behind, while the **Concourse Exhibition Center** in SoMa (864 1500) has a banquet facility that can feed the 5,000, with meeting space for 1,500 people.

Courier Services

Local messenger and delivery services include the 24-hour **Priority Express** (788 6611), which promises under two-hour delivery to locations within the Bay Area; **Quicksilver Messenger Service** (495 4360), famous for its daring bikers; and **Aero Special Delivery** (495 8333), which specialises in statewide message and parcel delivery. The Post Office can deliver overnight to most US cities and, in some neighbourhoods, delivers express parcels on Sundays. Check the Yellow Pages for more companies.

DHL

(1-800 225 5345). **Open** 24-hours daily. **Credit** AmEx, DC, MC, V.
One of the most competitive delivery companies; ring for details and drop-off deadlines.

Federal Express

(1-800 238 5355). **Open** 7am-9pm Mon-Sat. **Credit** AmEx, DC, MC, V.
One of the biggest courier services, with five downtown offices and distribution warehouses near the Moscone Convention Center and at both the San Francisco and Oakland airports.

UPS

(1-800 742 5877). **Open** 7.30am-8pm Mon-Fri. **Credit** (deliveries by air only) AmEx, MC, V.
Account holders can phone anytime during the business day for a pick-up; non-account holders must phone a day in advance. Ring for more information.

Hotels

In 1992, the Nob Hill Lambourne, a 20-room, upmarket inn, introduced new standards for commerce-friendly service. Now most of the major hotels in the city – the Hyatts, the Hilton, the Sheraton Palace, the Marriott and the Ritz-Carlton – have high-tech rooms or can make computer equipment and office supplies available to their guests (*see chapter* **Accommodation**).

Nob Hill Lambourne

725 Pine Street, CA 94108, between Powell and Stockton Streets (433 2287/1-800 274 8466/fax 433 0975). Bus 38/Powell-Hyde, Powell-Mason cable car. **Rates** *rooms from $145-$225.* **Credit** AmEx, DC, JCB, MC, V.
All rooms have a top-speed desktop computer, equipped with word processing, colour graphics and spreadsheet software, as well as an 'on-line concierge' providing information and directions to tourist attractions, restaurants, theatres and other services. In addition, each room has its own fax machine, voice mail, modem and access to the Internet and the Lexis/Nexis Information Service – a virtual library of government documents, business and legal data and a seemingly limitless catalogue of newspaper and magazine articles from most major worldwide publications. Downstairs in the hotel business centre, a printer can put your work on the page for that day's presentation. In the coming year, Lambourne management has hinted, some of the in-room computers might be removed in favour of laptop models, to be issued during check-in.

Libraries

As major city public libraries go, San Francisco's Main Library must rank among the nation's best equipped for business research. And it's bound to get better: in the spring of 1996 the library's new, bigger home will open down the street from its present convenient but cramped location. Other specialist libraries can also help the business traveller.

Law Library

401 Van Ness Avenue, at McAllister Street (554 6821). Bus 5, 42, 47, 49. **Open** 8.30am-5pm Mon-Fri.
Open to visiting lawyers for research, but only San Francisco-based lawyers can borrow books and materials.

Mechanics Institute's Library

57 Post Street, between Montgomery and Kearny Streets (421 1750). BART Montgomery/Muni Metro F, J, K, L, M, N/2, 3, 4, 30, 45, 76 bus. **Open** 9am-9pm Mon-Wed; 9am-6pm Thur, Fri; 1pm-5pm Sat, Sun. **Admission** $2 day pass.
This private, non profit-making organisation offers many of the same data sources found at the Main Library, especially CD-ROM-based search tools, but in only a fraction of the space. Its true source of fame, however, lies in its chess room (open from 11am-11pm, Mon-Fri), which has long been considered one of the best places in town for a quiet game. Out-of-town visitors can get a library pass for $2, provided they have ID showing that they hail from outside the city limits.

San Francisco Main Library

Old Library: corner of Larkin and McAllister Streets; New Library: corner of Larkin and Fulton Streets (main switchboard 557 4400/business reference section 557 4488/borrower services 557 4363). Bus 5, 19. **Open** 10am-6pm Mon; 9am-8pm Tue-Thur; 11am-5pm Fri; 9am-5pm Sat; noon-5pm Sun. **Admission** (to borrow books) $25 3-month visitor's card.

The Main Library offers access to annual reports from most major US and Bay Area corporations; Standard & Poors evaluations of publicly-owned companies; the Dunn and Bradstreet Business Database (which details a company's financial history and current well-being); Securities and Exchange Commission data on American businesses; computerised private service and government-offered information on population and commercial demographics; US Census information; environmental compliance records; medical news and statistics. Visitors can also gain access to the Lexis/Nexis service and its business databases. You don't need a library card to do in-house research or read back-dated newspapers and magazines. The research desk's librarians are among the best trained in the business and information professionals – journalists in particular – often seek them out for help.

Message Services

American Voice Mail
(923 1666). **Open** 5am-7pm Mon-Fri; 7am-4pm Sat.
Credit (after first payment only) MC, V.
Set up your own confidential voice mail service for unlimited phone messages, 24 hours a day.

Mail Boxes Etc USA
2269 Chestnut Street, between Scott and Pierce Streets (922 4500). Bus 28, 43, 76. **Open** 9am-6pm Mon-Fri; 10am-4pm Sat. **Credit** AmEx, MC, V.
The complete service runs to mailbox rental, mail forwarding, packing and shipping.

Office Services

Flip open the Yellow Pages to find dozens of companies hiring computers for home or business use; copy and printing shops; photographic services; architectural draughtsmen – everything that a visiting business person might need. But you can always use one of these:

Kinko's
201 Sacramento Street, at Davis Street (834 0240). BART Embarcadero/Muni Metro F, J, K, L, M, N/1, 41 bus. **Open** 24 hours daily. **Credit** AmEx, MC, V.
San Francisco's numerous Kinko's copy centre outlets are strategically located and offer an array of user-friendly business machines for temporary hire (phone for your nearest branch). Services include on-site use of computers, typesetting, printing, photocopying, fax facilities and overnight mail delivery and collection via Federal Express. This Financial district branch shares its building with a 24-hour Nautilus physical fitness centre; guest rates are under $15 per day.

Office Depot
855 Harrison Street, between Fourth and Fifth Streets (243 9959). Bus 27, 30, 42, 45, 76. **Open** 8am-8pm Mon-Fri; 9am-6pm Sat; 11am-6pm Sun. **Credit** AmEx, MC, V.
Photocopying, printing, desktop publishing, custom stamps, engraved signs, fax devices and every office product on the planet can be found at this enormous superstore.

Publications

Although not on a par with London or New York, San Francisco is still blessed with a number of top-quality periodicals that business travellers can use to gain useful, cheap information about the city's business community. *See also chapter* **Media**.

The San Francisco Stock Exchange.

Newspapers
On the daily front, the city has the *San Francisco Chronicle* (50¢) and the *San Francisco Examiner* (25¢), both century-old newspapers with lively business sections. *Chronicle* business reporters are aggressive and offer comprehensive coverage of Bay Area commerce, while the *Examiner* has a smaller, but flashy business section that focuses on technology, retail and tourism. Both publish annual statistical profiles of the city's 100 top businesses (available upon request). The *New York Times* ($1), the *Wall Street Journal* ($1), and the technology-oriented *San Jose Mercury News* (35¢) also offer good coverage of the local business scene.

Business publications
The *Daily Journal* ($1) and the *San Francisco Recorder* ($1) are the best daily newspapers for legal news in this lawyer-laden town and available at newsstands and racks around the city. The *San Francisco Business Times* ($1) focuses exclusively on corporate news once a week; pick it up at newsstands downtown and in the Financial district.

Computing/Technology
The computing magazine industry is dominated by *MacWorld* ($4.95), *PC Week* ($3.95) and the locally produced weekly *InfoWorld*, all of which closely follow business in the city and nearby Silicon Valley. *InfoWorld* is available only via subscription but is kept in the main library. The weekly *MicroTimes* and bi-weekly *Computer Currents* magazines are available free from news racks all over the city. San Francisco is also home to the monthly magazine *Wired* ($4.95), one of the fastest-growing publications in the country; its interactive reach and hip technological bent has attracted a worldwide following.

PIERS/Journal of Commerce
Suite 2450, 425 California Street, at Sansome Street (1-800 824 7537). Bus 41, 42/California cable car. **Open** 8.30am-5pm Mon-Fri. **Credit** AmEx, MC, V.
Port Import-Export Reporting Service can quickly produce detailed chronicles of North American cargo manifest reports, US Census data and worldwide trade statistics and shipping information (report costs vary so call in advance for an estimate). PIERS also publishes some of its reports in the daily (Mon-Fri) *Journal of Commerce* ($1.50), a specialised trade publication available at larger newsagents.

Children

Aquariums, babysitters, circuses... here's the ABC of kids' entertainment, suitable for children of all ages.

Swinging in **The Jungle**.

If you thought San Francisco was for grown-ups only, you're in for a pleasant surprise. This is a child-friendly city where under-fives travel free on public transport, many hotels provide babysitting facilities (*see chapter* **Accommodation**) and kids get a great fuss made of them in what is a predominantly Latino-Asian culture.

If you're looking for fun excursions with children, start by walking (or driving) down Lombard Street, the 'Crookedest Street in the World', riding a cable car and taking the lift up the Transamerica Pyramid or Coit Tower. The Bay Area – and northern California in general – is also a terrific place for kids interested in animals and marine mammals, especially sea lions, whales, otters and seals. As well as trying out the suggestions listed below, grab the pink Datebook section of the Sunday *San Francisco Examiner & Chronicle* and check the listings under Children's Events.

For more ideas, *see also chapters* **Sightseeing, Sport & Fitness** *and* **Trips Out of Town**.

Animals, Circuses & Carousels

For an enjoyable family outing, there's plenty going on at San Francisco Zoo, as 1.2 million visitors per year attest. Travelling circuses come to San Francisco all year round – watch out for the beautiful French-Canadian **Cirque du Soleil** every second summer – leaving swarms of fans in their wake. **The New Pickle Circus** (544 9344) is the friendly local group, which usually performs in San Francisco in December and sometimes has other performances in the Bay Area; look for advertisements or phone to find out the schedule.

San Francisco is also a great place for carousels; there's one in the Zoo, one in Golden Gate Park and a two-storey Venetian Carousel on Pier 39.

The Jungle, Fun and Adventure

555 Ninth Street, between Bryant and Brannan Streets (552 4386). Bus 19, 27, 42. **Open** 10am-9pm Mon-Sat; 10am-8pm Sun. **Admission** *unlimited play* $4.95 Mon-Fri; *2 hours play* $5.95 Sat, Sun. **Credit** MC, V.
This is an indoor children's play centre for kids from six months to 12 years-old, aimed at helping out weary shoppers. There's a tangled macaroni maze of colourful tubes to slide and crawl through, netting to climb and tanks full of coloured balls. In the Parents Only room you can grab a cappuccino while the employees look after the kids.

Make-A-Circus

Fort Mason Center, Building D, Marina Boulevard (776 8477). Bus 22, 28. **Open** office *mid-June to end-Aug* 10am-5pm Mon-Fri. **Admission** free.
The place to learn circus skills during the summer. Free all-day events for families include clowning, stilt-walking, juggling, and acrobatics workshops.

Marine Mammal Center

Marin Headlands, Golden Gate National Recreation Area, Sausalito (331 7325). Golden Gate Transit bus 28, 76/north off Highway 101. **Open** 10am-4pm daily. **Admission** donations welcome. **Credit** AmEx, MC, V.
In this animal sanctuary, just across the Golden Gate Bridge, sick or injured seals and sea lions lie around in tubs being fed and nursed back to health by young volunteers.

Paramount's Great America

Great America Parkway, Santa Clara (1-408 988 1776). BART Fremont, then County Transit bus to Santa Clara. **Open** *June-Aug* 10am-9pm Mon-Thur, Sun; 10am-11pm Fri, Sat; *Sept-Oct* 10am-8pm Sat, Sun. **Admission** $26.95 adults; $18.95 senior citizens; $12.95 3-6s; free under-3s. **Credit** AmEx, MC, V.
One of the nicest (and biggest) carousels is at this amusement park, 56 kilometres/35 miles south of the city at Santa Clara. The vast double-decker roundabout has fairytale animals, including a camel, a griffin and a huge black cat, plus a sort of chariot for toddlers. Check out the Nickelodeon 'Splat City Slime Zone' attraction, where you have to dodge buckets of green sludgy stuff and water while you run through a maze. Even more adventurous kids can try the Top Gun and Demon rides, both of which involve whizzing around upside-down, or The Edge, in which punters free fall 100 feet through space while their stomachs stay behind. Water rides include the infamous Logger's Run and Tidal Wave – you won't stay dry but, since it's hot in summer few complain. Admission price includes all rides.

San Francisco Zoo

Sloat Boulevard, near 45th Avenue (753 7061/recorded information 753 7083). Muni Metro L/18, 23 bus. **Open** 10am-5pm daily. **Admission** $7 adults; $3.50 12-15s; free under-12s. **Credit** AmEx, MC, V.
With more than 1,000 species of mammals and birds, there's

If you thought Twin Peaks *was weird, take a trip to the* **Exploratorium**.

a lot to see at the zoo. Koala Crossing (this is one of the few zoos in the US that has koalas), Musk Ox Meadows, Gorilla World (inhabited by two young and five adult gorillas), Tuxedo Junction for penguins and Wolf Woods all beckon. Children-oriented features include feeding times at 2pm daily; the Zebra Zephyr train; an Insect Zoo; and a great choice of creatures in the Petting Zoo, with some 'show and tell' information on pet care. The lions don't get fed on Mondays, by the way – but if *you* get hungry, there's a barbecue joint across the road with ribs and sweet potato pie.

Babysitting/Childcare

American Child Care Service
(285 2300).
An upmarket child care agency serving the downtown hotels. The agency will also take children on excursions to the Zoo, Exploratorium and so on. Rates are $10.50-$12 per hour.

Bay Area Baby Sitters Agency
(991 7474).
In business for over 48 years, this agency serves all the major hotels, vets sitters very carefully and won't employ anyone under the age of 30. The rates are $7 per hour plus transport, which probably means $30-$40 for a child-free evening.

Libraries

All local library branches have regular 'lap readings', where young children can sit on the knees of a local lady – especially recommended are the multilingual Mission (695 5090) and Chinatown (274 0275) branches.

San Francisco Main Library
Old Library: corner of Larkin and McAllister Streets; New Library: corner of Larkin and Fulton Streets (main switchboard 557 4400/business reference section 557 4488). BART Civic Center/Muni Metro F, J, K, L, M,

N/5, 19 bus. **Open** 10am-6pm Mon; 9am-8pm Tue-Thur; 11am-5pm Fri; 9am-5pm Sat; noon-5pm Sun. **Admission** $25 3-month visitor's card.
At the time of writing due to open in spring 1996, San Francisco's new Main Library boasts an entire floor for children with 52 little cubbyholes; books, videos and audio tapes in 40 languages; a children's multimedia and electronic discovery computer unit; a fairytale and folk collection in the Story Telling Room; a 'creative centre' for live performances and crafts; and a Teenagers' Drop-In section. Visitors without a library card can use the facilities but can't take out books.

Museums

There's no shortage of museums in San Francisco, but the following are particularly good for children, with plenty of hands-on exhibits. The **Cable Car Barn Museum**, **Cartoon Art Museum** and **Oakland Museum of California** are also worth a visit; for details of these and other exhibition spaces, *see chapter* **Museums & Galleries**.

Bay Area Discovery Museum
557 East Fort Baker, near north end of Golden Gate Bridge, Sausalito (487 4398). Golden Gate Transit bus 63 at weekends only/drive north on Highway 101 to Alexander Avenue exit and follow signs. **Open** 10am-5pm Tue-Sun. **Admission** $7 adults; $6 1-18s; free under-1s. **No credit cards**.
This collection of historic army barracks has been sensitively and imaginatively transformed into a stimulating series of rooms aimed at two to 12 year-olds, including an art room where two year-olds learn how to paint and model; a series of distorting mirrors and light shows; a showtime centre where children can sing and dance; a Media Center for older kids with a chance to practice Apple Mac graphics; and the San Francisco Bay Room where children squeeze through an underwater tunnel to emerge onto a boat. There is also a pleasant café and outside picnic tables.

Exploratorium

3601 Lyon Street, between Jefferson and Bay Streets (563 7337/24-hour recorded information 561 0360/ Tactile Dome 561 0362). Bus 22, 28, 29, 30, 43. **Open** *summer* 10am-6pm Tue-Sun; *winter* 10am-5pm Tue-Sun; 10am-9.30pm Wed. **Admission** $9 adults; $5 6-17s; $2.50 3-5s; free under-3s; $5 disabled; $7 students, seniors; everyone free first Wed of the month. **Credit** MC, V.

It's not just the science-mad who put the Exploratorium at the top of their list. The favourite attraction here is the geodesic Tactile Dome, which is a hemisphere of total blackness, where you fumble around in the dark touching different objects. It's so popular that it attracts noisy crowds, so book in advance.The primary aim of the Exploratorium is to encourage an inquisitive mind, with over 700 hands-on experiments (a guide at the entrance explains that you can touch *everything*). Other popular items are the Golden Gate Video, a computer which simulates your 'flight' over San Francisco, and Going to Pieces, a way of fracturing and reassembling your own image. The shop is full of educational and interesting scientific toys.

Lawrence Hall of Science

Centennial Drive, near Grizzly Peak Boulevard, Berkeley (1-510 642 5132). BART Berkeley, then AC Transit bus 8, 65. **Open** 10am-5pm daily. **Admission** $6 adults; $4 7-18s, students, senior citizens; $2 3-6s; free under-3s. **Credit** MC, V.

This fascinating science museum in Berkeley offers plenty more buttons to push and computers to try, as well as a replica of the Challenger spacecraft's nose cone outside the back door (cockpit open for tours); a Wizard's Lab; a planetarium; a biology lab with small mammals to pet; and a huge DNA model to scramble over. Climb up here to see the great view and use the giant telescope to check out those pink spots on Jupiter.

Museum of the City of San Francisco

The Cannery, 2801 Leavenworth Street, at Beach Street (928 0289). Bus 32. **Open** 10am-4pm Wed-Sun. **Admission** free.

Features include a special earthquake display, a huge Goddess of Liberty head from the pre-1906 quake City Hall and regular story-telling sessions. Curator Gladys Hansen is on hand to show you her great-aunt's sewing machine, which was saved from the flames of the Great Fire, and to tell you tales about the survivors.

Randall Museum

199 Museum Way, at the southern tip of Masonic Avenue (554 9600). Bus 37. **Open** 10am-5pm Tue-Sat. **Admission** free.

This small and friendly museum is scenically located above the city in Corona Heights Park, and has a modest petting zoo with lambs, raccoons, hawks and a lovely pair of San Francisco garter snakes. There are art workshops and an elaborate model railway that enthusiasts run on the second and fourth Saturdays of the month. Perfect for small children.

Park Amusements

As well as the attractions of Golden Gate Park, you can go cycling in the **Presidio** or take a picnic and watch the kite-flyers on **Marina Green**. The **Musée Mécanique** in the Cliff House is also worth a visit (*see chapter* **Museums & Galleries**). At the **Seal Rocks**, below the Cliff House, and at nearby **Point Lobos**, seals gather day and night; the ones with little ears are California seals; the shiny graceful ones are Harbour seals.

Golden Gate Park

Park between Fulton and Stanyan Streets, Lincoln Way and the Great Highway. Bus 5, 7, 21, 33, 44, 66, 71. **Open** dawn to dusk daily.

California Academy of Sciences, *Music Concourse (750 7365/24-hour recorded information 750 7145). Bus 44.* **Open** 10am-5pm daily. **Admission** $7 adults; $4 12-17s; $1.50 6-11s; free under-6s. **Credit** AmEx, MC, V.

If got just one day, spend it in rolling green acres of Golden Gate Park. It's also full of more organised fun – rollerskating, horse riding, boating, hothouse palm forests and museums.

Older kids can visit the California Academy of Sciences, which houses the Steinhart Aquarium and Morrison Planetarium, all for one admission fee. Experience the Safe Quake, look at African natural history dioramas and visit the Discovery Room for Children, with its hands-on nature exhibits. The Steinhart includes an alligator pit, an eye-level dolphin tank, the Fish Roundabout (a 100,000 gallon round tank with small sharks and tuna that encircles the room) and a Touch Tidepool where children can pick up starfish, sea snails and crabs. The Morrison Planetarium has shows like Star Death, the Birth of Black Holes and there's rock music for teenagers in the evening in the Laserium.

At the eastern corner of the park, opposite Kezar Stadium, there's an old-fashioned carousel, tree house and swings in the Children's Playground, with summertime Punch and Judy shows. At Stow Lake you can hire rowing boats, paddle boats and bicycles. Near the west end of the park, opposite Spreckels Lake at JFK Drive, is the Golden Gate Park Riding Academy (668 7360), which offers pony trails through the park for kids. There are also windmills, a buffalo herd and the beautiful Japanese Tea Garden, where you can have a pick-me-up jasmine tea over the goldfish ponds after a hard day's play. *See also chapter* **Sightseeing**.

Shops

Chinatown is ideal for children, with its baskets full of small toys and trinkets on display on the pavements. The San Francisco Shopping Center and Embarcadero also do well by kids. For children's clothing, *see chapter* **Shopping & Services**.

Basic Brown Bear

444 De Haro Street, at Mariposa Street (626 0781). Bus 19. **Open** 10am-5pm Mon-Sat; noon-5pm Sun. **Credit** AmEx, MC, V.

There are stuffed bears galore and free tours (at 1pm daily plus an extra 11am tour on Sat) of this teddy bear factory.

Chinatown Kite Shop

717 Grant Avenue, at Sacramento Street (989 5182). Bus 1, 15. **Open** 10.30am-9pm daily. **Credit** AmEx, MC, V. Hundreds of different kites, for flying or decoration. Other shops include **Air Time of San Francisco** (759 1177), for stunt kites; **Kite Flite** (956 3181), in the touristy Pier 39 arcade; and, in the East Bay, **Highline Kites** (1-510 525 2755).

FAO Schwartz

48 Stockton Street, at O'Farrell Street (394 8700). BART Powell Street/Muni Metro F, J, K, L, M, N/38, 45 bus/Powell-Mason, Powell-Hyde cable car. **Open** 10am-8pm Mon-Sat; 11am-6pm Sun. **Credit** AmEx, JCB, MC, V. Everything from Davy Crockett hats to rocking horses can be bought in the mother of all toy shops.

Imaginarium

Laurel Shopping Center, 3535 California Street, between Locust and Spruce Streets (387 9885). Bus 1, 4. **Open** 9.30am-7pm Mon-Fri; 9.30am-6pm Sat; 11am-5pm Sun. **Credit** AmEx, MC, V.

A very hands-on and child-friendly toy shop.

The Waterfront & Islands

The waterfront isn't all overpriced kitsch. At **Pier 39** you can see – and hear – the colony of gallumphing great sea lions, which arrives in January, and there are street performers here and at **Fisherman's Wharf** and **The Anchorage**.

Trips to the islands in the Bay are also a good diversion. Visit the prison on **Alcatraz** and ask Ranger John to slam the door behind you in one of the prison cells – he won't, because of the insurance problems, but it'll give him a laugh and give you shivers up and down your spine. Or take your bicycle to **Angel Island**, the largest island in the Bay, and cycle around the old barracks at Camp Reynolds. In December, take a boat to look for whales around the **Farallon Islands**.

For more information on Alcatraz and Angel Islands, *see chapter* **Sightseeing**; for bicycle hire and whale watching *see chapter* **Sport & Fitness**.

Hyde Street Pier

Jefferson Street, at the west end of Fisherman's Wharf. (556 2904). Bus 32/Powell-Hyde cable car. **Open** *summer* 10am-6pm daily; *winter* 9.30am-5pm daily; free first Tue of the month. **Admission** $3 adults; $1 12-17s; free under-11s, senior citizens. **No credit cards**.
This is somewhere that adults can enjoy as much as kids. Several ships are docked along the pier, including the *Balclutha*, a three-masted square-rigger built in 1886. Next door is the *CA Thayer*, a schooner built in 1895 and, on the other side, the *Eureka*, a paddle-wheel ferryboat that commuters used across the Bay in the 1920s.

Jeremiah O'Brien Liberty Ship

Embarcadero, at end of Brannan Street (441 3101). Bus 32, 42. **Open** *office* 9am-5pm Mon-Fri; *ship* 9am-3pm Mon-Fri; 9am-4pm Sat, Sun. **Admission** $5 adults; $2 10-18s; $1 under-10s. **No credit cards**.
You can explore this ship's engine room, officers' bunkrooms and a three-inch 50-calibre gun, as well as the foghorn. It's located on the south side of the Ferry Building.

National Marine Corps and Coast Guards Museum

Building 1, Treasure Island (395 5067). Transbay Terminal T bus. **Open** 10am-3.30pm Mon-Fri; 10am-4.30pm Sat, Sun. **Admission** $2 donation. **No credit cards**.
A great museum for those interested in navy paraphernalia, weapons, uniforms, lighthouse lenses and anything to do with shipping or the military.

National Maritime Museum

Aquatic Park, at Polk Street (556 2904). Bus 32/Powell-Hyde cable car. **Open** 10am-5pm daily. **Admission** free.
Built to look like an Art Deco ship, this museum of maritime history is full of photos and memorabilia; check out the Steamship Room with all its model boats.

Sea Trek

Schoonemaker Point Marina, Libertyship Way, Sausalito (488 1000/332 4465). Bus Golden Gate Transit 10, 50. **Open** 9.30am-5.30pm Mon-Fri; on the 'beach' *during season* 9am-5pm Tue-Sun; *winter* 9am-5pm Sat, Sun. **Rates** beginners' class $80. **Credit** MC, V.
You can kayak from Sausalito to Ayala Cove on Angel Island with Sea Trek, which runs summer camps and trips for kids. *See also chapter* **Sport & Fitness**.

USS Pampanito

Pier 45, Fisherman's Wharf (920 0202). Bus 32. **Open** 9am-8pm daily. **Admission** $5 adults; $3 children, senior citizens. **No credit cards**.
This is the only naval submarine from World War II that you can thoroughly explore, to see what it was like to spend the war years underwater in these cramped quarters.

Outside San Francisco

About 113 kilometres/70 miles south of the city on beautiful Highway 1 is the picturesque seaside resort of **Santa Cruz**. Its historic Boardwalk boasts 27 rides including the rattling and slightly ramshackle Big Dipper which first ran in 1924, as well as some great pinball machines that date back to the 1920s.

At **Año Nuevo State Reserve**, 20 miles north of Santa Cruz, trunk-nosed Elephant Seals gather and fight at breeding season in a magnificent pitched battle; it's dangerous to get too close and if you want to see them, you have to reserve a spot on the dunes (October-March only). Phone 1-800 444 7275 for more information.

For spotting otters and other sea mammals, head 80 kilometres/50 miles south of Santa Cruz, to Monterey, home of the National Marine Sanctuary protection area of Monterey Bay and the **Monterey Aquarium** (1-408 648 4888). Connoisseurs of great aquariums have plenty to choose from in the US, but this is the aquarium-fancier's aquarium, the best of them all, set in the old cannery building that John Steinbeck wrote about in *Cannery Row*.

For more information on Santa Cruz and Monterey, *see chapter* **Trips Out of Town**.

Marine World Africa USA

Marine World Parkway, off Highway 37, Vallejo (1-707 644 4000/643 6722). BART El Cerrito Del Norte, then Vallejo Transit link bus 90 Mon-Fri, 70 Sat/Blue & Gold Fleet ferry from Pier 39, then Vallejo Transit bus 85. **Open** *summer* 9.30am-6pm Mon-Fri; 9am-6.45pm Sat, Sun; *winter* 9.30am-6pm Wed-Fri; 9am-6.45pm Sat, Sun. **Admission** $25.95 adults; $21.95 senior citizens; $17.95 4-12s; free under-3s.
Credit AmEx, JCB, MC, V.
This park features the Shark Experience, a great oceanarium with a moving walkway. There's also an Australian Outback compound, a Walrus Pool and a fabulous flying owl that performs somersaults. The best view of orcas is likely to be at the Killer Whale and Dolphin Show, guaranteed to get the audience very wet.

Monterey Bay Kayaks

693 Del Monte Avenue, near Fisherman's Wharf, Monterey (1-408 373 5357/1-800 649 5357). Greyhound bus (1-800 231 2222). **Open** 9am-6pm daily. **Rates** $25 equipment rental; $40 kayak class; $45 bay tour. **Credit** AmEx, JCB, MC, V.
Hire a kayak and explore the bay. In the summer you can go out at sunset and watch the pelicans dive, seals pop their heads up and stormy petrels skim by. Kids must be at least 1.4m/4¹⁄₂ft tall and weigh no less than 36kg/80lbs to participate, whether on a tour, in a class or when renting equipment. Smaller children can go on guided tours only, but they can be just as much fun.

Gay & Lesbian San Francisco

Where to camp it up in the queer capital of the world.

Given San Francisco's adoration of the outrageous, the daring and the non-conformist, it's hardly a surprise that the city boasts one of the most vibrant and eclectic gay communities in the US. Gay people and the gay 'lifestyle' are such an integral part of life in the city that it's difficult at times to tell where straight San Francisco leaves off and gay San Francisco begins. While there are certainly gay districts, gay bars and clubs and specifically gay events, gay people don't feel the need to restrict themselves to these, just as many straight San Franciscans enjoy going out in the Castro or attending the Freedom Day Parade.

This kind of freedom didn't arise overnight: it has been hard won by the pride and passionate politics of the San Francisco gay community over the past 25 years, often with a tragic price. The 1978 assassination of openly gay Supervisor Harvey Milk is still a rallying point for a community which takes its politics in deadly earnest. The onslaught of AIDS, which has taken the lives of thousands of San Franciscans since the early 1980s, has also acted as a catalyst, bringing the community together, both in anger and compassion, to fight the disease and support those who are living with it.

GAY ABANDON

Although San Francisco may not quite be Utopia by the Bay, there is a quality of life here which is the envy of gay people around the country and the world. Which is, of course, exactly why everyone wants to come here: politics and pride aside, this is also the most entertaining place to be if you're gay.

The action is centred in the gay districts, among which the Castro reigns as queen. Based around the intersection of 18th and Castro Streets, it is more than just a place to go out drinking, dancing and cruising. It is also a vibrant neighbourhood of boutiques, restaurants, cafés and gorgeous Victorian flats, having lost much of the ghetto feeling it had in the 1970s – partly because its popularity with straight San Franciscans has grown and partly because it continues to spread to the surrounding Duboce Triangle, Noe Valley and Inner Mission neighbourhoods. The best way to experience the Castro is just to walk around: the

streets are usually packed and in a few hours you'll not only have seen a microcosm of the gay scene in the city, you'll also be loaded down with club invites, political fliers and (if you play your cards right) a phone number or two.

The Polk (Polk Street between Washington and Post Streets) is more of a poor relation to the Castro; it's seedier and lacks the surrounding gay residential areas but still has numerous gay bars. It's better to visit at night than during the day. Also more fun at night is SoMa, the former warehouse district that has been getting trendier and hipper with each passing year. It's not a gay district per se, but there's a healthy queer presence. There are also gay venues in the Mission, Pacific Heights and the Lower Haight as well as bars and clubs worth visiting all around the Bay Area, particularly in San Jose and the East Bay.

FESTIVALS & EVENTS

Of all the festivals and events which mark the gay calendar in San Francisco, the most famous and best-attended is the Freedom Day Parade in June. Commemorating the 1969 Stonewall Riots in New York and the beginning of the modern American gay liberation movement, this huge celebration draws participants from around the Bay Area and

Dykes on Bykes lead the Freedom Day Parade.

curious onlookers from around the world. The parade runs down Market Street, led by the Women's Motorcycle Contingent (formerly Dykes on Bykes), and culminates in a huge street fair at its terminus.

Other gay events worth attending if you're in town are the Gay and Lesbian Film Festival in early June, the Folsom Street Fair (September), the Castro Street Fair in October (*pictured below*) and Hallowe'en in the Castro (31 October). It's not the unbridled bacchanalia it was in the 1970s, but still a red-letter day; as always, the Sisters of Perpetual Indulgence, the international activist drag group, steal the show. (*See also chapter* **San Francisco by Season**.)

Help & Information

The best sources for up-to-the-minute info on new clubs, shows, films, events and general gay news are the free newspapers, which can be found in almost every café or in boxes on street corners. Look for the *Bay Times,* the *San Francisco Sentinel, Odyssey, SF Weekly* and the *Bay Guardian.*

For the **AIDS-HIV Nightline** and the **San Francisco AIDS Foundation Hotline**, *see* **Health & Medical** *in chapter* **Survival**.

The **NAMES Project**.

Gay and Lesbian Medical Association
Suite C, 211 Church Street, at Market Street (255 4547). Muni Metro F, K, L, M/22 bus. **Open** 9.30am-5.30pm Mon-Fri.
Over 1,600 gay, lesbian and bisexual physicians and students make up this organisation which publishes guides, holds forums, advocates rights of gay and lesbian physicians and offers medical referrals.

The NAMES Project
2362 Market Street, between Castro and Noe Streets (863 1966). Muni Metro F, K, L, M/8, 24, 35, 37 bus. **Open** noon-7pm Mon-Wed, Fri; noon-5pm Sat, Sun. **Credit** AmEx, MC, V.
A visitor's centre and shop for the AIDS Memorial Quilt, made up of over 25,000 panels, each one commemorating a person who has died from AIDS.

Operation Concern

1853 Market Street, at Guerrero Street (626 7000).
Muni Metro F, K, L, M/8 bus. **Open** 9am-5pm Mon-Fri.
A counselling service for gay men, lesbians and bisexuals,
dealing with issues ranging from substance abuse to HIV.
Callers can set up an appointment for an initial consultation.

Parents, Families and Friends of
Lesbians and Gays (P-FLAG)

(921 8850). **Open** 24-hour answerphone.
Helpline offering support for families and friends of gay and
lesbian teens and adults.

Westside Crisis Clinic

888 Turk Street, at Gough Street (353 5050). Bus 31,
42, 47, 49. **Open** 9am-9pm daily; last admission 7pm.
A drop-in clinic for people with psychiatric emergencies.

Bars

See also chapter **Bars & Cafés**.

Alta Plaza

2301 Fillmore Street, at Clay Street (922 1444). Bus 1,
3, 12, 22, 24. **Open** 4pm-2am Mon-Sat; 10am-3pm,
5.30pm-10pm, Sun. **Credit** AmEx, DC, MC, V.
This is the BMW of San Francisco gay bars, as befits its
location in ultra-yuppie and monied Pacific Heights. From
the suited lawyers and doctors to the aproned and well-
groomed staff, the Alta Plaza is the classiest gay bar in
town. If you want to splurge a bit, try the excellent restaurant upstairs.

Badlands

4121 18th Street, at Castro Street (626 9320). Muni
Metro F, K, L, M/8, 24, 33, 35, 37. **Open** 10.30am-2am
daily. **No credit cards**.
One of those bars that is popular for no apparent reason.
Usually packed with a varied crowd playing pinball, pool,
or just cruising. Not a place to visit if you're particular about
smoke – the air gets awfully thick on weekend nights. The
Beer Bust on Sundays is also very popular.

Detour

2348 Market Street, at Castro Street (861 6053). Muni
Metro F, K, L, M/8, 24, 35, 37 bus. **Open** 2pm-2am
daily. **No credit cards**.
High-decibel music, chainlink fence and angst-ridden Gen-
X boys with piercings galore – this is a place to look rougher
than you feel and get away with it. Pool and pinball are side-
lines to ferocious cruising. Check out the $1 beer and shots
on Sunday afternoons.

The Eagle

398 12th Street, at Harrison Street (626 0880). Bus 9,
12, 42. **Open** 4pm-2am Mon-Fri; 2pm-2am Sat; 1pm-2am
Sun. **No credit cards**.
The row of motorcycles always parked out front signifies
that the Eagle is the centre of San Francisco's leather community. Dress to the cat-o'-nines and check it out.

Elephant Walk

Corner of 18th and Castro Streets (252 8441). Muni
Metro F, K, L, M/8, 24, 33, 35, 37 bus. **Open** 8am-2am
daily. **Credit** (food only) MC, V.
More sedate than most of the Castro bars, but you can almost
always find a place to sit down. Elephant Walk may not be

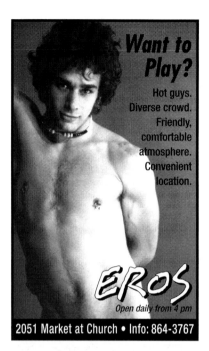

the trendiest place, but it's an excellent spot to meet some-one you don't know: it's simple to find and small enough to rapidly check out the faces. Live piano and show tunes on Thursday nights.

Esta Noche

3079 16th Street, at Mission Street (861 5757). BART 16th Street/14, 22, 26, 49, 53 bus. **Open** 1pm-2am Mon-Thur, Sun; 1pm-3am Fri, Sat. **No credit cards.**
Unpretentious and easily over-looked, Esta Noche is one of the city's hottest Latin bars – particularly on Friday nights when it hosts an evening of Latino striptease. Definitely worth a closer look.

Giraffe Video Lounge

1131 Polk Street, at Post Street (474 1702). Bus 2, 3, 4, 19, 76. **Open** 8am-2am daily. **No credit cards.**
Perhaps the most popular of the Polk Street bars, the Giraffe is generally low-key and friendly – a good place for pool or pinball. Rather dead during the week, but hopping at the weekend.

Hole in the Wall

289 Eighth Street, between Howard and Folsom Streets (431 4695). Bus 12, 19. **Open** noon-2am Tue-Thur; 6pm-2am Fri-Sun. **No credit cards.**
Rapidly becoming one of the most popular hangouts of the Gen-X queers who are turning their backs on the clone-scene of the Castro. Drop in to compare tattoos with hot boys in torn clothing – a real San Francisco experience.

The Lion Pub

2062 Divisadero Street, at Sacramento Street (567 6565). Bus 1, 24. **Open** 3pm-2am daily. **No credit cards.**
Largely frequented by the sweatered professionals of the sur-rounding Pacific Heights, the Lion also catches some of the younger crowd on their way to the clubs. Friendly bartenders and a good happy hour.

Lone Star Saloon

1354 Harrison Street, between Ninth and Tenth Streets (863 9999). Bus 19, 27, 42. **Open** noon-2am daily. **No credit cards.**
As the name indicates, this is a western/leather bar with a big following and an important centre for San Francisco's leather scene. Serious looks, serious scene and some serious fun.

The Metro

3600 16th Street, at Market Street (703 9750). Muni Metro K, L, M/8, 37 bus. **Open** 2.30pm-2am Mon-Fri; 1pm-2am Sat; noon-2am Sun. **Credit** (food only) MC, V.
Perched above a busy intersection, the Metro's balcony is a great place to have a drink and watch the boys heading in and out of the Castro. Can get very crowded on weekend nights – the weekday happy hour is more sedate. The attached Chinese restaurant is also worth a try.

The Midnight Sun

4067 18th Street, between Castro and Noe Streets (861 4186). Muni Metro F, K, L, M/8, 33, 35 bus. **Open** noon-2am daily. **No credit cards.**
A popular video bar and a good cruising spot. Generally packed for the after-work happy hour (two-for-the-price-of-one cocktails, 4pm-7pm, weekdays), and crammed full on the weekends. Frequented by a fairly young crowd which enjoys chanting along with favourite movie or TV clips.

The Mint

1942 Market Street, between Laguna and Buchanan Streets (626 4726). Bus 8, 26. **Open** 11am-2am daily. **No credit cards.**
The Mint's main attraction is its karaoke – watch the musical

theatre queens come out of the woodwork. It's rather a hit or miss spot as it can be unbearably slow on some evenings, though it's well worth a visit when it's hopping.

Moby Dick's

4049 18th Street, at Hartford Street (no phone). Muni Metro F, K, L, M/8, 24, 33, 35 bus. **Open** noon-2am daily. **No credit cards.**
Sort of a cross between a neighbourhood pub and a gay bar, Moby Dick's is most popular with pool players (although there is only one table) and pinball addicts (four machines in the back). Big windows make street cruising easy.

QT

1312 Polk Street, at Bush Street (885 1114). Bus 2, 3, 4, 19, 76. **Open** noon-2am daily. **No credit cards.**
Another Polk bar worth a look, and like its neighbours, slow during the week and packed at the weekends. Growing in popularity with the young Gen-X crowd.

Cafés & Restaurants

San Francisco doesn't have many gay restaurants: gays and lesbians are a mainstay of the restaurant scene and gay diners are welcome pretty much everywhere. The restaurants which might best be termed gay are located in the Castro, but be warned: if you've been lured to San Francisco by stories of fine cuisine, don't expect to find it in the Castro. Brunch is another matter: it's a Castro tradition to check out who picked up whom the night before over tofu scramble and a mimosa. Josie's Juice Bar and Cabaret (*see page 218* **Entertainment**) is a good brunch spot. The café scene is also very popular – San Franciscans take their coffee very seriously and enjoy lingering over a cup of joe. *See also chapter* **Bars & Cafés.**

Bagdad Cafe

2295 Market Street, at Noe Street (621 4434). Muni Metro F, K, L, M/22, 35, 37 bus. **Open** 24-hours daily. **No credit cards.**
Diner-type food and generous portions can be found here (try the Desert Fries). It's perfect for a late-night snack after a hard evening in the bars.

Cafe Flore

2298 Market Street, at Noe Street (621 8579). Muni Metro F, K, L, M/22, 35, 37 bus. **Open** 7.30-11.30pm Mon-Thur, Sun; 7.30pm-midnight Fri, Sat. **No credit cards.**
The one San Francisco café where the patrons spend more time studying one another than their books. Always popular and always crowded, the Flore and its surrounding gar-den is the see-and-be-seen centre of the Castro. The food is good and the coffee excellent. Try to get a table outside for maximum viewing potential.

Hot 'N' Hunky

4039 18th Street, between Hartford and Noe Streets (621 6365). Muni Metro F, K, L, M/8, 33, 35 bus. **Open** 11am-midnight Mon-Thur; 11am-1am Fri-Sun. **No credit cards.**
An exception to the normal ho-hum Castro dining, the Hot 'N' Hunky burger joint – along with its brother, Hot 'N' Chunky – is a perennial favourite. Ignore the 1980s' décor and sink your teeth into one of the best burgers in town – a place for carnivores to revel in their blood-lust.
Branch: Hot 'N' Chunky, 1946 Market Street, at Duboce Avenue (621 3622).

Mad Magda's Tea House

579 Hayes Street, at Laguna Street (864 7654). Bus 21.
Open 8am-9pm Mon-Tue; 8am-midnight Wed-Fri; 9am-midnight Sat; 9am-7pm Sun. **No credit cards.**
A uniquely San Franciscan spot – all the artsy funk of Hayes Valley with a queer, in-your-face twist. Go for Russian pastries and tea in the garden or have your Tarot read by the psychic by the door. A perfect cap to an afternoon's browsing in the surrounding shops and galleries, Magda's also hosts a range of evening 'events', many of which defy description; call for details.

Muddy Waters

260 Church Street, between Market and 15th Streets (621 2233). Muni Metro F, K, L, M/8, 22, 27 bus. **Open** 6.30am-11pm Mon-Thur; 6.30am-midnight Fri; 7am-midnight Sat; 7am-11pm Sun. **No credit cards.**
A café which takes its name from its unusually strong coffee – they will gladly water it down for the faint of heart. Lots of students and people reading the free newspapers, as well as interesting rotating exhibits by local artists.

Patio Cafe

531 Castro Street, between 18th and 19th Streets (621 4640). Muni Metro F, K, L, M/8, 24, 35 bus. **Open** 8am-10.30pm Mon-Fri; 8am-11pm Sat, Sun. **Credit** AmEx, MC, V.
The most popular brunch spot in the neighbourhood, so be prepared to queue. The Patio's seating is in a greenhouse-like structure off the street, a soothing place to recover from a hangover. It's tricky to find the entrance; look for the corridor leading behind the shops.

Pozole

2337 Market Street, at Castro Street (626 2666). Muni Metro F, K, L, M/8, 24, 35 bus. **Open** 4-11pm Mon-Thur; noon-midnight Fri-Sun. **No credit cards.**
Pozole's serves Mexican food with a healthy, contemporary twist – although the boys who eat here and the wild décor tend to overshadow the menu.

Sparky's

242 Church Street, at Market Street (626 8666). Muni Metro F, K, L, M/8, 22, 35 bus. **Open** 24-hours daily. **Credit** AmEx, MC, V.
Open 24-hours a day and particularly popular late at night. If you're craving hash browns at 4am, this is the place to go. There's a large menu and relatively low prices.

Clubs

Dancing is a San Franciscan passion and the club scene is always changing as new clubs appear and old ones fade away. The places listed below are likely to be around for some time to come, but the scene is in such a state of flux that it's wisest to pick up a copy of *Odyssey*, the club scene magazine, to found out the latest on what's in and who's wearing what to go where. *See also chapter* **Clubs.**

The Box

715 Harrison Street, between Third and Fourth Streets (972 8087). Bus 15, 30, 45, 76. **Open** 9pm-2.30am Thur. **No credit cards.**
Thursday nights at the Kennel Club: a San Francisco institution and domain of legendary DJ Mistress Page Hodel. The Box is all things to all people and prides itself on making everyone welcome – diversity is the watchword at this club. Plan to dance and sweat until you drop.

The Café

2367 Market Street, at Castro Street (861 3846). Bus 35, 37. **Open** 12.30pm-2am daily. **Credit** MC, V.
Once the neglected Café San Marcos and bitchily dubbed the 'lesbian airport lounge', the Café is now the most popular dance club in the Castro. It has two bars, a dance floor, a patio as well as pool and pinball – plus some of the hottest young things (male and female) in town. Expect to queue on Friday and Saturday nights, and wear something lightweight (and revealing) because the temperature soars as the night gets going.

Club Universe

177 Townsend Street, at Third Street (985 5241). Bus 30, 42, 45, 76. **Open** 9.30pm-7am Sat. **No credit cards.**
A big warehouse-type club with an emphasis on house sounds, that operates on Saturday nights only. Popular with gay and straight clubbers, it's a good place to go with a mixed group of people. Check *Odyssey* for a given week's 'environment'.

El Rio

3158 Mission Street, at Cesar Chavez Street (282 3325). Bus 12, 14, 27, 49. **Open** 3pm-midnight Mon; 3pm-2am Tue-Sun. **No credit cards.**
A mixed club featuring international and Latino music. Good fun, but try to get there before 9pm – the line can be one of the longest and slowest you'll find on a Friday night. *See also chapter* **Clubs.**

The End-Up

Corner of Sixth Street, at Harrison Street (487 6277). Bus 27, 42. **Open** 9pm-3.30am Wed; 6am-2am Sun. **No credit cards.**
If Saturday night has turned into Sunday morning and you're still going strong, the party continues at The End-Up, starting at 6am. There's a great dance floor in a large space, and the Sunday 'tea dance' is a perennial favourite. If you don't go, you can't say you've really seen gay San Francisco.

Pleasuredome

177 Townsend Street, at Third Street (985 5256). Bus 30, 42, 45, 76. **Open** 8.30pm-6am Sun. **No credit cards.**
The longest-running gay club in the city and still going strong. More bare pectoral muscles than you can shake a stick at – if you've been faithful in your gym attendance, here's the pay-off. Sunday nights only.

Rawhide II

280 Seventh Street, at Folsom Street (621 1197). Bus 12. **Open** 4pm-2am Mon-Thur; noon-2am Fri-Sun. **No credit cards.**
A truly authentic country and western bar full of – almost – authentic cowboys. There are free western dance lessons in the early evenings (makes for a good date). Leather night on Thursdays.

The Stud

399 Ninth Street, at Harrison Street (863 6623). Bus 19, 27, 42. **Open** 5pm-2am daily. **No credit cards.**
A San Francisco institution, buried in SoMa (plan to take a cab both ways), the Stud has one of the most varied crowds: from college students out for an exploratory evening to hardcore muscle boys posing in the corners. Sunday night is 1980s retro, but Wednesday night is the customary time to just drop in.

Entertainment

If the men don't provide sufficient diversion, gay San Francisco offers other equally theatrical

The **Castro Theater**: *for camp classics.*

alternatives. You'll be told to see *Beach Blanket Babylon* (do it) and probably the drag show at Finocchio's (don't – it's really aimed at awestruck Midwestern tourists), but check out the venues listed below as well. *See also chapters* **Film** *and* **Theatre & Dance**.

Castro Theater
429 Castro Street, off Market Street (621 6120). Muni Metro F, K, L, M/8, 24, 33, 35, 37 bus. **No credit cards.**
An ageing queen of a movie palace, the Castro Theater is one of the city's finest repertory cinemas, but truly comes alive for the great gay and camp classics. Until you've seen *Mommie Dearest, Valley of the Dolls* or *All About Eve* in a queer-packed theatre with full audience participation, you haven't really lived. Call for titles and times, or drop by the theatre to pick up a three-month schedule.

Josie's Juice Bar and Cabaret
3583 16th Street, between Market and Pond Streets (861 7933). Muni Metro F, K, L, M/8, 37 bus. **Open** 9am-9pm Mon-Thur; 9am-midnight Fri, Sat; 9am-10pm Sun. **No credit cards.**
The best place in town to catch gay comics, one-man and one-woman shows or performance pieces. The house is small, so get tickets in advance. The garden at the back is also a favourite weekend brunch spot.

Theatre Rhinoceros
2926 16th Street, at South Van Ness Avenue (861 5079). BART 16th Street/14, 22, 33, 49, 53 bus. **Performances start** 8pm or 8.30pm Tue-Sun. **Credit** MC, V.
Many other venues offer gay plays, but Theatre Rhino is the city's only truly gay theatre. A wide variety of shows are performed, many of them original plays. Check the listings in any of the free weeklies for what's on during your stay.

Bookshops

Almost any good San Francisco bookshop – of which there are droves – has a good gay and lesbian section, both new and second-hand. The best by far is **A Different Light** (489 Castro Street, at 18th Street; 431 0891), the SF branch of the national gay chain. If it doesn't stock what you're looking for, it probably isn't available. Around the corner is **Jaguar Adult Books** (4057 18th Street, at Hartford Street; 863 4777), which offers a wide selection of the 'other' gay literature: porn mags and books. Other stores with good sections are **A Clean Well-Lighted Place for Books** (601 Van Ness Avenue, at Golden Gate Avenue; 441 6670) and the famous **City Lights** (261 Columbus Avenue, between Broadway and Pacific Avenue; 362 8193). *See also chapter* **Shopping & Services**.

Working Out

The fitness craze has hit San Francisco as much as any other city and the question is no longer 'Do you work out?' but 'Where?' The city abounds in gyms, but some are more gay-friendly than others. Below are some of the most popular, which also offer day or short-term passes. *See also chapter* **Sport & Fitness**.

City Athletic Club
2500 Market Street, at 17th Street (552 6680). Muni Metro F, K, L, M/8, 35, 37 bus. **Open** 6am-10pm daily. **Admission** $10 per day; $30 per week. **Credit** AmEx, MC, V.

Market Street Gym
2301 Market Street, at Noe Street (626 4488). Muni Metro F, K, L, M/8, 37 bus. **Open** 6am-10pm Mon-Fri; 8am-8pm Sat, Sun. **Admission** $8 per day; $30 per week. **Credit** AmEx, MC, V.

Muscle System
2275 Market Street, between Sanchez and Noe Streets (863 4700). Bus 8, 37. **Open** 6am-10pm Mon-Fri; 9am-8pm Sat; 10am-6pm Sun. **Admission** $8 per day; $27 per week. **Credit** MC, V.
Branch: 364 Hayes Street, between Franklin and Gough Streets (863 4701).

Accommodation

It's not as necessary in San Francisco as in some cities to make sure that your lodgings are gay-friendly because most are either welcoming or indifferent. You can stay in any of the big hotels downtown without worrying about supercilious looks from the desk staff, but there are some specifically gay lodgings as well. *See also chapter* **Accommodation**.

Alamo Square Inn
719 Scott Street, CA 94117, at Fulton Street (922 2055). Bus 5, 24. **Rates** single $85-$110; suite $175-$275. **Credit** AmEx, MC, V.
One of the most charming and comfortable guesthouses in

the city, located on Alamo Square, across from the famous row of painted Victorians that shows up on almost every postcard of the San Francisco skyline. All rooms are no-smoking, breakfast is included and there is free parking.

Beck's Motor Lodge
2222 Market Street, CA 94114 , at 15th Street (621 8212). Muni Metro F, K, L, M/8, 37 bus. **Rates** *single* $69-$86; *double* $76-$93. **Credit** AmEx, MC, V.
Your typical American motel, down to the hideous carpets and glasses sealed in plastic, but with relatively cheap rates and very near the centre of the Castro scene, hence its popularity. A word of warning: the management frowns on cruising from the balconies overlooking the parking lot, so behave yourself. There are some no-smoking rooms, free parking and the rates are cheaper in winter.

Black Stallion Inn
635 Castro Street, CA 94114, between 19th and 20th Streets (863 0131/fax 863 0165). Muni Metro K, L, M/8, 37 bus. **Rates** *single* from $80; *double* from $95; *Wolf Den room with fireplace and garden view* $95-$110. **Credit** AmEx, MC, V.
This black-coloured Victorian, located in the groin of the Castro, deems itself 'San Francisco's only leather/Levi/Western bed-and-breakfast'. Eight minimalist rooms, a communal lounge with TV and VCR and a dining room make up the two-storey B&B. The ground floor is a uniquely Castro 'social club' where you can chat until the small hours or just watch the action. Services include breakfast, limited parking, fax and voice mail. Ask for a *Time Out* discount.

Gough Hayes Hotel
417 Gough Street, CA 94102, at Hayes Street (431 9131). Bus 21. **Rates** *single and double* $47 per night, $184.80 per week. **Credit** AmEx, MC, V.
On the edge of Hayes Valley and near to the Opera and Symphony Halls, this is a pleasant, gay-run little pension. Car parking is available nearby for $3.50 per day.

Inn on Castro
321 Castro Street, CA 94114, at Market Street (861 0321). Muni Metro F, K, L, M/8, 24, 35, 37 bus. **Rates** *single* from $80-$105; *double* from $85-$115; *suite* from $115-$150. **Credit** AmEx, MC, V.
This beautifully restored Edwardian building has been San Francisco's premier gay and lesbian hotel for nearly two decades. It has eight rooms, each with a private bath, original modern art and a profusion of elaborate flower arrangements. The highlight of the stay is the full breakfast, including home-made muffins and piles of fresh fruit. The hotel is no smoking, except on the back patio, and there are rooms for disabled visitors .

24 Henry
24 Henry Street, CA 94114, between Sanchez and Noe Streets (864 5686/1-800 900 5686). Muni Metro F, K, L, M/24, 37 bus. **Rates** *single* from $55-$80; *double* from $75-$90; *apartment suite* from $95. **Credit** AmEx, MC, V.
Geared toward gay vacationers but welcoming everyone, 24 Henry offers traditional San Francisco charm in the heart of the Castro at a very reasonable rate. Each of the five guest rooms within the Victorian has a private phone line with voice mail and a shared or private bath.

Willows Inn
710 14th Street, CA 94114, between Sanchez and Church Streets (431 4770/431 5295). Muni Metro F, K, L, M/ 22, 37 bus. **Rates** *single* from $70-$88; *double* from $78-$96; *suite* from $105-$125. **Credit** AmEx, MC, V.
The Willows offers 11 nice rooms in a 1904 Edwardian building, breakfast in bed and a location just outside the craziness of the Castro. All rooms have shared bath facilities and there's limited off-street parking for a nominal charge.

Lesbian San Francisco

The centre of lesbian San Francisco is the western Mission district – warm and sunny Valencia Street stretching from 16th to 22nd Streets. Although women patronise the Castro's bars, cafés and restaurants, the more affordable neighbourhood to the east provides a home for many of the city's lesbians, particularly younger women. Although longtime landmark Amelia's bar closed in 1991, leaving the city with, amazingly, not one specifically lesbian bar or club, the district is now bordered by Red Dora's Bearded Lady café, Good Vibrations, the renowned women-run, sex toy emporium, and Osento women's bathhouse.

Socialising in the 1990s is organised more around cultural events than bars or parties, and it's always wise to phone or check the local papers once you've arrived. The *Bay Times* contains the most complete calendar for lesbian events and, it is said, the most lively lesbian personal ads in the US. Newspapers and guides with lesbian listings can be found at the Women's Building, as well as on the streets and in the shops in the Castro and western Mission districts. *See also chapter* **Women's San Francisco**.

Help & Information

Community United Against Violence
(333 4357). **Open** 24-hours daily.
See **Help Lines & Agencies** *in chapter* **Survival**.

Lyon-Martin Women's Health Services
1748 Market Street, at Valencia Street, between Octavia and Gough Streets (565 7667). Muni Metro F, J, K, L, M, N/8 bus. **Open** 8.30am-5pm Mon-Fri. **Credit** MC, V.
Named after two of the founders of the modern lesbian movement in the US, the Lyon-Martin clinic offers affordable health care for women in a lesbian-friendly environment. Phone first to make an appointment.

Women's Building
3543 18th Street, between Valencia and Guerrero Streets (431 1180). BART 16th Street/26, 33 bus. **Open** 9am-9pm daily, depending on events.
The building is home to many women's organisations and also a central place for newspapers, bulletin board postings, events and information. The rich colours of the newly-created mural that covers the outside of the building have made the centre a city landmark.

Cafés & Restaurants

Many of the restaurants along Valencia Street (and new ones open every week) are populated with lesbians. Simply walk down the street to sample the choice of different kinds of food and price ranges. For the popular **Cafe Flore**, among other gay and lesbian hang-outs, *see page 217. See also chapters*

Bars & Cafés *and* Restaurants. We've listed some of the highlights of the lesbian scene below.

Just For You
1458 18th Street, at Connecticut Street (647 3033). Bus 22, 53. **Open** 6.30am-2.30pm Mon-Fri; 9am-3pm Sat, Sun. **No credit cards.**
It's a bit off the beaten track, but worth the trip. This tiny dyke-run restaurant serves a hearty New Orleans-style breakfast and lunch. Most of the seating is at the counter overlooking the cooking area, where muscled women prepare your delicious meal.

Red Dora's Bearded Lady
485 14th Street, at Guerrero Street (626 2805). Muni Metro F, K, L, M/26 bus. **Open** 7am-7pm Mon-Fri; 9am-7pm Sat, Sun. **No credit cards.**
The Bearded Lady is a café by day and, often, a performance space by night. The walls are hung with work by lesbian artists, and at the counter you can order anything from espresso to pesto eggs to breakfast cereal favourites.

Val 21
995 Valencia Street, at 21st Street (821 6622). Bus 26. **Open** 5.30-10pm Mon-Thur; 5.30-10.30pm Fri; 10am-2pm, 5.30-10.30pm Sat; 10am-2pm Sun. **Credit** AmEx, MC, V.
The menu here includes some of the best vegetarian fare in San Francisco. It's a bit pricey, but the cooking is innovative – in a gourmet, Californian way – the waiting staff friendly and the atmosphere elegant and warm.

Clubs & Bars

The **Café**, once the main gathering-point for lesbians, has become very popular with gay men as well at the weekends, though it remains a lesbian favourite. **The Stud**, a long-standing gay men's bar, is now home to several women's clubs, including the Girl Spot (G-Spot) on Saturday nights and the ever popular Junk on Thursdays, while **El Rio** shouldn't be missed as the ultimate San Francisco experience *(see page 218 for all three). See also chapters* Bars & Cafés *and* Clubs.

Blondie's Bar & No Grill
540 Valencia Street, between 16th and 17th Streets (864 2419). BART 16th Street/22, 26, 53 bus. **Open** 4pm-2am Mon-Sat; 6pm-2am Sun. **No credit cards.**
On Tuesdays and Sundays, Blondie's is filled with hip young women ready to dance, cruise and watch each other. During off-peak hours women frequent the bar's low-key pool tables and on weekend nights you'll often find a mixed clientele watching a good jazz or blues band.

Club Q
177 Townsend Street, at Third Street (974 6020). Bus 15, 30, 42, 45, 76. **Open** 9pm-3am, first Friday of each month. **No credit cards.**
One of the longest-running women's clubs in San Francisco, Club Q features fun music, girls galore and a hard-dancing, culturally-varied crowd. If you're in town while it's happening, this is highly recommended.

Covered Wagon
917 Folsom Street, at Fifth Street (974 1585). Bus 12, 27. **Open** 4.30pm-2am Mon-Fri; 8pm-2am Sat; 9pm-2am Sun. **No credit cards.**
Another club where certain nights are aimed at women. Muffdive (Sundays) draws a tattooed, pierced and sometimes slam-dancing crowd, while Faster Pussycat (Wednesdays) remains a popular favourite. *See also chapter* Clubs.

Wild Side West
424 Cortland Avenue, at Mission and Elsie Streets (647 3099). Muni Metro J/14 or 9 bus, then 24 bus. **Open** 1pm-2am daily. **No credit cards.**
This place has been around for ever (although it used to be located in North Beach), and the story goes that Janis Joplin would hang out and pick up girls at the very same wooden bar that now graces its Bernal Heights location. The walls are a shifting art installation and the clientele is a mixture of lesbians and locals. Fabulous juke-box of classics – you can count on hearing Joplin, Patsy Cline and, of course, Lou Reed's *Walk on the Wild Side*.

Entertainment

For the **Theatre Rhinoceros**, a theatre devoted exclusively to lesbian and gay plays, and **Josie's Juice Bar and Cabaret** *(the* place to see up-and-coming lesbian and gay comics) *see page 219. See also chapter* Theatre & Dance.

Brava! for Women in the Arts
2180 Bryant Street, at 20th Street (641 7657). Bus 22, 23, 27. **Open** *office* 10am-6pm Mon-Fri. **Performances** start 8pm. **Admission** $8-$12. **Credit** MC, V.
The results of women's performance and writing workshops are featured in the small theatre space. Brava! has encouraged the work of women playwrights and writers for years, and although it can be hit or miss, you may get a sneak preview of great work to come. Ring for performance details.

LunaSea
Room 216c, 2940 16th Street, between Capp Street and South Van Ness Avenue (863 2989). BART 16th Street/33, 53 bus. **Performances start** 8pm. **Admission** $8-$10. **No credit cards.**
You'll find experimental and sometimes cutting edge work by local lesbian performance artists and writers, as well as a supportive, interested and creative audience here. Shows are usually every Fri and Sat; ring to find out what's on while you're in town.

Shopping

See also chapter Shopping & Services.

Good Vibrations
1210 Valencia Street, at 23rd Street (550 7399). Bus 26. **Open** 11am-7pm daily. **Credit** AmEx, MC, V.
Good Vibes, as this women's erotica store is affectionately known, features a vibrator museum, all sorts of sex toys and a video collection. It also sponsors readings and workshops.

Modern Times Bookstore
888 Valencia Street, between 19th and 20th Streets (282 9246). Bus 26. **Open** 11am-8pm Mon-Thur; 11am-9pm Fri, Sat; 11am-6pm Sun. **Credit** AmEx, MC, V.
A collectively-owned progressive bookstore with an excellent women's and lesbian section, featuring writers from all over the world. A very friendly place to stop in and say hello.

Old Wives' Tales
1009 Valencia Street, at 21st Street (821 4675). Bus 26. **Open** 11am-7pm Mon-Sat; 11am-6pm Sun. **Credit** AmEx, MC, V.
Stocks a huge range of books, periodicals and music by and about women. Check the calendar for the on-going series of readings and events. It's also a good place to check for flyers and postings about cultural events.

Once dubbed the 'lesbian airport lounge', **The Café** *is the most popular Castro dance club.*

Scarlett Sage
3412 22nd Street, at Guerrero Street (821 0997). Bus 26. **Open** 11am-6.30pm Tue-Sat. **Credit** AmEx, MC, V.
Stop in to experience the comfortable and soothing atmosphere of this lesbian-run store. Wares include organic bulk herbs, herbal extracts, flower essences, bodycare products and a wide selection of books on herbs and homeopathy.

Stormy Leather
1158 Howard Street, between Seventh and Eighth Streets (626 6783). Bus 12. **Open** noon-6pm Mon-Thur; noon-7pm Fri, Sat; 2pm-6pm Sun. **Credit** AmEx, MC, V.
A woman-owned leather, fetish and sexual fantasy shop with everything from leather and latex bustiers to finely crafted whips and paddles. Friendly, helpful staff and interesting art exhibits.

Fitness & Health

For details of bath houses (including the popular women-only **Osento**), spas and retreats, *see chapter* **Shopping & Services**; for general sports facilities, *see chapter* **Sport & Fitness**.

The Women's Training Center
2164 Market Street, between Church and Sanchez Streets (864 6835). Muni Metro F, K, L, M/8, 37 bus. **Open** 6am-10pm Mon-Fri; 8am-8pm Sat; 10am-5pm Sun. **Admission** $10 day pass; $40 two-week guest pass. **No credit cards.**
Work out travel kinks at this women-only (and largely lesbian) gym. A pass includes free weights, basic aerobic equipment, dry sauna, showers and lockers.

Accommodation

See also page 221 **Beck's Motor Lodge** *and chapter* **Accommodation**.

San Francisco International Hostel (AYH)
Fort Mason Building, 240 Fort Mason, CA 94123 (771 7277/fax 771 1468). Bus 28, 47, 49. **Rates** $14. **Credit** MC, V.
This hostel may be off the beaten track for lesbians, but it is affordable and near public transport. Located on the San Francisco Bay, it provides a beautiful view of the Golden Gate Bridge and the hills of Marin County.

House O'Chicks Guesthouse
(861 8949). Muni Metro F, K, L, M/8, 24 bus. **Rates** *single* $50 per night, $300 per week; *double* $75 per night, $500 per week. **No credit cards.**
Two rooms in this seven-room flat are available for female visitors to the city. It caters to a mostly European clientele, and features a continental breakfast and shared bath. Not a stuffy B&B – there are notes and scrapbooks compiled by past guests, as well as guidebooks and current lesbian listings for around the city. Ring in advance to reserve a room and get the address.

Nancy's Bed
(239 5692). Muni Metro J, K, L, M to Forest Hill/36, 43, 44 bus. **Rates** single $25; double $45. **No credit cards.**
There are two rooms available in this private home, which is close to the Castro area and public transport. Ring in advance to make a booking and get the address.

Students

The Bay Area laid bare for radicals, preppies and eternal students.

University life in the Bay Area today has the reputation of being sedate and apolitical: at San Francisco State University students throng to business classes and it's known as a 'commuter campus' – most students work full- or part-time, drive to class, and leave immediately afterwards. You would hardly guess that during the 1960s, the concept of student activism was practically invented at the University of California's Berkeley campus, which became sufficiently radical at one point in the late 1960s, to prompt the then State Governor Ronald Reagan to send in the National Guard.

THE RADICAL SIXTIES
At the beginning of the 1960s, Berkeley was a large, old-fashioned campus (it was founded in 1873) with a 90 per cent white, mostly middle-class student population. In 1961 the House of Representatives Un-American Activities Committee (HUAC) held one of its infamous 'hearings' at San Francisco's City Hall. Thirty-one Berkeley students (along with about 30 others) were arrested after occupying City Hall. The following day, in a remarkable display of solidarity, more than 5,000 demonstrators showed up outside City Hall, forcing the hearing to be cancelled, and proving to the McCarthyites that student activists could tap mass support if they were able to identify and exploit popular issues.

The civil rights struggle in the South came to a head in the early-1960s and a number of Berkeley students spent the summer of 1964 working in Mississippi registering black voters. On returning for the autumn term they were dismayed to find that new rules prevented any student activism from taking place on or near the campus. Skirmishes followed the announcement and the Free Speech Movement was born. Sit-ins and mass arrests were commonplace and the general environment of rage and alienation mirrored the anarchy on college campuses around the country. The struggle in Berkeley culminated in the occupation of Sproul Hall, the administration building. Nearly 800 students were arrested in the largest mass arrest in California history.

By the late-1960s, the anti-Vietnam war and Black Panther movements had further radicalised and divided the campus. A student strike in protest at US military involvement in Vietnam shut down San Francisco State University; many of the strikers now teach at San Francisco State, or occupy prominent positions in the Bay Area. The town itself seemed to some to have become an anarcho-hippie commune.

Today, though the reputation remains, Berkeley is a thriving, multicultural university of 30,000 students. Affirmative action has swelled the number of Asian and Hispanic students on campus; whites are now in the minority, but much of the radicalism has dissipated and, as at San Francisco State, Berkeley students, pursuing their studies in law and business, lack the radical aspirations of their predecessors.

Where to Study

The California higher education system operates as a hierarchy, with publicly-funded community colleges and city colleges at the lower end of the scale, followed by California State Universities (CSUs) which cater primarily to undergraduates and do not grant doctorates, and the University of California establishments (including UC Berkeley), which tend to be formal, research-oriented universities with

The campus square at **UC Berkeley.**

*Can you take a skateboarding degree at **UC Berkeley**? Not yet, we're told.*

rigorous entry requirements, at the top. There are also private – and expensive – universities such as Stanford and the Jesuit University of San Francisco.

In general, American universities are much more flexible about part-time studying than their European counterparts, perhaps because many American students put themselves through college by working while studying. Each university has a different definition of part-time requirements; check with the college you're interested in. Non English-speaking students might have to pass a TOEFL (Test of English as a Foreign Language) test, and most students have to show proof of financial support.

Academy of Art College

79 New Montgomery Street, CA 94105, between Mission and Market Streets (274 2200). BART Montgomery Street/Muni Metro F, J, K, L, M, N/2, 3, 4, 5, 9, 30, 71, 76.
Foreign students flock to this visual arts college offering graduate and post-graduate courses in fine arts, history and graphic design.

Art Institute of San Francisco

800 Chestnut Street, CA 94133, between Jones and Leavenworth Streets (771 7020/1-800 345 7324). Bus 15, 41/Powell-Hyde cable car.
A hip and prestigious art school where 'alternative' is the word and black the colour to wear. The Institute offers the spectrum in fine arts including painting, film, photo, sculpture and new genres. Expensive, but well-respected.

City College of San Francisco

50 Phelan Avenue, CA 94112, at Ocean Avenue (main switchboard 239 3000/international students 239 3837). Muni Metro K, M/15, 29, 36, 43, 49 bus.
The largest community college in the US, City teaches more than 80 subjects on its eight campuses and 150 satellite sites in the city. It's the most affordable place to study and a good choice for a foreign language or computer class over the summer.

Mills College

500 MacArthur Boulevard, Oakland, CA 94613 (admissions: graduate 1-800 876 4557/undergraduate 1-510 430 2135; Study Abroad programme 1-510 430 2083). BART Coliseum, then AC Transit bus 58 to main entrance at Richards Gate/N bus from Transbay Terminal to Richards Gate.
A prestigious liberal women's college in Oakland and, like Stanford, an expensive place to study. Founded in 1852, Mills now admits men at graduate level. It offers excellent MFA courses in art and creative writing. For information on exchange programmes, call the Study Abroad number.

San Francisco Conservatory of Music

1201 Ortega Street, CA 94122, at 19th Avenue (564 8086). Bus 28.
Full- and part-time students study music at this independent conservatory. Tuition costs about $10,000 per year and there is no on-campus housing. Musical proficiency is the most important criterion for being admitted.

San Francisco State University

1900 Holloway Avenue, CA 94132, at 19th Avenue (admissions 338 1113). Muni Metro M/17, 26, 28 bus.
Undergraduate classes here are always full and many students have to be turned away at the beginning of each semester, so it can take five or six years to complete a degree. English, business and biology are particular strengths.

Stanford University

Stanford, CA 94305-3005. CalTrain to Palo Alto, then free Marguerite shuttle to campus (admissions: graduate 723 4291/undergraduate 723 2091).
A private college that is out of many students' league, with tuition, room and board running to about $25,000 a year. Academically, Stanford is highly competitive, known for its courses in business, law and medicine. Its turn-of-the-century campus near Palo Alto houses some internationally

known institutions, such as the Center for International Studies and the Hoover Institution (a conservative political think-tank) as well as special laboratories for electronics, nuclear engineering and physics.

UC Berkeley

Office of Undergraduate Admissions, 110 Sproul Hall, UC Berkeley, CA 94720-5800 (admissions: graduate 1-510 642 7404/undergraduate 1-510 642 3175/ international students 1-510 642 3246). BART Berkeley, then walk up Center Street.

The oldest campus in the nine-campus University of California system, some 30,000 students attend Berkeley, including 9,000 postgraduates. Famous for its law and engineering faculties, Berkeley also runs a controversial nuclear research laboratory in Livermore, an East Bay suburb. The campus is a strange mixture of urban (Telegraph Avenue stretches right up to the university) and rustic (the UC Botanical Gardens are open to the public and a stream runs through the campus). *See also chapter* **Trips Out of Town.**

UC Berkeley Extension

English Language Programme, 55 Laguna Street, CA 94102, between Haight and Market Streets (course information and registration 1-510 642 4111). Bus 6, 7, 8, 66, 71.

Berkeley Extension in San Francisco and other Bay Area sites offers night and weekend courses which can be taken by working adults for college credits, although it does not offers degree courses. It also has an excellent array of spring, summer and autumn courses in such subjects as film, the Internet, writing and women's studies.

University of California, San Francisco

400 Parnassus Avenue, CA 94143, at Fourth Avenue (476 4394). Muni Metro N/6, 43, 66 bus.

A health and sciences university with schools of medicine, dentistry, pharmacy and nursing.

University of San Francisco

2130 Fulton Street, CA 94117, at Masonic Avenue (admissions 666 6563/financial aid 666 6303). Bus 5, 43.

One of 28 Jesuit universities and colleges in the US, with a pleasant campus near the Haight district and a liberal, humanistic ethos. Foreign students make up 10% of the intake. Undergraduate tuition costs $13,000 per year and international students must show proof of financial support.

Visas & ID Cards

To study in the Bay Area (or anywhere else in the US), you must apply for either an F-1 visa (for exchange students) or a J-1 visa (for full-time students enrolled in a degree programme). Both are valid for the duration of your course and for a limited period afterwards.

Most colleges have admissions offices that give advice and information on studying in the US, including visa requirements, fees and student accommodation.

Foreign students should have an International Student Identity Card (ISIC) as proof of student status. This can be brought from your local travel agent or student travel office. In San Francisco, an ISIC costs $18 at Council Travel (530 Bush Street, at Grant Avenue; 421 3473) – just show your university ID to get one. Council Travel also offers low fares, especially on round-trip flights to London.

Student Accommodation

Cheap short-term accommodation is limited in San Francisco and even more difficult to find in Berkeley. However, both full- and part-time students at Berkeley can live in dorms or use the useful student housing information service (the Community Living Office, 1-510 642 3642) to find off-campus lodgings. Undergraduates tend to live on campus, while postgraduates usually live in shared housing nearby.

Berkeley also offers summer visitor housing in its dorms from 1 June-14 August (call the conference office on 1-510 642 4444 for more information). *See also chapter* **Accommodation.**

Globe Hostel/Inter-Club

10 Hallam Place, CA 94103, off Folsom Street between Seventh and Eighth Streets (431 0540/fax 431 3286). Bus 12, 19, 42. **Rates** *single* from $10. **No credit cards.**

Bright, cheerful hostelry in the centre of the trendy SoMa district.

San Francisco International Hostel (AYH)

Fort Mason Building, 240 Fort Mason, CA 94123 (771 7277/fax 771 1468). Bus 28, 47, 49. **Rates** $14. **Credit** MC, V.

Run by the American Youth Hostel system, this hostel offers wonderful views of the Bay and is near to the theatres and museums of Fort Mason. There's a two-week limit for staying here on consecutive nights and the hostel isn't open for daytime use (it's open between 4.30pm and 9.30am). *See also chapter* **Accommodation.**

YMCA Golden Gate

220 Golden Gate Avenue, CA 94102, at Leavenworth Street (885 0460/fax 885 5439). Bus 5, 19, 31. **Rates** phone for seasonal rates. **Credit** MC, V.

A YMCA open to both men and women, though the grim Tenderloin environment may be enough to encourage you to look elsewhere. There's a large gym.

Food & Drink

Cheap restaurants abound in San Francisco: the best are usually Mexican, Thai or Chinese. Most cafés offer good food and often beer and wine. The bar scene is thriving, but beware: if you are under 21 and look it, you will not get served. Always bring identification (a student card is fine) and be prepared to try elsewhere.

Apart from the places listed below **Cafe Babar**, **Mad Dog in the Fog** and **Vesuvio's Café** in North Beach are all hangouts popular with Generation X'ers (*see chapter* **Bars & Cafés**). *See also chapter* **Restaurants** for a selection of the best cheap eateries.

Café Intermezzo

2442 Telegraph Avenue, at Haste Street, Berkeley (1-510 849 4592). BART Berkeley, then bus 40 or walk. **Open** 7.30am-11pm daily. **No credit cards.**

One of the most impressive Berkeley eateries, serving healthy organic soups, salads and huge, delicious sandwiches on home-made bread. The staff, however, are consistently sullen.

Café International

508 Haight Street, at Fillmore Street (552 7390). Bus 6, 7, 22, 66, 71. **Open** 7am-11pm Mon-Thur, Sun; 8am-midnight Fri, Sat. **No credit cards**.

This café has a pleasant, earnest and almost European feel, and poetry slams are held here regularly.

Mel's Drive-In

3355 Geary Street, at Parker Street (387 2244). Bus 38. **Open** 6am-1am Mon-Thur, Sun; 6am-3am Fri, Sat. **No credit cards**.

A slightly bizarre throwback to the 1950s in both appearance and attitude; the menu encompasses hamburgers, milkshakes and tuna melts, but it's cheap and good.

Pancho Villa

3071 16th Street, between Mission and Valencia Streets (864 8840). Bus 14, 22, 49, 53. **Open** 10am-midnight daily. **Credit** AmEx, MC, V.

You'll get some of the best – and fattest – *burritos* in the Mission here; the fruit drinks change daily and are also great. Try the *horchata* (a sweetened rice drink). Noisy and packed at lunch-time.

The Pub

1492 Solano Avenue, at Santa Fe Avenue, Berkeley (1-510 525 1900). BART North Berkeley, then walk. **Open** noon-midnight Mon-Wed, Sun; noon-1am Thur-Sat. **Credit** AmEx, MC, V.

Berkeley bars tend to be packed and noisy with an emphasis on beer and sports. By contrast, the Pub in North Berkeley, near the Albany cinema, is a cosy neighbourhood hangout with a good range of imported beers and ciders, and an outside deck.

Bookshops & Libraries

As the city which spawned the poetry and novels of the Beat Generation, San Francisco is well endowed with bookshops selling new and second-hand titles. The mecca for second-hand bookshops is the Mission district: check out the **Adobe Bookstore** (3166 16th Street, between Valencia and Guerrero Streets; 864 3936), **Forest Books** (3080 16th Street, at Valencia Street; 863 2755) and **Dog-Eared Books** (1173 Valencia Street, between 22nd and 23rd Streets; 282 1901). In Berkeley, **Cody's** (2454 Telegraph Avenue; 1-510 845 7852) for new titles and alternative magazines and **Moe's** (2476 Telegraph Avenue; 1-510 849 2087) for second-hand books. Both are located conveniently near the campus. For information on other bookshops, *see chapter* **Shopping & Services**.

If you reckon you need books, try **Cody's**.

Berkeley Central Library

2090 Kittredge Avenue, at Shattuck Avenue (1-510 644 6100). BART Berkeley. **Open** 10am-9pm Mon-Thur; 10am-6pm Fri, Sat; 1pm-5pm Sun.

Entry to Berkeley's public library requires some proof of residence, although a supervisor at the registration desk might give you a card under special circumstances; it's worth a try.

San Francisco Main Library

Corner of Larkin and McAllister Streets (557 4400). Bus 5, 19. **Open** 10am-6pm Mon; 9am-8pm Tue-Thur; 11am-5pm Fri; 9am-5pm Sat; noon-5pm Sun.

Despite recent budget cuts, the old Main Library is a surprisingly good resource for books, music and videos (there's a great selection of foreign-language films). If you have a fixed address in San Francisco, you are eligible for a card. The very new **New Main Library** (at the corner of Fulton and Larkin Streets) more than doubles the space of the old library, with five times the seating capacity. It includes a shop, public meeting rooms, special collections (including a gay and lesbian archive) and increased computer access.

UC Berkeley Bancroft Library

UC Berkeley campus, near the bell tower (1-510 642 6481). BART Berkeley, then walk up Center Street. **Open** 9am-5pm Mon-Fri; 1pm-5pm Sat.

Contains an important collection of manuscripts and rare books. Show your International Student Card to get in.

Shops & Cinemas

There is a multitude of ways for penniless students to spend their money in San Francisco and Berkeley. The latter is very much a university town and the long stretch of Telegraph Avenue south of the campus is packed with music stores, bookshops, boutiques and coffee houses, all catering to the student population.

In the city, **Community Thrift** (623 Valencia Street, between 17th and 18th Streets; 861 4910) is a huge second-hand store, with clothes, books, electronics and kitchen equipment. Just down the street at **Clothes Contact** (473 Valencia, between 15th and 16th Streets; 621 3212) you can find vintage clothing sold by the pound. For more stylish second-hand gear, try **Buffalo Exchange**'s outlets at 1555 Haight Street, 1800 Polk Street and 2512 Telegraph Avenue in Berkeley.

Rough Trade Records (695 Third Street, at Townsend Street; 543 7091) specialises in alternative music and also sells concert tickets for the Fillmore auditorium without charging a service fee. In Berkeley, **Mod Lang** (2136 University Avenue, at Shattuck Avenue; 1-510 486 1850) and **Amoeba Records** (2455 Telegraph Avenue, at Haste Street, 1-510 549 1125) offer a vast selection of CDs and LPs, many of them imports or indies.

Naked Eye News and Video (533 Haight Street) is great for alternative videos and magazines. For serious filmgoers, the **Pacific Film Archive** in Berkeley (2625 Durant Avenue, between Bowditch Street and College Avenue; 1-510 642 1412) shows foreign and obscure but worthy American films. *See also chapters* **Shopping & Services**, **Museums & Galleries** *and* **Film**.

Women's San Francisco

Women-friendly bars and restaurants, useful resources and information in a city with a strong feminist voice.

In San Francisco, the old adage that the women are strong and the men are beautiful rings true. The Bay Area is one of the most woman-friendly spaces in the country, less rugged and macho than other western states such as Texas and Montana, less dangerously urban and frenetic than New York or Chicago. Perhaps this is why many career women, often successful single women with young children, have chosen to live here. On the political front, women make up half of San Francisco's governing Board of Supervisors (and two members at the time of writing were 'out' lesbians). California has anti-discrimination employment legislation which forbids companies from denying work on the basis of race, gender or sexual orientation, and women are fully integrated into the workforce, including the fire and police departments.

*The **Women's Building** in the Mission.*

POLITICAL ADVANCES

San Francisco has moved from being a thriving port with a large working-class population to becoming a dynamic, business-oriented modern city. This shift can be partly credited to Dianne Feinstein, who brought money and jobs to the downtown area when she took over as Mayor after the tragic deaths of Mayor George Moscone and Supervisor Harvey Milk in 1978 (*see chapter* **History**). She was an influential mayor for two terms and is now one of the two US Senators for California; the other is Barbara Boxer. The success of these two Jewish female Democrats symbolises the great strides that women have made in political life here, especially since the feminist movement exploded in the early 1970s.

The Bay Area is also home to some acclaimed women writers with strong, feminist, multicultural voices: Amy Tan, author of *The Joy Luck Club*; Alice Walker (*The Color Purple, In Search of Our Mother's Gardens*); Isabel Allende (*The House of the Spirits, Paula*); Terry McMillan (*Disappearing Acts, Mama*); and Anne Lamott, a Marin writer whose recent bestseller, *Operating Instructions*, describes the sorrows and joys of being a recovered alcoholic and single mother in harrowingly comic detail.

San Francisco women are free to enjoy the fruits of the feminist movement without much fanfare, and international visitors will notice the positive atmosphere. Former radicals and socialists of the 1960s are now happily ensconced in positions of power: for example, Angela Davis, once hunted by the FBI and a controversial figure in the late-1960s' black power movement, teaches women's studies classes at San Francisco State University. There is something of a leadership vacuum among young feminists, but Naomi Wolf, author of *The Beauty Myth*, is a San Francisco resident and typifies the educated, politically aware yet down-to-earth young women of today.

Lesbians will find a thriving gay community in San Francisco. Women-only spaces tend to cater mostly to lesbians, but straight and bisexual women are always welcome. San Francisco is a tolerant city and in general sexual harassment and homophobia are frowned upon. The Mission district, which is the centre of the lesbian scene and houses a lot of women-owned businesses and spaces, is less affluent and more ethnically diverse than the mostly gay, male Castro district, and women may experience some hassle on the street. It's best to stay away from the intersection of 16th and Mission Streets after dark, but adventurous women travellers should take advantage of the delights offered by the Valencia Street area south of 16th Street. (*See also chapter* **Gay & Lesbian San Francisco**.)

Information & Resources

For information on women-related and lesbian events, head for the **Women's Building** (3543 18th Street, between Valencia and Guerrero Streets) in the Mission. Owned by a Latina lesbian, this huge building with a shiny new mural outside has a multicultural slant, a library of feminist books and is a good place to find out about women's organisations, publications, housing and so on. **Old Wives' Tales** (1009 Valencia Street, at 21st Street) is a large women's bookstore in the Mission, run as a co-operative, which holds weekly readings and has listings and flyers. **Good Vibrations** (1210 Valencia Street, at 23rd Street) is a sex shop with a clean, women-positive atmosphere. The friendly, laid-back staff (all women) make shopping here a great experience. For full listings for all three, *see chapter* **Gay & Lesbian San Francisco**.

Gaia
1400 Shattuck Avenue, at Rose Street (1-510 548 4172). BART Berkeley, then 7 or 43 bus. **Open** 10am-7.30pm daily. **Credit** MC, V.
A women's bookshop in Berkeley specialising in books on spirituality, goddess worship, nature and sexuality. Gaia hosts weekly readings by local and national authors.

Health & Fitness

San Francisco has no shortage of women's clinics, but in general health care in the US is expensive and rather inaccessible. The **Lyon-Martin Women's Clinic** (1748 Market Street, at Valencia Street, between Octavia and Gough Streets) caters especially for lesbians, and offers safe-sex kits and information, HIV testing and examinations. There is a sliding scale of payments. If you are really broke and in need of health care, the **Women's Needs Center** at the **Haight-Ashbury Free Clinic** is the place to go; it offers low or no-cost medical care for women. (For details of these and other clinics, hospitals and emergency rooms, *see chapter* **Survival**.)

The AIDS epidemic has hit San Francisco very hard, and women should be aware of the need to practise safe sex. San Franciscans are generally very knowledgeable about sexuality – they have

to be. Holistic medicine is becoming more popular in the US in general and California in particular. Homeopathic treatments are available at health food stores such as the **Real Food Company** (look in the Yellow Pages for your nearest branch).

For details of bath houses, spas and retreats, *see chapter* **Shopping & Services**; for general sports facilities, *see chapter* **Sport & Fitness**.

Planned Parenthood Clinics
815 Eddy Street, between Van Ness Avenue and Franklin Street (441 5454). Bus 19, 31, 42, 47, 49. **Open** noon-7pm Mon, Wed; 4pm-7pm Tue; 9am-noon Thur; 9am-4pm Fri. **Credit** MC, V.
These clinics offer the most efficient and comprehensive health care service for women in San Francisco. Abortion information and procedures, contraception, gynaecological examinations and pre-natal care are available, all at a reasonable cost.
Branch: 222 Front Street, at California Street (765 6905).

Quan Yin Healing Arts Center
1748 Market Street, at Valencia Street (861 4964). Muni Metro F, J, K, L, M/6, 7, 8, 66, 71 bus. **Open** 11am-6pm Mon; noon-6.15pmTue-Thur; 11am-5pm Fri; 10am-2pm Sat. **Credit** MC, V.
This woman-owned centre is the best in town for acupuncture treatment.

Safety

Although it is a much safer city than New York, muggings are not uncommon here. Drugs are a problem in certain areas, and gang-related shootings are on the rise. Take the precautions you would in any large city, and avoid wandering through certain areas after dark: lower Haight Street (east of Fillmore Street); Mission Street from 13th to 22nd Streets; the Civic Center area on Market Street; the Tenderloin; and Hunter's Point.

If you are attacked, don't resist. Call 911 and report the incident immediately; the police will be able to transport you back to your lodgings.

Rapes are decreasing in San Francisco, but they are taken very seriously by the police. If you are the victim of a sexual assault and wish to make a report, call the police, who will escort you to an Emergency Room for a check-up. Or call one of the numbers below for advice. *See also chapter* **Survival**.

Good Vibrations: *for sex, not surfing.*

Old Wives' Tales. *See page 229.*

Bay Area Model Mugging
Mailing address: *629 Blair Island Road, Suite 104, Redwood City, CA 94063;* classes held at: *Avenue Ballroom, 603 Taraval Avenue, at 16th Avenue (366 3631/1-800 773 4448). Muni Metro L.* **Rates** introductory day $125; boundaries workshop $49. **Open** *office* 9am-5pm Mon, Tue, Thur, Fri. **Credit** MC, V.
Women's self-defence classes have become very popular in recent years. Model Mugging offers courses in which women learn effective defence techniques, using full force against padded male 'attackers'.

SF Rape Treatment Center
(206 3222). **Open** 24-hours daily.
See **Helplines & Agencies** *in chapter* **Survival**.

Women Against Rape Crisis Hotline
(647 7273). **Open** 24-hours daily.
See **Helplines & Agencies** *in chapter* **Survival**.

Eating & Drinking

San Francisco is full of coffee houses and cafés that serve food (and usually alcohol), many of them catering to students and under-employed young people. The line between a restaurant and a café is hazy, as is the distinction between a café and a bar.

There are few lesbian bars in San Francisco, but **Wild Side West** (424 Cortland Avenue, at Mission and Elsie Streets) is a great 'women's bar', with a cosy, eccentric, neighbourhood atmosphere, pool table, outside patio and large garden. It's not exclusively lesbian and men are also welcome. **Cafe Babar** (994 Guerrero Street, at 22nd Street) is a bohemian bar in the Mission, while **Hamburger Mary's** (1582 Folsom Street, at 12th Street) in SoMa is a popular drinking spot, famous for its surreal atmosphere. It's usually packed with gay men and lesbians. **Mad Dog in the Fog** (530 Haight Street, between Fillmore and Steiner Streets) is a loud, fun, sort-of-English pub which offers imported beers, ciders and pub grub; it's a good place to meet people. The **Bagdad Cafe** (2295 Market Street, at Noe Street) serves great sandwiches, pies and coffee, stays open late, and is a fun, high-energy place to go after a movie at the Castro Theater. *See chapters* **Bars & Cafés** *and* **Gay and Lesbian San Francisco** for more details on all of these.

The following bars, cafés and restaurants are recommended for their atmosphere and friendly, low-key service – they are all easy-going places to go if you're a woman on your own.

Amazing Grace
216 Church Street, at Market Street (626 6411). Muni Metro F, K, L, M/8, 37 bus. **Open** 11am-10pm Mon-Sat. **No credit cards.**
One of the few vegetarian restaurants in San Francisco, Amazing Grace is popular with women and gay men; the food is sometimes a bit unimaginative, but the helpings are huge.

Cafe Istanbul
525 Valencia Street, between 16th and 17th Streets (863 8854). Bus 26. **Open** 11am-midnight daily. **No credit cards.**
A charming Mission café right around the corner from the Roxie cinema. Istanbul serves incredibly strong Turkish coffee and often has a belly dancer performing.

Chloe's Cafe
1399 Church Street, at 26th Street (648 4116). Muni Metro J. **Open** 8am-3pm daily. **No credit cards.**
Chloe's serves a great Saturday and Sunday brunch and is always packed. It's popular with women and local Noe Valley residents.

Pauline's Pizza Pie
260 Valencia Street, at Brosnan Street, between Duboce Avenue and 14th Street (552 2050). Bus 26. **Open** 5pm-10pm Tue-Sat. **Credit** MC, V.
A woman-owned pizza parlour that's highly recommended for its speciality pizzas.

Radio Valencia
1199 Valencia Street, at 23rd Street (826 1199). Bus 26. **Open** noon-midnight daily. **Credit** MC, V.
This is a great place to go if you want to linger over a cup of coffee, hear good music and eat healthy food. Valencia has an arty atmosphere and stays open late, seven days a week.

Clubs

The best way to find lesbian clubs (which often change name and location without much warning) is to look for advertisements in the *Bay Times*, the city's free lesbian and gay fortnightly newspaper. Also check the free weekly arts and entertainment papers, *SF Weekly* and the *Bay Guardian*, which can be picked up from newsstands around the city. The Datebook 'pink' section of the *Sunday Examiner & Chronicle* has comprehensive live music listings. *See chapter* **Gay & Lesbian San Francisco** for a selection of the more long-standing lesbian venues.

Women-friendly clubs include **El Rio** (315a Mission Street, at Cesar Chavez Street), which has live music and a friendly gay-oriented atmosphere. **Cafe du Nord** (2170 Market Street, between Church and Sanchez Streets) offers live jazz and blues, and salsa lessons on Tuesday nights; it's popular with a young, mixed, hip crowd. **The Café** (2367 Market Street, at Castro Street) is a loud, trendy gay hangout, populated by mainly lesbians and bisexual women. *See chapter* **Clubs** for a full list of good clubs in San Francisco.

Trips Out of Town

Trips Out of Town

Whether it's untamed nature, Californian wineries, or the Wild West that draws you, the great outdoors is just a bridge away.

Escape across the Bay to Alcatraz – along with 4,000 other eager trippers each day.

Bordered by a bay on two sides and an ocean on another, San Francisco is ideally situated for easy getaways. Within an hour's drive, ride or boat trip are beaches, islands, mountains and other distractions, ranging from the small towns of the wine country to the big cities of the East Bay. A little further afield lie the dramatic slopes of the Sierra Madre, the celebrated golf links of the Monterey Peninsula, the protected shoreline of Marin County, and the wineries and spas of the North Bay.

That's the good news. The bad news is that these areas are ill-served by public transport. If you can't hire a car, you can use the Bay Area Rapid Transit (BART), which connects the city with the East Bay (via an underground tunnel), or the Golden Gate Transit, which has a regularly scheduled bus service to and from many Marin County destinations, and a less frequent service to Sonoma County. In addition, you can try the Greyhound Bus Lines, Amtrak (the nearest train

station is in Oakland), a charter tour, or one of the ferries that run frequently to the North Bay during the day.

Though few locals can remember their names, the Bay Area consists of nine counties. For the record, they are San Francisco, Alameda, Marin, Sonoma, Napa, Solano, Contra Costa, San Mateo and Santa Clara. They might all belong to the Bay Area, but each county has its very own political set-up, geography, weather and transport system. About the only thing they have in common is language (and even that's debatable at times). There's no overall tourist authority, and service varies drastically from one county to the next, as does the availability of accommodation.

All telephone numbers listed in this chapter are for the 415 area code unless otherwise stated.

*A tree-hugger's paradise: try one of the 800 year-old redwoods of **Muir Woods** for size.*

Heading North

Marin County

Crossing the world-famous **Golden Gate Bridge** is something everyone must do at least once in their life – ideally twice, unless you're not planning to return. The span is definitely not a good place for sightseeing, unless you're on foot or on a bicycle. If you're in a car, stay in the right-hand lane and pull off at the first exit north of the bridge, at **Vista Point**. From there the city seems almost close enough to touch.

Marin is full of spine-tingling views. To the northwest of the bridge, a couple of roads traverse the **Marin Headlands**. Most Americans are familiar with these vistas because the Headlands are an extremely popular location for automobile commercials which use San Francisco and the Golden Gate as a backdrop.

Starting with the Headlands, directly north of San Francisco, the county offers the best hiking and biking – mountain or otherwise – in the Bay Area. Thanks to state and federal legislation, a large percentage of the county is devoted to open space. The most famous parcel of land is **Point Reyes National Seashore**, part of the vast **Golden Gate National Recreation Area** (GGNRA) that extends north from San Francisco along most of the Marin coastline.

One of the strange things about Marin is its lack of a real centre. **San Rafael** is its biggest town, but it's also the least interesting to visit, though it's worth making a short detour to see 'Big Pink', the grand **Marin Civic Center** designed by Frank Lloyd Wright. There are still hippie enclaves like **Fairfax**, a quaint town called **San Anselmo**, where the shopping and eating are very good, and some odd spots such as **Bolinas**, the stand-offish coastal town where residents go out of their way to discourage tourists.

The southernmost Marin town of **Sausalito** may not be as quaint as its reputation claims, but it is undeniably picturesque, with a maze of tiny streets stretching from the shoreline up to Highway 101 far above. The charming bungalows, well-kept gardens, bougainvillea-covered fences that characterise the district, and the sensational views from just about every position, are best appreciated on foot.

Jampacked with tourists from all over the world during the summer months, Sausalito reclaims its waterfront in winter. The population is an intriguing mixture: there are boatbuilders, the yachting crowd, business people who commute from their houseboats to downtown San Francisco five days a week, and a sizeable population of artists and writers. The latter help support a fair share of coffee shops, cheap eateries and saloons along the water. The harbour is a good spot to 'window shop' for fabulous sailing boats and yachts that dock in Sausalito's protected waters – the strong winds and treacherous tides further out near 'the Gate' can be disastrous for the inexperienced sailor.

Despite its chilly waters, Sausalito is a centre for bay kayaking and windsurfing. A tiny beach is the launching pad for such watersports. Sales, rentals and lessons are available at **Sausalito Sailboards, Inc**, 4600 Bridgeway (331 9463).

To get a sense of the old Sausalito, stop for a cocktail or meal at **Casa Madrona**, the part-Victorian, part-modernised hotel that cascades down the hill from Bulkley Street to downtown Sausalito. Its restaurant and rooms all have fabulous views, not only of Richardson Bay but, in some cases, of the San Francisco skyline. Across Richardson Bay is the **Tiburon peninsula**, where a tiny old-fashioned downtown brings daytrippers over on the ferry from San Francisco.

The commercial district of Sausalito largely straddles **Bridgeway**, though some diners and shoppers are lured to **Caledonia Street** one block inland. Along north Bridgeway, opposite Spring Street, is the turn-off for the **Bay Model Visitors Center** (*see chapter* Museums & Galleries), a scale model of the San Francisco and San Pablo Bays. Travel north to where Bridgeway merges with Highway 101 for another worthwhile stop.

With all the Bay Area's bridges, islands, peninsulas and waterfronts, it can be hard to get your bearings. If you want to see the lie of the land from above, take an excursion with **Commodore Seaplanes** (332 4843). The company flies out to the coast, over the Golden Gate Bridge and along the San Francisco waterfront, which is especially romantic at sunset.

Marin County is dissected by the north-south Highway 101, which runs virtually the length of California. It may be the most popular route for public transport, but it's also unrelentingly boring. The other main road is Highway 1, aka the Coast Highway or Shoreline Highway, which leads out of Mill Valley, skirts the lower elevations of Mount Tamalpais, and reaches the coast at Muir Beach, where it turns north. For the full-fledged trip over Mount Tam, take the Panoramic Highway, a beautiful two-lane road with lots of hairpin bends leading through sun-dappled forests to the coast at Stinson Beach. From either Highway 1 or Panoramic, you can reach the turnoff to Marin's main attraction, Muir Woods.

MOUNT TAMALPAIS & MUIR WOODS

Visible from as far away as Sonoma, **Mount Tamalpais** soars to nearly 793 metres/2,600 feet. Its dramatic rise is so steep it seems to be even taller. It dominates and defines recreational life in southern and central Marin County. Mount Tamalpais

*The **Pelican Inn**: a slice of Surrey in the heart of Marin County.*

State Park covers some 2,511 hectares/6,200 acres. You could wander the area for months, but you can get an idea of its charms by heading directly to **Muir Woods**. The coast redwoods growing here are mostly between 500 and 800 years old and as tall as 72 metres/236 feet. The shade cast by these giant sequoia sempervirens creates excellent hiking on some six miles of trails (a short path is accessible to the disabled). **Redwood Creek** is lined with oak, madrone and buckeye trees, wild flowers (even in the winter), ferns and mushrooms. Deer, chipmunks and a variety of birds are frequently sighted in the sun-dappled spaces beneath the redwoods. Open daily, **Muir Woods National Monument** has a gift shop and toilets. The Ranger Station can be contacted on 388 2595.

You can take bicycles on the ferries as well as on some of the buses run by Golden Gate Transit. The roads that snake over Mount Tamalpais are great for bicycling, but unless you are a marathon athlete, don't expect to cover much ground.

Panoramic Highway leads past a number of trailheads, some of them near the **Mountain Home Inn** (810 Panoramic Highway, Mill Valley; 381 9000), a good stop for coffee, lunch or an overnight stay. There is a small parking lot directly across the road from the inn.

The **Mountain Theater** is a 5,000-seater amphitheatre, set 610 metres/2,000 feet above sea level. It affords spectacular views of both the San Francisco and Richardson Bays, Alcatraz and Angel Islands, the Golden Gate Bridge and, on clear days, the East Bay hills. This is the site of an annual Mountain Play each spring.

From Muir Woods, you can drive or bike to the coast and head on north from Muir Beach. There's a delightful Tudoresque pub called the **Pelican Inn** (Highway 1, at Muir Beach; 383 6000/6005), a good place to re-fuel. Its terrace and lawn make it an especially attractive lunch spot in good weather.

The Panoramic Highway dovetails into Highway 1 (the Coast Highway) at the town of **Stinson Beach**. Stinson is the closest you'll get to the classic idea of California beach life popularised by the Beach Boys and other surf groups. The water is chilly but the public beach is fabulous, a long curve of clean sand open all year round.

The Larkspur ferry docks near **Larkspur Landing**. The Larkspur Landing Shopping Center and its first-rate pub, the **Marin Brewing Company**, aside (*see chapter* **Bars & Cafés**), the

The birthplace of California's wine industry. See page 237.

only point of coming here is as a brief stop-off on the way to **San Quentin Prison** and its museum, about three quarters of a mile east along Sir Francis Drake Boulevard.

Just 5.3 kilometres/3.3 miles north of the sole stoplight in Stinson Beach is the **Audubon Canyon Ranch** (4900 Route 1; 868 9244), a 405 hectare/1,000 acre preserve on the shore of the Bolinas Lagoon. Of the 90-odd species, the big draws are the egrets and great blue herons that nest here. The **Alioce Kent Trail** leads a short way up to an observation point where telescopes are mounted for viewing the birds in the rookery. Other trails lead through redwoods and fir trees where squirrels, grey foxes, badgers, bobcats and deer roam free, all protected. Headquartered in a nineteenth century white frame house, Audubon Canyon Ranch houses environmental exhibits and a wonderful natural history bookshop located in an old milking barn at the back. The ranch is open at the weekend from 1 March until 4 July. Donations are welcome.

North of Stinson Beach, at Olema, is the turn-off for the fantastic **Point Reyes National Seashore**. This vast peninsula, now protected by federal law, is a natural treasure worshipped by just about everyone in California. Certainly it is an unforgettable place, with fresh sea winds, wild animals, sea mammals, incredible waterfowl, waterfalls, miles of unspoiled beaches, a highly variegated terrain, campsites and one lone café.

The towns of Olema and Inverness, as well as Inverness Park, are good places to refuel before heading out to the coast.

If you're coming to bathe, it's best to bypass the beaches of this windswept coast and head along Tomales Bay on the eastern edge for tiny beaches like **Heart's Desire** where tides are mild and the water's not so cold.

Hikers flock to **Mount Wittenberg**, where miles of hiking and riding trails crisscross the mountain, where chaparral, wildlife and fog are facts of life. There are excellent vantage points here and elsewhere for sighting migrating pacific grey whales off the coast during winter, as they pass on their round trip from Alaska to Baja California. A lighthouse stands on a dramatic promontory, and the **Miwok Indian Village** is near by. Before setting out, stop by park headquarters at **Bear Valley** (663 8522) to obtain maps, the latest weather information and tips on fishing, clamming and horse riding.

Getting There

By Car

Sausalito is 13km/8m and Muir Woods 24km/15m from San Francisco.

By Bus

Golden Gate Transit (453 2100) buses link the city to Marin County.
Marin Headlands: Take Golden Gate Transit bus 2 (it leaves from Pine and Battery Streets and from the Golden

Gate Bridge Toll Plaza Mon-Fri; on Sundays you can take Muni bus 76 from Market and Montgomery Streets.

Golden Gate Transit bus 10 leaves from the Transbay Terminal, Civic Center and the Toll Plaza to **Sausalito** at the weekends and on national holidays.

Except for charter tour buses, there's no direct public transport to **Muir Woods**; take BART to Walnut Creek and then change onto the County Connection bus 116 which runs to Muir Woods between 10.30am and 3.30pm Mon-Sat. Golden Gate Transit bus 63 takes you to trailheads at the weekend. It's a long bike ride to the coast, but if you go around the mountain, via Sir Francis Drake Boulevard, you'll see a lot of fabulous scenery. Golden Gate Transit bus 63 also stops at **Stinson Beach**, the **Bay Area Discovery Museum**, and **Audubon Canyon Ranch**.

To get to **Point Reyes**, take the Golden Gate Transit bus 24, which leaves from Market and Mission Streets.

By Ferry

Golden Gate Ferries (923 3000/332 6600) depart from the Embarcadero Ferry Building and travel north to **Sausalito** and **Larkspur** (on separate schedules) daily, with more trips on weekdays than on weekends or holidays. The Sausalito ferry takes about 30 minutes to cross the bay and is one of the best cheap thrills in the Bay Area. On board are snack and cocktail bars. The lower deck is better in bad weather, but on most days you should ride on the top deck for unsurpassed views of the San Francisco waterfront, the Golden Gate Bridge and Alcatraz Island. The boat docks in downtown Sausalito, close to dozens of shops and restaurants. A **Red & White Fleet** (546 2628) leaves from Pier 43 at Fisherman's Wharf, to **Tiburon**.

Blue & Gold Fleet Ferries (705 5444) offer various tours, including trips to Vallejo, home of Marine World/Africa USA. They operate from Pier 39 (Beach Street at Embarcadero).

Tourist Information

Muir Woods National Monument
Information (338 2595). GGNRA Headquarters, Fort Mason, Building 201, San Francisco (556 0560).

Point Reyes Visitor Information Center
Off Highway 1, Point Reyes, Marin County (663 1092).

San Rafael Chamber of Commerce
817 Mission Avenue, San Rafael (454 4163).

Sausalito Chamber of Commerce
333 Caledonia Street, Sausalito (332 0505).

Where to Stay & Eat

Stinson Beach Motel
3416 Highway 1 (868 1712).
Simple accommodation in a good location.

Casa del Mar
37 Belvedere Avenue (868 2124).
A simple, elegant small inn with good art and great breakfasts. Moderate to expensive.

Inns of Marin
(800 887 2880).
A service which books accommodation at 25 locations in West Marin.

Camping
The 1,053 hectare/2,600 acre Samuel P. Taylor State Park (488-9897) has 65 campsites and 75 picnic sites, and is located less than a mile west of the town of Lagunitas.

The Wine Country

When Californians say 'wine country', they usually mean Sonoma and Napa, no matter how many wineries open in Mendocino, Monterey or Santa Barbara. The state's original and best-known wine-producing region is so close to San Francisco that one can see skyscrapers from certain vantage points. Once in the vineyards, however, it's hard to believe the big city is less than an hour's drive to the south.

Sonoma and Napa Counties are both agricultural and scenic, but they share little more than a mountain range and a common passion for winemaking. Sonoma County is a sprawling, largely rural area stretching from the ocean to the Napa County line. The dress code leans to blue jeans and cowboy boots, so sometimes it's hard to tell a successful vintner from a poor farmer. The social life is somewhat more formal in the Napa Valley, where people still dress up for special occasions, though it has been described as 'antiseptic' by comparison to Sonoma Valley.

To avoid confusion, bear in mind that the names Sonoma and Napa can refer to towns, valleys and entire counties.

SONOMA COUNTY

At 4,138 square kilometres/1,600 square miles, Sonoma County is larger than the entire state of Rhode Island. Grapes are planted in every corner of the county except right along the Pacific Ocean, so touring it can take days or even weeks. The three major areas are the Sonoma Valley, which runs about 37 kilometres/23 miles north from San Pablo Bay; the Alexander Valley/Dry Creek area around the east and northwest of Healdsburg; and the Russian River Valley, which stretches from Highway 101 along the river towards the ocean. The recently designated Carneros district traverses the southern edge of both Sonoma and Napa.

One of the principal attractions of a Sonoma wine tour – besides the wine itself – is driving along winding roads with sometimes breathtaking, sometimes sweetly rural views of vineyards and farms. The **Sonoma County Wineries Association** is located near Highway 101 in Rohnert Park, one of the few towns with no wineries at all. It organises vineyard and winery demonstrations and daily tastings.

The Carneros district straddles southern Sonoma and Napa. Here you will find wineries such as the **Viansa Winery and Italian Marketplace** (25200 Highway 121, Sonoma; 1-707 935 4700). A scion of one of the state's oldest wine families, Sam Sebastiani and his wife Vicki built a Tuscan-style winery on a knoll facing the Sonoma Valley. Their spacious tasting room also sells Italian foodstuffs and there are picnic tables set out beneath trellises outside, overlooking the Sonoma Valley.

World Series

Amsterdam Berlin Budapest London Madrid New York Paris Prague Rome San Francisco

The city of **Sonoma** was founded in 1823 as the Mission San Francisco Solano, the last and northernmost of the Franciscan missions. It developed around a Mexican-style plaza and in 1846, the Bear Flag was raised on this plaza to proclaim the independent Republic of California (*see chapter* **History: Frontiersmen & Trappers**). The town celebrates its 150th anniversary in 1996. The plaza is now flanked by adobe and Western-style false-fronted buildings which house restaurants, bookshops, barbershops and plenty of places to grab picnic supplies, including a cheese factory and a bakery. The central plaza has hundreds of shady trees and a dozen or so picnic tables.

The **Sonoma Valley Visitors Bureau** (*see page 240*) distributes leaflets on walking tours of the historic downtown area. For more than a decade, the whitewashed adobe **Sonoma Mission** (1-707 938 9560, open 10am-5pm daily) on West Spain and First Street, served as an outpost for the Mexicans. Now restored, it houses a variety of historical relics.

The **Sonoma State Historic Park** includes the Mission building as well as the Toscano Hotel and the Sonoma Barracks where the troops under the control of Mexican General Mariano G Vallejo were stationed.

A good stop for children is **Sonoma Train Town**, about a mile south of the plaza, which offers a 20-minute ride on a miniature steam train past scale models of buildings, a petting zoo and a couple of waterfalls.

The history of Sonoma is intertwined with that of the California wine industry, which began here. Hungarian count Agoston Haraszthy planted the first European grapevines in Sonoma in the 1850s at **Buena Vista Carneros Winery and Vineyards** (18000 Old Winery Road, Sonoma; 1-800 926 1266). Like the Napa Valley, Sonoma Valley is hotter in the summer and colder in the winter than the open acreage towards the coast, where the climate is moderated by the ocean. Fog, generally from San Pablo Bay, does creep into the valleys during the summer months, doing much to extend the growing season but casting a deep chill on summer nights.

Of the 35 wineries in the Sonoma Valley, several are near the Sonoma Plaza. A great picnic choice is **Bartholomew Park Winery**, which has a museum and a relief map dedicated to the appellation.

The villages of **Kenwood** and **Glen Ellen** north of Sonoma would be hard to find, were it not for the presence of some of the best wineries. Jack London – adventurer, farmer and the most prolific author of his day – made his home in Glen Ellen. A mansion full of memories and the charred remains of Wolf House make **Jack London Historic State Park** (1-707 938 5216) one of the valley's top attractions (*see also chapter* **Literary San Francisco**). It's a nice place to stroll among oak and madrone trees; most of the park lies in shade during the heat of the day. Near the entrance to the park, the **Sonoma Cattle Company** leads guided tours of the area on horseback (1-707 996 8566).

One of the most popular stops in Kenwood is the **Kenwood Winery**, at Warm Springs Road and Highway 12, Kenwood (1-707 833 5891). The original old barn, now the tasting room and shop, dates from the pre-Prohibition days of the early 1900s. This is a friendly, classic Sonoma winery known for its grapes which are grown on Jack London's former ranch.

Northwest of Kenwood is the county seat of **Santa Rosa**, which offers little for the wine tourist. Due north, **Healdsburg** is like a miniature Sonoma, with an unusual number of good restaurants and boutiques for its size, and an enviable location at the intersection of three wine valleys – Alexander, Dry Creek and Russian River.

A much cooler winegrowing region than Sonoma Valley, the **Russian River Valley** is crisscrossed by several tiny roads, including West Side Road, which runs along the river for a distance through towns so small that most don't even have stop signs. The largest, **Guerneville**, is popular for river rafting and as a summer resort for San Francisco's gay community. The Russian River is also a good bet for fishing. There are bait shops in Guerneville and Healdsburg (you need a licence to fish in California, obtainable from most fishing and camping shops).

NAPA COUNTY

Napa Valley wines are the number one attraction in the county, with food a close second. Besides sipping and dining, there's fishing and boating on remote **Lake Berryessa**, mud baths in Calistoga, horse riding, bicycling, or riding the rails. The **Napa Valley Wine Train** (*see below* **Getting Around**) runs daily lunch and dinner trips up and down the valley. The best way to get an overview is from a hot air balloon, a thrilling pre-dawn experience that absolutely demands several rolls of film and a mastery of any fear of heights. For a closer look, several companies offer horse riding tours.

The 40 kilometre/25 mile-long **Napa Valley**, running almost parallel to the Sonoma Valley on the other side of the Mayacamas Mountains, is the heart of the Napa wine industry. Highway 29 runs up the middle and is usually crowded because the largest wineries, including Robert Mondavi and Beringer, are on or near it. Boutique wineries are mostly to be found on the **Silverado Trail**, or on one of the lanes that crisscross the valley, or along a winding road up a hillside.

Getting There

By Car

The wine country is roughly an hour by car (71 kilometres/44 miles) over the Golden Gate Bridge along Highway 101; turn off at Ignacio onto Route 37 and then take Route 121, taking Route 12 for Sonoma, or Route 29 for Napa. Though traffic can be hellish, particularly over the Golden Gate Bridge, travelling by road is the best way to get to the wine country.

By Bus

Golden Gate Transit operates buses as far north as Petaluma (bus 90 goes to **Sonoma**, stopping at San Rafael on the way). Within the county, Sonoma County Area Transit and The Vine, Napa's bus service, provide local transport. Several San Francisco operators run Wine Country Tours: contact the Visitor's Information Center in San Francisco, or one of the tourist offices listed below for more information.

You can also take BART to El Cerrito and then the Vallejo bus to **Napa**. Phone the Napa Valley Transit Authority (1-707 255 7631) for more information.

Tourist Information

Sonoma Valley Visitors Bureau
453 First Street East, Sonoma (1-707 996 1090).

Sonoma County Wineries Association
5000 Roberts Lake Road, Rohnert Park (1-800 939 7666/707 586 3795).

Napa Valley Conference and Visitors Bureau
1310 Napa Town Center, Napa (1-707 226 7459).

Napa Chamber of Commerce
1556 1st Street, Napa (1-707 226 7455).

Russian River Region, Inc
14034 Armstrong Woods Road, Guerneville (1-707 869 9212/1-800 253 8800).

Getting Around

By Balloon

This is one of the best ways to see the wine country. Several companies offer packages, such as flights for two with champagne, or balloon, brunch and lodging at a local hotel and spa. In Sonoma, try **Sonoma Thunder** (1-707 538 7359) or **Wine Country Balloon Safaris** (1-800 759 5638/1-707 829 7695). In Napa, try the **Bonaventura Balloon Company** (1-800 359 6272) or **Balloon Aviation** (1-707 944 4400).

By Train

Wine Country Wagons: for a different kind of vineyard tour in the Sonoma Valley, try a horsedrawn carriage (707 833 1202) or the **Napa Valley Wine Train** (1-800 522 4142/1-800 427 4124 from California).

Where to Eat: Sonoma

For more places to eat in the wine country, *see page 121* **Restaurants**.

Babette's
464 First Street East, Sonoma (1-707 939 8921).
Innovative French cuisine with an idiosyncratic wine list to match in an intimate, chef-owned setting. Expensive.

Bistro Ralph
109 Plaza Street, Healdsburg (1-707 433 1380).
An unusual menu is served in this spruced up shopfront. Great list of wines by the glass. Inexpensive to moderate.

The General's Daughter
400 West Spain Street, Sonoma (1-707 938 4004).
Large portions are served from a limited menu in this restored Victorian mansion. Moderate to expensive.

Juanita, Juanita
19114 Arnold Drive, Sonoma (1-707 935 3981).
The food is fresh Mex with a California twist. Inexpensive.

Kenwood Restaurant
9900 Highway 12, Kenwood (1-707 833 6326).
The Kenwood serves classic wine country fare concentrating on seafood and pasta. There's outdoor seating, a bar, an open fireplace and the emphasis is on local wines. Moderate to expensive.

Where to Eat: Napa

The Diner
Washington Street, Yountville (1-707 944 2626).
Fabulous breakfasts, great lunches and good dinners. The emphasis is on Mexican dishes. Inexpensive.

French Laundry
6640 Washington Street, Yountville (1-707 944 2380).
Sophistication in the country; *très* French. Very expensive. *See chapter* **Restaurants**.

Mustards Grill
7399 St Helena Highway, Yountville (1-707 944 2424).
A longstanding favourite, serving dependable California cuisine. Moderate to expensive. *See chapter* **Restaurants**.

Tra Vigne
1050 Charter Oak Boulevard, St Helena (1-707 963 4444).
An expensive, but great place on a sunny day. There's a large, outside terrace and an excellent selection of local wines available by the glass or bottle. *See chapter* **Restaurants**.

Where to Stay: Sonoma

Camellia Inn
211 North Street, Healdsburg (1-707 433 8182).
An Italianate Victorian inn near the heart of town, and one of the wine country's first and foremost bed and breakfasts. It's elegant but friendly, and the proprietor makes his own award-winning wines on the premises. Moderate to expensive.

Kenwood Inn
10400 Highway 12, Kenwood (1-707 833 1293).
New and elegant, the Kenwood has many spa services and a pool.

Sonoma Hotel
On the Plaza at West Spain Street and First Street West (1-707 996 2996).
An historic hotel, and excellent value.

Sonoma Mission Inn and Spa
18140 Highway 12, Boyes Hot Springs (1-707 938 9000).
A topflight resort with a full-service spa located in a turn-of-the-century Mission Revival complex.

Sonoma Valley Inn
550 Second Street West, Sonoma (1-707 938 9200).
Part of a souped-up motel chain with big, attractive rooms and a pool.

Where to Stay: Napa

Auberge du Soleil
180 Rutherford Hill Road, Rutherford (1-707 963 1211).
A top of the line hotel, with many services and amenities.

Cross Roads Inn
6380 Silverado Trail, Napa (1-707 944 0646).
A contemporary bed and breakfast with fabulous views and moderate rates.

Vintage Inn
6541 Washington Street, Yountville (1-707 944 1112).
The Vintage has great looking rooms and is close to shops and restaurants. There's also a pool. Probably the best value in the Valley.

Wineries & Wine Shops

Most wineries offer complimentary tastings of four different wines. Some charge for additional samples or for older vintages.

Château Montelena
452 Tubbs Lane, Calistoga (1-707 942 5105).
An 1882 château overlooking a Chinese garden complete with a lake, teahouses and bridges, and an ancient Chinese junk.

Domaine Chandon
California Drive, Yountville (1-707 944 2280).
The first of the French wine growers to invade California, Domaine Chandon continues to offer one of the best tours, with clear explanations of '*méthode champenoise*'. The restaurant is good enough to make reservations essential.

St Supéry Winery
8440 St Helena Highway, Rutherford (1-707 963 4507).
The knowledgeable tours guides make a point of de-bunking the mystique of wine tasting and growing, and there's an excellent wine discovery centre.

Wermuth Winery
3942 Silverado Trail, Calistoga (1-707 942 5924).
This is a charming example of a small, family-owned winery run by a former doctor whose love of the grape is infectious.

Wine Exchange of Sonoma
452 First Street East, Sonoma (1-800 938 1794).
Up to 15 California and European wines (plus beers) are available for tasting daily.

Calistoga & Harbin Hot Springs

The volcanic ash from neighbouring St Helena Mountain is the magic ingredient in the mud baths that draw the health-conscious as well as the plain curious to **Calistoga**. More than any other town in the wine country, Calistoga really looks Western. It's got saloons and a wide main street often festooned with banners promoting beer tastings or mustard festivals or other celebrations of the California good life.

The granddaddy of the mud bath spas is **Dr Wilkinson's Hot Springs** (1-707 942 4102/6257), but Lincoln Avenue is lined with smaller facilities offering massages and similar services. The town got its name in the mid-1800s, when San Franciscan Sam Brannan created a resort near St Helena Mountain and instead of proclaiming that the spa would be 'the Saratoga of California' (referring to the New York resort), said it would be 'the Calistoga of Sarifoma'.

At the end of the avenue, furthest from the highway is a **glider port** (Calistoga Gliders, 1546 Lincoln Avenue; 942 6000) where gliders take off on sightseeing tours of the surrounding countryside. The views are spectacular, and you can see much of the Napa Valley and the forested mountains that flank it.

Dioramas depicting nineteenth century Calistoga life, along with photographs and other artefacts, are displayed in the **Sharpsteen Museum** (1311 Washington Street; 1-707 942 5911). A mile north of town, on Tubbs Lane, **Old Faithful** geyser erupts about every 40 minutes. Water comes from an underground river and heats to about 177°C/350°F before spewing high into the air. Another quirk of nature is the **Petrified Forest**, eight kilometres/five miles west on Petrified Forest Road. The giant petrified redwoods make an unusual backdrop for a picnic here.

Several wineries are located in and around Calistoga. People get a kick out of the tram ride up to **Sterling Vineyards** (1111 Dunaweal Lane, Calistoga; 1-707 942 5151). Famous for its Cabernet Sauvignon and white wines, this hilltop winery has commanding views of the countryside and an excellent self-guided tour.

Robert Louis Stevenson, who honeymooned near here, included some of his experiences in both *Treasure Island* and *The Silverado Squatters*. The **Robert Louis Stevenson State Park** is 11 kilometres/seven miles north of Calistoga on Highway 29 (1-707 942 4575). The **Silverado Museum** (Library Lane, St Helena, Napa County, 1-707 963 3757) in nearby St Helena contains memorabilia of the author (*see also chapter* **Literary San Francisco**).

On Highway 29 near Calistoga, the **Bale Grist Mill State Historic Park** is a good place to stop for a picnic.

HARBIN HOT SPRINGS

Highway 29 does a lot of twisting and turning as it makes its way from Calistoga to Middletown. The latter is home to one of the best-known New Age retreats in California – and it's not short of competition. There's a school of massage and an educational centre on this 470 hectare/1160-acre property in the shadow of Mount Harbin in Lake County, but most people think of it as a spa resort. Like many hot springs in the area, this one is said to have been sacred to the Native Americans who believed in the healing properties of the water.

Today the resort is run by the Heart Consciousness Church, and you'll find a little theatre, organic vegetable gardens and a vegetarian restaurant, as well as enough hiking trails to make your calves cry for mercy. It's a good thing the pools are nearby. Harbin is a good place to discard any inhibitions about public nudity; it's *the* thing here, and while it's not mandatory, some people do begin to feel self-conscious in their clothes. There's a massage pavilion where you can get massaged in the great outdoors (by a nude masseur, if you like).

The place has an excellent reputation for acceptance and 'good vibes'. It draws people from all over the world, who come as much for the ambience as the reasonable rates. Other than Harbin, there's not a great deal to do in the area. Further up the road is Clear Lake, a major destination for people with RVs (those cumbersome and horribly popular Recreational Vehicles) and motorboats.

Getting There

By Car

From Napa (*see p240*) take Highway 29 to **Calistoga**. Continue on to Middletown, turn left onto Highway 175, then right on Barnes Street to Harbin Springs Road for **Harbin Hot Springs**.

By Bus

Greyhound Bus Lines (1-800 231 2222) run daily services from San Francisco to Calistoga and Middletown near Harbin Hot Springs.

Tourist Information

Calistoga Chamber of Commerce

1458 Lincoln Avenue, Suite 4, Calistoga (1-707 942 6333).

Where to Eat

All Seasons Cafe

1400 Lincoln Avenue (1-707 942 9111).
Fresh, delectable and local food and an award-winning wine list.

Cafe Pacifico Mexican Bar & Grill

1237 Lincoln Avenue (1-707 942 4400).
Upmarket Mexican food.

Catahoula Restaurant and Saloon

Mount View Hotel, Lincoln Avenue (1-707 942 2275).
Cajun-inspired California cuisine.

Where to Stay

Brannan House Cottage

100 Wapoo Avenue (1-707 942 4200).
An historic building on a quiet corner. The rates are moderate.

Comfort Inn

1865 Lincoln Avenue (1-707 942 9400/1-800 228 5150).
Inexpensive motel.

Harbin Hot Springs

Harbin Springs Road, Lake County (1-800 622 2477/1-707 987 2477).

The **Napa Valley Wine Train**. *See page 240.*

Heading South

Half Moon Bay State Parks District Office
95 Kelly Avenue, Half Moon Bay (330 6300).

Compared to the wine country and the Monterey Peninsula, the California coast just south of San Francisco is fairly low key. But this doesn't mean that it hasn't been 'discovered'. The centre of the action is the town of **Half Moon Bay**, just off Highway 1, a veritable boomtown ever since the city leaders decided to promote pumpkins for the Hallowe'en season.

There are a couple of golf courses, riding stables, bike paths and beaches in this appealing coastal town. Main Street has experienced a boom: now bookstores and boutiques compete with old-fashioned grocery stores and feed barns for space downtown. Half Moon Bay is known as an agricultural region and the countryside is worth exploring.

May and June are two of the best months for foraging about the farm tracts that dot the surrounding countryside. Just south of Half Moon Bay, **Phipps Ranch** (879 0787) sells berries and other fruit and vegetables throughout the year, which can be eaten on the ranch at picnic tables or packed into the car.

Before you get to Half Moon Bay, **Princeton-by-the-Sea** is a lofty name for a tiny town and a terrific little harbour. Languishing behind most coastal development, Princeton-by-the-Sea attracts mostly day-trippers who come to fish off the two long jetties or to charter boats for off-shore angling (and, in winter, for whale-watching expeditions). The busy little harbour, the fresh sea breezes and the surf that breaks along the beaches to the south imbue this former rum-running outpost with a distinctive flavour. It's a town for aimless ambling and perhaps a lunch at a laid-back restaurant.

Travelling further south on Highway 1, a string of beaches stretch up the coast between Pescadero and Half Moon Bay. Best of the lot is probably **San Gregorio State Beach**, a strip of white sand distinguished by sedimentary cliffs and a proximity to the nude beach further north.

Getting There

By Car
Half Moon Bay and Princeton are about a 30-minute drive south of San Francisco on Highway 1.

By Bus
SamTrans (1-800 660 4287) buses travel between Half Moon Bay, Pacifica and the Daly City BART Station, among other points.

Tourist Information

Half Moon Bay Chamber of Commerce
520 Kelly Avenue, Half Moon Bay (726 8380).

Where to Stay & Eat

Pillar Point Inn
Princeton-by-the Sea (728 7377).
Snappy nautical décor and generous breakfasts in an inn overlooking the harbour.

San Benito House
356 Main Street, Half Moon Bay (726 3425).
A hotel in a restored building in the heart of town, with lots of antiques.

Santa Cruz

This is a quintessentially quirky California beach town, known for being laid back and politically progressive. It is just recovering after suffering extensive earthquake damage in the late 1980s. The home of the University of California at Santa Cruz, it has a young population that keeps things lively, as well as plenty of longtime residents who are fiercely protective of the town's liberal heritage.

The closest you can come to recapturing the excitement of driving down Highway 1 is aboard the Giant Dipper, the classic roller coaster that, along with the nearby 1911 carousel, has been proclaimed a National Historic Landmark. A nice hybrid of tacky and nostalgic, the **Santa Cruz Beach Boardwalk** (400 Beach Street; 1-408 423 5590) offers 25 different rides and a rambling arcade with games, shops and places to eat. Bumper cars and tilt-a-whirls are as hard to come by in this world as sunny central coast beaches, but Santa Cruz offers all these attractions and more. The long beachfront here faces south, and is thus ablaze in sunshine on days when the Monterey Peninsula is shrouded in fog so thick you need radar to follow your golf balls.

In the old days, the boardwalk and the **Cocoanut Grove Ballroom** (1-408 423 2053) were links in a veritable chain of beachside entertainment complexes, including the late, lamented Playland-at-the-Beach in San Francisco. Remnants of that heyday can still be enjoyed on weekends, when a mixture of big bands and local rock/pop groups like Joe Sharino play for dancing on weekend nights.

The town's popularity as a beach resort dates back to the mid-nineteenth century, and if it keeps up, perhaps there will be talk of reinstating the old Sunshine Special train between San Francisco and the city named 'Sacred Cross'. Meanwhile, it's possible to trace the early days of this century at the little **Surfing Museum** (1-408 429 3429), located on Lighthouse Point, where old photographs and vintage boards tell the story of the Hawaiian sport that has become an entrenched part of the Santa Cruz scene.

Getting There

By Car

Santa Cruz is 119 kilometres/74 miles south of San Francisco: about two hours's drive down Highway 1.

By Train

CalTrains (1-800 660 4287) leaves from the station on Fourth Street and King Street and from 22nd Street and Pennsylvania Avenue every half hour. Take the train to San Jose Amtrak station, from where a shuttle bus goes to Santa Cruz.

Tourist Information

Santa Cruz County Conference & Visitors Council

701 Front Street, Santa Cruz (1-408 425 1234).

Where to Eat

Aldo's Harbour Restaurant

616 Atlantic Avenue, Santa Cruz (1-408 426 3736).
Coastal Italian food in casual surroundings. Prices are moderate; no credit cards or reservations.

Dharma's Natural Foods

4250 Capitola Road, Capitola (1-408 462 1711).
Possibly the oldest veggie restaurant in the US. Very low prices.

Pontiac Grill

429 Front Street, Santa Cruz (1-408 427 2290).
The ultimate diner experience, where Chuck Berry and the Drifters provide jukebox accompaniment while you eat burgers of all kinds.

Where to Stay

Babbling Brook Inn

1025 Laurel Street, Santa Cruz (1-800 866 1131/1-408 427 2457).
A luxurious bed-and-breakfast inn set in wooded grounds in the heart of town.

New Davenport Bed and Breakfast

32 Davenport Avenue, Santa Cruz (1-408 425 1818).
Away from the bustle, with ocean views and beach access.

Monterey Pensinsula

Jutting out into the Pacific between the fun-loving town of Santa Cruz and the dramatic coastline of Big Sur, the Monterey Peninsula is one of the best attractions on the coast. Writers and artists have been drawn to the area for decades, and the **Monterey Jazz Festival**, held each September, draws the top names in jazz and blues (contact the Visitors Council for more information). The area is perhaps best known for its spectacular golf courses, where golfers forgive the treacherous greens in exchange for some of the most compelling scenery in the world of sports. It's a great area for fishing and cycling as well.

The three major cities are Monterey, Pacific Grove and Carmel, where Clint Eastwood recently completed a stint as mayor. Also here is Pebble Beach, site of some of the most beautiful, famous and challenging golf courses in the country.

Carmel is a love-it-or-hate-it sort of place. Quiet, yet crammed with artists and craftspeople, it is also chock-full of mediocre shops. If you can find it, the beach is nice, but there are more interesting sights elsewhere.

Just south of Carmel Highlands is one of the most beloved parks in California, **Point Lobos**. Plan to spend an entire morning or even a whole day exploring its nooks, crannies, beaches and awesome promontories.

A trip to this peninsula is not complete without a few hours at the **Monterey Bay Aquarium** (886 Cannery Row; 1-408 648 4800, open 10am-6pm daily). If the area had a mascot, it would be the sea otter. Time your visit to coincide with one of the regularly scheduled feeding times of these irresistible sea mammals. There is much more to see at the aquarium, however, including sharks, an 8.5 metre/28 foot-deep

kelp forest and a hands-on exhibition on tidal life. At the weekends, the beach near the aquarium is busy with novice divers working towards their SCUBA certification. There are several dive shops in the area, but remember, once in the ocean both visibility and temperatures are quite low.

The aquarium is the class act along seedy **Cannery Row**, a neighbourhood made famous by native son John Steinbeck. Today it's full of tacky shops and disappointing restaurants housed in former canneries that were abandoned in the 1940s when the commercial sardine population mysteriously disappeared, presumably fished out.

The capital of Alta California during Spanish, Mexican and American governments, Monterey is one of the state's most historic cities. The chamber of commerce distributes free maps to adobes, gardens and other attractions to help you explore. Popular spots include **Colton Hall**, where California's first constitution was written (in 1849), the **Maritime Museum**, and the **Monterey State Historic Park**, seven acres containing various artefacts relating to the area's architecture and history.

Carmel, Monterey and Pebble Beach are so often mentioned in the same breath, that they sound like a single destination. But these three sisters have a fourth, shy sibling: **Pacific Grove**. Founded in 1875 as a camping retreat for the Methodist Church (in fact inspiring a similar effort in Carmel), Pacific Grove has remained true to its roots. It's best known lodging site, the **Asilomar Conference Center** (800 Asilomar Boulevard; 1-408 372 8016), still has a sort of ascetic ambience that characterises the entire town.

Sharp protruding rocks along much of the town's shoreline discourage most swimmers. The undeveloped shoreline, carpeted in native plants, is thus a wonderful place to stroll unhampered by throngs of frisbee players and picnicking families. The **Point Pinos Light Station**, the oldest operating lighthouse on the coast, is one of dozens of older structures still in good repair. There's an old saying that helps distinguish the three towns: it's Carmel by the sea, Monterey by the smell, and Pacific Grove by God.

It's understandable that Santa Cruz and **Capitola** (which bills itself as the oldest Pacific seaside resort) have been overrun. While it's almost impossible to drive to the most popular beaches, it is possible to walk to them. Especially from **Aptos**, a village located across the highway from two of the best beaches, **Seacliff** and **Rio del Mar**.

Aptos is a good back-up choice for lodging on popular weekends such as the **Great Monterey Squid Festival** held late in May. The cry of the wild calamari is a siren song for thousands of fans of this delectable treat, which is served in dozens of ways by local restaurants during a long weekend of music and entertainment. Aptos also has some weird distinctions, despite its diminutive size. It is home to an endangered colony of long-toed salamanders, and it boasts the World's Shortest Parade, sponsored by the Aptos Ladies Tuesday Evening Society, usually on the weekend closest to 4 July.

Getting There

By Car
Monterey is 214 kilometres/133 miles (about two and a half hours by car) from San Francisco. Take Highway 1.

By Train
Take the **CalTrain** (*see p243* **Santa Cruz**) to San Jose Amtrak station, where a local bus connects with Monterey. Amtrak (1-800 872 7245) runs the Coast Starlight Train along the coast, stopping in nearby Salinas.

By Bus
Greyhound buses connect San Francisco with Los Angeles, with regular services to Monterey via Salinas. Although there is local transit, this area is best explored by car.

Tourist Information

Monterey Peninsula Chamber of Commerce
380 Alvarado Street, Monterey (1-408 649 1 770).

Pacific Grove Chamber of Commerce
584 Central Avenue, Pacific Grove (1-408 373 3304).

Where to Eat

Fandango
223 17th Street, Pacific Grove (1-408 372 3456).
Mediterranean food, best enjoyed on the patio. Inexpensive to moderate.

Gernot's French Cuisine
649 Lighthouse Avenue, Pacific Grove (1-408-646 1477).
Heavy-duty continental classics are served in a restored Victorian house. Expensive.

Rio Grill
Highway 1, at Rio Road, Carmel (1-408 625 5436).
Fish, pasta and high style.

Where to Stay

Gosby House
643 Lighthouse Avenue, Pacific Grove (1-408 375 1287).
A terminally cute bed-and-breakfast in a great location.

Green Gables Inn
104 Fifth Street, Pacific Grove (1-408 375 2095).
A waterfront Queen Anne-style house.

Lone Oak Motel
2221 Fremont Street, Monterey (1-408 372 4924).
Clean, and cheapest during the week.

Seacliff Inn-Best Western
7500 Dominion Court, Aptos (1-408 688 7300).
An inexpensive, charmless motel in a fabulous location.

Heading East

Berkeley

Built in 1936, the Oakland-Bay Bridge changed the way of life in the San Francisco Bay Area, connecting the peninsula to the eastern mainland. One of the East Bay's most interesting attractions is the **University of California at Berkeley**, a sprawling campus that was the scene of a lot of political disruption during the 1960s (*see chapter* **Students**). That legacy remains to some extent, influencing the way politics and business are conducted in the city of Berkeley. On campus are the **University Art Museum** and other points of interest, including **Sproul Plaza**, the **Paleontology Museum**, the **Bancroft Library** and the impressive **Botanical Gardens**. The Visitors Center is a useful source of maps and brochures.

Bookshops, understandably, are a major attraction in Berkeley. Don't miss **Cody's** (2454 Telegraph Avenue, at Haste Street; 1-510 845 7852), **Moe's** (2476 Telegraph Avenue, between Haste Street and Dwaight Way; 1-510 849 2087) or **Black Oak Books** (1491 Shattuck Avenue, at Vine Street; 1-510 486 0698), all near the university.

Getting There

By Car
Head across the Bay Bridge and turn north on Interstate 80, following the Berkeley exits. The university campus is 19 kilometres/12 miles from downtown San Francisco.

By BART
Berkeley has BART stops at North Berkeley and Berkeley.

Tourist Information

Berkeley Convention and Visitors Bureau
1834 University Avenue, Berkeley (1-510 549 7040).

Where to Eat

Berkeley is a foodie's paradise, and is not only home to the famous Chez Panisse, but also several excellent farmer's markets (*see chapter* **Shopping & Services**) and the excellent and jam-packed Cheese Board collective (1504 Shattuck Avenue; 1-510 549 3183), among the other food emporiums, many on or near Shattuck Avenue.

Bette's Ocean View Diner
1807A Fourth Street, Berkeley (1-510 644 3230).
An all-American spot, with lunch and terrific breakfasts.

Chez Panisse
1517 Shattuck Avenue, Berkeley (1-510 548 5525).
Home of California cuisine. *See chapter* **Restaurants**.

Spenger's Fish Grotto
1919 Fourth Street, Berkeley (1-510 845 7771).
Hopelessly tawdry, with big crowds and surprisingly good food. Inexpensive to moderate.

Venezia Caffe & Restaurant
1799 University Avenue, Berkeley (1-510 849 4681).
A delightful setting and Italian specialities on the menu.

Where to Stay

Gramma's Rose Garden Inn
2740 Telegraph Avenue, Berkeley (1-510 549 2145).
Cute and cosy, in a nice setting.

Hotel Durant
2600 Durant Avenue, Berkeley (1-510 845 8981).
A good sized hotel one block from the university campus. Inexpensive.

Oakland

Oakland is still step-sister to San Francisco, though its port is more active. To spend a relaxing day, head to **Lake Merritt** and rent a paddleboat, perhaps packing a picnic along. Nearby is **Children's Fairyland** (1520 Lakeside Drive; 1-510 238 6876), a low-tech park for kids with a merry-go-round and puppet shows, as well as the Lakeside Park Garden Center, which is packed with native flowers and plants.

The socialising mecca **Jack London Village**, named after the writer who grew up in Oakland, is a hotchpotch of shops and restaurants. It's at the foot of Broadway, in downtown Oakland.

Getting There

By Car
To reach the East Bay by car, head across the Bay Bridge; turn north on Interstate 80 and continue onto Interstate 580 to get to Oakland. Downtown Oakland is 10 kilometres/16 miles from San Francisco.

By BART
There are three BART stops that serve Oakland: 19th Street, Lake Merritt and Oakland City Center 12th Street.

Tourist Information

East Bay Regional Parks District
2950 Peralto Oaks Court, at 106th Street, Oakland (1-510 635 0135).
Provides information and maps covering the numerous regional parks and trails in the Oakland hills.

Oakland Convention and Visitors Bureau
1000 Broadway, Suite 200, Oakland (1-510 839 9000).

Where to Eat

Lantern Restaurant
814 Webster Street, Oakland (1-510 451 0627).
Great dim sum in the heart of Oakland's Chinatown.

Where to Stay

Claremont Resort and Spa
Ashby and Domingo Avenues, Oakland (1-510 843 3000).
A luxurious and historic property, with a spa, tennis courts and much more. Expensive but worth it. *See chapter* **Shopping & Services**.

Further Afield

Lake Tahoe

No one knows how deep Lake Tahoe is. The locals call it Big Blue, and it's everything you could want in a lake. Flanked by snow-capped peaks most of the year, the lake is a prime recreation destination among Californians for skiing, waterskiing, fishing, hiking and – just over the state line in Nevada – legal gambling at a number of casinos that line the main drag in Stateline (gambling is illegal in California).

The scent of pine trees is wonderfully pungent in warm weather. During most winters, the entire area gets blanketed with snow on a regular basis. It is only recently that resorts have installed snow-making machinery to draw thousands of skiers during warmer winters, who pay hefty prices for lift tickets, snacks and rental fees.

The north end of the lake is about a three and a half hours' drive from San Francisco, unless there's heavy snow on Interstate 80. The other route, via Highway 50 (which shoots off from Interstate 80 at Sacramento), leads to the South Shore, where hotels are usually packed, either with skiers in the winter or gamblers any time of year. From March to early November, it's easy to drive the 116 kilometre/72-mile perimeter of the lake (much of it serviced by public transport). On the California side of the lake are attractions such as **Sugar Pine Point State Park**, near Meeks Bay, and a little further south **Emerald Bay State Park** overlooks the bay of the same name. Here is the only island in the lake, and its only campsite where you can arrive by boat as well as by car.

There are plenty of beaches around the lake: **Sand Harbour**, **Zephyr Cove** and **Camp Richardson** are all on the water. An important fact to bear in mind is the temperature of the water. Fed by snow and surrounded largely by mountains, Lake Tahoe is comfortable for swimming only in August and September, when the water has warmed slightly. At least, if you're planning to waterski, you'll have the added motivation to get up and stay up on your skis.

Around the lake and in nearby communities, accommodation ranges from luxurious resorts at places like **Squaw Valley** (1-916 583 6955, site of the 1960 Winter Olympics) to cheap roadside motels or campsites. Lakefront property is exorbitantly expensive, so most lodging is located a block or two from the lake.

Lake Tahoe straddles the state line with Nevada. The north and east sides are less fully developed than the south and west. **Truckee**, an Old West town about 19 kilometres/12 miles north of the lake, has board sidewalks and wood-frame shop fronts that make it look like a backdrop for a John Wayne film. It's not that big a place, but because of the tourist trade there are saloons and a growing number of restaurants. Nearby **Kings Beach** and **Tahoe Vista**, both beach towns, are headquarters for the outdoors set, complete with ski shops and bike rental shops. Unfortunately, Route 28 is usually jammed on summer weekends.

South Lake Tahoe is the same, only with wider streets and a lot less atmosphere, unless neon is your idea of ambience. This is the neighbourhood for innumerable chain motels. A good place to start exploring Tahoe is in **Truckee**; it's a great town for poking around. Take Highway 89 south to the lakeshore at Tahoe City and you will pass both Squaw Valley and Alpine Meadows, two of the most popular ski areas in the west. Skiers tend to prefer one or the other, but not both. Alpine is a bit more family-oriented, while Squaw is glitzier and has more exciting runs. There are dozens of other ski areas, including small ones like Boreal Ridge. In South Lake Tahoe, the **Heavenly Valley** ski lifts operate for sightseeing in summer (1-916 541 7544). In addition, Squaw Valley has an indoor climbing wall in its cable car building called the **Headwall Climbing Wall** (1-916 583 6985, ext 322), as well as ice skating and tennis at the **USA Ice Rink** (1-916 583 6985).

The **North Lake Tahoe Chamber of Commerce** (*see p248*) has information on boat launching facilities. Rapidly changing weather conditions can spell disaster for even seasoned sailors, so Lake Tahoe is no place for enthusiastic beginners.

For jet skiing, canoes, kayaks and other activities, try the **Lighthouse Watersports Centre** in Tahoe City (950 North Lake Boulevard; 1-916 583 6000). **Tahoe Whitewater Tours** in Tahoe City (1-916-581 2441) offers guided tours on five Sierra rivers as well as kayak tours of Emerald Bay and the nearby lakes.

The best way to get out on the lake without incurring risk is to book a cruise on the *MS Dixie II* paddlewheeler out of **Zephyr Cove** (1-702 882 0786/588 3508). There are daily scenic cruises as well as day cruises and dinner-dance cruises aboard this and several other tour boats.

For a bird's-eye view of the area, a trip with **Mountain High Balloons** (locations in Truckee and Tahoe City; 1-916 587 6922/1-800 251 6922) takes you soaring over the Sierra in style, and it includes a champagne celebration upon landing. There are numerous other outfits to take you up and away: the tourist office will supply details.

All the casinos are located on the Nevada side of the lake, mostly at South Shore, but if you are headquartered at North Shore, the closest casino is the **Cal-Neva Lodge** in Crystal Bay (1-702 832 4000).

In Tahoe City, you can visit the interesting **Gatekeeper's Log Cabin** at 120 West Lake

Boulevard (1-916 583 1762), a museum of Tahoe history including Native American artefacts, early pioneer logging and railroad equipment and vintage photographs. It's only open during the summer.

Getting There

For an update on road conditions, phone 557 3755.

By Car

It takes just over three hours to reach the Lake from San Francisco, traffic permitting. To reach the north shores, follow Interstate 80 over the Bay Bridge, which continues as far as Truckee and Reno. To reach the south, take I 80 as far as Sacramento, and then turn off onto Highway 50 to South Tahoe.

By Air

The **Reno Cannon International Airport**, 93km/58m north-east of the lake, is served by several airlines. The **Tahoe Casino Express** offers daily scheduled transport to South Lake Tahoe (1-800 446 6128).

By Train

There is an **Amtrak** station in Truckee (1-800 872 7245).

By Bus

Greyhound Bus lines (1-916-587-3822) stop in Truckee, South Lake Tahoe and in Reno (Nevada).

Tourist Information

Incline Village/Crystal Bay Visitors and Convention Bureau

969 Tahoe Boulevard, Incline Village, NV 89451 (1-702 831 4440).

Lake Tahoe Forest Service Visitor Center

Highway 89, between Emerald Bay and South Lake Tahoe (1-916 573 2674).
Beach access, self-guided nature trails and a helpful staff that distributes the necessary wilderness permits for the Desolation and Mokelumne wilderness areas. It's closed in the winter.

Lake Tahoe Visitors Authority

Box 16299, South Lake Tahoe, 95706 (1-800 288 2463/1-916 544 5050).
Information and lodging reservations for the South Shore.

North Lake Tahoe Chamber of Commerce

245 Highway 28, Tahoe City (1-916 581 6900).

South Lake Tahoe Chamber of Commerce

3066 US 50 (1-916 541 5255).

Tahoe North Visitors and Convention Bureau

950 North Lake Boulevard, Suite 3, Tahoe (1-800 824 6348).

Where to Eat

Boulevard

6731 North Lake Boulevard, Tahoe Vista (1-916 546 7213).
Northern Italian food served for dinner daily, all year round.

Fire Sign Café

1785 West Lake Boulevard, Tahoe City (1-916 583 0871).
Homestyle cooking served at breakfast and lunch.

Log Cabin Caffe

8692 North Lake Boulevard, King's Beach (1-916 546 7109).
Serves espresso, griddle cakes and waffles, as well as outrageous dishes like Cajun eggs benedict. All to the tune of Grateful Dead tapes playing in the background. Inexpensive.

La Playa

7046 North Lake Boulevard, Tahoe Vista (1-916 546 5903).
Serves creative seafood in a beach atmosphere. Lunch and dinner are dished up daily in summer; dinner from Thursday to Tuesday between September and May.

Sunnyside Restaurant

1850 West Lake Boulevard, Lakefront (1-916 583 7200).
Seafood specialities and a classic 'Old Tahoe' ambience. Prices are moderate.

Wolfdale's

640 North Lake Boulevard, Tahoe City (1-916 583 5700).
Asian/California cuisine and a seasonal menu.

Where to Stay: North

The Tahoe North Visitors and Convention Bureau will book accommodation. In addition to resorts, country inns and motels, the bureau also handles condominium referrals.

Mayfield House

236 Grove Street, Tahoe City (1-916 583 1001).
Bed and breakfast in an Tudor-style home.

Olympic Village Inn

1909 Chamonix Place, Olympic Valley (1-916 581 6000).
Intimate suites near hiking trails.

Resort at Squaw Creek

400 Squaw Creek Road, Olympic Valley (1-916 583 6300).
Top of the line hotel, with tennis, golf and horse riding facilities.

River Ranch

Highway 89 and Alpine Meadows Road, Tahoe City (1-916 583 4264).
A longstanding favourite on the Truckee River, with more funk than flash.

Sun 'n' Sand Lodge

8308 North Lake Boulevard, Kings Beach (1-916 546 2515).
A renovated motel on the beach.

Where to Stay: South

Camp Richardson

1900 Jameson Beach Road, South Lake Tahoe (1-916 541 1801/1-800 544 1801).
Lakefront cabins and hotel rooms catering to an active young crowd. Inexpensive to moderate prices.

Kirkwood Ski and Summer Resort

PO Box 1, Kirkwood CA 95646 (1-800 967 7500).
A family-oriented resort with many amenities, 56km/35m south of Lake Tahoe. Moderate to expensive prices.

Survival

Survival

All you need to know to survive the Barbary Coast in style, from shaking through a quake to finding a room to let.

San Francisco is, for the most part, a friendly city. Ask its residents for advice on anything and everything that's not listed below and they'll happily tell you the inside scoop. For essential tourist information, *see chapter* **Essential Information**; for transport information, *see chapter* **Getting Around**.

All 1-800 numbers can be called free of charge from within the US, although many hotels add a surcharge for use of their phones, whatever number you call.

Emergencies

Ambulance, Fire Brigade or Police
Dial **911** (toll-free from any phone booth).

Pacific Gas and Electric Company (PG&E)
(Emergency customer service 1-800 743 5000/ information hotline 1-800 743 5002). **Open** 24-hours daily.

Poison Control Center
(1-800 523 2222). **Open** 24-hours daily.
Provides information on poison intake ranging from too much medication to chemical exposure. The centre offers home treatments or refers patients to 911 in an emergency.

Water Department City & County of San Francisco
(Emergency Service 550 4911). **Open** 24-hours daily.

Help Lines & Agencies

Alcohol/Drug Abuse

Alcoholics Anonymous
(621 1326). **Open** 24-hours daily.
Phone for a schedule of meetings throughout the city.

Center for Substance Abuse Treatment
(1-800 662 4357). **Open** 9am-4pm Mon-Fri.
Substance abuse treatment, information and referrals.

Drug Crisis Line
(362 3400/781 2224 833 for hearing-impaired). **Open** 24-hours daily.
Call this number if you need someone to talk you through a bad drug trip or want to know the effects of a particular drug, an overdose remedy or how to get into a treatment programme.

Haight Ashbury Free Clinic
Drug Detox, Rehab and After Care Project, 558 Clayton Street, at Haight Street (565 1908). Muni Metro N/6, 7, 33, 37, 43, 71 bus. **Open** 10.30am-6.30pm Mon-Thur; noon-6.30pm Fri; 24-hour answerphone.
Prospective patients must attend in person to be evaluated by intake councillors; those accepted participate in a 21-day outpatient detox clinic, focusing on counselling.

Narcotics Anonymous
(621 8600). **Open** 24-hours daily.
Drug addicts man the phones here, offering solace, camaraderie and information on support groups throughout the city to those in crisis.

Child Abuse

Family Service Agency of San Francisco
Talk Line Child Abuse Prevention Center (441 5437).
Open 24-hours daily.
Trained volunteers counsel children suffering from abuse or parents involved in child abuse, and provide follow-up services.

Crime Victims

Community United Against Violence
(333 4357). **Open** 24-hours daily.
A counselling group assisting gay and lesbian victims of domestic violence and hate crimes.

Victims of Crime Resource Center
(1-800 842 8467). **Open** 8am-6pm Mon-Fri; voice mail Sat, Sun.
This information referral service advises victims of their rights and refers them to local resources.

Domestic Violence

Domestic Violence Prevention Hotline
(1-800 540 5433). **Open** 24-hours daily.
Trained counsellors act as an information and referral service and counsel victims as well as batterers.

La Casa de las Madres
(333 1515). **Open** 24-hours daily.
This safe home for abused women counsels and provides emergency housing.

Men Overcoming Violence
(777 4496). **Open** 10am-2pm Mon, Wed; 24-answerphone rest of time.
Support and counselling for men who batter.

Legal Help

Lawyers Committee for Civil Rights & Immigrant and Refugee Rights Project
(543 9444).
Legal services are provided on a case-by-case basis for those seeking political asylum.

Lawyer Referral Service and Volunteer Legal Services Program
(764 1616).
Legal interviewers refer callers to experienced attorneys and attorney mediators for all legal problems, including criminal, business and immigration.

Psychiatric Emergency Services

San Francisco General Hospital
(206 8125). **Open** 24-hours daily.
Those suffering from a psychiatric breakdown or those looking for someone who has been taken by the police or paramedics for acting out of control should contact this hotline.

Rape

Child and Adolescent Sexual Abuse Resource Center
(206 8386). **Open** 24-hours daily.
Crisis service for sexually-abused children under 18 years of age. Patients must be residents of San Francisco or victims of a crime occurring within the city.

SF Rape Treatment Center
(821 3222). **Open** 24-hours daily.
Call here within 72 hours of a sex crime and nurses or social workers will guide you through medical and legal procedures. Patients must be residents of San Francisco or victims of a crime occurring within the city.

Victims of Crime Resource Center
(1-800 842 8467). **Open** 8am-6pm Mon-Fri.
Legal information and community referrals are extended to victims of all crimes, from violent crime to child abuse.

Women Against Rape Crisis Hotline
(647 7273). **Open** 24-hours daily.
Counselling and support service for sexual assault victims and their partners.

Runaways

Huckleberry House
(621 2929). **Open** 24-hours daily.
Hotline and crisis shelter that aids runaway and homeless 11-17 year-olds.

National Runaway Switchboard
(1-800 621 4000). **Open** 24-hours daily.
Teens who have run away, are considering it or need a place to stay are informed of their options by trained volunteers.

Suicide

Drug Abuse Hotline
(1-800 222 0469/1-800 234 0216/1-800 444 9999).
Open 24-hours daily.
This suicide prevention hotline has trained counsellors offering local referral services. In an emergency, they will alert authorities and remain on the phone until help arrives.

Suicide Prevention
(781 0500). **Open** 24-hours daily.
Trained community volunteers lend a sympathetic ear.

Communications

Post

Post offices are open 8am-6pm Mon-Sat. Phone 284 0755 for your nearest branch.

Poste Restante
General Delivery, Civic Center, 101 Hyde Street, San Francisco, CA 94142 (441 8329). BART Civic Center/Muni Metro J, K, L, M, N/5, 9, 19, 42, 47 bus. **Open** 10am-2pm Mon-Sat.

If you need to receive mail in San Francisco and you're not sure where you'll be staying, have it posted to the General Post Office. Mail is kept for 10 days from receipt and you must present some ID to retrieve your mail.

Telegrams

Western Union
(1-800 325 6000). **Open** 24-hours daily.
Telegrams are taken over the phone and charged to your phone bill (not available from pay phones). You can also get advice on how to get money wired to you and where to pick it up at one of a dozen San Francisco locations. You can wire money to anyone outside the state over the phone, using your Visa or Mastercard.

Telephone Directories/Enquiries

Directories are divided into Yellow Pages (classified) and White Pages (business and residential) listings. These directories are available at most public phones and in hotels. If you can't find one, dial directory assistance (411, free from a phone booth, but not from a private phone) and ask for your listing by name.

For directory assistance anywhere in the US outside the San Francisco 415 area code, dial the area code you would like to reach followed by 555 1212. For more information on the US telephone system, together with a list of telephone hotlines *see chapter* **Essential Information**.

Foreign Consulates

For a complete list, consult the Yellow Pages, or phone directory assistance (411).

Australia *362 6160*
Britain *981 3030*
Canada *213 346 2700*
Commission of the European Communities
1-800 852 0262
France *397 4330*
Germany *775 1061*
Republic of Ireland *392 4214*
Italy *931 4924*
The Netherlands *981 6454*
New Zealand *399 1455*

Car Services

For information on renting a car, the rules of the road and parking, *see chapter* **Getting Around**.

California Department of Consumer Affairs Automotive Repair Bureau
(1-800 952 5210).
Investigates complaints related to repair and smog inspection services.

CalTrans Highway Information Service
(557 3755). **Open** 24-hours daily.
You must have a touch-tone telephone to access this automated service, which gives out information on the latest in highway conditions. If you don't, phone 916 445 1534 and listen to the recorded message.

Surviving homelessness with humour on the streets of San Francisco.

Breakdown Services

AAA Emergency Road Service

(1-800 400 4222). **Open** 24-hours daily.
Members receive free towing and roadside service. If you're not a member and are not with someone who is, but belong to a motorclub at home and have your card with you, AAA might honour your card: phone to check.

Golden Gate Towing Company

(826 8866). **Open** 24-hours daily.
If you don't have a motorclub card, telephone this company for roadside service. They also recommend repair shops.

Car Parks

Although there are some low-cost garages in the city, prices increase dramatically for long-term parking. Phone in advance for rates (which can range from $5-$20 a day), check the posted prices before you park, and inquire about discounted (or 'validated') rates and times.

Ellis-O'Farrell Garage

123 O'Farrell Street, between Powell and Stockton Streets (986 4800). **Open** 5.30am-1am Mon-Thur, Sun; 5.30am-2am Fri, Sat.

Embarcadero Center Parking

250 Clay Street, in Embarcadero Center (398 1878). **Open** 24-hours daily.
At certain hours, having your ticket 'validated' at an Embarcadero establishment will decrease the hourly rate.

Fifth & Mission Garage

833 Mission Street, between Fourth and Fifth Streets (982 8522). **Open** 24-hours daily.

Japan Center Garage

1660 Geary Boulevard, at Webster Street (567 4573). **Open** 6.30am-2.30am Mon-Thur, Sun; 24-hours Fri, Sat.

Lombard Garage

2055 Lombard Street, between Webster and Fillmore Streets (567 4915). **Open** 7am-1am Mon-Wed; 7am-2am Thur; 7am-3am Fri, Sat; 7am-midnight Sun.

New Mission Bartlett Garage

90 Bartlett Street, near 21st and Mission Streets (821 6715). **Open** 6.15am-midnight Mon-Sat; 8.30am-midnight Sun.

Portsmouth Square Garage

733 Kearny Street, between Clay and Washington Streets (982 6353). **Open** 24-hours daily.

St Mary's Garage

433 Kearny Street, between Pine and California Streets (956 8106). **Open** 6am-10pm Mon-Fri.

Sutter-Stockton Garage

444 Stockton Street, between Sutter and Bush Streets (982 8370). **Open** 24-hours daily.

Vallejo Street Garage

766 Vallejo Street, between Stockton and Powell Streets (989 4490). **Open** 7am-2am Mon-Sat; 9am-midnight Sun.

Union Square Garage

333 Post Street, enter on Geary Street between Stockton and Powell Streets (397 0631). **Open** 24-hours daily.

Petrol

You'll find petrol stations on almost every corner in San Francisco. Prices are usually displayed (if not, it's probably because they're ridiculously expensive) and vary from station to station. Most stations offer full- or self-service. Stick to self-service and save a bundle – if you don't mind checking your own oil and washing your windshield yourself.

Consumer Information

(*See also chapter* **Shopping & Services**.)

Better Business Bureau
(243 9999).
Provides information on the reliability of a company or service and provides a list of companies with good business records. The Bureau also has referral listings for anything from plumbers to auto repair and is the place to telephone to file a complaint about a company.

California Attorney General's Office Public Inquiry Unit
(1-800 952 5225).
Reviews consumer complaints. Call to make a complaint on consumer, law enforcement or any other agency.

Disabled Information

(*See also chapter* **Getting Around**.)

Braille Institute
(1-800 272 4553). **Open** 9am-4pm Mon-Fri.
Volunteers answer anyone who has reading difficulties due to visual impairment or physical disability with services for the blind throughout the US.

Crisis Line for the Handicapped
(1-800 426 4263). **Open** 24-hours daily.
A talk line and referral service offering advice on topics ranging from transport to stress.

DIRECT LINK for the disABLED
(1-805 688 1603). **Open** 8am-1pm Mon-Fri.
Information on disability-related needs and referrals to local, state and national resources.

Gay & Lesbian

(*See chapter* **Gay & Lesbian San Francisco**.)

Health & Medical

(*See also page 250* **Help Lines & Agencies**.)

Clinics

Haight Ashbury Free Clinic
558 Clayton Street, at Haight Street (487 5632). Muni Metro N/6, 7, 33, 37, 43, 71 bus. **Open** 10.30am-6.30pm Mon-Thur; noon-6.30pm Fri; 24-hour answerphone rest of time.
Free primary health care is provided to anyone who needs it. Specialty clinics include chiropody, chiropractics, pediatrics and HIV antibody testing. Appointments must be made in advance.

St Anthony Free Medical Clinic
107 Golden Gate Avenue, at Jones Street (241 8320). BART Civic Center/Muni Metro J, K, L, M, N/6, 7, 8, 9, 21, 66 bus. **Open** drop-in clinic 8.15am-10am Mon-Fri.
Free medical services for those with or without insurance.

Complaints

Physicians Complaint Unit
(1-800 633 2322).
Once a complaint is received by the Physicians Complaint Unit, the process takes up to six months for it to be sent to the medical board for investigation.

Medical Society
(561 0853).
The Society investigates complaints from those who feel they've been overcharged for medical services.

Dentists

Dental Society Referral Service
(421 1435). **Open** 24-hours daily.
Referrals are made by the Society, based on geographic location and the services desired.

Drugstores (Late-opening)

Walgreens Drugstore
3201 Divisadero Street, at Lombard Street (931 6417). Bus 28, 43. **Open** 24-hours daily.
Prescriptions and general drugstore purchases.
Branch: 498 Castro Street, at 18th Street (861 6276).

Emergency Rooms

It has been known for some hospitals, emergency rooms and ambulance services to turn away people without medical insurance. So it is essential to make sure you are insured before you travel to the US (*see also chapter* **Essential Information**).

Davies Medical Center
Castro Street, at Duboce Avenue (565 6060). Muni Metro N/24 bus. **Open** 24-hours daily.

San Francisco General Hospital
1001 Potrero Avenue, between 22nd and 23rd Streets (206 8111). Bus 9, 33, 48. **Open** 24-hours daily.

Saint Francis Memorial Hospital
900 Hyde Street, between Bush and Pine Streets (353 6300). Bus 1, 27/California cable car. **Open** 24-hours daily.

Health Advice

Planned Parenthood
815 Eddy Street, between Van Ness Avenue and Franklin Street (441 5454). Bus 19, 31, 42, 47, 49. **Open** noon-7pm Mon, Wed; 4pm-7pm Tue; 9am-noon, Thur; 9am-4pm Fri.
The morning-after pill, contraception and abortions are charged on a sliding scale. Insurance is accepted.

AIDS-HIV Nightline
(434 2437). **Open** 5pm-5am daily.
Crisis hotline offering emotional support.

San Francisco AIDS Foundation Hotline
(863 2437/1-800 367 2437 from anywhere in California). **Open** 9am-9pm Mon-Fri; 11am-5pm Sat, Sun.
A multilingual hotline that offers the most up-to-date information related to the HIV virus and safe sex, taken from an enormous database of Californian services.

Seismic Seizures

Earthquakes are an even greater San Francisco phenomenon than the Forty-Niners' legendary Joe Montana. And although ol' Number 16 recently retired, the city is still waiting for the Superbowl of quakes. After the 1989 earthquake shook the life out of the World Series and devastated the Bay Area, San Francisco got serious and trained for the Big One. Although it's very unlikely that a major earthquake will occur during your stay, it's a good idea to be prepared. Advice for what to do during a major earthquake includes:

•If indoors, stay there. Get under a desk or table or stand in a corner.
•If outdoors, get into an open area away from trees, buildings, walls and power lines.
•If in a high-rise building, stay away from windows and outside walls. Get under a table. Do not use elevators.
•If driving, pull over to the side of the road and stop. Avoid overpasses and power lines. Stay inside until shaking is over.
•If in a crowded public place, do not rush for the doors. Move away from display shelves containing objects that could fall.

American Red Cross
(202 0600/202 0675 for hearing-impaired). **Open** 24-hours daily.
Information on earthquake and disaster preparedness and the function of the American Red Cross.

Earthquake Safety Hotline
(1-800 286 7233/1-800 660 8005 for hearing-impaired). **Open** 24-hours daily.
Call this automated service to receive a brochure explaining what to do before, during and after an earthquake.

Hospitals

Davies Medical Center
Castro Street, at Duboce Avenue (565 6000). Bus 24.

Kaiser Permanente
2425 Geary Boulevard, at Divisadero Street (202 2000). Bus 24, 38.

Saint Francis Memorial Hospital
900 Hyde Street, between Bush and Pine Streets (353 6000). Bus 1, 27/California cable car.

San Francisco General Hospital
1001 Potrero Avenue, between 22nd and 23rd Streets (206 8000). Bus 9, 33, 48.

Medical Referrals

SF Medical Society Referral
(561 0853).
American Medical Association referrals.

Left Luggage

Amlock Travel and Baggage
(877 0422). **Open** 7am-11pm daily.
Located at the San Francisco International Airport, this company will store anything from a carry-on piece to a bike or oversized box. Prices range from $2 to $10 per piece.

San Francisco is one of the most accommodating cities for the disabled.

Lost Property

San Francisco Police Lost Property
Bryant Street, between Sixth and Seventh Streets (553 1377). Bus 27, 42. **Open** 8am-4.30pm Mon-Fri.
Make a police report and cross your fingers that you have Buddha's karma, because the likelihood of someone turning in a lost item to the cops is as good as winning the California lottery. But if you have a local address and phone number marked on your possessions, you never know – it could be your lucky day.

Public Transport
If you have left something on **Muni** transport, phone its lost-and-found office on 923 6168. For **BART**, phone 1-510 464 7090, for **AC Transit** 1-800 559 4636, **Golden Gate Transit** 923 2000 and **SAMTRANS** 1-800 660 4287.

Money

(See also chapter **Essential Information.***)*

Emergency Cash
If you run out of cash, there's always plastic. Almost any bank machine dispenses cash advances against your Visa or Mastercard – as long as you know your PIN number. Phone the following numbers for ATM (cashpoint) locations: **Cirrus** (1-800 424 7787); **Wells Fargo** (1-800 242 4932); **Plus System** (1-800 843 7587). If you don't remember your number or have somehow de-magnetised your card, most banks will dispense cash to card holders. Try **First Interstate Bank** (765 4511), which offers advances at any of its branches. If all else fails, you can have money wired to you through **Western Union** (1-800 325 6000).

Sing hallelujah and praise the lord at the Glide Memorial United Methodist Church.

Lost/Stolen Credit Cards

American Express Card
(1-800 528 2121). **Open** 24-hours daily.

Mastercard
(1-800 826 2181). **Open** 24-hours daily.

JCB
(1-800 366 4522). **Open** 24-hours daily.

Visa
(1-800 336 8472). **Open** 24-hours daily.

Lost/Stolen Travellers' Cheques

American Express
(1-800 221 7282). **Open** 24-hours daily.

Visa
(1-800 227 6811). **Open** 24-hours daily.

Public Toilets/Restrooms

These can be found in tourist areas such as Golden Gate Park and Fisherman's Wharf, and in shopping malls. Otherwise, don't hesitate to enter a restaurant or a bar and ask to use its facilities. In keeping with its cosmopolitan standing, San Francisco recently installed its first self-cleaning, French-designed, Decaux lavatory on the corner of Market and Powell Streets. Nineteen more of the forest-green commodes are due to be erected on select street corners within the city soon. Admission is a mere 25¢ for 20 minutes; after that,

you may be fined for indecent exposure, since the door opens automatically.

Religion

San Francisco is teeming with churches, whether Baptist or Buddhist, Jewish or Jehovah's Witness, Nazarene or New Age. For a full list, consult the Yellow Pages.

Calvary Presbyterian
2515 Fillmore Street, at Jackson Street (346 3832) Bus 3, 22, 24, 83.

Congregation Emanu-el (Jewish)
2 Lake Street, at Arguello Boulevard (751 2535). Bus 1, 4.
Jewish.

First Congregational Church
495 Post Street, at Mason Street (392 7461). Bus 2, 3, 4, 30/Powell-Hyde, Powell-Mason cable car.
United Church of Christ.

Glide Memorial United Methodist Church
330 Ellis Street, at Taylor Street (771 6300). Muni Metro J, K, L, M, N/27 bus.

Old St Mary's Cathedral
660 California Street, at Grant Avenue (288 3800). Bus 1, 15, 30/California cable car.
Roman Catholic.

St Paul's Lutheran Church
950 Gough Street, at Eddy Street (673 8088). Bus 31.

St Vincent de Paul
2320 Green Street, at Steiner Street (922 1010). Bus 22, 41, 45.
Roman Catholic.

Vineyard Christian Fellowship
*1098 Harrison Street, at Seventh Street (558 9900).
Bus 42.*
Charismatic.

Zen Center
400 Page Street, at Laguna Street (863 3136). Bus 6, 7, 71.
Buddhist.

Rented Accommodation

Finding housing in San Francisco isn't difficult, but it'll cost you. Look through the combined Sunday edition of the *San Francisco Examiner/Chronicle* classifieds or the Yellow Pages for apartment or house rentals, and you'll get an idea of what to expect. There are good deals to be found in the city, but you've got to search for the real gems. Shared housing is more affordable. As a last resort, roommate referral services will connect you with someone with a similar lifestyle. *See also chapter* **Accommodation**.

B & B Reservations
(696 1690).
Holiday rentals of private homes, apartments and inns.

Metro Rent
(563 7368).

For a fee, you'll get daily updates (even by fax) on availability in the area and price range of your choice.

Roommate Network
(441 2309).
Refers professionals and graduates to apartments, houses, flats, studios and shared rentals.

Work Permits

It is difficult for foreigners to find legal work in the US. Some people get illegal 'under the table' jobs (in restaurants, bars, on building sites), which offer no security or benefits and are hard to come by. If you want to work legally, an American company must sponsor you for an H-1 visa, which enables you to work in the country for five years. To be approved, your employer must convince the Immigration Department that no American is qualified to do the job as well as you.

Students, however, have a much easier time. Your student union should have information on US working holidays. For information on studying over the summer, contact the Council on International Education Exchange (CIEE), Work Exchanges Dept, 205 East 42nd Street, New York, NY10017, USA. *See also chapter* **Students**.

Size conversion chart for clothes

Women's clothes									
British	8	10	12	14	16	•	•	•	•
American	6	8	10	12	14	•	•	•	•
French	36	38	40	42	44	•	•	•	•
Italian	38	40	42	44	46	•	•	•	•
Women's shoes									
British	3	4	5	6	7	8	9	•	•
American	5	6	7	8	9	10	11	•	•
Continental	36	37	38	39	40	41	42	•	•
Men's suits/overcoats									
British	38	40	42	44	46	•	•	•	•
American	38	40	42	44	46	•	•	•	•
Continental	48	50/52	54	56	58/60	•	•	•	•
Men's shirts									
British	14	14.5	15	15.5	16	16.5	17	•	•
American	14	14.5	15	15.5	16	16.5	17	•	•
Continental	35	36/37	38	39/40	41	42/43	44	•	•
Men's shoes									
British	8	9	10	11	12	•	•	•	•
American	9	10	11	12	13	•	•	•	•
Continental	42	43	44	45	46	•	•	•	•
Children's shoes									
British	7	8	9	10	11	12	13	1	2
American	7.5	8.5	9.5	10.5	11.5	12.5	13.5	1.5	2.5
Continental	24	25.5	27	28	29	30	32	33	34

Children's clothes
In all countries, size descriptions vary from make to make, but are usually based on age or height.

Further Reading

Fiction & Poetry

Francisco X Alarcon: *Body in Flames (Cuerpo en Llamas)*
Collection of poetry in English and Spanish from leading Chicano/Latino literary activist.
Ambrose Bierce: *Can Such Things Be?*
Tales of horror and the downright horrible.
Marci Blackman, Trebor Healey (eds): *Beyond Definition: New Writing from Gay and Lesbian San Francisco*
Poetry and fiction from a cross-section of queer SF.
Ann Charters (ed): *The Penguin Book of the Beats*
Excerpts from novels, short stories and songs.
Philip K Dick: *The Man in the High Castle*
Japanese victory in WWII creates a very different San Francisco.
Allen Ginsberg: *Howl and Other Poems*
The rant that caused all the fuss.
Dashiell Hammett: *The Maltese Falcon*
One of the greatest detective novels, set in a dark and dangerous San Francisco.
Bret Harte: *Selected Stories and Sketches*
Adventurous tales from the gold-rush era.
Jack Kerouac: *On the Road, Desolation Angels, The Dharm Bums*
Drink, drugs and sex in San Francisco and around the world from the most famous Beat of them all.
Ken Kesey: *One Flew Over the Cuckoo's Nest*
Tragic, heroic yet frequently comic story of the inmates of a mental institution.
Maxine Hong Kingston: *The Woman Warrior*
Colourful childhood and family history of a Chinese-American.
Jack London: *Tales of the Fish Patrol, John Barleyworn*
Early works, set in London's native San Francisco and the Bay Area.
Cyra McFadden: *The Serial*
Macramé and mind-expansion in 1970s Marin County.
Terry McMillan: *Waiting to Exhale*
The life of a strong and cynical African American woman.
Armistead Maupin: *Tales of the City* (6 volumes)
Witty soap opera on the lives and loves of a group of friends in the sexually liberated 1970s and sobering post-AIDS 1980s.
Frank Norris: *McTeague*
Working class life and loss set in unromanticised Barbary Coast days.
Thomas Pynchon: *The Crying of Lot 49, Vineland*
Funny, wild novels set in Northern California, by one of the most enigmatic writers alive.
Vikram Seth: *The Golden Gate*
Verse novel about San Francisco yuppies.
John Steinbeck: *East of Eden, The Grapes of Wrath*
Grim tales of California in the Depression.
Robin Stevens (ed): *Girlfriend Number One: Lesbian Life in the 90s*
Fiction written for performance at Red Dora's Bearded Lady Café, a centre of the Spoken Word scene.
Amy Tan: *The Joy Luck Club*
Exploration of the lives of several generations of Chinese, and later Chinese-American women.
Mark Twain: *The Celebrated Jumping Frog of Calaveras County, From Scotland to Silverado, Roughing It*
Brilliant tales of San Francisco and early California.

Tom Wolfe: *The Electric Kool-Aid Acid Test, The Pump House Gang*
Alternative life-styles in trippy, hippy, 1960s California.

Non-fiction

Walton Bean: *California: An Interpretive History*
Anecdotal account of California's sometimes shady past.
California Coastal Commission: *California Coastal Access Guide*
Accessible and comprehensive guide to the coastal regions.
Carolyn Cassidy: *Off the Road: My Years with Cassidy, Kerouac and Ginsberg*
Not the most enlightened of feminism, but an interesting alternative examination of the North Beach Beats.
Randolph Delehanty: *The Ultimate Guide: San Francisco*
Meticulously researched compendium of 13 walking tours through the city.
Joan Didion: *Slouching Towards Bethlehem, The White Album*
Brilliant essays examining contemporary California.
Lawrence Ferlinghetti and Nancy J Peters: *Literary San Francisco*
One of the better accounts of the literary circles that have always been part of the city's history.
James Forbes: *Café San Francisco*
Helps you choose which slackers to hang out with.
James D Hart: *A Companion to California*
Hefty tome listing almost every category imaginable from the origins of street names to literary history.
Gladys Hansen: *San Francisco Almanac*
All the SF trivia you never needed to know, from weather patterns to bridge and tunnel statistics.
Don Herron: *The Literary World of San Francisco*
Vital and precise account of San Francisco's literary history.
Jamie Jensen: *Built to Last: 25 Years of the Grateful Dead*
History of the city's own cult offering to the rock world.
Oscar Lewis: *San Francisco: Mission to Metropolis*
Vintage photos and paintings, with a commentary on the natural and urban environment.
Malcolm Margolin (ed): *The Way We Lived: California Indian Stories, The Ohlone Way*
Accounts of the Bay Area's first inhabitants.
Randy Shilts: *The Mayor of Castro Street*
On the rising political career of the city's first openly gay elected official, and the development of gay politics.
Sally Socolich: *Bargain Hunting in the Bay Area*
A must for shopaholics.
Gertrude Stein: *The Making of Americans*
Autobiographical work that includes an account of her early childhood in Oakland.
Robert Louis Stevenson: *An Inland Voyage, The Silverado Squatters*
Autobiographical narratives describing the journey from rural Europe to western America.
Ronald Takaki: *Strangers from a Different Shore: A History of Asian Americans*
A survey of immigration in North America.
Hunter S Thompson: *The Great Shark Hunt, Hell's Angels*
Drug and alcohol-fuelled accounts of political campaigns, popular culture and chain-whippings.
Sally & John Woodbridge: *San Francisco Architecture*
The best of many books on the city's architecture.

Index

San Francisco Guide
Advertisers Index
Please refer to the relevant sections for addresses/telephone numbers

Maps

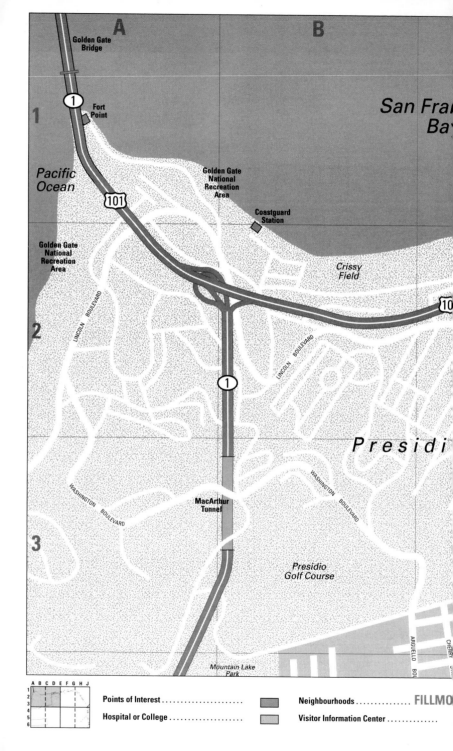

A

B

Golden Gate
Bridge

①

Fort
Point

1

*Pacific
Ocean*

101

Golden Gate
National
Recreation
Area

Golden Gate
National
Recreation
Area

Coastguard
Station

San Fra
Ba

*Crissy
Field*

10

LINCOLN   BOULEVARD

LINCOLN   BOULEVARD

2

①

P r e s i d i

WASHINGTON   BOULEVARD

WASHINGTON   BOULEVARD

MacArthur
Tunnel

3

*Presidio
Golf Course*

ARGUELLO   BOU

CHER

*Mountain Lake
Park*

A B C D E F G H J

Points of Interest . . . .

Hospital or College . . . .

Neighbourhoods . . . . **FILLMO**

Visitor Information Center . . . .

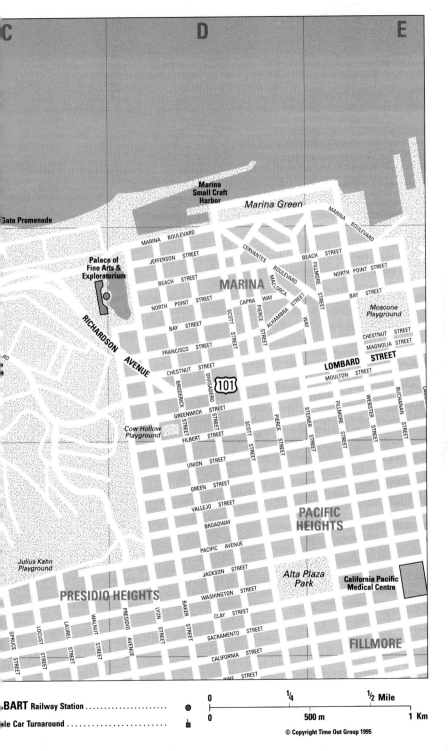

C　　　　　　D　　　　　　E

Marina
Small Craft
Harbor

Marina Green

MARINA BOULEVARD

iate Promenade

MARINA BOULEVARD

Palace of
Fine Arts &
Exploratorium

JEFFERSON STREET

CERVANTES

BEACH STREET

NORTH POINT STREET

BEACH STREET

MARINA

Moscone
Playground

RICHARDSON AVENUE

NORTH POINT STREET

CAPRA WAY

MALLORCA

BOULEVARD

FILLMORE STREET

BAY STREET

CHESTNUT STREET

BAY STREET

PIERCE STREET

ALHAMBRA STREET

WAY

MAGNOLIA STREET

FRANCISCO STREET

SCOTT STREET

CHESTNUT STREET

LOMBARD STREET

DIVISADERO STREET

101

MOULTON STREET

BRODERICK STREET

BUCHANAN STREET

Cow Hollow
Playground

GREENWICH STREET

FILBERT STREET

SCOTT STREET

PIERCE STREET

STEINER STREET

FILLMORE STREET

WEBSTER STREET

UNION STREET

GREEN STREET

VALLEJO STREET

BROADWAY

PACIFIC
HEIGHTS

PACIFIC AVENUE

Julius Kahn
Playground

JACKSON STREET

Alta Plaza
Park

California Pacific
Medical Centre

PRESIDIO HEIGHTS

BAKER STREET

LYON STREET

PRESIDIO AVENUE

WALNUT STREET

LAUREL STREET

LOCUST STREET

SPRUCE STREET

WASHINGTON STREET

CLAY STREET

SACRAMENTO STREET

CALIFORNIA STREET

PINE STREET

FILLMORE

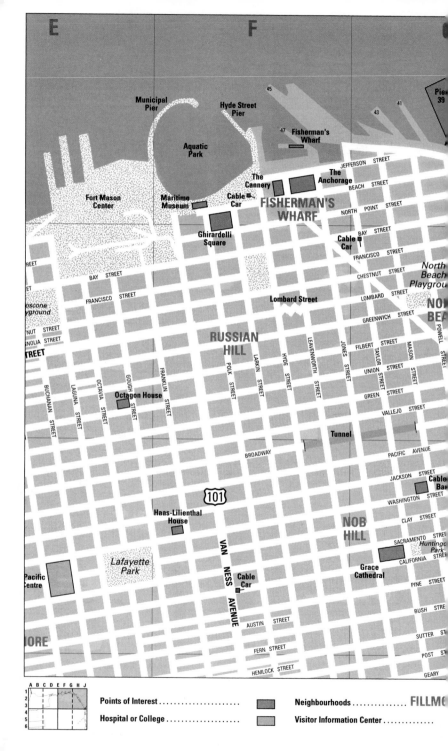

E

F

G

Pier 39

45

43

41

Municipal Pier

Hyde Street Pier

47 **Fisherman's Wharf**

Aquatic Park

JEFFERSON STREET

The Cannery

The Anchorage

BEACH STREET

Fort Mason Center

Maritime Museum

Cable Car

FISHERMAN'S WHARF

NORTH POINT STREET

BAY STREET

Ghirardelli Square

Cable Car

FRANCISCO STREET

REET

BAY STREET

CHESTNUT STREET

North Beach Playgrou

oscone yground

FRANCISCO STREET

Lombard Street

LOMBARD STREET

NO BEA

NUT STREET

GREENWICH STREET

POWELL

NOLIA STREET

RUSSIAN HILL

FILBERT STREET

MASON

TREET

STREE

LARKIN STREET

HYDE STREET

LEAVENWORTH STREET

JONES STREET

TAYLOR STREET

STREET

UNION STREET

FRANKLIN STREET

GOUGH STREET

OCTAVIA STREET

LAGUNA STREET

BUCHANAN STREET

Octagon House

GREEN STREET

VALLEJO STREET

Tunnel

BROADWAY

PACIFIC AVENUE

101

JACKSON STREET

Cable Ba

Haas-Lilienthal House

WASHINGTON STREET

CLAY STREET

VAN

NOB HILL

SACRAMENTO STREE

Huntingt Park

NESS

Lafayette Park

Cable Car

Grace Cathedral

CALIFORNIA STREE

Pacific entre

AVENUE

PINE STREET

BUSH STRE

AUSTIN STREET

FERN STREET

SUTTER S

ORE

POST S

HEMLOCK STREET

GEARY

A B C D E F G H J
1
2
3
4
5
6

Points of Interest . . . .

Hospital or College . . . .

Neighbourhoods . . . . **FILLMO**

Visitor Information Center . . . .

H   J

San Francisco
Bay

1

35 Cruise Ship
   Terminal

33

31

27

2

GRAPH
HILL

Coit
Tower

19

17

15

9

7

SANSOME STREET

BATTERY STREET

THE EMBARCADERO

5

3

MONTGOMERY STREET

FRONT STREET

DAVIS STREET

1

BROADWAY

FINANCIAL
DISTRICT

Jackson
Square

Golden Gateway
Center

DRUMM STREET

Ferry Building

TOWN

Portsmouth
Square

Transamerica
Pyramid

Embarcadero Center

Justin Herman
Plaza

BATTERY STREET

Wells Fargo
Museum

Bank of
California

FRONT STREET

DAVIS STREET

Cable
Car

Old St Mary's
Church

Merchant's
Exchange

SANSOME STREET

Muni
Metro BART
Embarcadero

STEUART STREET

San Francisco
Oakland Bay
Bridge

3

Bank of
America

Stock
Exchange

SPEAR STREET

80

Chinatown
Gateway

MONTGOMERY STREET

KEARNY STREET

MARKET STREET

MAIN STREET

BEALE STREET

24

Transbay Terminal
& Greyhound Bus
Depot

FREMONT STREET

26

nion
uare

Crocker
Galleria

GRANT AVENUE

STOCKTON STREET

1st STREET

28

Muni
Metro BART
Montgomery St

MISSION STREET

2nd STREET

30

BART Railway Station ....   ●

ble Car Turnaround ....

0   ¼   ½ Mile

0   500 m   1 Km

© Copyright Time Out Group 1995

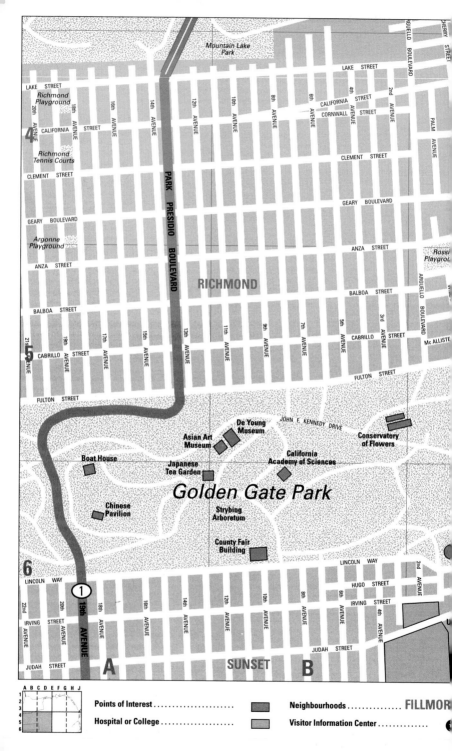

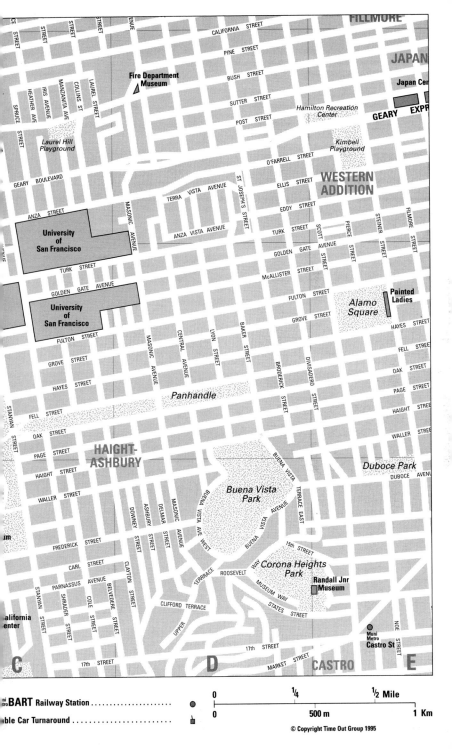

0	¼	½ Mile

0	500 m	1 Km

© Copyright Time Out Group 1995

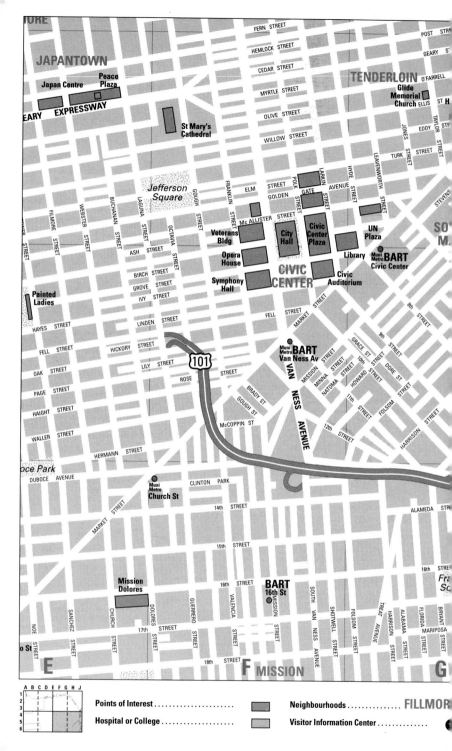

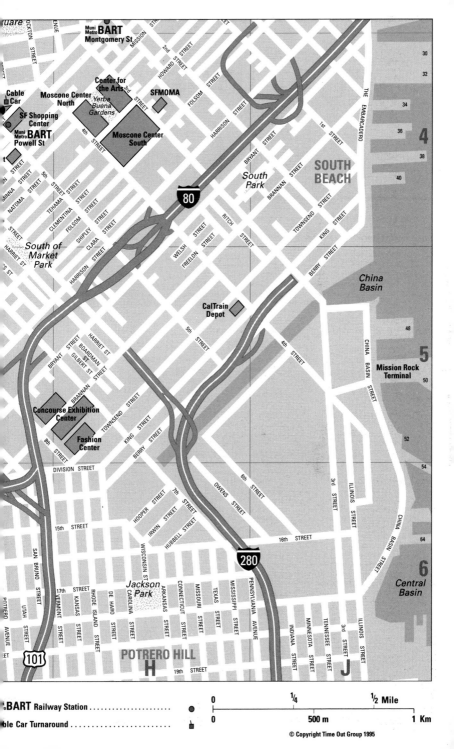

Street Index

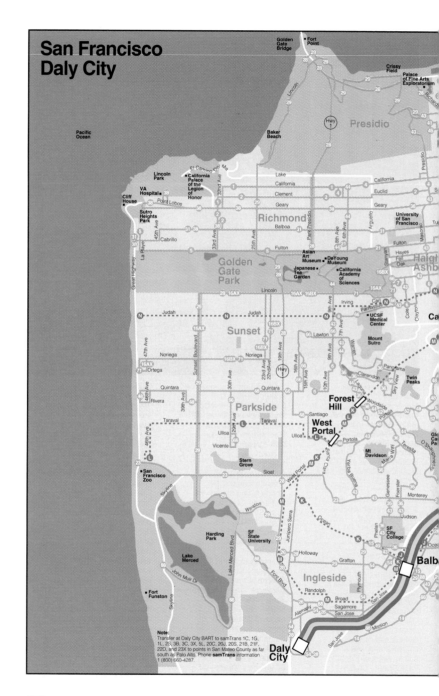

San Francisco
Daly City

Golden Gate Bridge

Fort Point

Crissy Field

Palace of Fine Arts
Exploratorium

Pacific Ocean

Presidio

Baker Beach

Lincoln Park

California Palace of the Legion of Honor

VA Hospital

Cliff House

Point Lobos

Sutro Heights Park

Lincoln

Lake

California

Clement

Geary

Euclid

California

Richmond

Balboa

University of San Francisco

Cabrillo

Fulton

Golden Gate Park

Fulton

Asian Art Museum

DeYoung Museum

Japanese Tea Garden

California Academy of Sciences

Hayes

Haight Ashbury

Lincoln

Judah

Judah

UCSF Medical Center

Sunset

Lawton

Mount Sutro

Noriega

Noriega

Ortega

Clarendon

Panorama

Twin Peaks

Quintara

Quintara

Forest Hill

Rivera

Parkside

Santiago

West Portal

Woodside

Taraval

Taraval

Ulloa

Ulloa

Portola

Mt Davidson

Vicente

Stern Grove

San Francisco Zoo

Sloat

Monterey

Judson

Winston

SF City College

Harding Park

SF State University

Holloway

Lake Merced

Grafton

Balboa

Fort Funston

Ingleside

Randolph

Broad

Sagamore

San Jose

Alemany

Daly City

San Jose

Mission

Note: Transfer at Daly City BART to samTrans 1C, 1G, 1L, 2G, 3B, 3C, 3X, 5L, 20C, 20J, 20S, 21B, 21F, 22D, and 23X to points in San Mateo County as far south as Palo Alto. Phone **samTrans** information 1 (800) 660-4287.

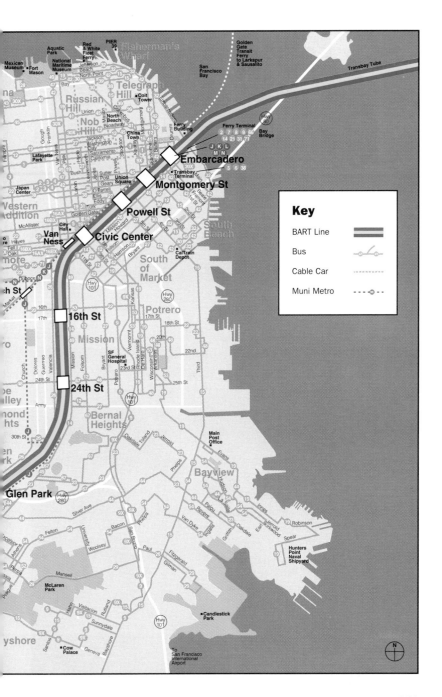

Key

BART Line

Bus

Cable Car

Muni Metro

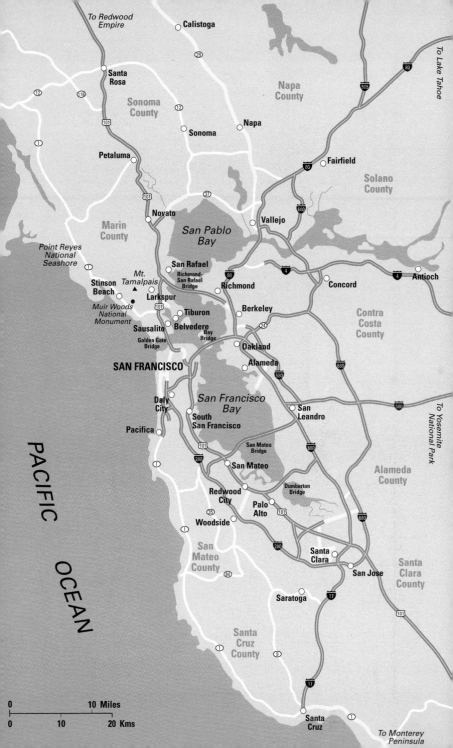

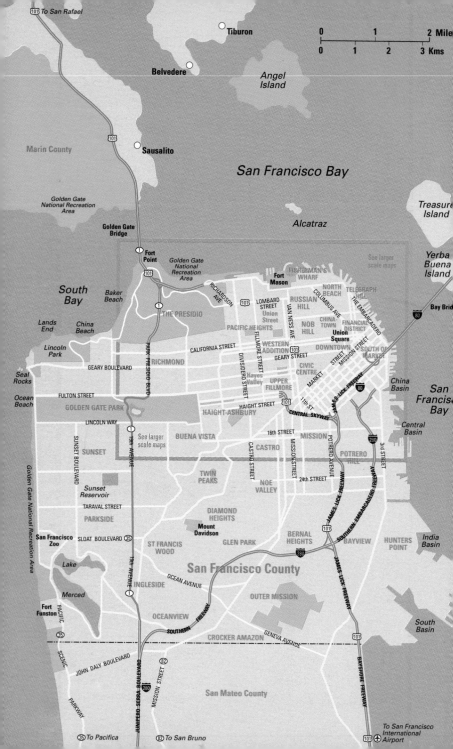